KAZ COOKE

GIRL STUFF

for ages

13+

2020-21 edition

Your full-on guide to the teen years

VIKING
an imprint of
PENGUIN BOOKS

CONTENTS

Intro 1

PART 1: BODY

1 CHANGE 9

So what are you in for? 11
Breasts 15
Your girly bits 21
Clear or white stuff 25
Your period 26

2 SKIN 39

The skin on your face 40
Pimples and blackheads 45
Skin colour 52
The sun and your skin 54
Skin marks 56
Sweating 58
Piercing and tattoos 60

3 HAIR 63

Looking after your hair 64
Body hair 72

4 BODY IMAGE 78

Your body shape 79
What's healthy? 80
Not liking your bits 95
Growing out of obsessions 100

5 FOOD 104

What you need 105
What you don't need 116

6 MOVE 124

Physical activity 125
Finding your own activity thing 128
Activity problems 133

7 BODY HEALTH 137

Managing your health 138
Girls' and women's health 144

PART 2: HEAD

8 CONFIDENCE 153
Not feeling confident 154
Getting confident 155
Who are you? 165
Growing up strong and smart 171

9 FEELINGS 178
Moods 179
Feeling embarrassed 180
Feeling angry 182
Feeling worried and stressed 184
Feeling down 189
Feeling optimistic and strong 192

10 DRINKING 195
Stuff you need to know about alcohol before drinking 196
Deciding whether or not to drink 202
Being drunk 204
Taking control of drinking 213

11 DRUGS 216
Cigarettes 217
Legal drugs 221
Illegal drugs 223

12 MIND HEALTH 236
Your brain 237
How to get more sleep 244
Good mental health 248
Mental health problems 249
Severe anxiety 254
Depression 256
Bipolar disorder 258
Self-harm 259
Eating disorders 260
Suicide 266
Psychosis and schizophrenia 268

rummage, rummage...

PART 3: HEART

13 FAMILY 273

Happy families 274
Not-so-happy families 281
When families break up 288
Different family combos 291

14 FRIENDS 296

Good friends 297
Friends on social media and your phone 301
Changing friendships 305
Groups of friends 309
Meanness and bullying 313

15 LOVE 331

Falling in love 333
Hooking up, dating, or going out with someone 338
Being 'differently attracted' 344
Relationships 352

16 SEX 359

Becoming a sexual person 360
Sexual touching 363
Deciding whether or not to have sex 365
Going all the way 373
Safe sex 383
Contraception 389
Sex and love 396
Sex without consent 398

17 PREGNANCY 402

Being pregnant 403
Pregnancy termination (abortion) 409
Becoming a young mum 413
Adoption 417

PART 4: AND THE REST

18 SCHOOLWORK 421

Homework and study 422
Learning stuff 428
After school 434
Education and careers 436

19 PAID WORK 443

Looking for a job 444
Applying for a job 446
The job interview 449
Being a good employee 452
Your rights as a worker 455

20 MONEY 458

How to hang onto money 459
How to spend money and not get into debt 463

21 SHOPPING 471

The tricky persuaders 472
Going shopping 479

22 CLOTHES & MAKE-UP 484

Clothes 485
Face 498

23 EQUALITY, FRIVOLITY 510

Why we had to fight for our rights 511
Why we still need women's rights 513

24 CARING 527

What people believe in 528
How to change the world 538

Acknowledgements 546

Index 551

Intro

This book is designed to be your friend through the teenage years – it will tell you the whole truth and let you make up your own mind about things. It doesn't care if you're in the cool group, or whether you need new pants, or about something that happened three months ago that still makes you blush.

GIRL STUFF 13+ is on your side.

You start your teens as a kid, and you leave them as an adult. In between, there's heaps of change, and it's not just that your favourite colour isn't Barbie pink any more.

I'm an adult now, so how do I know what girls want to read about? I set up a Girl Stuff website with a survey, and there were more than 4000 responses. Girls said they wanted to know about body changes, food, exercise, hair, their brain, their feelings, drinking, drugs, family, love, sex, confidence, what to believe in, helping other people, school, work, money, shopping, clothes, make-up, and their rights.

Then I asked a whole bunch of health and other experts what they thought girls should know. More than seventy generous and adorable ones lent this book their time and knowledge, often answering many follow-up questions. All of them wanted to help get girls the most up-to-date and useful info possible.

Being a teenager can be the most exciting, fun time in your life, when you sometimes can't stop laughing, you make great friends, and you get to work out who you are and some of the things you want to do with your life. But it also has its challenges. GIRL STUFF 13+ is about how to make the most of being a teenager, and how to handle some of the problems that can turn up and make you want to scream into a pillow. The book covers a lot of 'problems'. But don't worry – that doesn't mean you'll necessarily have any or all of the problems, or that they'll happen all at once. It just means there's lots of info on everything in case you do need help.

Some advice in books for teenage girls starts at periods and ends with 'moods', on the way referring vaguely to hormones without explaining them. Others say, 'Be confident!' – but nobody seems to explain how. Or they suggest that you find out what your body shape is, then use that info to work out how to relate to people, become incredibly popular and marry a European prince.

Some books and magazines for teenage girls are full of pictures of rich models who look as if their whole life is one long beach holiday (because everyone can relate to that, right?). And some seem to say that your eyebrow shape is more important than whether or not you're happy.

Then there are the adults who suggest teenage girls are evil, selfish fiends. Some people don't respect girls. Sadly, this is a problem you'll strike all through your life – you just graduate to meeting people who don't respect women either. The best revenge is to try to make them irrelevant to your life. This book talks about how to grow up to be a strong, independent young woman, and how to find out what you're good at and make the most of your life, not just your eyebrows.

Some adults see teenagers as a 'problem': they think girls are a bunch of bubble-headed idiots who don't care about anything but themselves. I don't agree – although I'm sure we've all met a couple of airheads in our time. I think most girls are smart and funny, and that they care about the world and what they can do to make a difference to others and build a great future for themselves. They're creative, emotional, thoughtful, loving and, yes, sometimes self-centred. But who wouldn't be, faced with a new body, new feelings and a media culture that urges us to hero-worship some of the most self-centred women on the planet?

It's up to you to decide whether you're old enough to hear about, or you're ready for, certain things. If you're not interested in drinking or drugs or sex, for example, that's absolutely fine. You can either leave those chapters until some time in the future, or read the stuff now so that you can make good decisions later. Knowing about something doesn't mean you should do it. Sometimes knowing about stuff means you understand it's a good idea *not* to do it, or *not* to do it yet.

intro

As the saying goes, 'Knowledge is power', and you need that power to make smart and informed decisions about your life.

The quotes used throughout this book are from the thousands of girls who filled in the survey on the Girl Stuff website. They're all real. But if you think you know somebody who's quoted – you don't, unless it was you. Lots of names have been changed to protect girls from possible embarrassment, or from getting into trouble with parents or teachers. We're keeping everybody's secrets.

Hello and welcome to all trans girls reading this book. Some kids are sure they're a boy, even if they are born with a 'female' body, and some kids are sure they're a girl, even if they're born with a 'male' body. This can be known as being 'trans'. Other kids feel that they're somewhere in between male and female, or neither. For help on how to be your best self, see 'More Info' on identity and different sexuality on page 347.

The four parts of GIRL STUFF 13+ each has a theme: Body, Head, Heart, And the Rest. You don't have to read the book all in one hit, from start to finish, like a story. You can use the Contents list (at the front) or the Index (at the back) to just pick the bit you're interested in at the moment. I've included some websites, books and other information at the end of sections or chapters so that if you want to find out more about a specific subject you've got a head start. Books, even if they're published overseas, can be ordered through your neighbourhood bookshop. Local libraries and school librarians can also help you chase things up or give you other useful recommendations.

Where possible I've suggested Australian and New Zealand websites, or the best ones from overseas. Please be smart when going online: beware of people being creepy, or trying to sell you stuff or get you onto a list so they can send you hundreds of advertising emails. I've tried to choose non-commercial websites (those that aren't trying to sell stuff). If one is a commercial site, I'm *not* recommending whatever it's selling, I'm trying to help you find some good info on it.

Some of the stuff explored in this book is covered by magazines and websites. Many of their stories are really helpful and well researched, but you can't rely on sites and mags and advertisers to give you totally independent advice. There *are* no beauty or fashion 'essentials', whatever they say. That's just a way to get you to buy things. What you'll find in GIRL STUFF 13+ is the lowdown, without the hard sell (or the hidden sell).

And this book, unlike a magazine, doesn't give you 173 tips on nail polish. Because frankly, it would bore us half to death. So dive in, anywhere you like, and start finding out about GIRL STUFF 13+.

Kaz x

intro 5

PART 1

BODY

1 **CHANGE** Understanding the new you 9

2 **SKIN** Don't put up with acting up 39

3 **HAIR** Cutting, curling, shaving and hairdo misbehaving 63

4 **BODY IMAGE** One size doesn't fit all 78

5 **FOOD** Sorting out feelings and food 104

6 **MOVE** Finding the groove 124

7 **BODY HEALTH** Taking care of yourself 137

CHANGE 1

I'm sorry to break it to you like this, but Mother Nature can be entirely random and completely nuts. Some natural things can be a pain in the butt – such as going through the changes of 'puberty'. These include growing hair in places where there wasn't any, getting periods, changing body shape and feeling new emotions.

Some girls start puberty at age 8 or 9, others at 15 or 16, but most begin around 11 or 12. Luckily the various changes happen over a few years until you've reached your full height, as early as 14 or 15 or as late as 18 or so.

Mother Nature doesn't care what problems you have on the way through puberty – she couldn't give a flying frittata if you get pimples, miserable or pregnant. In fact her job is pretty much confined to trying to **GET** you pregnant. It's okay, though, because you also have a brain you can use while you're growing from a girl into a woman. And the changes are gradual. Getting your first period doesn't mean you're ready to have sex, or a baby, or run your own airport maintenance business.
You're still a girl.

This chapter should smooth out any worries and questions you might have. Let's get down to it.

9

Reasons you may not want to change

Puberty can sound freaky and scary before you go through it. The natural changes can be confusing or annoying if you don't understand them or don't feel ready. Here are some of the common worries.

It seems gross at first

The changes can freak you out when they're new, but after a while you get used to your new body, and having a period every month, and don't really think about it any more.

Someone gets weird about you changing

Sometimes parents or other relatives find the idea that you're growing up very confronting and might say to you, 'It's too early. You're too young.' Remind them that it's obviously the right time for you, it doesn't mean you're a woman yet, and you need their support. (Or show them this paragraph.) Some adults have forgotten what it's like to go through the changes, so they say thoughtless things.

You don't have somebody to talk to about it

If you can't talk to your mum, try your big sister, dad, aunty, cousin, older friend, teacher, school nurse or counsellor, local doctor or friend's mum. This book should also answer most of your questions.

You're the first or the last of your class or friends to begin the changes

You won't always be the first or the last to go through a stage: things even out in the end.

Don't feel you have to talk to anyone of your own age about any of it if you don't want to.

You don't want people to look at you or comment on the changes

Well, they shouldn't. Most people who say rude things are either ignorant and determined to annoy you, or trying desperately to draw attention away from their own changes or lack of changes.

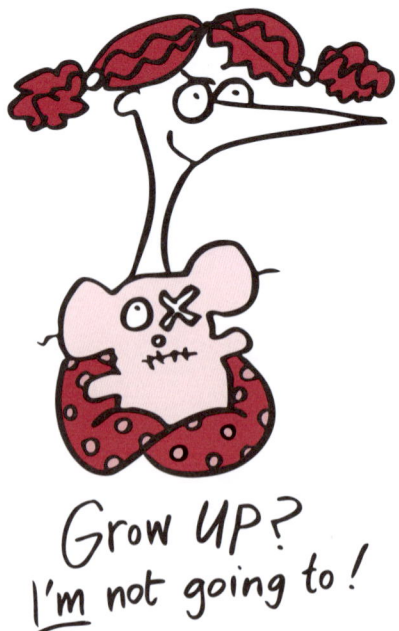

Grow UP? I'm not going to!

10 BODY ✸ change

So what are you in for?

During your teen years there are major changes you can see, and others happening inside your body that you can't see.

You get bigger

You might get taller steadily through the teen years, or have a few growth jumps or one big growth spurt. Some girls grow several centimetres in a year; usually the time of quickest growth is around 12 or 13.

Your hands and feet are the first to grow bigger, followed by your arms and legs, and then your spine lengthens. Over the teen years, you double the size of your bones. Your muscles get bigger and stronger. For some girls these changes are gradual; for others they seem to happen overnight. Changing quickly can affect your sense of balance, and make you feel awkward or clumsy while you get used to your new self, but you'll adjust quickly.

Anything you have two of will be slightly different sizes (this includes hands, feet, breasts, ears, the lot). Because you're paying such close attention you can think this is obvious, but almost certainly nobody else could tell or would ever notice.

Your breasts, hips and thighs will probably get bigger and rounder. Some girls will be curvier than others, but getting larger is a natural process. Teenage girls often worry about their tummy 'sticking out'. This bump is natural for many girls. It's normal to have a flat or a rounded tummy. Some girls will stay lean and not very curvy, even when they're fully grown, and that's fine too.

Inside, your girly bits, including your ovaries and uterus, are also growing (there's more coming up on those in a moment).

You get fluffier

By the end of your teen years you'll have:
- underarm hair
- pubic hair, which grows between your legs and on the pubic mound – the bump at the front
- leg hair that's more noticeable
- hair on your forearms (below the elbows) that also may be more noticeable
- perhaps some extra hair here and there.

Body hair is usually about the same colour as your eyebrows or a bit darker (there's more info in Chapter 3, Hair).

You get leakier

I know this seems appalling at first, but you just get used to it because it's normal. Your skin and hair may become oilier, and you sweat more (see Chapter 2, Skin, and Chapter 3, Hair). And you'll see that your vagina (the middle opening between your legs) leaks some clear or whitish fluid now and then, and also some blood, known as a period, for several days every month. (More on all this later on.)

You get moodier

During the teen years various organs in your body make some new hormones; these chemicals then faff around your body, causing the physical changes but also messing with your brain and helping to cause different moods. You can feel sad, angry, weepy or wildly happy without exactly knowing why (see Chapter 9, Feelings). Some girls get crabby or emotional and teary before their period.

What to say to rude comments about your changes

'Ooh, look, you've got boobies!'
'Oh, is that what they are. I thought I was getting antlers.'

'Show us ya tits!'
'Show us ya brain!'

'Oh, aren't you getting taller!'
'Yes, I believe it's compulsory.'

'You're getting a big butt.'
'What's the matter with you? Why are you looking at my bum?', or
'So what? *You're* getting ruder and more stupid.'

'You're becoming a woman.'
'Actually I'm just becoming a teenager/I'm not even a teenager yet. But if you really think I'm grown up, how about a car?'

'Ooh, you have put on weight.'
'Yes, the alternative is to wither away and die – so, tough decision', or
'Yes, lucky isn't it? Otherwise I'd look like a 9-year-old all my life.'

When I was first developing breasts, hair, etc I was VERY self-conscious about it and DIDN'T want it to happen, but then I got used to it and now it's not a problem. But I remember it was hard getting used to it.   Megan, 15, Kambah, ACT

The order of the changes

Here's the order that the changes usually go in, taking about four to six years to get from little-girl body to full-on young-womanly one.

The secret stage   This can happen any time between the ages of 8 and 11. Glands and organs inside (such as your ovaries) start getting bigger and sending hormone messages.

Your hands and feet may get bigger and you may grow taller.

The bosom stage   Breasts usually 'start' any time between 9 and 14. First you get breast buds, a hard little lump under each nipple (often one comes before the other). Months, or even years, later the nipples push out, and your breasts start to grow.

You can also have a growth spurt, getting taller and bigger all over.

The pubic hair stage   This usually happens a little while after the budding bosoms stage. About one in five girls gets some pubic hair before she sees any bosom action, which is also normal. The first hairs start out fine and straight. Some girls start getting wisps of pubic hair as young as 8 or so. Eventually you'll have a 'map of Tassie'–shaped 'triangle' of pubic hair.

The period stage   Usually about a year or two after the first sign of bosom business, you'll get your first period (doctors call this first one the menarche – pronounced men-ark – but we won't bother). Most girls get it at 12 or 13, but thousands of girls get it earlier or later (any time between 9 and 15) and the difference is no big deal. (See your doctor just for a check-up if it hasn't come before your sixteenth birthday.)

Your breasts keep growing, and your pubic hair usually gets a little thicker, darker and curlier. Your body is still growing taller and, although you can't tell, your vagina is enlarging (which helps if you want to use tampons during your period). You're probably also noticing a small amount of the clear or whitish fluid on your knickers, which comes from your vagina.

At first you think you're weird because your breasts grow oddly and you begin to get wild hair and your period becomes out of control, but really you're just like everyone else.
Sarah, 14, South Hurstville, NSW

The underarm hair stage   This usually happens any time between 10 and 16, and on average at 13 or 14.

The nipple area will also develop at this time, and inside you your ovaries are releasing an egg now and then, but probably not yet regularly once a month (see 'Insidey Bits' later in this chapter).

The it's-all-going-on stage Usually by about the age of 16, your breasts and body hair are 'finished', and you're at or near your adult height. Your period comes about once a month, and you regularly release an egg inside about halfway between each period.

> I started hating my body for being different. It might have helped if someone had told me that sooner or later the other girls would catch up.
> Annie, 16, Glebe, NSW
>
> If girls are worried that they're late bloomers – don't worry, it'll happen!
> Manda, 17, Wellington Point, Qld

More info on body changes

Your local doctor (GP) or community health centre or school nurse can answer any questions about your physical changes and whether you're on schedule (Chapter 7, Body Health, has info on seeing a doctor).

likeitis.org.au
Website with info about puberty and periods: interactive girly-bits diagram; heaps of Q and A.

🥝 New Zealand Government
Healthline: 0800 611 116
Qualified nurses can answer your questions.

I didn't really notice any changes straight away. It all happened really slowly, which I guess is good, 'cause I didn't have a real awkward stage.   Cate, 18, Prospect, SA

It can be embarrassing if you're the first one of your friends to go through it.
Alex, 13, Bayswater, NSW

You will get used to your body! It's ok to be embarrassed about the new bits. Stop stressing about what has happened and what hasn't and just enjoy the ride!   Suzie, 15

Breasts

Bosoms, boobs, bazoombas: call 'em whatever you like (but maybe not norks, jugs or rack). Once they start growing, breasts usually take three to five years to get to their final size. If you have a baby one day, your breasts will make milk. (There's no milk in your breasts now.)

Nipples

Nipples, the pointy bit of your breasts, have tiny hidden holes like a sprinkler system so the milk can come out.

During the teen years the nipples and the coloured area surrounding them can get darker, and they become darker still during pregnancy and stay darker (probably so they are easier for a hungry baby to see and latch onto).

Nipples can get erect – harder and pointier – when it's cold, when you are having sexy thoughts, or when you touch them. This is perfectly normal. Some girls worry about their nipples being seen through their clothes. You can try wearing a crop-top or tank-top (singlet) or a thick bra under your clothes, and a patterned top (rather than a solid block of colour) or a loose shirt.

Innies and outies   Some girls have nipples that always stick out. Some have turned-in ones, called inverted nipples (which are also normal). Inverted nipples usually pop out and say hello if they're cold or you're having sexy thoughts.

Colour   The coloured area around each nipple is called the areola (pronounced arry-ole-ah); the plural is areolae (pronounced arry-ole-eye). When they're growing, each areola forms a slightly mounded shape that will either stay that way or go back to looking flat. Some areolae (often on fair skin) are a very light pink or apricoty colour; others are dark plum or deep brown. The shape of the areolae can be round, oval or almost oblong.

> I woke up one morning and I swear my boobs just grew over night.
> Amy, 18, Ryde, NSW

> It's stupid how people want bigger breasts when most guys don't really care.
> Zoe, 13, Alice Springs, NT

Ouchy ones   Sometimes your tender new nipples get rubbed sore from bouncing around and rubbing against your clothes. You can wear a firm-fitting crop-top or a bra under your clothes to stop them bouncing so much. You're most aware of your breasts when they're 'new'. They may feel fuller and even a bit sore before your period.

Lumps and bumps Many girls and women have naturally lumpy breasts. Most lumps and bumps have absolutely nothing to do with breast cancer, which is very rare in young women, although it does happen. If you have a sudden or unusual lump you must see a doctor straight away – within a day or so (there's more on how to check for lumps in Chapter 7, Body Health).

> One breast is always bigger than the other!!!! Aaagghhhh!!
> Lucy, 14,
> Bangalow, NSW
>
> I hate guys liking me for my breasts, rather than myself.
> Kelli, 16,
> Perth, WA

Your breast size

Your breasts will probably start and finish growing at different times from your friends'. Most people have one breast slightly larger than the other. Frustratingly the two may grow at different rates (it's the same for your feet). Nobody ever notices this about someone else.

The size and shape that your breasts are meant to be is programmed, before you're born, by the genes you inherit from both sides of the family. There's nothing you can do to make them bigger or smaller or firmer, and this includes exercises, diet, pills or 'firming' creams and ointments. People make claims in advertising that you can, but liar, liar, their pants are on fire.

After your breasts are fully grown, their size will only change when you gain or lose weight; before a period and when you're on the contraceptive pill (the Pill) – they get slightly bigger; and during pregnancy and breastfeeding (bigger again).

Littlies Some girls worry that their bosoms aren't growing fast enough or big enough, but there's no such thing as 'too small'. Your breasts are just right for you. If any teasing goes on, remind yourself that girls with big breasts get teased about theirs, and girls with middle-sized breasts get teased about something else or are told their breasts are too big or too small.

Companies make bras that hoist breasts up, pull them together to create 'cleavage' or pad them, not because there's anything wrong with small breasts but because, if they can make you think you need those bras, they make more money.

Big 'uns Bosoms are right there, out the front, and difficult to hide. Teenage boys and the odd man tend to stare at bigger breasts. It's just plain rude if someone can't see past your boobs to talk to your face and discover the person behind them. Some people also assume a girl with large breasts is older and more sexually experienced than she is (of course they are utter morons, but still it's annoying).

Some girls with very big breasts can develop a protective shyness and physical problems. Big breasts can be uncomfortable when it's hot, change a girl's balance while she gets used to them, and get in the way of activities such as sport. For some girls with very large breasts, carrying their weight can create headaches and back, neck and shoulder pain.

Girls with big breasts who feel they need physical support should get bras with wide shoulder straps and be professionally fitted by an assistant in a lingerie shop or section of a department store (see the 'Getting a Bra' section coming up). (Lingerie is French for underwear and is pronounced lon-jer-ray.)

A few women make the big decision to have breast reduction surgery: girls need to wait until their breasts have stopped growing (see the 'Cosmetic Surgery' section in Chapter 4, Body Image).

Love the ones you're with So any combo of size, shape and colour is normal, and you may as well learn to love or at least be friendly to your breasts no matter what they look like, and whether they point east, west, north or south-south-west. Don't waste time wondering why they don't look like your friends'. Your knees aren't the same either. (And whether or not you care what guys think, they love breasts no matter what size, shape and colour they are.)

> I am very 'slow-developing' in terms of breast size. They are virtually non-existent, even though all the other 15-year-olds around me have 'developed'. I am also very short, which makes me rather self-conscious. Lara, 15, Balmain, NSW

Do you need a bra?

Hundreds of millions of dollars are spent each year on ads telling you to buy bras. The lacier and prettier they are, the more bras usually cost. Companies get supermodels, singers or actresses to put their names to their bras (and matching undies) in the hope that you'll buy them thinking some of the glamour might rub off on your nipples.

But the basic reason for a bra is simple: to stop jiggling and bouncing, especially during strenuous activity. Bouncing breasts can cause pain, be annoying or attract unwanted staring. Only a bra made of metal could stop *all* jiggling, which would be uncomfortable and weird, so bras are really jiggle minimisers, not jiggle killers. (If you start a band called the Jiggle Killers please invite me to your first gig.)

Many girls only need a bra when they're doing bouncy things such as exercising, dancing or playing sport. If you don't mind a bit of bouncing, then you don't need one.

Bras don't stop your breasts from sagging when they get older, or from changing shape after pregnancy. The body ligaments that support your breasts should be allowed to do their work sometimes, instead of never being used because a bra is doing the work for them.

> If you are flat-chested you will get picked on and if you have got big boobs you'll get picked on.
>
> Rhonelle, 17, Springwood, NSW

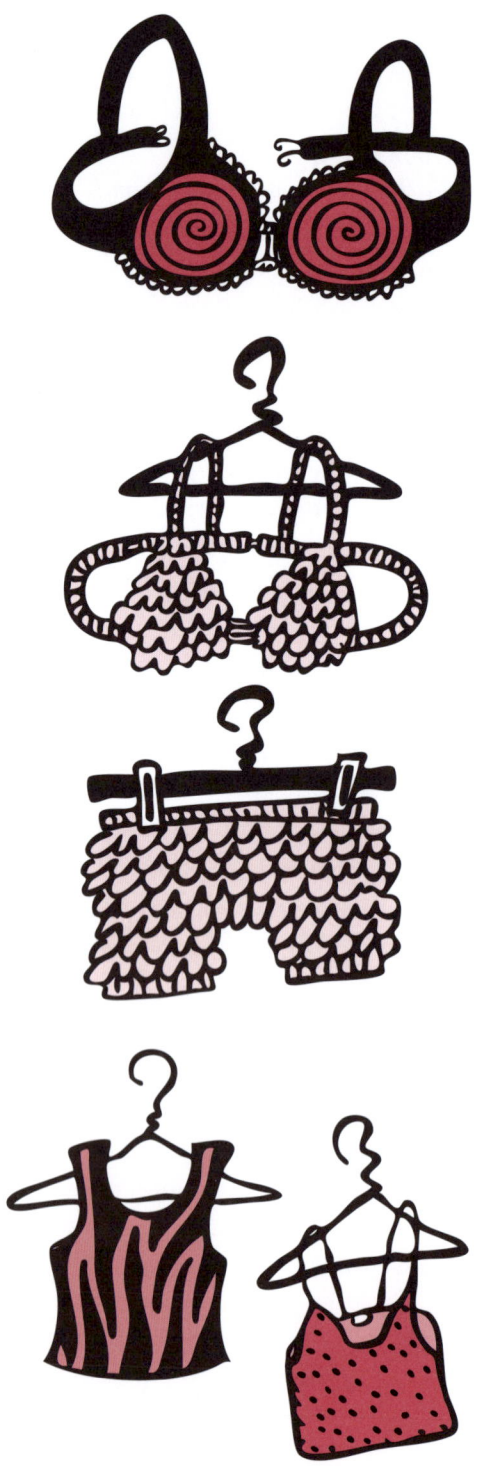

Bra alternatives Instead of a bra you can wear a camisole (a top with little straps) made of some stretchy fabric, or a crop- or tank-top. Some now have a double layer of fabric in the breast area, sometimes with a little elastic 'shelf' underneath, to cut down concern about visible nipples and the jiggle factor.

Getting a bra

A bra should be comfortable and not dig in or leave red marks when you take it off.

Bra sizes There are two parts to a bra size: the chest–back size and the cup size. It's important not only that the cups are the right size for your breasts, but that the bra is not too tight or too loose around the back. Most bras have adjustable shoulder straps, as the distance between shoulder and bazoomba varies. Your size will keep changing until your breasts stop growing.

> Let nature do what it has to do!
> Jennifer, 16, Christchurch, NZ
>
> People pay so much money for larger breasts but, I'm telling you now, being a DD is not that fun!
> Michelle, 17, Dandenong, Vic.

Some bras and crop-tops are sold as Small, Medium or Large, but most are sold in general clothes sizes (such as women's sizes 8, 10, 12, 14, 16 and so on), plus a cup size related to breast size (AA being the smallest, then A, B, C, D, DD – 'double D' – and so on through the alphabet). This means your size might be something like 10A or 12DD or 14B.

You can measure yourself with a tape measure, but translating your measurements into the right bra size can be tricky. Always take two measurements: one underneath the breasts and all the way around your body to get the general size; and the other all the way around your body from the largest point of your breasts for the cup size.

Many bra-selling websites will calculate your size once you've put in your two measurements (search Bra Size Calculator); but although cup sizes are the same the world over, clothing sizes aren't. If you're a 12 in Australia you'll be a 34 in American and UK brands and a 75 in European brands (except in France, where you'll be an 85, and Italy, where you're a 3).

> It just seems unfair that it happens to some girls so young. I was 7 when I first started developing breasts. I wasn't ready for it. Sophie, 15, Sydney, NSW

Having a bra fitting Ask an assistant in a lingerie department or shop to help you work out your size. Sales assistants do this all day long, fitting thousands of women a year. Just say, 'Hi, I need some help to work out my bra size.'

An experienced bra fitter will measure you accurately, make sure the size you get is right, and suggest styles or brands that suit you. Don't be afraid to ask for something cheaper or simpler.

More info on bra sizes

berlei.com.au/bra-size-calculator
You can work out your bra size, if you have a tape measure.

It's really upsetting when guys go 'She's hot, she's got a huge rack', when you just want them to look at your face and comment about your personality for once ... I also hate going shopping. Nothing fits me right and I end up leaving the mall with zero confidence.   Veronica, 15, Preston, Vic.

I love the changes that took place now. I would never have said that though while they were happening!

Ruby, 16, Orange, NSW

It was annoying that it [changing] was made a big deal. It happens to all girls so I didn't understand why everyone around me made it a big deal.
Billie, 17, Coffs Harbour, NSW

Older people constantly say they envy us for our youth, but what is the point of youth when you are so freaked out at your own body?

Sian, 15, Wollongong, NSW

I was comfortable with the changeover process from girl to womanhood as I felt it was relatively quick and barely noticeable.   Rachael, 17, Bendigo, Vic.

Your girly bits

Otherwise known as the Female Reproductive System, your girly bits include inside organs, and outsidey parts called genitals (pronounced jen-it-tals) by very serious medical staff, who need to loosen up and wear a party hat occasionally.

Even though you don't need all the female equipment inside you yet, your body is making sure it's ready in case one day you want to have a baby. Already it has been producing hormones with particular jobs to do. The main hormones for girls and women are:

- oestrogen (pronounced ees-tro-jen)
- progesterone (pronounced pro-jes-ter-own).

When your body starts to produce a lot more oestrogen it triggers the puberty changes. In a way the hormone tells your physical bits what to do.

The main hormone for guys and men is testosterone (tes-tos-ter-own), but we girls have a little bit of it too (and guys and men have some oestrogen).

Insidey bits

The following are the girly bits hidden away inside you.

- **Ovaries** These are two little glands that start off the size of a raisin (or an almond, depending on the snack habits of the doctor you ask) and grow to about walnut size in your teens. During pregnancy they will be the size of a fruit-and-nut chocolate bar. (No, I made that up.) Ovaries make the oestrogen and, on instructions from your brain, send it out around your body. Each ovary contains thousands of eggs smaller than this full stop. Each egg is called an ovum (the plural is ova). The ovaries' job is to ovulate: one of them releases an egg each month into a fallopian tube (they usually take it in turn).
- **Fallopian tubes** These two tiny, narrow tubes lead down from the ovaries to the uterus. They are usually 7 to 12 centimetres long, and as thick as a strand of wool on their outside but as narrow as a piece of cotton inside. If, on its way along one of the tubes, an egg is fertilised by a sperm, you'll become pregnant. This can happen if you have sex with a guy without using contraception (more on this in Chapter 16, Sex).

Being 16, in the middle of my teen years, I can slowly see myself becoming a young woman.   Donna, 16, Vic.

- **Uterus** (pronounced you-ter-us) Also known as the womb, the uterus grows during your teens from the size of a thumb to about the size of a (hollow) upside-down pear. If you ever have a baby in there, the uterus will grow along with the baby so that it always fits, and then shrink back to pear size afterwards.
- **Cervix** (pronounced ser-vicks) This spongy disk at the bottom of your uterus has a small opening leading into your vagina. The opening will stretch to about 10 centimetres wide during childbirth, to allow the baby to pass from the uterus into the vagina and out into the world. (This stretching doesn't happen at any other time.)
- **Vagina** (pronounced vaj-eye-nar) This is a passage of stretchy skin leading into your body from the middle opening between your legs (the one between the openings for wee and poo). This is where your period blood comes out, it's where a penis will go if you have sex with a guy, and it's where a baby will come out if you have one (unless it's delivered by a caesarean operation).

> ### Don't harass your vagina
>
> In the 1950s, women were told in ads to scrub their vulva in nasty, stinging disinfectant. Oh, they were such amateurs back then. Only one product to sell women by convincing them their lady garden needed weed-whacking, pesticide spraying and some lanterns strung up for a party? There's now a whole list of cosmetic vagina products, all of which are a baaaaad idea.
>
> Some women even subject their vulvas to 'deodorants', waxing, shaving, plucking, exfoliators, labia dyes, make-up, even stuck-on 'crystals' and sequins. Often they're literally buying themselves a problem: usually infections and itches.
>
> Your vagina is 'self-cleaning' and doesn't need any extra decoration, perfumes, or faffing with.

Outsidey bits

You can see your pubic mound – that plump, roundish area of skin where your pubic hair is going to be or is already – if you stand in front of a mirror, especially if you look at yourself sideways.

You can look at your girly bits between your legs with a small hand-mirror. You may want to lock the bedroom or bathroom door before making your inspection: this isn't a good time to be surprised by a visitor. 'I'm just plucking my eyebrows' isn't really going to be all that believable when the hand-mirror is between your thighs. Okay, now let's take a guided tour.

- **Vulva** This is the name for the whole area between your legs. Look at that, all pink and sort of glistening and possibly hairy here and there. Ignore hair-removal product claims, porn pics (they're altered to make some things less hidden) and advertisers of the totally dodgy idea of cosmetic genital 'surgery'. Unless you are getting a physical problem from your bits, you're totally in the range of 'normal' when it comes to hair, various sizes of bits, etc.
- **Labia majora** (pronounced lay-bee-ah ma-jor-rah), **or outer labia** These are the large 'lips' that surround and protect the vagina's entrance (and the front opening, where wee comes out). Pubic hair grows here too. A lot of girls think their 'lips' are too big, or too small, or too uneven – but all variations are absolutely normal. When you have sexy feelings there is a rush of blood to this area and it can feel tingly, tender and hot.
- **Labia minora** (pronounced lay-bee-ah my-nor-rah), **or inner labia** If you pull your outer labia lips open you will see that inside there are two other lips, which don't have hair on them. They look a bit like two teeny tongues. They may be barely visible or long and thick, they can range from light pink to purplish or dark brown, and one lip can be bigger than the other. The labia are like curtains that can be parted, and make a nice spongy covering over your vagina opening. (Lots of artists have portrayed the entrance to the vagina as a beautiful, delicate flower.)
- **Vagina opening and hymen** The hymen is a stretchy piece of skin, with a few blood vessels, which surrounds and perhaps covers some of the vagina opening, found between your labia. Your hymen has one hole or a few holes in it so that period blood can come out, and over the years it stretches or 'tears' painlessly. After that's happened – usually when you're dancing or playing sport of some kind – it looks sort of like a little scrunchie, or a donut with a hole in the middle. Most girls don't even feel it when their hymen stretches or breaks. (Some girls don't have a hymen at all, which is not a problem, so don't worry if you can't see yours.)

> As the years go on, you get more and more used to talking about things like that.
> Bianca, 15, Lake Macquarie, NSW

🌀 **Clitoris** (pronounced kli-tor-iss)   This is a small round bump that all girls have. At the front where the inner labia meet there's a skin fold called the clitoral hood, which connects to your clitoris. If you pull the hood up with your fingers you can get a better look at the little bump. Its only purpose is to make you feel good when it's touched in the right way (you don't have to make use of it yet, but it will be there when you need it). This is the most sensitive part of your body – made from the same sort of skin as the tip of a penis. If you touch your clitoris with your finger you'll probably feel a slight tingle. If you gently rub it you'll probably feel a harder bit underneath, which is its shaft.

While you're down there with your hand-mirror you may also see your urethra (or, if you prefer the classier title, wee-hole): between the clitoris and the vagina opening is another hood-like shape housing the teeny urinary opening (so teeny that you may not be able to see it easily), where your wee comes out.

Furthest towards your back you'll be able to see your anus, or bottom hole, where your poo comes out. It's separated from the vulva by a little area of flat skin called the perineum (pronounced perry-nee-um).

More info on your girly bits

Most diagrams and photos of girly bits are a bit over the top – they're either medical-textbooky or show very unusual, diseased or strange girly bits.

So What is a Vulva Anyway?
Booklet made for young girls with a better class of diagram, available by searching the title at brook.org.uk. Made by the British Society for Paediatric and Adolescent Gynaecology and the Brook organisation for sexual health for young people. Other vulva pics are at labialibrary.org.

en.wikipedia.org/wiki/Vulva and en.wikipedia.org/wiki/Clitoris
Diagrams and facts about girly bits and real photos (unless somebody's hacked in and left a picture of the Prime Minister).

If you're worried, a good place to get your girly bits checked out is your local GP or your nearest Family Planning clinic.

familyplanningallianceaustralia.org.au
Choose services, then select your state or territory to find your nearest clinic.

🥝 **familyplanning.org.nz**
Family Planning Association NZ. From the main page choose Find a Clinic.

After 3 years of despising my vagina I learned that everything I was terrified of and running away from was all inside my head.

Clare, commenting at labiaproject.com

Clear or white stuff

You'll start to notice on your undies the clear or white secretions (pronounced sec-ree-shuns) that come out of your vagina. All girls and women have these secretions. Around the time of ovulation, when there's an egg ready to be fertilised, the stuff is usually clearer and thinner (easier for sperm to swim through). When it dries on your underpants it can look yellowy and dusty.

These secretions are always a small amount, like a dab of clear jam – nothing that anyone else would ever notice – but they're why companies try to sell you 'everyday pads' or 'panty pads' so you can feel 'fresh'. The pads just soak up the little bit of stuff. These pads have only been around for the last few years: they're expensive and you don't have to use them. As long as you wear new undies and wash every day you will be fresh and clean.

If you have a very thick, lumpy secretion (sometimes called a discharge) or one that smells kind of 'off', and your vulva feels itchy or as if it's burning when you wee, these could be signs of an infection that needs treatment to make it go away. (You don't have to have had sex for this discharge to happen.) Any secretion that's unusual for you, or happens between periods and seems red, brown or another tinge or colour, should be checked by your local doctor or nearest Family Planning clinic. There's more info about infections in Chapter 7, Body Health.

> Girls find it hard to talk about things like this. Even though we are all going through the same thing you still feel a little uncomfortable. Now that I'm 15 my girlfriends and I, we joke about it. We are so over it! **Leisl, 15, Stratford, Vic.**

> **I think that it sucks that you go through all of these physical changes in the first twenty years of your life, then the rest of it is just boring.**
> Kelly, 16, Kelso, Qld

> At first I found the changes in my body scary and alien – almost disgusting. Now I've grown used to it I am sort of happy to look like a woman rather than a girl.
> Amy, 15, Sydney, NSW

> A lot of girls will actually be so upset when they have to mature! **Alysha, 17, Alton Downs, Qld**

> **Is there any way that I can hurry the process up?**
> Shell, 15, Camden, NSW

Your period

Here's a reminder of why you get a period. About once a month after the oestrogen call has gone out – 'Release the egg!' – and one of your ovaries has popped out a teeny egg, the egg tootles off, heading for the uterus.

The call goes out to the ovary...

Although it only has 10 or so centimetres to travel down the nearest fallopian tube, the egg can take about two or three days to get there – your eggs may be potentially miraculous but they are not speedy. The egg hangs around in the fallopian tube in case a sperm turns up to fertilise it. If this doesn't happen, the egg finally gives up, dawdles down into the uterus and dissolves away to nothing.

While it has been waiting for the egg, your uterus has grown a lovely soft lining of endometrium (pronounced endo-me-tree-um). A fertilised egg can implant itself and grow in the special blood cells of the endometrium. If the egg isn't fertilised, or if it is but your body decides it isn't a good one, the uterus packs it all in and sends the lining down the chute, as a period. The endometrium slowly breaks down into blood and begins to slide away, down the walls of the uterus, through the cervix into the vagina, and then out between your legs.

A menstrual (pronounced men-strewl) period, which is the technical term, usually lasts four to six days. Five to nine days after your period finishes, another egg is released from an ovary and the whole palaver starts all over again.

When to get ready

Because most girls get their first period anywhere between the ages of 9 and 15, as you've seen earlier, it's a good idea to be ready by having some pads in your bedroom or bathroom, and school bag.

> It's much less exciting once it actually happens to you. I can't believe I was so worried that it would never happen!
> Gillian, 15, Kareela, NSW

> **Periods suck!!!** Clare, 15, Vermont, Vic.

> **FACT**
>
> **Other names for periods** Menses (doctor-speak); the monthly (very old-fashioned Nanna word); Fred; a little visitor; having the painters in; women's troubles; and the curse (calm down, everybody!). I've even heard of Rebooting the Ovarian Operating System, but I think we can stop right there.

What to expect

The first time it happens you'll see the red period blood on your undies. Sometimes you'll feel the blood come out of your vagina or sense some wetness between your legs, but often you won't.

How much blood comes out during a period? Although it may seem as if a lot of blood is coming out, the actual amount is very small. Your whole period is about 2–3 tablespoons of liquid.

Some girls will bleed only a little; others more, or will have some clots (which look a bit like dark red jam) – this is just because some of the endometrium cells are clumped together rather than being liquid.

Generally the amount of blood is heaviest at the start, then gets less and less and finally fades to nothing. More than two-thirds of a period's total blood usually slides out in the first two or three days.

If it seems to you like the bleeding is too much or going on for too long, or there's a lot more than usual, see your doctor.

What colour should the blood be? Often on the first day of your period the blood is bright red, then it can become rust-coloured or browner towards the end as it gets 'older'. As blood dries on a pad it also goes browner.

Does period blood smell? Period blood does have the very faintest of odours – but nothing that another person would be able to smell as long as you change pads and tampons every 2 to 4 hours during the day and wash regularly. It's only 'old' blood that tends to smell noticeably as the air gets to it.

> I was the first at my school to get my period and it was so embarrassing. Marnie, 14, Yarraville, Vic.

Attitudes to periods

There are two extremes when it comes to the image of periods and menstrual blood. One is the ludicrous superstition and centuries-old ignorance and misunderstanding that says it's unclean and dirty, even evil or impure. These attitudes persist today in some cultures.

At first, having your periods can seem dirty or weird: it isn't. Having your period is natural, and after the first few times it actually just seems a bit boring and routine.

The other extreme attitude to periods is a deeply hippie, goddess-based nature worship that says everything about any period is natural and divine, the menstrual cycle is an airy-fairy oobly-doobly mystery that doesn't bear tampering with under any circumstances, and anything that interferes with that 'natural' process is wrong and bad, even if you're in pain. (And if you were more in touch with your 'natural womanliness' you wouldn't feel the pain or have a problem.) These people hate the Pill or any other ways of altering the menstrual cycle.

God knows I'm all in favour of vulvas, and heartily approve of any menstrual cycles that are working properly and don't hurt, and I believe we should all be entirely comfortable with our menstrual blood, but if there's a problem, see a doctor, because no amount of 'I just need time to go on a campfire retreat chanting and positive thinking' will cure a physical problem you need some medical help with.

Period tracking

Using an app on your phone, or your school diary, a calendar or a personal organiser, you can keep a record so you know when to expect your next period. Count twenty-eight days on from the first day of your last period, then record 'period due' (or you can mark the due date with a half moon or other secret symbol). Obviously if you find your period tends to come on Day Twenty-nine, or follows some other pattern, count and mark accordingly.

Some period app makers can share your information with other companies such as when you missed a period or when you note having sex. They can also use the info to target you with ads. To avoid this, check privacy settings or don't use a period app.

If you want to be old-school, you can use a photocopy or scan of the period calendar given on the page opposite. You can also record different symptoms on it, using a code (which is helpful for a doctor if you have period pain or other worries).

Period calendar

Circle each day you have your period and you'll soon see if it's 'regular' and how long it usually goes for. You can also add little notes in code to record other symptoms.* Add whatever else you want to factor in.

Jan 1	29	26	25	22	20	17	15	12	9	7	4	2	30
2	30	27	26	23	21	18	16	13	10	8	5	3	31
3	31	28	27	24	22	19	17	14	11	9	6	4	Jan 1
4	Feb 1	[29]	28	25	23	20	18	15	12	10	7	5	2
5	2	Mar 1	29	26	24	21	19	16	13	11	8	6	3
6	3	2	30	27	25	22	20	17	14	12	9	7	4
7	4	3	31	28	26	23	21	18	15	13	10	8	5
8	5	4	Apr 1	29	27	24	22	19	16	14	11	9	6
9	6	5	2	30	28	25	23	20	17	15	12	10	7
10	7	6	3	May 1	29	26	24	21	18	16	13	11	8
11	8	7	4	2	30	27	25	22	19	17	14	12	9
12	9	8	5	3	31	28	26	23	20	18	15	13	10
13	10	9	6	4	Jun 1	29	27	24	21	19	16	14	11
14	11	10	7	5	2	30	28	25	22	20	17	15	12
15	12	11	8	6	3	Jul 1	29	26	23	21	18	16	13
16	13	12	9	7	4	2	30	27	24	22	19	17	14
17	14	13	10	8	5	3	31	28	25	23	20	18	15
18	15	14	11	9	6	4	Aug 1	29	26	24	21	19	16
19	16	15	12	10	7	5	2	30	27	25	22	20	17
20	17	16	13	11	8	6	3	31	28	26	23	21	18
21	18	17	14	12	9	7	4	Sep 1	29	27	24	22	19
22	19	18	15	13	10	8	5	2	30	28	25	23	20
23	20	19	16	14	11	9	6	3	Oct 1	29	26	24	21
24	21	20	17	15	12	10	7	4	2	30	27	25	22
25	22	21	18	16	13	11	8	5	3	31	28	26	23
26	23	22	19	17	14	12	9	6	4	Nov 1	29	27	24
27	24	23	20	18	15	13	10	7	5	2	30	28	25
28	25	24	21	19	16	14	11	8	6	3	Dec 1	29	26

*Code   S: spotting   B: bleeding   HB: heavy bleeding   DP: dull pain   C: cramps   BC: bad cramps
T: tearful   G: grumpy   SB: sore bosoms

change ☀ BODY   29

Your menstrual cycle

The pattern of hormonal changes, egg release and periods is called your menstrual cycle, and each cycle has a period about every twenty-eight days – but some people have cycles that are a bit longer or shorter than this, or vary a bit from month to month. Day One of your menstrual cycle is Day One of your period.

Even though you will usually have a period each month, it may not be like that when you start. You may get the first one, then go for a couple of months before the next one, and so on. That's fine – eventually you'll settle down.

See the 'Reasons to See the Doctor' box coming up if there's something about your cycle that you think you should maybe check out.

Pre-period hassles

After a while you may start to recognise when your period is on the way. Known as premenstrual syndrome (PMS), the symptoms in the few days before a period can include:

- feeling tearful
- being clumsy
- getting grumpy
- having fuller breasts and/or a bloated tum (don't worry, that's not because there's heaps of blood to come out but because your body is retaining other fluid).

Symptoms can vary wildly between people. If PMS is getting in the way of enjoying life you need help.

How to fight PMS

- To help reduce fluid retention, wee a lot. Drink plenty of water and cut down on dehydrating salty foods (check the ingredients on a packet and if salt, or sodium, is high on the list give the food a miss), caffeine (it's in coffee, chocolate, colas, and energy and guarana drinks) and alcohol.
- To stop fuller, tender breasts feeling sore, try a firm crop-top or bra.
- To keep your energy on the level, eat healthy snacks between meals (that doesn't mean a Snickers bar – it means a small handful of almonds and some vegies or fruit).

> To help with period pain either curl up with a book and a cup of something warm and a hot water bottle, or do some stretches. That helps. That and sleep. Sharon, 15, St Kilda, Vic.

Natural therapists and herbalists may prescribe a range of herbal, vitamin and mineral supplements to deal with the general symptoms, often with an emphasis on vitamin B6, magnesium, vitamin E and evening primrose oil. (Make sure your herbalist belongs to the National Herbalists Association of Australia. Natural therapists should belong to the Australian Natural Therapists Association.) Not all doctors agree that this can help. Homeopathic 'remedies' can't and won't help (see Chapter 7, Body Health, to find out why).

> When you first get your period you need someone to talk about it with. I needed that but didn't really have anyone.
> Rachelle, 15,
> Glasshouse Mountains, Qld
>
> Periods shouldn't be so secret.
> Antonia, 14,
> Malvern, Vic.

Doctors sometimes suggest going on the Pill (which adjusts hormone levels), but this usually has more effect on the length and heaviness of the period than on the PMS symptoms.

Period pain

Most girls don't have any pain for the first few years of periods. Some girls get pains called cramps, which are often a squeezy feeling, usually in the first day or so of their period. That's because the uterus actually *is* squeezing a bit, trying to help the blood slide out. Sometimes you can feel the individual cramps; sometimes there's a dull achy or draggy feeling in your lower tummy area (but it's nothing to do with your stomach where you digest your food).

Ways to deal with the pain

- Put up with it – this only works if the pain is slightly annoying rather than seriously hurty.
- Do some exercise – walking and swimming are good because they won't stress the body or bounce sore breasts too much. Exercising before your period's due is the best, and can stop some pain.
- Find some relaxing activities (cramps can be worse if you're stressed) – these can include

taking a nice warm bath, meditation, or gentle yoga over the month, but ask your yoga teacher which are the exercises not to do when you have a period because some make the pain worse.

- Put a warm (not boiling) hot-water bottle or wheat-bag on your tum.
- Take medicines that have an effect on the prostaglandin hormones causing cramps. Ask your doctor or chemist which one could be good for you. If the pain is bad enough for you to feel you need painkillers each month, see a doctor.
- Take herbal remedies prescribed by a qualified herbalist – some herbs make the uterus cramp less, some are 'warming' and some regulate hormones. Natural therapists may suggest supplements with omega 3 fatty acids, calcium and magnesium.
- Take the Pill if your doctor recommends it – many doctors prescribe it because it usually makes a period less painful and less heavy.

Stuff you need for periods

Otherwise known as 'feminine hygiene products', for gawd's sake, pads and tampons are the small, disposable items we use to soak up (absorb) period blood. You can buy them at all supermarkets and chemists and most corner shops, milk bars and convenience stores.

When they're just starting periods, most girls try pads first because they don't feel ready to use tampons, which are pushed up inside the vagina. (If you're a virgin a tampon doesn't change that – there's more on this in Chapter 16, Sex.)

Sometimes a pad or tampon will take in all the blood it can absorb within a couple of hours during those first days when most of the blood comes out (often called 'heavy' days), so you should change it every few hours.

There are pads and tampons made of cotton, with no chemical additives to help absorption, that are sold as 'natural' alternatives. These are way less absorbent than synthetic ones with chemical additives and may need to be changed a lot more often.

Pads

A pad is rectangular, with curved ends (sort of like a surfboard – one of its nicknames). It has a sticky strip on the back: you stick the back to the inside of your undies' gusset (the bit between your legs). Before ways to make them more absorbent were invented, pads of yesteryear were up to 4 centimetres thick: wearing one felt like having a single mattress in your undies. (And before they were invented, girls had to wear folded-up rags in their pants, which they then had to wash out by hand and re-use.)

When to change a pad On the heavier days of your period you'll need to change the pad up to every 2 hours, then later every 4 hours (whether there's much blood or not), to be fresh and clean. This can be hard when you're stuck on a school bus trip. Bigger, 'overnighter' pads are good for these times, but it's best not to wear any kind of pad for longer than 4 hours during the day.

Types of pads

- Panty pads/liners: these are just to keep your pants fresh and protected from non-period vaginal shenanigans (see the 'Clear or White Stuff' section earlier) and are definitely not absorbent enough to deal with the period flow.
- Ultra-thin pads: they are very thin but have a lot of absorbency.
- Regular, super and overnighter pads: the terms indicate their different degrees of absorbency, but all are more absorbent than the ultra-thins. During your first few periods you probably won't need anything more than regular, but see how you go.

Tampons

A tampon is a super-compressed roll of absorbent material. It has a rounded tip to make it slide more easily into the vagina, and a securely attached string at the other end, which you pull gently on to drag it out.

A tampon is less messy than a pad because it soaks up the blood before it comes out of your body. You can swim with a tampon in – you can't swim with a pad because it will swell up with water. Only one tampon should be used at a time.

PADS of yesteryear were much more obvious...

1978

Be careful where you put your adhesive strip...

When to change a tampon Like pads, tampons need to be changed every couple of hours on heavy days, and no kind of tampon should be worn for more than 4 hours max or all night because of the rare chance of the dangerous infection toxic shock syndrome (see the 'Reasons to See the Doctor' box opposite).

You need to wash your hands before you touch a tampon that you're about to use.

Types of tampons

- Slim, extra-slim and super-slim – these thinner-than-ordinary tampons are for young girls having their first few periods.
- 'Silky' ones – these are designed to slip in and come out more easily, and are also good for girls new to tampons.
- Light, regular (or medium) and super (or heavy) – the super ones (the most absorbent tampons) can be used during the first couple of days or for heavy periods.
- Tampons with applicators – each tampon has a small, disposable cardboard 'syringe' to push it up inside you.
- Twinpacks – these usually combine packs of super and regular tampons so that you can use the supers in the first couple of days, then move on to the regulars.

Getting a tampon in First lock the door of the bedroom, bathroom or toilet for privacy. It's easiest if you lie on a bed with your legs open, or you squat, or you stand with one foot on the toilet lid or the edge of the bath. Follow the instructions on the pamphlet inside the box of tampons, and unravel the tampon string before you start.

You may need to practise lots of times. Start with slimline tampons, and don't worry if you fluff up the ends of a couple trying to get them in. Just chuck them away.

Try to relax when you're putting in a tampon, and always point and push it slightly towards the small of your back, rather than straight up towards your head.

A tampon also needs to be pushed a little way up from the entrance of your vagina, otherwise it'll be uncomfortable all the time. When it's correctly in place you can't feel it. (Sometimes when you're wearing a tampon the string will end up in a position that annoys your vulva – you just need to get to a loo and move the string.)

You can't push the tampon in too far – you'll always be able to reach the string, even if it gets a bit bunched up just inside your vagina. You can't lose a tampon inside you because it's too big to get pushed up out of the vagina, through the tiny cervix opening and into the uterus.

Reasons to see the doctor

* You haven't had your first period before you're 16 (lots of girls don't so there's probably nothing wrong).

* You think there's too much blood; or there's more than usual (you have to change a pad or tampon more than every 2 or 3 hours).

* Your period lasts for more than seven days or less than three.

* You get pain that interferes with your life (you can't go to school or work or play sport).

* You have little bleeds or 'spotting' between periods. It's very common in teenagers, but can also be the symptom of something you need treatment for.

* Your periods, after becoming regular, stop for more than two months. This can be a sign of body stress, too much exercise, not enough food, some illnesses or pregnancy.

* Being a girl doesn't mean you have to get periods. Some girls never have any periods because of medical issues. Some girls and women take the Pill 'non-stop' for months or years, for medical or other reasons. You need to see a doctor to get a prescription. For more on the Pill, which isn't suitable for everyone, see page 389.

Toxic shock: a rare emergency

If you have the symptoms of **toxic shock syndrome** this is a medical emergency, so go straight to a doctor or hospital casualty department and say you need immediate help.

Toxic shock, a very rare infection, is caused by bacteria that can develop if you leave a tampon in for a long time.

Symptoms include a sudden very high fever, a rash similar to sunburn, vomiting, watery diarrhoea, confusion, muscle pain and headache.

Even if you don't use tampons, having those symptoms together means you need medical help absolutely immediately.

Always tell the doctor about any pills or medicines you have been taking, including herbal treatments and vitamin supplements.

If tampons still hurt when you're practising, try again with new ones another time – you can always use pads in the meantime.

When you want to change a tampon, pull gently on the string. If your vagina is dry and there is hardly any blood a tampon might feel a little resistant, but don't worry – the string won't break.

Menstrual cups

Menstrual cups are re-usable silicone cups you insert into your vagina that seal up against the cervix. They should be sterilised between periods. Follow the manufacturer's instructions on how to use and clean them: you'll need to practise at first. Because of the very small risk of toxic shock syndrome (explained on page 35), it's not recommended that you keep the same menstrual cup in for more than 10–12 hours. You can set a reminder on your phone in case you forget. Follow the cup manufacturer's instructions.

Absorbent period undies

You can buy absorbent period undies and swimwear with built-in pads. The pants can absorb 2–4 times as much as a tampon. You can also get re-usable pads. Washing instructions vary between brands: in most cases you just need a cold tap for rinsing and a cold-water machine wash. Order online to match your usual undies size.

Your period kit

You'll soon work out what you need, but here are some suggestions:
- tampons and/or pads or absorbent period undies
- baby wipes for washing yourself (although toilet paper is fine)
- spare undies in case you get blood on the pair you're wearing
- two or three folded-up small plastic bags for putting used pads or tampons in before you throw them in a bin
- two or three sandwich-sized brown-paper bags if you want to cover a see-through plastic bag.

Replace supplies the day you use them.

emergency period kits

'Emergencies'

If you're caught short without pads or tampons because you've run out of them, or your period has come unexpectedly, you can ask someone if they have a spare. (Women who

Disposal

Most public and school toilets have a sanitary bin next to each loo to put your used pad or tampon in. (Signs often call pads and tampons 'sanitary items'.) If there's no bin, you can put anything with blood on it in a plastic bag, then dispose of it in the nearest bin (or carry it in your period kit or bag until you can get to a bin at home). When you haven't got a bag with you, wrap the pad or tampon in toilet paper.

Don't try to flush a pad down the loo – this could cause an overflow, and a spectacular waterfall is not what you need right now. Tampons and baby wipes shouldn't be put down the loo either.

don't know each other often do this in public toilets.) Most adult women will carry tampons, but not pads.

A more reliable alternative is to make up a few little emergency period kits: a small make-up bag with a zip is perfect. You can keep one in your school bag, sports bag, backpack, school locker, work locker or desk, the glove box of the car, or a house at which you often stay – wherever you think would be handy. If all your friends also keep emergency kits you'll be able to help each other out.

Emergency clean-ups If there's a lot of blood on your undies and you think it could soak through onto whatever else you're wearing, take off your undies, fold them up as small as you can and put them in a plastic bag from your kit to take home to wash. Clean between your legs with your baby wipes (or tissues or toilet paper). Insert a new tampon, change into a new pair of absorbent period undies, or stick a new pad onto your emergency undies, and you're away.

Hiding bloodstains on clothes Sometimes blood can soak through to your outer clothes. Having a 'leak' or bloodstain on your clothes caused by a period is totally normal and nothing to be ashamed of. Some girls prefer to deal with it quickly and quietly. If you have a stain on your clothes that can't be privately or completely rinsed out, or you can't scoot home straight away to change, here are some possibilities:

- avoid wearing white or a pale colour on your lower half if you're expecting, or already have, your period
- wear a jumper or jacket tied around your waist
- keep something to wear in your locker as a spare (or an old uniform if at work)
- see a school nurse or counsellor – they should be able to help you get sorted out
- ask a friend or another girl at school, or a woman if you're in a public place, to

help you – most women have experienced this problem at least once
- if you're at a friend's house, borrow something to wear or ask their mum to help.

Stain etiquette If someone has a stain on their skirt or pants don't blurt the fact out in front of everyone. Talk privately and quietly to her. Help by lending her some clothes or giving her something from your emergency kit. Don't tell other people what's happened.

Make a pact with your friends that you'll keep on stain alert for each other, and that you'll handle telling each other discreetly. It's comforting to know that your friends are having the same experiences, and talking about them. And sharing information will help you deal confidently with the whole big deal of periods, and give you all an extra bond.

> Why does everyone think that getting your period is embarrassing? Everyone will get it.
> Alysha, 14, Wellington, NZ

> Periods. Must. DIE.
> Alice, 17, Mt Macedon, Vic.

More info on periods

Your local doctor or community health centre or school nurse can answer any questions about your period, and so can the Family Planning Australia Healthline (see 'More Info on Body Changes' earlier).

mum.org
A wacky online museum of historical products, names and attitudes to periods.

[At first it's] scary, but after a couple of years it's actually normal. It's just like: 'Another period, how annoying!' But it's no big drama.   Rachel, 15, Grovedale, Vic.

I was actually 9 and a half when I got my period.   Janne, 18, Thornbury, Vic.

At the time, getting my period was a terrible and scary thing, and I was fully developed by the age of about 14. It's something we all go through, and nothing to worry about.
Caitlin, 17, Geelong, Vic.

When I first got my period I noticed the pad so much and could feel it, I thought everyone would be able to see it: but no one can.   Jemima, 16

Periods are not that bad, just a bit annoying.   Jess, 15

SKIN

2

Skin wraps us up; helps to keep us warm or cool; sends us messages about what we're touching; and occasionally checks our diary and sees that we have an important event coming up, then immediately erupts into an obvious, **throbbing** red spot the size of Argentina, called a pimple, which makes us want to scra-heeeeeeam the house down.

Most of the billions of dollars spent on skin cosmetics every year comes from women wanting to look younger (but without the pimples). So your teenage skin is actually a **highly** fashionable commodity, dahling, I'll have you know.

39

The skin on your face

You've inherited your skin from your ancestors, which determines what colour it is and whether your face is prone to scarring, freckles, pimples, dimples or wrinkles. Cosmetics companies refer to skin 'types' on the labels of their products to try to convince people they need special stuff (which is sometimes true).

These skin types are:

- oily (also tactfully known as 'teenage', 'troubled' or 'problem') – shiny skin that may have larger-than-average pores (tiny openings in the skin)
- dry – lacks oil and moisture, and is more prone to flaking, rough, dry patches, or eczema
- normal – no problems (possibly fictitious)
- combination – a mix of oily, normal or dry patches on your face
- sensitive – the skin tends to react, with a rash or redness, to cosmetic ingredients, heat, allergens and alcohol (skin products that are non-fragranced and 'hypo-allergenic' are usually best for sensitive skin)
- problem – prone to pimples and blackheads. Products labelled 'oil free' and 'non-comedogenic' (won't block pores) are better for skin that's prone to pimples.

Skin products

Nobody needs to cleanse, tone and moisturise every day. You will probably just need to clean your face. You don't need a toner, and you probably don't need a moisturiser most of the time.

Cleanser Wash your face morning and night. Some people clean their face with soap as well as water, but soap can dry out your skin because it washes off the natural oils that skin needs.

> Some days it feels as though the oil crisis could be solved by the amount of oil on my skin.
>
> Charlotte, 17, East Doncaster, Vic.

The sort of cleanser to buy is one that's:
- mild and non-perfumed (or a soap substitute), and specifically for the face, not a body wash
- oil free, which will help cut down the oil on your face.

Moisturiser A moisturiser is used to stop skin getting too dry. Your skin can become too dry if you over-wash it, have very hot baths, wax or shave, go out in the sun or swimming a lot, or spend most of your time in air-conditioned or heated buildings. And when that happens your body can be fooled into making more oil, causing blockages and pimples.

A lot of people don't need a moisturiser for their face (or body). Most girls, especially those in humid climates, or those who drink lots of water and have enough oils in their diet from nuts and fish, probably won't need one. See Chapter 5, Food, for details on what to eat and drink.

When choosing a moisturiser for your face, buy one:
- from a mid-range known brand, not a mysteriously cheap one from the $2 shop – but don't assume expensive is better than mid-range
- with a sunscreen, of SPF (sun protection factor) 30+, unless you have very dark skin (see the 'Sun Protection for All Skin Types' box later in this chapter)
- matching your skin colour if it's a tinted moisturiser
- that's labelled for the face – body ones are more likely to block pores.

If you have very dry body skin you may need a body moisturiser: ask your doctor or chemist to recommend one.

Scrubs and exfoliators These have crunchy little 'beads', or particles, in them that are abrasive – rather like salt – so they scrub off dead skin cells. They're not good for skin that's sensitive. Most teens don't need to use one on their face: washing it twice a day, using a face washer, should be enough to get rid of dead skin cells.
- Don't scrub too hard – it can make you go red and flaky.
- Don't use a facial exfoliator more than once a week.
- Don't use a body scrub on your face.

Toner Nobody needs a toner (also called an astringent). Toners have chemicals to make your face feel briefly tingly

Beware of SCRUBS

Allergies and skin reactions

All chemicals and natural products, even organic ones, can cause a reaction. Some products that are claimed to be 'hypoallergenic' or 'all-natural' or 'low-allergy' could still cause a skin irritation or allergy. Essential oils and some skin medication can also cause a rash. You can test a product by putting it on a patch of your skin (many people use the inside of the elbow area because it's easy to dab and easy to see any reaction). Leave it there for forty-eight hours without washing it off, and see whether any reaction develops.

or tight, but don't do anything to change or protect your skin. Some contain alcohol, which is drying. Toners can't make your pores smaller or improve your skin, and don't get rid of blackheads. Toners are just an expensive, stinging, useless liquid.

Cosmetics companies' claims

Companies are competing for those billions of dollars in cosmetics profits, so they have to spend big money on advertising and make huge claims about their products (next to a picture of a girl who's never had a pimple in her entire life).

The more money a company spends on TV and magazine ads, the more they charge for their products – so the more expensive stuff isn't necessarily better for your skin.

Don't get sucked in by the companies' ridiculous claims. They can pretty much lie about what their products do because government authorities hardly ever bother taking them to court. I guess the authorities must be busy. Possibly getting their hair done.

There are a lot of ways in which big companies try to make you buy their products (see Chapter 21, Shopping, for the full lowdown). Here are some things to look out for in cosmetics ads.

Skin cream fibs Skin creams you buy at a supermarket or pharmacy (chemist shop) or order online can't change the way your skin grows, whatever the ads suggest. Stuff you put on your skin helps to clean it or stop moisture evaporating, or makes the very top layer a bit moister, but there is no magic ingredient that can alter the nature of your skin. Any real changes happen from the inside (see the 'Hints for a Healthy Skin' box on the opposite page).

Hints for a healthy skin

✱ Eat well: good nourishment shows in your skin (more in Chapter 5, Food).

✱ Drink lots of water: this helps your digestion and food absorption, and keeps your body and skin hydrated (although drinking more water doesn't stop pimples).

✱ Exercise regularly: this increases blood flow to the skin, which helps clean up and repair any skin problems (see Chapter 6, Move).

✱ Avoid cigarette smoke and smoking: they cause dull, discoloured skin and early wrinkles (see Chapter 11, Drugs).

'Natural' claims Some cosmetics companies sell 'natural' products. This doesn't automatically mean they're good.

Potions made from natural ingredients may be less effective than some synthetic ones, or just be a cheap lotion with an added natural fragrance (which is still a chemical) or a natural ingredient that doesn't really do anything but sounds impressive and so they can charge more for it. Natural products usually need to have chemical preservatives added so they don't go 'off' on the shelf. Many people are allergic to synthetic chemicals; others are allergic to common natural ingredients such as citrus, mint, tea tree and eucalyptus oils, and witch-hazel.

Don't fall for a claim made on the label that it's 'chemical-free'. Everything, even water and pure air, is made up of chemicals. Sometimes it says the product is 'free of harmful chemicals' – but that doesn't mean the other products *do* contain harmful chemicals.

'Organic' products can be made from ingredients or crops produced without pesticides, and can be better for the environment. But an 'organic' product won't necessarily work better and non-organic products are not automatically bad for you. (The same goes for hair products: see Chapter 3, Hair.)

More info on organic products

austorganic.com
Organic industry folk have rules and a logo on packaging that they say guarantees genuine organic products.

'Scientific' claims   Cosmetics companies tend to bang on hysterically about how 'scientific' their product is. If they'd really invented a cream that cured pimples in a day, or prevented wrinkles, it would have been on the news. The 'scientific breakthroughs' are almost always just a trick to get you to buy something new and expensive.

Most of the scientific-sounding ingredient names given in the ads are just completely made up by the company selling the skin product, like Enzyme B27 with Phyto-gel, New Dermfill Claro-spraunce with Cell-lift and . . . Well, you get the idea.

Exact percentages, kinda   You can't measure whether a skin is '86 per cent brighter', or a product has '93 per cent purifying efficiency' or is '71 per cent effective on imperfections'. This is just more advertising piffle. Sometimes I think three people stand in an elevator and make up numbers at random.

Claims you need a three- or four-step routine   A magazine or website may tell you that you need a complex three- or four-step beauty routine, using lots of products, because it's keeping its advertisers happy. The advertisers would *love* to sell you those products.

More info on looking after your face

choice.com.au
The independent Australian Consumers' Association site has product tests and info. For example, search Moisturisers or Acne.

Pimples and blackheads

As a teenager you can become so obsessed with looking at your new self, endlessly inspecting your body and face in the mirror, that you notice even a wee red dot and go through days of writhing torture thinking everyone is staring at your GIGANTIC PIMPLE: RULER OF THE UNIVERSE.

Some teenagers get just the occasional pimple or blackhead outbreak (which some doctors call acne), or the odd zit here and there. Others have a really big problem that they have to face in the mirror every day (often called severe acne). Nobody has to put up with a terrible pimple problem; there are ways of getting help.

These things DO NOT CAUSE pimples or blackheads:
- greasy food
- not exfoliating your skin
- not washing enough or properly
- not drinking enough water
- dirt or germs on the skin
- chocolate
- bad karma.

Getting pimples or blackheads is not your fault.

What causes pimples and blackheads?

If you have pimples or blackheads it's not because you're doing anything wrong, or failing to suck up to the Goddess of Clear Skin. You get teenage pimples and blackheads because one of your grandparents or parents had a similar problem: you inherited it (some disappointment if you were hoping for a small French castle instead).

For a blemish (pimple or blackhead) to form, you need a blockage in one of those tiny holes in your skin called a pore. Everyone has sebaceous (pronounced seb-ayshus) glands everywhere in their skin, which pump out small amounts of oily stuff called sebum (pronounced see-b'm). Sebum protects us. It's why when we get in a bath or go swimming we don't fill with water and puff up like a sponge. Well done, sebum. Fine work. Just leave it there, thanks. Sebum? Down, sebum! Down!

Damn. During the teen years you have more of the hormone androgen, which over-excites your sebaceous glands, which then pump out too much sebum, which then blocks the pores, causing pimples and blackheads.

Pimples

When a pore gets blocked by extra sebum, bacteria can grow underneath, causing inflammation – the pore gets cranky and turns red. Then as the bacteria build up white or yellow pus forms, which under pressure eventually rises to form a head on the surface of your skin. Now you have a pimple.

Or you may get what's called a blind pimple: it looks angry and red but never comes to a point. A blind pimple stays under the skin and the pus is eventually absorbed by the body.

Pimples can get worse during stressful times (such as before exams or a school dance) because hormones caused by stress make inflammation worse.

Can you believe that we have the greatest number of sebaceous glands on the *face*? I mean, why not the stomach, where at least we could hide them? You can also get pimples on your back, neck, buttocks, shoulders and chest. You know, just as a bonus.

Pimple scars Pimples can leave scars, particularly if you pick at them. Even blind pimples, which don't come to a head, can cause puckered scars. Scars can be very hard to hide or remove, so it's better to prevent them if you can.

How bad the damage is can depend more on whether a person is prone to scarring than on how many pimples they have or even whether they pick them. People with a tendency to scarring can include:

- those who get cysts (very deep pimples)
- anyone of Asian heritage
- those who know from childhood experience that they scar easily
- some people with sensitive skin.

Anyone prone to scarring should see an experienced dermatologist – a qualified skin specialist – as soon as they start getting pimples, and all scarring needs to be treated by one. Get a referral from a doctor (and see 'More Info' at the end of this section). Never go to somebody who advertises – good dermatologists don't need to advertise – or who calls themself a 'cosmetic surgeon' (they could be just a GP, not a skin specialist).

Fighting pimples   There are a few things you can do to try to stop pimples forming, or to hurry them along if they do arrive.

- Wash your skin every night to remove any excess surface oil and dead skin cells, which can clog your pores (but be gentle because too much washing and scrubbing can make your skin too dry, prompting your body to release more oil, and irritate any healing pimples). If your skin is very oily wash your face in the morning too.
- Make sure any gloop that goes on your face, whether it's make-up or a pimple lotion, doesn't clog pores (look for labels saying 'non-comedogenic' or 'non-acnegenic'; 'oil free' is also good).
- Wash sweat off after exercise or when it's very hot to avoid more blocked pores.
- Keep your hair clean and try to keep it off your face and neck, especially if you use 'product' (such as gels and moulding wax).
- Try not to touch your face, or rest your cheek or chin in your hand, as you will rub off any pimple cream you're using.
- Eat healthy food, which will help your immune system, which in turn will help your body fight bacteria (although it won't stop your sebaceous glands making the extra sebum). Eating oily or sugary foods doesn't *cause* pimples, but it doesn't help your system either.
- Avoid cigarette smoke, which blocks pores.

Squeezing pimples   Everyone says not to squeeze, and talks in hushed and horrified tones about scarring and bacteria, but don't be frightened, sometimes you need to 'pop' one. Remember, the body is trying to get the gunk out because there are bacteria underneath already and it's okay to help out if you don't want to go around with a throbbing, beacon-like, yellow-headed pimple.

Gently remove a 'head' that's ready to pop by lancing it carefully with a needle or pin tip. If you fancy, you can wipe it with a tissue or a little alcohol wipe afterwards to help it dry. But don't squeeze hard; if it isn't ready to go, stop. Otherwise you could cause a bigger problem that lasts longer than the pimple would have, by forcing the gunk somewhere else under the skin, or creating more redness, bleeding or a bruise.

> When my mum and sisters point out that I have a few pimples it affects me a lot because they are my sisters and mum.   Saskia, 16, Auckland, NZ

> This is my 7th year of having pimples. I have tried nearly everything but nothing seems to work. I'm just hoping for the day they disappear.   Evvie, 16

Covering up pimples   Any foundation make-up used to cover pimples should be oil free and matched to your skin colour. 'Cover sticks' made for adults are usually designed to disguise grey bags under the eyes so they're the wrong tint to hide red pimples.

Natural therapies   Natural therapists often suggest a vitamin supplement that includes B6 and zinc to reduce inflammation. Doctors say there's no evidence this helps. Herbal supplements and potions to regulate hormones must only be prescribed by a herbalist who is a member of the National Herbalists Association of Australia, or by a natural therapist belonging to the Australian Natural Therapists Association.

> I have some acne which I'm really touchy about. Even though nobody really cares, I do. People get like one pimple and go on and on about how bad it looks and they talk about it to me and my face is covered in them!!
> Sarah, 13, Sydney, NSW

Don't use a 'colloidal silver' preparation because it doesn't work and can be toxic (poisonous). It's very important that you don't use vitamin A except in a pimple preparation specifically prescribed by a doctor. Vitamin A supplements in the amount needed to attack pimples are toxic and can damage your liver. The vitamin A medications prescribed for pimples by doctors have had the toxic element removed.

Pimple washes and creams   Spend some time in the supermarket aisle or at the pharmacy working out which soaps, cleansers or pimple creams could be right for you. Talk to the pharmacist (the professional behind the prescriptions counter) about your skin, and ask them to show you different pimple stuff for your face in a range of prices. People go to the chemist all the time to ask for things to stick up their bum, so don't feel embarrassed asking about pimple creams. The chemist may recommend a cleanser or other face wash, and a pimple cream.

FACT

The girls in the pimple ads with amazingly clear skin?

Take no notice of them. They've either never had a pimple in their life – or they've had a 'mouse makeover' by a digital 'artist'.

A **facial cleanser**, a **soap substitute** or a special **facial soap** is usually better than a traditional soap, which can be too drying, especially if you then put on another drying product such as pimple cream. A gentle, oil-free cleanser is included in many ranges of pimple products.

Wash your hands well, foam up the cleanser or soap in them, massage it gently into your face, then splash it off completely with a few scoops of warm or cold water.

Common ingredients in cleansers for skin with pimples are salicylic acid, and alpha hydroxy acids (AHAs) such as glycolic acid. These are exfoliants, which help to loosen dead skin cells (although exfoliants can irritate some sensitive skin). If you are using a cleanser for pimples don't also use an exfoliator or scrub your skin.

Pimple creams can't do anything much to pimples you already have. They work to prevent new ones coming.

Most creams use chemicals to dry out the pimples already there, and have an antiseptic to kill surface germs that could cause further infection in broken skin. The drying ingredients include alcohol; sulphur; tea tree oil; and benzoyl peroxide, believed to be the most effective agent because it fights extra oil, bacteria and the clogging of pores. (Some people are allergic to benzoyl peroxide but think the red rash it causes is part of their pimple problem.)

- Don't start thinking about using pimple cream a couple of weeks before a special party: it won't have enough time to do its thing. Pimples take about six weeks to form before you see the end result.
- Test a small amount on your face first to make sure your skin doesn't have a bad reaction to it.
- Don't mix pimple creams or put different ones on at the same time: they can cancel each other out.
- Don't put too much on because all drying agents can cause flaking, peeling and dryness around the pimples.
- Apply it all over pimple-prone areas, not just on the visible spots, because creams work to prevent new pimples coming.
- Make using the cream a daily routine because if you miss a few days the treatment won't have a chance to work properly. Use benzoyl peroxide in the morning because it can leave bleach marks on bed linen. >

> I've acne problems and the like. They're little, and I know they'll pass, but sometimes I look in a mirror and just feel hideous.
> Nastacia, 17, Newcastle, NSW

- Continue using the cream once a day until you haven't had a pimple for a month, then stop and see what happens.

Hang in there with the pimple cream – it takes a number of weeks to see results. Not everyone's pimple problem is solved with stuff from the pharmacy, though. See a doctor if, after six weeks of using a pimple cream every day, there's been no sign of improvement.

> When do pimples leave your life???
> Shannon, 16, Wellington, NZ
>
> It doesn't last forever.
> Former pimple victim

Doctors' treatments for pimples   If you feel you're really losing your battle with pimples, your doctor may prescribe some treatments or refer you to a dermatologist for specialist advice. Medical treatments for pimples can take a few weeks to start working, and can include one or a mix of these:

- antibiotic pills to kill the bacteria from the inside and calm the inflammation
- antibiotic gels and lotions
- vitamin A gel or cream to help unclog the pores, which is best put on at night and washed off in the morning because it can cause sun sensitivity
- pills that reduce or counteract the amount of androgen, that pesky oil-producing hormone; a version of the contraceptive pill is often prescribed because the oestrogen in it suppresses androgen (if you need the Pill for contraception as well, see how to take it properly in Chapter 16, Sex)
- medication for a problem called polycystic ovary syndrome if you're diagnosed as having it – some cases of bad pimples can be a sign that your ovaries are misbehaving
- 'blue light' treatment – the Australasian College of Dermatologists says this 'treatment', which is said to reduce bacteria, isn't a great success and that your doctor should give you better and cheaper options to explore
- medication called isotretinoin, which is derived from vitamin A, only prescribed by a dermatologist for really difficult pimple cases, and available under different brand names, including Roaccutane. If you get pregnant while taking it, or in the month after you stop, it will severely damage the baby, so if there's any chance you'll be having sex you also need to be on the Pill and using a condom every time.

Isotretinoin causes side effects such as dry lips and being more prone to sunburn. A possible, very rare side effect is mood changes. Most doctors believe it's not the medication causing it, just that it's most often prescribed to teens and they're more likely to have problems with moods. And most teens experience mood improvement when their skin clears anyway.

Blackheads

Everyone has tiny blackheads, most of which nobody notices (and whiteheads, which are only noticeable on darker skins). Blackheads happen in pores blocked by sebum when a skin protein called keratin turns black after it's exposed to the air. So even though the pores look black, it has nothing to do with dirt or not washing.

- Only try to pop a blackhead if it is really obvious (wash your hands before squeezing gently). The blackhead should then come out easily, but if it doesn't immediately, stop.
- Scrubs may help, but you can't use them more than once a week. Exfoliators, toners and astringents do not cure blackheads.
- Those sticky strips that you press on and rip off may or may not take a few blackheads with them, but they don't stop blackheads forming.
- A 'comedome' or blackhead 'extractor' is usually just a tool like a pen with a little wire loop on the end that you press over a blackhead, which is supposed to squeeze it out of the pore. There's no need to buy one.

More info on pimples and blackheads

acne.org.au
This volunteer site by doctors and dermatologists has independent advice. Choose Treatment, then Treatment Steps, then Hormonal Acne for lots of tips.

dermcoll.edu.au
The Australasian College of Dermatologists site: choose A–Z of Skin for info on skin problems and how to find a skin specialist.

> At the moment I am on antibiotics to clear my skin of pimples. I am scared of my blackheads. Vanessa, 16, Northcote, Vic.

Skin colour

Years ago it was fashionable in many countries to have 'white' skin, to show that you were too rich and posh to have to work outside. Then it became fashionable to have a tan because it showed you were too rich and posh to have to do any work at all and could lie around in the sun all day. Then people realised the damage that too much sun can do to the skin, causing dryness, wrinkles and blotches, not to mention the whole skin cancer thing.

These days people realise it's fine not to have a tan – and to be whatever colour you were born, whether you have inherited the beautiful skin of people from Africa, Papua New Guinea and Aboriginal communities; the heavenly caramel skin of Polynesian Islanders; one of the gorgeous brown tones found in India, Pakistan and Sri Lanka; the attractive olive skin of folk around the Mediterranean Sea; the delicate prettiness of Asian skin; the moonlight-lovely pale skin and freckles found across Europe; one of the much-admired skin colours belonging to South America; or any of the equally enviable variations . . . ooh, I've come over all poetic.

Anyway, my point is: all skin colours have their own beauty. To insult someone about the colour of their skin reveals nothing except the nastiness and embarrassing stupidity of the person who said it.

While some people are desperate to look darker with a fake tan, others try to lighten their skin colour using bleaching creams and similar products. This seems very sad, and is also sometimes dangerous, as some of the creams and lotions can cause rashes and even damage or scarring. Others might try to use a skin lightener on a spot or patch of darker skin – but always discuss this with your doctor first (and see 'Skin Marks' coming up in a bit).

> The majority of people love that I'm Indian and brown. But u get some real a-holes that just don't know when to stop so, yeah, their comments can affect me. But usually I ignore it, or give them the one-finger salute.   Vinu, 15, East Perth, WA

> I come from an Aboriginal family, and coz I don't look very black people think it's cool to be racist.
>
> Emily, 17, Coraki, NSW

Sun protection for all skin types

Here's what the experts say.

For people with pale skin

* Try to avoid going out in the sun at the hottest time of day (between 10 am and 3 pm).

* Wear a hat that shades the neck and face, and preferably long sleeves and long skirts or pants if you can't avoid being in the sun for ages. Clothes and shade give more sun protection than sunscreen.

* Use a sunscreen with a SPF (sun protection factor) of 30+. SPF 30+ gives you the best, maximum protection available. Any SPF number higher than that doesn't offer you any extra protection worth having.

* Apply sunscreen half an hour before going out to give it a chance to have the chemical reaction on your skin that will protect you.

* Be aware that most people don't use enough sunscreen, or put it on often enough.

* Use a water-resistant sunscreen if you'll be swimming or sweating.

* Apply a toddlers' sunscreen if you have sensitive skin.

* If you get pimples use a gel sunscreen, which is less likely to block pores.

* Don't use a sunscreen that's way past its use-by date.

For others

Some Australians need *more* sun than they usually get. Girls with very dark skin (for example, those with two African parents) shouldn't use any sunscreen or wear hats. They, and girls who always wear scarves, veils and clothes that cover arms and legs, need extra sun and may require a vitamin D supplement. (Pale veiled girls still need to avoid sunburn.) If you live somewhere cold and cloudy, try to get more sunlight on you in winter.

The sun and your skin

We know too much sun is the biggest cause of skin damage, and also that Australia has the highest rate of skin cancer in the world caused by sun exposure. But a little bit of sunshine every day is good for you because it boosts your immune system and helps your body to heal and to make vitamin D, which is needed for healthy bones. People with naturally very dark skin need to worry less about sun protection, which is lucky because they need up to ten times longer in the sun than pale folk to make enough vitamin D.

Sunburn and skin colour changes caused by sun are the things to avoid. The more times you are sunburnt, the more chance you have of later developing skin cancer – sometimes as soon as your late teens or early twenties.

If you want to see the damage the sun does, ask a grandparent to show you a part of themselves that doesn't get any sun, such as their tummy, and compare it with their face or hands. The skin is the same age in both places: the only difference is one part looks older because it has sun damage – blotches and wrinkles. (Of course there aren't a lot of laugh lines on a tummy, but you get the picture.)

Freckles Freckles are small, pale to dark brown spots seen mostly on the face and arms because those are the areas most exposed to sunlight. Freckles look fine – except to some girls who worry about theirs. Freckles seem to be the first and last thing they see when they look in the mirror; this time will pass.

People who get lots of freckles have skin that's likely to burn so need to take extra care to protect themselves against the sun. Freckles can't be removed by exfoliating or home chemical treatments.

Wanting a tan

A suntan is evidence that the sun has damaged your skin. The tan is discolouring resulting from the skin trying to protect itself by producing more melanin (the chemical that causes pigment – skin colour). You can still get sunburnt if you have a tan.

Tanning salons: don't go there Cancer Council Australia warns that tans from tanning salons (also known as solariums or 'sun beds') are just as dangerous and damaging to your skin as lying in the sun for hours and hours – and probably worse, because the kind of rays they use penetrate further. That means quicker wrinkles, and a much greater chance of skin cancers. Because of the dangers, tanning salons are illegal in some places in Australia. If it's legal where you're on holiday or elsewhere, that doesn't mean it's safe.

Fake tans A fake tan is a dye that is rubbed, sponged or sprayed onto your body. We've all seen those celebrities who have overdone it and look like a beaming gigantic carrot wearing sunnies. Although a fake tan is a berzillion times safer than a real tan caused by the sun or a scary tanning salon, it does have other risks – for example, looking like a stripy gigantic root vegetable. Also, you can still get sunburnt if you have a fake tan on (and that increases your skin cancer risk).

Magazines mainly suggest you get a fake tan because the major cosmetics companies selling fake tan products spend millions of dollars a year on magazine advertising. The models in the magazines usually have a (professionally applied) fake tan: it's an easy way to get across the idea we should all look like that so we need to buy one. A company would threaten to pull out their advertising money if a magazine article said that fake tans were unnecessary, or that you should make up your own mind about whether you want one or whether it suits you, or that some fake-tan products are ridiculously expensive and practically impossible to get looking right.

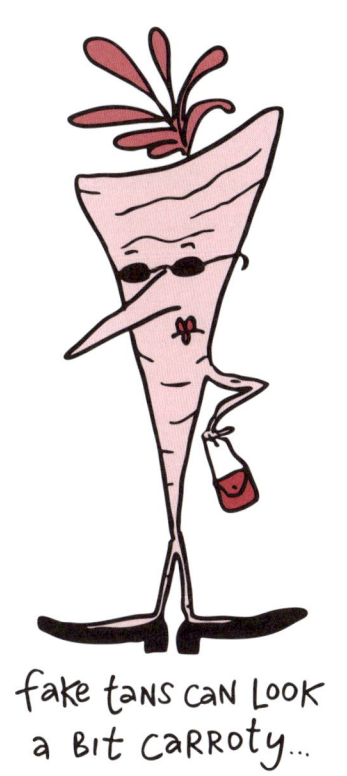

As well as fake tans you apply yourself, you can get one sprayed on at a salon. This can be very expensive, and if sprayed on the face can block pores and cause pimples. Spray-on tan has the same drawbacks as the stuff in bottles: it can smudge, stain and go streaky. It lasts for a few days, depending on how often you wash and with what.

fake tans can look a bit carroty...

More info on sun protection

You should only go to local (not overseas) websites for info on tanning or sun care.

sunsmart.com.au
The go-to Aussie site with good info on sunscreens, skin care, and skin cancer in young people. Advice line: 13 11 20.

sunsmart.co.nz
The official Kiwi site for sun info.

Skin marks

Everybody has moles, birthmarks or stretch marks – some people have more than others, or larger or smaller ones, or a skin colour that means they don't show up as much.

> I have this scar I got on my lip when I was 10 on my friend's trampoline. I'm self-conscious about it and want it to go away. People always ask if it's a cold sore.
>
> Deirdra, 16, Balwyn, Vic.

Moles

Moles are usually brown or black dots on the skin that can appear anywhere, either alone or in groups. They can be flat or raised, smooth or bumpy. They mostly appear in the first twenty-five years of your life, and it's normal to have between ten and forty moles by then. (No, don't count them. How bored would you have to be?)

Moles can change over the years, or even disappear, but it's important to keep an eye on them. Have your doctor or dermatologist check them every year or so.

Most moles are not dangerous, but if you notice that one has changed – grown, become red, or darker – or has edges that are itchy, bleed or have altered in some way, see a doctor immediately because misbehaving moles can lead to skin cancer. Moles that look as if they might be a skin cancer, or which get rubbed by, say, a bra strap, can be easily removed by a dermatologist.

Many people add a fake facial mole for glamour, using an eyebrow pencil or eyeliner. (It can be a little less glamorous when the real ones have hairs growing out of them – but if you like you can pluck the hairs out using tweezers.)

Birthmarks

A birthmark is any skin mark that you were born with or developed as a baby. Lots of people have them. Some of them go away as you grow older. There are marks that are blood vessels you're able to see under the skin, and others that happen because the body puts too much pigment in one area.

Birthmarks can range from small, light brown spots to a large area of pink or purple pigment. Most are harmless and there is no need to get them removed for health reasons, but it is always a good idea to get them checked out by a doctor.

People with a birthmark (or a scar) on their face can feel self-conscious. Some girls use make-up to tone them down, although others quite like them as a symbol of individuality. Some birthmarks are easily treated or removed; others aren't.

It's essential to see a dermatologist or a member of the Australian Society of Plastic Surgeons, not a 'cosmetic surgeon' or 'cosmetic physician', when you're seeking treatment. And never just pop along to a 'cosmetic centre' or 'laser clinic' because some people who use lasers and other skin techniques have much less experience and training.

Stretch marks

Almost everybody gets stretch marks. They're just the stripy lines left after your skin has had to stretch. They're most common on breasts, hips, thighs and tummies, and can happen when your body has a growth spurt or you put on a lot of weight quickly.

When they first happen they're often slightly raised and purply pink or red. Nothing – and no amount of rubbing with creams – will prevent them or make them go away. But the good news is they always fade to flat, silvery marks that blend with your skin colour and are often pretty invisible – or so faint you'd only notice if you were obsessing.

You usually don't notice them on other people: they're just not that obvious. Yet a lot of girls get self-conscious about them and hide their bodies. We're not used to seeing real naked bodies – just the computer-adjusted and make-up-slathered bodies of models in ads and magazines. (Yep, they use full body make-up to hide things like stretch marks.)

More info on skin marks

dermcoll.asn.au
On the Australasian College of Dermatologists site, choose Public, then Find a Dermatologist.

youngwomenshealth.org/facial_difference.html
Overseas site with good info, links and support for those with a facial difference, such as a birthmark or scars.

I have stretch marks on my breasts, upper thighs and so on. I get really self-conscious about it and have to wear less-revealing clothing, so my question is how do I get rid of them?? Essie, 15, Clapham, SA

Does everyone get stretch marks and how do I get rid of them? Peta, 16, Parkes, NSW

Sweating

You've always been able to sweat, even as a little tacker. You probably haven't been aware of it, but the sweat from your armpits, between your legs or buttocks, and in other areas where the air can't circulate, has always stayed wet longer than elsewhere.

Now, in your teens, you're suddenly sweating more (although not as much as guys), because you've been developing extra sweat glands all over your body. And guess where in particular you've got extra sweat gland activity? Under your arms and between your legs. (Gee thanks, Mother Nature, you maniac.) We do need to sweat: it cools us down if we get too hot because of the weather or exercise. And if we overheat we go purple and have convulsions. You'd probably prefer to sweat.

How much you sweat depends mainly on genetics. Some people just sweat less because that runs in their family, or because they're of Asian heritage.

You can sweat more if you're nervous. Extra sweat from nervousness often concentrates in your armpits and on your forehead, palms and feet.

Things that make you sweat more include stress; undies, pantyhose, socks, shoes and other clothes made from synthetic fabrics, which don't 'breathe'; shoes worn without socks; hats (sunhats are cooler if made from cotton or some other natural fibre and are a light colour); very heavy skin-covering lotion or make-up (because the skin can't 'breathe'); and hair around your neck and ears on a hot day.

Sweating too much

Some people have a sweating problem, even when they're not nervous or exercising. A GP should check: in most cases there's no illness, but the problem continues.

Expensive and radical treatments include Botox injections and surgery to remove the sweat glands. This major and tricky surgery can cause scars and have serious side effects as it involves removal of some nerves. Your body still needs to sweat, so if your sweat

> **FACT**
>
> **DIY** 'Intimate' sprays, vaginal deodorants, douches, perfumes, any kind of powder or talc or other smelly stuff shouldn't be put on, or up, your girly bits. Your vagina is self-cleaning.

58   BODY ✿ skin

glands in, say, your underarms are removed or disabled, then the glands elsewhere will sweat more to compensate. Make sure you get second opinions before doing anything major, and consider all your options.

Smell

Everyone gets BO (body odour) when they don't wash sweat off every day. Yours smells more now than it used to because of the hormonal chemicals released in it. The longer sweat is left on the skin, the more it can change smell because of the build-up of bacteria. 'Fresh' sweat usually smells fine.

Talcum powder, perfumes and body sprays don't stop or really disguise BO on bodies or clothes – washing every day with soap is the only way to solve it.

You don't really need to feel too disgusted at the prospect of the teen years being leakier, oilier, sweatier and smellier (not to mention the whole once-a-month period palaver) because luckily you can be in control of it all.

And it could be worse. You could have been born in the Middle Ages, when there was no plumbing. You'd be lucky to have a bath once a decade, your mossy teeth would go a fetching shade of brown before dropping out, and you'd probably snuggle up at night with a rat or two on some nice warm horse poo, in your pyjamas crocheted from sword grass and goat fur. Instead you've got toilet paper, so cheer up.

Deodorants and antiperspirants

Not everyone needs an underarm deodorant or antiperspirant. Some people only use it before exercising or on very hot days.

- An underarm deodorant uses a chemical to help neutralise the smell of sweat, but it won't stop wetness.
- An underarm antiperspirant temporarily plugs or seals sweat glands, usually with an aluminium-based substance.
- Some products combine an antiperspirant with a deodorant.
- If a deodorant or antiperspirant causes a rash or itchiness try another brand or type – maybe one that's hypo-allergenic or unscented.

More info on sweating

sweathelp.org
This US-based site is sponsored by companies that sell treatments. Get your own independent medical advice as well.

dermnetnz.org/topics/hyperhidrosis
The NZ Dermatological Society site on excessive sweating.

skin BODY 59

Piercing and tattoos

Piercing and tattoos have become more ordinary, instead of new and exciting, because so many people have them now. (There wasn't a lot of eyebrow piercing or tatts on my nanna, frankly.)

Piercing

It's possible, but not necessarily a good hobby, to pierce almost any area of the body. Check your local legal age for piercing.

Body-piercing facts

- It needs to be done by an experienced professional who uses a new needle, which is then thrown away, and who sterilises all other equipment in a machine called an autoclave. This is the only way to make sure you and other people don't catch one of the serious and possibly fatal viruses – such as HIV (the AIDS virus) and hepatitis B – that can be spread by unhygienic piercing. Some equipment, such as the gun piercers that work a bit like a stapler, can't be properly sterilised.
- Make sure before you have a piercing that you're up to date with your immunisations, especially for tetanus and the hepatitis variations. There's no vaccine for HIV.
- The Australian Dental Association is against lip and tongue piercing. Dentists see some of the results: swollen tongues, causing breathing difficulty; infected gums; and teeth cracked, chipped or broken by the metal. Lip piercing can also cause speech problems, including lisping.
- The more chance there is for bacteria to breed, the more chance there is of infection: nose, mouth and (Ow! Ow! Oww!) girly bits are the most likely places.
- You should never pierce yourself or get a friend to do it: a home job is much more likely to become infected or look botched.
- Take extra special care after you have your piercing done. The practitioner should give you instructions on how to treat it until it has healed properly, including regularly using disinfectant.

One of my friends just got her tongue pierced for a guy and she had to suck ice all week! DUMB, and to change for guys is wrong.
Salima, 17, Wodonga, Vic.

- If there's infection, which is common, minor or major scarring can result. And if you no longer use a pierced hole it will close over but can leave a small scar.
- Know what the symptoms of infection are so you can get it treated by a doctor very quickly. These include soreness, redness, swelling, and gunk coming out.

Tattoos

Before you get a permanent tattoo, you need to know some stuff.

- A tattoo is basically a wound that heals into a permanent scar. It hurts a lot.
- You'll need to go to a clean, licensed professional tattoo shop that sterilises its equipment in an autoclave, and uses a new needle for each client.
- If you're under 18 getting a tattoo is illegal. (It's 16 in New Zealand.) Good tattooists won't do illegal work, so that means if you're under 18 and a tattooist accepts you as a client you'll be getting inferior work by somebody without the right experience, equipment or skill. And if a tattooist doesn't observe the rule about asking you for ID proof of age, why would they observe the rule about sterilising equipment?
- You'll need vaccinations against hepatitis and other blood-borne diseases (but you can't be vaccinated against HIV).
- The tattooist may do it crookedly, or start in the wrong spot.
- Most people who have a tattoo have regrets later.
- It's very much harder to remove a tattoo than to get one, it hurts more, it can cost several thousand dollars and it leaves scars.
- The tattoo you want now may not be the one you'd have chosen five years ago. So would it be the one you'd choose in two, or ten, or twenty years' time? How do you think a tattoo looks on someone your mother's age or older? >

WILL YOUR TATTOOS LOOK GOOD LATER?

skin BODY 61

- A tattoo is distorted if the part of your body it's on gets smaller or bigger. (Has your body finished growing? Will you ever be pregnant? Will your size ever change, permanently or temporarily?)
- A tattoo may not always suit the sorts of jobs you decide to go for, or your lifestyle later on.
- Many tattooed symbols turn out to mean something other than what people believed, and many are not spelt correctly.
- You don't need a tattoo to remember a friend, relative or event.
- The tattooist should give lots of information on how to keep the wound clean afterwards that you can easily follow.

A possible solution: temporary tatts There are now lots of people, often at fairs, fetes, street markets and parties, and even at tattoo parlours, who can airbrush or paint on a 'temporary tattoo'. This means you can change the design any time you like. You can also buy supplies online or at some tattoo shops so that you can stencil your own.

Temporary tattoos are not always safe. Some of the dyes used in temporary tatts can cause irritation, allergic reaction and in serious cases, chemical burns. Some teens have ended up with scars from temporary tattoo dye reaction – many of them were 'tattooed' at holiday resorts overseas, but it has happened in Australia too. If you're not absolutely sure of what's in the dye, it's smart to give it a miss.

More info on piercing and tattoos

lawstuff.org.au
Check out the legal age for piercing and tattoos (and other things) in your state or territory.

youngwomenshealth.org/2013/08/07/body-piercing
Great for info on piercing and healing times.

3
HAIR

you have tiny hairs all over your body...

Hair insulates us from cold weather (though what a shame we're not as **furry** as a brown bear in winter), it helps to stop dust or grit getting into sensitive areas, such as eyes, and it allows us to indulge in a number of mind-numbingly **ludicrous** and embarrassing hairstyles until we find one that suits us. And everyone ends up with **extra** hair on their head, legs, arms, face, armpits and private bits. It reminds us that we are descended from shaggy cave folk. Lovely. Let's move on.

Looking after your hair

Like skin, the hair on your head is often divided into types – oily, dry and normal (this doesn't mean more normal than the other types, just neither oily nor dry). Don't worry too much about which type yours is because it's usually not a problem. For instance, your hair might be naturally dry but probably won't be 'too dry' (unless it's affected all the time by the sun, dyeing or hot hairstyling gadgets).

> **FACT**
>
> **Your hair's dead (sob)** Hair is made of the protein keratin (about 90 per cent) and water. Every strand has an outer layer (the one we see, which is a protective surface); an inner layer that's made of keratin and gives the hairs strength and texture; and a core of colour, which shines through the other layers. Hair is created in follicles under your skin's surface – but by the time it pokes out it's dead.

Shampoo and conditioner

Because your hair's dead, any shampoo and conditioner you put on it just strips off the oils ('cleans' it) and then adds a coating to make it easier to brush or comb and less frizzy or fly-away.

Shampoo and conditioner combos are hopeless. A shampoo needs to get stuff off your hair; a conditioner needs to put stuff on. Combining them in the one bottle means you neither wash nor condition your hair properly.

Shampoo facts

- Crap shampoo from a $2 or discount shop is likely to be just coloured detergent, which will strip too much of the natural oils from your hair.
- You don't need top-dollar, salon products. They're better for your hair than the really cheap shampoos because they contain gentler surfactants, the ingredients that make shampoo lather, but you can buy products just as good for less than half the cost.

- Most people use far more shampoo – and conditioner – than they need to. Try using only a little bit and see if that does the job.
- Most shampoos recommend you lather, then rinse, twice to make sure your hair is thoroughly clean, but really you only need to shampoo once. You get a better lather on the second go because your hair's already clean.

Conditioner facts

- Most conditioners are just a coating that makes the hair shinier, and also smoother so that knots comb out more easily – they don't change the hair itself.
- 'Leave in' or 'heat protection' conditioners usually have sealing chemicals to protect the hair from drying out too much when blow-dried.
- Sometimes conditioners cause a build-up of coatings, making hair look heavy and dull. To get these off you'll need to change your brand or type of shampoo or conditioner.
- If your hair is the oily type, try conditioning it only once a week; use a conditioner labelled for oily hair; or just condition the ends.

How to keep your hair looking good

- Eat lots of different healthy foods (see Chapter 5, Food), and don't go on diets. Hair is affected by what you put, or don't put, into your body. Dieting and unhealthy food can make hair grow out thin and weak.
- Wash your hair to get rid of dirt and any oil build-up: every few days is fine. Most people don't need to wash their hair every day unless it's very oily.
- Use a wide-toothed comb to untangle wet washed hair, and be gentle so you don't stretch and break the strands.
- If you need to use a hair dryer, stop before your hair is completely dry so you don't blast all the moisture out. If possible let your hair dry naturally.
- Wear a swimming cap in a chlorinated pool. The chemicals will make your hair drier, and possibly swamp green, especially if you're blonde.

I love my hair every now and then. Freya, 16, Auckland, NZ

Label check

- Shampoos and conditioners with 'natural' ingredients won't necessarily do anything better for your hair than ones with synthetic chemicals.

- Shampoos and conditioners that boast fruit or herbal ingredients usually just include chemicals that smell like the real thing.

- As with skin products, beware of 'scientific breakthroughs' or 'newly discovered' ingredients that have names made up by the hair product companies: 'revolutionary new Pro-enz serum' may mean nothing.

- Shampoos and conditioners that claim they 'thicken', 'volumise' or add 'body' just sit on the outer surface of your hair, making each strand look ever so slightly plumper.

- 'Baby', 'mild' or 'hypo-allergenic' shampoos usually have fewer ingredients known to cause skin reactions, but this is not a guarantee.

- 'Moisturising' shampoos have moisture that is absorbed into the outer layer of each hair. This can be useful if you blow-dry your hair a lot.

- 'Colour-enhancing' shampoos contain chemicals that help to prevent hair dye washing out. Sometimes they contain dye, but it isn't permanent.

- 'Protein' conditioners are said to strengthen your hair, but really they just leave a coating on it.

FACT

Chemicals versus organic hair products All substances contain chemicals – even water. Using common brands of shampoo and conditioner can't hurt you. If you'd like to use 'organic' products to help the environment that's fine, but don't pay heaps or expect it to do anything special to your hair – it won't. 'Natural', 'botanical' or other 'green' ingredients in your shampoo and conditioner may well just be fragrances or colourings made in a laboratory anyway.

66   BODY   hair

Different hair

Because everyone's different and has a cocktail of genes that decide how their hair will sprout, there's an amazing variety of head hair. It can be straight, wavy, madly curly, bouffy, thick, thin, fine, red, strawberry blonde, black, dark brown, light brown, or dyed iridescent purple to scare your parents. Many people who have blonde hair when they're little end up with brown hair as they grow up.

Straight A lot of people get bored with their straight hair and want to make it curly or fouffy. The best way to curl straight hair is temporarily. Don't get a perm. It's expensive, it uses a lot of strong, stinky chemicals and if it goes wrong you're stuck with it until it grows out or you cut it off. Instead you can experiment with cheap Velcro curlers: you wind damp hair around them and wait for it to dry. Or you can use heated curling tongs – but be careful not to burn yourself, and avoid repeated use because they'll dry out your hair. If you have a chance, get a professional to show you how to curl your hair, using your own tools.

Curly or kinky While people with straight hair often want volume or curls, some people with wavy or curly hair want it to be straight. Never try to iron your hair with a household iron. Seriously. It's a really quick way to sizzle your hair right off and burn yourself.

You need a tongs-like electrical hair-straightener, but good ones are expensive. Most hair-straighteners end up abandoned in the bottom drawer. Borrow one for a while if you can, to see if using it regularly suits you and your lifestyle, and try to get a professional to show you how to apply it. Being straightened all the time (with tongs or chemical products) will make your hair very dry and brittle, and may result in some of it breaking and falling out.

mine's boring

it takes 3 hours to comb

EVERYONE WANTS SOMEONE ELSE'S HAIR...

Frizzy Some people straighten their hair to avoid frizz. Other people don't find frizz frazzling.

Hot, humid weather means more moisture and less static electricity, so hair has more volume or looks frizzier. (But when the weather's hot and dry, frizzy hair takes in less moisture and has more static electricity, so the curls tend to flatten out.) Conditioners and sprays can keep the hair coated to try to beat weather effects.

> I find that my hair affects me a lot ... If my hair is looking especially bad and I know it the slightest comment on it can really darken my day.
> Bron, 16, Gympie, Qld

Hairstyles You'll notice that lots of ads in the magazines are for shampoo, conditioner, hair-styling products and hair dye. Each year women worldwide spend billions (yes, you read that right) on their hair. So all the companies are competing to get you to buy their products. And all the magazines and websites are competing to get the hair companies to advertise with them.

The best hairstyle isn't the one the ads or magazines say is the most fashionable – you know, the one needing lots of hair-care products. It's the one that suits your face, the natural tendencies of your hair, your life and how much time you want to devote to faffing about with your hair. If you need to spend an hour to get your hairdo looking the way you want it, you won't be able to move, swim or go anywhere that has weather.

Dyed hair In the Girl Stuff Survey a surprising 40 per cent of the 13- to 15-year-olds said they dyed their hair, and a whacking great 60 per cent of the 16- to 18-year-olds did too.

Dyed-hair maintenance will cost time and money. And don't forget that results are not guaranteed. Make sure you buy a colour that suits you, and that you understand how it will look as it grows out. You can get colour that will wash out after a few shampoos, or even one. 'Permanent' hair dye usually penetrates to the inner part of the hair, and you're stuck with it until you can cut off the dyed bit or put another dye over the top (not always possible).

Top six bad hairstyles

Avoid the latest celebrity hairstyle: it probably won't suit you, your hair or your wallet. And also avoid these six styles.

OVER-BLEACHED

Hair bleached to a hard white-blonde. Regrowth is quick and obvious, and the chemicals can make your hair break.

CUT BY AN AMATEUR

The DIY haircut or the one you let your untrained relatives give you. Just say no.

THE PERM

Fake, chemically tortured curls. Usually makes you look like a demented poodle.

THE MULLET

Short at the front and long at the back. Scarier than vampires and not controlled by garlic.

ASYMMETRICAL

Much shorter on one side than the other. Always looks like you fell into a blender, even if you paid for it.

BEEHIVE

A tower of 'teased' and hair-sprayed layers. Not for a young woman.

And don't get me started on bad dye jobs.

hair ✱ BODY

Some pretty hefty chemicals are used in hair dye. Avoid breathing them in. If you have a history of allergies make sure you do a patch test for a reaction, even in a salon. Never dye your eyebrows or eyelashes yourself – you could permanently damage your eyes.

If you dye your hair at home, from a packet bought at the chemist shop or supermarket, follow the pamphlet instructions absolutely exactly and get someone older to help. Your 6-year-old sister, despite being keen, might miss a spot or dye your ears.

I'll bet you a million dollars the women in the hair dye ads didn't dye their hair themselves in the backyard, wearing rubber gloves and a garbage bag, so don't expect to look like the celebrity in the ad or the girl on the packet.

Salon hair colourists can usually do a much better-looking hair dye job than you, using several colours to give a more natural effect, but can charge up to $200. Don't forget to ask how often you'll need a touch-up as it grows out.

FACT

Oops A home dye job may be cheaper but if you need a salon rescue when it goes wrong, then you pay twice.

Dandruff

Dandruff is a skin condition in which dead skin cells keep flaking off your scalp, often causing itchiness. Sometimes people's eyebrows also get dandruff.

Everyone has a bit of a flaky thing happening, but with true dandruff dead skin cells are stuck together with sebum (skin oil) and so bigger, more noticeable flakes come off. (Don't worry if a doctor says you have 'seborrhoeic dermatitis': it just means dandruff.)

Treating it First, make sure that you really do have ongoing dandruff, and that you're not just worried about normal bits of dead skin falling off.

- Try a specialised dandruff shampoo and conditioner from your chemist or supermarket, and follow the instructions.
- Try washing your hair every day to keep the oil level down a bit.
- Put conditioner only on the ends of your hair, not the scalp.
- Avoid hair-styling products such as gels, mousses, putties, and clays.
- Don't change your diet because that probably won't have any effect on dandruff.
- If your dandruff won't go away, see your doctor for a referral to a dermatologist specialising in hair (see 'More Info on Body Hair' at the end of the chapter).

More info on looking after your hair

Most hair websites try to sell you stuff, but have good info as well.

virtualhaircare.com
Every problem or hair scare you can think of is explained.

choice.com.au
The Australian Consumers' Association has tested shampoos, conditioners, straighteners and other hair-care products. Search Hair in the product A–Z guide.

austorganic.com
Organic industry folk have rules and a logo on packaging that they say guarantees genuine organic products.

adiosbarbie.com/feature-articles/hair-today-gone-tomorrow
An American page for girls with dark skin and kinky or curly hair.

teenvogue.com/beauty/hair
All the delicious shallow scoop on all sorts of hairstyles. While you're on the site, check out *Teen Vogue*'s excellent news and politics section (no ponytails).

SHAKE FOR DANDRUFF

My hair is really oily, I wash it then by the afternoon of the next day it needs to be washed again.   Vicky, 13

One day I just got sick of all my long hair and decided to just cut it off, best decision I ever made.   Grace, 17

hair ✿ BODY

Body hair

Everyone has body hair. Fair-haired and fair-skinned people often have less noticeable body hair than those with darker hair. Some people, such as those of Asian heritage, have less than others. Girls of Italian, Greek, Turkish or Arabic heritage can have more body hair than some others.

An excess of facial hair (and other body hair) can indicate a hormone problem such as the treatable condition polycystic ovary syndrome (bad pimples are another symptom). For most girls, the amount of body and facial hair they have is preordained by their genes, but if you feel it's really a bit out of control, see your doctor.

Downy hair can appear on the arms and back of girls who don't have enough body fat because they're starving themselves: it's the body's way of trying to keep warm.

Why do people remove their body hair?

Even though it is completely normal for girls and women to have body hair, there's a lot of pressure to remove it. Partly this is because of the idea that it makes us different from hairy men and therefore somehow more 'feminine'. But mostly it's because people make big money from selling us hair removal stuff. So the message girls end up getting is not 'Make up your own mind about if and when you do anything to your body hair', but rather 'You need to choose – right now – which product you'll buy to remove it or disguise it.'

Some girls have been so affected by the pressure of advertising and a desire to be more 'grown up' that they've started removing their body hair at a very young age. More than half the 13- to 15-year-olds in the Girl Stuff Survey plucked their eyebrows, and about three-quarters shaved their underarms and legs. This is way earlier than in past generations.

me too

every body has hairy legs

> I HATED getting underarm hair!
> Sonya, 13,
> Geelong, Vic.

> Why do you get bushes growing down there!?! I say that they should stay in the forest ...
> Susanna, 14,
> Brisbane, Qld

In the older, 16 to 18, age group even more girls in the Girl Stuff Survey were removing hair: three-quarters plucked their eyebrows, and about 85 per cent shaved their underarms and legs.

Most girls who remove body hair just do the legs below the knee and their underarms. Some people never remove any. In the United States people can be almost fanatical about removing body hair. Big US companies that sell hair removal products now also target us with their ads and products. Now there are a lot more salons that do hair removal too, so they all compete for our business as well.

It's part of wanting to look like the 'high-maintenance' actresses, socialites and other rich, often idle women lurking in the magazine photos. (It costs tens of thousands of dollars a year to keep that look up.)

UNDERARM HAIR IS USUALLY PRETTY SHORT

Some areas where you may not have expected a furry visit

✱ Your forearms (below the elbow).

✱ The snail trail: you might develop a line of darker hair going from your map of Tassie (the pubic mound area) up towards your tummy button.

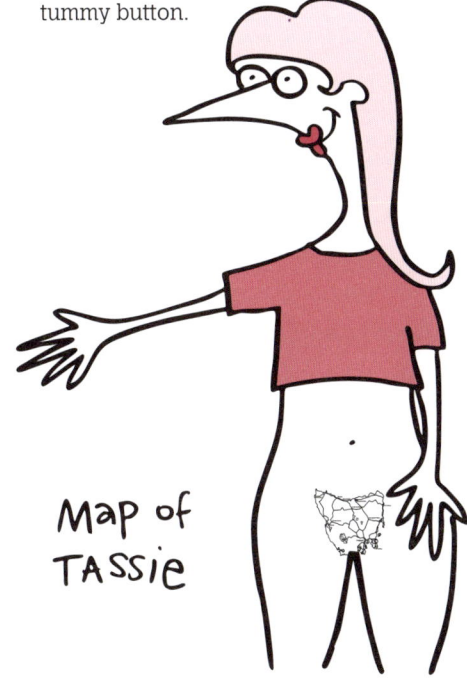

MAP OF TASSIE

✱ Top lip: all women have a little moustache.

✱ Nipples: as you get older you'll probably get the odd hair around them.

✱ Your bot: it's quite normal to have a little bit of hair around your anus and on your backside.

hair ✱ BODY   73

Pubic hair removal Some people shave or wax the outer edges of their pubic hair to remove a few straggly bits that might otherwise show when they're wearing bathers.

Removing all pubic hair was a fad for a while and is still done by a very small minority of women. But even if you use hair removal methods on other parts of you, let your pubic hair be free range. A little trim here and there with some carefully wielded nail scissors should keep you hiding your sprouty bits, or you can buy less brief bathers.

> Courtesy of my mother I have been so unfortunate as to receive the gorilla gene, and am nearly as hairy as my Italian boyfriend.
> Crystal, 18, Sunshine Coast, Qld

If you really want the edges of your 'pubes' waxed (called a bikini wax), don't do it yourself. Go to a busy professional salon, where they have a lot of experience, and be prepared for pain and expense.

Trying to remove all or lots of your pubic hair is a bad idea because it can result in:

- big-time pain if you wax – it's a very sensitive area down there
- irritation – shaving or waxing the pubic mound or hair between your legs can cause very painful rashes, redness and infected ingrown hairs; some skin conditions of the labia and other girly bits needing treatment by dermatologists can be originally caused by hair removal methods
- uncomfortable, day-long itching (shaved hair can itch like mad as it grows back) and scratching – not a good look
- ingrown hairs (when the removed hair attempts to grow again and is trapped under the skin, causing cysts or sores) – a sterilised needle or pair of tweezers can be used to relieve these, but pubic ones can be awkward or impossible to attend to yourself
- embarrassment – do you really want a stranger looking at your girly bits that closely if they're not a doctor?
- a bad look – pubic hair trimmed into unnatural shapes can look weird

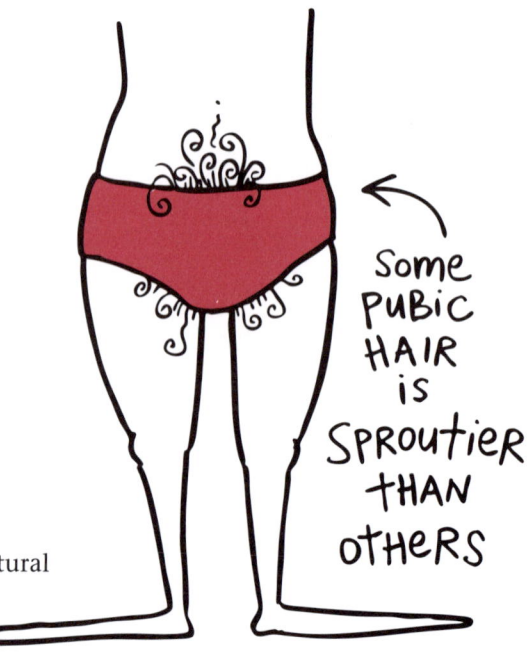

Some pubic hair is sproutier than others

- cost – because doing a pubic hair wax is not exactly a dream job for anyone, a full-on 'Brazilian' or 'XXXX' (whoops – that's a beer) is very expensive
- bald girly bits that make you look like a little girl – kind of creepy when you're not one. And as you get older it's extreeemely creepy if a guy wants you to look like a little girl down there. If a partner wants you to remove your pubic hair you can just say no and ask why he needs his sexual partner to look like a 7-year-old girl. Or suggest he first get his scrotum, chest, arms, face, legs, back and bot-bot waxed for you. I don't think you'll hear much more about it.

Hair removal methods

All hair removal methods should just remove hair, not skin.

Shaving The most common shaving areas for girls and women are their underarms and their lower legs below the knee – mostly because they're easy places to reach and, in warm weather, the most visible. Shaving is cheaper than other methods, but the grow-back is really fast. You can use a razor, preferably with warm water and a chemist's soap-free wash or a sorbolene cream, or a (more expensive) electric shaver.

Whatever 'they' say, shaving does not make the hair grow back faster, slower, thicker or darker. Regrowth feels coarser and sharper because it has a recently cut end.

Many people only shave the day before a leg-featuring event because shaving every day, even if it takes only 10 minutes, means more than an hour a week, which means more than three whole days a year! Bor-ing. Also stubble is always annoying.

Waxing, plucking and threading These are methods in which hair is pulled out by the roots so it doesn't grow back as quickly as when it's shaved.

With waxing, either hot or cold wax is poured on the region, then a strip of cloth is placed over the wax and ripped off, taking the hair with it. You can either do this yourself at home, using a product from the chemist or supermarket and following the instructions exactly, or have it done at a beauty salon by a professional, which is expensive.

Why is it expected of women to have plucked eyebrows, shaved underarms and waxed legs? It's painful and annoying yet we continue to do it. For men they have to shave their face (or not) and shower occasionally. One guy at school even found it appropriate to comment that I had forgotten to shave my legs. How dare he? Let's see him try ripping up his legs.   Lucy, 14, Ringwood, Vic.

Wax is most commonly used on the legs, armpits, eyebrows and upper lip. The upper lip area can be very sensitive and waxing anywhere can cause pimples and rashes. Never use hot wax near your eyes yourself – go to a salon. Waxing does hurt (sometimes a lot), and you'd need to do it every three weeks to a couple of months. (Some girls only wax once a year, before summer.)

Plucking with tweezers and threading are methods of pulling out single hairs by the roots. In threading, a cotton thread is twisted around the hairs to pull them out.

When hair is pulled out by the root it can damage the hair follicle so not as much hair grows back or hairs become ingrown. The regrowth will not have a flat stubble end, like shaved hair, so will feel softer. (See also the 'Eyebrows' section in Chapter 22, Clothes and Make-up.)

you can wax a moustache

Depilatories These are strong chemical creams or liquids that remove the hair by dissolving it so it can be wiped away. Even when used properly, creams can cause rashes and irritation. Never use them on your girly bits or anywhere else that has a body opening, including the eye and mouth areas. Ya-how! Sorry. Just thinking about it.

Other methods You might have heard of electrolysis. In this method hair follicles are damaged permanently, so they don't produce any more hair, by inserting a needle into them one at a time and zapping them with an electric current (for god's sake, who discovered that?). It is generally only used for small areas of hair, such as the top lip. Electrolysis must be done by a professional beauty worker in a salon. (Ask what experience they have had with using it.) You need to have several appointments, it can take many hours, it hurts and it's expensive.

Laser treatment is also used to reduce the amount of body hair. It destroys a hair follicle with high heat. It's not permanent, but it can take months for the hair to grow back. The regrowth should be finer and lighter coloured. A common claim is that about a third to a half of the unwanted hair is gone after about three treatments with six weeks between visits. It works best for dark hair on light skin. It's expensive, and if not done properly can cause skin discoloration and scarring. Most laser treatments won't work well on grey, blonde or pale red hair, or dark hair on dark skin. This is one that should be performed by an experienced, qualified dermatologist or a very experienced technician, not just any salon worker or a 'cosmetic surgeon'. How long have they been doing the procedure? How many do they do in an average week? What training have they had? A 'certificate' or saying they're 'qualified' doesn't mean they are good at it, or have the right experience and skill (see 'More Info' below).

It's not a removal exactly, but some girls bleach their dark hair blonde so it's less noticeable on paler skin. You can get special body hair bleach at the chemist. Follow the instructions carefully and try a tiny bit first to make sure your skin isn't allergic or reactive.

More info on body hair

dermcoll.edu.au
The Australasian College of Dermatologists site can help you locate a dermatologist who specialises in hair or operates a hair removal laser. Ask a GP to refer you.

hairfacts.com
A US consumer site on hair removal, with info on methods, side effects and dodgy products.

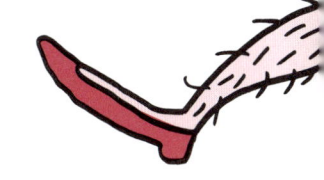

> I hate being hairy. I have more facial hair than the average teenage boy. Not just a mono-brow and upper lip hair either – it comes onto my cheeks and jaw. It's really annoying having to pluck it. I also hate the fine black hair all over my belly and back as well. Natasha, 14, Sydney, NSW

> Although I do, and a majority of girls remove hair, I want it to be stressed that hair removal is unnatural and has nothing to do with becoming a woman. It really upsets me when women are labelled and harassed when they are seen as not going to all the extreme measures to be more 'womanly' or desirable. Emma, 17, Newstead, Qld

4
BODY IMAGE

You look FINE, girl

Be your own best friend

Heaps of girls are unhappy with how they look. Large girls are unhappy, thin girls are unhappy, girls with **wide** hips feel afflicted, girls with **slim** hips feel short-changed, girls with **big** boobs are dissatisfied, girls with **little** breasts are crestfallen, girls with **curly** hair are disgruntled, girls with **straight** hair are troubled, tall girls feel peeved, short girls want a refund. And some girls are convinced their earlobes are wrong.

Your body shape

The 'ideal body' admired in the media is the shape of a very tall, thin girl aged about 10 but with big breasts. A tall man with fake bosoms and no hips, wearing false eyelashes, a wig, a dress and high heels (a 'drag queen') is closer to this so-called ideal than an actual . . . woman. So it's ludicrous. Very few girls or women are that shape. This means they tend to think there's something wrong with them. 'Why don't I look like that?' they ask, instead of 'Why is that shape supposed to be the only good one, anyway, and who says so? And, by the way, shut up.'

> I have a 'normal' build, and I found at high school most girls define this as fat.
> Abbie, 13, Melbourne, Vic.

You're the shape you are because of your genes. You could take after Mum or Dad, or look like someone else in the family – possibly Cousin Yuri. Or maybe Aunty Lorraine, who has spectacular sideburns.

A lot of girls have a negative body image, meaning they don't like the way they look. But there are billions of people on earth so it doesn't make sense to think there could be only one 'perfect' kind of body. Instead there are heaps of different kinds of beautiful.

Body types

You can see just by looking around that some people inherit genes that make them tall, lean professional basketball player types, while others are built like short, cuddly . . . amateur basketball players.

After you're fully grown, your size can be slightly affected by what you eat and how much you move your body around, but your shape will always be essentially the same. It isn't based on your star sign or any other ancient made-up system, or on the latest theory from someone trying to sell a new diet book. That's all piffle.

As well as different inherited body types, people also have different rates of metabolism and genes and other factors affecting their weight. Two people can eat the same food and exercise in the same way but still have different body shapes and sizes.

> It annoys me how the most beautifully shaped girls can say 'oh, I'm so fat, I'm not eating today.' It just doesn't make sense to me.   Marney, 15, Caloundra, Qld

What's healthy?

Healthy means having a body that lets you do all the physical activities you need and want to, and is able to fight off illness. So when the term 'unhealthy weight' is used it means there's too much weight – or not enough weight – for the body to be able to function well and too much strain is being placed on organs and other parts of the body, making injury and illness more likely, now or in the future.

Since it's obvious that there can't be one exact healthy weight for you or anyone else, a healthy weight should be expressed as a range of possibilities, based on several factors.

You need body fat

We female folk have to get over our unrealistic expectations about what's normal and natural when it comes to fat. Girls need to be putting on body fat as well as muscle during their teens – it's a natural part of becoming a young woman. It's healthy for fit, gorgeous mature girls and women (say, from the age of 16) to have 25 to 30 per cent of their body as fat. It's not a dirty word. It doesn't mean *too* fat; it means *necessary* fat.

We usually need about 17 per cent of our body weight as fat to be able to have any periods, and at least 22 per cent as fat to have them regularly. Speaking in averages, a 10-year-old girl needs and has 10 to 15 per cent more body fat than boys of the same age. A grown woman has 10 to 30 per cent more fat than a man.

This girly padding is mainly around our breasts, hips and tummy, and basically it's there to help our bodies in case we ever want to have a baby. If this body fat falls below a healthy level it can result in periods stopping, difficulty getting pregnant or breastfeeding, damage to bones (which can result in serious fractures) and other problems, including lifeless hair, bad teeth and dull skin.

'Cellulite'   Cellulite is a made-up word for dimples on the skin of thighs, bots and sometimes stomachs, caused by the natural fat underneath. Everyone has it, even thin people. It's not caused by toxins, it's caused by being female. No 'firming' or other cream, no amount of scrubbing or seaweed wraps or sweating, will get rid of it. Cellulite is just some-

What's your healthy weight range?

If you answer yes to all of the following questions it's likely that you're within your healthy weight range.

- Do you feel healthy and comfortable?
- Do you feel fit, strong, flexible and able to do any physical manoeuvres you might want to?
- Do you usually get some real physical activity every day? (See Chapter 6, Move.)
- Are you eating from a wide range of healthy foods? (See Chapter 5, Food.)
- Do you eat when you're hungry or at the usual times each day – rather than either ignoring your hunger and rigidly policing your food intake, or eating when you're bored, upset, already full or not hungry?

thing cosmetics companies would like us to obsess about so we buy useless expensive crap. The only cure for cellulite is not to care about it.

Being thin is okay too

You don't have to have big bosoms or wide hips to be a real woman. A lot of girls are genetically programmed to be small and thin or tall and thin. People can make rude and thoughtless comments (who loves being compared to a stick?) and even suggest that you have an eating disorder.

Thin girls are just as beautiful as girls with more curves. But if you feel that you're underweight and it's affecting your health and energy levels, ask a GP for a referral to a dietician for some hints.

If you're worried that you (or a friend) may be losing too much weight or obsessing about food, see 'Eating Disorders' in Chapter 12, Mind Health.

Assessing yourself

You can't judge yourself by:

- whether you look thin or not – having more fat than some people does not necessarily mean you're unhealthy. And being thin doesn't automatically mean you're healthy.
- whether anything wobbles. Next time you're watching an elite athletics race and the women runners are getting ready, notice how they wobble their muscles and skin – and they have even less body fat than is healthy. Everyone wobbles. If we didn't, we'd be skeletons. >

- doing a Body Mass Index (BMI) calculation – it's no good for anyone who hasn't finished growing (which sometimes isn't until you're 18 or so) and ignores many possibly relevant factors, such as how fit you are, how much of your weight is muscle (which weighs more than fat) and whether you're healthy.

And don't judge yourself by:
- reading the scales – weight gain can be natural because your bones are getting bigger, or be caused by your body making extra muscle (that's good), while weight loss may be caused by having gastro for a couple of days (that's not good). Even once you've stopped growing, you don't want scales ruling your life. Getting on them every day is misleading – everyone goes up and down a little depending on daily factors.
- consulting a weight-for-height chart – these are often outdated or based on men, and not scientific or individual enough for you to judge from.
- doing a fat-pinch caliper test. Sometimes gym assessors or coaches use a little set of tongs to pinch some fat, often at your waist, and measure it. It's invasive and humiliating, it doesn't tell them anything useful scientifically, and is often used

Comments people shouldn't make about weight

'You're getting fat. You need to go on a diet.'

Try not to be influenced by these comments. They can hurt your feelings (particularly if they come from your mother), don't help you to change even if you need to, and are often just plain wrong.

And be careful not to make these kinds of comments yourself. Many girls say such remarks started them on the road to an eating disorder, when they were a healthy size to begin with.

'You look great. Have you lost weight?'

People mean this as a compliment, but actually it's just as intrusive as 'You need to lose weight'. And it makes you think, What – did I look terrible before?

So don't link someone's looks to their weight: again it can hurt feelings and even trigger an obsession with getting thinner. Just compliment somebody on their hair or their clothes, or say they look pretty.

as a tool to intimidate you into buying a gym membership, or feeling you have to achieve a certain set of numbers on a chart. Don't bother.

- 'going up a size' – a teenage girl needs to double the size of her skeleton over a few years, and grow bigger organs inside her. You need to go up a few sizes between the ages of 11 and 18!
- the number on your clothes labels, because sizes differ a lot. Girls' clothes sizes (8, 10, 12, 14) are supposed to be related to age, but vary wildly from brand to brand; women's clothes sizes (8, 10, 12, 14, 16 and so on) are supposed to be based on a series of measurements taken a gerzillion years ago, but they vary wildly too, depending on shop and brand (or label). You can be a size 10 in one brand and a 14 in another, or a different size on the top and bottom.

> There is so much conflicting information about what is a healthy weight for certain heights. It's hard to know which one to believe.
> Sheree, 17, Carrum Downs, Vic.

And you absolutely *mustn't* judge yourself by:

- comparing yourself with other people – your height and hair colour are different from a friend's, and your weight will be too (unless the two of you are clones in a science fiction movie, and you eat exactly the same foods and move your body exactly the same number of centimetres every day and have the same metabolism). >

'size 10'   'size 14'   'one size fits all'

LaBeL SiZes don't meaN MuCH...

- comparing yourself with the fashion models. They are unusually tall, unusually thin women with unusually wide shoulders (they're more like hangers that the clothes are draped on), and some have fake breasts. As the saying goes, 'The only people who look like models are models.' If most women were shaped like a stop sign, with a big head and a pole-thin body, the advertisers would be selling strap-on bottoms, special pens to draw dimples on our thighs, spray-on hips and supplements to make us look bigger.

- comparing yourself with famous actresses – they exercise for hours and have full-time teams of minders and chefs to care for them. A lot of them are bored and hungry. And look like Bratz dolls. It's a miracle they don't take a bite out of their own agents.

- what a relative or anyone else says, even if it's your mum – these comments often come from ignorance about weight and eating, or from the person's own problems or bad feelings about food and body image. And I think we all know how mean brothers and sisters can be. Bullies too can be very good at finding something to say that they think will freak you out (but which isn't necessarily true).

Magazine HELL

> **QUOTE**
>
> 'Change your mind, not your body.'
> **Positive body image slogan**

Being too heavy

Some people are above their healthy weight, and this really restricts their life. We're not talking here of being big and healthy or naturally curvy and fit. We're talking about being too large to feel comfortable a lot of the time.

Girls who are very much bigger than they need to be can find it hard to bend, stretch and be flexible, their fitness levels may drop, and it could limit their choices of hobbies and career. They could also face a number of health problems that range from diabetes to finding it hard to get pregnant when they decide they want to have a baby. People who are above their healthy weight range can also find it hard to buy nice clothes that fit.

It can seem as if the whole world thinks you're lazy and have no 'willpower', and that it's okay to hurt your feelings. You can feel, wrongly, that it's your fault and you're less worthy than other people, and get sad and depressed.

Things to say when somebody comments on your size or shape

'Wow.'

'You do know you said that aloud, right?'

'Is it International Random Opinions Day?'

'I'm the right shape for me.'

'Mind your own body image.'

'Thanks, but I'm not interested.'

'Nothing personal, but do you think you could shut up?'

'I'm supposed to be getting bigger. I'm a teenager, not a puddle in the sun.'

'Who made you the Body Police?'

'No, I don't have anorexia. Do you have any manners?'

'Sorry, I can't hear you, I've got the idiot filter on.'

'Here, read this chapter.'

Obesity Being 'obese' means being at a much higher weight than you need to be. There's no magic line you cross, although many doctors use charts of heights and weights or weight ranges to work out whether you're a lot heavier or a little bit heavier than is healthy for you.

The word 'obese' was originally used by scientific researchers to describe a section of the population. Like 'fat', it can sound insulting applied to individual people and make them feel bad about themselves. We don't need to use these words about ourselves or anybody else. We can talk about 'being in a healthy weight range' or 'being above a healthy (or comfortable) weight range'.

Seeing a doctor about a suspected 'weight problem' If you are worried, check out the box 'What's Your Healthy Weight Range?' a few pages back. If you answer no to most of the questions it could be a good idea to see your GP – that's the only way to know for sure what you're dealing with. The doctor will probably weigh and measure you (which, as you can imagine, is not the most fun you're going to have that week). They should explain nicely what the healthy weight range is for you – not for your age group in general – and whether you're above it. Also ask around your relatives and tell your doctor if there's a family history of type 2 diabetes or other health problems associated with being over a comfortable weight.

> I would personally love to be healthier and to lose about 20 kg. At the moment I am 120 kg.

> I would like my hair to grow out and be its natural colour again. Irina, 18, Brisbane, Qld

Changing to a healthier life If you need to change some habits to get down to a healthier weight range:

- ask the doctor whether this means you need to lose weight – maybe instead you can stop gaining and stay the same weight until, when you've become taller, it's a healthy weight (you've 'grown into it')
- ask the doctor to refer you to a dietician, who will talk with you about the food you eat, the usual size of your food portions and the reasons why you eat; and about how to choose healthier food
- see Chapter 5, Food, for hints about food and eating, and Chapter 6, Move, to find a physical activity you like – no weight-maintenance or weight-loss program makes any sense unless it involves increasing your physical activity as well as decreasing certain kinds of foods
- don't 'diet' (see the 'Dieting' section below), and don't take 'weight-loss tips' from magazines, websites, well-meaning relatives or friends
- contact one of the eating disorder groups given in Chapter 12, Mind Health, if you feel that you can't control the amount of food you eat, that you binge-eat or that you can't stop eating even when you're not hungry – they have many people with the same problem in their support groups and can recommend counsellors and strategies
- accept that changing your life is going to take effort and work – it can be mentally challenging, and sometimes physically hard going
- give yourself regular rewards (think about ones that aren't food, such as pampering sessions, new clothes, money towards a holiday) – you deserve them for all your hard work

> People calling me 'fat': even if they're joking it hurts. And body image is like a huge thing these days – calling someone fat does not make it any easier.
> Lisa, 16, Melton, Vic.

- try to be as kind and understanding to yourself as a best friend would be
- go slowwwly and gradually – any successful and lasting change has to become part of the way you think and feel. Don't get furious with yourself for any straying from the path – just step back on, don't wander further off into the distance.

Losing weight means you're still you, but a healthier you with a lot more energy. One of my favourite stories is about a girl who had been over her healthy weight for years. After months of hard work she changed her life and lost the weight she needed to. A guy who had been her friend for many years suddenly wanted her to be his girlfriend. Instead of feeling grateful and thrilled, she told him where to go. 'If he wasn't interested in me before,' she said, 'when he knew me just as well, then he wasn't going to really love me for me.' That is a great girl with the right attitude.

Dieting

'Diet' can be such a confusing word. It even gets adults all mixed up. Some people use the words 'a good diet' to mean having good eating habits. But 'a good diet' can sound like 'going on a diet' is good. And it really isn't. A 'diet' or 'going on a diet' or 'dieting' or 'starting a diet' usually means something else: a short-term diet people put themselves on, which is a Very Bad Idea.

Going on a short-term diet, or strictly restricting food, almost always results in you ending up larger than when you started. Going on lots of diets is also a sign that you're more likely to develop an eating disorder (such as eating too much or too little). Diets are often a response to a body image fear or worry – a response that can make things worse.

don't worry if you step off the path occasionally...

Even if you're over a healthy weight, 'dieting', 'going on a diet' and short-term diets are not good for you, and don't work in the long term. You'll almost certainly lose some weight but then put on more than you started with. So then you think you need another one. So then you end up bigger again, and frustrated, and think it's your fault. This is sometimes called 'yo-yo dieting' (going up and down) or 'weight cycling' (going round in circles).

> Diets are stupid and make you fat and feel really crap about yourself!! Never go on one, ever!!! Diets are not fun, and anyone who tells you they are has problems and you should refer them to a counsellor.
> Emily, 14, Tylden, Vic.

So some people are very cross about the so-called weight-loss industry (which promotes certain foods and 'programs' as weight-loss solutions). They say such claims are misleading or even lies, because in the end almost everyone puts the weight back on, plus some more, after they 'diet'.

These days many people assume that thinner always means healthier, and that dieting is the best way to do that. Both of these things are untrue. There are so many pressures on girls to look a certain way, and so many weight-loss and other companies advertising their products by appealing to our body image fears. Sometimes, it's hard to realise that happiness isn't about the size and shape of your body but what's happening in your head. Don't go on diets just because magazines, websites, apps, books and weight-loss companies promote them as a way to lose weight.

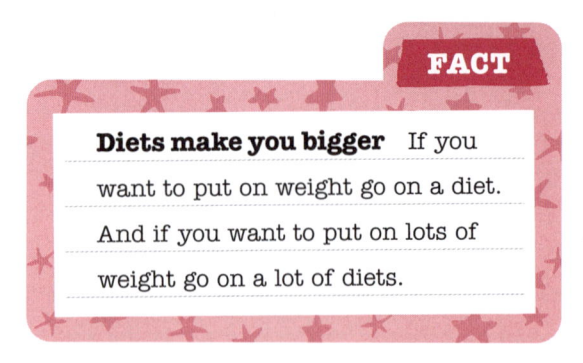

FACT

Diets make you bigger If you want to put on weight go on a diet. And if you want to put on lots of weight go on a lot of diets.

FACT

Healthy food plans It's so much better to start a long-term healthy eating plan than go on 'diets', which can damage your body and mess with your mind. 'Diet' drinks and food aren't always good for you (and usually aren't). Arghhh! So read Chapter 5, Food, for all the real facts.

Why don't diets work?

- When you severely restrict food the body thinks you are in starvation mode, so it starts conserving fat to create an emergency supply. It does this by making it harder for you to burn fat during exercise. It allows your body to lose water, but not fat. Your metabolism slows down, meaning you need to exercise more to burn the same amount of energy as you used to. And it starts sending you signals saying 'Feed me!' It's a survival thing.
- By saying, 'I will never eat a donut', you pretty much guarantee that that's all you'll think about. So you get cravings, go off the diet and overcompensate by eating too much.
- Dieters feeling sad and deprived of comforting food are far more likely to binge-eat than other people. Then later they feel guilty or depressed about 'failing'.
- Diets are almost always too hard to stick to. They can require people to devote masses of brain space and time to counting, measuring, weighing, following instructions, having strict shopping lists, buying foods that aren't in season and eating things they don't like or that are expensive and not suited to family meals.
- Crazes or fashionable diets that suggest that being overweight is caused by cheese, indigestion, mucus, eating the wrong things before 11 am or eating certain combinations of foods, your blood group or your body 'type' never last long term because they are too faddish, and dieters get sick of them. There's absolutely no scientific basis for them. You may as well base a diet on numerology, your horoscope, your hair colour or your favourite football team. >

> **FACT**
>
> **Healthy exercise plans** See Chapter 6, Move, for all the info you need on ways to enjoy getting fitter and more active.

> **FACT**
>
> **Epic fail** Short-term diets are guaranteed to fail you, while making you feel that you're the failure. If you go on one, or stop eating much for a couple of days, you will lose weight. So it will seem to be 'working'. The catch is – it can't last. The weight you lost will go back on, plus more.

Don't starve yourself.   Monique and Charlie, 14, NT

Believe me the diets aren't working.   Siobhan, 14, Clontarf, Qld

Why you shouldn't diet

* Dieting can stunt your growth and delay your development – fad diets that restrict you to one or only a few kinds of food deprive your body of the nutrients it needs.

* Dieting can cause hunger, tiredness, crabbiness, forgetfulness, inability to concentrate, headaches, muscle cramps, constipation, weak bones, vitamin and mineral deficiencies, dull hair and skin, bad breath and dehydration.

* Dieting is a known cause of depression – the more diets, the more severe the depression can be.

* Dieting is a known trigger for eating disorders (see Chapter 12, Mind Health).

* Dieting mostly doesn't factor in exercise as a must-do part of a healthy life, or provide enough energy for you to exercise without becoming exhausted or sick.

* Dieting can lead to futile 'yo-yo' dieting – a diet doesn't work so inevitably you try it again or another one (lose some, put more on, lose some, put even more on).

* Dieting can set you up for a lifetime of feeling out of control, and sad, bad and mad about food.

* Dieting makes you gain weight.

- Virtually no short-term diets are designed for an individual, so they don't suit anyone perfectly. They're too inflexible: the diet says you must eat fish and a salad tonight, but it's cold and you feel like chicken risotto.

- We're social beings whose world is arranged around eating together. Dieters have to slink off or aren't able to fully join in, and it can feel lonely and isolating.

Some don'ts

- Don't share dieting either with a friend or through a club, magazine or website. It can result in shared obsessions and competition about how much weight is being lost. (Everyone is different and competitions are dangerous.) It's especially unhelpful to go on a diet with an adult (such as your mum) because you have different needs. Share food, not dieting.

- Don't diet for an event, such as a wedding at which you're a bridesmaid, or your school Formal.

- Don't fast (have no food or fluids, or very little, for a day or more): it's dangerous and damaging for teenage girls. (Some people are required to fast for religious reasons, but religions will make exceptions and other arrangements for children, teens, pregnant women and women who are breastfeeding.) Never participate in charity diets or fasts. Show your support another way.

- Don't take diet pills. Most of these are a form of 'speedy' drug that makes you less hungry, or not hungry at all, and may make you feel buzzy, unable to sleep, cranky or faint. You could do damage to your body, make yourself more vulnerable to addiction, suffer from anxiety and exhaustion, and become deficient in basic nutrients.
- Don't take laxatives (drugs or herbs used to cause diarrhoea as soon as possible after eating). They don't result in any weight loss, because food is still absorbed on the way through, but taking them a lot or regularly can lead to you not being able to control when poo comes out. Bleeding from your bottom and dehydration are other results. >

Blame the diet

Girls tend to blame themselves when a diet fails. They think they didn't have enough willpower and that they just needed to stick to it – even when sticking to it is illogical and makes them unhappy. Blaming themselves means they're likely to feel even sadder. And that can be a trigger to eat to feel comforted, instead of when they're hungry.

Don't blame yourself – blame the diet.

FACT

Cigarettes Smoking doesn't make you lose weight.

Diets make you farty

Diets, in my opinion, are wrong. A healthy eating scheme and exercise plan are much better.

It gets me REALLY pissed off if my grandmother tells me about diets. Sofia, 18, Brisbane, Qld

'Health' products

Beware of anything that's marketed to you as a 'health' product – from a 'diet plan' to multivitamins to crappy so-called exercise equipment – you don't have to spend money on anything special to have a healthier lifestyle. Also beware of nasty self-hating messages that can be used to undermine your confidence. That's their special trick – if they make you feel like you have to look 'better', different, bigger, 'healthier', smaller . . . then they can sell you stuff they promise can help transform you, whether it's make-up, an 'eating program', so-called diet or low-fat food . . . whatever. See Chapter 21, Shopping, for more sneaky marketing tricks; Chapter 7, Body Health, and Chapter 12, Mind Health, for unbiased advice; and Chapter 5, Food, for what it's really healthy to eat.

- Don't take meal 'replacements' or 'supplements' (usually a powdered drink or a biscuit). No fun, not social, hard to stick to and just plain weird.
- Don't try patches or gels that are claimed to release a 'fat-burning' or 'fat-melting' substance into your system. No, they don't – there is no such thing. (Damn. You've been totally ripped off.)
- Don't over-exercise because it can get out of hand, and too much will cause many health and mental problems: your period may stop, stress bone fractures are common, and repeating one type of exercise over and over, whatever it is, can cause permanent physical damage.

THE DRESS HAS to fit YOU

school dance madness!

no! no! no! noooooooo!

do not 'diet' to fit into a dress!

being uncomfortable is your enemy

ow ow ow

PRom horror!

YOU DON'T HAVE to fit tHE DRESS!

More info on avoiding diets

choice.com.au
The Australian Consumers' Association site has reviews of fad diets, and diet products. Check out Food and Health.

ifnotdieting.com.au
The website and book (*If Not Dieting Then What?*) of Dr Rick Kausman, the eating behaviours expert, help people develop a good relationship with food and their body.

The last time I went on a diet was at the beginning of December for a major eighteenth party, where this boy I like was going to be. I lost about 5 kilos in two weeks and I'm still recovering from it and I've actually gained 10 kilos – currently I'm trying to do it slowly and one step at a time.   Grace, 17, Bentleigh East, Vic.

In year 9 I only ate dinner [*not breakfast or lunch*] because my parents were there and now as a sort of 'rebound' I suppose I've put on about 10 kilos. I do try to stay fit and healthy now, the proper way!   Sophia, 17, Boorowa, NSW

Diets are a waste of time. Skipping breakfast makes you put on weight because it slows your metabolism down. Diets wreak havoc to your immune system and your health and they don't help lose weight at all.   Emma, 15, Brisbane, Qld

I have just lost 10 kilos by eating healthy and exercising and have never felt better.   Geraldine, 18, Wallsend, NSW

Diets suck. They never work for me even though I try so hard.   Elise, 15, Penrith, NSW

When I went on the mandarin diet I would eat about eight mandarins a day and drink water and that was all. I got pretty sick and had diarrhoea.   Annabelle, 15, The Gap, Qld

Diets girls have tried that didn't work for them long term

Girls who answered the Girl Stuff Survey said they had tried:

stupid starvation diets ✻ eating and spewing!! ✻ stopped eating ✻ eating less carbs and fat ✻ currently attempting a high-exercise, low-junk-food diet – I am also failing miserably ✻ anorexic diet ✻ junk free ✻ **one with Mum** ✻ no wheat, meat, dairy, sugar, salt ✻ stupid one where u didn't eat much at all, but still junk and stuff – that's soooo stupid ✻ just lettuce ✻ starvation diet ✻ starving, binging, purging ✻ ciggies and diet coke ✻ apple and water – it is very draining, and made up by the girls at school ✻ Slim-Fast and it was horrible and didn't work at all ✻ **not eating lunch and brekky** ✻ think I have tried every one!!!! ✻ hardly-eat-any-food kind of diet ✻ Eat Right 4 Your Type, starve yourself ✻ just salad ✻ Weight Watchers, Atkins ✻ soup diet, but that didn't last very long ✻ fruit and yoghurt, lots of water ✻ a blood type diet for my eczema, many other diets ✻ not sugar, only vegetables and very little meat ✻ meal-replacement shakes ✻ bulimia ✻ South Beach ✻ **only eat what fits on a small plate** ✻ only eating fruit and plain bread ✻ water only, dinner only, one piece of fruit a day, six meals a week, breathing in when eating ✻ not eating for days and then pigging out (bulimia) ✻ **low GI one – it was working but I couldn't keep going** ✻ Fat Blaster Lite, Easy Slim, Slim-Fast, Optislim ✻ make up my own really: no bread, detox diet, only fruit ✻ wouldn't eat anything except dinner ✻ a kind of not-eating-and-throwing-up diet ✻ everything from tablets to starving myself ✻ CSIRO ✻ didn't eat for a while ✻ **starving** ✻ ate vegetables and fruit for three weeks ✻ anorexia and bulimia for the past two years; also binge eat a lot ✻ low-kilojoule ✻ no fat foods, but it didn't really work out ✻ just a diet my family put together ✻ stupid one I made up that would be skipping meals or cutting down the portion I ate ✻ tablets ✻ soup and fruit ✻ **strange, self-invented ones** ✻ only allowed to eat some stew ✻ crazy unhealthy one that made me lose too much weight ✻ liquid diet ✻ what sort have I not been on?!?!?! ✻ mostly salad and only tiny amounts of carb diet Mum once put me on ✻ only green things, no bread, extreme water, lots of chocolate ✻ Ultra Slim ✻ **made up my own! – starving usually (very silly)** ✻ some diet my mum had ✻ mainly starvation diets or throwing up after every meal ✻ tried to cut out carbohydrates – it didn't work! ✻ blood type ✻ detox, no sugar, brown bread ✻ starve myself ✻ **fat-free options** ✻ food-combining diet, and under 500 cal a day ✻ dinner-only diet ✻ used to cut out breakfast and lunch, but had no energy and used to faint regularly ✻ eat one piece of fruit or veg a day ✻ no bread.

Not liking your bits

When you spend a lot of time obsessing about how you look (otherwise known as The Teenage Years) you can develop wacky ideas about one of your bits. Some people hate their ears; others their nose. Some are convinced their ankles are the first thing everyone notices about them because they're the first thing about themselves *they* see when they look down or in a mirror.

> Once I didn't eat for 2–3 weeks and only ate apples and very little dinner. It sucked. I was sooo hungry and moody, and I often pigged out then felt guilty. Then I punished myself for eating.
> Bethany, 14, Goulburn, NSW

And yet if you asked a stranger to guess which bit you hated they'd probably never get it. Likely comments would include 'Your knees? What the hell's wrong with your *knees*?', 'But you've got GREAT hair!', and 'Huh? I've never even noticed your ears.'

Wanting cosmetic procedures

Talking through a body image problem with a trained psychological counsellor is more likely to make you feel better than assuming you need to be 'fixed'.

Cosmetic surgery The number of teenagers having cosmetic surgery in the US is rising every year. It's not so common in Australia and New Zealand, but certainly more girls here are thinking about it, wanting it and, in a small number of cases, having it.

Although the Australian Society of Plastic Surgeons doesn't have an official policy on surgery and teens, its spokes-doc says it's generally not a good idea unless there are special circumstances (such as really big breasts that are making life uncomfortable and difficult).

Some cosmetic procedures that a plastic surgeon may be happier to perform on a teen include removing large birthmarks or moles, and pinning back ears that stick straight out from the head. The operations that most reputable plastic surgeons wouldn't touch for a teenager include 'nose jobs' (rhinoplasty), liposuction and breast enlargement.

COSMETIC SURGERY IS PROBABLY NOT THE ANSWER

The downsides and dangers of cosmetic surgery

The downsides and dangers are rarely discussed when magazines and TV shows talk about cosmetic surgery. If you are under 18 your parent or guardian will have to approve the operation. Surgery isn't something to be taken lightly – as if it's just a quick, easy nip 'n' tuck.

- It is usually very expensive and, unless done for a medical reason such as breast reduction, won't be covered by a Medicare refund.

- The risks include complications under general anaesthetic (people have even died).

- Many operations involve breaking bones, the rearrangement of facial features and massive bruising. Recovery time and pain can be the same as for car accident injuries.

- Some mistakes made by surgeons are impossible, difficult or painful to fix, and the repair work needs to be attempted by a qualified plastic surgeon.

No cosmetic nurse or doctor should inject a teenager with cosmetic products either. If you do think you need cosmetic surgery or procedures such as Botox, please read the chapter Cosmetic Surgery & Procedures in my sequel to this book, for adults, called *Women's Stuff*. There are some special rip-offs and other concerns you need to be aware of.

Injections Some ludicrous people are claiming Botox injections in your twenties are a good idea to stop lines from forming. Botox is simply a toxic substance that paralyses areas where it is injected, for up to three months. Each 'unit' of Botox is a measure of poison that's enough to kill a mouse. Injections to paralyse an area such as the forehead can be up to 60 units – in other words, a lot of dead mice. You can see the effect of Botox on many actresses – the ones who can't move their foreheads or have a natural facial expression; the ones whose faces look like giant boiled eggs. Botox side effects can include a droopy eyelid for several weeks or months, not to mention the weird alien effect of not being able to frown, or of having a fake-looking smile because the skin around your eyes looks dead or plastic.

96 BODY body image

Teeth whitening Despite all those grinning Hollywood starlets' faces flashing shiny sets, teeth aren't supposed to be toilet-bowl white. Most people only require a whitening product if they have badly stained teeth. Don't be sucked in by advertising telling you that you 'need' one.

Many whitening toothpastes, chewing gum and other products sold over the counter take too long to, or don't, work because the amount of bleaching agent is too small, or can cause burns because the concentration is too high.

Teeth whitening using high bleach concentrations, the only effective way to whiten teeth, should be done or supervised by a fully qualified dentist. If your dentist agrees you need one ask them about products that won't hurt and will whiten your teeth safely.

Intense teeth-whitening procedures, where you sit in the dentist chair with whitening agent on your teeth while a laser light is shone onto your teeth for a few minutes at a time, can be really painful. It's the bleaching agent that hurts, not the light – which actually does nothing to make your teeth any whiter. A warm light just dries out your mouth, which makes your teeth look whiter until your saliva gets going properly again. Even having paid for this hugely expensive treatment, many people bail out halfway through.

Most independent dentists agree that the safest and most effective way to whiten teeth is to use an at-home tray treatment sold by your dentist, but this will require some dedication, doing it in shorter bursts over a few days to build up the bleaching, and isn't cheap.

Don't get conned

Some revolting characters in the cosmetic surgery business have been convincing women they need surgery on their girly bits. These operations are hardly ever necessary, are very expensive, cause pain and can cause side effects and damage.

Some girls and women can be vulnerable to this kind of advertising or suggestion because they're worried that their vulva area and labia look untidy, lopsided, odd or too big. Usually we don't get to see each other's girly bits, so we have nothing to compare ours with. There's a huge range of different shapes and sizes when it comes to the 'frilly edges'. (What you see in porn is no help because everything about those girls has been faked.) You can rest assured that your girly bits are both as individual and as normal as anybody else's, but if you're really worried ask your doctor to have a look and reassure you. You may feel more comfortable with a woman doctor.

Us Spanish people have a saying 'Para el gusto se hicieron los colores', meaning 'The colours were made for everyone's taste', as in people got different tastes and if one person thinks you are ugly another person may think your cute.

Alandra, 15, Brookline, Massachusetts, US

There's this one coach at my gym club that puts some of us down, particularly me, saying that I'm fat and overweight, when I know for a fact that I'm not, I'm in a healthy weight range, I eat good food (most of the time) and I exercise regularly.   Vera, 18, Anula, NT

I am a skinny girl and I get called stick, paper and anorexia.

Ange, 13, Lismore, NSW

I feel upset when people comment on my body. It's not theirs so why do they have to say anything?   Shoshana, 18, Townsville, Qld

I know I'm not fat but I still feel that I am sometimes.

Bonnie, 15, Wagga Wagga, NSW

I want to be smaller but my friends say I am perfect.

Sam, 15, Bathurst, NSW

How come even though I'm thin I haven't got a fantastic figure?   Simone, 14, Farrer, ACT

Why can't I put on any weight?

Erin, 14, Norton Summit, SA

I have to say that I get annoyed when girls my age complain about their belly mound – because it's NATURAL for all girls to have it! And I wish we could all stop being so self-conscious of it!

Natalie, 17, Wangaratta, Vic.

I hate seeing girls in magazines (you know, the ones in bikinis on the front of magazines). I get fidgety and anxious because I worry that I'm not good enough because I don't look like them. I know my boyfriend loves me but I still have this constant feeling that I have to look like a supermodel. It makes me sick.

Shaz, 17, Ballina, NSW

Whenever I go shopping with Mum and I need a size bigger, she always tells me I'm fat. Because I'm a size 14 and I need a 16 sometimes, it makes me feel really awful.

Anna, 14, Eltham, Vic.

I think everyone feels that there is something wrong with their body at one time or another. Madelyn, 15, Lithgow, NSW

I know I am not fat because people always comment on my thinness, but I want to be skinnier – I think it looks better. People always say how hot models are. Amanda, 17, Toorak, Vic.

What is the right size?
Teghan, 15, Quambatook, Vic.

I have a bit of trouble putting weight on. It does not help me to want to put weight on when girls constantly compliment me on my skinniness.

Lola, 15, Toowoomba, Qld

Sometimes being abnormal is the normal and being the normal is the abnormal.

Jude, 17, Masterton, NZ

If somebody says something about my body or appearance I get quite upset. I know in myself that I'm not 'fat' but sometimes it hurts to be called that all the same.

Prashanti, 15, Winmalee, NSW

My parents, mainly my mum, have been telling me since I was 13 that I should go on a diet despite being in the healthy weight range. It's screwed my thoughts on dealing with being healthy and maintaining a good weight and diet. Sometimes parents don't know what's best.

Cami, 18, Mooloolaba, Qld

I'm not very sure whether I'm overweight or underweight or anything. Victoria, 16, Brisbane, Qld

There's an insane amount of pressure put on girls to be thin, but most of it comes from themselves.

Taylor, 17, Adelaide, SA

Growing out of obsessions

Generally bit-hating feelings tend to get less as you grow into your body, and as you get older you don't obsess so much. And of course until you stop growing you don't know what your body is finally going to look like anyway.

Most obsessions that result in a girl wanting cosmetic surgery or some other physical treatment are actually cured by non-surgical methods: learning to like yourself the way you are; growing to realise your 'flaw' is quirky and attractive, or something that you hardly think about any more. One day soon you'll look back at yourself in a photo and think, Damn, I looked good, and I didn't even realise it at the time! Or at least, That was an awkward stage but it's all turned out fine. Many famous people were teased at school and even, early in their career, told to change something – only for their so-called 'flaws' to become trademark features. In the long run, the things that make you different are part of what makes you special.

Mirror, mirror, mirror, mirror, mirror . . . that's enough now

* Think about putting any full-length mirror on the inside of a wardrobe door, rather than somewhere in your bedroom where you can stare at yourself all the time.

* Have a mirror in the bathroom, but not on your desk.

* Avoid magnifying mirrors – they are really quite the evil item. Nobody ever sees you up that close.

* Don't spend ages looking into any mirror. You can always find something to worry about if you look long or hard enough.

Hey. I look nice

Judge yourself kindly

Take a compliment

When someone pays you a compliment – 'You look great', 'I love that skirt' or 'That haircut really suits you' – smile and say thanks.

Don't say anything negative about yourself or deny the compliment – none of that 'Aw, I look terrible', 'But what about this gigantic pimple?' or 'Shut UP, I so do not look okay.'

thanks

HOW TO TAKE a COMPLIMENT

More info on body image

Beware of 'health' pages on social media and other contact sites. Many have dieting and exercise 'tips' and 'advice' that can damage your body and mess with your head.

reach.org.au
The Reach organisation's Birdcage program offers workshops for schools and community groups on body image and self-esteem.

thebutterflyfoundation.org.au
Support and info about body image and eating behaviours, with extra info for parents and medical professionals. Follow their hashtag #TheWholeMe on social media.

kidshelpline.com.au
Advice line: 1800 551 800
On the website choose Teens 13-17, then scroll down to Developing a Positive Body Image.

betterhealth.vic.gov.au
To do a quiz, on this reliable Government health site choose Healthy Living, then click on Quizzes then Teenagers, then Girls and Body Image or Boys and Body Image.

about-face.org and **bodypositive.com**
Two US sites about how to be happy whatever size you are. About-face has a totally brilliant Gallery of Offenders: shameful ads and images.

theconversation.com
Search Body Image on the university-linked site for a series of reputable reports on body image issues, research, antidotes and more. While you're there, search Girls for more articles that might be relevant to you.

adiosbarbie.com
Fights stereotypes.

any-body.org
A coalition of good folk led by author and psychotherapist Susie Orbach has created a non-profit hub for body image info. Full of life-affirming, commonsense writing.

amysmartgirls.com
On this US website started by writer-performer Amy Poehler and her best pal Meredith Walker, search Body Image for a range of videos, articles, art projects, interviews and ideas about body feelings and positivity.

10 Steps to Positive Body Image list
Search that title on nationaleatingdisorders.com, a US site, for a good list.

FACT

We're all lopsided As pointed out in Chapter 1, Change, we all have features and 'matching' body parts that are of different sizes: eyes, hands, breasts, ears, feet – each is a 'pair' of slightly different sizes. In other words, 'unusual' is actually . . . normal! And what you think might be weird and obvious is probably not noticed by anyone . . .

My shape is not your business

I wish I had an ass.   Ange, 18, Dapto, NSW

You are what you are.   Kiara, 15, Darlington, SA

I don't like my thighs.   Jasmine, 14, Campsie, NSW

Be grateful for what you have, not what you don't have.   Rose, 16, Toorak, Vic.

My body is what it is. I'm extremely glad to be me.   Kirsty, 17, Brisbane, Qld

I hate the shape of my legs. They seem huge. Apparently they're not too bad but I still worry. I've been told there's nothing wrong with it and there isn't really anything to do about it. But I would like to know if there is something.

Leah, 14, Melton, Vic.

It makes me think, 'Hey I'm beautiful the way I am, I feel healthy and I'm in a healthy weight range and there is nothing wrong with my body. I am beautiful.' Rosie, 15

I wanna lose weight but my friends think I need to gain weight. Lexie, 13, Houghton, SA

Everyone thinks that everyone else notices every single flaw in them but really they're all too busy worrying about what other people think (of them). Elle, 15

Just don't take what people think too seriously – they're saying it because they're jealous that they aren't that confident with their own bodies. Ricki, 16, Richmond, Tas.

I think it would be nice to see some normal-sized girls being promoted and I don't mean a feature story on 'love your body' in Cleo or whatever, I mean just spread through everything. The mags say they are about promoting good body image but in reality it's very token. Ellen, 18, Melbourne, Vic.

Body image should be about you and how you want to project your self image! Others' opinions should never rule your life. 'Moraelin', 17

I haven't felt comfortable in my skin for years. Jasmine, 15

How can I get rid of my boobs? Fran, 17, Happy Valley, SA

My weight is good, I just don't like being tall! But that's OK, I guess ... Rosie, 13, Darwin, NT

I don't feel confident about my body – my mother tells me that I'm fat, but I'm only a size 10 (and 180 cm tall). I know that I'm not fat, but I still don't have much confidence. Allie, 16, Canungra, Qld

FOOD

5

I take your point

grrowwl

You gotta eat! Otherwise you might not grow to the height you should (your skeleton size doubles in the teen years). Or **fight off** germs. Or stay **brainy**. Instead you'll spend the rest of your days stunted, sniffly and staring at the wall **wondering** how the preferential voting system works, and what's the capital of Mongolia. (It's Wagga Wagga. Or Ulan Bator.)

What you need

You're going to need to work out what food is healthy and eat it. (Unless you're the heir to a string of luxury hotels or a Hollywood starlet who, in between being photographed and sliding off nightclub couches into a pile of their own underpants, exists mostly on room service, narcotics and red lolly snakes soaked in gin by a personal chef.)

So here's the lowdown on the food you need, when you need to eat it, and how to make sure you don't miss out on any of the good stuff.

Eating plans

You don't need to keep a food diary for weeks or obsess about how many 'serves' of which kinds of foods you've eaten every day. Just read the guidelines coming up and think about whether you need to make an effort to, say, eat more fresh fruit and vegies (yeah, probably). Trying to follow strict rules or diet lists or planning on Thursday exactly what you'll have for breakfast next Tuesday is too hard. And too boring. Lots of those lists don't even take into account what season it is, so they suggest turnips in summer and mangoes in winter.

Top ten hints for enjoying food

1. Eat food with fresh ingredients.
2. Make it for friends and/or family.
3. Prepare and cook it with friends and/or family.
4. Eat it with friends and/or family.
5. Don't watch TV or read while you're eating.
6. Don't stand up and walk around while you're eating.
7. Eat slowly instead of 'bolting'.
8. Don't diet. (And see Chapter 4, Body Image, for why!)
9. Don't think of some foods as 'forbidden' or 'naughty'.
10. Try lots of different foods.

FACT

Teenagers need more Teenagers need more fuel than children or adults because of the growing they have to do. So listen when your body says it's hungry.

food ✱ BODY   105

You need fruit

You need three to four pieces of medium-sized fruit each day, such as an orange, a peach, a mango, an apple, a small banana or quarter of a rockmelon. 'Half a piece' means something the size of a kiwi fruit, an apricot or a few lychees or berries. Different fruits have different vitamins, so go for a mix such as a fruit salad. Whole fruit gives you more fibre than juice, which your body needs (so you poo regularly), and it's cheaper.

> Can I eat too many vegetables? [*No.*]
> Jess, 14,
> Vermont, Vic.
>
> Are carbohydrates bad for you? [*No.*]
> Skye-Rebekkah, 15,
> Berwick, Vic.

You need vegies

You need at least five serves a day of vegetables and it's fine to have more. Vegies give you important vitamins and minerals, and fibre. One serve would be a medium-sized spud or half a cup of vegies such as broccoli, cauliflower, peas, spinach, carrot, turnip and pumpkin. Chips (hot or cold) are potatoes cooked in saturated oils and shouldn't be included, because they contain unnecessary fats.

A good way to get a mix of vegies is to have a bowl of steamed or stir-fried ones or homemade minestrone (vegies and bean) soup, or a plate of salad or raw sticks or slices. Try serving vegies different ways: with a splash of low-salt soy sauce, Asian style; as a pasta sauce, Italian style; or in a salad sanger. Add flavour with chopped fresh herbs, garlic, grated lemon peel or lemon juice, and pepper.

You need stuff made from grains

This means wholegrain bread, (unsweetened) breakfast cereals, pasta, noodles, rice, polenta and cous cous. (A sweet pastry is not a good grain food.) You probably need at least four to six serves a day of this stuff, even more if you're doing lots of exercise.

One serve is a cup of breakfast cereal, pasta or rice; or two pieces of bread or a medium-sized roll; or about a cup of cooked pasta or rice (or similar). To avoid confusion, a perfectly fine amount of grainy things to have each day would be a big bowl of porridge or unsweetened cereal for brekky, or a smaller

spinach, pumpkin, mushrooms, grapes, plum, banana — mix up your COLOURS

> **HINT**
> **Eat the rainbow** Try to eat fruit and vegies every day from all the five colour groups: blues/purples; reds; yellows/oranges; whites; greens.

bowl of porridge or muesli plus a piece of wholegrain toast with cheese and/or tomato; a sandwich or filled roll for lunch; wholegrain toast with cheese and/or tomato for an after-school snack; and a bowl of pasta or rice with a sauce containing vegies and meat, fish or tofu for tea or dinner.

Grain foods are the biggest source of our most important energy nutrient: carbohydrates. They're the fuel that make us go, physically. And our brains need carbohydrates too. Low-carb diets are bad for you. Especially when you're a teenager. And they make you FART a LOT.

> **FACT**
> **Recommended serves** The recommendations about what teenagers should eat from each food group differ depending on which website or book you read. Many were written some years ago, and in any case are a guide only. You don't have to be exact about it, or eat the same stuff every day. Because that's booooring.

You need protein

Ever since we were faffing around in caves, trying to make a cute pair of thigh-boots out of dead squirrels, we've been meat eaters. The human body is designed to run on lots of protein, which is found in lean meat (meaning with the fatty white parts cut off), poultry (chicken, duck and turkey) and fish.

Alternatives to meat include nuts, soy products, eggs and legumes. Don't ask me what a legume is, I'll have to look it up. (Okay, it's beans and peas, including chickpeas, soybeans and lentils. For some startling reason, a peanut is also a legume, not a nut.)

People eat too much junk food from the tuckshop and don't eat their own healthy lunch.

Lana, 13, Brisbane, Qld

You should have at least one or two serves of protein a day: that's two slices of roast beef or ham (about the size of your palm) in a sandwich; or two little lamb chops; or half a cup of bolognaise sauce; or up to 100 grams of some other meat such as a chicken fillet or 120 grams of fish (a piece of fish a bit bigger than your palm). One serve also equals a third of a cup of almonds, peanuts or legumes.

You should have red meat about three or four times a week (beef, lamb, pork or . . . well, I doubt you'll be having venison, which is deer meat). Red meat is the easiest source of iron and zinc, which girls and women need lots of.

One egg is half a serve (which makes a two-egg omelette one serve). A couple of eggs a week is plenty, but don't get hung up on counting exactly.

You need calcium foods

Dairy foods are an easy source of calcium, which is important for your growing bones. They are made of milk from moo cows (okay, it's getting technical now) and you should eat two to three serves of milk, cheese or yoghurt a day.

One serve would be a glass of milk; or a couple of thin, sandwich-sized slices of cheese; or a small tub of yoghurt. If you don't eat lots of dairy stuff go for the milk with extra calcium added.

Some non-dairy sources of calcium include soy yoghurt, soy milk and rice milk, with added calcium; almonds; tinned salmon, with bones; and tahini (made from sesame seeds).

You need fats and oils

You need to eat fats and oils to keep your skin and hair looking good and your hormones working properly, and to help some vitamins be absorbed effectively. This means making sure you eat useful fats, found particularly in some oils.

You need omega 3 oils from fresh or canned tuna and salmon, and some seeds and nuts. Other useful oils include canola, sunflower, corn and extra-virgin olive oil. Look for oils and spreads that are labelled 'unsaturated', 'monounsaturated', 'unhydrogenated' and 'polyunsaturated'. Cooking or salad oils should be 'cold-pressed' so they maintain their goodies.

You need water

Make water your main drink. It stops you from getting headaches, keeps your skin and hair looking good, and if it's out of a suburban, city or town tap should have fluoride, which protects you from tooth decay. Some bottled and filtered water has no fluoride. Make sure you have a drink as soon as you feel thirsty, and that you choose to drink water, not sugary soft drinks, flavoured water, fruit drinks or juices. A refillable water bottle is cheaper and better for the environment.

> I worry I'm going to injure or do some permanent damage to myself when I don't eat properly.
> Georgie, 17, Fremantle, WA

More info on drinking water

gotap.com.au
The campaign to get us to reduce pollution and save money by drinking tap, not bottled water.

tapproject.org
Millions of children around the world don't have access to unpolluted water to drink or wash in: this causes disease and death. You can start a fundraiser or donate to UNICEF to help.

You need vitamins and minerals

If you eat lots of fruit, vegies, protein and grains you should get enough vitamins and minerals. Many vitamins and minerals need other vitamins and minerals before they can be absorbed into the body – for example, calcium needs magnesium.

To get the most vitamins out of your vegies it's best to eat them raw, stir-fried, lightly microwaved or steamed. The more you boil vegies, the more vitamins and minerals are lost (and you end up with gluey grey stuff).

If you think you need a supplement ask your doctor to check your health first, before paying up for one. If a supplement is necessary they'll be able to recommend the right one. Some girls need a zinc, calcium and iron supplement, which they can get in a 'women's' multi-vitamin.

The way to go

Here are some ideas for a healthy way to eat, which will give you lots of energy.

Eat brekky Oh yes, you can. Try unsweetened DIY porridge made from rolled oats (cooked on the stove or microwaved with milk), and put sliced fruit or berries on top; or wholegrain toast topped with banana or peanut butter (from the health food store, with no added salt, sugar or oil). Even if you don't feel like eating a lot the moment you get up, or you're too busy rushing off to school, have a banana smoothie with yoghurt to get you through until a mid-morning snack.

If you skip breakfast it makes you crave sugary snacks or drinks during the day, means it's harder for you to concentrate, and causes shipping accidents and the raining of frogs upon the earth. Well, no. But have breakfast.

When time is the problem, get some things ready the night before. Soak some rice or oats for porridge, or lay out the bread and stuff you need next to the toaster. Mix some of the ingredients for a smoothie and store them in the fridge.

One of those high-sugar, high-fat processed 'breakfast bars' is not the answer. (And they cost more.)

Eat regular meals and snacks If you go too long without food your blood sugar level drops, and you can feel dizzy, tired and crabby. And if you let yourself get madly hungry you'll be more likely to grab something sugary or a fast food, which will only give you a quick burst of energy before you feel tired again. That's why eating three decent meals a day, with healthy snacks in between, is important.

The best snack foods create longer lasting energy rather than a sudden 'high' followed by a crash. These include dairy foods, soy foods, fruit and vegies, as well as rolled oats, legumes, basmati rice and pasta. In second place for snacks are rye bread, brown rice and cous cous. Snacks that travel well in a school bag or handbag include almonds, carrot sticks and hard fruits such as apples.

tHis is not a meaL. It's a ≈ SNaCK ≈

not a meaL ↓ Water 250 ML

TAKE AWAY LATTE
not, you'll be surprised to know, a meaL...

Eat unprocessed food The least useful grain foods are the ones that have been over-processed, such as pastries and factory-made biscuits. They lack fibre, vitamins and minerals.

Packet cereals are usually so over-processed that most of the nutrients have been removed. Some nutrients have to be put back (sort of like sticking ground-up vitamin tablets into the cereal flakes) and are harder for the body to absorb. The Australian Consumers' Association has rated Australia's most popular cereals and recommends only a few (see 'More Info' coming up).

Seedy multigrain bread is better for you than squishy whitey-white bread. Brown rice has more nutrients than white rice. Porridge is better than corn flakes. Know what you're eating, and use wholegrain when you can.

> I asked my canteen at high school why their menu wasn't more healthy, and the woman actually said this: 'Pizza is bread based, Cheezies are cheese based, and pies are meat-based.' How are teenagers meant to get to their right size when they can't order healthy and filling food?
> Rhiana, 16, Mandurah, WA

Eat food close to its original form A fresh pear is better than sliced pears in a can. Steamed vegies are better than a can of vegetable soup. Fish grilled at home is better than battered takeaway fish and chips or a packaged meal from the frozen section. (Snap-frozen vegies are fine.)

Learn to cook Because that way you get to eat more unprocessed, healthier, yummier, cheaper food. Your friends will want to eat with you, and return the favour. It's fun and relaxing, you learn heaps and it's something that's handy when you travel, are trying to impress somebody, live in a shared house or on your own, have kids or want a career in the hospitality industry.

Not LUNCH (one bite from sandwich)

I am not a meal. I am a lolly snake

not a meal (no, really)

Food and feelings

You need to listen to your brain and body, rather than your emotions, when deciding what to eat and how much.

✽ **Recognise non-hungry eating triggers** Non-hungry 'reasons' for eating can include being bored, sad or anxious; wanting a 'reward' or treat; finding the food is just plain available; someone else is having some; or you eat stuff you like whenever you see it. Those responses need another solution, not food.

✽ **Eat when you're hungry** Most of the time you need to let yourself get hungry and then respond by eating, stopping when you're full.

✽ **Use your judgement** Experiment with what's a good-sized portion for you. How hungry are you? Do you need a smaller or a bigger size right now? Shops and takeaway joints often serve stupid sizes, with buckets of oily popcorn as big as a hatchback and muffins that could house a family of guinea pigs if they didn't mind sharing a bathroom.

✽ **Have a relaxed attitude to food** Don't be upset if every meal isn't a perfectly precise balance of the right serves and measurements. It's not a good day if you have to weigh a mushroom.

✽ **Be adventurous** Food can be fun, not just fuel. Try new food and learn new ways of eating and cooking for yourself and friends. Try food from different cultures and new tastes. Sometimes you need to try something a few times to get used to it and to allow your tastebuds to change.

✽ **Don't ban foods** Food isn't 'bad' or 'naughty'. If you say you can't have chocolate ever, you'll start wanting a whole block. Learn to have just a bit, or eat it only sometimes.

✽ **Share** Rather than eating alone, or in front of the TV, and rushing things, try to make your meals a chance to catch up with family or friends.

I only eat every 2nd hour in a month with a Y in it... ...and NO eggplant before 7 pm!

=Strange food Rituals=

Vegetarians

Vegetarians don't eat meat, right? But what about vegans and all the other groups? Well, vegans avoid all food that comes from animals, including dairy (milk, cream, butter, cheese, yoghurt), eggs, meat (red or white) and fish. And pesco-vegetarians eat fish, dairy and eggs. And sorta-kinda-semi-vegetarians eat fish, dairy, eggs and white meat but no red meat.

Many people are vegetarian for moral reasons: they think eating animals is wrong. Some people think meat is unhealthy for them; some have religious reasons; and some are experimenting, just want something to talk about, or like rules about what they do.

Vegetarian and vegan special needs   Many girls 'go' vegetarian or vegan and then find they have no energy because they lack protein and minerals. Vegetarians and vegans need to find substitutes for the essential foods they've cut out. The 'What You Need' info earlier in this chapter gives good non-meat and non-animal alternatives.

- Vegetarians and vegans must replace meat each day with enough serves of other proteins.
- Vegetarians and vegans need an iron supplement because meat is the source of the most easily absorbed iron, which you need lots of. Some soy milks, cereals and breads have chemically added iron. Iron from vegetable sources is more easily absorbed by the body when combined with food or (sugar-free) juices rich in vitamin C, such as capsicums, and guavas, blackcurrants, mangoes, oranges and other fruit.
- Vegans (and vegetarians who decide not to eat dairy) need vitamin B12, which is only available in animal products, especially meat. Many soy milks and some other products have it as a chemical additive, and it is a common component in multi-vitamins and B-complex vitamins.
- Vegans (and vegetarians who decide not to eat dairy) need good alternative sources of calcium. Certain foods, such as some juices and soy products, have extra calcium added.

It can be hard to eat right as a teenage vegetarian. A bag of chips that have been deep-fried in oil might be vegetarian, but it's not good for you. Having just vegies without protein when you're eating at someone else's house won't give you enough nutrition and energy. The more anyone restricts their food choices the more difficult it gets, and the more obsessed they may become with food and rules about food.

If you're determined to go vegetarian or vegan talk to your doctor or a qualified dietician first, and get informed so you can convince your parents that you'll be getting enough nutrition. Don't forget that as a teenager you have more nutritional needs than adults. Most info for vegetarians and vegans on the internet and in books and handouts is for adults, and even the info for teens usually doesn't explain how much of the different foods you need.

> I am a vegetarian and any girls who think this helps you lose weight are VERY wrong!!! It's harder to maintain a healthy weight!!
> Bec, 16
> Happy Valley, SA

HINT

Home movies When you're watching a movie at home with your friends, try snacking on bowls of fruit salad or plain homemade (not pre-packaged) popcorn (go easy on the butter and salt).

I can have half a carrot!

I'll alert the media

you don't Have to CouNT youR fooD

More info on good eating, and recipe books

marketfresh.com.au
Info on what's in season (and therefore cheaper), and fun ways to cook or serve fruit and vegies.

choice.com.au
On the Australian Consumers' Association home page search Breakfast Cereals.

daa.asn.au
The Dietitians Association of Australia articles on nutrition and recipes, plus info on how to find a dietician. Click on Smart Eating For A Healthier You. (Anyone can call themselves a nutritionist – a dietician has a medically recognised university qualification.)

Calm Eating by Dr Rick Kausman
Dr Rick is an Australian doctor who specialises in eating behaviours. This little book has advice, tips and personal stories on getting control over eating and feelings. His site is ifnotdieting.com.au.

angry-chef.com
A funny (and sometimes rather cross) chef who blogs to expose the pretense of claims like 'clean eating' and other fads and fancies that aren't based on real experience or science and nutrition facts. He talks about how to find good ingredients and not fall for false claims and other faffery.

Many girls who are maybe a little overweight complain, but when you look at their diet, the majority is junk food. Rather than complain, they should accept some responsibility, but still realise thin does not necessarily equal beautiful. Loz, 18, Kiama, NSW

Growing up, my mum had an eating disorder, and because I watched her not eat I never thought it was unusual or unhealthy. When I was a perfectly healthy child my grandma ridiculed my weight a lot, so that nowadays I don't have the confidence to eat in public.
Tess, 18, Wynn Vale, SA

What you don't need

The body saves any sugars and fats it doesn't need as extra weight. In the past it was hard to get fatty and sugary foods (you couldn't exactly go out with a spear and hunter-gather a packet of chips, a gigantic muffin and a sweet drink), but now they're available all the time, everywhere, and they're cheap.

People have got into the habit of eating more sweet, fatty food than they need, and not doing much activity. And if they don't get out of this habit they end up at an unhealthy weight.

You may be amazed at the amount of fat and sugar in processed, takeaway and fast food. One takeaway hamburger or serve of fried chicken, or pre-packaged creamy curry from the supermarket frozen section, can be more than half or two-thirds of your whole day's energy needs, without providing much nutrition that your body can use.

If you want to eat this kind of food find out what's in it – and what's not in it – so you're informed.

> **FACT**
>
> **The fuss about weight** There's no 'perfect weight' for your height or your age. There is a healthy range for each individual. If you follow the guidelines in this chapter and Chapter 6, Move (about physical activity), you should stay within your healthy weight range. Chapter 4, Body Image, helps explain about sizes.

You don't need much sugar

Our bodies are designed to love the taste of sugar (it's even a pain reliever). The human body assumes, from its experiences in the tough old cave folk days, that sugar is hard to get so it craves more.

We used to have to make our own cakes from scratch to have something sweet. Now we can get sugar hidden in nearly every packaged and processed kind of food, so most of us eat way more of it than we need.

← 'health bars' can be just 'Fat 'n' Sugar Bars'

High-sugar products include cakes, biscuits, muffins, many breads, lollies, chocolate, ice-cream, bottled fruit drinks and juices, cordials, bubbly drinks and alcohol.

If you put a teaspoon of sugar on a bowl of processed breakfast cereal you're probably adding another one to the perhaps five teaspoons of sugar already in the cereal. Honey's the same as sugar so don't add it to everything either. Sugar is also a major cause of holes in the teeth.

Label check

- Sugars can be listed as glucose, fructose, lactose or maltose.
- If a label has sugar in the first three or four ingredients listed, that usually means a high sugar level.
- There are 4 grams of sugar in a level teaspoon, so if the label says one food serving has 12 grams of sugar in it, that's three teaspoons.
- Check out the fine print on the labels of foods you mightn't think would contain sugar.
- Look for things labelled 'no added sugar'.
- Don't drink products labelled as 'sports' or 'energy' drinks (they're usually really high in sugar, and caffeine) unless an accredited coach tells you to.

Are you the devil?

No, I am just a cakey

FACT

Cakey things Sometimes seen as treats or rewards, high-sugar and high-fat foods are okay occasionally – say, once or twice a week – but not every day.

food ✹ BODY 117

You don't need unhealthy fats and oils

You often hear about 'bad fats', as if there are tiny evil fats trying to take over the world and going 'Nyahahaha' in high, squeaky voices. 'Bad fats' means saturated fats and hydrogenated oils, which have no health benefits in large quantities and can eventually cause big health problems.

Unhealthy fats are mostly the ones from animals, such as cream (including butter) and the white bits on meat, but they are also found in coconut cream and the oils used for takeaway food, especially fried food.

A little bit is okay, but eating high-fat takeaway or fast food every day or several times a week can quickly take you above your healthy weight and put you at risk of diseases such as diabetes. They make your body do all the work of turning them into fat or poo without it getting anything useful on their way through.

> This girl at my school, all she eats is junk food and a lot of it. Seriously I have never seen her eat anything healthy.
> Natalie, 14,
> Terrey Hills, NSW

FACT

Weird but true The fatter the chip, the less fat it has absorbed. For guidelines on how your chips should be cooked see 'More Info' at the end of this section. Very few takeaway joints seem to have taken any notice of said guidelines.

Label check

- Check the labels on packaged food: anything with 20 grams of fat or more in a 100-gram serve is considered high fat.
- Food that's labelled 'low fat' or, say, '95 per cent fat free' usually has heaps of added sugar to make it taste better. Any extra sugar you don't need will be converted to fat in your body.

LEARN to READ LABELS

You don't need fizzy drinks and sweetened juices

Most bubbly drinks (except unflavoured soda or mineral water) and fruit drinks have an unbelieeeevably high amount of sugar in them: up to 6 to 8 teaspoons each. Juices from juice shops, in bottles or in tetra packs usually also have a really high sugar level.

Juice bars sell drinks that are hellishly expensive for the ingredients actually used, and have been told off by the government for claiming that additives in their juices could give you energy, help you lose weight or boost your immune system because this isn't true, or not proven.

Don't make a habit of bubbly or sweetened fruit drinks: try for none, or one a week, or only occasionally. Processed fruit juice is okay now and then, but as a daily habit could be way too sugary and cost you heaps. More sugar than you need causes holes and decay in your teeth, and unnecessary weight gain. Go for plain water.

Label check

- Fizzy drinks that are labelled 'low fat' could still have high sugar levels.
- 'Diet' versions are just expensive water that has been flavoured with chemicals. Some researchers believe that the fake sugar in 'diet' drinks can 'train' your body to crave more sugary things.

> **FACT**
>
> **Hard to believe** By drinking one sugary drink a day you could convert the unwanted sugar to 6 kilos of unnecessary body fat by the end of a year. Hold 6 kilos of potatoes and you'll get the idea.

You don't need too much salt

Salt, like sugar, is something the human body has evolved to want because in the past it was hard to get. (Cave folk didn't have packaged food or a salt-shaker.) Your body needs a little bit of salt, not a lot. Too much can make you dehydrated, bloated and tired, and put you at higher risk of heart and other health problems.

There's way too much salt in most canned and packaged foods. Savoury biscuits (especially rice crackers), bread, bought sauces (especially soy and barbecue) and spreads often have high levels. Even most processed sweet foods contain salt.

Label check
- Watch out for sodium or sodium chloride as one of the first or major ingredients (sodium chloride is the scientific name for table salt).
- 'Brine' on a label means salted water has been added, so buy canned fish in just spring water (or oil) instead.
- Choose 'no added salt', 'reduced salt' or 'low salt' versions of foods.

Ways to reduce salt
- Don't add salt automatically when you're cooking, or sprinkle it on food after it's cooked.
- Use herbs, spices and other condiments to brighten food up if it seems too bland without added salt, and wait until you're used to the new tastes. This may take some weeks, but after that when you taste salty foods you'll be shocked.
- Go for unsalted chips, popcorn and nuts.

4th long black

THERE IS SUCH A THING AS too PERKY

You don't need too much caffeine

Caffeine gives you a buzzy, more awake and energised feeling, but it can also make you restless and jittery, cause headaches and keep you awake at night. It makes your heart beat faster, your blood pressure rise and your body wee more. You can get 'addicted' to caffeine and it can mess up your sleeping patterns, especially if you have it in the afternoons or at night.

The highest levels of caffeine are in filtered or shop-made coffee, then 'energy' and some 'sport' drinks, then instant coffee, then cola drinks, then tea, then chocolate (that's why little kids go berserk at Easter). In New Zealand caffeine can be in non-cola bubbly drinks too.

A 1-gram dose of guarana (in 'energy' drinks) is usually about as strong as a medium cup of coffee. Lots of takeaway-style and coffee bought at cafes is stronger.

One weak coffee a day shouldn't do you any harm.

Label check

- The 'recommended serve' may be actually only a third of the can, and the number of grams in a serve will apply to that, whereas you'll usually drink the whole can (three serves).

Finding out what's in processed foods

Most manufactured foods and drinks have to have a label telling you what's in them. Labels show a food's energy content in kilojoules (kj) and its weight in grams (g), and list its protein, total fat, different types of fat, carbohydrate, sugars, sodium (salt) and any other relevant ingredients.

> Being healthy isn't always about what size you are or what other people think. Being healthy is when you feel comfortable with yourself, eating right, and feeling fit. Lana, 17, Broome, WA

Tricky claims on labels

- 'Light' or 'Lite' could just mean the product is light in colour or a fine, not thick texture: it doesn't necessarily mean it's low in fat or sugar (or 'energy').

- 'Barn-raised' or 'farm-raised' doesn't mean 'free range'. Any big building can be called a barn or a farm. Free range means animals are able to move around outside.

- The serving size can be misleading; for example, a manufacturer can decide a can of diet cola is 1.88 serves so that they can say it has 'only one calorie per serve'.

- 'Natural' or 'no added chemicals' doesn't mean organic. Organic means no chemicals are added to the soil or in the growing or feeding cycles when the food is produced.

- If an item claims to be, say, '93 per cent fat free' it means it contains 7 per cent fat, which is not considered a low percentage in food (3 per cent is considered a small amount).

- 'Baked not fried' sounds healthier, but the food may have been baked in just as much fat.

- 'Fresh' means the product hasn't been preserved by freezing, canning, high temperature or chemical treatment. It may have been refrigerated, processed and transported weeks ago.

Changing habits

If your family eats unhealthy stuff maybe you could suggest you all get together to plan how to change eating habits. Perhaps you could show your parents the websites in the 'More Info on Good Eating, and Recipe Books' earlier in this chapter; or see if you could go as a family to a dietician for advice about how to change the way you shop and eat.

> **HINT**
>
> **Out and about** Go for a salad and meat wrap and a water instead of a hamburger and a fizzy drink.

Some parents are so busy you might need to:

- help them to make fresh meals, when you can, rather than relying on takeaway or frozen meals or high fat, sugar and salt options
- make a list of healthy food choices and go shopping with them
- suggest that it becomes one of your jobs to check that the fruit bowl is always filled with a variety of fruit, and the same for vegies in the fridge crisper
- ask if you can have your own supplies, and get your own breakfast, make your own lunch and even cook a simple dinner for yourself, if your family really can't stop eating takeaway most nights
- keep talking to them about healthy eating, and learning together, rather than slagging them (and your siblings) off about their choices.

More info on fast food, additives and labels

choice.com.au
Independent info and tests on fat, salt and sugar levels. Search Fast Food or Food.

foodstandards.gov.au
Choose Food Consumer Information then Labelling. You can download a poster, 'Food Labels: What Do They Mean?'.

Choosing the Right Stuff: The Official Shoppers' Guide to Food Additives and Labels, Kilojoules and Fat Content by **Food Standards Australia New Zealand**
A book to carry with you when checking labels in shops: buy at a local or online bookshop.

> **FACT**
>
> **Skipping meals** People who skip meals usually don't lose weight – they lose energy and feel fainty, and just eat more stuff later.

122   BODY ✦ food

Food allergies and intolerances

Allergies and food intolerances need to be medically confirmed – you can't diagnose yourself. Symptoms of food intolerances or allergies can include rashes, a runny nose, nausea, trumpety farting, diarrhoea (not so amusingly pronounced 'dire rear') or constipation (not being able to poo), a bloating feeling, tummy ache, vomiting, wheezing or, in serious cases, a life-threatening allergic 'anaphylaxis' shock reaction. Your doctor can give you a referral, if necessary, to an allergy specialist or dietician. Natural health practitioners must not diagnose allergies, but they can help a lot with management, complementary therapies (which you must tell your doctor about) and lifestyle advice.

'Gut'-related symptoms can be very confusing and come and go. It can take time to work out what the problem is. It's important not just to assume something because it seems logical. Many things cause similar symptoms, including stress. Some people have assumed they're allergic to wheat, restricting themselves to a difficult diet for years, only to find out they didn't have an allergy at all, just an imbalance in friendly stomach bacteria, or stress causing tummy pains or nausea. If you've stopped eating a kind of food and then you eat a big whack of it and have a bad reaction, it may mean you need to reintroduce it in little bits, not that you're allergic. Anything you eat too much of is likely to make you feel odd and wrong.

Recovering from a food allergy   Many people will have an allergy or intolerance for life and learn to manage it well. Research shows that many children can overcome some allergies, with help from a medical allergy specialist.

More info on food allergies and intolerances

daa.asn.au
The Dietitians Association of Australia can help you find a specialist dietician.

allergyfacts.org.au
Anaphylaxis Australia's site has info, advice and support for serious allergies.

coeliac.org.au
Info, support, links and lists of friendly cookbooks and restaurants from specialist Australian dietician Dr Sue Shepherd. Also for people with gluten and lactose intolerance, fructose malabsorption and irritable bowel syndrome (IBS).

Food Intolerance Management Plan by Sue Shepherd & Peter Gibson and *Gluten-free Cooking* and *Gluten-free Kitchen* by Sue Shepherd
Books with info and recipes for IBS, and lactose, wheat, dairy and other allergies and intolerances.

AllergyPal
An app developed by the Murdoch Children's Research helps you manage your food allergy at home and away from home.

glutenfreegirl.blogspot.com
US site with links to other sites, bloggers, recipes and stories.

6

MOVE

Physical activity can 🌀 make you feel good 🌀 make you feel strong 🌀 make you happier 🌀 guard against depression 🌀 make you like yourself more 🌀 maintain your body in good condition 🌀 **be fun** 🌀 give you more energy 🌀 help you fight off illness 🌀 help to repair and heal your body 🌀 help you feel like you **belong** (to a team) 🌀 give you a sense of calm 🌀 help you concentrate better 🌀 help you get to sleep 🌀 help you make and hang out with **friends** 🌀 spice up your day 🌀 help make strong bones and muscles.

Physical activity

The point of physical activity is to feel healthy. If you don't do any you'll become unfit and feel stiff and heavy, cranky and tired; you'll be unhealthy and unable to fight off colds and other illnesses; and you won't burn up any extra sugars and fats as energy.

Why activity makes you feel good

When you do something active, especially suddenly (for example, running from a standing start), your brain releases 'good mood' chemicals such as endorphins and serotonin (see Chapter 12, Mind Health).

Probably the simple reason exercise makes most people feel good is that the body is doing what it's supposed to – moving around, pumping blood, getting oxygen in and out. And anyway, what's not to love about dancing? (Especially with the lights out and the door locked.)

The amount you need

National government guidelines suggest kids and teenagers should be having an hour of physical activity a day. It's something to aim for, not a rule to get upset about. The guidelines also say teenagers should:

- have no more than 2 hours a day combined screen time – looking at TV, games or a computer >

> Doing a little bit of exercise a day makes you feel better about yourself.
> Kylie, 14, Shepparton, Vic.

dancing fights stress

move ✱ BODY 125

=:⚾ baseball :=

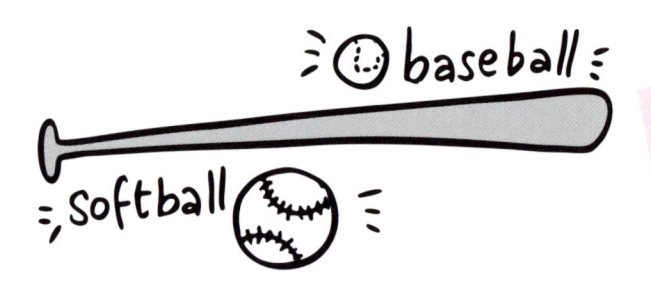

=: softball 🥎 :=

- be active every day in as many ways as possible
- try to do some moderate exercise every day (moderate means you're moving your body but not necessarily getting a much faster heart rate and faster breathing)
- get some regular vigorous exercise for at least 20 minutes three to four days a week. Vigorous exercise makes you 'huffy-puffy' – your breathing is quicker and it's hard to speak normally.

Moderate huffy-puffery includes walking (not ambling or strolling), going on a long bike ride, skateboarding, playing softball or volleyball in which you spend a bit of time standing still or waiting for your turn – that sort of thing.

Vigorous huffiesque activity is stuff that keeps your heart rate up for a while: playing basketball, hockey or soccer, swimming laps, running, walking fast, dancing full on.

> I always feel better after exercise. You feel like you've accomplished something.
> Iharna, 14, Donnybrook, WA

> I feel horrible if I don't exercise.
> Gemma, 15, Darwin, NT

Exercise is a great way to stay healthy and meet new people. Kelsey, 14, Kyabram, Vic.

Since I started playing rugby I have become more confident.
Lauren, 17, Auckland, NZ

walk to meet friends...

126 BODY ✹ move

Stuff girls do for fun and exercise

abseiling ✱ aerobics ✱ aikido ✱ aquarobics ✱ archery ✱ athletics ✱ Australian Rules footy ✱ badminton ✱ balinta wak (Filipino stick fighting) ✱ ballroom dancing ✱ baseball ✱ basketball ✱ beach volleyball ✱ belly dancing ✱ bobsledding ✱ bocce ✱ bodyboarding ✱ **bodysurfing** ✱ boogie boarding ✱ bowls ✱ building a tree-house ✱ building fences ✱ bushwalking ✱ canoeing ✱ capoeira ✱ cardio-boxing ✱ cardiovascular exercises in gym class ✱ carrying, not pushing, groceries ✱ circus skills ✱ cleaning vigorously ✱ climbing trees ✱ contemporary dance ✱ cricket ✱ croquet ✱ cross-country run training ✱ cross-country skiing ✱ curling ✱ cycling ✱ dance lessons ✱ dancing on your bed with the door locked ✱ delivering newspapers or pamphlets on foot or wheels ✱ digging holes and planting trees ✱ diving ✱ dog training ✱ elastics ✱ fly-fishing ✱ Frisbee ✱ fruit picking ✱ gardening ✱ getting up out of the chair ✱ gliding ✱ **going the long way round** ✱ golf ✱ gym machines ✱ gymnastics ✱ handweights at home ✱ hapkido ✱ hiking ✱ hiphop dance ✱ hockey ✱ horseriding ✱ hula hoop ✱ ice hockey ✱ ice-skating ✱ in-line skating ✱ Irish dancing ✱ javelin ✱ jazz dancing ✱ jogging ✱ **judo** ✱ jujitsu ✱ jumping ✱ karate ✱ kayaking ✱ kendo ✱ kickboxing ✱ kite boarding ✱ kite flying ✱ lacrosse ✱ Latin dance ✱ lawn bowls ✱ leaving the train/tram/bus early and walking the rest of the way ✱ line dancing ✱ long jump ✱ lunchtime walk ✱ marching ✱ modern dance ✱ mustering cattle ✱ netball ✱ orienteering ✱ Paralympic sports ✱ PE classes at school ✱ petanque ✱ Pilates ✱ **playing catch** ✱ playing sport with little kids ✱ playing the drums like crazy ✱ power walking ✱ power shopping ✱ pretend boxing ✱ pushing a pram ✱ quoits ✱ refereeing: the power! ✱ riding my bike to school ✱ rock climbing ✱ rollerblading ✱ rowing ✱ rugby league football ✱ rugby union football ✱ running ✱ running upstairs ✱ salsa dancing ✱ scuba diving ✱ shooting hoops ✱ shot-put ✱ skateboarding ✱ skiffle boarding ✱ skiing ✱ skipping rope – on your own or in a team ✱ snorkelling ✱ snowboarding ✱ soccer ✱ softball ✱ squash ✱ stacking shelves at work ✱ stair climbing ✱ stationary bike class ('spinning') ✱ stretching ✱ **surf lifesaving** ✱ surfing ✱ swimming ✱ swing dancing ✱ synchronised swimming ✱ tae kwon do ✱ table tennis ✱ tag ✱ tai chi ✱ taking the stairs, not the lift ✱ tap-dancing ✱ tennis ✱ touch football ✱ training ✱ trampolining ✱ trapeze ✱ treadmill walk or run at home ✱ tree planting ✱ tumbling (acrobatics) ✱ TV games like tennis you can do by yourself ✱ using a swing ✱ underwater hockey ✱ vacuuming ✱ **volleyball** ✱ walking dogs (part-time job) ✱ walking with Mum ✱ weight-training machines ✱ whitewater rafting ✱ windsurfing ✱ woodchopping ✱ wrestling ✱ yachting ✱ yoga ✱ Zorro-style fencing with swords (well, nobody said that but I had to have a Z).

Finding your own activity thing

Most girls try a few different sports or activities before they find the right one for them. Don't stick with something you hate or find boring. Sometimes it takes a while to find one you really love and are good at.

You might want a sport that's related to hand-to-hand fighting so you can scream a lot, or to belong to a team that believes winning is important. Or you might just be the sort of person who likes a 'hit and giggle' with friends, or a long walk listening to music. (See also the 'A–Z of Exercise' box on the previous page.)

Choosing an activity near home makes it quick and uncomplicated. Your local council and state government sports and recreation department can tell you about teams and clubs, dance groups, yoga and other classes, and bike and walking tracks in your area. You can also ask around or look in local newspapers, on shop noticeboards, or on the internet. Many teams and classes don't cost much to join.

Meet or take a friend so you motivate each other to keep going. Joining a group activity is a good way to catch up with old pals and to make new friends.

Team sports can be fun but not provide a lot of activity, depending on where you're positioned on the court or field (unless they have really active training sessions). So if you find that you're spending a couple of hours per game standing still in the outfield, you'll need to do something else that's actually active.

> Tae kwon do is GREAT exercise. Plus it teaches you great self-defence and body control. I would highly recommend it!
> Shell, 13, St Ives, NSW

Getting active

For some people any physical activity seems like a huge challenge – maybe they've never had good sports skills, or they've always felt clumsy, or they're embarrassed about people seeing them exercise. Other people like the idea of physical activity but just don't know where to start, or they need help to see how to jiggle it into their schedule.

> If you don't think of yourself as sporty, dancing can be great. Find a dance studio that's inclusive and friendly, try to avoid the uptight bitchiness of some professional dance studios. Jen, 16

Of course it's important to remember that if you're unfit, or above your healthy weight, you may get huffy-puffy very easily, or certainly quicker than someone who plays an hour of non-stop hockey every second night. Oddly, doing no exercise can make you feel tired so it can be harder to get started (but you feel better after you do).

Check out the list of possible activities just a page back and find one that suits you. Drag along a friend if that helps, or start with something you can do in your lounge room – like crazy dancing or using a screen game that requires activity. Just remember it isn't about being 'good at' something or what you look like doing it: it's about having a go and feeling better.

Some hints for starting

- Do more than nothing: do *something*, even if you don't feel you can do the recommended hour a day.
- Start slowly, perhaps with a 10- or 15-minute walk each day, then build it up by 5 minutes each time to 30 minutes, and finally by 10 or 15 minutes to an hour. It gets easier.
- Don't do the hour a day in one go. Try walking for half an hour in the morning, 15 minutes at lunch, 15 minutes to and from the bus stop, and around the block a few times with the dog when you get home (unless your block is a 456-hectare outback cattle station).
- Look for any opportunity to be active: walk to the local shops; get off the bus a stop or two earlier and walk the rest of the distance; choose a cafe a few blocks away from work for lunch; go the long way home.
- Keep in mind that everyday stuff is activity too: putting out the washing, walking to work or school, dancing, mucking around with friends outside, doing work such as heavy gardening or delivering pamphlets. >

> Exercise doesn't have to be a big workout or anything, just something that you enjoy that's active. I always like music to get me motivated.
> Lou, 15, Fremantle, WA
>
> I do lots of exercise because I enjoy it.
> Sarah, 14, Kew, Vic.

I really ought to exercise more. That's probably one of the reasons why I'm so short.
[*No it isn't.*] Sian, 15, Lakemba, NSW

I want to know exactly how many easy, quick exercises I can do for instant results.
[*Well, if anyone promises you that, they're lying!*] Meg, 17

- Choose an activity you like so you don't get bored. Or vary the activities.
- Try exercising before homework and tea or dinner, and not too close to bedtime: straight after school is a good time.
- Work out an exercise plan with your doctor if you have a medical condition such as asthma. (Asthma shouldn't stop you from being fit and active: many champion athletes have it.)
- Set targets, if that will help you get started, such as joining a team that has regular practice and playing times; or doing an hour's brisk walk four times a week. You can keep charts or reward yourself with flowers, a movie or nice undies (when you reach the little goals as well as the big ones).
- Walk with a pal or group of friends.
- Impress your parents and get out of other chores by walking the dog.
- Combine walking with someone and going somewhere you both want to go: talking and, say, window shopping is a way of being active without feeling it's a compulsory chore.
- Listen to music – it makes the time go quicker, if that's what you want. But leave off the earphones if you're riding on the road or crossing streets or driveways because music tends to distract you and block out other sounds (see the 'Hearing' box in Chapter 7, Body Health).
- Learn circus or dance skills – they can open up a whole new world.
- Have a box or basket of fun stuff – bats, balls, helmets – by the door or on the porch. Keep your bike and helmet together and handy (not in the attic) and keep the tyres pumped up.

HINT

Stre-e-etch? Exercise experts are divided about whether you should stretch before and/or after exercise. It probably doesn't prevent injury, but increases flexibility. It should never hurt.

BODY move

The goal is to make activity the normal part of your day that your body expects it to be.

And let's say it again: the point of activity is to stay healthy. It's not to be thin. Naturally thin girls who don't move their bodies around much and exist on custard donuts and coffee will not be anywhere near as healthy as heavier girls of the same height who eat well, are robust and full of energy and like to move their bot-bot. (And the rest of their bodies. Just moving your bot-bot would be weird, like one of those tragic girlies in music videos.)

Many girls think of exercise as a chore, something they have to do to 'work off' a chocolate biscuit. Exercising isn't a short-term 'fix' for anything or a punishment for eating. Think of food as fuel for all the things you need to do with your body, such as move it around, make cells and grow bones.

If you think of activity as something that's natural to the body and makes you feel good, you'll save yourself from a lifetime of grumpy, resentful exercise, and enjoy mucking around with friends and having a walk in the fresh air.

When it's hard When you haven't done much exercise for a while, or you're very unfit, it can feel as if you'll never get there, as if you'll never be fit.

The lone mover

Some people prefer to do physical activity by themselves. If you're one of those, options that might work for you include:

* swimming laps, hitting a tennis or golf ball or practising archery rather than taking up a team sport

* exercise at home – you can rent or buy DVDs on aerobics, yoga, Pilates and other disciplines

* a yoga or dance class or other activity where you don't have to know anybody or chat

* vigorous housework or a part-time paid job with activity

* walking or jogging in the bush or a park, along the beach or around the suburbs. If you don't want to be seen, go early in the morning or evening. Choose different places to walk to and explore your neighbourhood, if it's safe. Take a dog – even a neighbour's – if you feel like extra protection.

This is when self-discipline comes in: it sounds boring, and it can be, but the results are amazing. You'll feel proud of your achievement and healthier than you've ever been.

- You may have to try a little longer, get active a little more often than other people you know, and go a bit harder. Gradually your body *will* get stronger and more resilient, but it may be a while before you notice a difference.
- Don't overdo it; and if you do, rest the following day.
- Don't be cross with yourself if you miss a day: think about why you did and how you can change that, then try again tomorrow.
- Find a public pool, have a couple of swimming lessons if you need to, and then try some laps or a water aerobics class – being in water can make you feel lighter and more graceful, and puts less strain on your ankles and knees than some other activities.
- To check you're exercising in an efficient way that won't cause injury, work out a program with an accredited school PE teacher.

More info on finding your own activity

For any sports, martial arts or dance styles you're interested in, use your web search engine or contact your local council to find the nearest club or lessons. Use your own common sense about what kind of team or level of training is appropriate or useful for you – when in doubt, or if it hurts, or you hate it, stop and try something else.

ausport.gov.au
The Australian Sports Commission. Choose About Us, then Australian Sports Directory.

Women in Sport Aotearoa
This NZ women's sport organisation has a presence on social media and an email address: womeninsportaotearoa@gmail.com

---

My father comments about my weight. He started calling me fat when I was about 10. I had puppy fat but before that I was really active and sporty. Then I became really self-conscious about my body and refused to wear shorts or run because I thought I would jiggle. I've started jogging now but it took a long time.   Isobel, 17, Traralgon, Vic.

Activity problems

Some physical activities have downsides that you need to know about. Avoid:

- over-training – such as several hours a day
- any sport that has coaches or parents who shout at you
- something that often makes you feel like crying or think that you're a failure when you lose or you're never good enough
- any activity that causes repeated injury, especially in the same part of your body
- a sport that overheats you – choose sports and times carefully during hot weather and don't let yourself become dehydrated (drink water before and during exercise, whenever you feel thirsty)
- sports or activities that encourage you to lose weight or to stay at a certain weight or size. These include some ballet, gymnastics and modelling disciplines; although many kids are picked because they are naturally smaller or thinner than others, normal puberty and growing up can 'get in the way'.

Athletics and other sports practised at an elite level can impose severe and unhealthy weight controls. If you're told to weigh yourself as part of your sport it's probably time to get out. It's physically and mentally unhealthy to fight your natural body changes. It's not your body that's the problem; it's the attitude around you.

> I don't do any exercise as my mum can't be bothered driving me to places. She tells me to exercise around the house (no idea what that means).
> Kaylee, 14, Sydney, NSW

> Whatever I do I seem to have no time for it with all my schoolwork. Tanya, 14, Penrith, NSW

Exercises

Exercises and stretches are good for keeping your body flexible and your muscles strong. It's really useful to work the abdominal or core muscles, which help keep your back strong and supple: yoga and Pilates have these kinds of exercises or 'poses'.

A lot of gyms and fitness magazines provide specific exercises, done with or without equipment, to build up the muscles in certain areas, such as the arms, stomach or legs. That's fine, but daily exercises for a 'firmer bottom' or a 'flatter stomach' can have you obsessing about something that isn't a problem. If you are already fit and healthy your body is basically its natural shape.

Gyms can be expensive and intimidating places, but you don't have to join one to get fit or to do gym-style exercises. You can do exercises at home, perhaps with a hired or a bought instructional DVD and some basic equipment. Another option is to check whether your local council has a nearby youth or recreation centre with cheap classes or gym equipment that you can use for free or a small fee.

Injury first aid

If you've been injured, stop the activity immediately, get a diagnosis from a doctor if necessary and treat the injury. Often, treating a bruise or sprain with ice immediately will be a big help. Ice will take down the swelling and inflammation and reduce bruising. Anything that bleeds a lot or is a suspected broken bone will need fast medical attention. Continuing to train or play with any injury risks serious damage. Any sport that requires repetitive actions for hours can cause long-term or strain injuries. Any head injury or knock means you must come off the field or stop the activity and be monitored by a responsible adult with recent first aid training.

First aid for ordinary injuries

For bruises, bumps and sprains (like a hard ball to the shin or a twisted ankle) apply an icepack for 20 minutes (even a packet of frozen peas in a tea towel or T-shirt will do), then take it off for two hours, then repeat. When icing, and at other times straight after an injury, try to keep the injured body part elevated – i.e. put your arm on a cushion or table, or put your leg on a footstool or chair. Depending on how bad it feels, you can keep this up (except while you're asleep) for two or three days. Don't massage an injury, or put warm packs on it in the first two to three days. Don't ice an old injury before more exercise.

See Chapter 7, Body Health, for info on how to do a first aid course.

Screen time

People now move their bodies much, much less than people did in the past. (Compared with 100 years ago or more, we're practically as active as a building. I mean, do you know any hunter-gatherers?) What with homework, computer time, sitting-around-chatting time and getting-driven-around time, a lot of people miss out on physical activity (not to mention thinking and creating). TV and computer watching are probably the biggest munchers of the time that used to be spent on being active.

Changing habits

Your family may have no tradition of doing physical activity or exercising. This means you will probably have to work a bit harder to develop new habits. Here are some ideas on how to.

- Call a family meeting and start a discussion about whether family members would like to be fitter and healthier. You don't need to talk about anybody 'having to lose weight' or being 'overweight'

Suggestions for watching less TV

- Make a decision about how much you can watch a day. Maybe set a limit of one show a day, or two a week – 1 to 2 hours is a lot of TV time, even if it's less than normal for you.

- Cut down progressively: watch half an hour less a day for a week, then an hour less a day, and so on.

- Look at a TV guide to work out what you really want to watch instead of flicking through endless crap, hoping something good might come on – it usually doesn't.

- Record shows you like and watch them later, without ads.

- Don't watch TV in the morning – take the time to leave home earlier and walk further to school or work.

- Do an experiment – don't watch the TV for a week! Throw a rug over it, and see what you do instead.

FACT

Lost years If you watch TV for an average of 2 hours a day and have since you were 4, by the time you're 70 you'll have spent five and a half years of your life in front of the screen.

as this can seem like an accusation. Ask everyone for suggestions. Who can exercise together? What games or walks could you try together? Which activities would be good for weekdays and which for weekends? Where's the Frisbee?

- With family members, or by yourself, start doing half an hour's activity each day if possible and build up to an hour, even if it's in two or three lots (and check out the section 'Some Hints for Starting' earlier in this chapter).
- Talk to your parents and teachers about what can be done to allow you to exercise your human right to exercise. If your life is too busy for exercise, then there is something wrong and it needs to be fixed.

> I think a lot of us don't try because we're scared of what we look like when we do – guys don't do that. It's not feminine to be competitive or actually sweat. If we forgot about all that crap, it's so much fun, and so worth it!
> Dakota, 17, Stirling, WA

If nobody in your family wants to change, or can commit to being healthier and more energetic, don't let that be an excuse to hold you back. Find other groups or friends you can meet up with, or go your own way. Nobody can do it for you: it's your choice.

Yoga/Pilates is really good to just clear the mind and relax and enjoy life without really thinking about it.   Lusi, 15, Sandy Bay, Tas.

Do it! Just do it! It makes you feel refreshed and it helps you keep fit and you may even meet a cute guy!   Jodie, 14, Palmyra, WA

I think exercise is the perfect medicine. If you are upset or depressed, it releases endorphins, making you feel slightly more alive. If you are confused about something, a quiet walk can clear your mind.   Holly, 18, Lane Cove, NSW

It is essential to being healthy and happy, and beneficial to yourself, in that it increases your confidence and all good things like that.   Jess, 15, Fadden, ACT

It's good for you. I like running because I feel the wind.   Naomi, 13, Maui, Hawaii, US

BODY ✱ move

BODY HEALTH

Women and girls tend to understand that their body needs check-ups and regular maintenance, whereas most guys will only go to the doctor if their leg has fallen off – and even then they'll forget to bring the leg. **Good health** is partly about luck and genes, but it's also partly about taking care of yourself. Here's how.

Managing your health

It's normal to have various 'tummy bugs' and colds and viruses ('the flu') now and then. It's how our immune system learns to recognise germs and develop 'antibodies' to stop you getting the same illness again. You can build up a better immune system by eating well (see Chapter 5, Food) and exercising (see Chapter 6, Move). But no matter how healthy you are, you can still get sick sometimes. It isn't your fault. Blame the germs!

Almost every health problem can be better managed and is less serious if you take it along to a doctor straight away, as soon as you notice anything different or weird, or that hurts, or that doesn't seem to be going away. Report any strange symptoms to a parent or a school nurse.

> **FACT**
>
> **Mental health is just as important as physical health**
> See Chapter 9, Feelings, and Chapter 12, Mind Health, for lots of tips on how to stay calm and optimistic, and good websites and where to get help for any problems such as stress, depression, eating behaviour troubles and more.

Going to the doctor

Whether you want to go on your own or with a parent, you'll need a doctor you feel you can talk to. You can continue to see your usual family or local GP (general practitioner) or try a new one. Maybe a friend can recommend one. There are lots of great GPs: you just have to find one. Feel free to 'shop around'.

In the suburbs there are many women's clinics that specialise in girly health and problems (see 'Girls' and Women's Health' coming up). Girls in the country and remote areas may have the hardest time getting to choose a doctor they feel comfortable with, because there's less choice. Try your nearest community health centre or start with a school nurse if there is one.

Your Medicare card

Australia's national government health scheme, Medicare, is paid for by taxes. It means you can go to a doctor who 'bulk bills' without having to pay. The government pays a set amount (called the 'scheduled fee') for any service performed by a doctor. Some doctors charge more than the scheduled fee, so their patients have to pay the extra.

Your name is on a parent's Medicare card already, but when you turn 15 you can get your own by calling Medicare or registering online. You'll need to provide your date of birth and an address for the card to be sent to. It's also helpful to give the number of your parent's Medicare card, but not essential. (Simply knowing your full name and date of birth should be enough for a doctor to access your parent's card and bulk bill, if you don't have a card yourself.)

When you ring a clinic near you to make an appointment, as well as checking if it has doctors who bulk bill, ask whether any tests or procedures a doctor might recommend are covered by Medicare. If cost is a problem and the clinic doesn't bulk bill, ask whether the fees can be reduced.

medicareaustralia.gov.au
Infoline: 13 20 11
Apply for your own Medicare card.

It's normal for a doctor to check your breasts for lumps and suggest you have a regular smear test (again see 'Girls' and Women's Health'). If you'd prefer to see a woman doctor, ask to when you're making an appointment. It's also okay to ask if you can have somebody such as your mum, aunty or friend's mum, or a female nurse from the doctor's clinic, in the room with you for the examination. Always tell your doctor if you:

- have sex, or have ever had sex, and if you use or have used any contraception
- could possibly be pregnant
- have taken or are taking any medications, including herbal ones (see 'Complementary Medicines' coming up)
- are worried about anything, or have a question, no matter how silly it seems.

Privacy Doctors must keep all information about patients confidential, whether you ask them to or not. This means they're not allowed to discuss your condition with anyone (including a parent) unless you give them your permission. In very rare cases, if you are under 16, a doctor may have to tell somebody when they believe you are in danger from yourself or another person, or you may be a danger to someone else. But even in these rare cases it doesn't always have to be your parent who is told.

Health websites

Medical info on websites can be old, irrelevant to your own country, biased (pushing a particular line) or utterly made up. If you have a diagnosed condition or illness, it's always a safer bet to find a support group near you, which can tell you what the most reliable, relevant and up-to-date sites are (to search, enter the name of the disorder or illness, then Support and your state or territory). Rather than guessing what's wrong or which treatment might help, see a real doctor.

Here are some good health sites for girls. Also see all the 'More Info' sections in Chapter 16, Sex, and Chapter 12, Mind Health, for more.

healthdirect.gov.au
Health department websites and links: search a topic or use the A–Z list.

mydr.com.au
Scroll down to Health Information by Age and Gender and choose Kids' & Teens' Health or search an illness or health issue.

choice.com.au
For independent health info, from the Australian Consumers' Association site choose Food and Health, then General Health, then Conditions.

wwda.org.au
The Women With Disabilities Australia website has lots of info and links.

thewomens.org.au
The Royal Women's Hospital in Melbourne has lots of fact sheets on all sorts of health issues.

youngwomenshealth.org
US site of the Children's Hospital Boston's Center for Young Women's Health.

awhn.org.au
The Australian Women's Health Network has fact sheets under Publications and a list of Women's Health Services clinics.

familyplanningallianceaustralia.org.au
Choose services, then select your state or territory to find the nearest clinic.

canteen.org.au/young-people/my-parent-has-cancer
A site for young people who have a family member or friend with cancer.

womens-health.org.nz
A non-profit group aiming to improve women's health knowledge, rights and access. Choose Health Topics and choose what's relevant to you.

Immunisation

You should have had all your childhood immunisations (also known as vaccinations) by now to protect you against various diseases. You will need some teenage boosters (additional doses of injections you had as a child), and to have extra vaccinations if you travel overseas.

These diseases are very strong and very 'catchy'. Before immunisation, millions of kids died each year from them: in some places, hundreds of thousands still do, because they're not immunised. The following things will *not* protect you against infectious diseases if you come into contact with them: being breastfed as a baby, being healthy, eating organic food, 'homeopathic medicines', living in Australia. Only immunisation will protect against these lurgies.

You should already be protected against tetanus, diphtheria, whooping cough, polio, measles, mumps, rubella, hepatitis B, Hib, meningococcal C, chickenpox and the human papilloma virus (HPV). A lot of the vaccines are given in one injection, so you have a minimum number of jabs. You usually get teenage boosters (an extra jab) for some of these immunisations at your school, or you can go to your doctor.

Some of the vaccines may not have been available when you were little, so you may have to have them now. Ask your doctor what you need. Any immunisations on the government's recommended list (called the 'schedule') are free. Other vaccinations, such as extra ones you need for travel, are not free.

At about the age of 10 to 13 all girls (and boys) should have the HPV vaccine as it protects them from the most common causes of cancer of the cervix. If you're older than 13 and you haven't had the HPV vaccine already (this usually happens at school), ask your doctor about having it as soon as you can. You'll need to get a meningococcal disease booster at about age 14–16, probably at school.

First aid

Courses in first aid can be a great way to find out more about how the body works, and to learn how to save a life or deal with an injury in an emergency.

stjohn.org.au
St John Ambulance. Choose First Aid Training.

redcross.org.au
Choose First Aid Courses.

More info on immunisation

immunise.health.gov.au
Information line: 1800 671 811
Government info on diseases and jabs, and FAQ. Choose National Immunisation Program Schedule to see which jabs you need. To find out which ones you've had, get your vaccination record by calling 1800 653 809.

Hearing

You can do permanent damage to your ears (damage that can't be cured) by listening to music at high volume using earphones, or at live gigs and clubs; playing in a band, especially drums; or working in factories or computer rooms.

If you're somewhere where it's hard to hear people speaking, then the noise is enough to cause damage to your hearing. Carry industrial or super-strength earplugs and use them as soon as you notice a place is too noisy.

Earphones

Anything above about two-thirds of maximum volume on your headphones can cause hearing damage.

* Don't listen to a personal music device for more than an hour a day.

* Don't turn it up louder if you can't hear over traffic or public transport noise – upping the volume will cause hearing loss over time, and can cause accidents if you're walking (you need to hear traffic and other dangers).

Complementary medicines

For some illnesses and conditions 'alternative', 'complementary', 'naturopathic' and herbal remedies can help or even deal with the problem. But for others natural medicines alone will have no hope of helping (you wouldn't go to just a naturopath for a broken arm).

- Some natural and herbal medicines have very strong effects. They must be prescribed by a very qualified and experienced practitioner. Many alternative and herbal remedies can be dangerous (especially in pregnancy) at the wrong time or wrong dose.
- Tell your doctor about any complementary medicines or treatments you're taking, as some can have side effects or interfere with other medication.
- Some natural therapies aren't dangerous but may not do anything useful either, and can be expensive. Homeopathic 'treatments' such as 'rescue remedies' don't work any better than a spell or hope or a cup of tea, as they have no real active ingredients.
- There's no natural or alternative treatment that works like immunisation. It's a slight bummer to have injections but it would be a much bigger disaster to have any of the diseases they protect you against.

Teeth

You just need to:

- clean your teeth really thoroughly with toothpaste and a toothbrush morning and night
- use dental floss between your teeth every couple of days, when you can feel stuff stuck between your teeth or, let's face it, when you remember
- see your dentist every six or twelve months
- if you chew gum, always choose sugar-free gum (sugar-substitute chemicals, in large doses, can cause diarrhoea).

The biggest causes of holes in teeth are believed to be sugary fizzy drinks, cordials and fruit juices, and bottled water that doesn't have a tooth-protecting compound called fluoride in it. If you carry bottled water, keep refilling your bottle with tap water (filtered is fine). Tooth decay causes really painful holes, which can cost hundreds of dollars to fix.

See also 'Teeth Whitening' in Chapter 4, Body Image.

Bad breath

For at least a hundred years the companies that make breath-freshening mints, mouthwashes, toothpastes and chewing gums have paid for ads designed to make us squirmy and scared of having bad breath, or halitosis (which is pronounced hally-toe-sis).

What causes bad breath?

- Smelly bacteria in your mouth.
- Not brushing your teeth (and tongue) regularly: the bacteria tends to grow on little bits of food left in your mouth.
- Some foods: garlic and onion, for instance, can make your breath smell of them for a little while.
- Not eating for long periods: your saliva isn't being stimulated to wash bacteria and plaque away.
- Smoking.
- Low-carb and other diets.

How to get rid of bad breath

If bad breath isn't kept away by cleaning your teeth regularly, your dentist can help.

Girls' and women's health

You don't have to have had sex, or be planning to have sex, to look after your sexual health. And even if you don't intend to have a baby soon or ever, you still need to make sure all the equipment and procedures in the baby department are okay (that means periods, ovaries, and a few other bits and pieces). Girls have a lot more going on than guys in this department.

Male and female doctors see patients' girly bits all day long and are very used to it – one of the reasons they're able to tell you whether everything is normal is that they see so many different people's bits. Frankly, they'll find yours quite dull, I imagine.

People specialising in sexual stuff such as contraception, sexually transmitted infections (STIs), and pregnancy tests and options can be found at Family Planning clinics, which usually 'bulk bill' so the service is free (see also Chapter 16, Sex, and Chapter 17, Pregnancy).

There are medical specialists (called gynaecologists, pronounced guy-no-colla-jists) who deal with everything to do with sex, contraception, breasts, pregnancy, ovaries, the vagina, the uterus and the cervix. Your first stop is your GP (or a Family Planning clinic doctor), who can refer you to a gynaecologist if necessary.

Every year you should have a check-up at your GP, community health centre or women's health clinic. See 'Health Websites' earlier in this chapter for info on girls' and women's health.

Take care of yourself.   Rose, 17

Breast checks

All breasts have their quirks. A lot of girls and women just naturally have lumpy bosoms, and breasts may feel different around the time of a period.

Once you've developed breasts you should check them after each period for lumps, bumps or changes that don't seem to be just about them growing to their eventual adult size. Get your GP to show you how to do this and what to watch for. Doctors say girls in their teens should still look out for changes even though their breasts are supposed to change.

Be on the alert for:

- a lump, bumpiness or thickening in or on your breast that isn't normal for you
- puckering or dimpling of the skin
- unusual redness or other colour change to the breast
- nipple changes such as altered shape, sores or an ulcer, a different skin feeling (say, rough), more redness than usual, or an in-drawing of the nipple that wasn't there before
- liquid or anything else coming out of the nipple (little hairs are normal)
- unusual pain that's in only one breast and isn't your normal tenderness before a period.

Having any of the above symptoms does *not* automatically mean you have cancer or even a problem. Usually a lump is not cancerous, but any symptom must be checked out by a doctor as soon as possible – don't delay.

Breast cancer happens rarely in teenagers and young women, but, when it does, 'catching it early' will give you a very good chance of getting rid of it before it can get worse.

More info on breast health

bcna.org.au
The National Breast Cancer Centre site. Choose Breast Health Awareness.

Smear tests

The smear test checks for signs that cancer of the cervix could develop. Your cervix is the spongy bit between the top of your vagina and the uterus opening – see Chapter 1, Change). (The test is often called a pap smear or pap test because it was named after a doctor whose last name started with Pap.)

Any GP will do a smear test, and the test is also available at community health centres, women's health centres and Family Planning clinics (see 'Health Websites' earlier in this chapter).

A couple of months after the first time you have sex you should see a doctor and discuss when you need to have your first smear test and – maybe now, or maybe when you turn 18 or 20 – then one every two years. Most forms of cervical cancer are caused by variations of the human papilloma virus (HPV), a sexually transmitted infection. There is an injection that will prevent most forms of cervical cancer (see 'Immunisation' earlier), but to be safe teenage girls and women will still need a smear test every two years. A smear test will only guard against cervical cancer, not ovarian or other cancers.

What happens during a smear test It's less messy to do the smear test when you don't have your period, although if this is the only time you can go to the doctor it is better to do it then than to cancel. The test only takes 5 minutes or less, from beginning to end.

- You take off everything on your lower half, including your undies, and hop onto the bed in the doctor's office. The doctor should have given you a sheet to spread over you.
- The doctor will ask you to lie with your knees bent and your legs spread apart, but your feet together.
- The doctor will put a little lubricating jelly on a sterilised instrument called a speculum, which they will carefully push into the very start of your vagina and then gently open it to hold the walls of the vagina apart a little. Because your vagina is very stretchy, this shouldn't hurt, but it may feel odd and uncomfortable – and a bit cold compared to your body temperature.
- The doc will push up inside you a long, thin plastic stick (with no sharp ends), use it to gently swipe off a couple of cervix cells, then pull it out carefully and transfer the cells to a slide to be analysed by a laboratory. Again it can feel odd, but shouldn't hurt. Very occasionally afterwards there is a tiny amount of spotting or bleeding, which is absolutely fine.

Smear test result If the result shows you need treatment or another check-up the doctor will let you know. When you have the test done ask the doctor whether you're supposed to ring to get the result, or whether they'll just contact you if they want to see you again. Sometimes people need to have the test again because the result was unclear, but usually there's nothing wrong.

In some places the laboratory that processes your result will automatically send you a reminder before your next test is due. This is a handy service to sign up for.

Don't be worried if the test says you need a follow-up or more treatment: in most cases this just means they'll do more regular tests to 'keep an eye on things' or repeat the test because the results were unclear. It doesn't mean you have cancer. Even if a doctor mentions finding 'precancerous cells', this is good news as it means you can be treated so you won't go on to develop cancer.

More info on smear tests

papscreen.org
Lots of info on what to expect from the test and what the results mean.

Infections that aren't necessarily sexually transmitted

Many infections that affect your girly bits, give you a yukky discharge or make you itchy are not sexually transmitted at all: they're just things that girls and women get from time to time and need a bit of treatment for. Luckily, it's not like you get several at once. For details see the 'Common Infections of the Girly Bits' chart coming up.

Tests for common vaginal infections (and for STIs) can be done at the same time as a smear test, using a separate swipe-stick to collect some cells from your cervix or inside the vagina. As with a smear test, it can feel a bit undignified but shouldn't hurt. You can request a female doctor, a doctor you're familiar with, or a nurse to be in the room if you feel uncomfortable about having the test done. But don't dodge a medical examination, because it's important to get a diagnosis and treatment, as an infection is likely to get worse if untreated.

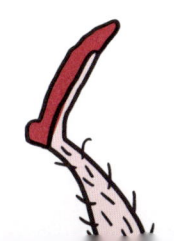

Common infections of the girly bits

You can get these infections of the vagina and vulva area without ever having sex, but sex can be one of the ways of making them worse or of passing some of them on. (For info on sexually transmitted infections (STIs), see Chapter 16, Sex.) The non-sexual infections listed below are all easily treated, and early treatment is always best. Vaginal infections are made worse by lack of air around your girly bits, so avoid G-strings, tight jeans and nylon or closely fitting undies. To help prevent infections and irritations, wash girly bits with a mild soap substitute, and don't use perfumes, powders or 'douches' in the area. Always wipe toilet paper back towards the anus, not from there towards the vagina.

Candida, or thrush

What is it? An infection of the vagina caused by unusually high levels of a natural organism (yeast) in the vagina. It's very common.

How you get it The organism can get out of balance in the vagina with antibiotic use, low immunity or yeast from the bowel entering the vaginal area.

Signs and symptoms Vaginal itch, a thick and clumpy discharge, and stinging when you wee.

How you know you have it A lab analysis of a swab from your vagina taken by a doctor.

Effects No long-term health risks or side effects. It's just incredibly annoying.

Treatment Antifungal cream or pessaries (dissolving pills or creams you pop up your vagina). Sometimes it goes away without treatment.

Bacterial vaginosis (BV), or gardnerella infection

What is it? An inflammation of the vagina caused by natural bacteria in the vagina.

How you get it The bacteria get out of balance.

Signs and symptoms Fishy smell, white or grey and watery discharge, and mild irritation.

How you know you have it A doctor can often tell by looking, or a lab analyses a swab from high in the vagina taken by the doctor.

Effects No big deal unless you have it during any internal surgery nearby, because it can spread infection, but it's worth getting rid of just because it's not nice to have.

Treatment Antibiotic pills, but it sometimes goes away by itself.

Urinary infections, including cystitis

What are they? Infections of the weeing system, including the urethra, urine and kidneys.

How you get one By micro-organisms getting into your body.

Signs and symptoms Wanting to wee all the time (even if only a few drops come out), burning when weeing, blood in your wee, and pain above the pubic bone.

How you know you have one A lab analysis of a wee sample, organised by a doctor or a nurse, to find out which infection you have.

Effects If the infection spreads to the bladder or kidneys, it can cause permanent damage.

Treatment Usually antibiotic pills as soon as possible. Early treatment can stop it spreading to the bladder or kidneys. Chemists' alkaliser powders stop wee stinging, but don't cure the infection.

Vulva problems

What are they? Inflamed or itchy skin around your girly bits.

How you get them They can be due to many things, including dermatitis (or eczema), tinea, psoriasis, vulvodynia (a painful condition of the vulva), waxing or shaving pubic hair or using anything else to remove hair there, perfumes, 'douches' and similar products used on the area. The most likely condition is a common skin rash, but it could be more serious so always ask a doctor to check.

Signs and symptoms Can include itchiness, broken skin, stinging, swelling, redness, lumps, scaly bits, pain, or an abnormal discharge.

How you know you have one A doctor can often tell by looking, or a lab analyses a sample of a discharge, or outer skin cells gently collected by the doctor or a nurse.

Effects Most skin conditions will have no long-term effects, but some can be symptoms of a more serious illness.

Treatment Usually ointments or creams, either prescribed by a doctor or bought over the counter from a chemist.

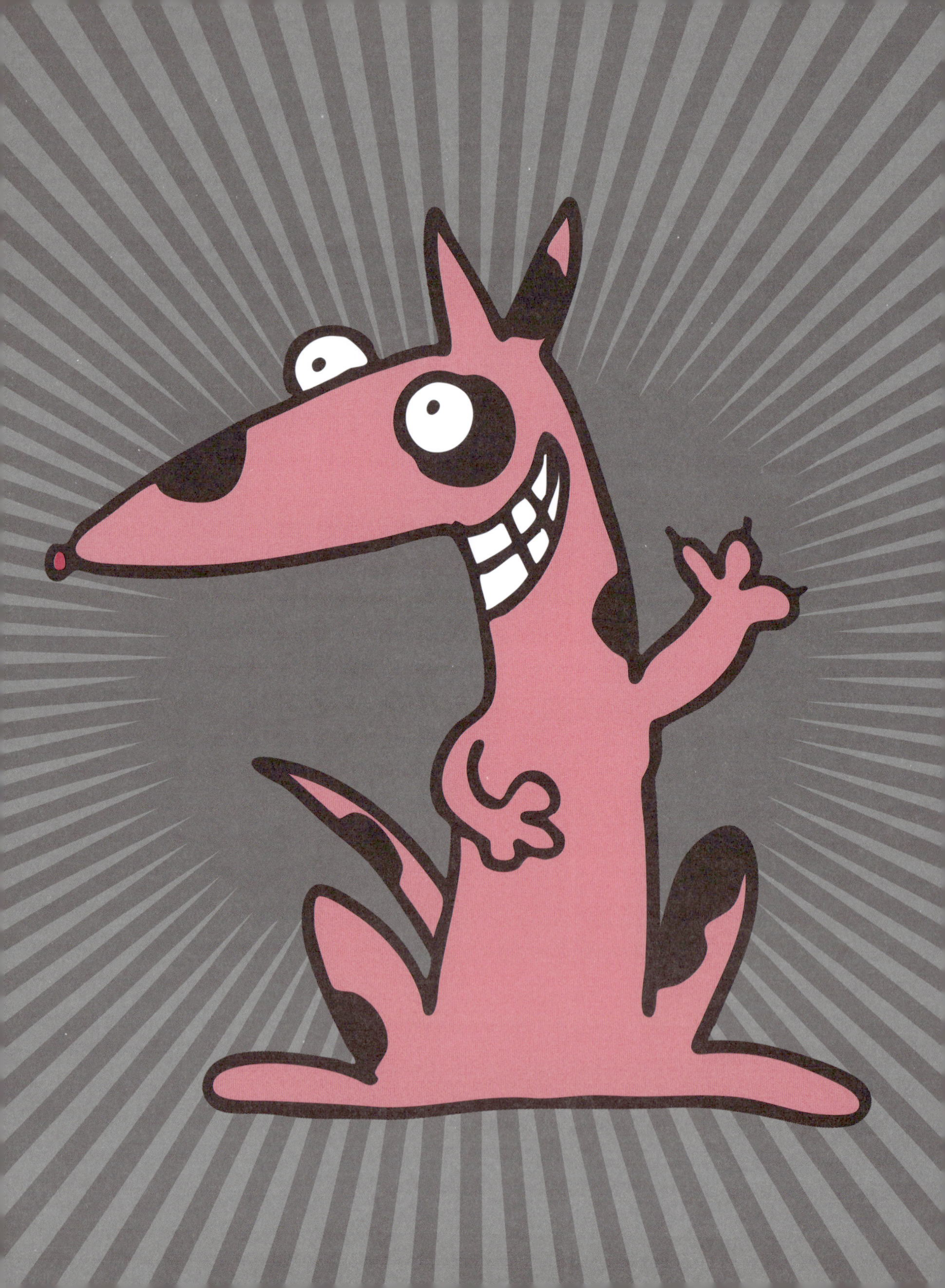

PART 2

HEAD

8 **CONFIDENCE** In search of the real cool 153

9 **FEELINGS** Up, down, all around 178

10 **DRINKING** Make your own rules 195

11 **DRUGS** Make up your own mind 216

12 **MIND HEALTH** Getting your head together 236

8

CONFIDENCE

Confident people believe, 'I'm okay, and it doesn't really matter whether you agree.' **Real cool** has nothing to do with fashion or money: it's a head thing.

Nobody expects you to have total confidence, or to get it all at once. But it's something to work towards. The more you can laugh at yourself, the more you don't care what you look like all the time, the more you don't obsess about what other people think, the freer and **happier** you'll be – and the cooler you'll seem.

Not feeling confident

It can be hard to feel self-confident when you're a teenager because:

- you usually haven't worked out everything about who you are, what you're good at and what you love doing (secretly lots of grown-ups haven't either)
- you may not want to be seen as special and different – some girls want to blend in and not be noticed
- it can be tough not caring about what other people say about you, even when they're just being mean.

> I guess what affects my self-confidence negatively would be myself, really, because sometimes it's hard to turn off that inner voice telling you something isn't good enough.
> Hannah, 18, Canberra, ACT

What girls don't feel confident about

Some of the girls in the Girl Stuff Survey said these things made them feel less confident:

People thinking I was a fool or a ditz – this makes me extremely self-conscious when I meet new people and prevents me from being myself! ✱ **other people's expectations** ✱ going to parties and being around others who are drinking or doing drugs ✱ being a bit shy ✱ **my ability to have or get a boyfriend** ✱ what I am going to do after school ✱ the opposite sex ✱ my body and how others see it ✱ pimples ✱ body image ✱ when I learn someone's name – I don't feel confident about saying it, just in case I get it wrong ✱ being around guys ✱ **my place in the world** ✱ going up to people and introducing myself – I absolutely hate that ✱ feeling as if I must please everyone – I hate that about me ✱ meeting new people ✱ the way others perceive me, especially how the opposite sex sees me ✱ **standing up to people – can't do it, never could** ✱ public speaking, speaking my mind, doing things by myself ✱ singing, dancing, performing, speaking in public ✱ exams! ✱ talking in front of groups ✱ my height ✱ talking to strangers ✱ I don't feel confident about being taken seriously by my mum ✱ meeting people for the first time – I always put my foot in my mouth ✱ putting forward ideas that could be cut down ✱ **pretty much everything** ✱ my appearance, my 'coolness' and some of my grades ✱ I feel a bit awkward around some people – guys mainly ✱ my friends.

Getting confident

Being confident means life opens up, you try new experiences and you have a more interesting time. Having self-confidence means wearing an invisible suit of armour against people who try to put you down, criticise or tease you.

Things you can do

Here are some steps on the way to feeling good about yourself and your strengths, talents and capabilities.

> If you have no self-confidence here is a little trick that helps me when I wake up in a bad mood: look at yourself in the mirror and find at least ONE thing you like about yourself (it doesn't have to be big), and tell yourself that it looks good, GREAT even.
> Kristan, 18, Townsville, Qld

Get some basic body confidence
- Stand up and sit up straight (seriously – it makes you look more confident).
- Let yourself be recognised – don't hide behind a hairstyle that covers your face, or baggy clothes.
- Stop being fussed about whether something's in fashion – wear what *you* like.
- Wear comfy clothes that are not about to trip you up, fall off, expose a nipple or show any underpantery.
- Realise that, although right now your changed body is new, you have a lifetime to get used to it. Keep reminding yourself that you really will adjust and feel comfortable 'in your own skin'.

I'll have what she's having...

do you want to hide, blend in, or stand out?

Encourage yourself

- Go easy on yourself: don't tell yourself you're hopeless if you make a mistake or do something others laugh at. Be your own best friend. What would you say to others to make them feel better about themselves? Tell it to yourself.
- Be content, knowing that for you, and for everyone round you, 'me' is a work in progress. It takes time to discover who you are and what you're going to be. Nobody is allowed to rush you. 'I don't know' is a perfectly fine answer to a lot of questions.
- Be still for a while. It's hard to work out what you think or how you feel if you're always with other people, watching TV, listening to music or on the computer. Sit or walk by yourself and give yourself time to think.
- If there's something you don't like about your personality, ask yourself how you can come to terms with it; or, if it's something you really hate, how you can change.
- Know that there are ways to become more optimistic (see Chapter 9, Feelings).
- Keep in mind that it doesn't matter if someone doesn't like you. Not everyone has to like you. Some people liking you is enough.
- Know that you can move away from friends who say mean things and find new ones (see Chapter 14, Friends, for how to do this).
- Trust that you will find Your People – people who think like you and like the same things. You just may have to wait until you leave school or move out of home. It's a much bigger world out there, beyond your school, your suburb, your town – there is a rightful place for you in it.

> When people say something nice to you appreciate it and take it on board because it makes you feel better about yourself. When you are having a bad day you can think about the things that are good about you.
>
> Jessie, 18,
> Wagga Wagga, NSW

Do something that makes you feel better about yourself

- If you live in a family where there is a lot of sarcasm, where nobody ever says 'I'm proud of you' or 'You did really well', it can be very hard to feel proud of yourself – but it can be done. First tell your family members, or a parent, how the put-downs are making you feel. If that doesn't work, you need to look somewhere else for validation: talk to friends, a teacher or another trusted adult.
- Don't be embarrassed or apologetic about your pastimes or hobbies – find a group or club with the same interests; or websites for all the people out there who like the stuff you do (just be careful about meeting 'Great Guy, 16' from the chatroom – he'll probably turn out to be 'Desperate, Creepy and Pathetic, 46').

- Do something for others – it will make you feel useful and that you're doing something important (see Chapter 24, Caring).
- Find something you really like doing and get better at it.

Practise being confident

- Role-play situations you might find yourself in: go over in your head things you could say, and practise them with a friend or parent, or on your own.
- Practise being strong, even if you don't feel so inside – real courage is doing things even though you're scared.
- Experiment with ways of walking, standing up straight, looking people in the eye and saying things such as 'I'd like to do it this way instead'.
- Exercise your right to try new things. As long as it's fun, give sports, arts and hobbies a go, even if you're not good at them straight away.
- Don't mind too much when you make a mistake. It's just an investment in a more confident future.
- Defy any labels or reputation put on you. You can change if you want to. Don't accept labels, such as 'not smart' or 'mean' or 'slut'. Show with your behaviour that you are your own person regardless of what's happened in the past or what people have said about you.
- Do public speaking or some kind of performance art – if it's too embarrassing to do it at school find somewhere out of school hours. Learn how to use confident body language, and how to project your voice suddenly for effect.

Don't listen to the people that put you down. The only ones that matter are the ones that make you feel good. Holly, 16, Bonner, ACT

Even if you aren't feeling very confident it's always good to pretend that you are: mostly no one will actually realise you're absolutely terrified if you act calm. Victoria, 13

I don't care what anyone thinks. People at school think I'm weird because I listen to punk/rock/emo/hardcore music but I don't care. I think it's funny they're teasing me when they're the ones listening to the crappy music. Fay, 13, Rouse Hill, NSW

Be assertive For some people being assertive doesn't come naturally. It means being able to stand up for yourself and what you believe in. It means being able to say no as well as yes. It means being able to make the right decision and act on it, even though the right decision is often not the easiest or most popular one. (It *doesn't* mean being loud and bossy or imposing yourself and your ideas on other people.)

- Ask adults to listen to your problems and help you. Don't let them say, 'Just ignore it.' Tell them that doesn't work.
- Read Chapter 10, Drinking, and Chapter 11, Drugs, to find out how you can make your own decisions, and excuses for saying no.
- Don't agree to something just to impress anybody else. Walk away if you need to (see Chapter 14, Friends, for ideas on finding a new group).
- Don't behave in ways that disrespect your own beliefs and intelligence – even if other people are pressuring you to. Leave rather than give in.
- Learn how to complain, protest and hassle your local media and politicians when you feel strongly about an issue (see Chapter 24, Caring).

Some ways to say no

'No.'

'Nup.'

'No thanks. It's not really my thing.'

'I'm pretty busy right now.'

'I'm not allowed.'

'I can't – I'm supposed to be home in 10 minutes or Mum will kill me.'

'I can't – I have to get home to take a phone call.'

'Maybe another time.'

'I've got too much on at the moment.'

'I'll let you know later/tomorrow/next week.' (This gives you time to think.)

um... NO!

Stop blaming yourself Tell a guy he stuffed something up and he'll bristle – 'That is CRAP!' – then be determined to improve or have another go – 'I'll show THEM!' – while a girl or a woman is far more likely to say, 'Sorry, sorry, sorry. You're right, that was terrible. I certainly won't try that again. Did I mention I'm very, very sorry? Yes, I probably did. Sorry.' Arrrghhh!

Getting things wrong is part of learning, practising and getting better at something, whether it's playing a guitar or finding new friends. Say you're learning to play table tennis – you don't have to apologise every time you hit a ball off the table. Sometimes you don't have to say anything. So if you get something wrong, or somebody tells you that you have to do something another way, don't always say sorry. Try these instead:

- 'Argghhh! Let's try that again.'
- 'Can you show me that again?'
- 'Okay, I'll keep practising.'
- 'This is hard, but I'm determined!'
- 'I'm gonna get this!'
- 'Ohh, this is better than the last time I tried.'
- 'Thanks for the feedback.' (If you say this, you don't have to do it their way. You're just saying thanks for the option.)

> I think acting confident is the best way to feel confident. If you do something for long enough it tends to become who you are.
> Dunja, 17, Adelaide, SA

Being less shy

When you're shy almost any social situation can seem excruciating and embarrassing. Many people are shy with those they don't know. Even if your natural tendency is to be shy life can become a lot easier with just a little extra confidence and poise. People used to do 'deportment' classes in which they would be taught how to confidently and slowly sit, stand, walk and eat – a good start. You can practise these yourself.

Be polite, but feel free to remain quiet until you've seen how you could warm up and be more outgoing, or how the social rules work in the unfamiliar situation. (You can dance on the table later if that seems like a good idea – although having two beers can make it seem like a good idea when it really isn't.)

> I don't usually care if other people don't like me because I like myself the way I am and I'm not changing who I am. Kendall, 14, Rosebud, Vic.

A lot of people use tricks and confidence boosters to overcome their shyness. Try:
- pretending to be yourself, only a more confident version
- getting drama or voice lessons to learn how to speak and move in front of other people without being embarrassed
- joining a drama, debating, performance, sports or any other group in which people are brought together by a shared goal or interest.

Actually I think the most annoying part of being shy is when adults point it out. As if you've never noticed.

Cool

Being confident isn't being up yourself, or thinking you're better than everybody else, or that you can put other people down. Real cool is not caring too much about what's in fashion or what other people think. What's cool right now will be uncool pretty quickly. Real cool lasts.

Really cool people don't need to feel better by criticising others. People who desperately want to be cool are the most judgemental.

Things that definitely aren't cool These can include:
- trying hard to be popular and fashionable
- being mean to other people so you can get into or stay in the 'cool group'
- being cruel to other people because they're different
- being rude to staff in shops or cafes
- sneering at everything, and everybody else
- being a snob.

The 'popular group' aka 'cool group'
This group always flounces around, acting cooler than anybody else. It's probably not much consolation right now, but here's the good news: the popular group is usually exactly the same bunch of people who, at the school reunion ten years from now, turn out to be the biggest losers of all time.

And then one day, I realised all the people in the 'cool group' behaved like chimps...

iiii

Still snotty, of course, but with absolutely NOTHING to be snotty about. You realise they're such a bunch of has-beens you wonder why you ever cared, for a microsecond, about what they thought or did.

Responding to horrible comments

The best revenge against a consistently mean person is to make them as irrelevant to your life as possible. Sometimes that's really hard when they're at the same school or even in the same class or, for some poor souls, in the same family. Get help from friends and adults as you need it. Sometimes, a thoughtless or even deliberately cruel comment can come from a total stranger. Always remember: whatever they're targeting you for, that is not the problem. There isn't a terrible problem with your appearance, or your personality, or that embarrassing thing you did, or the fact you didn't know what a word meant. All that is normal, or individual – and fine. Where the blame lies is with the attitude of the person who's giving you a hard time. They're (generally or temporarily) being stupid, ignorant, thoughtless, mean or, in some cases, honestly think they're a superior being who can ignore the rights and feelings of others.

This whole book is about finding out stuff that will make you feel more confident and how to deal with lots of different situations. Here are some suggestions for some specific bits, with info and support to raise your confidence in various situations when you could be a 'target':

- See all the ways to deal with mean girls and bullies in Chapter 14, Friends.
- See 'Feeling Embarrassed' in Chapter 9, Feelings.
- See how to deal with difficult family members in Chapter 13, Family.
- See info on feeling down or stressed and how to be optimistic in Chapter 9, Feelings.
- See help for depression, eating disorders and more in Chapter 12, Mind Health.
- See stuff about having different feelings for girls in Chapter 15, Love, and Chapter 16, Sex.

> Until year 7, I never cared what anyone thought of me. But then I cut my hair short (stupid idea) and moved up to high school and suddenly everyone was wearing cool clothes and talking about things that i didn't know about. That was a real hit on my confidence and I think that's when I started to be really self conscious – I never knew what i was meant to do.
>
> Sophie, 15

Sometimes when somebody says something horrible you can just feel embarrassed or angry or lost for words. Mean people are very good at picking something to say that would hurt anyone's feelings or 'sting': often about your appearance or possible 'flaws' that you might feel sensitive about. For those moments when you feel stunned or shocked, try these tactics:

- Ignore it, so you don't have to think of anything smart to say. But to absolutely triumph, laugh if you can, or try this devastating trick: just smile slightly, to yourself, as if you have a funny secret about them.
- Say, 'Yes, yes, you're always saying it and I'm still bored with it.'
- Just say 'Wow' and shake your head and look a bit surprised. Or try: 'Oh yeah, I heard you say random mean stuff to people. How are you going with that?'

If somebody gives you a backhanded 'compliment' or a comment that has a sting in it, such as 'You'd be pretty if you lost weight' or 'At least you have a nice personality' or 'I noticed your giant pimple but I'm sure he won't', try: 'Well, if that's your idea of a compliment, I can probably do without it.' Or just look at them and laugh.

If they say, after something mean, 'Well it's true', say, 'I don't know if it's true, but I do know you didn't have to say that' or 'It's also true that you didn't have to say it.' If they say, 'I'm just trying to help', try, 'It's not helping.' If they say, 'It was just a joke' you can say, 'It's not a real joke if it only makes *you* laugh' or 'You need some new material' or 'Nobody's laughing.'

If you keep your tone light, even friendly, feel free to get stuff out in the open:

- 'Are you trying to be mean, or did you just not think about that before you said it?'
- 'I'll get back to you about that. Maybe when I'm 30.'
- 'No, I'm not anorexic. Are you rude? Oh wait, I already know the answer.'
- 'Luckily I don't have to care what you think of me.'
- 'When I need your opinion I'll know I've lost my mind.'
- 'Mind your own body.'
- 'Hey, good luck with that attitude.'
- 'Congratulations. That's the stupidest thing I've heard all day.'
- 'You want to try that again?'

Self-confidence is something that you will achieve only when you find that what others think of you is not the be all and end all.
Sarah, 16, Townsville, Qld

When people give me compliments I don't take them in. I say thank you or whatever but it sort of goes in one ear and out the other. When I give someone else a compliment I genuinely mean it. Don't know why it's like that.
Chrissy, 18, Canberra, ACT

If you want to build up self-confidence you should find a talent and improve it. Other than that get friends that appreciate you. Henrietta, 16, Sydney, NSW

I think that teenagers need to stop looking at magazines full of supermodels! Some magazines even say they are showing 'real girls' but it looks like they have had makeovers and photo enhancement. It's hard to teach someone self-confidence – maybe you should get all your friends to write a list about the good things about you and make sure you read it every day to remind yourself how important you are. Ange, 18, Rockhampton, Qld

Adults being patronising – makes you wonder why you went through the whole toilet-training saga if only to be seen as a child.
Emily, 16, Florey, ACT

Don't listen to what people say, and don't believe the photos in magazines. Value you. Value what you have to offer to the world as a human being, not as a pretty face. There is more to being alive than spending a life on the scales, or in front of a mirror. No one else has the right to judge you for the importance or adequacy of your contribution to the world. And if they think they do, prove them wrong. Nicola, 16, Wangaratta, Vic.

Avoid negative thought patterns and remember life is what you make it, and not everything is always about you – no one is constantly taking notice of what you are doing.
Anonymous, 18, Toorak, Vic.

For nasty comments about somebody's race, skin colour, religion, sexuality or anything else that's off-limits, you can respond with:

- 'I'm allergic to racism – gotta go.'
- 'That's not funny, that's horrible.'
- 'Just in case anyone thinks I agree, I don't.'
- 'That says more about you than it says about her.'
- 'That's just cruel – and wrong.'
- 'If you really believe that, I don't want to be around you.'
- 'Oh my god, you sound like somebody from last century.'

Practise saying this kind of stuff with somebody close to you or just when you're alone. Don't try to memorise whole brilliant speeches, but just get used to the idea of using a word or a sentence to 'fight back' or at least stand your ground.

More info on self-confidence

amysmartgirls.com
Comedy legend Amy Poehler founded this great website and network for teenage girls about 'how to change the world by being yourself', with videos, problem-solving, music and much more.

Don't Sweat the Small Stuff for Teens by **Richard Carlson**
Some stress-busting help from this US psychologist.

Too Soon Old, Too Late Smart: Thirty True Things You Need to Know Now by **Gordon Livingston**
If you don't have a family whose wisdom helps you along in life, try this guy.

Think Confident, Be Confident for Teens by **Marci Fox, Leslie Sokol, Aaron and Judith Beck**
Self-help tips from clever counsellors.

I was the most unconfident person but when I drive, that all just disappears. Grace, 17

Being told I'm 'indie' or a 'hipster' as if it's a negative accusation is something I've come across more recently. It's always hard to have what you wear, do or listen to categorised into a little box . . . it's easy to shake off: 'I like what I like, deal with it.' Also, I recommend reading 'How Not to Care What Other People Think of You' by Tavi on rookiemag.com! Em, 16

Who are you?

As you grow from a kid into an adult you start to ask questions such as 'Who am I?' And 'Why do some guys have feet that smell like mouldy cheese?' And also 'How come I am not an international movie star with my own island?' But let's start with that first one.

> Being yourself can be hard. But it's a lot of fun. Once you have learnt about yourself, that's when it's easy.
> Billie, 13,
> Mt Waverley, Vic.

What do I know for certain?

You can say these things for certain:
- 'I'm a good person.'
- 'I have as much right to life and happiness as anybody.'
- 'I'm an individual and I'm okay.'
- 'Nobody's perfect. I don't have to be perfect.'
- 'I don't have to settle for something I'm not happy with.'

If it helps, you can say these affirmations to yourself regularly.

Is there a role model who would suit me?

A role model – somebody you admire – can be a useful person to learn from or to feel inspired by. But it can be hard for girls to find role models in a culture that mainly celebrates women for what they look like rather than their achievements.

You just may have to look a little harder. You'll need to seek out some women you can admire for what they've done – not whether they're rich enough to lie around getting fake tans and being photographed in 10-centimetre high heels, with weeny, bald dogs.

Think about women politicians; sports people; song writers and musicians; writers; businesswomen; actresses; brainy girls; kind girls; political activists; mothers; racing-car drivers; scientists; philosophers; grandmas; interviewers; paramedics; teachers; engineers; aunties; journalists; percussionists; artists; photographers; designers; comedians; small-business owners; chief executive officers of major corporations; political leaders; environmental activists; child-care workers; acrobats; councillors; builders; nurses; doctors; TV producers; farmers; daredevils; good girls; naughty girls; trailblazers; brave ones; feisty ones; ones who don't care what their hair looks like while they're getting stuff done. See Chapter 23, Equality, Frivolity, for some suggestions.

Some thoughts on role models

- Don't get so involved you want to be them, not you.
- Don't set them up as a goddess who's oh-so-perfect and then get disappointed when they try to break into a bar at 4 am, with no pants on. A role model may be good at acting, but not so good at dignity.
- Don't let regard for a role model blind you to other people and other options. It's good to have other role models too.
- Don't settle for role models who are being pushed in your face. Search outside the mainstream radio, TV and sports stars. Who else is doing something interesting? Important? Different? Out there? When I was researching the 'big sister' book to this one, *Women's Stuff*, thousands of women told me who they admired, from women politicians to fictional characters, sailors, mums, military pilots, farmers, surfers, prime ministers, comedians, girls with disabilities, sportswomen, geologists, Indigenous leaders, Björk, the Pankhurst Sisters, Marie Curie and Vivian Bullwinkel (look 'em up!).

Blend in or stand out?

One of the confusing things about being a teenager is that:

- in some ways you want to be just like everybody else – 'Don't notice little ol' me, I'm just going to blend in with the back wall here; in fact I'm going to paint myself beige.'

- yet in other ways you want to be so special and different that you can hardly stand it – 'Hey, check it out, I'm going to be FAMOUS!'

How can I find out more about myself?

To discover more about yourself why not try the 'Who Am I?' quiz opposite. (If you find the answers are depressing, or confuse you, talk to a trusted adult about it.)

You can photocopy the quiz first so you can do it again every few months. Maybe you'll be surprised at the things that change, and the things that don't. Keep the filled-in quiz sheets in a safe place such as your diary or a secret hidey-hole, and look back to see how you and your life change as time passes, and how much confidence you've gained.

> **QUOTE**
>
> 'When I was little I felt embarrassed about being different. Later I learned that the things that make you different make you special.'
>
> **Kylie Kwong**, chef, restaurateur, author

166   HEAD ✱ confidence

Who am I?

My name: _____

Date: _____

What do I love doing? _____

What interests me? _____

What am I good at? _____

What makes me happy? _____

When do I feel the most confident? _____

What do I believe in? _____

What are my biggest problems right now? _____

What am I afraid of? _____

What qualities do I like in people/friends? _____

Who are my closest friends? _____

If I wasn't in this group of friends, would I be different? _____

How do my friends treat me? _____

I need to find friends who are interested in: _____

I'll always love: _____

How am I like my parents? _____

How am I like my siblings or cousins? _____

In what ways am I different from my parents? _____

In what ways am I different from my siblings or cousins? _____

What's special about my family? _____

What makes me feel good about myself? _____

Who can I confide in with total trust? _____

What have I changed about my life? _____

What would I like to change about my life? _____

What would I like to stay the same? _____

What are my short-term goals? _____

What are my long-term dreams or ambitions? _____

confidence ✱ HEAD

What girls feel confident about

Here are some of the things the girls in the Girl Stuff Survey said made them feel confident or that they feel confident about:

my sporting ability * **my morals and personality** * my hair * I'm good at acting so even if I don't FEEL confident I act as though I am * I'm not bad looking; I know I can make people laugh; I can walk in heels * **that I am a good person, that I am intelligent and healthy, and not too ugly** * my friends * speaking in front of my class mates! * Um . . . everything basically * not much * nothing * **my intelligence** * being able to enjoy myself * doing school work and playing sport * drumming * answering teachers' questions – sounds stupid, I know, but people think I do that well * that I can walk the streets at any time of day and feel that if I am attacked I will be able to defend myself * I'm a good listener; I live to help friends and I'm confident that in some ways I can help * **how I look when I am wearing clothes my mum says suit me** * talking to people * my reading/writing ability; performing * don't really feel confident about anything, I just love to give everything a go * sports * nothing – but I can deal with nerves okay * I try to look and feel confident about everything * my image, my friends, meeting new guys * that I am going to be happy and successful in whatever path I choose to follow in my life * my face * **my family loving me no matter what** * my swimming and my legs – love my legs! * that I can look after myself and young children * my personality and those who I can trust * my dancing * asking for assistance; talking to adults; ability to do well at school; trying new things * outdoor stuff * people always say I'm a nice person * **I can always make my friends laugh** * I am good * playing wing defence in netball, and making a fool of myself for a laugh * my family loving me * **my life, and I am doing the best I can to live life to the fullest** * mixing with new and different people * I'm not popular and I don't want to be so I can just be myself because my friends accept me for who I am * **sailing, and having a laugh** * art * being around my friends and my family * everything * my calves * my tae kwon do abilities * wearing what I feel comfortable in * my hair (sometimes) * everything except public speaking and talking to guys * **getting where I want to be** * I have a larger vocabulary than my friends 'cause I like to read – this makes me feel special * **who I am on the inside** * I am good at netball and people like me (most of the time!) ✲ my fringe ✲ that I can talk to strangers now ✲ basically everything but my appearance ✲ **my attitude** ✲ the way I dance; I'm a good friend; schoolwork ✲ being gay ✲ **making new friends and not caring about what people think or say about me** ✲ everything – I'm an overly confident person ✲ cycling ✲ cooking, and standing up for my rights ✲ designing! ✲ **helping people sort out their problems** ✲ acting – it's when I can be a different character, not me any more! ✲ my intelligence ✲ my personality ✲ being myself; trying hard at everything ✲ I am a good person ✲ I'm able to hide my insecurities from myself and others so that I may be confident ✲ riding motorbikes ✲ singing ✲ when I am in a group of people ✲ my mum – we have a good relationship ✲ **my image – I'm different and I like it** ✲ showing people the movies I make; talking to little kids ✲ my smile ✲ my clothes ✲ I feel that I am very good at science and I'm the best in my class ✲ I want to become a journalist and I'm confident that I will become one ✲ **everything** ✲ I feel confident when I am laughing ✲ karate and music and school ✲ my strength ✲ that I will go somewhere in life and succeed ✲ **that if anything bad happens there will always be someone to support me** ✲ looking after my siblings when Mum and Dad go out ✲ my long legs because I spent most of my life hating them and got sick of it so I made myself love them!! ✲ **I believe that if you're good at something, you don't need to say 'Oh, I really suck.'** ✲ my abilities to listen, be a good friend, sing ✲ kickboxing ✲ speaking my mind ✲ my choice in fashion ✲ my family will always love me no matter what I do or what I look like ✲ **my fashion – I know most girls my age are afraid to wear some things that I do** ✲ my water-skiing and my artwork ✲ that my pets will always love me even when I make mistakes ✲ my organisational abilities ✲ parenting; labour ✲ being able to help people in most circumstances; and telling people how I feel ✲ **my health** ✲ talking to people and dealing with customers; most of myself; being able to handle any type of horse ✲ **my academic abilities** ✲ my artworks ✲ my face ✲ **I can cook!** ✲ **saving my money** ✲ speaking different languages ✲ my ability to have interesting conversations with older age groups (55 plus) ✲ work (only part-time but still) ✲ being silly – I can laugh at myself and really not care ✲ **working and earning** ✲ one of my friends always looks confident and I think it is due largely to how she walks so now I try to walk confidently! ✲ **the way I think**.

Growing up strong and smart

In your teens, you grow from being a girl-child into a young adult woman. You might think that's scary (don't worry, you have years to get used to the idea) or you can't wait (it'll happen!). How do you get a parent to give you more independence and freedom? By showing them you have the well-placed confidence you need to handle challenges. You need to know what they worry about, and show them you have plans to deal with unexpected or even unlikely situations.

See also Chapter 23, Equality, Frivolity, for info on your rights as a young woman, and how to make sure you're not treated like a second-class citizen; the 'Abusive and Controlling Relationships' section in Chapter 15, Love; and the 'When Sex is Scary' box and 'Sexual Assault' section in Chapter 16, Sex. Feel free to show these to your parents and discuss them, so they know that you're not ignoring any dangers. Now read on, strong girl-womany-type person.

Changing the rules

Most families have fewer rules as you get older – parents love it when you show them you can be trusted, and that your confidence is backed by knowledge.

Here are some possible ways to get rules changed or relaxed.
- Get acceptable marks at school.
- Always be reliable when you say you'll call or you'll be home at a certain time.
- Don't lie to them about where you're going or where you'll be staying.
- Have sensible friends, who they can get to know.
- Do a self-defence course or martial arts training so you won't seem so vulnerable.
- Drop any bad toddler habits, including tantrums, rolling your eyes and saying, 'What . . . ever.'
- Ask them for their advice on how you could have made a situation better: 'How could I handle something like that next time?'
- Tell them what you think you learnt from a mistake or an experience, good or bad.

You so have a point

HOW to TALK TO PARENTS WHEN YOU WANT SOMETHING

> I've learned that parents aren't always right.   Faith, 16, Richmond, NSW

- Talk about the difference between rights and responsibilities. (You have the right to be treated respectfully; you have the responsibility not to frighten your parents by staying out all night without telling them.)
- Say in a reasonable voice that you think you're ready for more independence: 'Can I tell you why I think things have changed?', 'I think I can act responsibly because [*give reason*]', 'What can I do to reassure you that I'm ready for [*whatever it is*]?'
- See if you can reach a compromise – if the rule is you can't ever go out at night, how about only Friday or Saturday nights as long as you're home by a certain time and they know where you are?

Gaining confidence and independence

Because you'll be going out more and more as you get older it's smart to be clued up on avoiding trouble when that's possible. There are lots of tips coming up about different situations, but here are some general pointers:

- always keep your phone charged and in a safe place in your bag or a pocket
- have somebody you can always call on – see 'Your Emergency Rescue Crew' coming up
- call 000 if you believe that you're in real immediate danger (or you're in need of medical help and an ambulance)
- do some self-defence classes – local councils and schools should have details of, or can arrange, classes.

Look confident

- Stand up straight, walk purposefully and look like you know where you're going.
- Don't wear silly high shoes or clothes that tend to fall off or get in the way.
- If you need help, don't act little-girl or stupid. 'Hi, can I borrow your phone, I need to make a quick call' is better than 'Oh my god, I have no idea where I am and my parents don't know either.'

Sound confident

- Practise different ways of saying no, and how to keep saying it even if there's a lot of pressure. See 'Peer Pressure' in Chapter 14, Friends, for hints on how, and also the list of ways to say no in Chapter 10, Drinking.
- Practise saying something or asking for something in a voice that sounds firm and certain. Say the same sentence as a question and as a statement, to see how much

more grown-up you sound when it's a statement: 'Um, I was just wondering if I could ask something? What if we . . . I mean can we go home? Soon? Shall we say goodbye to everyone, or? What do you think?' is very different from 'Okay, I'm going now. See ya later.'

Security tips

A lot of security tips just become part of your routine and then you don't have to think about them any more. And there are some 'stranger dangers' worth knowing (even though most people who are assaulted are attacked by someone they know, not a stranger).

Never let anyone say, 'You're being paranoid', or 'You worry too much.' Don't agree to go somewhere or do something that seems dangerous, such as into a dark, scary place where there are no people to be seen. Guys tend not to worry about that stuff because they've been taught all their lives not to react to physical pain or aggression, especially on the sports field. And they're not targeted for sexual assault as often as girls. So do what's best for *you*.

Home alone or with younger kids

- Make sure people outside can't see inside.
- Get a spy hole in the front door, and if you're home alone don't answer the door to anybody who's not a close friend or relative.
- Don't leave windows open at night, even when it's hot, unless you have bars on them, or another security feature.
- Don't give your key to friends.

Out and about

- Try not to walk home (or be on public transport) when it's dark or there are few people around. When in doubt, head for the crowds and bright lights of open shops, restaurants and other public places.
- Vary your routine – such as where you jog early in the mornings or when you leave work – and change the journeys.
- Be aware that a surprising number of attacks happen in the early morning, not just when it's dark.
- Try to take a dog or a friend if you walk or jog.
- Always walk or run against the traffic so that you can see what's coming.

- Think about not using earphones up loud – music or talk in your ears means you can get distracted and step onto a road without hearing unexpected traffic coming. You also can't hear someone coming up behind you.
- If a strange adult takes a picture of you with their phone, take their photo too (if it's safe to) and keep it to show to a parent.
- If someone is acting creepy or following you, make sure you get a good look at their face, and that they know you have. Or take a picture of them with your mobile phone (if you can safely) and send it straight away to a friend or a family member. This way the person knows they can be identified.

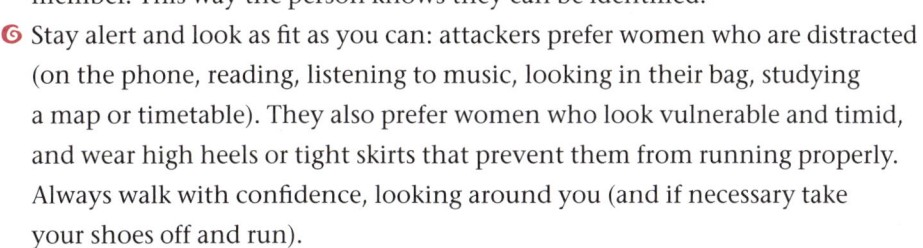

Take a DOG

- Stay alert and look as fit as you can: attackers prefer women who are distracted (on the phone, reading, listening to music, looking in their bag, studying a map or timetable). They also prefer women who look vulnerable and timid, and wear high heels or tight skirts that prevent them from running properly. Always walk with confidence, looking around you (and if necessary take your shoes off and run).
- Have a spare key hidden outside your house (but not somewhere obvious such as under the mat or a pot plant or rock) so that even if you haven't got your own key you can get inside quickly.

Out and about on public transport and in cars

- If you're on an almost-empty train, sit in a corner – that way you can see everyone who gets on or off, and nobody can get behind you. Always try to be in, or get to a place that's crowded and busy: there's more protection there. On an empty bus or tram, sit near the driver rather than right up the back.
- Obviously, avoid being alone with a creepy person. Sometimes you don't know why you think there's something odd. Doesn't matter. Trust your instincts: if someone or somewhere seems dodgy they probably are. It's more important to be safe than worry about whether you've been rude or overreacted.
- Always call and order a cab instead of hailing one on the street, if you can. This means the taxi company will have a record of who the driver is, and he's less likely to do anything rude or horrible.
- Keep some taxi money at home for emergencies in case you lose your handbag or wallet. (This means you'll need a spare house key hidden in a very safe and

Your emergency rescue crew

Have at least one or two emergency contacts for late-night or other rescues. These are people – a parent, friend's parent, aunty or uncle, brother or sister – who'll come and get you at any time, or organise to call a taxi and pay for it if necessary. You can use them when or if your only alternative is getting into a car with people who are drunk, or if there's some other situation you know you should get away from. It's a good idea to:

- Put their numbers on speed dial.
- Memorise their phone numbers in case you can't call them on your own phone.

The deal is you try never to get yourself into a stupid, dangerous situation – and the emergency person never screams at you for waking them up in the middle of the night.

unobvious spot, too. My mum taught me to hide it in a tiny plastic container in a neighbour's garden. I thought she was mad until I needed it at 2 am once, and was out there digging in their front yard by street light, like an insomniac puppy.)

- Don't enter a car park if it's empty or really late, or you feel weird about it. Get a security guard or a person you trust to walk you to your car.
- Never go over to a man in a deserted car park who says he needs help. Get in your car, lock the doors and use your phone to ring the emergency number for him.
- Don't faff about looking for your car or home keys: always have them ready when you get to the door.
- Lock all car doors, whether you're in or outside the car, so someone can't jump in. This goes for daytime as well as night-time journeys, and sitting in the car reading a mag while eating takeaway before a meeting. Make it a habit: if you're in the car, the doors are locked.
- If a car pulls up when you've broken down in a deserted place check all your doors are locked and the windows up. Call a roadside service company, family member or close friend to come and get you. If you don't have a phone, open the window a crack

ooh, no you don't...

If it feels weird it PROBABLY is... time to BACK out

174   HEAD ✱ confidence

and ask the person to make the call for you. Don't get out of the car or let them in. You can wait.
- Never, ever hitchhike. It's illegal – because it's dangerous.
- Never get into a car when ordered to by a man, even if he has a weapon – resist (see the 'Resisting Force' box coming up).
- Generally avoid getting into a car or going somewhere with a group of young men. Groups tend to be more dangerous than a guy on his own.
- Have a rule for yourself that you won't get into a car with a driver you don't know, a driver you think could be unsafe, a drunk driver, or somebody who's been drinking and may be over the limit, and that you won't get into a car that doesn't have a working seatbelt for you.

Be prepared

Practise some 'what if' scenarios with a parent or a friend's parent, or workshop ideas with a teacher in class. What are the best things to say and do in these situations?
- You want to look confident on public transport.
- A friend or a guy you like says to get in the car and they'll drive you home. You know they've been drinking.
- All your friends have accidentally left you behind at a party and you don't know the address.
- You find yourself stranded in a park, after midnight, and you're not allowed to be there.
- You're at a friend's party when gate-crashers arrive and a fight breaks out.

Partying

- Don't go outside or down the road or to a park – stay where there are friends, or parents, nearby who can help you if things get nasty. (See also Chapter 10, Drinking, and Chapter 11, Drugs, for good hints.)
- If something seems off or wrong about a guy, and the way he looks at you or speaks to you (he seems extra intense in a weird way or too charming to be true), be extra careful. Don't forget – you may not be interested but an older guy may have creepy ideas about you (even a really old one, like your parents' age or beyond).
- If you're at end-of-school celebrations or at a club or other function watch out for 'toolies' – older guys who hang around hoping to find girls drunk enough to assault.

Resisting force

If you're attacked or physically restrained, whether it's by a stranger or somebody you know, resist. It's good to practise this with a parent, friend or older sibling, so you're ready to react with confidence if it happens to you.

* Scream, fight and run away if a guy tries to corner you or stop you getting away – and keep screaming. He'll be looking for an easy target, and is more likely to give up.

* If somebody attacks you, always fight back if it's possible – biting, kicking and punching – and make a lot of noise. Attackers want someone who is quiet and no trouble. If you hurt his testicles, you're trouble. Remember this is a guy who will definitely hurt or rape you if you don't fight. If you do fight, you may get away.

* 'Weapons' you can use include keys, sharp edges of heavy books, even your teeth, hands, the heel of a shoe.

* If struggling and screaming doesn't scare him off shout, 'Dad!', 'Mum!' or 'Help! Fire!', to attract other people's attention and make him think somebody is just nearby.

* Break away and run into a shop or anywhere else that's crowded, and yell for help. Always choose crowds with women as well as men if you can.

* It's worth having some training in self-defence. Ask your school if you can have a self-defence class as part of your sport lessons. Sometimes local police can come and give a talk about self-defence too.

And when the party's at your place:
- go to the local police station at least a week beforehand and let them know the date of the party and your address – if anything goes wrong they'll be there quicker, and they'll also see you as a responsible person they want to help (which is handy if there are thirty scary gate-crashers who won't go away)
- if your parents are away for the night don't tell lots of friends or word will get around and you'll suddenly have a house full of unwanted guests. If scary people you don't know do arrive, leave the house (taking friends with you). Go to a neighbour's and call the police. Your parents will be pleased the uninvited guests got chucked out before any damage was done – to you or to their house.

More info on parties

Search the following state and territory police sites for more ideas on safe parties and a 'party notification form' you can download, print out and give to your local police station with the details of your party. This means they'll get there quickly and protect you if there are gate-crashers.

police.act.gov.au

police.nsw.gov.au

pfes.nt.gov.au/police.aspx

police.qld.gov.au

police.tas.gov.au

police.vic.gov.au

police.wa.gov.au

'There's a stranger called Bevan throwing up in your dad's underwear drawer'

FACT

Your legal rights Be confident in knowing your rights. Check out lawstuff.org.au, a site from the National Children's and Youth Law Centre, which answers common questions from teens based on local laws, plus provides info on the UN convention on the rights of the child. Kiwis, try youthlaw.co.nz.

9

Aaarrghh!

FEELINGS

There are some days when a mood ring on a teenager would be flashing about 273.5 colours for **different moods**, and you'd have to carry around a dictionary-sized chart to decode every one from awkward but charming, through vivacious but proud, to brave but slightly baffled. Not to mention giggly, creative, clever, annoyed, and dying to lie down in a hammock.

This chapter shows how to deal with negative thoughts and moods such as being worried, angry or embarrassed, and how to get through a time of sadness. Being a teen can also mean lots of fun and laughter. So just in case you need it, there's info on how to feel more cheerful, too.

Moods

Adults get moody too (especially supermodels and socialites, who throw shoes at their assistants), but teenagers have a reputation for moodiness because it's a contrast to the more even, little-kid years (not counting toddler tantrums).

Reasons for being moody

There are several possible reasons for feeling up and down and all over the place.

- Your brain hasn't had enough sleep – this can make you cranky.
- The brain's chemicals are out of whack, which can happen during the teenage years. They need to be in balance for you to feel calm and happy.
- Teenage hormones – up and down moods are often blamed on these. For instance, higher oestrogen in girls and women can trigger extra dopamine (that brain chemical that makes people feel happier), but when the oestrogen falls, as part of the monthly cycle, the dopamine does too and they can suddenly feel less happy. High levels of progesterone, just before and during a period, make some feel flat, tired, grumpy, tearful or anxious (see Chapter 1, Change, for info on PMS).
- You're thinking too much about your own problems.
- The stressful stuff that can happen when you're a teenager – moodiness can be a logical response to all that.

If your moods seem really extreme or your feelings seem very troubling, and it seems relevant, check out the sections in Chapter 12, Mind Health, including 'Depression', 'Severe Anxiety' and 'Eating Disorders'.

bewitched...   bothered...   bewildered...

Feeling embarrassed

The level of embarrassment you suffer between the ages of 12 and 18 pretty much goes through the roof. (It's crashed back down to earth by the time you get to old age, when you're quite happy to go shopping in a hairnet, overcoat and socks with thongs, singing show tunes at the top of your voice and hitting annoying people with an umbrella.)

You can be so freaked out wanting to be perfectly normal that falling over, or blurting out something during a silence, can seem SO embarrassing you have to move to another country and live in a tree for the rest of your life.

Part of the embarrassment is that during these years you're intensely self-conscious and always super-aware of what you're doing and how you might be seen. Actually nobody else is noticing you as much as you think they are – they're probably too concerned with how everyone else is seeing *them*.

All you can do in the face of hideous humiliation is apologise, if necessary, hold your head high and move on gracefully, then get behind a closed door, cry, think about it 1 647 474 times and get the embarrassment out of your system. You'll remember it long after everyone else has forgotten (in about 10 minutes).

> A girl in my year had embarrassing photos put online recently and nobody looks at her differently now. Don't waste time regretting what happened, everyone makes mistakes, don't let them hold you back.
>
> Elle, 15

Blushing A common side effect of being embarrassed is blushing. This is because the stress triggers the release of the hormone adrenaline, leading to blood being pumped rapidly to all parts of your body (so that you're ready to run away from a mammoth if necessary). The extra blood close to the surface of your skin makes you look redder. (The adrenaline can also cause you to suddenly sweat more, especially on your palms, and your mouth to go dry.)

I wonder if my head will explode?

Handy recovery lines for an embarrassing situation

'Maybe I'll take my foot out of my mouth.'

'This might be a good time to move to Iceland.'

'Or I could actually say something far less embarrassing. I'll get back to you on that.'

'But now I must go and find my identical twin [*insert your own name here*], who never gets herself into a situation like this.'

'Did I just say/do that? I guess I've been possessed by that damned alien again.'

'Somebody press rewind.'

'Does anyone have a hole in the ground I can get into now?'

Laugh. Blush. Be embarrassed. Then move on.

> I worry about embarrassing myself in front of people.
> Emily, 13,
> Lenah Valley, Tas.

> I blush.
> Lily, 14,
> Forestville, NSW

As well as going bright red with embarrassment, you can blush because someone has accused you of something (blushing is never proof that a person is 'guilty'), or they've given you a fright or even just looked at you. You can also blush when you're angry, self-conscious, nervous or surprised. Most people won't even notice that you blushed, even though you're super-aware of it.

Some people find that their blushing or hand sweating in nervous situations seems to be really severe. See a doctor if this sounds familiar. (There's more on sweating in Chapter 2, Skin).

> There was a time when I was afraid of walking around the schoolyard because I was scared of getting embarrassed – but then I thought I'd try something different. If something embarrassing happened to me that wasn't insulting or anything, just cringe-worthy (eeek!), I would laugh it off. I felt so much better and the next time something embarrassing happened it just came naturally to me and I was admired for it! Now anything can happen to me and I don't feel like I'm going to fall over and die! Of course if the embarrassing thing just isn't funny I tell the person and they usually get the message. Kirsty, 15, Mildura, Vic.

Feeling angry

Girls can get the idea that they're not allowed to be angry, that it's not ladylike or it's too disruptive. Not admitting you feel angry, and bottling it all inside, can lead to more stress and random outbursts that don't seem related to what you're really cross about. (You're angry with your parents but you take it out on your little brother.) If you don't acknowledge and talk about your anger, it will still be there.

Sometimes, though, teenagers don't realise that what they're experiencing is anger. Writing down your thoughts and feelings can help you recognise your anger. Talking to someone is also a good way to work out what's going on inside you.

It really is okay to be angry, and some of us need help with expressing anger – but also sometimes with managing it.

More info on feeling angry

See also the info on family abuse in the Chapter 13, Family.

kidshelpline.com.au
Kids Helpline: 1800 55 1800
If you'd like to talk about a parent or friend's anger, or your own, call the helpline. There's a web counselling service: check online for available times – choose Teens 13–17 or Young Adults 18–25 from the home page.

relationships.com.au
Relationships Australia lists anger management courses or groups.
For nearest main office call 1300 364 277.

kidsline.org.nz
NZ Kidsline: 0800 543 754

> *Sometimes when people say things that hurt you it has nothing to do with you, but how they feel about themselves. Figuring that out helped me brush off nasty comments.* Hannah, 17, Perth, WA

> I find sport the best way to relax and you can let all your anger and frustration out without hurting the people close to you. Ashleigh, 15, Burpengary, Qld

Dealing with anger

Try these useful ways to handle anger:

* work out the feeling behind the anger – is it a sense of being unfairly treated or ignored, or is it a reaction to seeing a general injustice such as racism?

* admit it when you're not sure why you're so angry, and talk about it

* talk about how a situation has affected you ('I feel . . .' or 'I had trouble understanding why . . .' rather than blaming or accusing – 'You did this to me' or 'It was your fault')

* explain that in a discussion you need to have your turn, even with parents

* allow yourself to 'come down' from the brain chemical high that anger causes, before you make any important decisions

* do something really physical – sometimes running, dancing or playing sport can help dissolve angry feelings (see Chapter 6, Move)

* think and talk about ways to avoid the situation that caused the anger, and about a more positive response to the situation

* ask a calm, sensible friend or relative for advice about how to handle a problem – don't feel you have to tackle everything on your own

* take a quiet moment (or days) to collect your thoughts before trying to resolve a problem with somebody so that you're not confrontational

* admit a mistake or say sorry – this makes it easier for others to do the same with you

* follow the old saying that 'Living well is the best revenge', which means that when somebody does the wrong thing by you, get on with enjoying your life instead of brooding or plotting against them.

Try to avoid anger that's only negative, which can make you (and others) feel worse and won't fix anything. Unhelpful responses include:

* refusing to speak

* breaking or damaging things

* shouting or swearing at somebody

* ignoring or snubbing somebody

* being mean to or bullying someone

* being constantly sarcastic

* damaging yourself (self-harm)

* being violent

* focusing on 'punishing' whoever you're angry with.

Feeling worried and stressed

Anxiety is the feeling of nervousness, worry, concern or fearfulness about things that might or will happen. In severe cases it can lead to panic attacks, in which you feel terrified or 'frozen'. Severe anxiety needs to be treated (see Chapter 12, Mind Health).

Stress is the feeling that you can't cope with or control everything you have to do, or live up to expectations. Although stress is more about feeling under pressure, while anxiety is more about being worried, sometimes they feel kind of the same.

As well as these feelings, you can experience physical symptoms with anxiety and stress, which can include a faster than normal heartbeat, sweating, trouble sleeping, and lots of colds and infections because your body's too busy with the anxiety or stress to keep up a healthy immune system. Some girls get headaches, pains in the stomach or nausea (feeling squirgly, as if you might throw up).

People often go to great lengths to avoid anxiety-making or stressful events, such as facing a bully.

Beating anxiety and stress

Here are some good ways to tackle anxiety or stress:
- talk about your feeling with Mum, Dad, friends, your aunty, a doctor or nurse, a friend's mum, a counsellor or teacher, or anyone else you feel comfortable with
- do some physical activity each day – it can help you be a calmer person
- drop something (not a priceless vase) – a subject, an unrealistic expectation of yourself, or a friend who teases you and causes anxiety
- distract yourself – instead of staying home all afternoon thinking about your difficulty, see a movie with friends

> I have a lot of trouble with standing up in front of groups of people, no matter how big or small. I sweat, shake and stutter. My breathing speeds up quite significantly and I have become physically sick on a number of occasions.
>
> Anna, 16,
> Forestville, NSW

- analyse how you can get out of the stressful or anxious situation, and try to avoid it happening again. What's the worst thing that could happen? Who can help you with that?
- read Chapter 8, Confidence
- avoid caffeine (in coffee, cola and 'energy' drinks) – it tends to make you hyper and more jittery
- get more sleep, which will help you cope better with everything
- breathe slowly – this is a quick, simple way of heading back towards calm. Breathe in for a count of six (or four or whatever you can manage). Pause, then breathe out for a count of six, if you can. Repeat for a minute or so. Learn yoga to find out more about the deep relaxation possibilities of breathing techniques.

I blow bubbles when I'm stressed

You're weird ... Actually, can I have a go?

CHANGE. It's the one thing that scares me. Change always seems to take over and make people and life different and sometimes more difficult. Amelia, 16, Bundeena, NSW

School is important but it's critical to have fun: don't take life too seriously, you only live once! Juliet, 15

What girls worry about

Here are some of the things that the girls in the Girl Stuff Survey said they worried about:

boys, love, friendship, grades, the usual stuff ✱ whether my mum, who got breast cancer last year, will die ✱ exams ✱ **change, and hurting myself** ✱ money shortage and my family ✱ whether it's going to rain on my school shoes 'cause then my socks will get wet and I will have to walk home in soggy socks ✱ being attacked by random people in the street; animals that are kept in tiny cages; our family not having enough money ✱ **the snow season being bad!** ✱ I'll never be healthy ✱ people and friends seeing me as a slut or a skank or thinking that I try to be popular ✱ now I am 15 I am seen as an adult and I feel as if my childhood is over ✱ my friends, my appearance, school, what others think of me, jellyfish etc. – so much stuff ✱ I might get pregnant at the age of 15 ✱ what's going to happen to me at school today – am I going to fall over in front of everyone or do something embarrassing? – and my brothers because they both do drugs ✱ **my mum drinking too much** ✱ my year 10 Formal ✱ everything (catching the train, going to parties) – there's just so much to worry about, and I worry about forgetting something important I should be worrying about ✱ Am I pretty enough? Am I fat? Why am I different to everyone else? Is my family wealthy enough? Do I have cool enough clothes and are they expensive? ✱ my father killing me and my mother ✱ my grades and assignments; disappointing people; having fights with friends; ending up alone; SPIDERS ✱ people not taking me seriously so I look like an idiot; people not liking me ✱ nothing much ✱ **I don't get over 95 per cent in my tests** ✱ what I'll get for my birthday/Xmas/Easter/any present occasion ✱ global warming; money and my parents running out of it coz of me ✱ my parents finding out interesting facts about me that they didn't know! ✱ BAD HAIR DAYS ✱ what's going to happen to this country – I have already seen a huge increase of racism just in my school ✱ everyone else liking the same bands as me, and that my acne won't go away ✱ death, my stomach (it could be flatter I think – but it's okay, I guess) ✱ going somewhere new because I fear that I will not be accepted ✱ just about everything, but I pretend I don't really care about anything ✱ falling for someone hard and them never having the same feeling back ✱ my parents – I know they are both depressed, have money issues and will probably get divorced soon ✱ **the Formal** ✱ Mum finding out all the naughty things I've done ✱ boys, clothes, and that huge zit that always pops up before a big night ✱ Mum finding out about my boyfriend ✱ my bizarre-looking toes; the amount of time it takes to straighten my hair ✱ my son's father, because I'm scared he will want to take him away, and whether my baby will be okay when he's born, and if I will be able to take care of him properly ✱ pimples.

Feeling overwhelmed?

Time to get underwhelmed. Don't blame yourself for feeling stressed and think you just need to cope better – maybe too much stress is a logical response to your life right now, and that means your life needs to change.

Ever feel like it's just too much, what with puberty, schoolwork, homework, sport, home chores, body image worries, friend or guy troubles? Or in other words, 'Arrghhhhhhh!' Feel free to drop something that will make your load lighter (a third sport commitment, for example, or a sarcastic boyfriend, or a late-night TV show you can record for the weekend instead). Talk to a parent, friend or sympathetic teacher about how you can deal with too much stress.

Talking to someone   The girls who answered the Girl Stuff Survey said they find it helpful to talk to people about their worries. Many girls spoke to lots of different people: about two-thirds spoke to their friends, and about a third spoke to both parents. About a quarter of the girls talked to their mum but not their dad, and a handful of girls only talked to their dad. Other people who girls talked to included sisters, brothers, aunties, uncles, cousins, grandparents and God. Some girls suggested speaking to a psychologist, a school counsellor, a favourite teacher or a doctor; telling a pet; chatting to internet friends, a journal or a blog (but be careful about your privacy: see info about online safety in Chapter 14, Friends).

it HeLps to talk aBout worries

Sadly, nearly one in ten girls said they didn't talk to anybody about their worries. Whatever you do, pick somebody to talk to. And if that experience isn't good, pick somebody else until you find help.

FACT

Perfect isn't always great If you're always feeling that you're a failure, but you're passing tests and doing okay, think about the standards you're setting yourself. If you expect 'perfection' or 100 per cent or an A+ every time, then you'll see anything else as a failure when in fact in means you're doing exceptionally well. Did you learn something? Did you have fun doing an art project? Did you lose a leg in the process? There are other ways to judge things, you know . . .

More info on feeling anxiety and stress

If relevant, also see the help offered in all the 'More Info' sections in Chapter 14, Friends, covering being different, gossip, meanness and bullying.

If you feel really up against it, your GP can refer you to a counsellor experienced in techniques for avoiding anxiety and stress, but here are some starting points. There's more on anxiety in Chapter 12, Mind Health. See also the info on yoga in Chapter 6, Move.

kidshelp.com.au
Kids Helpline: 1800 55 1800
A 24-hour counselling line you can ring anonymously. Check out their web counselling, too (click on Teens & Young Adults).

reachout.com
Info, blogs, online chats, and fact sheets to help with negative feelings and lots of other things.

> I feel that people will judge me on everything I do. Even the performance of simple daily tasks, such as walking or eating, can provoke the feelings of being watched and make me feel as if I may do these tasks 'wrong'. Carly, 16, East Kew, Vic.

Feeling down

'Feeling down' covers different emotions such as grief, sadness and depression.

> Magazines (with perfect models on every page) make teenage girls feel like crap even though we don't realise it.
> Anonymous, 16, Melbourne, Vic.

Grief

Grief is the word used for the intense feelings caused by a severe emotional loss, such as a death; a family or relationship break-up; the upheaval and separation resulting from war or another trauma; the departure of somebody; or a life-changing illness.

Different people grieve in different ways – even those in the same family or a group who lose someone they all love.

The swirling feelings of grief can include lots of responses, all normal:

- **Crying** 'Every time I think about our old life I start crying', 'I don't seem to be able to stop crying since Dad left.'
- **Denial** 'She didn't really die. She'll walk in the door tonight.'
- **Questioning** (to make sense of the loss) 'Why did this happen?', 'Why us?'
- **Anxiety** 'I don't know how to cope', 'I can't work out what to do', 'I can't stop thinking about it.'
- **Self-blame** 'If only I hadn't said/done that, maybe Mum and Dad would have stayed together.'
- **Anger and frustration** 'How could you leave me?', 'You've never lost anyone so how could you possibly understand what it's like?'
- **Loneliness** 'I'm the only one who really understands how this feels to me.'
- **Depression and loss of interest in life** 'I'm not getting up and going to school today', 'Whatever. I don't care what we do.'
- **Sadness** 'I wish my mum was here for my birthday party', 'I don't think I'll ever see my homeland again.'

> You just hit 'one of those days' and you're down for no apparent reason. Danielle, 17, Myrrhee, Vic.

> I'm sad when I am tired. Lisa, 18, East Albury, NSW

Ten things to avoid when you feel down

1. Thrash-trash-death-puke metal or country music.
2. Eating fifty-six Tim Tams.
3. Tragic movies that make you cry so much that snot comes out.
4. The news.
5. Staring at yourself in the mirror.
6. Wearing clothes that are the wrong size.
7. Deliberately avoiding sleep.
8. Documentaries in which animals eat each other's head off.
9. Asking someone if your bum looks big in whatever you're wearing.
10. Cutting or dyeing your own hair.

As well as these reactions many grieving people experience physical symptoms, including headaches, an upset stomach, tiredness, trouble sleeping or sleeping too much.

In the early stages of grief it's totally okay just to think about what to do in the next hour, or the next day. You don't have to sort out everything right away, or even soon. Everyone who grieves needs some help and other people to talk to. Taking each day as it comes, one step at a time, and getting help is a good way to move forward.

Nobody should expect you just to 'get over it'. You need time to grieve properly, and then find a way to take your sadness with you into the next phase of your life where you can feel more positive, without having to forget someone or pretend an important event never happened.

See the section on feeling strong and optimistic, coming up.

More info on grief

grief.org.au
Inquiries: 1300 664 786
Help to find a counsellor.

Teenagers and Grief by Doris Zagdanski
An Australian book for teenagers and for their friends, parents and teachers who want to help.

reachout.com
Choose Tough Times then Loss and Grief for fact sheets, real stories and help.

skylight.org.nz
This non-profit grief organisation has advice specifically for teens experiencing grief: choose Young People.

Motherless Daughters and *Letters from Motherless Daughters* by Hope Edelman
US books about losing or living without your mum: the feelings and practical things.

Sadness

Grief is an extreme, not an everyday, emotional experience, whereas sadness can be a less intense feeling that you might have quite often, about many things. At the risk of being blindingly obvious, it's okay to feel sad sometimes – if you didn't, you wouldn't really care about anything, and that would be worse. It's when sadness becomes your usual mood no matter what happens, or you feel an ongoing depression or blankness, that you need to watch out.

> If I am feeling sad or bad about myself (and I have some money) I will go and buy some chocolate, come back home and watch a movie or read a book.
> Sofia, 18, Brisbane, Qld

FACT

Depression Like sadness, depression isn't only experienced in times of grief. 'Being a bit depressed' usually means a temporary mood: feeling rather flat after a big excitement has ended, being 'blue' for a couple of days, or having 'a good cry' here and there after something rather sad happens. It's part of everyday life. 'Clinical', or major, depression is different: it's a constant crushing feeling of hopelessness that it seems will never lift – there's more on this and lots of help and advice in Chapter 12, Mind Health.

Give yourself a reality check when you feel one comment or incident wearing you down. Mentally list ten things that make you special, beautiful, desirable, different. Chloe, 17, Mosman, NSW

Don't say 'It's too hard, nobody can help me.' Try this: 'It will get better, and I can help myself.' If you admit to yourself you're on the way up, people can help again.
Katie, 17, Wangaratta, Vic.

> Sometimes I'll sit in front of my mirror and I play my iPod and just sing some of my favourite songs, and because a lot of the songs are meaningful, something about them just makes me feel beautiful and loved.
> Chelsey, 15, Port Norlunga, SA

If I have a bad day I just take it all out in my sports training which makes me feel so much better afterwards. Erin, 16

Feeling optimistic and strong

Almost everyone goes through bad patches, experiences moody phases and has times when they feel down. Some have the ability to 'bounce back' quickly. They're optimistic: they expect that things will, or are likely to, turn out well. If that's not you, you'll be relieved to hear that you don't have to be born with optimism – you can learn it. You can also learn resilience: the buzz word that means you are strong; a survivor who can face hard times and come through it all okay; the sort of person who can take a disappointment, instead of going off to brood for days or weeks.

You can *learn* not to let the pain of a rejection stop you from making new friends. You can aim to be a girl who doesn't take crap from anyone, who when 'one door closes' in their face will kick down a few more. Or at least think about knocking politely.

Getting strong

Here are some ways to get strong.

- Like yourself. If you try to be a good person who isn't mean and nasty, then you can feel good about yourself. When a bad thing happens you'll know it's not your fault.
- Have a support team. It could be family or friends or both. Being part of a team, club or neighbourhood helps.
- Have a list of people, activities, DVDs, books and music that cheer you up.
- Think about great times you've had. Think about bad times you went through that got better.
- Recognise that sometimes things don't get better by themselves – you may have to take action or ask for help. Sometimes you have to persevere before things improve.
- Face fears and hard times because they do have a positive side. You'll be more experienced at solving problems, feel braver, maybe get to know yourself and your limits, and be better prepared for obstacles in life.
- Try to be realistic. Instead of saying 'Nothing will ever change', set an achievable goal.
- Don't be a catastrophiser – that's a person who turns the smallest problem into a catastrophe by panicking, shouting, being a drama queen or complaining to everyone. Save your energy to deal with real problems.

Happy, happy, happy!

If my sister and me bake cookies together I forget my problems and have fun. Sara, 13, Haberfield, NSW

Stop stressing about the little things, believe me, you will get through it. Kate, 15

Ten things to help you cheer up

1. Laughing – with friends, at a movie or show. If necessary, get in a water or pillow fight.

2. Fresh air and light – proven mood lifters.

3. Affirmations: use a diary, sticky notes, posters or your own thoughts to remind yourself of your good points and things you enjoy or want to achieve.

4. Exploring your creative side – express your feelings in writing, drawing, music, performance, cooking.

5. Having things to look forward to. Check your schedule this week: is there any time for fun? If not, start to schedule it for coming weeks.

6. Taking time out – try to get some time all to yourself. Just lie there in silence or listen to some soft music.

7. Doing 'good works'. This could include helping to look after an animal, or volunteering some time or money to a charity (see Chapter 24, Caring).

8. Telling someone you love them – and doing them a favour.

9. Having a big clean-out of your room: chuck out stuff you don't want that's cluttering your space, rearrange things the way you want them and start afresh. If it's too big to tackle all at once, do one bookshelf or one wall at a time.

10. You choose. Some people want to spend every spare moment with other people, liking to be 'kept company', but others prefer to have some time on their own.

- Stand your ground on fixing the big things, even if they are not big to someone else.
- Even while you are dealing with a problem, make sure you have breakfast and two other good meals a day, and that you keep up your general grooming (no need for elaborate hairstyles with a tiara, but don't stop showering for a week).
- Check just in case there's a funny side to the problem you're dealing with.

> Looking back I wish that I had been braver and instead of worried about all the new things happening, I should have just gone with it, accepted it and enjoyed it.   Arabella, 15

> Looking back I realise that life changes, people change and you'll change, whether you like it or not.
>
> Rosie, 17

Girls often focus on their weaknesses, the bits of themselves that 'need work' or 'could be better'. How about your strengths? Can you make a list in your head, or on paper, of your good points? If not, you either need to think harder or to cultivate some (see Chapter 8, Confidence, for hints).

Here I come!

future

≥ optimism ≤

More info on feeling optimistic and strong

Letting It Go: Attaining Awareness Out of Adversity by Bev Aisbett
Australian counsellor and cartoonist on self-esteem and mood strategies.

Don't Sweat the Small Stuff for Teens by Richard Carlson
Self-help advice.

A For Attitude and *Attitude in Action* by Julie Davey (available from aforattitude.com.au)
Bite-sized positive mottos and an easy-read guide to planning a happier life.

rookiemag.com
Positive teen girl site.

There are so many positive things about being a teenager. We meet new people, watch new movies, read new books, have new experiences every day.   Amy, 17

While teenagerhood can be really bad it can also be really GOOD. Now's the time you can make life-long friends and can wear what you like and have a great time – adults will still judge you but you can say – Hey, I'm just a teenager!   Mina, 15

I always used to be worried about how people see me and I never just relaxed and had fun without being self conscious. I'm learning to be happy and not care what people think.   Delia, 15

10 DRINKING

Some people have this image of a whole generation of wasted girls rolling about in their own wee on the floor of the nearest house where the parents are out, or performing upside-down sex acts, hanging from a light fitting by their underpants, after skolling a six-pack of ready-to-drink fizzy, raspberry-flavoured vodka, and throwing up in hot pink. The **truth** is a little more complicated.

Most teenagers drink at some stage. A lot of teenagers will have a drink or two but don't get drunk because they **don't like** the out-of-control feeling. Some can get drunk a couple of times and then stop. Others will drink every day, hurting their brain and their body. Many girls 'binge-drink'. Some teenagers develop a psychological dependency on, or a physical addiction to, alcohol (doctors can use either word to describe someone who **can't** or won't stop drinking). Some teenagers aren't interested in drinking at all.

Stuff you need to know about alcohol before drinking

Alcohol is a legal drug – but not because it's necessarily safer than other kinds of drugs. Like other drugs, it affects your mind temporarily and has physical side effects (see also see Chapter 11, Drugs, next). It can make you feel good, make you feel terrible, and damage your body. (Although the ads for alcohol seem to suggest it will make you crazy-happy, find you a boyfriend and cause you to have much bouncier hair and a gold dress, you've probably worked out this isn't true.)

The alcohol industry has been around for a couple of centuries and in Australia is worth tens of billions of dollars a year, so the national government makes millions and millions from it in taxes: *that's* why it's legal. The government uses part of that money to cover the cost of some of the health and social problems caused by alcohol abuse.

What alcohol is

Alcohol is the liquid that results from controlling the way chemically treated fruit or vegetables go mouldy (ferment) over time.

> **FACT**
>
> **The legal age for drinking** The legal age in Australia for buying alcohol is 18 years old. It's usually illegal to give alcohol to anybody who's under 18. Drivers of cars in their first years of being licensed (and aeroplane pilots!) must have a zero blood alcohol content (BAC). If you're in charge of a boat or jet ski and under 20, you should also have a zero BAC. Details of the laws and penalties can vary between states and territories. New Zealand's legal drinking age has been 18 since 1999, but there's a campaign to raise it again to 20. In the US the legal drinking age is 21.

Half of my friends have, half haven't drunk alcohol.   Jessica, 14, Caroline Springs, Vic.

People say they get drunk all the time but sometimes
I think they're just showing off.   Lizzy, 14, Melbourne, Vic.

Alcohol percentages   The average percentage of alcohol in different drinks is:
- beer (made from fermented grain) – 5 per cent
- light beer – up to 3.5 per cent
- wine (made from fermented grapes, and includes red, white and sparkling) – 12 per cent
- fortified wine (heavy, more concentrated wine; for example, port and sherry) – 18 per cent
- spirits (concentrated, distilled alcohol; for example, whisky, vodka, gin and bourbon) – 40 per cent
- liqueurs (highly flavoured, extra-concentrated spirits; for example, whisky and cream, or brandy and coconut) – from about 15 to 60 per cent or more
- cocktails (a mix of one or more spirits with flavourings, liqueurs and sometimes fruit juice) – about 40 per cent.

> My mum lets me drink, as do most of my friends' parents. The only rule is that I have to drink only what she buys me. However, that doesn't usually happen.
> Annabelle, 16, Bunbury, WA
>
> Hangovers suck.
> Alison, 15, East Lindfield, NSW

How alcohol affects the body

When you have a drink the alcohol is taken very quickly into your bloodstream from your stomach. Within an hour nearly all of it has been absorbed by your body (which is why you're still drunk even if you throw up).

Alcohol travels all around the body but a lot of it hangs about in the brain, liver and kidneys. The liver and kidneys try to process it and get the waste elements out of the body.

Teenagers have less developed livers than adults so they get drunk quicker on the same amount of alcohol and process it more slowly. It's now thought that a teenager only needs to drink half as much alcohol as an adult for it to have the same effect. Yet teenagers take longer than adults to become sleepy or seem clumsy when they're getting drunk, so they may not recognise the early warning signs.

Alcohol is often said to be a depressant, not a stimulant – in other words it's more of a downer than an upper. But in teens, especially in a social situation, at first it does work more as an upper. Some of this may be psychological: people hanging out together and expecting to feel an effect will also get louder and excitable and 'act' drunk even when they're not. The depressant factor still kicks for teens: it can just take you another drink or two to get there. Drinking affects people differently: it's impossible to say exactly how much will be a danger to an individual.

Oddly, given it's a liquid, alcohol causes your body to dehydrate. This can become a life-threatening problem in extreme cases.

How much alcohol is in one standard drink?

A 'standard' drink is surprisingly small: it contains 10 grams of pure alcohol. Almost all glasses of wine or champagne poured at home or in a pub, almost all ready-mixes in a can or bottle, and all average cans of full-strength beer have more than one standard drink in them. The whole idea of a 'standard drink' is really confusing because it actually bears no relation to what fits into a glass or even the amount usually served. If you want to do an easy demonstration to see what a real standard drink is, into the kitchen with you, jugs out (oh dear) and here we go.

'Standard' drinks can vary a lot...

Pour one or some of the following amounts (using water) into a baking or medicine measuring cup. Everyone gets a surprise at how little makes a standard drink for the different alcoholic beverages.

A standard drink in Australia is:

- about half to two-thirds of a usual glass of wine poured by someone at home (100 millilitres)
- one small nip of vodka, scotch or another spirit (30 millilitres – only 6 teaspoonfuls)
- one-third to three-quarters of a ready-to-drink small bottle or can of, say, vodka and flavoured fizzy drink, rum and cola or whisky and cola (depending on the bottle or can size and the percentage of alcohol)
- two-thirds of a bottle or can of ready-mixed spritzer, breezer or other wine mix (250 millilitres)
- 470 millilitres of low-strength beer, or about one and a half schooners
- one can of mid-strength beer (375 millilitres)
- three-quarters of a stubby or one middy or pot (pub glasses) of normal-strength beer (285 millilitres)
- half a can (190 millilitres) of extra-strong beer (depending on alcohol percentage)
- one very small glass of sherry or port (60 millilitres – 12 teaspoonfuls)
- one-sixth of a cocktail, depending on the ingredients.

cocktail = 5 or 6 standard drinks, maybe...

How alcohol affects the teenage brain

Research has revealed that alcohol works more quickly and has more effect on a teenage brain than an adult one because it's still developing up to the age of 20 and beyond (see Chapter 12, Mind Health); and when a teenager is really drunk the alcohol probably does more damage to the areas of the brain controlling vocabulary, memory, judgement and the ability to learn things.

New research shows that a teenager is far more likely than an adult to develop a dependence on (addiction to) alcohol.

> I often can't remember the night before, and for a while I didn't know if I was a virgin.
> Stella, 16, Napier, NZ
>
> I once drank champagne by myself, without eating much before. I have never thrown up so much in my life.
> Alana, 18, Mosman Park, WA

The right age Many experts say that the more they find out about alcohol's effect on a developing brain, the more they think teenagers shouldn't drink alcohol at all until the legal age of 18 or even later, and should try not to get drunk before their brain has finished developing, say, after 20.

That's probably pretty unlikely to happen, so what they say is: don't start drinking until you're at least 16, and then try not to get drunk. The most important thing is not to binge-drink (drink to get drunk), which definitely risks damaging your brain.

Why girls tend to be more affected by alcohol than they planned

Girls tend to be more easily affected by alcohol than they planned to be for heaps of reasons, which are to do partly with their bodies and partly with the way they drink.

- Girls naturally have more body fat and smaller livers than guys, and this means that they almost always get drunker on the same or a smaller amount of alcohol than guys. The greater your percentage of body fat, the more susceptible you are to alcohol. But even if you're a thin girl you still have a different percentage of body fat from guys and a smaller liver. The simple fact is that if you're female your body processes alcohol at a different rate.
- Girls can soon get beyond the low-risk level of alcohol without realising it (see 'What's the Right Amount?' box coming up).
- In some groups girls tend to drink wine and spirits, while guys tend to drink beer. If you're drinking a ready-mixed vodka and fizzy drink you'll be having the equivalent of two or three drinks to his every

What's the right amount?

There is no recommended amount of alcohol for teenagers.

Because it's not known what the safe level is for a brain that is still developing, it's never going to be recommended that you drink early, often or a lot.

'Officially' adult women should have no more than one standard drink an hour, and no more than two drinks a day. Having more than four drinks in one day is dangerous. Female bodies are also not supposed to have alcohol every day – you need several alcohol-free days a week, even as an adult.

Experts say the official recommendations for women doesn't apply to teens, who shouldn't have any alcohol at all.

They do know that the earlier the age you start drinking or getting drunk, the more likely you'll develop an addiction or other problem with alcohol.

There's no recommended safe level of drinks during pregnancy so girls and women are advised to stay off it completely through pregnancy and until they've finished breastfeeding.

one – which means that, being female, you're going to be four or five times drunker than he is. (Not a good look.)

- If girls are drinking bottled or cask wine they often have their glass refilled before it's empty – this makes it harder for them to keep track of how many standard drinks they've had.
- Bubbly alcoholic drinks affect people quicker than 'flat' ones because the high oxygen content takes the alcohol to the brain faster. This is risky for girls, who often choose 'bubbly' not realising they'll get horribly drunk quickly.
- Most wine and champagne glasses hold much more than a standard drink. Each glass of wine could actually be two or more standard drinks, not one.
- Because many premixed drinks are sweet, girls drink them faster.

Other reasons girls get drunk quicker than they meant to are:

- cocktails look pretty, but because one cocktail can have up to five or even six standard drinks in the one glass they are way, way over the safe limit
- many more alcohol ads are now aimed at young women and they try to make it look glamorous to drink a lot

- once anyone has a couple of standard drinks they start to lose their judgement, so they're more likely to keep drinking
- some girls drink a lot, quickly, because they want to get 'out of it'
- teenage girls often haven't experienced the different factors that can affect how drunk they get; drinking on an empty stomach, drinking quickly, without leaving time between drinks, and not alternating alcohol and water – all these things can greatly increase the effects of alcohol
- some girls under the legal pub or club drinking age drink in parks, on beaches, or at someone's house when the parents are out or don't care what their kids are doing. This means there's often no experienced person to say, 'Hey, you've really had enough.'

> **FACT**
>
> **Alcohol and a healthy weight**
>
> Alcohol is high in sugar so people who drink a lot often put on unwanted weight, as well as having other health problems.

More info on alcohol

darta.net.au
doingdrugs-darta.blogspot.com/ and
Teenagers, Alcohol and Drugs by Paul Dillon
An Aussie authority has useful info for teens and parents in his book, and in his school and community programs and presentations.

adf.org.au/drug-facts/
The Australian Drug Foundation's Drug Info Clearinghouse has info on lots of aspects of alcohol, and on parties. Click on Our Publications then Fact Sheets.

Alcohol Drug Helpline
Alcoholdrughelp.org.nz
0800 787 797
You can ring anonymously to talk about a problem you have, or somebody else has, or check out the info on the site.

> **A few friends have had their stomachs pumped and I've been arrested for over-intoxication and possible harm or damage to myself and others.**
>
> Jen, 17, Nightcliff, NT

Deciding whether or not to drink

Lots of teenagers don't drink. In some friendship groups nobody or hardly anybody ever drinks. In other groups almost everybody does, a lot.

Before you have a drink, ask yourself why you want it. Here are some common reasons – not necessarily good ones – teens give for drinking: they think it will make them more grown up; to help them relax; because they're allowed to; because they're not allowed to; everyone else is; someone just gives them a drink so they have it; they don't know how to have fun without it; they think you have to on every possible occasion; they want to 'wipe out' their feelings temporarily; they have a dependency problem – any teenager who drinks every day, or gets drunk every week, has a serious alcohol problem, whether or not they admit it (there's more on this later).

> **QUOTE**
>
> 'One reason I don't drink is that I want to know when I am having a good time.'
>
> **Lady Astor**

A sneaky strategy for not drinking

If you're going somewhere and feel worried you'll get hassled about not drinking, or that you'll lose control, here's a trick to try:

* get your parents or another adult to buy you a couple of mixed alcoholic drinks in screw-top bottles
* carefully unscrew the tops
* pour out the contents and replace them with lemonade, flavoured mineral water or cordial (whatever looks the same as the original)
* screw the tops on again
* take the bottles with you as your 'personal drinks'.

non-alcoholic

Things to say when you're not drinking (even if you're fibbing)

'No thanks.'

'I don't feel like it tonight.'

'I'm not feeling too good.'

'I'm allergic to the preservatives in alcohol.'

'One's/two's my limit.'

'I'd rather have water, thanks.'

'My parents are picking me up.'

'I don't like being drunk.'

'I can't – I promised my friends I'd stay sober to keep an eye on them.'

'That's not my drink, thanks.'

'Yuk, sorry, but I hate the taste of those.'

'I usually like to stop before I fall over and poo my pants.'

'I'm taking it slow tonight.'

'I like a water in between.'

'Not for me, thanks.'

'No more for me, thanks.'

'I've had enough.'

'I have this test/game/family thing early tomorrow morning.'

'My mum is going to call me soon.'

'Maybe later.'

'I like to know what language I'm speaking in.'

'I have to call my dad every hour and let him know where I am.'

'I'm not in the mood.'

'I'm off it at the moment.'

'I need to have a blood test tomorrow and I don't think they like it when it's half vodka.'

'I'm not drinking tonight/today/this week.'

'I had a few before I came.'

'Not unless you want me to be sick all down your front.'

'I hate throwing up on my hair and I haven't got an elastic band so I can't keep it in a pony tail and . . . I'm boring you, aren't I?'

going to throw up...

Being drunk

Roughly speaking, drunkenness follows certain stages, although not everyone gets drunk in the same order after the same number of drinks, or continues until they pass out.

Stages of drunkenness

If you keep drinking, the stages go more or less in this order.

Up to and past the legal driving limit of .05 per cent blood alcohol

- You feel good – warm, relaxed, confident, friendly, and chattier and less inhibited than normal.
- You have less judgement and control, and your mental and physical reflexes are slower – you're clumsier.
- You may not be noticing any of these changes.

All of the above only more so

- You have emotional swings, possibly becoming affectionate or aggressive: 'I love you', 'Shut up.'
- You lose judgement about what's a risky behaviour or a dumb idea ('Why don't I photograph my bosoms and text the picture to my ex! Wheee!').
- You're excitable and loud.
- You don't listen and you keep repeating yourself.
- You're having a real problem with balance.

Body and brain really not working properly
- You're confused and sleepy.
- You're dizzy and staggering, and your speech is slurred.
- You're having very big emotional swings or extremes – you're sloppily affectionate or more aggressive or violent – and no one can reason with you.
- You're not seeing straight – your sight is blurred.
- You can hurt yourself and not notice the pain.

Horribly drunk
- You can't manage the simplest physical tasks, such as getting a key in the door or walking.
- You don't respond to pain, prodding or voices.
- You could be vomiting, weeing or pooing.
- You fall asleep or become unconscious.

Unconsciousness
- Your body temperature and blood circulation are lowered and your breathing is repressed.
- You vomit, wee and poo without knowing it.
- You could progress to coma and, if you'd really drunk a stupid amount, even death.

> **FACT**
>
> **Why does alcohol make you throw up?** Your body recognises an excess of alcohol as poison and tries to get rid of it by throwing up, weeing a lot, sweating, having diarrhoea, or all four (for an extra-classy bonus).

My best friend had a massive go at me when she was drunk. We didn't talk for two months after as I was so hurt. We are back on track now. Kim, 16, Bendigo, Vic.

I usually have really good experiences when I'm drunk cos I get really happy and fun. A friend always gets depressed, and finds something to talk about, and the majority of my friends act like hussies and blame it on the alcohol the next day. Sarah, 17, Bundoora, Vic.

My friend was an alcoholic when she was 11, but she got help. Lisa, 13, Cronulla, NSW

My friend's dad tried to crack onto me while I was drunk. And my friend spewed on me once. Natalie, 16, Armadale, Vic.

I enjoy getting drunk. It's my choice and any 'consequences' I can deal with.

Judith, 15, Punchbowl, NSW

I absolutely hate alcohol and can't even bear the smell so I don't go near the stuff – not even at parties! Emily, 15, Elizabeth, SA

I used to have a group of friends but now I don't like hanging out with them. They are too shallow and immature. All they do is go to parties and drink. I'd rather do my own thing now.

Tess, 17, Fremantle, WA

Guys blackmailed me by sending photos of me drinking and pashing a friend to my parents. Kelly, 17, Gympie, Qld

I think it's sad to watch all the smart people I know slowly be dumbed down by alcohol and drugs. As far as I can see they're spending all their money so they can act like arseholes, throw up a lot and then have a really bad headache. Wow. Top night out.

Maddison, 17, Blackheath, NSW

My friends get happy and start dancing and then they just fall asleep. Jody, 13, Banks, ACT

The risks of getting drunk or being near drunk people

Sometimes you don't even have to be horribly drunk for something bad to happen, such as an accident, but you increase the risk by being drunk or being with drunk people. Alcohol is also involved in most of the drug-related deaths of young people.

An average-sized 16-year-old who drinks solidly (one drink after another) could damage herself very seriously within an hour.

People who are drunk take more risks. You're more likely to do or say something that you don't mean, or that you'll regret, or that will be an embarrassment. You are also more likely to be assaulted, or otherwise in danger.

Unwanted sex   Drunk girls are vulnerable to sexual experiences they don't choose or fully agree to. (They are also less likely to use contraception or to make sure the guy uses a condom as protection against sexually transmitted infections.)

Many girls do things (or have things done to them) that they don't want and would never do when sober and safe. Many regret that their first sexual experiences were drunken encounters that they can barely remember, with people they didn't really like or who didn't respect them.

In the answers to the Girl Stuff Survey a lot of girls aged 13 to 18 said they or a friend had been raped when they were drunk – often by somebody they knew. It might have been that there was no hitting but force was used, or the girls were not capable of stopping the guy even though they didn't want to have sex.

It's smart to try to minimise your risk in ways you can control, but it's important to know that sexual assault is never the girl's fault, no matter how out of it she got or what she was wearing: there's more on this in Chapter 16, Sex. Being too drunk to say no doesn't mean she said yes. Don't fall into the trap of saying that somebody 'asked for it' because of their behaviour. The blame and the shame is always on the attacker or the person who does something sexual without consent.

> My friend got drunk at a party and passed out in a bed and was raped. I'm the only one she's told but she still drinks.
> M-L, 14, Ringwood, Vic.

Cars   Alcohol is involved in many, if not most, serious car accidents. It's safest not to drink *any* alcohol if you need to drive a car because it's hard to guess your own blood alcohol level. Police can test your breath or blood at any time.

If you are over the legal limit in your area (usually 0.05 per cent) that result will be used against you in court. Penalties include heavy fines, losing your licence, and jail. P-platers must maintain a zero blood alcohol content – and that really does mean zero.

Getting in a car with a drunk driver, or a driver who has been drinking, increases your chances of injury or death by a huge margin. It doesn't matter if a driver says they are not drunk or they don't seem drunk. If they have been drinking, don't get in the car. Call an adult who has agreed to come and pick you up no matter what time it is (see the 'Your Emergency Rescue Crew' box in Chapter 8, Confidence).

> If you're drinking at a party make sure you know where your friends are and that you look out for one another.
> Jacqui, 13, Brighton, Vic.
>
> I was lucky not to have any real damage done.
> Maeve, 17, Perth, WA

Drink spiking Some people at pubs, clubs or parties have had drugs added to their drinks, which make them woozy or even unconscious, and they have then been taken elsewhere and assaulted or raped. Although this is rare, it's a good idea never to let your drink out of your sight. Most girls who think their drink was spiked have probably underestimated how quickly and severely they got completely 'out of it' on the alcohol alone. (A sexual assault is never your fault, no matter how drunk you were – see 'Unwanted Sex' on the previous page – but it makes sense not to get so drunk you put yourself at greater risk.)

You're more likely to accidentally get too drunk than have your drink spiked

Drowning Many drownings, whether at the beach or in a pool, lake or river, involve alcohol. If people are drinking don't let them go in the water, especially at night. (Guys in particular tend to want to do this.)

Violence The more alcohol drunk, and the more guys present (especially ones who don't know each other), the greater the risk of violence at a festival, an event or a party or on a weekend or a holiday. Added elements may be previous tension, and hot or humid weather.

> One of my friends went home drunk and then threw up on her dad at their front door. Bobbo, 14, Rosebud, Vic.

Drunk people

Sometimes things can go very wrong when people are drinking. If you can see a potential problem, or at the first sign of ugliness – big talk, threats, pushing, shoving, someone leaving and threatening to get revenge (and perhaps returning with reinforcements), rumours of a big gate-crash – leave, taking your friends with you. What seems exciting and dramatic in theory is actually nasty and terrifying in real life.

> Getting drunk causes a few problems with relationships!
> Alex, 14, Melbourne, Vic.
>
> My dad is an alcoholic.
> Suze, 15, Mt Isa, Qld

Coping with a drunk person   The first rule is to make yourself safe. If doing any of the following – or any of the actions outlined in the 'When to Call an Ambulance' box coming up – means that you are at risk of injury, then your first priority is to keep clear and call for help from somewhere else.

If the drunk person is conscious but very drunk and out of control:
- don't leave them behind or alone, or believe them when they say they'll be fine or can get home on their own
- take them to a safe place where there is no alcohol available (home, for example) or take all alcohol out of their reach (basically, remove them from the party or remove the party from them)
- don't try to reason with them – if necessary lie and tell them you are taking them to a place where they can get another drink
- if you feel you can't control the situation, find a responsible person who has not been drinking or call your emergency person to come and get you
- before you leave the drunk person at the safe place to 'sleep it off', make sure they're only asleep and can be roused, not unconscious.

> I'll never forget when I drank so much wine I threw up all over my best mate's house, IN FRONT OF MY CRUSH, and then passed out.   Tori, 15, Berwick, Vic.

> I don't drink: I am definitely in a minority, at least in my social circles.
> It can be hard – sometimes people don't believe you – but in the end it's not a struggle.
> It gives me a lot of pleasure to know I can spend the money I earn on things that are actually worthwhile, not just on a night out I may not remember.   Audrey, 17

When to call an ambulance

Call 000 and ask for an ambulance if the person has:

* not responded to you trying to wake them up by nudging or pinching them a few times and shouting at them (but not shaking, punching or kicking them)
* blue lips or face
* eyes rolling back into their head
* foam on their lips
* stopped breathing
* anything else that doesn't seem normal and is scaring you.

Waiting for the ambulance

If the person is lying down and has vomited or is vomiting, or is unconscious, make sure you quickly clear any vomit out of their mouth and throat with your fingers and move them onto their side so they don't choke to death. Put them in a safe place; for example, off the road.

* Don't leave the person alone. They could wander off later, or otherwise be in danger.
* Keep watching the person until the ambulance arrives, unless you are in danger, and ask an adult or a sensible person who hasn't been drinking to help you.
* Ask if anybody knows what the person has been drinking and any details of drugs taken, whether legal or illegal (what, when, how much or how many), so you can tell the paramedics (ambulance medical staff).
* Medical helpers will need to know what has been drunk or taken so that they can save the person's life – they're *not* interested in telling anybody's parents or the police. Treatment varies according to the kinds of drugs or alcohol, and the quantities.

> I've had to look after people who are throwing up and/or passing out. They have done stupid things and regretted them the next day, or not remembered them at all. Yet they still continue drinking. This has added to my reasons for being uncomfortable about drinking.
>
> Shelley, 14, Craigieburn, Vic.

A drinking problem

Some people are more likely to develop a dependency on, or an addiction to, alcohol than others. Signs that someone has a problem include:

* drinking has caused problems but the drinking continues
* drinking every day
* getting drunk once a week or more, or regularly (but getting drunk at all risks brain damage for a teenager)
* anger if it's suggested they need to cut down or they might have a problem
* dark moods, sarcasm, abuse, a bad home atmosphere or violence associated with the drinking
* drinking to forget or wipe themselves out temporarily
* drinking alone
* drinking at every social gathering
* drinking more and more
* drinking secretly or hiding alcohol.

If you think that you are experiencing any of these signs – or that a parent or friend is, which can be very scary – you need to speak to an adult you trust or ring an anonymous helpline about what you can do (see 'More Info' coming up). The treatment options suggested can include counselling, finding strategies, a withdrawal program, support groups, and sometimes medication prescribed by a doctor.

With a dependency or an addiction, giving up alcohol or even cutting down is not really possible alone – everybody needs help with the 'how to', no matter how good or determined a person they are.

More info on help with alcohol problems

State or territory contact numbers for alcohol help:

ACT Health Service Line:
(02) 6207 9977

NSW Alcohol and Drug Information Service:
(02) 9361 8000 or 1800 422 599 (rural)

NT Alcohol and Drug Information Service:
1800 131 350

Qld Alcohol and Drug Information Service:
1800 177 833

SA Alcohol and Drug Information Service:
1300 131 340

Tas. Alcohol and Drug Information Service:
1800 811 994

Vic. Alcohol and Drug Information Service:
1800 888 236 (direct line);
1300 858 584 (drug info);
1300 660 068 (Family Drug Helpline)
Youth Substance Abuse Service Line:
(03) 9418 1020 or 1800 014 446 (rural)

WA Alcohol and Drug Information Service:
(08) 9442 5000 or 1800 198 024 (rural)
Parent Drug Information Service:
(08) 9442 5050 or 1800 653 203 (rural)

al-anon.alateen.org/australia
For young people with a friend or relative who's a problem drinker.

NZ Alcohol Drug Helpline:
0800 787 797

alcohol.org.nz and **fade.org.nz**
Both these NZ sites have info and links for problem drinking.

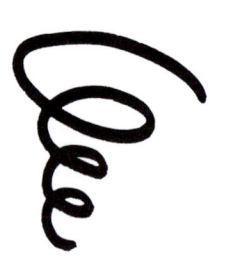

I've had an uncle who was an alcoholic (he's recovered now) and I saw him mess up my family's life. I never, ever want that to happen to me. Mary Ann, 13, Adelaide, SA

The most fun I've had in my life was when I was drunk. I don't regret a minute of it.
Gabby, 13, Wollongong, NSW

I don't like it when my dad gets drunk because he promises things to people like my little sister and then doesn't keep these promises as he doesn't remember. My sister then gets really upset and Mum ends up getting blamed. Amy, 15, Mackay, Qld

I worry about my dad catching me drunk (which I am for every party). Meghan, 15, Perth, WA

Taking control of drinking

Some researchers say that teenagers drinking at home with their parents learn to drink alcohol responsibly; others think that's sending the wrong message and is more likely to lead to problem drinking. Probably it has more to do with the way your parents use alcohol.

Think about how alcohol is used in your family: maybe a parent has a glass with dinner a couple of times a week. Or perhaps drinking is the only way your parents know how to celebrate or wind down, or they drink to get wiped out, which are more dangerous ways to use alcohol.

If your parents don't limit your alcohol intake you will need to, unless you want to get regularly sick and embarrassed.

Make your own drinking rules

You can vary the rules on different nights, but here are some examples you could think about.

- Don't drink at all until you're at least 17 or 18.
- Don't feel that because you started early you have to keep drinking – leave it alone for a couple of years.
- When you do start to drink, set your own limit.
- Work out how many standard drinks are in whatever glass, bottle or can you're drinking.
- Have no more than half a standard drink an hour.
- If you lose count or control assume that you've had more than two standard drinks and stop drinking.
- Don't drink every day.
- Don't aim to get drunk.
- Ask for help if you have a problem.

A safer drinking environment

Some people are going to get drunk. They will do more damage to themselves and others if they don't choose to do it in a safe environment.

- Stay in a house or other environment where sober friends, parents or other people are within reach. Don't go out for a drive, down the road to a park, or to another house or party.
- Always go out in a group. >

- Organise to have a couple of friends who'll stay sober and look out for you, or do the same for them.
- Make sure you stay with at least one really close friend. Assault by a stranger can be a real danger, but most sexual assaults are carried out against somebody who has met their attacker. Don't go into a room or to a more private place with somebody where you can't be heard or seen by others.
- Don't aim to get drunk. (This is likely to result in you getting so drunk you can't speak or move properly.)
- Make sure you always have a working phone or are with a friend who has a working phone, and that you have the number of an adult who will come and pick you up at any time (see the 'Your Emergency Rescue Crew' box in Chapter 8, Confidence).
- Don't accept a drink that you didn't ask for or from somebody you don't know.
- Don't mix taking any kind of prescription or non-prescription or illegal drug with drinking alcohol – the combination can cause unexpected and dangerous reactions, including coma or death.
- Don't ever get a lift with somebody who's been drinking, even if they say they're fine to drive. Call your emergency contact instead.
- Never leave anyone behind, even if they are too drunk to move. They will be vulnerable to assault, injury or arrest.
- Make sure that no drunk person is left unconscious on their back or in any other position in which they could choke to death on their own vomit.

Smarter ways to drink

- Eat something in the hour before you drink. A fistful of something is a good idea – pasta, a sandwich, left-over rice, even a fast-food hamburger or serve of hot chips is better than nothing. If there's no food, a glass of milk will do.
- Eat substantial food while you're drinking, even if it's just nibbles and snacks, but try to avoid the salty ones as they'll cause more dehydration. If the nibbles and snacks are salty and you get thirsty, drink something non-alcoholic.
- Start with a non-alcoholic drink so you're not thirsty. Being thirsty means you will probably drink alcoholic drinks too fast.

- Work out how many standard drinks are in what you're drinking and how much will be within your safe limit (see the boxes 'How Much Alcohol Is in One Standard Drink?' and 'What's the Right Amount?' earlier in this chapter).
- Never drink alcohol with bubbles on an empty stomach, or quickly.
- Always finish your glass before putting more in it: that's the only way you can measure how much you have drunk. And stop someone else 'topping you up' from a jug or bottle.
- Stop when you get to the limit you set yourself no matter what anyone else says.
- Take your own water because it may not be available. To cut costs, refill bottles from the tap at home.
- Don't touch the party 'punch' – a mixed drink in a big bowl or tub. There's a reason it's called punch – you usually have no idea what's coming and it'll hurt.
- Dance – then you don't have to stand around for hours with a glass in your hand. Drink water when you get thirsty.
- Dilute your drinks with water, melting ice, soda water or juice.
- Have a non-alcoholic drink in between alcoholic drinks.
- Drink low or light alcohol drinks.
- Stick to one kind of alcohol: beer OR wine OR the same spirit with the same mixer.
- Don't get involved in 'shouts' or buying rounds of drinks as it means someone will buy you another drink when you don't want it (and you end up spending more money).
- Don't get involved in drinking that's a contest, a bet or a game.
- Don't 'skol' drinks or encourage others to.
- Don't gulp down alcoholic drinks. They're supposed to be sipped.
- Don't drink liqueurs – they're too ridiculously alcoholic.
- If you're given a drink you don't want, get a non-alcoholic one and ignore the alcoholic one, or walk away and 'lose' it, or pour it out on the ground (if you're outside).
- Don't hang out with people who hassle you to drink more.

drink water in between any alcoholic drinks

> There should always be one person who doesn't drink who can keep their eye out for the others and to drive.   Milly, 18, Lower Templestowe, Vic.

DRUGS

Some herbal and chemical compounds can do **amazing things** – stop pain, help healing, prevent an anxiety attack, cause an anxiety attack, block or boost certain hormones, put you to sleep, make you feel wide awake. Nearly every culture has fiddled with nature to create substances that will make them feel more relaxed, dreamy or excited. But **none of it** comes for free. Every drug has risks and side effects. The more drugs you take, whether legal or illegal, the more you risk damaging yourself. The most common drugs you'll come into contact with are cigarettes and alcohol. We've just had the full bottle (sorry) on drinking, so here's what you **need to know** about tobacco and other drugs.

Cigarettes

Why do people start smoking? They probably have their first cigarette to be rebellious because it seems wrong and forbidden. Many girls have their first cigarette because they're with older guys who smoke – just as many girls give up when they fall for someone who doesn't like smoking.

Why does almost everyone *keep* smoking? Because they're physically addicted. The essential ingredient of cigarettes is nicotine, one of the most addictive substances ever discovered. Even more addictive than mobile phones and chocolate.

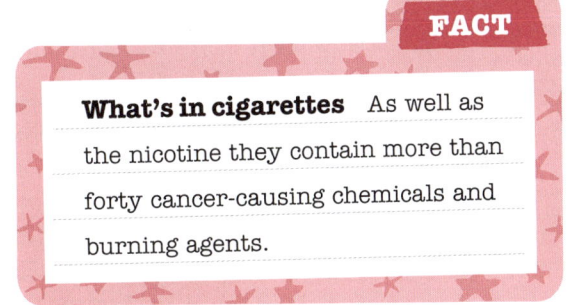

FACT

What's in cigarettes As well as the nicotine they contain more than forty cancer-causing chemicals and burning agents.

Things you need to know about cigarettes

Smoking can seem attractive because you're not allowed to do it as a kid so it seems like an adult thing to do, and it often gets associated with freedom, taking a break or partying, but there's no upside to its effects on your brain and body. Here's what it does.

Straight away
- Your hair, clothes and breath smell of smoke.
- Your sense of taste and smell is reduced.
- Your brain and nervous-system activity is stimulated for a short time.
- If you feel temporarily calmer that's because you're already addicted.
- You possibly experience dizziness, nausea, watery eyes, increased acid in the stomach, and a sudden urge to poo (because the body wants to get the poisons out of your system).
- Your lungs are damaged by every cigarette you smoke.
- If you're pregnant, your unborn baby 'smokes' too (through the bloodstream) and their health is damaged with every cigarette.

SMOKERS SMELL

> Getting drunk helped me start smoking.   Amy, 16, Albany, WA

After a little while

- You're addicted.
- Your skin, hair, breath and clothes smell strongly of smoke – although you can't smell it any more.
- Your sense of taste and smell is suppressed.
- You develop yellow or orangey stains on your fingers and teeth, and dryer skin.
- You are short of breath and have a cough – regular or heavy smoking causes lung damage that may not be reversible.
- You find it harder to walk, run, play sport, go upstairs or dance without feeling unfit.
- You get more colds, coughs and chest infections, and take longer than non-smokers to recover.

Long term

- Your hair, breath, hands and clothes constantly stink of smoke.
- Your skin develops 'smoking' wrinkles.
- You may suffer from a disease called emphysema (pronounced em-fiz-eema), which starts as shortness of breath and progressively makes breathing harder until you need an oxygen mask or you can't get enough air to survive.
- You may develop cancer: smoking is a proven cause of, or contributing factor in, many cancers, including those in the lungs, throat, mouth, bladder, kidneys, pancreas, cervix and stomach.
- You may have a stroke or a heart attack, or have to have your toes, feet or legs amputated: smoking is a big cause of these because it narrows the arteries and veins, restricting blood flow.

> I know a group of girls in my class smoke. They always stink of smoke when they come into the classroom.
>
> Joelle, 13, Townsville, Qld

Remind me again - what's the point?

um....

FACT

Not just cigarettes All tobacco products and anything else smoked will damage your body and your lungs – including 'roll your owns', cigarettes with and without filters, all pipes, shared hookah pipes and 'passive' smoking (breathing in smoke from other people's smoking).

How to give up smoking

The best way is never to start. Because it's way addictive it's really hard for some people to give up 'on their own'. Stopping smoking causes cravings for cigarettes (because the person is addicted), possible weight gain (only short term) and grumpiness.

You will need one or some of the following while you are giving up smoking:

- a reason to stop, such as liking a guy (or girl) who doesn't like smoking; finding that smoking is affecting your sports performance or general fitness; fighting an illness; being pregnant, breastfeeding or not wanting smoke to damage your baby; being frightened of getting cancer later in life
- advice and support from a GP or a helpline (see 'More Info' coming up)
- friends and family who help and encourage you
- goals such as saving the 'cigarette money' for a big treat or trip instead
- hypnotherapy
- nicotine gum or patches
- a smoke-free environment (stay away from people who smoke)
- determination and mental strength.

Stuff the cigarette companies don't tell you

- Smoking causes more damage to women than men. Researchers are not yet sure why.
- 'Light' or 'mild' cigarettes contain as many damaging chemicals too.
- Herbal cigarettes are not good for you.
- You can have all the ill-effects of smoking by breathing in the smoke from other people's cigarettes when you're in a house, car or public place with them (this is called passive smoking).
- Cigarette companies make huge, huge profits – in the billions of dollars – even though most of each packet's price goes to the government in taxes.
- Menthol cigarettes are not better for you.

> I smoke but it's such a bad habit! I started because my friends thought it was really cool – but four years later and I'm still smoking.   Brooke, 18, Mill Park, Vic.

Things to say when you don't want to smoke (even if you're fibbing)

'Not for me, thanks.'

'My mum/dad always smells it on me.'

'No thanks, I've given up.'

'No thanks, I'm trying to cut down.'

'I'm in a netball/hockey/soccer team and need all the lung power I can get.'

'No thanks, I don't like it.'

'I can't – it gives me asthma.'

'I hate menthol/rollies/filters/unfiltereds.'

'I can't because it gives me a lung infection.'

'No thanks, I've never been into it.'

'No thanks, it's not my thing.'

'I already have seven bad habits and I need to concentrate on those.'

'No, I only smoke Cuban cigars.' (Okay, that might be a bit hard to make convincing, but you get the picture.)

'No thanks, I was addicted and I don't want to go there again.'

'No thanks, I'm sick of it.'

More info on smoking

cyh.com
A SA government site: choose Teen Health then search Smoking.

quit.org.au
Helpline: 137848
Help to quit smoking.

ask for help

> Most of my friends are smokers. My dad is dying of lung cancer. However, we all drink and smoke pot simply because it is part of our social culture, a way for us to relax. We're just imitating what we see our parents and the rest of society doing.
>
> Zoe, 16, Coburg, Vic.

Legal drugs

Apart from the main legal drugs in Australia – alcohol and cigarettes – there are heaps of prescription drugs, and stuff you can buy without a prescription at the chemist and even the supermarket, that are very dangerous if not taken in the right way or by the right person. Nicotine is the most addictive drug but other legal ones are right up there, including alcohol and some prescription drugs.

> Almost everybody I know drinks, smokes cigarettes and weed, and takes different medications to get high. They steal prescription drugs all the time.
> Jolie, 15,
> Bullhead, Arizona, US

Just because a drug is legal doesn't mean it's safe for you – in fact it almost certainly won't be unless it was prescribed specifically for you by a doctor or suggested by the pharmacist (not a shop assistant). Some over-the-counter drugs (meaning not needing a prescription) can only be sold to you after a pharmacist has explained them to you.

Problems with legal drugs

You should never take more of a drug than the dose prescribed by your doctor for your age or weight and written on the chemist's label on the packet. And always read the manufacturer's information given in the leaflet inside. (See also 'More Info' coming up.)

Most prescription medications are for an illness or symptom that is specific to one patient – this means if you take someone else's drug you may not know what you've really taken, and you won't know how it is going to affect your body and brain.

Some people may 'only' take two or three pills but that's more than their particular body can handle. Don't accept any pill not prescribed for you, even if it's a family member offering it: it could be wrong for you or even damage you. Likewise, if you have a medication prescribed for you, don't give it to anybody else.

If not used correctly many common, supermarket-bought painkillers can cause massive damage to internal organs, such as lungs, heart, liver and kidneys.

The results of taking more legal drugs than you are supposed to include incontinence (not being able to control when you wee or poo), brain damage and being unable to walk or speak.

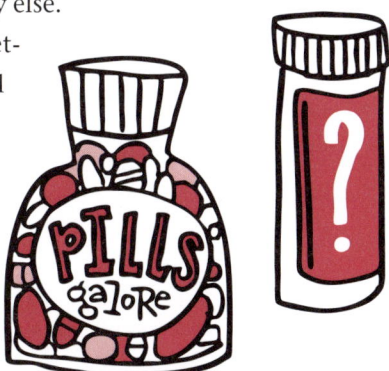

Mixing alcohol with either prescription or over-the-counter drugs makes them more dangerous.

See the box 'When to Call an Ambulance' in Chapter 10, Drinking, for the signs and symptoms that mean someone needs emergency help, and info on what to do while waiting, and ring 000.

If you are worried that you, a friend or a family member may have a psychological dependency on or be addicted to a legal drug, see the section 'How to Help Somebody with a Drug Problem' at the end of this chapter.

More info on legal drugs

'More Info on Drugs and Help with Drug Problems' at the end of this chapter lists helplines that also deal with legal drugs.

National Prescribing Service: 1300 633 424
Info on the safety and use of prescription drugs, and over-the-counter and herbal preparations.

I take drugs. No one knows and I don't hang around many people who do, other than my dad.   Missy, 14, Yarraville, Vic.

Pot ruined my friend's life. Now he is schizophrenic. You never know what it can do to you.   Valentina, 14, Byron Bay, NSW

I took E. Nothing much really happened. Maybe it wasn't what they said it was.
Louise, 17, Glenelg, SA

I'd like to know where you can get drugs.   Leah, 14, Chirnside Park, Vic.

I used to want to try cannabis but now I am going to wait for a few years.
Gina, 15, Melbourne, Vic.

Some of my friends have overdosed and even died from drugs.   Judith, 17, Albury, NSW

Illegal drugs

The best known illegal drugs include cannabis, methamphetamine, ecstasy and heroin (see the 'Illegal Drugs' chart coming up for more info).

Teenagers are not the biggest users of drugs – people in their twenties and thirties are – so you may not see or be offered any for a while, or ever. But it's probably a good idea to be prepared just in case you are, so that you'll have some idea of what the drug is and whether you think it's smart to go ahead.

Things you need to know about illegal drugs

Despite scary-pants stories, taking a drug once isn't going to make you addicted, and smoking a joint won't lead you directly to harder drugs and a heroin 'habit'. But it is true that things can go very badly wrong even the first time.

The upside of taking illegal drugs is that they can cause some people to forget any troubles for an hour or two, feel high and happy, or floaty and out of it, and experience a different way of thinking. But they don't work like this for everyone, and they're never risk-free. The reverse side is that individual brain chemistry produces different reactions. Some people who smoke cannabis (weed) get terrified and worried instead of giggly; some people who take heroin throw up instead of feeling floaty; some people who take cocaine don't feel high and chatty and smart – they feel paranoid (sure that everyone, or someone, is out to get them). Other problems can include feeling down the next day after a high; running out of money because you're spending it on drugs; and seeming like a loser who's only interested in drugs.

There are some really big downsides to drugs. Immediate ones, even the first time you take a drug, can include suddenly getting so out of it you can't protect yourself from sexual assault; and an accidental overdose causing a medical emergency, brain damage or death.

Longer term downsides if you're a regular, repeated or heavy illegal drug user include not being able to keep up with schoolwork or sport; the development or sudden onset of a severe mental illness; several serious physical illnesses; 'ruining your looks' because of the side effects; dependence and addiction; losing friends or boyfriends because you've developed a drug problem; and legal difficulties (such as being arrested).

Many girls find they need to break up with a guy when he gets involved in heavy or regular drug use, especially of 'weed' (aka cannabis), and he becomes incredibly boring.

> Girls need to realise what they are doing to their bodies and how it can affect them later in life, even if they stop using.   Talula, 17

The risks of illegal drug use The only way to avoid risk with illegal drugs is not to take any. Because everyone's brain and body are different, even the same batch of a drug will affect people in different ways. While a friend may have a good time on a drug, and encourage you to use it, that doesn't mean you'll have the same result, even if it's the same dose. Illegal drugs aren't like prescription ones; they don't come in accurate doses, so you'll have no idea how much you're getting. In most cases when you're deciding whether or not to take or smoke something, it will be impossible to know precisely what's in it, its strength or its likely effects.

If you have any predisposition to mental illness, including depression and psychosis, illegal drugs or misuse of legal drugs can trigger episodes of the illness. Anybody can have a predisposition, regardless of their family history. And the first time their mental illness shows itself may be triggered by their first ever drug use. Having a relative (especially a parent) who has or has had a mental illness makes a predisposition more likely, but not automatic. If you have a predisposition, it's not something you can know beforehand (because it's something locked in your brain, not something you can see).

If you have drug or alcohol abuse in your family history, this can be a big advantage for you. Instead of thinking it's inevitable you'll have the same problem, you can guard against temptations and danger signs. You can control your own destiny. If you have a family or personal history of mental illness, including depression or anxiety, avoiding drugs and alcohol will dramatically decrease your risk of problems.

For many people common results of drug taking are vomiting, stomach cramps, sweating and diarrhoea, all symptoms of the body trying to get rid of the drug as soon as it can. More severe reactions can include convulsions (jerking and foaming at the mouth), unconsciousness, coma and death.

Many problems, emergencies and overdoses happen because people combine taking a drug with alcohol or other drugs, or take them within a day of each other.

The legal risk Penalties vary, but generally the lowest are for use or growing a small amount of cannabis, and get more serious for possession and trafficking (buying and selling drugs, taking them from one place to another). Penalties range from a warning, to a fine, to a short or very long jail sentence. What gets you a warning or fine in some places may mean jail in another (see the 'Travel and Drugs' box opposite).

Travel and drugs

The laws of other countries can differ hugely from Australia's. Prescription drugs that are legal in Australia can be illegal in some countries.

Many countries have mandatory (automatic) life sentences or death sentences for using the smallest amount of an illegal drug; having any amount on your body or in your pockets, handbag or a room where you are or have been; and selling or trafficking.

An offence such as cannabis possession in Australia might result in a warning or a fine – in another country it could mean you never come home again.

* Never travel with illegal drugs on a plane, whether locally or overseas. If you don't get caught the first time, your risk gets bigger each 'next' time. If you travel with prescription drugs, keep them in their original packet and take the prescription with you.

* Never go somewhere unknown with a stranger to buy drugs. (Strangers can act friendly to win your confidence.)

* Never assume the Australian government can get you off a drugs charge in another country – it can't. It can only advise you of available lawyers. It won't pay for them.

HOW NOT to tRaveL

FACT

What's a safe dose? There's no known safe dose for any illegal or unregulated drug – that's why the 'Illegal Drugs' chart doesn't go into details about how to take a drug, or in what dose.

Postal services regularly screen for drugs in letters and packages. Police can search your car if they stop you on the road, but they must say they have 'reasonable cause' (which could be there's a smell of drugs or someone has a drugged appearance).

Random roadside drug testing (of saliva) has been introduced across Australia and drivers can be made to take further tests, which can detect some drugs in your system for hours, days or even weeks after you've taken them. Penalties for drug driving can include cancellation or loss of your licence and you being charged with drug offences.

Deciding whether or not to take drugs

Most people don't take drugs. The reasons given by those who do – not necessarily good reasons – include wanting to feel relaxed; wanting to feel nothing; trying to cure or help an illness; curiosity; not wanting to be left out; boredom; being rich enough to afford drugs; feeling indestructible; wanting emotional or physical pain to go away for a while; not realising, or denying, the risks; pressure from a friend or group; a dependence or an addiction.

Before you decide to take a drug, think about why you want to. Is it because you want to fit into a group or impress somebody? (Because that's a bit tragic.) Is it because you want to get or keep a friend? (Because, even if that works, it's not a good basis for a relationship.) Are you sad and hoping it will wipe out your pain? (Because the pain will still be there a few minutes or hours later, and there are other ways of making sad feelings go away – see Chapter 9, Feelings.)

> Why let something take control of you? What could happen whilst you are 'tripping'? Who knows? That thought scares me.
>
> Julie, 15,
> Port Adelaide, SA

Get informed before you decide. See the 'Illegal Drugs' chart coming up, and some of the websites recommended in 'More Info' at the end of this section.

Not taking drugs   Reasons not to take drugs include:
- different brains have different reactions
- some drugs are known to trigger mental illness in somebody with a predisposition, but nobody knows beforehand if they have a predisposition

WANTING to feeL NOTHING MeaNS you NeeD HeLP...

- all drugs have side effects and some of them are major
- it's impossible to tell how strong or pure the drug is just by looking at it – this means you are more vulnerable to a bad reaction or an overdose
- you can become dependent or addicted
- by being a drug consumer you are part of an industry that exploits, cheats and kills
- some illegal drugs are very expensive because people take risks to get them to you without being caught by police
- it's illegal.

If you think you'd feel too embarrassed or seem uncool refusing drugs, see the list in Chapter 10, Drinking, of things to say, and also the one in the 'Smoking' section earlier in this chapter. If friends seem to be going in a direction you don't want to follow, you may want to see Chapter 14, Friends, for ideas on ending a friendship and finding a new group.

> Pot should be legalised. It's so cheap and easy to get already it's not like it would make a difference.
> Kayla, 16, Sydney, NSW

> Friends that were smoking weed felt isolated even when surrounded by friends.
> Erica, 16, Sheidow Park, SA

what are we smoking?

I can't remember

> Don't do drugs: they can't take your pain away permanently. Brigid, 13, Darwin, NT

> My uncle died from a drug overdose. Jane, 14, Innisfail, Qld

QUOTE

'Speed: it will turn you into your parents.'
Frank Zappa, US musician

Illegal drugs

The known facts about the drugs listed here could change, and some drugs aren't included, so check out 'More Info' at the end of the chapter for websites that can keep you up to date. There are no details below on how to take a drug and in what dose, because there's no one-size-fits-all safe dose of any illegal or unregulated drug. All drug use by someone who is pregnant or breastfeeding can damage their baby. Illegal drug use and abuse of legal drugs up to your early 20s can cause particular damage to your own, still-developing brain.

Cannabis

Also known as marijuana, weed, dope, grass, pot, skunk, reefer, joint, mull, cone, hash, spliff, ganja, and buddha.

What is it? Cannabis is a depressant drug that in some cases can cause changes in perception of sounds and vision and, in rarer but disturbing cases, trigger hallucinations or delusions. It comes in various forms, all from the cannabis plant. Crushed leaves (the least potent part of the plant) or the stronger buds and flowers (heads) are smoked in a hand-rolled cigarette (joint), or in 'cones' in a pipe or a bong (like a vase with a pipe attached). The resin or oil from the plant (hash) is the most potent part, and is added to a joint, or baked and eaten, usually in biscuits (this creates more of an overdose risk). Cannabis is the most common illegal drug. Many teenagers will come into contact with it and about a quarter will try it. In some areas or friendship groups most people will use it.

Why do people take it? It can make them feel calmer, floaty, temporarily less shy, and like laughing. A puff of a joint can be enough to feel 'stoned'.

Side effects and problems Effects depend on how much you take and which part of the plant is used. Many people believe cannabis grown with chemicals is more likely to cause problems. Side effects include red eyes, enlarged pupils, hunger and sleepiness. Cannabis is far from a 'harmless' drug, and is particularly damaging to a teenage (still-developing) brain. It is now firmly linked to disordered thinking, memory problems, depression and serious mental illness. Teen use may double the risk of panic attack in your twenties. Heavy use can cause panic attacks, severe depression, paranoia and psychotic episodes. Regular or heavy cannabis users tend to seem boring and antisocial. The smoke causes the same damage as cigarettes

Dependence and addiction Some people become psychologically dependent; and some become physically addicted, despite what was once thought.

Speed and ice (methamphetamines)

Also known as whiz and goey. Ice is also known as P (for pure), crystal meth, meth, glass, and shabu.

What is it? Speed, as it sounds, is a stimulant, which speeds up the activity of the central nervous system. It comes as a powder, which can be white, yellow or brown, and usually other chemicals are added as filler to make it go further. Ice is a much, much purer kind of speed in crystal form. (Ice is up to 90 per cent pure and speed is up to 20 per cent.) It looks like transparent rice grains or tiny glass shards, sometimes with a yellow or brown tinge. Speed and ice are usually snorted through the nose, smoked or inhaled as the powder is heated, or possibly injected.

Why do people take it? To try to block feelings of hunger or tiredness (it's often used by people who want to stay awake) or to feel a sudden 'rush' or high.

Side effects and problems Side effects for both include jittery feelings, aggression, exhaustion, feeling invincible, blurred vision, dry mouth, fast breathing, enlarged pupils, headache, nausea, anxiety, 'high' mood, talkativeness and repetitiveness. Regular or heavy users tend to become paranoid and confused, which can lead to mood swings, depression, extreme anxiety, severe mental illness (psychosis), and sudden violent acts.

Ice has especially nasty side effects. It's more physically damaging than speed and has more extreme effects on behaviour, health and lifestyle. It badly damages the skin and hair, and causes teeth to rot and fall out.

Speed or ice mixed with filler chemicals can be poisonous if injected. Injecting puts you at greater risk of diseases, vein damage and overdose. Some users end up turning to crime or sex work to pay for the drug, which also puts them at risk of violence, exploitation and jail.

Dependence and addiction Regular or heavy users will become addicted. Ice is *extremely* addictive (much more so than speed) because of its purity.

→

GHB (gamma-hydroxybutyrate)

Also known as GBH (grievous bodily harm), fantasy, and liquid ecstasy or liquid E (although in fact it isn't like ecstasy, which is a stimulant).

What is it? A depressant, GHB comes as a liquid, which is swallowed or, rarely, injected.

Why do people take it? It can cause a 'rush', then calm.

Side effects and problems Has a reputation as a drink-spiking drug but it has a distinct and strong taste and smell, so it's more likely to be used on somebody already too drunk to notice that something's weird about their drink. Side effects include sleepiness, calm, nausea, headache, intense sense of touch, dizziness and memory loss. Heavy use can cause extreme vomiting, worry and confusion, muscle stiffness, breathing problems, coma, convulsions and death. The difference between taking enough to get an effect and enough to kill you is very small. A 'safe' dose of GHB is very hard to calculate: accidental overdose causing death is a very high risk.

Dependence and addiction Regular or heavy users will become addicted.

Heroin

Also known as smack, skag, dope, H, harry, horse, hammer, and gear.

What is it? It's a depressant and painkiller chemically derived from the opium poppy. Most commonly it's injected into a vein. It is also smoked ('chasing the dragon') or snorted.

Why do people take it? Because it can give them a floaty feeling that temporarily wipes out bad feelings. But most continue to take heroin because they are physically addicted to it.

Side effects and problems Can include feeling sick and vomiting, sweating, itching and weeing a lot. Heroin slows the breathing system, blood pressure and heartbeat: users can doze off. As with ice, some users end up turning to crime or sex work to pay for the drug, which also puts them at risk of violence, exploitation and jail.

Medical problems include self-neglect, malnutrition and needle infections (including hepatitis C and HIV/AIDS). The overdose risk is high because the dosage is hard to estimate.

Dependence and addiction A hugely addictive drug, both physically and psychologically.

Ecstasy (methylenedioxymethamphetamine – MDMA)

Also known as E, and XTC.

What is it? Ecstasy belongs to both the stimulant family (like speed) and the hallucinogen family (like LSD). It comes in tablet or capsule form: most of the tablet could be filler or other drugs (such as speed). Some users poke the tablet up their anus, which is called shafting, plugging or shelving.

Why do people take it? Because it can temporarily heighten the senses, boost energy and create feelings of belonging, social confidence, closeness and a 'happy high'. It's often taken at clubs or dance parties, where it can intensify music and light with hallucinogenic effects.

Side effects and problems Faster heart rate, raised body heat, possible jaw clenching, shaking, nausea, anxiety and sweating. In the days afterwards: feeling down, cranky, listless and unable to concentrate. Ecstasy is associated with anxiety and panic attacks, and with depression, possibly in people who have an unknown predisposition.

So far there's not enough scientific data about ecstasy use. We don't yet know the long-term effects of ecstasy, but we do know it can change and harm your brain. Accidental overdose or mixing it with other drugs or alcohol can cause convulsions, hallucinations (seeing or hearing imaginary things), brain damage and heart failure (death).

Ecstasy shouldn't be taken by anyone with their own or a family history of brain problems, heart disease, blood pressure, or mental illness, or by anyone taking prescribed drugs. Some teenagers have died after taking ecstasy, either because of an underlying medical condition they didn't know they had or from accidental overdose.

See the information about drugs and drinking water, which follows this chart: some ecstasy users have become dangerously dehydrated or have accidentally drunk a life-threatening amount of water.

One of the tricky things in advising on ecstasy is that most of what's sold and claimed to be ecstasy isn't – it's a mix of speed and other powders, or a mix of more dangerous ingredients.

Dependence and addiction From what we know so far, it appears most users don't become physically addicted but may develop a psychological dependence.

Cocaine

Also known as coke, snow, nose candy, Charlie, blow, dust, white, and toot.

What is it? Cocaine, derived from the coca plant, is a stimulant. It looks like salt crystals and is usually arranged in a 'line' and 'snorted' up the nose. It can also be smoked but this is rarer, and known to cause quicker and more dangerous dependence. Intensely addictive 'crack' cocaine, also known as rock or freebase, is usually smoked in a pipe, but is rarer in Australia.

Why do people take it? To try to get a fast high, and to feel buzzy, super-alert and confident. Cocaine also makes them talkative. It blocks hunger, but users always eat later.

Side effects and problems Can include fast heartbeat, raised body heat, enlarged pupils, anxiety, wild behaviour, aggression, sleep problems, paranoia, severe mental illness (psychosis), and heart attack or failure. Long-term use is linked to depression, eventual permanent destruction of nose tissue, panic attacks, possible heart problems and brain damage. People with their own or a family history of heart or mental problems should avoid it.

Users can't tell by looking how pure the cocaine is, or whether it has been 'cut' with other white substances (such as baking soda or talcum powder) to make it go further. This can mean an increased risk of accidental overdose.

Dependence and addiction Known to cause heavy dependence and addiction.

Inhalants

Also called sniffing, sniff, and chroming.

What is it? The fumes of chemicals (often glue, paint or petrol), which are inhaled, causing a depressant effect.

Why do people take it? They want to feel numb or 'wiped-out'.

Side effects and problems Inhaling can cause nose bleeds, sore eyes, nausea, flu-like symptoms, stinky breath, stains around the nose and mouth, stumbling, zombie-like staring, vision and hearing problems, and passing out. Ongoing problems can include lack of energy, confusion, crankiness, and serious eye, organ and brain damage. Some users have died when they inhaled before physical activity. Others have suffocated.

Dependence and addiction Can cause psychological dependence addiction.

'Minimising' the harm

If you have decided to take a drug (which is not recommended, obviously!):

- never take it when you're alone
- take too little rather than too much – this is always better because you can never know exactly what's in the drug
- never take anything without telling a friend what you're taking, and how much or how many (also always find out exactly what your friend has taken, and how much or how many)
- always have at least one designated sober person (no drugs and no alcohol) – this is really important. You need someone on watch who's completely together. Talk to your friends about what they should do if things go wrong.

Have a plan so you don't panic if things go wrong...

Drinking water Experts disagree on exactly how much water party and club goers need to drink. Too little or too much water combined with some drugs can cause serious damage to your body or (in rare cases) death. Be smart: drink if you're thirsty and also take your moisture loss as a guide – if you're weeing a lot, or sweating, drink more water even if you don't 'feel thirsty'. Drink it regularly in sips and small swallows, rather than gulping it all in one go. Take rest breaks and don't dance non-stop for hours.

Reaction and overdose

If someone has an adverse reaction or overdoses it's really important that they receive professional help as soon as possible. A quick response can save their life.

See the box 'When to Call an Ambulance' in Chapter 10, Drinking, for the signs and symptoms that mean someone needs emergency help, and info on what to do after calling 000.

> One time my friend became paralysed and started throwing up. It really scared me.
>
> Marg, 15, Samford Valley, Qld

drugs ✱ HEAD   233

> **FACT**
>
> **Some don'ts** People who have taken drugs certainly shouldn't drive, swim, look after children or operate machinery because of the risk of an accident or of being unable to react properly in an emergency.

How to help somebody with a drug problem

Many people with unlimited access to a drug they like will develop health problems and an overuse or dependency problem (although they will often deny it).

- Listen to what they have to say, and be there for them, but don't compromise your own decision, values or safety.
- Friends (and relatives) can be angry, even mean, if you raise the subject of their drug (or alcohol) problem. Share your worries with a trusted adult, or with a friendly doctor or a counsellor on one of the anonymous helplines listed opposite in 'More Info' (they're not interested in telling the police – their job is to help the person).
- Have some information, such as fact sheets on drugs from one of the websites found in 'More Info', and some of the helpline numbers listed, so that in a crisis, or when the person is ready to seek help, you've got something useful on hand.
- Accept that unless and until they want help there's nothing more you can do. Their drug problem is not your responsibility and you can't fix it. If it starts to affect your own enjoyment of life, step back and distance yourself (while assuring them you'll be there if and when they need you to help them tackle their drug problem).

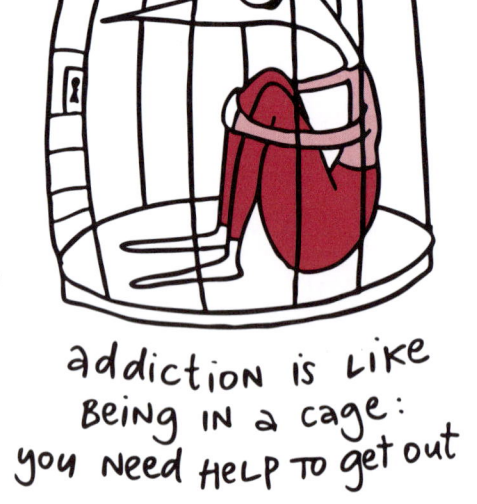

addiction is like being in a cage: you need help to get out

More info on drugs and help with drug problems

Kids Helpline: 1800 55 1800
National Drugs Campaign
(for info and help): 1800 250 015
ACT Health Service Line:
(02) 6207 9977
NSW Alcohol and Drug Information Service:
(02) 9361 8000 or 1800 422 599 (rural)
NT Alcohol and Drug Information Service:
1800 131 350
Qld Alcohol and Drug Information Service:
1800 177 833
SA Alcohol and Drug Information Service:
1300 131 340
Tas. Alcohol and Drug Information Service:
1800 811 994
Vic. Alcohol and Drug Information Service:
1800 888 236 (direct line);
1300 858 584 (drug info);
1300 660 068 (Family Drug Helpline)
YoDAA (Youth Drugs and Alcohol Advice):
1800 458 685
WA Alcohol and Drug Information Service:
(08) 9442 5000 or 1800 198 024 (rural)
Parent Drug Information Service:
(08) 9442 5050 or 1800 653 203 (rural)

adf.org.au/drug-facts
The Alcohol and Drug foundation has heaps of info, articles and fact sheets on all drugs.

campaigns.health.gov.au/drughelp
The National Drugs Campaign offers real-life stories, facts and help.

darta.net.au and *Teenagers, Alcohol and Drugs* by Paul Dillon
An Aussie authority has useful info for teens and parents in his book, and in his school and community programs and presentations.

adf.org.au/insights/drugs-and-driving
The Australian Drug Foundation's page on drugs and driving.

🥝 Alcohol Drug Helpline
alcoholdrughelp.org.nz
0800 787 797
You can ring anonymously to talk about a problem you have, or somebody else has, or check out the info on the site.

I believe that MOST people will try drugs/alcohol at least once in their life and I think that if you are going to try them make sure you are with/around people that you can trust and are going to look after you if it gets out of hand.   Tash, 18, Devonport, Tas.

I wish I had known that my friends who tried to force me to do things I didn't want to do, like smoking and stuff, weren't really my friends, particularly when they ditched me. Rosie, 17

I have had ecstasy about four times. On my second time I OD'd. I could have died. I regularly take speed and smoke bongs. I also have been smoking cigarettes since I was 11. My ex-boyfriend also is currently doing this thing where he is staying high for two weeks.   Kath, 16, Traralgon, Vic.

12

MIND HEALTH

Although 'mental health' (the usual term for mind health) sounds a bit strange, **it's a good thing**. It means you're feeling optimistic, capable, confident, and pretty happy about life, and that you can deal with most problems and **keep things in perspective** (not feeling utterly furious or bursting into tears because you broke a fingernail).

Good mental health allows you to cope pretty well with the stress that everyone experiences, have **fairly stable emotions** rather than wild mood swings, and react rationally to things, which helps keep relationships from turning into confusion and fighting.

Your brain

Brain researchers are perpetually blowing their own minds with what they're finding out. Experts used to think brains were fully formed by the time we were 12, and that we knew everything about them. Now they know that there's lots we don't know yet. But we do know what can scientifically be defined as 'some stuff'. Here it is.

We know that a teenager's brain is not as fully developed as an adult's. You're more likely to have mood swings, react emotionally, not recognise other people's feelings, and get into an argument with someone who's telling you what to do. When you're a teenager some of your brain still needs some work: the parts that make judgements and decisions, plan, organise, and assess risks and consequences.

The upside of all this is you have a big excuse for doing dumb things: 'It's not my fault – my brain's not finished yet.' But if you use that excuse your parents and teachers can say that's why they can't let you make important decisions for yourself: 'Until your brain is finished, I can still treat you like a kid.'

Hmmm. Let's see if we can get around this.

Use it or lose it

Your brain did most of its growing before you turned 3 years old. By the time you were 6 your brain was already nearly adult-sized, although the contents still aren't finished, even when you're in your teens: it's as if you have the computer but the software hasn't finished downloading.

Right through childhood and the teenage years your brain is making new connecting pathways so that you're quicker and more efficient with your memories, ideas, plans, understanding and conclusions. So the more you challenge your brain, and the more you have to think about different things, the more your brain needs to keep its pathways open and make more.

When you're a teenager your brain is busy chucking out information to make room for new stuff – it destroys any connections it thinks it won't need. Experts reckon that teenagers 'prune' (cut back) their brains without knowing: if you spend a lot of time smoking weed and watching TV, instead of being creative or studying, your brain shuts down the bits you don't use. But the good news is if you use your brain it gets smarter, and you can always start building it up again even after an injury or you've ignored it for a while.

Guy and girl brains

Guys' brains are likely to be bigger than girls' (by about 10 per cent), but this doesn't mean guys are smarter than girls. Girls' brains develop more quickly than guys', but that doesn't mean girls are necessarily smarter either – maybe just less likely to take crazy risks.

We're really in the very early stages of understanding the common differences between the male and female brain: boys are more likely to be diagnosed with brain-related conditions such as attention deficit disorders, autism disorders, and dyslexia (a brain problem that makes it harder to learn reading and spelling). This may be because boys with these conditions tend to be seen as 'misbehaving' so people investigate more, whereas girls are more likely to be 'quiet' and not ask for help.

Many people believe that women are better at understanding and dealing with emotional situations and negotiations. But of course it also depends on an individual's genes, personality, abilities, skills and education.

I may look like I'm staring into space, but I'm pruning my brain...

What's in your brain

Everyone's brain has a left and a right side. The left hemisphere controls all the movements you make with the right side of your body. The right hemisphere controls your left side.

Here are some of the main brain bits.

- **Frontal cortex**   This is your sensible bit. You use it to work out what's important and logical, and to decide and plan. In a teenage brain it's not so well developed yet. It's the frontal cortex that guys are not using when they staple their scrotum to a fence to see what will happen. (They cry.)
- **Corpus callosum**   This is a big cable connection of nerves linking the left and right hemispheres. The better the connection the more creative you can be, and the better the solutions you'll think up. If it could light up it would go on like a light bulb when you had an idea.
- **Amygdala** (pronounced a-mig-d'lar)   This sits in the middle of your brain, underneath the corpus callosum, and is the emotional, reactive part that teenagers tend to use more than the logical frontal cortex. It plays a role in risk taking, mood swings, decisions based on sudden 'gut reactions', and having trouble when trying to recognise the emotions of other people. Some researchers think most girls use the frontal cortex more than most guys, who rely more on the amygdala. While the science in this area is still new, brain researchers now believe that the amygdala is active when we feel emotions, such as fear or falling in love.
- **Hippocampus**   This little bit of your brain, right next to the amygdala, is the memory centre – it would light up, if it could, when you smelt coconut sunscreen reminding you of a beach holiday. It's the bit that your brain rummages through to remember an answer for your science exam.
- **Cerebellum** (pronounced serra-bell-um)   This is at the back of your brain above your spine. Scientists used to think it was only used to run your muscles and physical movement, but now they think it also influences how you co-ordinate your thoughts. Scientists think that it keeps developing until your early twenties.

Is it your fault or your brain's?

So can you blame your teenage brain when you do risky or dumb things? Maybe.

But what excuse do adults have when they behave like idiots?

If you're going to take risks and act on impulse, try to:

* restrict those times to actions without life-or-death consequences – such as cooking experiments, ill-advised celebrity crushes from a distance and orange eyeshadow
* access your fast-developing frontal cortex when deciding important stuff with potentially huge consequences such as whether to steal something and whether to get into a car with a drunk or show-offy driver.

After all, you're not stupid. It's just that your brain's still growing.

My brain's still growing. What's your excuse?

mum

Brain chemicals Brain chemicals zoom about between nerve cells, making lightning-quick electrical connections and helping to control your moods, your body and your actions. The chemicals include:

- **Serotonin** The right amount, or a bit extra, of this keeps moods even and helps you to feel calm and able to make judgements, and to go to sleep. Not enough means you're more likely to have depression, anxiety and impulsive reactions and behaviour.
- **Dopamine** High levels make you feel cruisy or on a 'high'. Not enough and you can feel depressed. Too much probably contributes to psychosis, a mental illness that involves delusions. Dopamine also helps to control your physical movement and balance.
- **Endorphins** These are pumped around your brain during vigorous exercise, childbirth or a trauma – whenever your body needs to override stress or pain and create a kind of high.

240   HEAD ✳ mind health

Keep your brain healthy

You've got to look after your brain to make sure you don't end up with the mental powers of a demented guinea pig. Luckily there are lots of things you can do to keep your brain healthy.

- Eat 'brain foods' such as fresh fruit and vegies; fish and other sources of healthy omega 3 oils; and lots of protein (see Chapter 5, Food).
- Exercise. Moving yourself about, whether in organised sport, dancing or whatever, will release your feel-good brain chemicals (see Chapter 6, Move).
- Relax. Stress and depression give you brain strain and make it harder for your brain to develop. Get help if you live in a stressful home situation or often feel anxious or scared (see Chapter 9, Feelings).
- Get regular sleep (see the info coming up).
- Avoid brain injury. It can sometimes be improved but not always cured. Wear a helmet if you're doing fast or impact sport, or riding a bike. Avoid high-risk vehicles: tractors, motorbikes and 'quad bikes'.
- Don't let a coach or parent put you back into a game after a head knock or injury: go straight to a doctor.
- Protect your brain from outside chemicals. The most dangerous time to use alcohol and drugs is while your brain is still developing – that's now (see Chapter 10, Drinking, and Chapter 11, Drugs).

Keep your brain exercised

Maybe in the future there'll be a pill or a slot-in brain card to keep us smart. In the meantime keep using your brain for thinking and creating, instead of just letting it hang out up there between your ears.

Here are some suggestions (inspired by the Brain Foundation of Australia) for making your brain work better.

- Change around your hobbies and habits – learn new dances, card and board games and puzzles (ask an oldie); learn how to do something new, whether artistic, sporty or musical; help a littlie build something out of plastic blocks, wood or even paper; find out how to fix or create something you're interested in (an engine, a story, a sculpture); turn off the TV and the computer (aside from homework) for a week as an experiment. >

- Try not to totally specialise in school subjects or hobbies until later in your teens. Do a little bit of lots of things, instead of *all* science or nothing but swimming. (I can tell you from personal experience that if you don't use the maths pathways they become overgrown with brambles, like the ones outside Sleeping Beauty's castle. No prince is ever going to come along and teach me what nine times eight is.)
- Daydream: it's creative, not a waste of time. Think about ways to solve the world's problems – both social and physical. What would you do if you were the ruler of the world/stuck down a pit without a ladder/born with green skin? Make plans for hypothetical events or overseas trips, design your dream home, imagine what you'd do if you were trapped on a deserted island and which five things you'd want to have and why.
- Talk: have discussions with friends, family or others about politics, ethics, the way advertising is trying to manipulate us all, and the Big Questions of Life.

Be proud of your brain

Some girls pretend to be stupid, thinking that it will attract guys. It's a shame these girls don't realise that only dumb guys would want dumb girls, and who wants a dumb guy?

While you're pretending to be dumb you may really be getting dumber, switching off brain pathways and making it harder to get smart later on when you want a high-paying job or to work out the best way to get that amazing trip overseas.

Smart people can pretend to be dumb, but dumb people can't really pretend to be smart. Or not for long. Smarter is always going to work better for you, throughout your whole life, no matter what you decide to do. I'm not saying you have to be brilliant at exams and schoolwork. Or a whiz with words, or a physics genius.

everyone's BRAINY at something...

Some other ways to be clever include being:
- a practical problem-solver
- good at building and making things
- creative and artistic
- able to understand other people and their needs and motives ('emotional intelligence')
- able to make and stick to a plan to achieve or escape something
- an observer who learns from watching others
- good at physical or mental games.

Your brain is one of the great things about being a teenager. Your brain is better and faster at adapting to new situations and learning stuff than an adult's brain. In a few more years you'll be better at risk assessment and more experienced at understanding what's happening in your life or why somebody behaves the way they do. But right now you've got the perfect brain to help you get better at stuff you love doing and want to find out about. It can make you feel confident, optimistic and full of energy. Your brain helps you figure out how you can change the world for the better and how you can have the best life.

You're young and so, if you choose to, you can still get smarter and more interesting every day – take that, adults.

More info on your brain

brainfoundation.org.au
Choose Healthy Brain for tips (that seem mostly for adults but will work for you, too).

All In The Mind
This ABC podcast has great stories and reports on the wonders of the brain.

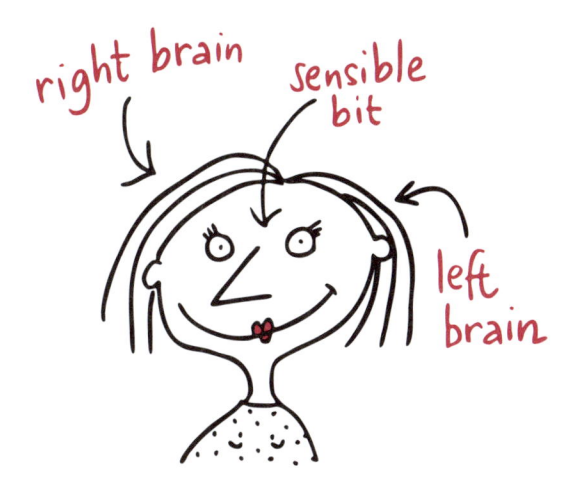

How to get more sleep

At this time of your life your body starts making more of a hormone called melatonin, which 'sets your body clock', telling you when to be sleepy and when to be awake and alert.

You have more melatonin zapping about in the morning than adults and less late at night, which means you're likely to feel awake late at night and tired in the morning, as if you had jet-lag. If you don't get enough sleep you can feel cranky, irritable and a teensy bit dull-witted.

Why you need sleep Between the ages of about 12 and 18 you are having those growth surges and most of the action happens in your deepest phase of sleep. (Yes, you *can* kind of grow a bit in the night.) If you don't get enough of this deepest phase of sleep you won't achieve your height potential.

Everyone's brain also needs to dream each night, although dream researchers don't agree on exactly what role dreams play. Some think they're a way that the brain helps us to learn, memorise and

> **FACT**
>
> **ZZZ** Teenagers need more sleep than adults because they're still growing.

dreams are not REAL. Sometimes we dream in symbols

> **FACT**
>
> **How much sleep is enough?** Teenagers need at least 9 or even 10 hours a night for their brain and the rest of their body to develop properly. That means that if you have to get up at 6 am, for sports training or school transport, you really should be asleep by about 9 at night. And if you have to get up at 7 am to do chores, you should be doing the horizontal slumber by 10 pm.

Some ideas to help you sleep at night

- Sorry, I know it's truly appalling, but Bad News Alert: you should probably have a bedtime to aim for.

- Go to bed before you get overtired.

- Turn off all devices, including TV, screen games, computers and your phone ideally at least an hour before bedtime. Keep them off all night so they can't twoot, swoosh, phoof, ding, ring or any other thing. Record TV shows to watch earlier the next night.

- Listen to relaxing music (not thrash metal) in the hour before bed. Some girls like to listen to burbly radio, relaxing noises or music to get to sleep; for others, this keeps them awake (see 'More Info on Sleep' coming up).

- Do sport, exercise, yoga or dancing – but finish at least a couple of hours before bedtime or you'll be too alert.

- Be aware that coffee, tea, colas, energy drinks, chocolate (all have caffeine) any time during the day or food late at night can disrupt your sleep and wake you up in the night. A huge glass of water before bed means many wee trips.

- If you readjust your daily schedule don't suddenly change your bedtime by an hour: gradually move it by 10 or 15 minutes a day. Try this before a daylight saving change, too.

- Stay warm: being cold can make it hard to fall or stay asleep.

- Make sure your bed isn't too hot either – dreams can get weird if you're overheated. A lot of people sleep better when they swap to using a sheet and a couple of blankets instead of a doona (some doonas are designed for arctic winters and are equivalent to eight blankets).

- Make your bedroom as dark as you can – any light tells your brain it's not time to be asleep. Red digits on a clock are less disturbing than green.

- Don't take sleeping tablets: they're bad for the teenage brain, and can make you feel awful the next day. Used repeatedly, they can cause serious psychological and physical problems. Never take sleeping tablets prescribed for anyone else.

When zzzz means arghhhh

Do you usually snore a lot, or really loudly? This can be a sign of sleep apnoea (pronounced ap-nee-ah). If you have sleep apnoea your airways narrow during sleep, not enough air gets in, and your brain keeps waking you up as a bit of an alarm response. In this way you can get a bad, 'broken' night's sleep every night and not even know it – this can cause you to be tired and have accidental mini-naps in the daytime, which can be dangerous. So it's off to the GP for any snorers, to get checked.

find solutions to problems. Others believe they show a person's sub-conscious (underlying) thoughts. And some think dreams are the 'rubbish bin of the mind': that the brain replays the useless bits of images and information it doesn't need. Try to just get over bad dreams, but tell your doctor about any recurring nightmares or if you often wake up feeling very scared.

If you're sleep deprived you're going to find school and work harder, and be more likely to get depressed and anxious. It also means you could be likely to use caffeine to stay alert, which makes it even more likely that you won't sleep, setting up a vicious cycle and possibly damaging your physical and mental health.

When you're really overtired it's 'normal' to have odd thoughts. You may dwell on scary or disturbing thoughts or images. Try doing some more physical exercise in a day so it's easier to fall asleep at night.

> **FACT**
>
> **Can you pay back a 'sleep debt'?** No. 'Sleep binges' only confuse your body clock. Have an extra hour or two of sleep on the weekends if your body wants it, but avoid 'marathons'.

More info on sleep

Check out chill-out and relaxing music, deep-breathing techniques or guided meditation podcasts or sessions to download or buy as a phone app. You can make your own playlist for free from your own music library. Research apps with relaxing sounds to see if they're your idea of calm: one has seagulls bleating, which just makes me feel anxious that my fish and chips are about to be stolen, and the sound of wind chimes makes me quite murderous.

Beware of phone apps to 'track' your sleep that you literally have to sleep on and are claimed to wake you in the right 'phase' of sleep. Most people have to get up at a certain time of the morning anyway rather than in the right 'phase'.

vuir.vu.edu.au/467
Download this Australian e-book by Professor Dorothy Bruck for info on teen sleep problems and solutions. Links to many other sites on sleep strategies.

sleep.org.au
The Australasian Sleep Association has lots of fact sheets and medical links.

radiolab.org
Fun science podcasts: search Sleep and Dreams.

Lack of sleep can make you CRANKY

Good mental health

Good mental health, or mind health, means you have a mind that can rev up and be alive with thoughts and ideas, then wind down and relax when you need time out or sleep. It means you'll still face challenges but feel able to tackle them and work your way through.

Self-help tips

These hints can help you enjoy life and get through any mind health problems.

- Talk about it and ask for help.
- Be around other people – keep communicating.
- Try to remember that bad thoughts are not necessarily true, but part of the problem or illness. Maybe you could make a poster or list to remind yourself of the good things about you and life.
- Have a routine so you don't have to think about what time to eat and go to bed.
- Eat a healthy diet (see Chapter 5, Food). Your brain needs good food. A multi-vitamin supplement can be a useful idea.
- Exercise can help control mood swings and depression (see Chapter 6, Move).
- Get more sleep – at the right times (see earlier in this chapter).
- Try some relaxation techniques such as meditation or yoga. Your local council, gym or community noticeboard should have details of classes, or you can find a website.
- Avoid smoking, drugs not prescribed for you, and alcohol.
- Keep a diary to see how your moods change. It might be best to keep this private, rather than tell the whole world on your social media page, but it's up to you!

Above all, always be kind to yourself. How would you treat a best friend going through a difficult time?

Five mind health affirmations

1. Say to yourself: 'I can control and manage my own mental health. I will ask for help and accept good support and medication if necessary.'

2. 'For most people a mental health problem is only temporary.'

3. 'By acknowledging a problem I've already started work on fixing it.'

4. 'If it's not all fixed straight away, I'll keep trying. Failure isn't caused by setbacks, it's caused by not trying any more.'

5. 'New research, medication and other treatments are being developed all the time.'

Mental health problems

It's normal to feel down, overwhelmed or sad sometimes, especially as a teenager, and most people have the skills to bounce back after a 'low'. Chapter 9, Feelings, talked about how being moody is part of growing up. Most of us go through emotions, sometimes without really knowing why, or have a healthy reaction to stuff that life throws into our path. This doesn't mean we're mentally ill. There's lots in Chapter 9, Feelings, about how to deal with ordinary embarrassment, sadness, grief, anger, stress, worries and feeling down, and how to be more strong and optimistic.

If feelings are out of control or seem like they're ruling our life, they can be a symptom of a mental health problem we need to have assessed and then get some help to fix.

Getting help for mental health problems

Pretty much everyone, at some time in their life, will experience a mental health problem themselves, or have contact with a friend or family member who has the problem. For most people it can be just a stage in their life that they overcome with time, treatment and good support. There are lots of ways available now to recover from or manage a mental health problem, and the earlier you get onto it the better. Many mental health problems can first appear in the teen years. These can include depression, severe anxiety or stress, an eating disorder, wanting to harm yourself, or psychotic disorders, which are all explained later in this chapter.

If you recognise some of those feelings and problems in yourself or a friend or family member, reach out for help. A good idea is to start by talking to your parents, a friend, a relative, a friend's parent, your doctor, a teacher or school counsellor, or even a confidential helpline counsellor. Some local councils also have youth officers who can refer you for help.

It's important to have a professional assessment so you know what you're dealing with. A doctor can refer you to a counsellor (therapist), or a psychologist who is trained in talking about mental health problems and helping people work out strategies to overcome them.

> **FACT**
>
> **Mental health websites** Some websites are wrong, simply ill-informed opinion or out of date. So find a big, reputable, local mental health site that's updated often, such as sane.org (see 'More Info on Mental Health Problems' coming up soon).

Only a psychiatrist – a medical doctor who has specialised in problems of the brain and mind – or a specialist psychologist can diagnose a mental illness (see 'Mental Illness' below).

Don't be afraid to try another specialist if the first one doesn't work out for you. Go back to your GP and ask for another recommendation.

There are a range of options for treating mind health problems, including:
- talking therapy (counselling)
- cognitive therapy – learning strategies to manage or change feelings and reactions
- possibly drugs (which can only be prescribed by a doctor or a psychiatrist)
- alternative treatments as part of a combined medical approach (these might include yoga, relaxation techniques, vitamins and herbal preparations) – but you need to tell your doctor which ones you are using or have used.

> ## Some facts about mental illness
>
> * These days we know that having a mental illness is common and nothing to be ashamed of.
>
> * Mental illness has happened throughout history, in all countries, to all sorts of people.
>
> * Somebody with a mental illness can't just 'pull themselves together'. The illness is not their fault. Something is out of balance in their brain.
>
> * With help, most people can find ways to control and live with, or recover from, a mental illness.

All treatments for mental health problems take time. There'll be good days and bad days and some steps backwards, but you'll know you're heading in the right direction.

Mental illness

A mental illness is at the serious end of mind health problems and needs specialist medical help. Mental illnesses that teenagers can experience range from severe anxiety, major depression, bipolar disorder (huge ups and downs), obsessions (with eating, body image or other things), and self-harm, through to the rarer psychosis (not being able to tell what's real from what isn't).

Most mental illnesses cause a person to be unable to keep things in perspective.

Who to tell about a mental illness

There is such a high level of ignorance in the community about mental health that you may want to keep a mental illness to yourself – not because it's shameful, but just because you don't want to be 'labelled' or feel like answering questions about it. Your doctor and family will have to know so they can help and support you. You can make the decision together about who to tell, and who can help share your worries.

For example, a depressed person will think nothing is ever going to be fun or interesting again; a person with anorexia may think they're 'fat' when they're dangerously thin; and a person suffering from psychosis may believe they can hear voices.

To the person with the mental illness, these things are absolutely real. They're not pretending, or just trying to be special or different.

What causes a mental illness? Mental illness is often associated with an imbalance in brain chemicals. Often the trigger for the first episode of mental illness is some kind of stress: family trouble, severe illness or other worries, perhaps social or financial. It's now known that alcohol and illegal drugs can also trigger a mental illness in somebody with a predisposition (see Chapter 10, Drinking, and Chapter 11, Drugs). Some people may have the predisposition but it is never set off, perhaps because they avoid drugs, have a personality that minimises stress or are just lucky.

Does mental illness 'run in the family'? Some people have a family history of mental illness, and this can make them more predisposed to mental illness themselves.

Just coz I'm bipolar doesn't mean you will be

I don't want your fashion sense either!

mind health ✱ HEAD 251

The predisposition may never become an illness, but is more likely to if there's a trigger such as severe stress or drug use. Most people with mentally ill relatives never develop the illness themselves, and have the advantage of knowing they need to avoid common triggers.

Diagnosis of mental illness Your doctor, and the psychiatrist you're referred to, will talk to you about:
- what you're thinking and feeling
- your medical or psychological symptoms
- your family, school or work.

Perhaps after two or three visits to the psychiatrist you'll be given a diagnosis – in other words a name for your problem – and some ideas about what treatment might be most useful. (Sometimes the diagnosis varies depending on the psychiatrist.)

At first for some people it's a little scary getting a diagnosis because it means you have a recognised problem. But it's also a huge relief: 'I have recognised symptoms, and now I can get help to manage my problem.'

Living with someone who has a mental illness

Living (or being friends) with someone who has a mental health problem can be hard, disruptive and even heartbreaking at times. When they're struggling it can be very difficult for you to know what to do or say.

Often it can seem as if the attention is on them all the time, and that no one is thinking about what you need. This can leave you feeling angry and frustrated, and maybe then guilty and upset. But it's normal to feel these things.

If it's a parent who is having trouble sometimes the kids are expected to take on all responsibility. If you have a single parent who is mentally ill it's a good idea to try to find another adult who you trust, to talk to and to help you out with day-to-day things when needed. *You* deserve support and help too (see 'More Info' opposite for services).

> My brother has got a brain injury and my mother has manic depression. I'm a young carer so that takes up my time. Gracie, 17, Coraki, NSW

More info on mental health problems

sane.org
Helpline: 1800 187 263
SANE is Australia's biggest mental health info place, with lots of fact sheets and stuff on where to go for help. SANE also offers confidential advice and a referral service. You can email questions, which will be answered within three days.

copmi.net.au/kids-young-people
Children of Parents with a Mental Illness: especially designed to help kids whose parents are living with a mental illness.

au.reachout.com
Help with all sorts of mental health problems, including depression, moods, loneliness, worries, eating disorders and more.

headspace.org.au
The National Youth Mental Health Foundation has links and info for young people, and tells how to get easier and cheaper medical help. Choose from Real Stories, Find information or Getting Help.

beyondblue.org.au
Best known as a depression hub, BeyondBlue has fact sheets on various problems and info on help.

For help with living with someone else's mental illness try these:

youngcarers.net.au
Support Line: 1800 242 636
For young people who care for, or help care for, relatives with mental or physical challenges and other health issues. Forums and help.

Kidsline: 0800 543 754 and **Youthline: 0800 376 633 (youthline.co.nz)**
NZ confidential counselling services.

urge.co.nz
A Kiwi youth site that covers mental health issues.

Severe anxiety

It's normal and sometimes even helpful to feel anxious about exams, a sports event or performing in a play. But severe anxiety gets in the way of enjoying life. It can be a feeling of possible imminent disaster, or an overwhelming sense of worry, fear or embarrassment. It can include symptoms such as:

- faster breathing and heartbeat
- trembling and sweating
- having to rush to the toilet all the time
- feeling 'frozen' – unable to move or talk.

Some anxiety disorders

Severe anxiety includes a number of disorders, which share some of the symptoms just listed but also have particular feelings and behaviours.

Panic attacks If anxious feelings get worse they can turn into panic attacks – sudden feelings of terror or complete weirdness. Sometimes a place or situation will cause one: for example, going over a bridge or being caught up in a crowd.

During a panic attack a person may feel:
- their heart beating rapidly
- dizzy
- short of breath
- sick in the stomach
- disconnected from reality or 'out of body', as though they've lost control of their body and mind.

> I used to have panic attacks from getting worried so much. I don't get as worried but I do get worried mostly over tiny things like my maths teacher expects me to finish five pages in one night. People might say something like: 'Don't do that, you'll get radiation poisoning and die!' At night I worry the most.
> Jasmine, 13, Urunga, NSW

Obsessive compulsive disorder (OCD) With OCD the anxiety results in repeated thoughts or actions, which the person can't stop no matter how much they want to. Common repetitive behaviour can be many things, including:

- washing hands
- knocking a certain number of times before entering any room
- counting things.

Post-traumatic stress disorder A terrible or sad event can cause anxiety-related symptoms, including:
- 'flashbacks' (sudden interrupting memories of the event)
- nightmares
- fear of the event happening again.

> I think I might worry about food poisoning more than anything else. I worry not that something will happen to the people I love, but more that something already has and they haven't told anyone about it.
> Sarah, 18, Newcastle, NSW

Trichotillomania People with this form of anxiety pull their hair out by twisting, tugging or plucking: it can be the hair on their head, or their eyebrows or eyelashes.

Treatment for anxiety

If you feel anxious, see your GP. People who tend to become severely anxious usually need professional help to make changes in their life, and to become less shy, if that's what they want.

If you have an anxiety disorder
- Your GP should be able to refer you to a specialist or counsellor who can help.
- You may have cognitive behaviour therapy – talking about new strategies you can use.
- You may also find that short-term medication is helpful.

More info on severe anxiety

See 'More Info on Mental Health Problems' earlier in this chapter, especially sane.org and ranzcp.org for contacts.

betterhealth.vic.gov.au
Search 'Anxiety-treatment Options' for important advice. Also search Anxiety Disorders, Panic Attack, Social Phobia and Breathing to Reduce Stress.

Depression

Diagnosed depression is different from the odd day of feeling 'blue' and a bit down that everyone experiences, and which Chapter 9, Feelings, talked about. People who are seriously depressed often lose interest in everything and have no hope that things will ever get better. Being severely depressed is like having all the lows and none of the highs of life, as if someone pulled a plug at the bottom of your mind and let all the fun run out.

> I have depression, so often I struggle to stay positive and keep going. I am sad when I get bad marks for schoolwork, or when I fail at anything I give a decent shot at. Anything as small as a fight makes me really upset because I tend to worry about the worst that could happen.
> Isabel, 16, Mt Macedon, Vic.

Almost everybody will know somebody who goes through periods of depression.

Warning signs of severe depression

People who are severely depressed may:
- feel 'empty' or 'numb' inside; be angry, irritable or sad all or most of the time; cry a lot; and lose their temper over what other people would think were small things
- believe they are ugly, wrong, useless and unlovable
- lose interest in everything they usually like (favourite foods, school, work, hobbies, sports, friends, family), have no energy, and feel really tired all the time and that they can't be bothered doing anything
- have trouble with sleep – usually wanting to sleep most of the time, or perhaps not getting much but instead lying awake worrying or feeling blank
- be unable to concentrate, remember things or finish tasks
- experience the bad feelings for days, weeks or even months
- have recurring or constant thoughts about dying or what it would be like to die, or think everyone else would be better off if they were dead (see 'Suicide' later in this chapter).

> One of my closest friends now has depression and it's really, really painful for me to watch her go through this. Samantha, 15, Fairfield, Vic.

What causes depression?

There usually isn't one cause of depression but rather a combination of things beyond a person's control, which pushes them over the line. Sometimes it's not obvious what the cause might have been.

Contributing factors may include:
- an imbalance of brain chemicals – the mood-regulating chemicals may be out of whack
- drugs or alcohol, usually with repeated use
- a stressful or traumatic event such as trouble in the family, abuse, continual bullying or the death of somebody close
- a recurring or chronic illness
- a family history of mental illness.

Treatment for depression

Depending on your symptoms, these treatments can be combined or used separately:
- counselling, with practical advice on strategies and coping
- drugs to correct the brain chemical imbalance.

More info on depression

All the services listed under 'More Info on Mental Health Problems' earlier in this chapter have specific info on and help for depression.

Depression is common. Some girls (me) are too scared to tell anyone and just paint on a happy face. Belinda, 16, Redcliffe, Qld

I had depression. I became paranoid and self-obsessed, 'everyone in the world is out to get me'. It affected every part of my life, and I was suicidal for a bit. My mum dragged me to counsellors and in the end I went on drugs to help me get through it. I'm glad I did. I try my very best to be there for others and to raise awareness among peers and adults that depression is an illness, not a sign of a bad person. Ellie, 18, Mt Waverley, Vic.

I have my own counsellor and I can sit in there and talk to her about me for an hour or more straight, which is very therapeutic. Alicia, 16, Sydney, NSW

Bipolar disorder

Bipolar disorder (formerly called manic depression) is a kind of mental illness known as a mood disorder. It's made worse by drug and alcohol use.

A person with bipolar disorder has wild, seemingly random mood swings, with very down and listless periods and high, or 'manic', madly busy ones. The swings can happen within a period of days, or one phase (high or low) can take over for weeks or even months.

High phases

During a manic period a person may:
- not sleep much
- have grand ideas and a sense of superiority
- get crabby a lot at little things
- have trouble slowing down thoughts, even to go to sleep
- rush into wild projects and actions that make no sense to anybody else
- behave recklessly, over-spending and acting out of character
- even experience psychosis so that they are not able to tell what's real and what's a delusion.

More info on bipolar disorder

All the places listed in 'More Info on Mental Health Problems' earlier in this chapter have special info on, and help for, bipolar disorder.

Depression can feel like 'NOTHING'

Self-harm

Sometimes people deliberately hurt themselves, usually in secret, and try to hide any marks with their clothes. Examples of self-harm include cutting, burning, hitting, scratching or biting parts of the body, or using drugs or alcohol to put themselves in danger.

Self-harm is usually a way of trying to cope with painful or difficult feelings – often because the person finds it hard to put their feelings into words or to ask for help. It's most common in the mid to late teens and early twenties. It's also more common in girls or women who've been abused, attacked or assaulted. If this could be relevant, for extra help see 'Abuse and Control' in Chapter 15, Love, and the section on sexual assault in Chapter 16, Sex.

Treatment for self-harm

If you harm yourself:

- it's very important that you see your GP for a referral to a psychiatrist or a psychologist who specialises in this problem
- talking therapy can help you to change the way you think and to find strategies so that self-harm does not become a habit or the usual way you deal with something. Many girls have great success with talking therapy.

More info on self-harm

See all the services listed in 'More Info on Mental Health Problems' earlier as well as the sites below.

sane.org, au.reachout.com and ranzcp.org

All these reputable mental health sites have specific helpful info about self-harm. Search the phrase Self Harm from their main pages.

I just thought I was worthless and nobody loved me. I'd run to my room and cry. Then I started cutting myself when nobody would come to my rescue. Georgia, 17, Sydney, NSW

A lot of girls who do it feel like freaks, or like they are the only person doing it, and don't know how to stop. Georgie, 17, Burleigh Heads, Qld

I have been doing this for the last five years and it has only been in the last month that I have been able to talk to anyone about it, and this only was by chance. Encourage people to talk to someone about their problems. Maz, 17, Adelaide, SA

Eating disorders

Eating disorders are not just about being concerned with food, being 'vain' or going a bit too far with diets. They are complicated mental disorders that also affect the body.

Disordered eating behaviours are driven by emotions. They usually begin with thinking about weight, dieting, food control or exercise, and are accompanied by anxieties such as guilt, obsessive thoughts and a sense of being out of control. People who have an eating disorder are very unhappy, whatever their weight or size.

> I was diagnosed with anorexia at 13, but have since come the full cycle and now I binge eat and throw up everything.
> Elsa, 16,
> Pascoe Vale, Vic.

Disordered eating includes having very strict rules about foods and a wide range of unusual or otherwise odd behaviours – basically food weirdness. These can include:

- repeated dieting
- talking and obviously thinking about food a lot
- increased or obsessive monitoring of food (for example, checking fat content and kilojoules on all food labels)
- lying about not being hungry or having eaten already
- compulsive and strenuous exercising to lose weight
- trips to the toilet after or during eating, to try to purge food
- eating huge amounts or tiny amounts (sometimes restricting food to starvation levels)
- trying to ignore hunger or welcoming it
- drinking water before every meal, or instead of eating, to try to 'fill up'
- taking 'health' ideas to the extreme, such as aiming for no fat, instead of less fat; or only eating fruit and vegies, instead of including proteins and carbohydrates
- only eating one sort of food
- only eating some meals
- inventing eating rituals, such as only eating in the same spot or with a certain spoon.

FACT

Eating well, being active and being happier with yourself See Chapter 5, Food; Chapter 6, Move; and Chapter 4, Body Image, for related stuff and how to be fitter, have fun with food, and make friends with your body.

Other warning signs that someone has an eating disorder can be:
- weight changes
- fainting, tummy pain or headaches
- mood swings
- increased anxiety, depression, sadness or crankiness
- intense shame about their body image (often they wear baggy clothes to cover up), or guilt after eating
- involvement in elite athletics, ballet, gymnastics, modelling or another pursuit that focuses on body shape, weight or size
- they're a celebrity or a person who is constantly examined or commented on.

The two biggest risk factors for an eating disorder are low self-esteem and dieting. Disordered eating can start with a confidence problem, and be triggered by harsh self-criticism or unkind comments by somebody else – often a family member – about body shape or size. Girls don't usually choose to develop an eating disorder, but choosing to go on diets, restricting foods, making rules about eating or rigidly controlling food intake does make a disorder much more likely to develop.

The most common eating disorder Known as 'Eating Disorder Not Otherwise Specified', the most common eating disorder is a level of odd behaviour that includes some or many of the signs just listed, but is not full-on anorexia, bulimia or binge-eating (all explained below), although it might include a milder form of one of them, such as repeated dieting.

These dieting and food obsessions can be seen by some friendship groups and families as normal, but they are not normal and not healthy.

Anorexia nervosa

This is one of the most visible eating disorders because the person with anorexia eats as little as possible and often becomes very thin, haggard and bony. Eventually they look and are very, very sick. Anorexia often begins in the early to mid teens. People with the disorder usually have a very disturbed body image, seeing themselves as 'fat' even when dangerously underweight.

> We're doing eating disorders in school and sometimes I wish I could just lose that much weight and look like a model. Eleanor, 14, Paddington, NSW

At any weight anorexia causes severe sadness, self-loathing and an obsession with food and sometimes over-exercise. Signs of anorexia, apart from weight loss, are usually not obvious, but can include:

- tiredness
- dizziness when the person stands up
- stomach pain and headaches
- stopped periods.

Long-term effects can include:

- stunted growth
- an inability to become pregnant
- easily broken bones
- heart or other organ failure.

> If you see someone you know losing weight really fast do something about it before it is too late. Don't tell them they look good. Tell them they are unhealthy and will get very sick and tell someone who you can trust. It is a mental disease, not something to tease them about or to join in on.
> Lisa, 17, Bilgola Plateau, NSW

Few people with anorexia actually die from it, and the majority can recover when they get help (see 'Treatment for Eating Disorders' coming up soon). But most people with anorexia won't seek help themselves – it takes intervention from family and friends to move somebody towards treatment and recovery. Parents and friends will need to guard against online sites (and 'friends') that encourage the illness.

FACT

Not a 'girls only' problem There's so much publicity about eating disorders and young actresses that lots of people think only girls develop this problem, but guys and older women can too.

Bulimia nervosa

Bulimia nervosa is more common than anorexia nervosa, and also more hidden. Often it begins in the late teens or early twenties.

Bulimia is a cycle of binge-eating (eating a lot more than the person needs), guilt and purging. Girls who develop it often have a history of dieting or restricting their food. Eventually they give in to cravings and eat what they think of as 'bad' food – usually lots of it.

They then feel ashamed of 'losing control' and worried about gaining weight, so they try to get rid of the food by purging.

Purging efforts can include vomiting, over-exercising, fasting (not eating) and taking laxatives. None of these methods really works because the body has already taken in at least half of what it needs from the food before vomiting or pooing happens. Fasting as self-punishment just means the hunger will eventually tip into another binge.

As well as the feelings of shame and being trapped, bulimia can cause:
- stomach and bowel problems
- damaged teeth (because vomiting carries stomach acids into the mouth)
- dangerous heart problems.

Binge-eating disorder

Binge-eating disorder is similar to bulimia. The difference is that people with binge-eating disorder don't try to purge the food and are often above a healthy weight. Bingeing becomes a way of dealing with their negative or difficult emotions. They often eat alone and feel ashamed of the amount they've had and of feeling out of control.

But the good news is that many, many girls recover from bulimia, with help.

Treatment for eating disorders

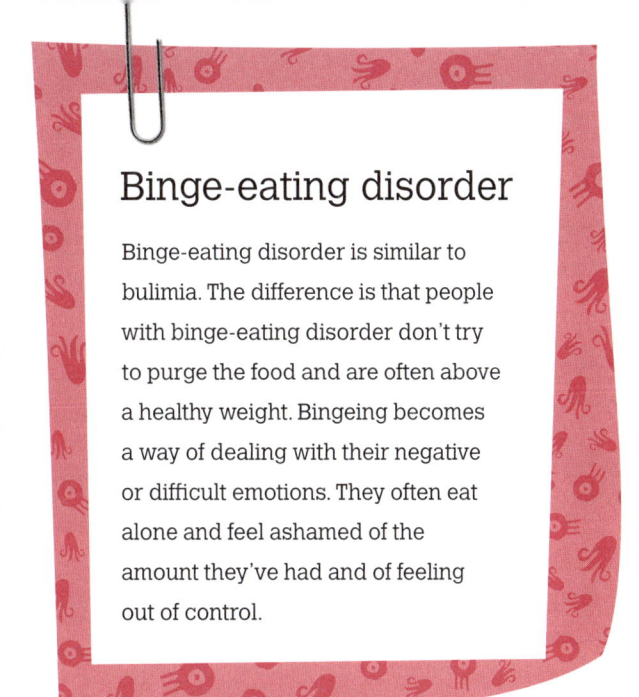

People with an eating disorder need to be treated by a specialist doctor with experience in the area. The ones with the best chance of recovering are those who ask for help or are given help as early as possible – but part of the mental illness is that the sick person may not want treatment.

If you have an eating disorder The most important thing to understand is that you can recover – but not by yourself. First, speak to a trusted adult.

Here are some steps to recovery.
- Ask your local doctor for a referral to a specialist in eating disorders, if that's possible. You may have combined help from a psychiatrist or a psychologist, a dietician, and a specialist eating-behaviours counsellor. The help will usually be regular and ongoing, and may include attending special programs such as individual or group therapy. >

Helping someone with an eating disorder

If some of these warning signs remind you of a friend or family member, ask the person whether they would like some help or information. Eating disorders support groups all have info and advice on how to approach a friend or relative you think may have a problem with eating (see 'More Info' opposite).

- Contact an eating disorders support group or foundation for help. It's a great place to start to talk with people who are going through the same thing (or have already been through it), so they can understand and support you while you decide what you're going to do, and afterwards. (To contact one see 'More Info' opposite.)
- Short-term medicine may be prescribed to help change your feelings of depression or to correct chemical imbalances or protein, vitamin and mineral deficiencies.
- You may need a short stay in hospital for treatment if you are very sick.

Recovering from an eating disorder is often a long and hard road, but there's a much calmer place at the end of it, where people can declare a truce in the war against their body and find a way not to think about food all the time.

> I learnt the hard way that the only person my weight matters to should be me.
> I was anorexic. Zara, 16, Newcastle, NSW

> My friend became anorexic on a diet. I hate diets. Anna, 15, St Kilda, Vic.

More info on eating disorders

thebutterflyfoundation.org.au
Info, links and news for girls and families. Lots of practical and emotional help by experts and people who've been through it.

eatingdisorders.org.au
Fact sheets about support groups for all states and territories, and interstate contacts. Run by Eating Disorders Victoria. Phone: (03) 9885 0318; country callers: 1300 550 236 or email edv@eatingdisorders.org.au.

ed.org.nz
Helpline: (09) 5222 679
The Eating Disorders Association of NZ has links and advice.

I first started myself out on a low-calorie diet. But things just declined from there. I became extremely obsessed with losing weight and eating less/losing extra weight by the day. I was admitted to hospital 6 times in the matter of a year and a half. I'm still struggling today. Don't make the mistake I did.
Jade, 18, Ipswich, Qld

I am recovering from an eating disorder which is a very difficult road. It has been tricky because it did not spawn from any perception of myself as 'fat' or 'overweight'. I think it has been more about control and a fear of growing up, for me. Mia, 18, Isaacs, ACT

I've had Bulimia for about 3 years and even though I am aware of this and understand that it's a sickness and everything, I do not want to change it. I am terrified of getting fat and even though I'm at my healthy weight I'd still like to lose more. Eve, 17, Broadbeach, Qld

Suicide

Lots of teenagers think about what it might be like if they were dead, but most of them won't try to kill themselves.

Most people who commit suicide believe, always wrongly, that they are doing the best thing. If teenagers die they never find out how great the future could have been, or how devastated family and friends are by their death – how haunted they are by guilt and sadness, sometimes for the rest of their lives. Lots of people think about committing suicide but don't carry it out, and are happy later that they didn't.

Suicide is never the right answer.

Worried about a friend or family member?

If you are worried that a friend or family member might try to commit suicide tell a calm, sensible adult you trust. Your friend or family member may insist you don't tell anybody, but it's more important to help save their life than keep a secret. You can also ring a helpline for advice (see 'More Info' opposite).

If you're having suicidal thoughts

You need to know that the thoughts:
- are a sign that your mind is not quite right at the moment, even though the thoughts seem logical to you
- can be caused by sleep deprivation
- are just thoughts – they don't mean you have to act them out
- won't go away with drugs and alcohol – these usually make them worse
- can be changed and won't always be there, even if you have them again, or a few times, or for a while. It may not seem that way, but you *can* be happy again.

Getting help

You have lots of options.
- Talk about your thoughts with someone. If they dismiss them, talk to somebody else. School counsellors, doctors, nurses and helpline staff are experienced in talking about this stuff.

- Promise yourself you'll never do anything at night to harm yourself, but instead will wait for the next day and talk it over with somebody: problems always seem harder at night.
- To get you through a bad night, call a friend, listen to music that's optimistic, or ring a 24-hour helpline (see 'More Info' below).
- Talk to your GP or community health centre staff, who will know how to help you find ways to get to a happier place in your mind. Your doctor can refer you to a psychologist or a psychiatrist.
- Try coping strategies, which can include making a list of things you can distract yourself with when you have suicidal thoughts; writing your thoughts and feelings down; setting small day-to-day goals that you can manage; and removing access to any dangerous items such as weapons or drugs.
- Read this book's section on Depression (earlier in this chapter), Grief, and Optimism (in Chapter 9, Feelings) and self-help tips under Good Mental Health (earlier in this chapter).

More info on suicide

Kids Helpline: 1800 55 1800
kidshelpline.com.au
Free counselling and help.

Lifeline: 13 11 14
More free 24-hour counselling.

Suicide Call Back Service: 1300 659 467
24-hour helpline.
Free, immediate counselling, with further sessions available.

After Suicide by Dr Sheila Clark
This Australian book explores the feelings and questions of the family and friends left behind.

LifeLine: 0800 543 354
lifeline.co.nz
Kiwi counselling service.

Youthline: 0800 376 633
youthline.co.nz
Counselling for teens. You can also email talk@youthline.co.nz or text 234.

My friend is really depressed and he says that he wants to do things to hurt himself – this worries me a lot! Millie, 13, Gympie, Qld

A friend of mine told me she was going to kill herself then told me to keep it quiet. I told an adult at school and then my friend found out and said if she ever killed herself it would be my fault. I felt terrible but I would rather have a friend who hated me but was alive than a friend who still liked me and was dead. Toni, 17, Hampton, Vic.

Psychosis and schizophrenia

Psychosis (pronounced si-koh-sis) is a severe form of mental illness caused by a brain chemical imbalance that mucks up a person's thoughts and causes them to be unable to tell reality from what's only happening in their mind. The most common time for the first 'psychotic episode' to happen is in the late teens or early twenties, most often after a period of severe stress or using drugs, including cannabis (weed), speed, ice and ecstasy. Schizophrenia (pronounced skitz-oh-freen-ee-a) is the most common psychotic illness.

Warning signs of psychosis

Psychotic symptoms can appear slowly and usually build up to a psychotic episode.
- The person's ideas and conversations become stranger as time goes by.
- During an episode a person with schizophrenia can see or hear things that aren't really there. They might try to make sense of it by thinking the voices are coming from a TV, or that another person is projecting or intercepting their thoughts. Other hallucinations can involve smell or visions. (Schizophrenia doesn't mean 'split personality'.)
- Many people with schizophrenia also have delusions of being very important or having secret knowledge. Or they're afraid that someone or unseen forces are trying to hurt them. The delusions seem utterly real to the person having them.

Other signs can include:
- a habit of pacing (walking back and forth)
- complete withdrawal from family and friends
- neglecting to wash or clean themselves
- unusual sleeping patterns, such as sleeping in the day and being awake at night.

FACT

Mental illness 'treatments' Some people think severe mental illness can be 'cured' by vitamins, a healthy lifestyle, 'willpower' or religious exorcism. It can't be. It must be treated by a psychiatrist.

Treatment for psychosis

Somebody with symptoms of psychosis needs help quickly. Treatments are much better now than they used to be, and most people can recover well when they find the right treatment and support.

- Many people with schizophrenia manage their condition by recognising their need to take the right medication, and take advantage of community services and rehabilitation programs. (Sadly sometimes a symptom of the illness can be rejecting the need for medication.)
- Most people who have schizophrenia can learn to prevent psychotic episodes by avoiding their likely triggers (these include most illegal drugs, alcohol and stress). Many people with schizophrenia have 'normal' family and work lives, like anybody else. Statistically, someone with schizophrenia is far less likely to hurt someone else than themselves, as part of their illness.
- Sometimes a hospital stay is needed while the right drug combination is tested. There's no 'magic' pill or pills for everyone.

More info on psychosis and schizophrenia

See 'More Info on Mental Health Problems' earlier, especially sane.org.

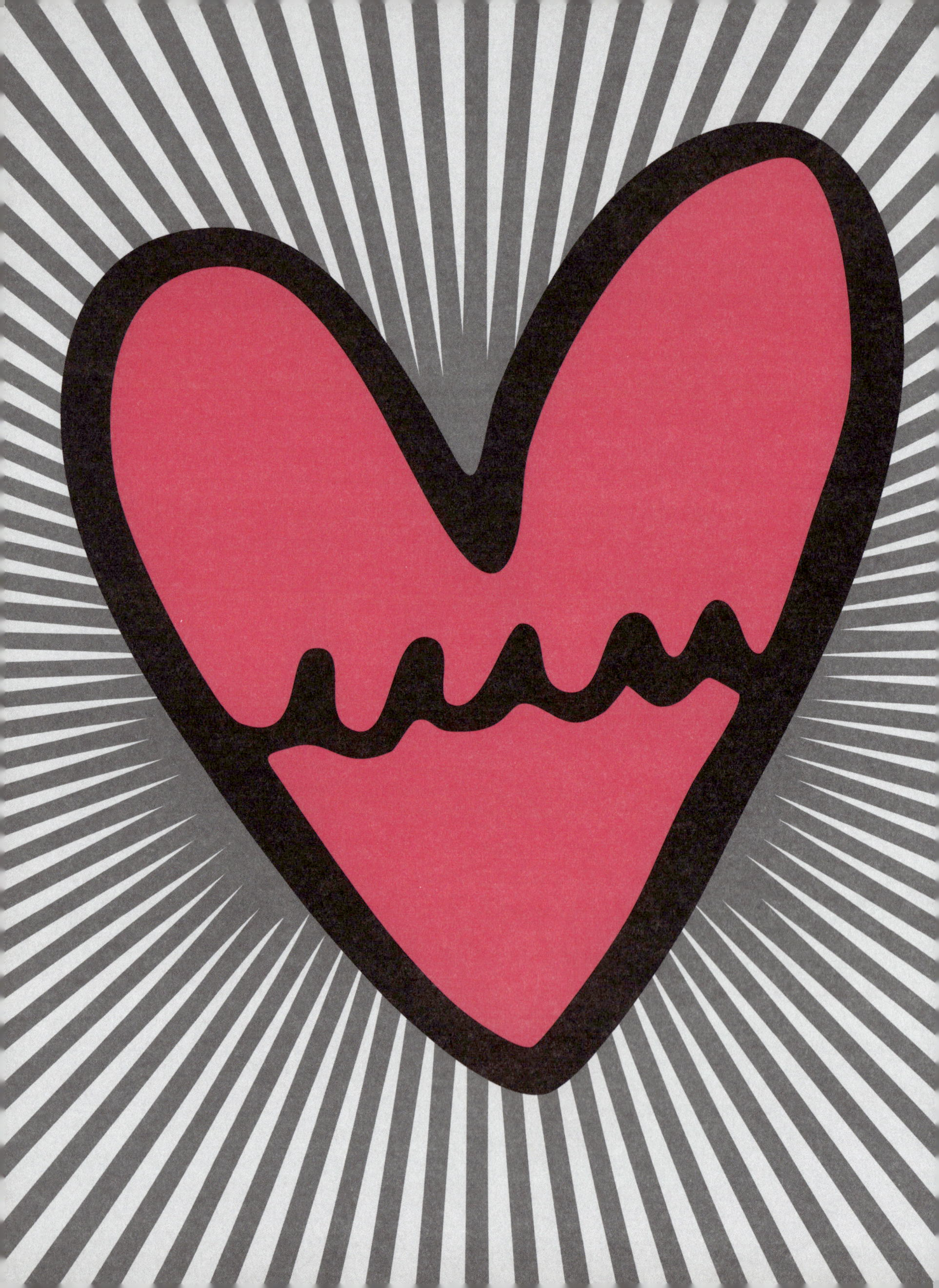

PART 3
HEART

- **13** **FAMILY** Getting on and moving on — 273
- **14** **FRIENDS** Good ones, bad ones, and downright enemies — 296
- **15** **LOVE** When it's real, what's the deal — 331
- **16** **SEX** What goes on, how you feel, and why — 359
- **17** **PREGNANCY** What to do and where to go — 402

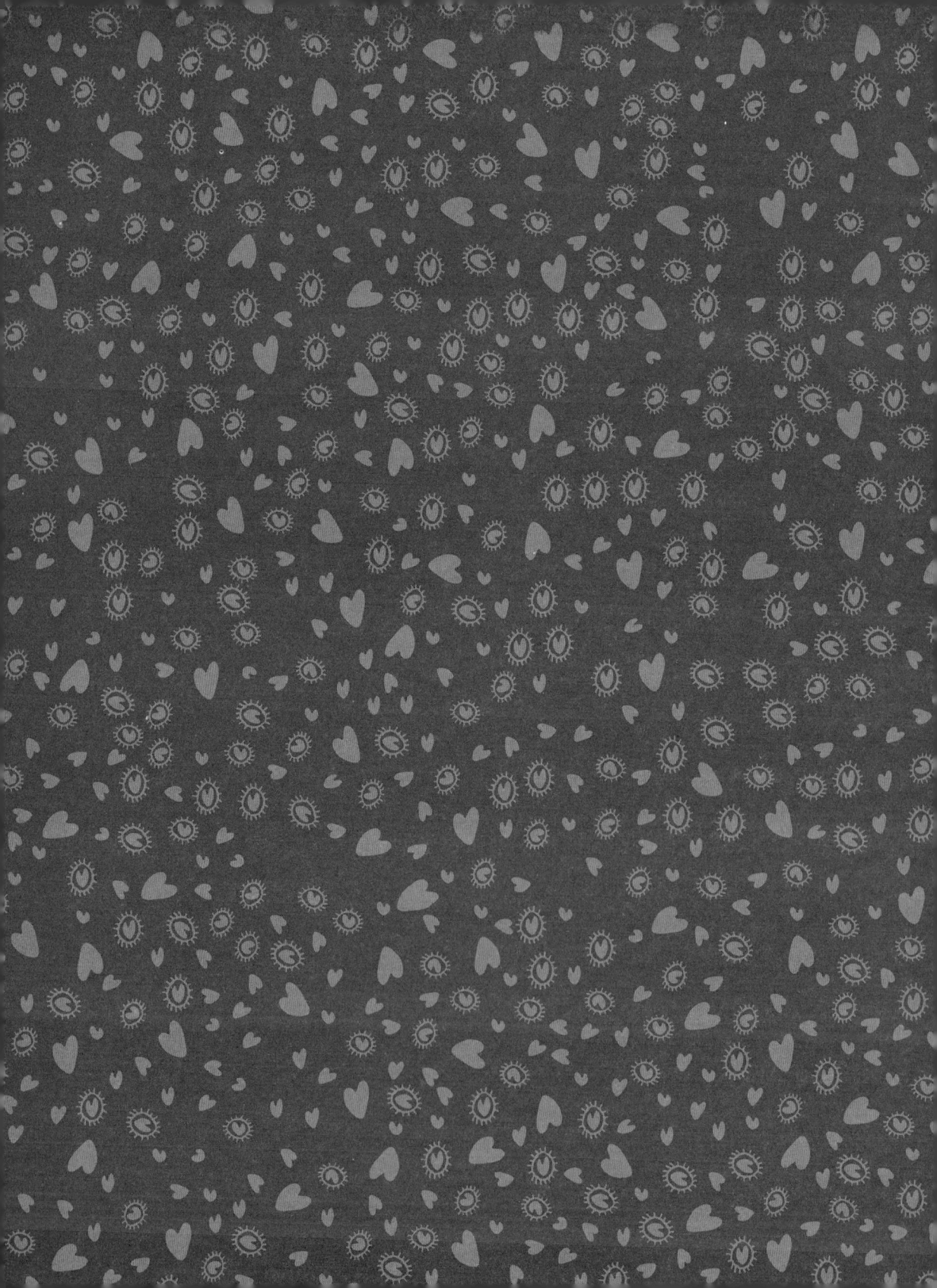

FAMILY

13

there are many kinds of family...

Some families are happy havens where you go when you need help and cuddles. Others are sad or bad, and you spend most of your time trying to avoid them.

When you're little you think that **all families** are the same – that all parents do what yours do, and that all families eat the same food and have the same problems. As you grow up you start to realise that families can be very different, and that your parents may not be as smart as you thought – or as stupid.

Happy families

Happy families seem to share some of the same elements. Not every family can achieve these, but working towards them can make family life happier.

In a happy family people tend to:
- love each other and show it
- like and respect each other
- communicate honestly and openly with each other
- spend time together
- solve problems together
- get through bad times together
- not have serious stresses such as mental or physical illness, drug or alcohol abuse, war or a history of distressing events
- have an okay financial situation so that they are not worrying about money all the time – this is not necessarily about how much money a family has, but its attitude to money
- be willing to find ways to get on better together.

> We've had some great and awful times. But we've always pulled through them together. No matter what happens I know they'll be there for me. I love them.
>
> Cassie, 13,
> Narre Warren, Vic.

Getting on with a parent

If you get on with a parent everything is easier. Letting them know you well is an important part of this. Tell them what you think about, what your hopes and worries are. Tell them when you find something difficult, when you're trying your best, when you are happiest. And tell them that you want them to be proud of you.

Try to be honest. If you let them know how you feel they won't have to guess (and maybe get it wrong): 'I guess I feel angry because I really, really wanted to go.' Let them know that when they start panicking or yelling as soon as you tell them worrying stuff (such as someone offered you drugs) it makes you feel you don't want to tell them anything.

You don't have to tell a parent everything – you are entitled to your privacy and thoughts – but it will help you to get on better if they know how you think and feel.

It also helps if you make an effort to understand where *they*'re coming from (which can be hard to do if your parent or parents are away from home a lot or otherwise busy or distracted).

How to get to know a parent

- Offer to team up with them for a walk some days, before or after their work. It will give you a chance to chat.
- Help to get the evening meal, and sit down together to eat it.
- Take the time to get to know the parent you spend less time with (even if you have to do this by message, emailing or texting).
- Go on family outings and holidays (you can trade these off for other occasions when you want to do something else).
- Show support by offering to help them with extra chores when they're going through a rough time.
- Go to their work or to sporting events if they want you to: this makes it more likely they'll return the favour when you need it.
- Let them know that you appreciate what they do for the family and that you're proud of *them*.
- Accept apologies from them as you would want them to accept yours. You're old enough to know that your parents aren't perfect: they make mistakes and can handle things the wrong way.

> I can talk to my mum about anything and I know she won't judge me.
> Hailley, 17,
> Devonport, Tas.

When a parent isn't there for you

- Ask for their attention, in a nice way. Try a suggestion like, 'Mum/Dad, can we do something together soon, such as make a cake/see a movie/play Frisbee?'
- Explain that you understand they're very busy, but you don't want to turn into one of those kids who only get attention when they do the wrong thing. That'll scare 'em.
- If they're busy, or in the middle of a temporary project, ask to make an appointment with them for an activity or a talk later on and stick to it.
- If they're always busy, ask them when they think that might change, or what you could do to help change it.
- Wait for the right moment to talk to them. Don't interrupt them when they're on the phone or in the middle of something else (including an intersection).
- Learn a few parent-friendly phrases such as 'I'd really like your advice', or 'I think you could help me with this', or 'Can I come with you and help?'
- Try a regular 'appointment' with a parent – such as Sunday brunch or a Friday-night walk.

Conversation starters with a parent

Ask them:

- what they loved when they were your age
- what naughty things they did as teenagers
- whether their life turned out the way they thought it would
- what makes them happy
- what makes them sad
- what they'd like to accomplish in life
- what their ideal holiday would be
- what they have to do at work and whether they like it.

Dads shouldn't make stupid comments about their daughters' looks. It affects them and families should remember to tell each other you love each other and that you are proud of each other.

Gabriella, 18,
Strathfield, NSW

Family rules

Most families have rules about safety, schoolwork and responsibilities, and ones to avoid fights and to let kids know how to behave. A lot of people think the rules are the same for all families, but they're not. One girl who wrote to the Girl Stuff Survey was amazed somebody had even asked what her family's rules were: 'Duh, the usual rules – no horses in the house.' This will come as news to folk who never thought of popping a pony in the pantry.

family RULES
1. no undies on heads
2. feed the ferret

It seems to some teenagers that their families are nothing but rules, with laws laid down on even what opinions they're supposed to have. (And if parents live apart there may be a different set of rules in each house.) Others think their family has hardly any rules at all, leaving them to find their own way to adulthood with not much more than a can opener and a couple of pairs of socks provided.

Negotiating family rules If you want a clearer understanding of the rules that seem to be operating at home, or you'd like fewer rules or some input into them, ask if the family can have a meeting.

- Ask your parents to write down the important rules – or perhaps you can do it together.
- Ask politely for the reasons behind the rules ('Could you please explain why my brother is allowed to do something, but I can't?'), and show that you appreciate some of their concerns: 'I understand that you're trying to protect me.'
- Ask them to explain what will happen if you break the rules: 'Will I be grounded, or yelled at, or what? And will the consequences be the same if I break the rule accidentally?'
- Ask if any of the rules have exceptions or are open to interpretation. (To you 'Keep your room tidy' may mean you know where everything is. To them it may mean there has to be nothing left on the floor.)
- Tell them if you don't think a certain rule is fair and why: 'I think this rule is fair, but that one doesn't seem to be because [*give reason*]', 'I'm feeling frustrated because none of my friends has that rule in their family.' >

Common family rules
- No hitting.
- No disrespectful talk or swearing.
- Everyone must sit down together for the evening meal.
- No going out wearing a skirt smaller than a packet of chips.
- No TV until homework is done.
- Everyone except the adults must keep their room tidy.
- No wet towels to be left on the floor.
- Kids must bring their dirty clothes to the laundry and put them in the washing basket.
- Half an hour of phone time a night.
- Parents should always know where the kids are.
- No alcohol before 18.
- Kids must not take illegal drugs.
- Kids must be home before dark or call to say they are in a place the parents are happy with.
- Kids will be grounded when they lie.
- Kids must do chores for their pocket money.
- Kids must pay for their own mobile phone calls.
- Kids must be in bed by a set time but can then read for half an hour or an hour.
- No stealing Nanna's wig.

> I'm shocked to see how different my friends' families are to mine. Usually the kids get whatever they want, yet have no close relationship with their parents and just think of them as a free meal. It makes me really value my own family.
> Phoebe, 14, Glossodia, NSW

> Mum and Dad work 24/7 so I have to cook tea and look after my sister and I hate it.
> Erin, 14, East Malvern, Vic.

> My parents give my younger brother privileges I wasn't allowed at his age.
> Laura, 17, Wentworth, NSW

If you feel a rule is too strict or unfair, but your parents won't change it, perhaps there is a relative, a teacher or one of your parents' friends who could talk to them about loosening up a little (with or without you being there).

FACT **You can change the rules** See Chapter 8, Confidence, for more on how parents and kids can get together to change family rules as you get older.

> I had no rules. My mum never asked me where I was or what I was doing.
> I could disappear for days and walk home in the middle of the night.
> It was like she just didn't care what happened to me.
> Jessica, 17, Torrens Park, SA

Brothers and sisters

How you get on with your siblings (brothers and sisters) can depend on your ages; personalities; whether one needs more health care than the others; and whether you are seen as equal and individual (you may not be treated the same, but you can be treated with equal fairness and love).

Good things about brothers and sisters

- They understand where you are coming from.
- They can be an ally against your parents.
- They can be loyal friends when you need them.
- They can give you a feeling of belonging.
- You can share lots of secrets and memories.
- Younger ones look up to you.
- Older ones do some of the hard work with your parents on gaining freedoms before you have to.
- You don't usually stay mad with each other for long.

Annoying stuff about brothers and sisters

- They can seem the favourite.
- You may have a personality clash.
- They may take your stuff.
- They're in 'your' space (or face).
- People assume you're the same.
- People expect you to 'follow in the footsteps' of an older one.
- People expect you to take responsibility for the actions of a younger one.
- People assume because of your position in the family you'll have a certain personality.

Training parents

You can train parents to treat you more like a grown-up (actually some grown-ups are totally dippy). If you build up trust over time and show you can be honest and look after yourself, in most cases they'll let you have more independence. See Chapter 8, Confidence for lots of ways to look after yourself, so you can discuss them with your parents. This will make you sound – and be – more prepared for any difficult or dangerous situations they imagine you might end up in. This is how you get the rules changed as you get older.

I used your lipgloss

SIBLING CRISIS

> I absolutely ADORE my little brother.   Jade, 15, Centenary, Qld

> My mum expects me to be as good as my sisters.   Madison, 15, Sydney, NSW

What girls say are the strict rules in their family

Mum won't let me out at parties unless she calls the parents first ✱ **every day 24/7 we must show respect to our older relatives, and rebellion is as bad as murder** ✱ if a boy sleeps over they cannot sleep in the same bed ✱ sensible actions. Think ✱ no dog upstairs, no games before homework, no out on the streets after dark ✱ don't wag or get pissed ✱ no chat rooms ✱ I am not allowed to shave my legs or buy *Dolly* magazine ✱ **I can't have a boyfriend** ✱ I have curfew for the phone: 8 pm ✱ my dad is in charge – don't annoy him ✱ not allowed to tell any one we are on the dole ✱ I can't date, go to parties where there are boys, sleep over at friends' houses, wear miniskirts or low-cut tops ✱ **no slamming doors, no saying shut up** ✱ nothing with preservatives to eat ✱ don't eat meat ✱ no parties!!!!! It is the WORST rule! And no make-up ✱ not allowed on the net during the week ✱ **can't go out on school nights** ✱ no mobiles till you're 18, can't leave church till you're 18, no dating till you're 16, can't leave home till 18, can't dye your hair till 18 ✱ I have to do maths for one hour every day ✱ call if you are running late home ✱ always tell Mum where I'm going and when I'll be back and who I'm going with ✱ **no kissing the rat too much and no tormenting the rat** ✱ no cat on the table ✱ don't go in cars with drink drivers, or friends with their learner or restricted licence. No drugs, drinking ✱ whenever Dad makes up rules he forgets them a week later. Ha ha ✱ **NO BOYS IN THE BED (except when my parents don't know and they are SLEEEEEEPING!)** ✱ my parents have a lot of faith in my brother and me. We do what we think is right, and if it isn't they put us back on the right path ✱ **my mother just says no to everything** ✱ to tell my mum if I have sex ✱ no wearing heels with a miniskirt ✱ my parents say if there are no parents where I'm going, or they can't speak to them beforehand, then I CANNOT GO. They are good about most other things but usually places I go are unsupervised so it means a lot of sneaking around them and lying! ✱ **I'm only allowed to take two alcoholic drinks with me to parties** ✱ don't dress like a man, don't have short hair, don't discuss Muslims, Christians, the economy, feminism, gay rights. Don't speak to Dad unless you're spoken to, don't talk back to Dad, don't disagree with Dad. No parties, no short clothes, no boyfriends or boy friends (girlfriends for boys okay) ✱ we have no rules.

Not-so-happy families

Every family has its tensions, its secrets, its roles for each member (the clown, the peacemaker, the naughty one), and some families are dysfunctional (don't work properly) and full of tension and strife. Many families, though, can learn how to turn fights and arguments between generations, or between siblings, into (reasonably!) calm discussions.

Taking the heat out of arguments

Perhaps your family can agree to a few guidelines that will help calm a disagreement. Here are some examples.

- Anyone can make an appointment to discuss something with another family member or call a family meeting.
- No interrupting. Everyone waits their turn to speak and listens respectfully.
- Nobody is allowed to end a discussion without hearing everything the others want to say – but a discussion can be suspended until everyone has calmed down.
- No shouting or insults.
- No physical hostilities.
- No pouting, sulking, flouncing, theatrical sighing or slamming of doors.
- Discussions must be conducted without sarcasm, mimicry or other meanness.

If it feels as if a discussion is getting off track, try to get the family to refer to this plan: somebody raises a problem, then everyone talks about their ideas on how to solve it and the possible drawbacks they see to each solution, and finally everyone agrees on a solution.

Maybe you have a parent who is stressed

> My mother and I don't talk and haven't for nearly a year.
> Nic, 17,
> Kambah, ACT

> My parents aren't around much.
> Alana, 14,
> Prestons, NSW

Tension breakers for yourself (and other family members)
- Scream into a pillow.
- Do something that makes you laugh.
- Have a bath.
- Go for a walk.
- Dance madly in your room for 15 minutes.

Conflict between partners

All partners have arguments (even if they try to keep them from you). It's a natural part of a relationship and doesn't necessarily mean they're going to break up. But it can be horrible for you to hear arguments, especially if they sound mean or they're violent.

If the fighting does upset you, try explaining to the grown-ups (when they're not fighting) how it makes you feel. Ask them to make an effort to argue when you are not around.

Sometimes the fights involve the children of the family as well. When conflicts never get resolved, family counselling services can help. Many talking therapists (counsellors) specialise in getting families together and helping them to find solutions to their problems and better ways of listening to each other.

Step 1: get a pillow
Step 2: scream into it

When parents are hopeless

Not everyone has kind, generous or useful parents. Some parents do not know how to properly look after and care for their children – or even how to show love. Many parents themselves were brought up in sad, cold, abusive or violent homes, and some don't know how to change. If you need to avoid home, try to find another family that you can go to for relief and to see people relating in healthier ways.

It can be comforting to know that lots of people who have been brought up in a bad home situation eventually form new 'families' with groups of friends. You may not have met yours yet, but one day you'll be out of there and off to find them.

In the meantime you can get advice on how your family life might improve by calling the Kids Helpline (see 'More Info' coming up soon). Call it if you or your brothers and sisters don't feel safe, or you're very worried.

> My dad makes me sad. He doesn't realise how much what he says affects me. I've tried to tell him, but he chooses not to hear it. Bethany, 17, Oregon, US

Dumb things to say in an argument

The following statements will either make a parent (and anyone else) even more furious, or will make you seem like a little kid who can't argue on a grown-up level.

'That's not fair', 'You're so unfair.'

'You hate me.'

'I hate you.'

'You never let me have any fun.'

'Piss off.'

'You suck.'

'You don't have a clue.'

'You're trying to ruin my life.'

'It's different since you were a kid.'

'Everyone else is going.'

'You are so.'

'Shut up.'

'You can't make me.'

'Anyway, nerny ner ner.'

'What would *you* know?'

'I *said* sorry.' (That doesn't suddenly make it okay.)

'That haircut makes you look like a baboon's arse.'

Unhelpful 'body language'

Also avoid body language that could make a parent (or anyone else) even crosser. (It may be entertaining, but it won't help you get what you want.) Try to steer clear of:

* 'closed poses' such as crossing your arms, lying rolled into a ball, turning your back, refusing to make eye contact, shrugging, turning your body away

* grunts instead of replies (which are so Neanderthal and non-verbal as to be almost body language)

* aggressive or hostile poses such as standing too close to someone, or looming over them if they're sitting down; clenching your fists; making violent movements; putting your hands on your hips; or staring in a challenging or angry way.

UNHELPFUL BODY LANGUAGE

Useful things to say in an argument

Get yourself an advantage by sounding responsible and smart, and able to listen and take in what a family member is trying to say. Something like these will help:

'I disagree, but I don't think it's worth fighting over so we'll do it your way.' (Save your energy for an argument you really want to win.)

'Let me get this right: what you mean is . . .'

'What are you feeling?'

'Are you angry, or worried, or both?'

'I didn't know that's how you felt.'

'I hear you.'

'I never thought about it that way.'

'Can we talk about this later after I've thought about what you've said?'

'Could we please sit down and talk about this because I'm confused.'

'Let's talk later when we're not upset. Maybe after school?'

'Is it my turn to speak now?'

'I'm sorry.'

'Can we try and work it out together?'

Family abuse Family abuse can include emotional, physical or sexual abuse. Some families are so dysfunctional that almost everyone abuses everyone else, although of course the children are always the most vulnerable. Abuse can be by a dad, mum, brother or sister, or a relative from outside the home. The person being abused can be a child, a parent or a grandparent.

Abuse is wrong and never the fault of the person being abused, even though it can feel that way.

My family is very broken. It's hard. I think it's had a great effect on me and my sis and bro. All I can say to others out there is, keep ur friends close, they're the ones that are gonna help u thru it all.
Lila, 15, Chatswood, NSW

More info on not-so-happy families

Kids Helpline: 1800 55 1800

au.reachout.com
A website for young people going through tough times.

relationships.org.au
Relationships Australia runs courses for kids and parents and can refer the family or the adults for counselling.

frsa.org.au
The Family & Relationship Services Australia site has links to communication courses and counselling.

theinsite.org
Relationships Unlimited US. Choose Relationships Unlimited, then Parents, or Sibs, or whatever else you're interested in.

I think we have the funniest moments together, especially when we go on holidays, camping. Hannah, 13, Epping, NSW

My mum is a judgemental person, so I don't feel comfortable sharing personal details with her, as much as she'd like me to. Cassandra, 16, Darwin, NT

Families are freaky, weird things! Everyone thinks only their families are the most dysfunctional, but there's always one out there that tops you ... And there's no such thing as a perfect or totally happy family, even if it seems that everybody else's family is more together than yours. Heather, 16, Northcote, Vic.

I hate the thought of moving away from my mother even though I know it is a normal thing to do. Amelia, 18, Brisbane, Qld

I can always rely on Mum to understand me, and Dad to give me stuff. Natasha, 13, Blackburn, Vic.

My mum acts like she doesn't even like me sometimes, and she acts like I do and say everything wrong. Tess, 13, Devonport, Tas.

Family abuse

In a family the abuse might be against a partner, the kids or the whole family. Physical abuse is often called domestic violence and, because it involves physical threats or injury, often with shouting and loud noises, it is the abuse most often spotted by outsiders. But emotional abuse can also be used in a family; for example, a mum might be controlled by the fear of her child being hurt, or a child controlled by the fear of their mum being hurt.

Sexual abuse of children and teenagers also occurs within some families. The abuser can be a parent, a parent's partner, an uncle or grandparent, a sibling or another relative (or a teacher, coach, religious leader or some other adult trusted by the family), who might:

- do things to the child or teenager's private parts, or make them do something to the abuser
- look at their private parts in a sexual way
- insist they look at pictures (on a computer, TV or somewhere else) that seem wrong and make them feel uncomfortable
- do or say something else that feels wrong or creepy
- make the child or teenager touch them sexually or have some kind of sex with them.

The abuser might say things such as 'It's normal', 'Don't tell anyone', and 'It's our secret.' Often they might threaten to hurt the kid (or somebody else), or to shame them if they tell anyone what's going on. Or the abuser might say that nobody will believe the kid if they tell. But there are people who can help you and make the abuse stop.

If you are being sexually abused you need to know that, no matter what they say:

- it's not your fault: it's never your fault
- it's against the law
- it's never normal or right
- and, no matter what they say, it's not your fault – by doing this to you they have betrayed your trust in them and that is very wrong
- you can get help and protection.

Sexual abuse can be confusing, especially when the person doing the abusing is someone you love or have been taught to obey. It doesn't happen because a person 'can't control their sexual urges', or because the way you look 'makes' them do it. You might feel guilty or ashamed, but you are not the person responsible for the wrong thing. The abuser knows what they are doing and has made a choice. You can get help and support to realise you don't need to be ashamed.

What to do about abuse in a family

It can be very hard to know what to do or who to trust after emotional, physical or sexual abuse. But you can go one step at a time, without anyone in the family finding out at first. In some families, people want to keep the abuse secret. You need to tell a trusted adult – perhaps another relative, a teacher or school nurse, a doctor, your friend's mum – or call a helpline. It is scary to take this step, but it's the first step to making it stop – and it must stop.

You can't fix this by yourself, but there are ways to make your life safe, and there are people who will help you: reach out to them.

More info on abusive families

One parent abusing the other is also a form of child abuse because they're not making the child's home a safe or happy place to be.

These places will help with emotional, violent or sexual abuse.

Kids Helpline: 1800 55 1800
Free 24-hour counselling and advice: you can call without giving your name.

burstingthebubble.com
Info, advice and links on what to do about violence and abuse in your family and how to help a friend.

reachout.com
For teens having a hard time.

🥝 **LifeLine: 0800 543 354**
Anybody of any age can call, 24 hours a day, for free advice and help.

Legal rights of children and young people

All kids and young people have human rights. Australia signed the United Nations' Convention on the Rights of the Child (CROC) way back in 1990, agreeing to its contents. The convention sets out and protects the rights of children up to the age of 18. Under it you have the right, among other things, to:

❋ freedom from economic and sexual exploitation

❋ have your own opinion

❋ education

❋ health care

❋ a safe place to live

❋ economic opportunity.

> I don't live at home because my dad assaulted me, so I live with my best friend's family.
> Alex, 16, Burra, SA

family ♥ HEART 287

When families break up

Lots of teenagers have parents who separate or divorce (the legal version of separation). Often the people separating are very sad, and sometimes also feel angry with each other, guilty about the break-up of the family and worried about the future. There might be another adult involved because one of the partners has started a new relationship, but sometimes the two people separating just don't want to be together any more.

Family breakdowns can happen really quickly, and you might have had no idea that anything was wrong before you were told. This can make it hard for you to understand why your parents want to separate, or make you believe that it isn't necessary, but usually adults have thought long and hard about it before they've decided.

Sometimes former partners stay friends, even taking holidays together as a family. Sometimes the parents don't like each other any more but, because they respect each other and their kids, they're always polite and never criticise each other in front of their children. But sometimes the conflict, hurt or anger between them is so strong that they say bad things about each other and continue to fight, or refuse to communicate.

And if the parents can't work out how to share the parenting there may be a case at the Family Court to decide on the custody arrangement, as it's called. Because the court's main aim is to do what's right for the kids, you may be asked to see a court worker, usually a trained counsellor, to talk about how the conflict is affecting you, and how you can divide your time between the two parents or which one you'd like to live with.

Talking it through

There are a lot of important things you'll want your parents to discuss with you about the separation. You can:

- ask them why they have agreed to stop living together – they may have decided not to discuss this because they're afraid it will upset you to talk about it, but you may want to hear the answers even if it is upsetting (have these conversations at a calm time, not when they're having an argument)
- say you prefer them not to go into the details of what they fight about, or what one 'did' to the other or didn't do

> My mum is my best friend and I never fight with my dad. Although my parents are divorced, I see my family life as more stable and healthy than a huge percentage of my friends' families whose parents are together.
> Alice, 17, Coburg, Vic.

- tell them you can't take sides
- make it clear you won't be the 'messenger' between them, or pass on info about what the other partner is up to
- ask them not to say anything negative about the other one when directly talking to you, or where you can hear it.

Speak up if you're not happy with the living arrangements they've decided on and you'd like to spend more or less time with a parent. You don't have to make a decision suddenly or quickly: you can just say how you'd like the arrangements to be for a month or longer, and then change them later.

Often after a separation or divorce one or both of the parents will have less money. One may give you presents and money to reassure you they still love you, but a parent who can't afford lots of presents still loves you.

Go easy on yourself as this isn't something you just get over immediately. Your parents are upset, and you're upset. You're not in control of the situation, and it's normal to feel angry and to grieve for what life used to be like (see Chapter 9, Feelings). It will take time to adjust to the new situation, and it can help to talk about how you feel.

Things to know about separation and divorce

- Separation or divorce is not caused by you, even if your parents sometimes argued about your behaviour. It's caused when adults don't want to be together any more, and that's never a kid's fault.
- You have a right to be upset about such a huge change in your life, which you did not ask for or cause.
- You shouldn't be asked by either parent to 'take sides'.
- You have a right to ask one of your parents not to criticise the other in front of you.
- Your parents are separating from, or divorcing, each other but they will always be your parents.
- You have a right to continue to see both parents, and both sets of grandparents, if you want to.

I get very upset about not seeing my dad.
Flick, 13, Doncaster, Vic.

I think my dad is a jerk and I don't really want anything to do with him. Rosie, 15, Frenchs Forest, NSW

The upside of separation

- Your parents will probably be happier apart.
- Your parents may be more honest with you.
- Your home life may not be so stressful.
- You may get a better understanding of your family and yourself (talking therapy can help).
- It can be a reminder that, no matter what the family goes through, your parents still love you.

More info on when families break up

All this info is helpful for parents who are separating or have separated. Ask one or both of your parents to get some of this info to help them – and you – through this tricky time.

familyrelationships.gov.au
Choose Publications, then download the booklet 'Children and Separation'.

A Step Up for Stepfamilies by Marcia Watts
A thoughtful guidebook on the practical and emotional issues of a blended family, by a mum and step-mum who's also a relationships counsellor. At stepfamilies.com.au.

justice.govt.nz/courts/family-court
Family Court of New Zealand. Choose Publications, then Pamphlets and Resources, then download 'Teenagers' Guide to Family Separation' or 'Teenagers' Guide to the Family Court'.

My parents divorced when I was 5, and what really shits me about society is how they think divorce is SO terrible. They rarely understand that in a lot of cases divorce is a very, very good choice to make. Alex, 16, Narraweena, NSW

I love my family. Even though it's small, it's great. My mum is a champion, and she does a wonderful job as a single parent. Emily, 15, Sandringham, Vic.

My parents fight all the time even though they don't live together any more. Sky, 13, Nambour, Qld

290   HEART ♥ family

Different family combos

There are nearly as many kinds of family as there are families.

Any of these combos can make a family

Mum and kid; dad and kid; mum and kids; dad and kids; mum and kid and 'weekend' dad; dad and kid and 'weekend' mum; mum and dad and kids; mum and step-dad and her kid; mum and step-dad and his kid; mum and step-dad and her kids; mum and step-dad and his kids; dad and step-mum and her kid; dad and step-mum and his kid; dad and step-mum and her kids; dad and step-mum and his kids; mum and dad and his kids and/or her kids and their kids together; mum and mum and kid; dad and dad and kid; mum and mum and the kids of both; dad and dad and the kids of both; mum and mum's boyfriend and her or his kids; dad and dad's girlfriend and his or her kids; mum and mum's girlfriend and kids; dad and dad's boyfriend and kids; nanna and grandkid; grandma and grandad and grandkids; kid living with an aunty or uncle; kid living in aunty's or uncle's family; kid and adult brother or sister; kids living with a friend of the family; kid living with their friend's family; mum and grandma and kid; mum and grandma and kids from different dads; dad and grandma and kid; mum and dad and pop and grandma and kids and Great-aunty Fanfaronada; mum or dad and kid or kids, with various other relatives and a bunny.

And I wouldn't be surprised if there was a family with a step-bunny.

FACT

Gay parents The main problem with having a gay parent is having to explain it about 96 573 times to people: 'Yes, Mum has a girlfriend. No [*sigh*], it doesn't seem weird to me' or 'Yes, two Dads'.

Sole-parent families

For some or all of your life you may have known or lived with only one parent. It may be because your other parent died or can't come to this country; but sometimes it may be because one parent decided from the start that they didn't want to be involved in a family, or they drifted away after a separation or divorce.

Some parents don't want to be in their kid's life. This is never the kid's fault. Some adults can't handle the responsibilities of bringing up children or never learnt how to make a good family. It's okay to be angry about feeling let down by one of your parents, but it helps to talk to someone about it. Be proud that you're part of a successful team with one parent.

Being adopted

Finding out suddenly that you're adopted can be confusing. It's usually easier when your adoptive family is open and honest about it from the start.

If you feel you want to find your birth parents you may decide to wait until you've left home because you don't know how to talk about it with your adoptive parents and don't want to hurt their feelings. Many people decide to wait until they're 18 to meet their birth parents.

The agencies that reunite you are not allowed to give your contact details to anyone searching for you until you give your permission.

Some reunions with birth parents are successful, and some aren't. There's a lot to think about, and no way to predict the outcome. You may want to have a continuing relationship, or you may just want to meet once.

'Partner parade'

When your parents are no longer together you can often have their temporary (or ongoing) new partners in your life.

Some parents have a series of partners who come, then go. A new partner can be very hard for you to accept, especially if you don't like the person; feel they're in your space or don't respect you; resent them taking your other parent's place; or fear they'll put you through another break-up.

You have a responsibility to be polite and to behave well towards new partners, but you also have the right to ask your parent:

- to keep the details of their love life, particularly their sex life, to themselves
- whether their partner is allowed to tell you what to do, or whether that's your parent's responsibility alone

> I don't like having two different houses to go to. Stella, 14

- for the privacy and space you need, and an assurance that you won't have to deal with a shared bathroom that doesn't have a lock on the door
- not to expect that you'll consider the partner your new parent or call them Mum, Dad, Aunty or Uncle. First names, used respectfully, are perfectly fine.

'Blended' or 'step' families

Most parents who separate will make new families straight away or within a few years by taking up with a new partner – and sometimes that partner has their own kids or will have a baby with your parent. So there'll be a 'blended' or 'step' family situation – with all kids living in the same house all the time or moving between their parents' houses.

Getting your head around the idea of a new family is a pretty big project, especially if it happens before you've absorbed the shock of your original family coming apart. Sometimes it's the upsetting point at which you really understand your own parents will never get back together.

Before you become part of a step-family You need to discuss with your parent the issues outlined in 'Partner Parade' opposite, and also talk about:
- what your parent expects of you
- who will tell your other parent about their ex's new relationship
- where each person will live
- what will happen if you don't like the new family members
- what will be the response if any of the new family members are mean to you
- who your parent will side with if you have a disagreement with their partner
- whether you will have to change school or house
- whether you will have to share a room with anyone
- whether you will have new responsibilities such as looking after younger step-siblings
- what will happen if this partnership breaks up too.

It can be heart-breaking when you finally realise that mum and dad are NOT getting back together. Lauren, 14, Brisbane, Qld

The ups and downs of step-families

Downside

* Your other parent might be jealous and angry about the new family and ask you questions or say mean things about it, or make you feel disloyal.

* It might be hard to adjust to a new family and/or a new house.

* You might feel you're missing out on your parent's attention as they try to make the new relationship work and welcome the other kids.

* You might feel left out, especially if there are more of 'their gang' than 'our gang'.

* You might have to share a bathroom with more kids, which is especially difficult if one is a guy who's the same age or older.

* It takes time to get used to your parent being affectionate to someone new.

* It's confusing if your parent is acting differently with this partner from the way they acted with the previous one.

* Try as you might, maybe you won't be able to like your parent's partner or their children.

* You might resent your new step-parent telling you what to do.

Upside

* There can now be more people in your family gang who will be loyal to you and look out for you.

* It can be fun to have 'new' brothers and sisters.

* Your parent will probably be happier and there is now someone else to love and look after them, which can take pressure off you.

* It can give you another opportunity for some happy family life.

* The cost sharing can mean there's a bit of extra money for fun things.

* You can share thoughts on the situation with step-siblings.

* Your new step-parent loves your parent so they will want this to work. With luck, they'll want to be your friend, while understanding they're not a replacement for your other parent.

* More presents!

You do have to be reasonable and you can't deliberately sabotage your parent's new relationship. Your parent will appreciate you making an effort to give it a go.

You also shouldn't 'spy' on the step-family for your other parent.

But you don't have to adjust to the idea of a new family the first time it's suggested. You need time to get used to the idea. And you do have rights that need to be respected, including the right to have any new rules or responsibilities explained.

You may even end up being connected to two new blended families, one with your mum and one with your dad, and find you've suddenly got a lot of instant step-relatives. (And if the new partners were to break up you'd end up with a lot of ex-step-relatives.) Don't even start on what happens at Christmas. But then Christmas can be a pretty full-on time for any family.

More info on step or blended families

If you're having trouble in a step-family, convince one of the adults to check this out:

relationships.org.au
Search Stem Family on the site of Australia's premier relationships support service.

stepfamily.org.au
A non-profit research, help and education hub. From the main page choose Parenting Help, Books, Tip Sheets or Research.

Since my elder brother moved out to live with my dad, I like the female energy mum and I have in our household. Denise, 17, Adelaide, SA

I don't think of them as my half brother or sisters but as normal brothers and sisters. Theresa, 14, Hamlyn Heights, Vic.

My dad had an affair. Mandy, 14, Melbourne, Vic.

I hate my dad's girlfriend. She makes me want to move out. I wish she'd die. Janice, 15, Hobart, Tas.

Mum has a boyfriend as well as a husband. Jaimie, 14, Rossmoyne, WA

My step-sisters are so much fun!
Alex, 14, Hurstville, NSW

I hated my step mum at first but then I realised she wasn't there to take my mum's place, she was there because she and my dad were happy. Mel, 14, Vermont, Vic.

FRIENDS

14

good friends can make you laugh 'til cry...

Some days life – and school – seems all about friends. Do you need a **best friend**? Are you in the right **group** of friends? How can you tell a real friend from a **frenemy**? How do you break up with a friend, make new ones, keep your phone and social website pages free of snark, triumph over a **bully**, or stop yourself from being the mean one? It's all here . . .

Good friends

Having friends can make life so much easier and more fun. It means laughing so much you nearly wet your pants (or you actually do wet your pants – but enough about me). It means hanging out together, and having secret codes and words that only you understand. It means writing songs or plays together, borrowing each other's stuff, going places together, being there to help each other through bad times, having someone you can blather on to about absolutely anything.

> I can rely on my best friends for everything. It doesn't matter if I make a total idiot of myself with them because I'm confident that they will always be there for me.
> Steph, 15, Melbourne, Vic.

It's about having a safe place to go, except that the safe place is a person or a group of people.

How to be a good friend

Good friends are reliably good company and share jokes and opinions – but easily tolerate or enjoy each other's differences. They make an effort to stay in touch. Good friends fall back into easy patterns of having fun and chatting when they've been apart.

Real friends will be sincere when they say sorry – and other good friends will forgive slip-ups. Being mean on purpose is something else: see the 'Meanness and Bullying' section later in this chapter for more on this.

Real friends are tactful and don't want to hurt each other's feelings. That means you don't tell somebody, 'There's a giant pimple on your nose.' I think she may have noticed already. Try to think before you say something: do you really need to say it out loud? If you do, will it hurt somebody else?

If a friend asks your opinion, think of kind ways to reply that are also true. 'Does my bum look big in this?' could be answered with: 'An ant's bum would look big in that – it's not very well made', or 'I think the blue one suits you better', or 'Stop thinking about your bum, it looks amazing and matches your eyes. Not your bum, the dress. Oh, I give up.'

What makes a good friendship?

Real friends:
- genuinely like each other
- can be themselves when they're together
- keep each other's secrets
- like doing some of the same things
- make time for each other – and not just when it's convenient for them
- really listen and try to understand each other's feelings
- are loyal, stick up for each other and never join in when others are being mean
- accept that friends have different opinions, clothes and interests.

a good friend doesn't blab your secrets

More info on good friends

Check out the 'Friends Online and on the Phone' section coming up for how to stay safe with real friends.

au.reachout.com
The Inspire Foundation website.
From Wellbeing choose Friends and Family, then Friendships for info on getting along.

rookiemag.com
Click on Categories then Live Through This for real stories on this US teen site.

> I feel confident about my relationship with my friends. Surround yourself by a good group of friends. They always see the good bits, the important bits.   Kat, 16, Ballarat, Vic.

> **My closest friends remain my closest friends. I feel confident that I am loved for who I am, and that I am the most comfortable with them, which gives me confidence that I'm doing something right!**   Jane, 18, Adelaide, SA

> I often feel like it's hard to make friends because I am quiet. People don't give me time to open up and instead they write me off straight away.   Megan, 18, Wantirna South, Vic.

Choose your friends

Just by being yourself you will often attract people who like the same things. And sometimes you 'click' with somebody without really knowing why (although you can't always tell when you meet someone for the first time whether they are going to become a good friend).

But don't sit back passively, waiting to be chosen. You're better off 'toughing it out' for a while until you find a good friend, rather than letting yourself be chosen by someone who's too bossy, boring or not nice to you. And don't go to all the bother of pretending to be different in an effort to be liked by someone – it's too hard to keep up the act. (The section 'Making New Friends' later in this chapter has tips to help you.)

Sometimes somebody you choose won't be interested in being friends with you. That can be hard, but you have to move on. It's still heaps better than just waiting there, like a box of muesli on the shelf, for somebody – anybody! – to pick you.

Not everyone has to like you or be your friend. A couple of friends are enough.

In our early teens kids can be so cruel, it's hard to remember you are beautiful. Surround yourself with positive, supportive people. Liz, 17, Melbourne, Vic.

I just want lots of good friends, not a best friend. Maddie, 14, Adelaide, SA

I am in year ten and have just found a couple of people who I can really connect with. Nic, 15, Lavender Bay, NSW

You need to surround yourself with people who love you and can keep you really positive about every situation you get in. They will keep telling you that you can do it and help you to become a strong person. Chelsea, 18, Mosman, NSW

Guy friends

Some good things about guy friends

✽ They can be just as loyal as girlfriends.

✽ They're like your secret agents in Guy Land – they can tell you how guys think and what they're saying.

✽ They help you to be less nervous around guys.

When you have a guy friend

✽ Be yourself – don't suddenly be girly or flirty, or all tough and footy-pants, if that's not the usual you.

✽ Don't treat him as a substitute boyfriend who gets dropped when the 'real thing' comes along.

✽ Don't expect him to hang out with your boyfriend, but don't ever let a jealous boyfriend tell you who you can't be friends with.

✽ Don't touch him in a girlfriend way: no kissing on the lips or lingering hugs.

✽ Don't ever expect a gay guy to 'turn' for you and become your boyfriend – it's a waste of time and offensive to try to change somebody's sexuality.

✽ Be honest with yourself about whether you really want to be 'just friends'. Imagine him kissing another girl, and see if you wish it was you.

✽ Be kind if he wants 'more than a friendship' and you don't. Say that you don't feel the same way. If he finds it hard to be 'just friends' take a break for a while till he gets over it. (Never tease him about it or joke that you might change your mind.)

If you do want to make the transition from friends to something more, see Chapter 15, Love (next in the book).

Friends on social media and your phone

If you're grown-up enough to use a phone and social media sites to contact friends, you can guard against some dangers. Avoid being a target for mean people, scams or creeps. Get help when you need it from a teacher or parent or other trusted adult.

Most social websites say you can't join until you're 13, but many girls join earlier. When you first sign up, ask an adult to help you adjust your settings and profiles. As you get older, here are some important ways to avoid embarrassment or worse:

- Always pause to think before hitting 'send', 'submit' or 'upload': anything, including a text, message, pic, email, post, tweet, blog, status change or link, can be instantly resent to thousands of people. Do you really want this out there?
- Only let family members or close friends map, check in or log your location. Otherwise – 'don't allow'.
- Make sure any of your webcam vision and video chat can only be seen by you and your own chosen friends.
- Some nasty types take advantage of being anonymous to 'troll', harass and threaten girls and women online, sometimes in a sexual way. Block them if you can. Responding personally will probably encourage them to keep trolling. Keep a record (eg screen-shot) in case you need to, or you want to report or take it further with the site or service provider. See the 'Confidence' and 'Equality Frivolity' chapters for more ideas and support.
- Don't give your password to anyone except a parent.

Phones

Everyone has a phone but nobody wants phone trouble. Here are some ways to avoid it:

- Don't let your phone out of your sight. Someone could use it to make a prank call that can be traced to you, or to send or upload something illegal. Set a secret PIN (personal identification number) on your phone.
- If someone is using texts or calls to be mean to you, see the info coming up under 'Meanness and Bullying'.
- See the info on sending and receiving pics, also coming up.

Social media and friendship sites

- Don't add friends from requests if you don't know them, or if you're not friends.
- Adjust your privacy settings. Check your settings often because the website may change them. >

- Be careful what you post. Even if it's on a private page, anything you post could become public. It may be legally owned by the website, which can move it to other sites or keep it public for years.
- Keep details out of it: many criminals and creeps go online to find last names, birthdays, addresses and schedules, which helps them to steal money or know where you are.
- Bear in mind that many people have potential access to your current or past pages, including parents, grandparents, teachers and potential bosses, new friends or people you hook up with.

Nude and private pics

Some people send nude pics of themselves but that doesn't make it a good idea. Accidentally or on purpose, those pics can be shown or sent to someone else, who could also share it. Pictures meant to be private have been sent to friends, parents, in emails sent to multiple adults, and publicly on social media.

A person who makes a private picture more public, or sends it to someone else, is doing something much worse than taking a nude pic of themselves. But once it's 'out there' you can't 'get it back'. You'll have no control over who sees it or how it's used, whether it shows your face or not. So here's the best advice that could help save you from some real drama.

- Don't send or post a photo of yourself that you wouldn't show everyone you know and everyone you haven't met yet.
- Never allow anyone to take video or a picture of you that you don't want shown to everyone or anyone. If someone tags you online in any photo you object to, remove the tag. Change your settings so others can't tag you.
- Don't take photos of a friend and post or tag them without their permission.
- Don't keep any embarrassing pictures on your phone that someone could send deliberately or accidentally.
- If an embarrassing pic of you is posted or texted, don't despair. Ask friends to delete it, get help from an adult to deal with any wider problems, and put it down to experience. A photo can't ruin your life, define you as a person or create a reputation that stays forever.

Porn stuff and sexting

- Even as a joke between friends, never allow anyone to take a picture of you nude, topless or showing private parts. Never take or send such a pic of yourself (this is often called 'sexting').
- Never send or resend anyone a pic of you or anyone else under 18 who's undressed or showing private parts. It can result in police investigation, charges and a criminal record. If somebody sends you a nude or sexual photo, show it to a trusted adult then delete it.
- Remind yourself that any sexual message you send to a friend, even as a joke, can be sent on accidentally or deliberately and end up being seen by parents or teachers.
- It's illegal for anyone to send you porn pictures, messages, links or info by email or text, or otherwise display it or send it to where you live, work or study.
- If you get a porn or harassing message or pic, report it to your parents or a teacher.
- If porn sites or pics 'pop up' on your computer, tell a parent, teacher or boss (depending on where the computer is).

Online scams and creeps

While we're on the subject of online friends, it's time to talk about enemies, too!

Scams

- No matter what you're promised (prizes, celeb pics, whatever . . .) never give any contact details (email, phone, postal address, etc.) in a phone call, text, email or on a website. These can be used to rip you off or harass you. Never put in a friend's details. Ask a parent to help you buy anything online (and see Chapter 21, Shopping, for more).
- Never give banking or other financial details or numbers by text, phone call, email or online, even if you're asked for them in an official-sounding way. This is *always* a scam (and see Chapter 20, Money).
- Only give your phone, website, locker or any other passwords or PIN numbers to parents – never to friends or anyone else.

Creeps You may think you're chatting online to a cute young guy or a friendly teenage girl you've never met, but it may be a dirty old criminal man typing with one hand and fiddling with his willy with the other. Euwwww!

Creeps research bands, books, TV shows, movies, gaming, interactive websites and other stuff teenagers like, so they can sound younger. Their aim is to meet you or find out where you live, or watch you or keep talking to you.

They can be good at pretending, by using fake profile pics, spending weeks or months turning you against friends and family; saying they're the only one who understands you; telling untrue stories of illness or bullying to make you feel sorry for them; promising you money, exciting holidays or presents; making you believe they're a celeb or a hot guy falling for you; or blackmailing you by saying they'll tell your parents something bad (believe me, they're bluffing).

They can:
- get a kick out of seeing you in your room on video chat, or talking with you online
- try to get you to talk about sex, or listen to them do it
- tell you to dress or look a certain way.

If anything like this happens you need to tell a trusted adult about it straight away. Even if you can see what they're up to, a younger or more trusting kid could be in danger next time. Your parent or teacher can report the incident to the internet service provider, relevant website and the police.

Never go alone to personally meet somebody you met online. Girls have been threatened or sexually assaulted by men they met who'd been pretending to be their friend online. If an online friend wants you to keep a meeting secret, don't go. Immediately tell your friends, parent and/or a teacher about any invitation or request.

Photos and videos on social media

You already know the way people present themselves in photos and videos is not 'real'. They use filters and body-editing apps, and can give a made-up idea of their pretend life. Some people try to make you feel bad so you buy something they're being paid to promote. Others are just wrong, giving dangerous or useless advice. Unfollow anything that makes you feel uncomfortable, or 'less than', or not beautiful enough. And don't forget to read the Body Image chapter starting on page 78, you gorgeous creature!

More info on social media and phones

www.esafety.gov.au
Tips on how to use social media without being trolled; the place to report bullying or harassment.

staysmartonline.gov.au
How to secure your mobile phone, and join social media websites safely.

Changing friendships

Some friendships are good for a little while, or even a long time, but then it's best to move on. Sometimes you need to decide if a good friendship has permanently gone bad, or if it has just been damaged but can be repaired. Many girls find it too intense to have a best friend, or only one close friend.

When a friendship goes bad

The giveaway signs are that the 'friend':
- makes you feel used
- treats you differently at different times, depending on who else is around
- doesn't keep your secrets and confidences
- dumps you when they get a boyfriend or a 'better offer'
- makes you feel uncomfortable, nervous or frightened
- is possessive or clingy – always jealous of your other friends and insisting on being with you
- makes you feel you're being controlled or manipulated to do what they want
- promises a lot of things but doesn't come through
- gossips and judges a lot, creating a negative atmosphere
- thinks only of themselves
- seems to compete with you all the time.

It's time to let a friendship go instead of trying to patch it up when:
- a friend has let you down so badly that you don't feel you can trust them again
- you don't really want to make up – you're just avoiding conflict or being polite
- the other person doesn't really want to make up (although it can be really hurtful, you have to accept rejection and move on)
- you can forgive, but you don't want to be close again
- it's only other people who want the two of you to be friends again
- you'd only be agreeing to be friends again to stop the tension of constant fighting. A relationship in which one person has to give way all the time isn't really a friendship.

> I used to try and 'fit in'. Right clothes, act the right way, talk the right way. But when I learned to be a green-loving freak, I was so much happier. BE YOURSELF. Try not to worry about what people might think of you. Be proud of who or what you are!!
>
> Lalli, 17, Rutherglen, Vic.

Fixing a friendship

A friendship is worth saving if you:
- really want to be friends again and the other person does too
- can forgive them, or want them to forgive you
- want it to be okay again, even if you know it won't ever be quite the same
- understand that you expected your friend to be perfect and that wasn't realistic
- accept that you were blaming your friend for everything, but perhaps should share some responsibility for what happened.

How to fix a friendship Make a few attempts to talk through whatever is making you or your friend angry or upset, and see if you feel there's a friendship worth saving. If there is, invite your friend somewhere, or suggest doing something together, and see what the reaction is. Spend a little more time together and gradually you may find the friendship is back on.

Sometimes it's just time that hammers out the dents left on a friendship by a misunderstanding, a bad mood or a mad moment of meanness. Friendships can be up one week and down the next, or even on different days.

How to leave a bad friendship

The following suggestions may make it sound easy, but ending a bad or unsatisfying friendship is always hard. The whole thing can be very messy and upsetting. It can make you feel anxious, give you tummy aches and cause tears. One way to get through is to focus on what you really want, such as new friends who don't tease you, or friends who do stuff instead of just sitting around gossiping. Keep reminding yourself that the pain you're going through is worth it because your life will be so much better.

Doing the drift You can just let a friendship wind down by gradually spending more time on other things and with other people.

> **FACT**
> **The jealous kind** If one friend demands all your time or criticises all your other pals, explain that having other friends doesn't mean you're disloyal.

- Explain nicely that you have a new hobby, lunchtime theatre rehearsals, something to study in the library or sports training.
- Get a parent to say you're not allowed out so often, or you have to make a wider group of friends. (If you want, one of your parents can contact one of theirs.)

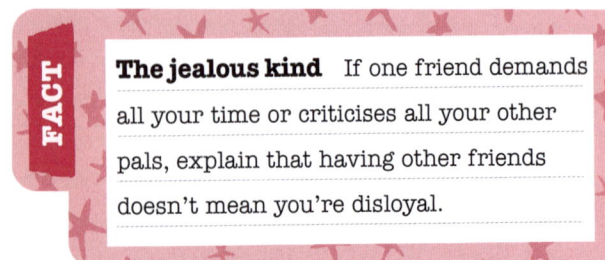

Stopping a friendship cold Sometimes you need to end a friendship straight away. But it seems mean and too dramatic to just stop talking to someone and walk away whenever they approach. Here are some other ways:

- Say 'I'm sorry, but I just don't want to be close friends any more. I don't like the way you talk to me', or 'I don't want to fight with you any more so let's take a break from seeing each other out of school', or 'I think I'm going to sit with different people at lunchtime for a while.'
- If you end up in a huge fight try to stay calm enough to say the things you want to, such as 'I was so hurt when you told people my secret. I just feel I can't trust you again', or 'You yelling at me like that is one of the reasons I don't want to hang around with you any more.'

> **FACT**
>
> **Say it, sister** If you have something important to say to a friend, like a complaint or an apology, say it out loud in person, not in a text or email that could be shown or sent to other people. If face-to-face confrontations are hard for you, write a list of the things you want to say, make a phone call and cross off points on the list as you go.

Making new friends

Making new friends can be hard, especially if you're shy. (And who isn't a bit shy and slow to warm up around someone new?) The most obvious place to make friends is at school, but there are plenty of other places too.

Getting started Making friends usually involves some effort. Unless you're the sort of person who can set up a booth with a sign saying 'Apply Here to Be Friends with Me: $5' and wait for a customer, you'll need to develop some 'small talk' skills. The best thing is to quickly hit on something that you're both interested in and get chatting about it (see the 'Starter Sentences' box coming up for some suggestions).

Making good friends, rather than acquaintances (people you know but aren't close to), takes time. Don't go telling people your deepest, darkest secrets when you first meet them, or asking them really personal things, as this could scare them off. ('Hi. Ever had a sexually transmitted infection? Hey, where'd everybody go?')

Where to look for new friends

- Is there someone you see around but have never got to know? It could be someone you've seen at the bus stop reading a book you love.
- What about your local neighbourhood? Can you reconnect with kids you knew at primary school who went to different schools?
- How about cousins or friends of friends, or the kids of your parents' friends who you haven't seen for a while?
- Is there a part-time job you could take that would mean new people as well as new skills?
- If you're old enough to be on safe game or fan websites, can you make connections there?
- Can you think of a sport team, band, bushwalking club, film-making class, or circus-skills, art or martial arts group you could join? (See Chapter 24, Caring, for heaps more ideas.)

Saying sorry

If you're the one who has behaved badly in a friendship, you need to apologise sincerely, not just with a 'Yeah, sorry.' Show that you know what you did and the effect that your actions or words caused: 'I'm so sorry. I did the wrong thing and I can't take it back. I hope you can forgive me or at least give me another chance.'

One solid apology should be enough. You don't have to grovel, but you do have to accept that if you let your friend down again (or a third time) they will be wise to move on. And you too can have a two-or-three-strikes-and-you're-out policy.

If you're on the receiving end, accept a genuine apology gracefully by saying something like 'Okay, then. Thanks for saying sorry', and either patch up the friendship or choose not to.

FACT

Frenemies A frenemy is someone who says they're a friend but acts like an enemy, often someone who tends to use 'compliments' or 'helpful suggestions' that are actually rather insulting. You should feel happier after talking with a friend, not worse.

My best friend often ditches me for a boy. Antonia, 14, Malvern, Vic.

308   HEART ♥ friends

Groups of friends

Some people love the sense of belonging so much, or feel so attracted to an image or lifestyle, that they join a group that almost has a uniform, code of conduct and headquarters. This 'tribe' might be the goths, nerds, surfs, cool group, art gang, musos (musicians) or whatever else is going at the time. These small worlds can give you a strong sense of belonging and being among friends who understand you – but they can also make you feel you're living in a little box.

Other people choose to be friendly with lots of people rather than joining one group: they're natural diplomats who don't need intense friendships. Not everyone is like that, but even when you're someone who wants a special group of friends it's good to be able to get along with other groups or different people outside your own circle.

Starter sentences

Here are some ways to kick off a conversation with someone new.

'Mind if I sit here?'

'Did you have any idea what that science experiment was supposed to do this morning?'

'What are you listening to?'

'Help! I don't know anyone else at this party and I'm about to talk to the pot plants.'

'Hi. Where'd you get your shoes? They look great.' (Don't overdo this or it will be sucky. One compliment a conversation is plenty.)

'Hi. Have we met?'

'Can we talk? I've been texting all day and I don't know if I remember how to have a conversation any more.'

Hang around with friends that don't make you feel like you have to conform or act in a certain way. Joey, 17, Brisbane, Qld

Actually my friends don't really like me. Andrea, 13, Brunei

The problems I have experienced with friends are that they are self-absorbed little … Jen, 17, Bundaberg, Qld

A girl used to swear at me and I felt sad and left out because she was in our group and everyone was on her side. Can you still be someone's best friend when you don't like them? Kathy, 13, Aspley, Qld

Fitting in

It's great to feel you fit in, but you should be able to without having to be exactly the same as everybody else. If you hang out with positive people who don't mind your little differences or eccentricities, it makes you feel more positive too.

In a good group of friends you should be able to:
- feel proud of your own interests
- keep (or change) your opinion even if it's not the same as everyone else's
- choose your own clothes and how you look
- admit to feeling unsure about something
- feel as if there isn't a group leader who makes the rules for everyone else
- make your own decisions about where to go and what to do
- feel confident your friends won't ridicule you.

'Peer pressure'

'Peer group' is a term that can mean a particular bunch of people of similar age, background and interests: say, the drama group at school. (It can also mean all people of similar age and experience – teenagers, for example.) Sometimes being in a group means all the members deliberately or unconsciously start doing the same things and looking alike (lots of piercings, blonde with a fake tan or whatever).

Bad peer groups make you feel as if you have to do and say the 'right' things or you'll get frozen out. Being seen hanging out with the popular mob may not be as much fun as it looks. In fact it may be like being a puppet in hell.

'Peer pressure' is the pressure you feel to change your behaviour, your appearance or what you have to say because you want to impress your friends or be more acceptable.

Peer pressure can be:
- **Direct**   Somebody orders you around.
- **Implied**   You know that if you don't wear what the others are wearing people will mock you or be cruel to you.
- **Manipulated**   Advertising and other kinds of marketing make you feel that if you don't have the latest thing you won't be cool (see Chapter 21, Shopping).
- **Internal** (comes from within you)   Because you're unsure of yourself, you copy others to feel you're more likeable and doing the right thing.

Peer pressure can give you logic-fade. Remember when you were little you could get into soooo much more trouble if you were with a friend, brother, sister or cousin than if you were on your own? Because when you were together something could seem irresistible: decorating the couch cushions with mashed banana, 'borrowing' Mum's lipstick, or feeding the dog beer. The same thing can happen to you as a teenager, or even when you're grown up. 'It seemed like a good idea at the time' may be completely true, but it isn't the brainiest philosophy of all time.

How not to be controlled Always have a few good comebacks ready for when you're being pressured into something you don't want to do or say. In Chapter 10, Drinking, and Chapter 11, Drugs, there are lists of things to say that can be useful in other situations. Chapter 8, Confidence, has ideas on how to feel strong and good about yourself and ways to say no.

> I have never really fitted into a particular group anywhere. I'm friends with lots of people in different groups. Trudi, 15, Preston, Vic.

> I have tried to exclude girls I don't like from entering my group of friends at school. Sarah Jane, 14, Bellevue Hill, NSW

> My friends always bitch about each other. It makes me wonder what they say about me! Lauren, 17, Mooroolbark, Vic.

> In year 7 my 'best friend' decided she didn't want to hang out with me any more. I can easily say that was the biggest grief I had ever had to deal with. The loss of that comfort zone was devastating. Zoe, 18, Kyneton, Vic.

> **I just kept my head down and rode it out. Found some new friends that I'm still best friends with today.** Kathryn, 18, Frankston, Vic.

> I spent six months alone when I left a mean friend. Sitting on benches, reading. Now I have a best friend and other friends. I don't need her any more, and I don't need to feel bad when she sneers at me or makes up more rumours. I'm strong now. Jules, 13, Adelaide, SA

> I would like a best friend who I can share all my thoughts with and who would be able to share her thoughts with me. Not having a best friend makes me feel kind of lonely. Lee-Anne, 15, Maroubra, NSW

Moving to a new friendship group

If you're in a group pressuring you to conform, if you're threatened by, frightened of or being frozen out by people in the group, or if you feel restricted, or that you can't be yourself, or that you don't like what they do, consider moving groups. Have a look at the tips given earlier in the 'Changing Friendships' and 'Making New Friends' sections.

The breakdown of your relationship with a group is a really confusing and upsetting time, and can make you feel like hitting somebody with a plank or hiding in the library forever. And the changeover to a new one can be difficult and take a while, but in the end you'll have new friends who are more fun to be with.

I completely changed friendship groups, which was the hardest and best thing I have ever had to do. You worry about what the people you were leaving behind will think, and whether the people in the group you want to be a part of want you there. Win, 16.

Do something outside of school so you make friends away from your school groups and stretch your comfort zones. Phoebe, 14, Armadale, Vic.

I think that it is about year 9 when people begin to realise who you are (and there was some nastiness). I knew I had to move on. I am now in a group with 6 other girls (I also have friends from other groups) and I love them all. Mia, 15, Parap, NT

I just can't find a friendship group that suits me. I have had at least 5 different friends groups during my life. Alicia, 13, Launceston, Tas.

I made a pact and said that next school year I'm getting out of this group even if it means I'd be alone for a while. I made loads of awesome new friends and am really happy. Katherine, 13, Melbourne, Vic.

Meanness and bullying

Have you ever spoken to an adult about somebody being mean to you and the adult said, 'Oh, just ignore it'? If this happens to you again, ask the adult, 'Who was the mean kid in your year at school?' I'll bet they can remember the person's whole name and everything else about them. It will remind the adult that mean stuff sticks with you. It's not trivial, and they need to take your problem seriously.

Meanness is the flip side of friendship and can even come from someone who claims to be your friend. Being mean is something that can be done carelessly or deliberately. It's nasty to say something cruel to somebody's face, and it's cruel to say something nasty behind their back. Meanness includes nasty comments, harsh or unnecessary criticism, and spreading rumours or gossip. We've all had it done to us. Sometimes we've been guilty of meanness ourselves.

> **FACT**
>
> **Stuck in the middle** No friend should ask you to ignore another friend, or to 'take sides' in a disagreement. You have the right to stay neutral. You don't have to stop talking to one friend because another friend says so. You can say: 'I don't want to get involved', or 'I know you're hurt/angry/upset about this, and that's bad, but I won't ignore her.' You can also say, 'I think she said the wrong thing, but she said she's sorry, and I still want us all to be friends.'

So what's the difference between meanness and bullying? How severe it is, really, and whether it keeps going rather than being a one-off. Bullying is ongoing meanness from somebody or a group, targeting one person or more. It could be regular, often or constant, or organised. Bullying using phones or social media website pages can be called 'cyberbullying' – which just means it's done using electronics, not 'in person'.

Bullying is a big cause of sadness, depression and self-harm in teenage girls. Some who are targeted even think about taking their own life, as a number of girls told the Girl Stuff Survey. The rest of this chapter has heaps of suggestions for what you can do and where to go for help – so read on! If you're feeling in despair, go straight to the end of the chapter to read the 'More Info' section and ring the Kidsline number.

Some people just stay mean all their lives, so it's good to know how to deflect their meanness. (Because leaping at them from trees and trying to strangle them is apparently illegal. I checked.)

About two-thirds of girls aged 13 to 18 who responded to the Girl Stuff Survey said they had been bullied, although when they described what had happened the behaviour ranged from awful, repeated bullying that had lasted for years, to someone saying a mean thing once.

All the things on this list are mean. If they become repeated, ongoing or relentless, then it's bullying:

- nasty comments and insults
- teasing
- mean 'jokes', such as telling you the wrong room to go to
- rudeness when you're talking (rolling of eyes, sighing, sarcastic comments, whispering, mimicking, mocking, or smiling in a mean way as if they're laughing at you)
- spreading gossip and rumours (more coming up)
- the Intentional Freeze-out (coming up)
- intimidation – following you, looming over you, staring at you
- threats
- sexual comments, rumours, insults or pornographic pictures shown or sent to somebody
- damage to your things
- physical violence.

Being different

Being 'different' can make you feel like a target. You can get used to hearing: 'You're weird.' (Let's not even get into how the logical answer to this is: 'You only think that because you're boring.')

Mean people can be jealous, racist, otherwise ignorant or stupid, or just freaked out by anything 'different'. In the end, the joke's on them because everyone's different – and that's one of the joys of life.

Differences can include skin and hair colour, disabilities, sexuality, hobbies, even taste in music and clothes. The more you embrace your differences, the more successful and happier you can be. Your identity is precious. It could well be the thing that makes you famous, or just happy, and fun to be with.

You may feel you're not accepted by your family, school, friendship group or town. That doesn't make you weird and wrong – it makes you special. And right now, there are others like you, or who will understand you, in the same situation in other families and schools and places. They're out there. And you'll find them. Use these websites as a starting point.

bornthiswayfoundation.org
Lady Gaga's foundation to fight bullying. Stories of bravery.

igba.org.au and **itgetsbetter.org**
A video project with messages saying it's okay to be gay.

Nasty tactics

Gossip and rumours Gossiping can be a way of catching up with friends' news, a way of keeping in touch. But nasty gossip can do terrible harm to somebody's reputation and self-esteem. People often make a rumour sound more likely by claiming to have a close connection with it – their cousin 'saw it' or a friend of a friend was involved.

Unless you know for sure that something is true – *and* you have a real reason for telling somebody else about it – you're better off ignoring it and not becoming part of the gossip chain.

Why you need to avoid mean gossiping and spreading rumours

- The gossip you're passing on may be a lie.
- Making up a rumour is not only wrong, in some cases it's illegal.
- Cruel gossip hurts people, even if they're not there when you gossip.
- It makes people feel it's fair enough to gossip about you.

If you get caught gossiping you should apologise sincerely. Don't make it worse by making excuses.

If the gossip is about you The gossip could be a made-up rumour about you or a secret of yours that somebody has told. You have several options.

- Ignore it by remaining 'above it all'. Instead of an Invisibility Cloak, you have the Invisible Cloak of Dignity.
- Distract yourself. Get on with whatever you're doing. Don't drop everything to investigate and brood.
- Deny it, and just stick to your story. Rumours get distorted or more complicated as they pass from person to person, so usually at least some of it's wrong. This can make it easier for you to deny it.
- Confront the original source or the spreaders of the gossip, alone, if you can find them. Tell them to stop it.
- Tell a parent or a teacher who you think could help you.
- If the rumour or gossip is about something that's true and that can't be avoided, take the sting out of the gossip part. Just shrug and say, 'Yeah, what's the big deal? Why are people gossiping about it? I'm not trying to hide anything.'

> I worry that when I am myself my friends won't like me. Smita, 17, Devonport, Tas.

The Intentional Freeze-out

Most people will go through a freeze-out at least once – at some point they get left out of a group.

Of course sometimes it happens accidentally: for instance, people forget to save you a seat. But sometimes you can be hit with the ugliest of mean tactics, the Intentional Freeze-out. You know the kind of thing: people turn their backs or walk away when you arrive, ignore what you say, give you dirty or cold stares, make sure you catch them whispering about you.

The central point of the Intentional Freeze-out can be that nobody will tell you why they're freezing you out. And if you ask, 'What did I do?', the answer is, 'You KNOW what you did.'

It can go on for a lunchtime, a day, a week, or in rare cases even longer. Of course all the time the group is careful not to let adults see what they're doing. What they're doing is bullying you.

There was one main ringleader and she always caused trouble for me. I was never good enough, I felt worthless and I didn't have anyone to be close to.
Suzette, 17, Grafton, NSW

I was being controlled by a person and the person wouldn't let me make any other friends. Deena, 13, Harkaway, Vic.

I was bullied for three years, people stole my things and called me names, they wouldn't let me sit with them and the boys often beat me up.
Bronwyn, 16, Emerald, Qld

I'm always scared to show them the real 'me'. Caz, 13, Adelaide, SA

Ignorant guys/girls make comments about me being in a wheelchair and being able to walk. They call me a fraud and yell out stupid comments about me.
Kate, 13, Yagoona, NSW

There can be any number of reasons for the Intentional Freeze-out:
- the 'leader' of a group is testing her muscles by ordering the action (possibly you have angered Her Majesty by being more interesting than her, or by standing up to her)
- maybe there's a rumour going around about you
- you said something and now everybody's mad
- you didn't say anything, but somebody's boyfriend said they liked you
- some girl decided Thursday was International Intentional Freeze-out Day.

Don't ask, 'What have I done wrong?' It could be *anything*. Or nothing. Ask yourself, 'How can I find some nicer friends?'

If you're doing the freezing out   The least you can do when you're mad at someone is have the decency to tell them why. And make an agreement with your friends that it's no way to treat anybody in the group – otherwise you could be next.

Why meanness happens

People who work as counsellors tend not to like the word 'bully' because they think it unfairly labels somebody. 'Mean girl' seems like a similar label. I understand that idea but I think we all know that some girls (and guys) are mean. We're all capable of being mean. Some people choose to keep being mean, some choose to stop.

People being mean can be loners or part of a group. They can be someone your own age, or older, or sometimes even younger. Mean people can include your friends, a family member, a boyfriend or girlfriend, a teacher or a boss.

> Girls started rumours about me because they thought it was funny. It got out of control and we stopped talking for a while. It's sorted out now, though.   Francesca, 13, King Island, Tas.

friends ♥ HEART   317

It doesn't always matter why they do it. You don't have to know why somebody's being mean or bullying, but sometimes it will help you work out the best way to make them stop.

Some people might tell you that being bullied is part of the 'real world' and that everyone has to put up with it at some time in their life and everyone survives it. But we all have the right to live without harassment and discrimination. No one deserves bullying, and no one 'asks for it'.

Bad excuses for being mean
- 'I was just telling the truth.'
- 'I didn't do it on purpose.'
- 'I was just joking – they should get the joke.'
- 'Everyone does it.'
- 'They were mean to me so I was mean back.'
- 'It's what girls do.'

That last one's the biggest bad excuse of all. Lots of girls and women support each other, as friends and in the workplace, and it's not fair or true to say that all girls and women are mean to each other.

I spread rumours I knew weren't true.   Amy, 17, Lane Cove, NSW

Sometimes I worry that people must talk about me behind my back as the people I do it to are so oblivious it could be happening to me too.
Annabelle, 15, Brighton, Vic.

I was in a group at school and thought everything was fine, then one day they all just literally stopped talking to me, and now they are talking to me again and I asked why but no one ever gave me an explanation.   Ruby, 17, Armadale, Vic.

You don't realise how much it hurts until it happens to you.   Lulu, 14, Nightcliff, NT

318   HEART ♥ friends

The real reasons for meanness

Different people can have different reasons, or more than one reason (which still doesn't make it okay!). Why are people mean, or become bullies? Here are some possibilities:

- They don't care about other people's feelings.
- They feel entitled and superior.
- They feel inferior and insecure and want to feel more powerful.
- It makes some them feel better about themselves to make others feel bad.
- They seem to be easily led by someone else who's being mean.
- They choose a victim because otherwise they're scared they'd become a victim.
- They wanted to fit in or join the group being mean.
- They're unhappy and lashing out.
- It's 'learned' behaviour from somebody in their family.
- Nobody stopped them.
- They're bored and don't have enough going on in their life so they stir up drama to entertain themselves.
- They're boring and unimaginative, so they feel challenged by people who are 'different'.
- They set impossible standards for themselves (an A is a 'failure' because they 'should' have got an A+), and this harshness spills over into their treatment of other people.
- They think they don't have to face the person they're being mean to if they do it online.

When you're the mean one

In the replies to the Girl Stuff Survey, about 70 per cent of girls aged 13 to 18 said they had been mean to somebody else, although many also said they regretted it. Probably almost everyone has done it at least once: the important thing is not to get into the habit. Even if it has become something you do a lot, you can stop.

friends ♥ HEART

I tend to make fun of people to make myself feel better.
Emma, 16, Brisbane, Qld

I had this friend who was really mean. I was willing to do anything to make her think better of me. So I turned into a really mean person. I feel so bad. I probably made more than one person's life hell.   Lucy, 17, Agnes Water, Qld

I am often a bitch to people before I actually know them.
Georgina, 16, Subiaco, WA

I've excluded people and insulted people, although mostly jokingly.
Chrissie, 15, Geelong, Vic.

I can be bitchy. I feel really sick afterwards. I'm trying to be nice now and just being an all-round nice person to everyone makes you feel better inside.
Liz, 13, Torquay, Vic.

Maybe I'll try to stop ... I think I will ... It's harder to be nice, but more rewarding.
Mary, 17, Yarra Junction, Vic.

Time for a new shirt...

TEAM MEAN

I talked about people behind their backs and made fun of them to their faces but as it happened to me also I realised I was really hurting people. I am now much more careful about things I say.   Felicity, 17, Bendigo, Vic.

320   HEART ♥ friends

Why you should stop being mean

- It's the right thing to do.
- You'll like yourself more, and so will other people. The alternative is that people don't trust you and don't like you.
- Otherwise you may feel guilty about it, even after you become an adult.
- If you keep going you'll be caught and probably punished. Any text, message, posting or email you've written will be evidence against you – even if you used a fake name you can be traced.
- Parents may confiscate your phone. At school you may be given detentions, be suspended or even expelled in serious cases.
- Internet connection and phone companies have all cut off access to people for being mean or bullying. In serious cases there can be a criminal charge.

How to stop being mean or a bully

* Stop and think before you speak, write or send. Is there any point, apart from being mean, to what you're about to say?

* Get busy. Have some activities to do so you talk about a show you saw, or how your team's going, or something else.

* If you're sent mean texts about someone else or horrible comments are posted on social media pages, ignore it, delete it, or say something like: 'I don't want to hear about it', or 'Don't send me that stuff.'

* Get happier. Mean people are often unhappy. (See 'Feeling Optimistic and Strong' in Chapter 9, Feelings).

* Make a pact with friends not to do it. If somebody starts, say 'No bitching!', and stop.

* Help spread the word to others that it's not okay. Say you once used to be mean and now you regret it. Don't repeat the mean stuff.

* Even if you don't like somebody, it doesn't mean they deserve to be picked on.

Speak up when it happens to someone else Practise a few things to say to at least let others know you don't agree with it. Possibilities include: 'Stop being so mean', 'I don't agree with that stuff you're saying', 'Why are you being so mean?', 'Not this crap again' and 'I don't want to be part of this: see you later.'

If it happens right in front of you, walk away alone or with the person who's being picked on. You don't have to be best friends with them forever – the point is to do the right thing at the time.

If you feel trapped in a group of friends, see the sections earlier in this chapter such as 'How to Stop Being Mean', 'How to Leave a Bad Friendship', and 'Making New Friends'.

> She always makes fun of me, 'cos I'm smart. She does this stupid voice and imitates what I say if I use a big word, and it makes me feel really bad about myself. Pru, 13, Adelaide, SA

> **They call it being 'brutally honest', but sometimes I feel that some comments should be kept to yourself.** Pip, 16, Bankstown, NSW

> Sometimes friends have this voice that sort of makes me wonder if they respect me [or are] making fun of me. Grace, 13, Blackburn, Vic.

> **Despite the saying 'sticks and stones may break my bones, but names will never hurt me' words hurt, equally as much as actions.** Jessica, 17, Perth, WA

> My friend told me 'all the weight I'd put on' really suited me. It made me feel so angry, because I couldn't do anything back because it was said nicely, but it was so mean. Sam, 14, Sydney, NSW

How to deal with meanness and bullying

Each person being mean and every bully may have different reasons for being horrible – so there isn't one magic answer. But you're about to read heaps of good suggestions for all sorts of things to try and places you can get help.

Ignoring meanness is hard: it doesn't always make it go away, and it doesn't stop it hurting. Even if you walk away or don't show a reaction of course you can still feel crushed or furious. And that's an understandable and normal reaction.

Self-defence against meanness and bullying DIY (do-it-yourself) tactics can be your first line of defence. Sometimes these tactics work, but sometimes they don't. I know some of these methods won't work in all situations, or on some bullies. (I mean, how can you 'avoid them' if they're in four of your classes every day?)

You may have to try a few ideas until you get one that seems to work. If these strategies don't help, you'll need help (suggestions for that coming up soon).

- Ignore them. Don't react, don't reply, look right through 'em, walk away.
- Be assertive: stick up for yourself.
- Imagine them standing there with a big dog poo on their head they don't know about, or silently repeat to yourself: 'You pathetic worm, you pathetic worm, you pathetic worm.'
- Fight back by saying something smart or sarcastic to show they haven't hurt you (suggestions coming up, and there's more in Chapter 8, Confidence).
- Confuse them. Sing loudly, recite poetry or comedy, shout: 'Yes, the lobster army is marching! To the barricades!' They'll say 'You're crazy' but then you can say 'Ooh, woolly hats akimbo!' Just never say 'Your mother' to a giant bald guy with tattoos.
- Stay positive: focus your mind on people who love you, good times you've had and all the things you like about yourself.
- Threaten to tell an adult.
- Learn a self-defence martial art so you feel more physically confident about defending yourself if necessary.
- Hang out in a group: several people confronting a bully can be more powerful than an individual.
- Challenge them. 'Really? This is how you want other people to see you?', 'Why are you doing this?', or even 'Please, stop embarrassing yourself.' Keep it short and simple as if you have better things to do. >

- Tell the harasser in person, when they're alone or with a parent, to stop. If you have to tell them in a message, decide what you're going to say and make it unemotional, impersonal and clear: 'Any further harassment/messages/emails from you will be reported to the school/your parents/police/your phone company/the website used.'
- Some teachers suggest you just need to explain to the person being mean that they've hurt your feelings and they'll stop. Unfortunately, some people will be perfectly thrilled to know they've hurt your feelings, so I reckon at least have a plan B. (Plan Bs coming up!)
- As explained earlier, if an embarrassing photo of you is sent to other people or posted on a website, it's only a temporary humiliation. It doesn't define you as a person and it won't 'ruin your life'. Get help and support from friends, parents, trusted teachers or a school counsellor. Being the target of meanness reflects far worse on the people who are doing it than it does on you. You will get through this, and come out stronger.

Protecting yourself
- Tell friends, family and teachers if the meanness is ongoing or threatening rather than a one-off that seems to have resolved itself.
- Keep your email address and phone number private – only give them to friends, and always keep your phone secure.
- Block caller ID to hide your number when you call someone else. You can change your number by calling your service provider: ask your parents to help.

Keeping evidence of bullying
Like any good detective, you need to build your case:
- Keep any handwritten notes you're given.
- Take photos of any damage done to your property by mean people.
- Use your school diary or your phone to write down the dates, times and things people said or did.
- Show any obscene or horrible texts, website or email messages to a trusted adult so they know what's going on and can support you.
- Keep the messages sent to you and, if your phone or computer doesn't record the time and date they came in, keep a list of those details.

Getting support against meanness and bullying

Asking for help isn't a sign of weakness: it takes courage. If the first person you tell isn't helpful, keep trying until you find someone who can make things happen.

Help from home Sometimes it's just helpful to talk about stuff that's annoying or upsetting, even if nothing actually gets 'solved'. Brothers, sisters, cousins, aunties, uncles and parents may be able to help you by sharing problems and talking things through.

In cases of ongoing meanness or bullying, ask a parent for help. If your mum or dad can't seem to see that it's tough for you, ask them to think back and remember the bullies at their school. Explain that ignoring the bullying doesn't work and ask them to help you. You can show them the stuff for parents in 'More Info on Dealing with Meanness and Bullying' at the end of this chapter.

Ask your parents to agree that if you ever tell them about being given a hard time online or on your phone, or you think you've been contacted by someone creepy, they won't 'punish' you by restricting your access to the phone or computer pages. In return you'll always be honest with them about it.

Get your mum, dad or big sister or brother to answer any horrible phone calls or texts. This can give the caller a fright, especially if your parent says calmly, 'I know what you're doing and I'll speak to your parents/the school/the police if this ever happens again.' It's important for them to speak politely and firmly, not swear or yell, make no physical threats, and hang up without abuse. Your parents can also send a calm text with the same idea, or ring the parents of the person giving you a hard time. If none of this works, or instead as the first option, they can contact your school to ask for help.

Feeling overwhelmed by bullying

If you feel in real despair, or it affects you a lot, or you feel dread or anxiety about it, tell somebody else right away. Try a parent, friend's parent, teacher or school nurse. You can call the Kids Helpline (for under 18s) on 1800 55 1800.

There's lots of info in this chapter to help you. You might also like some of the stuff in Chapter 9, Feelings, about how to deal with stress, sadness and anger, and how to feel more optimistic and cheerful. See Chapter 12, Mind Health, for info on serious mental health issues such as self-harm and depression.

> I started acting tough. Suze, 16, Dayboro, Qld

Help from friends Tell a friend or friends what's happening. They might be able to be with you at danger times, or speak up for you. They may also agree to be with you to provide support when you tell a teacher or a parent.

If you know any older students at the school, such as a brother or sister or friend, see if they have any useful suggestions. Ask them or some other friends to hang out with you at danger times for a while. Often students are much better at seeing meanness that teachers can seem blind to.

Help at school Talk to a trusted teacher or school counsellor. A lot of girls who responded to the Girl Stuff Survey said there was no point telling teachers because they didn't seem to want to do anything or take it seriously. But other girls said that when a bully was told off by a teacher or knew that teachers were watching, the problem stopped. In other words, some teachers are really great, and a few are pretty useless – but you already knew that, right?

Schools are now required to have 'bullying policies' for behaviour by their students at school and elsewhere, which can cover the unacceptable use of computers and phones, even outside school hours. Ask for a copy of the policy and see what the rules say about how teachers or a principal must help. There should be a teacher at school who is in charge of dealing with this stuff: if this is a good teacher they'll be experienced and really helpful. If the school is dodging its responsibility, get your parents to contact the education department in your state or territory to complain.

Last-resort help Ask an adult to help you with these more serious responses. If harassment by phone or texts continues, you can change your phone number or email address, or inform your service provider. They can investigate and take steps to stop harassment. Social websites can ban the accounts of people who break the website's rules of conduct.

If this doesn't work, or if the messages are constant, threatening or obscene, contact your local police directly and they'll investigate.

> You have to work really hard to keep their antagonistic voices out of your head.
> Sandi, 17, Wantirna, Vic.

> Ignore comments from those peers who don't have two brain cells to rub together: ie the majority of the 'popular' people at school.   Jo, 16, Katoomba, NSW

Snappy comebacks

If ignoring cruel comments or teasing doesn't work, or you don't feel like being silent, try a few snappy comebacks. Sometimes this can cause it to 'escalate' or get worse because they enjoy the reaction or want to crush your resistance to seem more powerful. But it shows that you're not just going to take it, and can be really satisfying. Use your own judgement. Sometimes a secretive smile or rolling your eyes or laughing at them (not with them!) can be just as effective.

There's heaps more suggested things to say in the section called 'Responding to Horrible Comments' in Chapter 8, Confidence. That chapter also has heaps of hints on feeling stronger and raising your self-esteem.

You can come up with your own snappy replies to mean comments, and practise so you can deliver them easily. If you can raise one eyebrow, or say 'Wow' with a level stare, practise that, too. Here's some sample snappy comebacks:

They say: 'Can't you take a joke?'
You say: 'Can't you stop being mean?'

'It was just a joke.'
'If that's a joke you'll never get a comedy gig' or **'That wasn't a joke, that was an insult in a bad disguise.'**

'You need to toughen up.'
'I don't think I should have to change just because you want to say more mean stuff to me.'

'You're too sensitive.'
'I'm not oversensitive, I'm just over it.'

'I'm just telling you the truth'
'No, you're just being mean.'

'Friends tell each other the truth and I'm your friend'
'Wow. It doesn't sound like friendship to me.'

'Well, it's true.'
'Saying it's true doesn't make it true.'

'I'm just saying . . .'
'Have you tried thinking before you do that?'

Changing the feelings caused by bullying

Bullying can cause stress, fear, low self-esteem, illness, physical injury, loneliness and depression. But some of these feelings can, in time, be turned around. Instead of each of the common thoughts below, try the ones in bold.

First thought: 'It must be my fault somehow.'
Better thought: 'No, it's not my fault.'

'It's never going to stop.'
'There are things I can do to try to make it stop – and I'll start right now.'

'I have to face it alone.'
'I must talk to an adult who can help.'

'Nothing can help me.'
'There are lots of people and strategies that can help.'

'Nobody likes me.'
'I need to find some of My People. These are not My People.'

'I don't fit in anywhere.'
'This is not a place where I would want to fit in. But somewhere there is a place where I can be different and still fit in, and I can find it.'

'I'm scared to go to school or where the bullies are, but I can't escape.'
'I can escape: I need help to stop this, or to move to another school.'

'I should hurt myself so I can keep control of that hurt.'
'Their bullying shouldn't cause me to want to hurt myself. There is help available to turn these thoughts around, and better ways to control my thoughts.'

'I feel rejected and depressed.'
'I need to find some friends and get some help so I don't feel rejected and depressed. It will take some time, but I will start feeling better and be back on the way to happiness.'

'I need to pretend I'm fine and make lots of jokes.'
'I don't have to pretend that what's happening is okay. It's not a joke if only one side laughs.'

'I should pick on someone else so that they do too, and leave me alone.'
'I refuse to let them turn me into one of them.'

'I'm ashamed of myself, my family and my culture.'
'I'm proud of myself, my family and my culture. It's the bullies who have the problem.'

Taking a break

As well as fighting back, you can run, you can hide, and you can get a fresh start if necessary. Even small breaks from stress can be really useful.

- Don't keep being drawn back to people who are mean. You don't have to try to make them like you.
- Here's a handy motto: if 'friends' are mean, it means they're not friends. Don't try to laugh it off or think it's normal if your feelings are constantly hurt. Start planning your escape. See the sections 'How to Leave a Bad Friendship' and 'Making New Friends' earlier in this chapter.
- When you can, turn your phone or computer off for a few hours to give yourself a break. Keep them charging in another room when you're asleep.
- Ask friends, brothers and sisters, older students or parents to help protect you during danger times such as recess or after school for a while.
- Feel free to take people off your 'friend' list on your social media website pages. It's better to have a small group of close friends with access to your pages. Don't give in to pressure to add people you don't know or don't like: you don't have to explain yourself to anyone.
- In some really bad cases, after you've tried everything else, you may be able to move schools and make a fresh start. This works wonders for some people.

I get teased and put down all the time. Occasionally I get threats of physical violence – it really scares and worries me. Rain, 13, Perth, WA

These two girls humiliated me publicly and no one did anything to stop it. It feels really disorienting, you start to question your self worth. You wake up fearing the day and go to sleep planning revenge. Meena, 17, Brisbane, Qld

I was hanging around with the popular group, and one girl decided she didn't like me so like sheep ... the rest follow. I felt not wanted and like no one cared. Dani, 14, Mooroopna, Vic.

I got teased & bashed up. Felt like no one cared about me any more. Just felt like I was nothing. Anonymous, 14, Mt Colah, NSW

More info on dealing with meanness and bullying

See also Chapter 8, Confidence, and Chapter 9, Feelings. There's info on self-harm and depression in Chapter 12, Mind Health.

Kids Helpline: 1800 55 1800
kidshelpline.com.au
Free counselling help and advice: you can call without giving your name.

bullyingnoway.gov.au
Info from, and for, students, parents and teachers.

Mean Girls and *Clueless* (a 1990s take on Jane Austen's *Emma*)
Each of these movie DVDs has something to say about gossip and bitchiness.

If your school or parents need help to fight bullying:

ncab.org.au/bullyinghurts
The National Centre Against Bullying has lots of fact sheets.

bounceback.com.au and *Bounce Back! A Wellbeing and Resilience Program* by Dr Helen McGrath and Dr Toni Noble
A program for students about friendship and bullying and accompanying book.

> There has been a lot of bitching in my life but I left that clique. Now I don't have to worry about walking away for a few minutes and have the whole group bitching about me, it's great!
> Ashlee, 16, Drouin, Vic.

15

LOVE

Is it gastro, or love?

Imagine a little alien has landed on your shoulder and asked you to explain **love** on your planet. 'Well', you might begin, 'I really **love** avocado on toast, and I **love** this guy who's the lead singer of my favourite band but I've never seen him – I just **love** his music and the way he looks and everything about him – and I **love** my goldfish Martine and, well, obviously I HATE my parents because they won't let me go to Dylan's party on the weekend, but I sort of **love** them, but I'll never **love** my little brother, but I guess I kind of do, and I **love** purple, and sunsets, and my friends, but not Mel because she told Ashleigh what Jake said (did I tell you I'm in **love** with Jake?), and obviously I **love** Grandad, even though he died, oh and I **love**, **love**, **love** having my ears tickled and – hey, where are you going? Alien?'

Different kinds of love

Family love
'They drive me crazy.' (But you probably love them anyway.)

Pet love
'I love all my pets, but I love Sparky best.' (It's usually easier to love a dog than a fish. Why is that?)

Friendship
'I *love* my friends.' (Until they're not your friends any more.)

Fair-weather friendship
'Some of my friends only seem to love me when they need something.' (So not really friends then.)

Attraction
'Hmmm, he's cuuuuuute. I don't even know his *name*. Am I blushing? I'm blushing.'

In-person crush
'There he is. He's still there. Now he's moved his left foot slightly. I think I'm going to throw up. In a good way. No, that's not good.'

Celebrity crush
'Oh, my GOD. I'm cutting a picture out of a magazine.'

Unrequited love
'I love you, but you don't love me.' (Or the other way round. Bummer.)

Romantic love
'I'm so happy I could SING it from the rooftop. But that would be weird. But I don't CARE.'

Lust
'I *really* want to do things with this person when the lights are off. Or on. I'm not interested in lighting.'

Relationship love
'We've been together six months. I don't know if we'll be together forever, but right now we want to be with each other and we have heaps of fun.'

Lasting love
'I've loved this person for years. We get along well and have similar ideas about some important things, and we're comfortable together and I never seem to want anyone else.'

332 HEART ♥ love

Falling in love

You'll probably have heaps of relationships in your life, particularly since girls these days generally wait longer to settle down and have kids (or even to move out of their parents' house). In your romantic life you'll get dumped, you'll do some dumping, you'll have some so-so relationships, make some bad choices, break hearts, have your heart broken, think you've found The One, be betrayed, betray, get over it, make mistakes and then fall in love again.

Attraction

What makes us feel attracted to certain people? Nobody really knows. Different theories say it's all about:

- **Genetics**   This idea says we're programmed to choose people we want to have stronger, cuter children with. It doesn't explain why some people prefer short brunettes with big legs, and others are crazy for nerdy-looking guys with glasses.
- **Sexuality, or gender preference** (even though you may not have had sex yet) Most girls are heterosexual: they're attracted to guys. Some find themselves more romantically interested in girls (they're gay – homosexual). And some are attracted to both guys and girls (they're bisexual).
- **'Type'**   The first guy who was ever lovely to you was a tall redhead with hairy knees. Ever since then you've been a sucker for big Scottish chaps with a furry middle leg area.
- **'Me want pretty one'**   It's like wanting a shiny toy. You choose a good-looking one, whether or not they have any brains or are useful as well as decorative.
- **Repeating what you know**   You pick someone who somehow looks or acts like your dad, or someone else in your family.
- **Playing nursie**   You pick people who are in trouble or need looking after, or who have no energy and need some of yours. >

> Don't rush in. They have to be a friend not just a partner.
> *Mayz, 16, country WA*

> I think I'm getting more fussy.
> *Sara, 16, Mildura, Vic.*

- **'Some day my prince will come'** You want the whole romantic package. If somebody agrees to take care of you while you stay home and file your nails, then your work is done.
- **Finding your comfort zone** Some people just 'fit right' with you – like an old security blanky or a pair of tracky daks.
- **'Danger: falling person'** 'Oooh, some people are just so exciting! They make stuff happen! You never know what to expect! Take me with you on that adventure!'
- **'Danger: falling expectations'** 'Oh, pick me, because I'm getting desperate. I'll settle for anyone.'
- **Getting conned** You'll take anyone who can talk you into it because you just want to hear those sweet nothings.
- **Physical messages** Mysterious hormones and scents called pheremones (pronounced fare-em-owns) attract you to a guy without you knowing why – it's almost a subconscious decision.

Symptoms Falling in love symptoms can include a racing heartbeat; sweaty palms; flushed cheeks; tingly bits; nausea; enlarged eye pupils; not being hungry; wild feelings of happiness and crushing disappointment; utter self-consciousness; knowing exactly where the person is, even if you're pretending not to notice; not being able to think about very much else; an inability to concentrate.

Of course these symptoms also apply to a fleeting attraction, a crush, and several tropical diseases.

> A lot of my boyfriends have been sort of unsure about what they are supposed to be doing, and it seems they only 'make a move' because their friends keep hassling them.
>
> Denise, 17, Newport, Vic.

> I lost my best friend of all my life because I'm a girl and he's a boy. He got a girlfriend, and that didn't bother me, but his girlfriend didn't like us being friends. That ruined our friendship.
>
> Didi, 17, NZ

Crushes Getting a crush on someone means you're attracted to them but don't necessarily ever do anything about it: you just admire them from afar, blush when they come anywhere near you – and then get a crush on someone else one day.

Most girls get at least one crush on someone they don't know. Usually the crush is on a celebrity such as a singer, sports person or actor. The 'celebrity machine' makes this easier for you by doing stories and publishing pin-up pictures of 'boy bands' and 'pretty guys' (not giant, hairy ones) who are not too adult-looking and therefore likely to appeal to teenage girls. Some girls are prone to 'serial' crushes, one after the other, some stay 'loyal' to a heart-throb for years, and some girls get crushes on horses, or fictional characters instead.

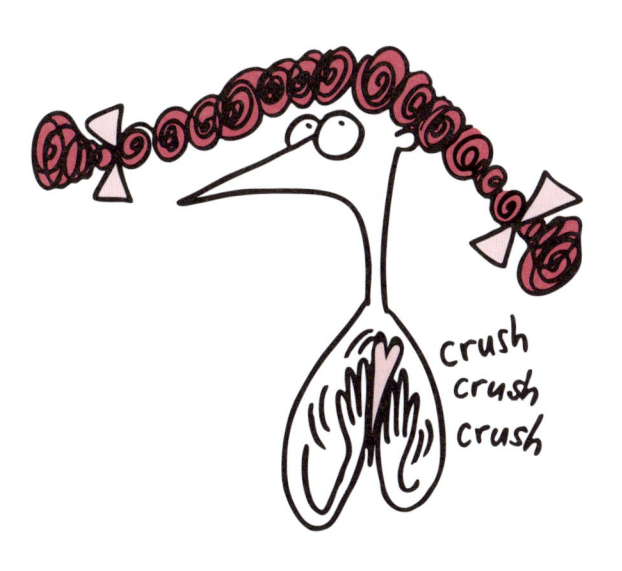

crush crush crush

Texting dramas

There are lots of ways to flirt or continue a relationship using phone calls, texts, social media pages, other messaging and email. Just remember that anything you send can be sent on to other people.

Don't write or send anything unless you could stand it being sent to somebody else – or everybody else – by mistake or deliberately.

Danger areas include over-the-top lovey-dovey babble-on, baby talk (oh please, noooooo), sexy talk and embarrassing photos (why yes, now that you ask, that does include nudity!).

'Sexting'

Some guys suggest or insist you send a nude or raunchy pic to show you trust them or really love them. That's called 'emotional blackmail': don't fall for it.

Any 'sexting' (sending nude or raunchy pics) can result in criminal charges and a permanent criminal record that prevents you from ever working with children. See Chapter 14, Friends, for more on safety online and on the phone.

love ♥ HEART   335

Guys

Now we pause for some faff-on about guys. (If it's girls you seem to be romantically interested in there's stuff on that later in this chapter – and all the dating and relationships info coming up is for you too.)

Stuff to know

- There is no perfect person for you, no Mr Right. There are lots of Mr No Ways, plenty of Mr Approximates, quite a bunch of Mr Okay For Nows, a small gang of Mr Nearly Rights and a handful of Mr You'll Do Me, Sunshines.
- If you change your personality to impress a guy, and he starts spending time with you, you won't be able to keep up the act. (Be yourself. If he likes you, yay. If he doesn't, bzzzt. Move on.)
- If you judge a guy by looks alone, you may end up with a creep.
- Don't give up your girlfriends or spend all your time with a boyfriend.
- Don't fall for a guy who is with someone else, especially a girl you know. Try to have a radar that will only go into full-on Possible Boyfriend mode if he's single.

Bonus facts about guys

- Guys your own age are probably more immature than you are.
- They're going through their own body changes, insecurities and self-esteem struggles.
- Guys are all potential friends, not just potential boyfriends.
- Guys are not aliens. Most of them like doing the same stuff you do – going to movies, watching TV, playing sport, eating, breathing.

Guys to avoid

- **The racist, rude or otherwise stupid guy** Life's too short to hang out with an idiot of small brain and big mouth.
- **The arrogant strutter** A guy who thinks he's 'it and a bit' will never respect you because in his own head he's king.
- **The stud** He acts as if he's made a conquest.
- **The blabberer** Who needs a guy they can't trust?
- **The mean guy** Maybe he has a hard home life. That's sad, but it's not your responsibility to fix it, or to take abuse from him of any kind.
- **The risk taker** He'll always love the risk/drink/drug more than you, and you can get damaged if you're drawn into it with him.

- **The little boy**   He can come back when he's grown up. Gross jokes and uncontrollable giggling ain't that entertaining.
- **The vampire**   Look out for the tragic soul who'll drain your energy.
- **The boy who wants a trophy girlfriend**   Yes, he thinks you're pretty, but does he listen to you or just show you off like a new toy?
- **The trophy boy**   Yes, he's handsome and cool and used to go out with that popular girl, but you're really just using him for show, aren't you?
- **The mummy's boy**   This guy's mother does everything for him and is always hovering over him like a helicopter.
- **The friend's boyfriend**   Out of bounds.

HINT

How to make a guy like you

For this you will need to study the ancient discipline of hypnotism. You will need about six years of study and various trinkets to give as bribes (such as shiny baubles, large-screen televisions and vehicles with sound systems the size of a fridge). Oh, and a guy.

Hints that a guy might be a good one

- He asks you about yourself and what you want to do.
- He likes his mum.
- He doesn't change his behaviour towards you depending on who's around.
- He makes you laugh.
- He's never mean to you.
- He's not mean to other people to try to impress anyone.
- He admits that he finds some things scary and doesn't know stuff.
- He doesn't blab about things you tell him.
- He doesn't try to pressure you into stuff that you don't want to do.
- He uses deodorant and otherwise looks after himself, without thinking he's a movie star.
- Other girls like him as a friend.
- He's generous.

Hooking up, dating, or going out with someone

> I think it is important for girls to know that they don't have to do everything a guy says and that they shouldn't spend their whole lives wondering what they can do to make them happy etc.
>
> Robyn, 17, Gorokan, NSW

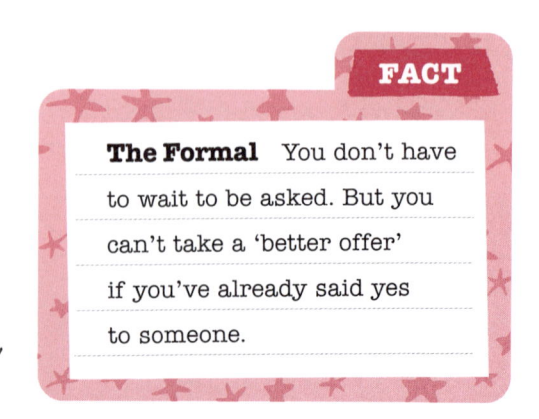

If you like teen mags and websites you've probably already read about a frazillion words on going on dates. Here are some more, briefly, before you lose consciousness from boredom.

- Going on a date, or out with a group and pairing off with someone, doesn't mean either of you are in love, or will have sex, or anything else. It just means you go out.
- You have to communicate about this stuff. When you ask someone out make it clear whether it's a date or you just want to be friends (studying or going to band practice together).
- Think about making a first date going out with a group (unless you don't want other people watching you) and maybe to see something (a movie or music gig) so that you don't have to talk for hours. If you like how it went you can go for a second date, alone, later.

Asking and being asked

There is no reason why girls can't ask someone out on a date. Guys, in fact, are usually pretty awkward and shy, and if you sit around waiting for them it may never happen.

Asking someone out

- Best to ask face to face if you can. Find the person when they're alone and say something along the lines of 'Would you like to go out some time?' That way they can let you know if they're interested or not. Always have something in mind in case they say, 'Sure. What and when?'

FACT

The Formal You don't have to wait to be asked. But you can't take a 'better offer' if you've already said yes to someone.

- If you don't know them very well, see if you can get their phone number and ring. But don't send an email or other message unless you're sure it would be kept private.
- Don't ask them in front of friends of either of you – this could be embarrassing for both of you.
- If the other person says no in a rude or mean way, be assured they're a first-class arse and it's lucky you found out now. If they say no nicely, smile and move on.

When someone asks you out

- Only say yes if you really want to. Otherwise you're just giving false hope.
- Don't rush giggling to tell your friends in front of the person.
- If you're sent a message or email keep it private.
- Only ever say no in a genuinely nice way (see 'Rejection' below).
- If you can't go to a specific event but you're interested in the person, make that clear: 'I can't go because I have hockey practice every Saturday lunchtime, but if something else comes up ask me again', or 'I can't because I have to go to this family thing. But maybe another time?'

Rejection

Nearly everybody gets rejected at some point in their life, no matter how smart, gorgeous or popular they are. Sometimes rejection, like attraction, doesn't really make sense – it's not about how likeable we are, or how attractive, funny or adorable.

How to handle rejection

- Keep your dignity. Try not to make a scene, throw yourself on the ground, burst into tears, abuse them, sneer or say something rude. You can do all those things alone in your bedroom later.
- Don't try to figure out why – it's not because you are fat, ugly or stupid, its just because they can't feel any 'chemistry' or they have their own quirky reason. It means it wouldn't have worked out – so move on. >

what if I beg?

HOW NOT to 'HANDLE' RejectioN

love ♥ HEART   339

- Don't wallow in self-pity, and make sure you're not obsessing about them just because you can't have them. Hold out for someone who'll really like YOU.
- Get on with something else to take your mind off it.
- Give it time: I guarantee you that after a while you'll notice things that will make you glad you didn't go out with that person.

> Don't rush into anything. Boys are not the world. I am 17 and I have never had a boyfriend and I don't feel less of a person because of it.
> Maddy, 17, Springsure, Qld

HINT

The best dating advice ever If the other person isn't interested, GIVE UP NOW. Anything else is a waste of time and liable to end with you feeling humiliated or dissatisfied.

If you do the rejecting

- Tell them simply and make it short: 'That's really nice of you but, I'm sorry, I don't feel the same', or 'That's really nice of you but, I'm sorry, I'm kind of interested in someone else at the moment.' Honesty and kindness are always best.
- Don't try to make them feel better about the rejection by sending confusing signals such as flirting with them or saying, 'Maybe next week.'
- Don't faff on, explaining why or giving excuses.
- End the conversation nicely: 'I'm sorry that I'm not up for that, but it's good to be friends, and I hope I'll see you around.' Then leave them so they can have a moment to get over the rejection without you watching them.
- From then on, when you run into them, say hi and don't ignore them.

On a date

First dates can be a bit nerve-racking but here are some hints to help things go more smoothly.

- If it's just to the movies don't dress like you're going to your Formal. Choose a favourite outfit that you feel good in (and use deodorant).

> It sucks when the feeling's not mutual!!! Holly, 16, Geelong, Vic.

340   HEART ♥ love

- Work out beforehand if one of you is paying or you're going halves. If the other person's paying for what you eat, or you're splitting the bill, don't order the most expensive things.
- Be safe: tell an adult where you're going and when you'll be back, and carry enough money for a taxi. Don't go anywhere that feels dodgy or dangerous. And if you begin to get a bad feeling about the person, or don't know them well, stay in crowded places (see Chapter 8, Confidence).
- Don't do stuff you wouldn't normally do such as drinking something really unfamiliar.
- Think of some things you could talk about if the conversation dies. Have a few conversation starters, such as a mutual amazing friend's latest news, or a TV show or movie. Ask them about something you know they're into.
- When you ask them questions about themselves, listen to the answers. Seems obvious, but people can get caught up with nerves and end up not listening to what the other person has said.
- It's sometimes a good idea to admit that you are nervous, because they will be too. Always make light of it if things go wrong (say, someone spills something).
- Don't agree with everything they say if you don't, but be polite. Better to say, 'I've never thought about it like that', or 'That's interesting – I have a pretty different opinion . . .', than 'You great hulking moron, that's the stupidest thing I ever heard.'
- Turn off your phone while you're together.
- Don't talk about your ex, don't bitch, don't put yourself down, and don't pretend you're not hungry. >

> Younger girls need to know that boys don't only care about your looks. The good ones actually care about what is on the inside.
> Tamara, 18, Tweed Heads, NSW

HINT

Date blabbing Don't tell everyone you're going on a date, and don't tell everyone everything that happened. Respect the other person's privacy, and your own.

love ♥ HEART 341

- Try to have a good time instead of looking for faults or becoming negative.
- Never dump the person you came with and go off or home with someone else.
- If you've had a good time, say so at the end of the date. If you haven't, just say thank you. Have a few casual back-up lines in case they try to kiss you and you don't feel like it: 'I never kiss on the first date', or 'I think I'm coming down with a cold and I'd hate to give it to you.'

Kissing

No matter how old you are, you're usually going to be a bit nervous about the first kiss with someone. Don't expect your first kiss to be that spectacular: like most things it takes a bit of practice. And it's not all about you – the other person could be a shocking kisser. Some things that will help you:

- fresh breath – just so you won't have to worry about it, brush your teeth regularly, and before you think there's going to be a smooch don't eat garlic or raw onions

A second date

If you want to date someone again

- Tell them at the end of the first date that you'll be in touch or that you'd love to hear from them, but don't push to make firm plans.
- If you haven't heard from them within three days send them a text or ring and say, 'Hey, I had a great time the other night', without actually asking them out.
- If they don't respond, or sound uncomfortable or not very interested, back off and move on.

If you don't want to date someone again

- It's important to try to avoid hurting their feelings.
- Don't give false hope. Say, 'Thanks, that's really nice of you, but I don't think I really want to get into dating right now', or 'I'm going to be pretty busy for a while, but maybe we'll bump into each other some time.'

> I went out with a guy who was 16 when I was 17 and he was only interested in what he could get out of me and motor bikes. Madeleine, 18, Cooktown, Qld

- moist lips – use a fairly standard lip protector as too much gloss can make them sticky and lipstick might get smudged all over both of you
- the right position – stand or sit close to the person, lean in and tilt your head slightly to one side (if you see the other person tilting their head one way, go for the other side so you don't bump heads)
- closed eyes – not compulsory but can help you focus on the feeling (open them as soon as the kiss is over)
- breathing – remember to (through your nose when your lips are busy)
- the Tongue Thing – you can keep your lips closed, or open them slightly for a deeper, more sexy kind of kiss. The tongue gently licks the other person's lips or tongue. This is what's known as 'French kissing' or 'pashing'. It can be awkward at first, but after a time will feel natural.

Kissing takes practice

Kissing problems

- Sucking at the other person's lips or face – most people don't like it.
- Lovebites, 'hickeys' or bruises, created by suction or biting – they look tacky.
- Pash rash around your mouth, which can happen if you kiss your partner for so long that your skin is rubbed red – not a good look, and especially painful and long-lasting if he has shaving stubble.
- If your partner does any of the above, or otherwise kisses like a demented washing machine – all thrusting wet tongue – or does scared little nibbles that you don't like, stop and say, 'Let's try kissing like this', and do something a bit more slow and sweet.

> Always be in a relationship with someone who makes you feel good about yourself and understands when you want to do girly stuff with friends.
> Sally, 18, Adelaide, SA

> I've realised that I have never dated a guy my own age, they have always been a couple of years older. The maturity level is much greater. Pippa, 18, Thornlie, WA

Being 'differently attracted'

As long as we've been humans, some women fall in love with women (lesbians), some guys prefer boyfriends (gay men), there are folk who fancy both genders (bisexual) and people not interested in any of it (asexual).

Some people are transgender which means they feel they're in the 'wrong' body and must live as the other gender. It sounds complicated but is really just about knowing who you are.

Working out your sexual identity is a part of growing up, and questioning your sexuality is totally normal. You might already have a clear idea of your gender and sexual identity. But if not, you don't have to decide now. It's not as if you get to be a teenager and suddenly have to choose which door to walk through.

Your sexuality is up to you to decide, not for other people to 'diagnose'. Despite what some extreme religions believe, or even what people you know and love might say, being gay or bisexual is not wrong or bad, or a disease or illness that needs to be 'cured'. It's just how some people are. Sexual orientation is in-built and not something that can, or should, be changed.

You probably already know or have met some lesbian people. You can't tell they're lesbians by looking – they don't all dress the same, have the same haircut, like the same music or give a secret handshake.

It's entirely legal to be homosexual, and gay people have the same community responsibilities and most of the rights of other people. Shamefully, Australian law still doesn't recognise same-sex marriages.

How do you know if you're gay?

The physical and emotional changes of puberty can be pretty confusing. A lot of girls experiment with their sexuality while they work out how they feel and what their preferences are. (Having bisexual feelings can be particularly confusing and put you under pressure because some people want you to 'make a decision – straight or gay': you don't have to.)

Having a crush on someone of the same sex, such as a schoolteacher or a friend's older sister, doesn't necessarily mean you are a lesbian. Touching or experimenting or having sex with a girl doesn't 'make' you gay, even if the other girl considers herself a lesbian. And having sex with a girl or a guy isn't a 'test' that tells you whether you are gay or heterosexual, because there is no test.

Some girls 'just know' from an early age, or it kind of dawns on them they only ever have crushes on, or are romantically interested in, girls. Others try to suppress their real feelings and then finally accept them when they're adults.

If you think you might be a lesbian take it slow and don't worry – even if you don't know any others now, you will. There are lots of places, festivals and clubs where people won't be shocked or tease you, and you'll find lesbian and straight friends you can be yourself with.

The important thing as you're discovering your sexuality is to find a non-judgemental person or people you can talk to without them betraying your confidence.

Being a lesbian

It can be hard as a teenager to find other girls who feel the same because they are often still working it out or scared to say anything. Lesbian relationships can also be difficult because of the ignorance and prejudice experienced: could you hold a girl's hand without being shouted at in the street? And it can be difficult to tell parents because they may have trouble sorting out their feelings and their fears that a lesbian daughter will face a lot of prejudice and may not later have children.

You may have to reassure some girl friends that you don't want to be their 'girlfriend', and give them a little time to realise it's still the same old you. But they need to get used to this new aspect of your life.

Some people are gay: that's their business

I kissed a few girls and the word got around. I spent a lot of time denying the rumours, but got sick of it. That's who I am for now. Who knows? Who cares?   Elaine, 16, Charters Towers, Qld

I have plenty of friends who are lesbians and they're as happy as Larry. (Larry's happy.)

Lesbians do not have to act like men or pretend they're men, and I don't know any who do. You don't have to dress outlandishly as a lesbian or have really short hair. You can be any sort of lesbian you like: you can wear lipstick and dresses and be interested in cooking and flower arranging, or motorcycles or rainfall averages. Don't be frightened by some images of lesbian life you might see on the web, in magazines or in porn – none of it's compulsory, and there's no one way to be a lesbian, or bisexual.

Coming out Coming out usually means to declare your sexuality. Don't feel you have to make a big announcement. (Some people have done this and then changed their mind about their sexuality.) You may just want to tell family and one or two close friends. You may want to be out in the family and in at school or vice versa, but remember that can be impossible to control.

LGBTQA+: who's who

LGBTQA+ stands for different ways of not being straight. ('Straight' means heterosexual, or opposite-sex attracted). Gender identity (whether you identify as a girl, guy, somewhere in between or neither) is not the same as your sexuality (who you may be attracted to).

Lesbian means gay woman.

Gay means homosexual man. Lesbians are also 'gay'.

Bisexual describes a person who's attracted to people of both genders.

Trans means someone is born with the anatomy of a boy or girl but how they feel inside about their gender identity doesn't match.

Intersex is a person who's born not typically male or female.

Asexual means someone who can be in love but isn't interested in sex.

Non-binary is an identity that is somewhere between 'male' and 'female'.

Queer just means not 'straight'. Anyway, all you need to know is, if you're LGBTQA+, that's OK and you're not alone! (See contacts on the opposite page.)

Being gay or transgender at school   Your school should enforce a policy that protects the rights of gay and transgender students, and takes fast and firm action against bullying.

Some schools unfairly insist on rigid different-sex couples at school formals, and generally won't support or accept their gay students, even recommending that gay students try to change their sexuality through religious courses (this doesn't work).

You should have the right to be out and gay without bullying or discrimination at school, but of course that isn't always the case in reality. And of course some people just love the drama of accusation or name-calling. Gay students can often feel a sense of enormous relief after 'coming out' and being able to act almost 'gayer than gay' for a while as a reaction against being hidden or to rebel against the idea that it's a shameful thing.

'Out and proud' can be a positive change, but it can also make you a target, or seem like the biggest thing ever in the history of the world for you (until it settles down and just becomes another variation on 'normal' again). In some schools, with a bullying or a punishingly religious culture, it may not be safe for you to come out. Before anything else, keep yourself safe, and reach out for help and support, anonymously if you want to (see 'More Info' below).

More info on identity and different sexuality

qlife.org.au
Free webchat and support phoneline (usually late afternoon and evening hours) at 1800 184 527.

minus18.org.au
Australia's biggest youth-led LGBTIQ+ site.

scarleteen.com/article/sexual-identity
Q and A about coming out, having same-sex crushes, gay parents and transgender matters.

transcendsupport.com.au
Parent and trans peer support, info and more.

gendercentre.org.au
Choose Groups, then Transtopia Youth and scroll down to download a booklet made by and for trans young people. Or, choose Resources then Kits & Fact Sheets.

pflag.org.au
Parents and Friends of Lesbians and Gays. Can advise on how to come out to your parents.

genderhelpforparents.com.au
pgdc.org.au
Parent-led support groups.

ry.org.nz
RainbowYOUTH group.

Fun lists for every stage of love

Here are some lists of songs and movie DVDs to celebrate romance and help you through heartbreak and other bad times. (Most are classics – oldies but goodies.) Add your own favourites to the lists. Check the film ratings for age suitability.

Classic romance movies

10 Things I Hate about You Huge teen hit based on Shakespeare's *Taming of the Shrew*.
An Affair to Remember Oldie but goldie, the inspiration for *Sleepless in Seattle*.
Bridget Jones's Diary Jane Austen, big undies and stupid jumpers.
Casablanca The black and white classic.
Eternal Sunshine of the Spotless Mind Forgetting and wondering.
50 First Dates Forgetting and believing.
Four Weddings and a Funeral True love, Brit-style.
Love Actually Love, everywhere.
Much Ado about Nothing Shakespeare rides again.
Muriel's Wedding Hilarious and touching.
The Princess Bride Silly and romantic.
Sixteen Candles and **Pretty in Pink** Teen romance and heartache 80s style.
Sleepless in Seattle Finding The One.
The Year My Voice Broke Aussie coming-of-age story.
Twilight series Team Edward? Team over it?
The Adjustment Bureau Fate, destiny and fighting for love.

Classic break-up wallowing songs

Always Something There to Remind Me Rebecca's Empire
Back to Black Amy Winehouse
Cry Me a River Julie London
Crying Roy Orbison or k.d. lang
Go Your Own Way Fleetwood Mac
I Don't Feel Like Dancin' Scissor Sisters
I Will Always Love You Dolly Parton or Whitney Houston
Poor Me Coldplay
Poor Poor Pitiful Me Linda Ronstadt

Somebody's Crying Chris Isaak
Somebody that I Used to Know Gotye (with Kimbra)
Someone Like You Adele

Classic movies for a good cry

Bambi Deer, dear.
Beaches Lifelong friendship, terminal illness.
Breakfast at Tiffany's Iconic Audrey Hepburn, sunglasses, cat.
Edward Scissorhands Trying to fit in and find love.
E.T. Phone home, for god's sake.
Ghost Nice husband, but dead.
Moulin Rouge Boy sings, villain twirls moustache, girl faints.
Rabbit-Proof Fence Two little girls try to get back to their mum.
Romeo + Juliet Classic Shakespeare in modern gangster setting.
Steel Magnolias Great cast, terminal illness.
Titanic Love floats, ship sinks.

Classic get-over-it songs

Don't Need You to (Tell Me I'm Pretty) Samantha Mumba
Don't Tell Me Avril Lavigne
(I Could) Wipe the Floor (with You) Lisa Miller
I Will Survive Gloria Gaynor
It's Raining Men The Weathergirls
Let Him Fly Dixie Chicks
No Man's Woman Sinead O'Connor
R.E.S.P.E.C.T. Aretha Franklin
Rolling in the Deep Adele
These Boots Were Made for Walking Nancy Sinatra
Since U Been Gone Kelly Clarkson
Smile Lily Allen
Strong Enough Cher
Where I Stood Missy Higgins
You're So Vain Carly Simon

Classic songs to get you in a good mood

Absolutely Everybody Vanessa Amorosi

Ain't No Mountain High Enough The Temptations

Bad Reputation Joan Jett

Beautiful Day U2

Born to Fight Tracy Chapman

Can't Hold Us Down Christina Aguilera

Celebration Kool and the Gang

Dancing with Myself The Donnas

Don't Change INXS

Everything Reminds Me of My Dog Jane Siberry

Express Yourself Madonna

Feelin' Kinda Sporty Dave Graney 'n' the Coral Snakes

For Once in My Life Frank Sinatra or Michael Bublé

Free Your Mind En Vogue

From Head to Toe Elvis Costello

Get Dancin' Disco Tex and His Sex-O-Lettes

Get Happy Judy Garland

Girls Just Wanna Have Fun Cyndi Lauper

The Glamorous Life Sheila E

Good Vibrations The Beach Boys

Here's Where I Stand Tiffany Taylor

Holiday Madonna

I Can See Clearly Now Johnny Nash

I Feel Love Donna Summer

I Kissed a Girl Jill Sobule

I'm a Believer The Monkees

I'm Coming Out Diana Ross

I'm Every Woman Chaka Khan

I'm Free Rolling Stones or The Soup Dragons

I'm Too Sexy Right Said Fred

Independent Woman Destiny's Child

Just a Girl No Doubt

Keep on Livin' Le Tigre

Man! I Feel Like a Woman Shania Twain

Move on Up Curtis Mayfield

My Boyfriend's Back The Spazzys

One Love Bob Marley and the Wailers

Precious Things Tori Amos

Respect Yourself The Staples Singers

Sisters Are Doin' It Eurythmics with Aretha Franklin

Shakin' the Tree (Woman's Day) Peter Gabriel and Youssou N'Dour

Stupid Girls Pink

Suddenly I See KT Tunstall

Sunshine on a Rainy Day Christine Anu

Take Me to the River Al Green

That's Not My Name The Ting Tings

There's More to Life than This Björk

These Are Days 10,000 Maniacs

Tubthumping (I Get Knocked Down But I Get Up Again) Chumbawamba

Turn Off the Light Nelly Furtado

We Are Family Sister Sledge

Wild Wild Life Talking Heads

You Can Get It if You Really Want Jimmy Cliff

Young Hearts Run Free Candi Staton

Video India Arie

Walkin' on Sunshine Katrina and the Waves

What a Wonderful World Louis Armstrong or Joey Ramone

Woman Neneh Cherry

Add some of your own favourites:

_____
_____
_____
_____
_____

✱ Now see the lists of movies and books with feisty heroines in Chapter 23, Equality, Frivolity!

Relationships

After you've been dating for a bit the two of you may decide you're a couple. Being in a couple involves both of you working out what it means and what the ground rules are.

Good relationships

When you're in a healthy relationship you:

- really like and enjoy each other
- trust and respect each other
- are honest with each other
- can be 'yourself' and don't have to put on an act
- keep communicating and listening to each other
- can argue or disagree without fighting all the time
- can both say sorry
- don't have to spend all your time together
- have some, not all, things in common
- agree about whether you can both still date other people or only each other
- agree also that each partner would 'call it off' before starting something with someone else or telling other people
- don't really care if the other person doesn't look like a movie star or wears awful shoes.

Wrangling partners and friends

- Don't drop your friends when you get a partner. Try to spend some time with both.
- Keep the full-on snogging and baby talk for private moments. Nobody else ever wants to see you all over each other or hear you call each other 'iddle wookums'.
- Be sensitive – don't faff on about your partner to your friends all the time as if they should have one too.
- Make sure you don't betray your friends' confidences to your partner, or your partner's to your friends.

- If your friends don't like your partner, or your partner doesn't like your friends, see them separately but ask yourself, Do they see something that I need to be concerned about?
- Don't expect a friend to tag along with just you and your partner – go out together in a group rather than a threesome.
- Try not to be jealous of a friend and your partner, unless you think either of them is flirting with the other, or you come across them behaving in a way they wouldn't if they knew you were there: kissing on the lips, being madly passionate or . . . I don't know, wearing each other's underpants on their heads. Somewhat suspicious, I'd call it.

> It's awesome when it's good, but when it's bad it turns you right off relationships all together.
> Linda, 17, Lisarow, NSW

FACT

If you think you'll have sex Just because you're madly in love and trust each other doesn't mean you should have a baby, or that you can't get a sexually transmitted disease. Always use a condom (see Chapter 16, Sex).

Problem relationships

Sometimes a relationship just isn't quite right. Some common aspects of an unhealthy relationship include:

- your partner is way older – it's generally not good when a young or mid-teenager goes out with anybody more than two years older (and can even be illegal in some states) and it's definitely not good for them to go out with someone older than 20 (sure, it can be flattering, but he also might be unable to get a girlfriend his own age, or be too controlling)
- friends and family say they are worried about the relationship in some way
- your partner is often critical of you or doesn't seem to really like or respect you
- your partner is over the top about love – says they can't live without you, is too possessive and wants to be with you *all* the time
- one or both of you is very jealous, which leads to accusations and lack of trust

- one or both of you is making the other 'prove' their love by doing things they don't want to
- you bring out bad rather than good things in each other
- you fight a lot, disagreeing on nearly everything.

Break-ups

Some relationships are only good for a little while; others break up because one of the partners wants to move on. Sometimes it takes time to recover, even if you made the decision yourself or you made the decision together.

If you're the dumper

- Do it face to face. Never send a message or a letter: it's disrespectful, and could be made public. If you absolutely can't face them, call. But make sure they're alone and can talk.
- Explain why you're breaking up with them.
- Talk about how you feel, rather than blaming the other person: 'I want to be single for a while', not 'You turned out to be pretty boring.'
- Make it a clean break, no matter how upset your partner is. If you're sure you have made the right decision don't get back together. This just prolongs everyone's agony.
- Don't gossip, spread rumours or talk about private moments you had with your ex.
- If you 'cheated', think about how not to get into that situation again. (Note to self: break up first, then get together with somebody else.)
- Don't expect the two of you to be best friends straight away. That's unrealistic. It might take weeks for your ex to get over you, and they might never want to be friends.

If you're the dumpee

- Don't argue, don't beg, don't disagree with their decision, but feel free to say, ' Of course I accept your decision that it's over, but I don't agree with those things you say.'
- Don't see your ex at all for a few weeks, if that's possible. If they're at your school or work just avoid them as much as you can.

- After that see if you want to be friends. Not being 'friends' is okay too. It doesn't mean you have to be enemies.
- Don't assume there's something wrong with you. You just weren't right for each other.
- It's all right to cry, get mad and feel humiliated – these are normal feelings. But do it in private with family and friends instead of your ex.
- Give yourself a few weeks to get over it. Take it one day at a time, and don't feel bad if you have an overly emotional day (especially before a period).
- Prepare yourself for seeing your ex with somebody else.
- Even if they've behaved badly, don't gossip too much about it, or badmouth them, or tell their secrets. That just makes you look bitter.
- If your ex says nasty things or spreads rumours about you, be dignified and don't get into public or private fights. Tell a few close friends the truth and send them out to counterbalance the gossip.
- Don't rush into a new relationship just so that you can feel that 'somebody' wants you.

Being single is fine

Many girls don't have a partner until they leave school. Others start panicking if they're single at 13. (Sit down and put your head between your knees and breathe slowly. For a few years.)

Being single is heaps better than being in a bad relationship. You're not automatically lonely just because you're not part of a couple.

Good things about being single include:

* you can do what you want when you want
* you can flirt with who you want when you want, and go on as many dates as you want
* you can focus on other things – friends, hobbies, sports, school
* you can plan great girls'-nights-in (or out!).

The best way to find someone, or to not mind about being single for now, is to be happy with yourself. So enjoy being single and get to know what you want and what makes you happy. One day it'll be as if your porch light has come on and all the moths are zeroing in. One day your moth will come. Until then don't settle for a cockroach.

Abusive and controlling relationships

Emotional, physical or sexual abuse is never right – in any kind of relationship – and must never be accepted. Unacceptable behaviour includes:

- always putting you down and being unkind to you
- making you wait on them and serve and fetch things, telling you what to do or what to wear and enforcing in other ways that they think men are the boss of, or superior to, women
- forcing or pressuring you into sex of any kind (see Chapter 16, Sex, for more on sex without consent)
- accusing you of flirting or being 'unfaithful', without evidence
- being unfaithful (even though you're 'not allowed' to be).
- making demands or ordering you around
- sulking or giving you the silent treatment if they don't get their way
- flying into unpredictable rages even if they apologise afterwards.

Many people in an abusive relationship start to think they deserve to be treated badly. This is never true.

Even though you may love your partner, if they treat you badly they need to change or you need to leave the relationship. You must escape from a partner who constantly puts you down, frightens you, or threatens, hits or otherwise hurts you, mentally or physically.

How to get out of an abusive relationship

- Tell a trusted adult what you are going through, and ask them for help – whether it's advice or just being there to support you and help protect you.
- If you want to give it another chance, tell your partner you don't like certain aspects of their behaviour – that it makes you feel upset and disrespected. Tell them that they need to change. If they agree or get counselling, that's a good sign. But put a time limit on the change, such as a couple of weeks (even if only you know about the limit), and if the change doesn't happen, then break up. Many people believe promises to change that never come true, or only a bit, so make sure you stick to your time limit. Don't keep giving them another chance. It's not enough that the person feels bad and says they love you – their behaviour must change.

* Write down the abusive behaviour so you have a list to remind yourself of what's really happening.

* Make a plan to end the relationship: work out where and when you will tell the person. Don't break up face to face and alone if you are scared the reaction will be violent or threatening. You can do it on the phone or have somebody with you.

* If you're threatened tell the person that you've told many people about the abusive behaviour, and that they'll be protecting you. Get an adult, a parent or a teacher to talk to the person and explain that they can't threaten or harm you in any way, and that they'll be watched.

* Remember that it's a crime when someone stalks you – repeatedly harasses, follows, intimidates or calls you without permission. Contact the police if necessary.

Don't be ashamed of yourself, even if you feel you stayed with them too long. Get help to stand up for yourself, and have support around you. You are not alone. Don't believe them if they say nobody else will like you or love you. Reach out and you'll find help.

More info on abusive relationships

If you're scared that you're in immediate danger call the police on 000.

Kids Helpline: 1800 55 1800

theline.org.au
Helpline: 1800 695 463
This site especially for young people explores what's 'crossing the line', including emotional and physical abuse in relationships. Videos, songs and stories.

lovegoodbadugly.com
Info about abusive or controlling relationships with boyfriends or girlfriends. Has good checklists, a warning signs quiz, help and support.

1800respect.org.au
24-hour Helpline: 1800 737 732
Free counselling from the National Sexual Assault, Domestic Family Violence Counselling Service. They can support and advise you. You can call anonymously. You can also call to talk about it, or get help dealing with any emotional, physical or sexual abuse or assault that happened in the past.

au.reachout.com
For teens having a hard time.

I had a boyfriend for 3 years. The break up was inevitably difficult, but I'm glad it happened cos I need to develop on my own, without a boyfriend's influence. Kylie, 17, Rockhampton, Qld

Heartbreak Breaking up happens to us all – even the rich and famous – that's why so many songs are about broken hearts. And while you're going through it, every heartbreak song seems to be about you. If you feel it's really making you depressed, talk to a counsellor – your GP can help you find one (and see 'More Info' below).

Otherwise listen to the songs, watch some sad movies, have a bit of a wallow and talk it out with friends. Then, when you're ready, switch to up, optimistic, girls-are-strong, kick-arse songs and movies (see the lists earlier in this chapter and the ones at the end of Chapter 23, Equality, Frivolity) and get back into life. It takes time to recover from a broken heart, but you absolutely will.

> I feel quite happy with my life at the moment being single. Maybe in a few years time I will feel the need to have a serious relationship.
> Kelly, 18, Albany, WA

More info on relationships

lovegoodbadugly.com
Everything from asking somebody out to being asked, quizzes on how it's going, what to do when it goes wrong, help to break up and lots of fun stuff about being single or in a relationship. Videos, quizzes, stories.

> If you know the relationship you're in isn't working then, trust me, stopping it is better than dragging it out. It hurts when you break up with people but the longer the relationship the more it hurts. Ayesha, 18, Geraldton, WA

16

SEX

You stand on your head, & I'll go into another room

totally safe sex...

You'll either look at that word sex and say, 'Euww, yuk', or you'll be interested in reading on. If you think the idea of sex is gross then **don't read this chapter until you feel ready**. Or you can read it just to be informed. It's okay if you're not ready to actually do anything about it yet.

The main reason people have sex is because it feels good, especially with somebody they're attracted to or in love with. Nature has equipped us to enjoy having sex so that we do it a lot and that way have lots of children and keep populating – kind of like in those documentaries where fish lay about 67 000 eggs. **Luckily** we don't have to behave like mad fish. We get to wait until we're ready, decide on the right person, use contraception if we don't want to get pregnant, and **protect ourselves** against sexually transmitted diseases or infections.

Becoming a sexual person

You become a sexual person at puberty, when your hormone levels change and your girly bits start to mature – usually long before you're ready to have sex with somebody. (Scoot back to the section 'Your Girly Bits' in Chapter 1, Change, so you know what sexual equipment you're working with, then come right back here.)

Sexual thoughts

As your body matures you start to have sexual thoughts and feelings, and to have crushes on and be physically attracted to other people. Everybody gets sexual thoughts or has sexual daydreams.

You don't have control over your sexual feelings in the way you do over your sexual actions. Sexy or curious thoughts can pop into your head at the most inconvenient times. Just as long as you know that thinking about something, or knowing about something, doesn't mean you have to do it, or that there's anything wrong with you.

Masturbation

Pretty much everyone starts to masturbate once they begin to have sexual feelings and become curious about their body. Masturbation means touching yourself for sexual pleasure. It's normal, healthy, shouldn't hurt, and everybody does it sooner or later (only not on the bus). Some girls do it once or twice a week; others have a craze on it every day for a while.

Girls usually touch and rub the area around the clitoris with their fingers or one finger. If they continue, the good feeling increases (they become 'sexually aroused') and the clitoris enlarges slightly. But touching yourself there doesn't necessarily mean you have to keep on doing it if you don't want to. If you don't feel like going on that's fine: don't.

To help with lubrication so you're not dry, which can cause soreness, you can use your vaginal secretions, spit or a little bit of any oil that's safe for the body. Massage or body oil can be good, although some can include ingredients that sting.

Me and my boyfriend are getting ready to get into that kind of stuff.
Pam, 14, Mt Ommaney, Qld

I want to know about the feelings and pleasure you get from it, but I guess that just comes with experience.
Anonymous, 15, Katherine, NT

Most girls masturbate while they are lying in bed or in the bathroom. (Lock the door first.) Some lie on their front and move their hips, others on their back and rub or gently flick their clitoris (for a bit of info on your equipment down there see Chapter 1, Change). There really aren't any rules – just whatever feels good.

Masturbation is very safe: you can't catch a disease or get pregnant. It helps you find out what you like and what's the best way to become sexually aroused – different things work for different people – so that eventually you can show a partner what you enjoy. And it's a good way to learn that sex is about what you feel, not what you look like.

Although it's the clitoris that will get you to orgasm faster and more effectively, some girls put an object in their vagina. Hospital emergency room doctors are always removing things from people's vaginas that shouldn't have been there in the first place, including vegetables. Think carefully before you look sideways at that zucchini – or anything else. Anything you put inside should be well washed, easily gripped, long enough so it can't go all the way in where you can't reach it, and easily removed. You have to be over 18 to buy a vibrator (a battery-operated plastic object usually shaped like a penis).

Stages

Usually the stages of becoming a sexual person go something like this (but it's not like a shopping list, and doesn't always go in this order):

- born with all girly bits present and correct
- go through the changes of puberty
- develop a regular period and ovulate once a month or so
- have some sexual thoughts now and again
- start being romantically interested in guys or girls (see Chapter 15, Love)
- have more sexual thoughts
- learn how to masturbate to see what physical sexual feelings are like
- start relationships slowly, with kissing and cuddling and holding hands
- eventually (hopefully) decide to have sexual contact with somebody who respects you
- move on to sexual touching of private parts (with fingers) or oral sex (with mouths)
- have vaginal sex
- negotiate a respectful and loving relationship with somebody you're happy to be with.

Signs of sexual arousal

Signs of arousal include:

* wanting to keep being touched

* breathing faster

* feeling warm, tingly and sensitive (especially the nipples and the between-the-legs department)

* the vagina creating slippery 'juices' (so that if sex happened it would be easier)

* getting hot and sweaty.

Feeling sexually aroused doesn't mean you have to have sex.

Orgasm

An orgasm is a big rush of sexual pleasure – the climax to sexual arousal. It's often known as 'coming'. It's followed by an intense feeling of release. Not everyone makes panting or breathy noises and then yelps, grunts, squeals or screams during orgasm. But because it's such a great feeling many people do 'let themselves go' and make a noise. It's okay either way. Afterwards you'll feel relaxed.

Usually masturbating, or being stroked or licked around or on the clitoris by a partner, is the easiest way for girls and women to orgasm. It is rarer for them to orgasm during penis-in-vagina sex because the clitoris isn't always stimulated while that's going on.

For guys, sexual stimulation, by masturbation or with a partner, leads to the penis becoming erect (hard). When a guy reaches orgasm he ejaculates (pronounced ee-jack-u-lates). This means the penis spurts out about a teaspoon of semen, a runny white fluid that contains sperm. The individual sperm in the semen are too tiny to be seen except under a microscope, but there are hundreds of millions of them in each ejaculation and it only takes one to make you pregnant (there's more on all this in 'The Penis' later).

Wait till you meet somebody nice.   Sally, 14, Forestville, NSW

One of my friends is going out with an older guy, and is thinking about having sex though she is far too young (12). I am really worried about her. All of my friends know too much about sex. We're still kids really so I don't like talking about masturbation and stuff. **I still find it a bit gross.**   Bobbi, 13, Brisbane, Qld

Sexual touching

In the same way that enjoying masturbation and having an orgasm doesn't mean you're necessarily ready to have sex with someone, enjoying kissing with a guy doesn't mean you're ready to have sex with him either.

What do people mean by 'sex' or 'having sex'? Most people mean penis-in-vagina or 'penetrative vaginal sex', otherwise known as 'going all the way' or 'doing it' (see 'Going All the Way' later in the chapter). But there are other forms of sex, such as oral sex (explained soon), and there can be many steps before – or instead of – 'the final destination'.

Taking your time

Becoming a sexual person is a big experience, and taking time to enjoy touching and exploring and being close to someone else is part of it. There are lots of pleasures to discover and finding out about them might follow this kind of order (or not):

- talking, going out, liking each other a lot
- holding hands
- kissing and cuddling
- open-mouth kissing
- stroking, kissing, licking or blowing on each other's neck and other places
- touching the breasts through clothes
- touching or kissing breasts
- hands down each other's pants, exploring.

You might decide you want to go out with lots of guys over the next few years, having fun and a bit of a kiss and cuddle. You might find that doing intimate physical things with someone is so new and such a big deal that you want to go slowly for a while, enjoying, say, having your breasts touched but not yet feeling ready to have your clothes off. You might have gone further with somebody than you felt comfortable about and now want to go back to an earlier stage for the time being. Or you might decide that you're really enjoying all the things you're doing with the other person, including the physical stuff, and

> Going to a Christian school we don't get the real nitty gritty [information]. When the time comes it would be nice to know exactly what to do!!
> Macquarie, 13, Torquay, Vic.

> I don't like to talk about sex.
> Tara, 13, Rockhampton, Qld

that if you keep liking being together you'll probably become more intimate and perhaps end up having sex.

Because teenage guys are new to sex too, they often get to – or want to get to – orgasm quickly, but most girls like taking time to learn about and enjoy different stages of touching. Make sure you're not rushed.

Different strokes for different folks Stroking can make us feel great. Having the private bits touched by a partner's hands can be part of 'foreplay' leading to having sex. But it doesn't have to go all the way, and touching can be to any part of the body. Stroking hand motions are usually sexier than patting ones. It should always be done gently, especially at the start. If you're ready, it can also feel warm and wonderful for the body, including the private parts, to be licked or sucked.

When two people stroke each other's private parts it's sometimes called mutual masturbation; licking and sucking is known as oral sex. Often partners take turns.

As part of touching, the girl's partner might softly stroke or lick around the vulva and clitoris area. Often just around rather than right on the clitoris feels better. (A guy may think girls are more thrilled about the idea of a finger inside the vagina, so you might have to tell him about the magic clitoris.) If it's what the girl wants, the stroking or licking can continue until she has an orgasm.

Touching or oral sex needs to be 'safe' (see 'Safe Sex' later in the chapter). Sexually transmitted infections can be passed on by hands, although the chance isn't as high as it is with oral sex. It's okay not to like giving oral sex or swallowing semen (which contains sperm). Oral sex is given as a favour; it's not compulsory.

> I've never even had a boyfriend and already heaps of people my age are having sex.
> Mari, 15, Frankston, Vic.

> I've heard of oral sex but I dunno what it is.
> Gaelle, 14, Penrith, NSW

I'm scared of sex in general, and tampons.   Bridie, 13, Deniliquin, NSW

I've only kissed a guy once.   Katrina, 16, Geelong, Vic.

I don't believe in sex before marriage and when I tell people I get weird looks.   Anna, 14, Kuranda, Qld

I'm becoming a nun.   Theresa, 15, Nakara, NT

Deciding whether or not to have sex

As you get older and know more people who have 'gone all the way' or 'had sex' (or *say* they have), and you see it in movies and on TV all the time, you could think that it's somehow compulsory. It isn't. (And don't forget that most people do it more than once in their life so we're not just talking about a one-off incident, but about beginning a lifelong sex life.)

A sexual relationship can be very intense, causing rushes of strong feelings about love and belonging. Even if you're not both in love, at the very least it should be fun and make you feel liked and respected.

The decision about when to have sex is not so much about how old you are or how developed your body is. It's about whether *you* feel really, really ready.

I'd rather stick a fork in my eye

You may not be interested in anything to do with sex

Not feeling ready to have sex

If you're unsure, you're probably not ready yet. And if you're not comfortable with kissing, caressing with your clothes on, being touched on your breasts or between your legs, then you're definitely not ready to have sex.

Even though most people think of 'sex' as 'intercourse' or 'penis-in-vagina happenings' (okay, nobody says 'happenings'), other things are sex too. So you may be ready to touch each other or yourself sexually, or have oral sex or give a guy an orgasm through touching (most of the terms used for this are not classy – for example, 'hand job' and 'wristie' – even worse is the term 'fingering', which is often used to describe what a guy might do to a girl). Or maybe even those words

> I like him, but do not want to have sex with him.
> Sash, 16, Belconnen, ACT

> I'd rather not have to think about sex.
> Hilary, 13, Epping, NSW

sex ♥ HEART 365

are enough to send you screaming into the distance. Luckily, your sexual experiences can be a lot more romantic and meaningful than the words a lot of people use. (See the box coming up about sexual terms and definitions.)

Deciding not to have sex

Not having sex is called abstinence, or celibacy (pronounced selly-bass-ee). If this is what you have decided on, nobody else's opinion should dissuade you.

Even though many girls are choosing to have sex at a younger age than in previous generations, you are not a statistic. And not all those girls were glad they did: many say they wish they'd waited. There's nothing wrong with not having sex until your late teens, early twenties or beyond. It's absolutely up to you.

But if you do decide to wait (say, until you're over 18, or married), make sure it's your own choice, not just what someone else expects of you. In some families, cultures and religions, having sex outside marriage is called a sin or a dishonour, even though it's natural to have sexual thoughts or to want to have sex.

It's okay to 'wait for the right person' – and it's okay to experiment, as long as you stay safe and are treated with respect and kindness. Sex isn't bad or wrong, and it doesn't make *you* bad or wrong.

Bad reasons for having sex

- You're afraid that your partner will find someone else unless you do.
- The other person wants to and expects it.
- Other girls you know have done it.
- You've done it already.
- You want to make somebody like you more.
- You don't care whether you do or not.
- You want to rebel against, or get back at, strict or religious parents.
- You're too drunk or out of it to say no.
- You're too shy or too scared to say no.
- Your parents won't find out, so if you can 'get away with it' you may as well.
- You're forced or pressured into it.
- You like the kissing and touching so you think that means you have to keep going.
- Somebody's keeping score in any way or saying you 'owe' them.
- You're looking for approval.
- You want to seem like you just don't care.

Even if you don't have sex it's a good idea to make sure you know about contraception and sexually transmitted infections. Researchers say that about half the teenagers who sign 'abstinence-until-marriage' pledges in the US have sex within the next year, and most don't keep the pledge until marriage. So it's best to be informed and able to use a condom if things do go further than expected and that's okay with you.

> I don't feel ready, personally. I have gone out with three guys in year 10 and every one of them have asked me for sex but I have always said no. One of them broke up with me because I wouldn't have sex with him.
> Emma, 14, Central Coast, NSW

Virginity Technically you are a 'virgin' if you have never had a guy's penis inside your vagina.

You may have heard that you're a virgin until your hymen is 'broken'. This is not true. (Your hymen is that bit of skin surrounding the entrance to the vagina described back in Chapter 1, Change.)

Over the years most girls have probably done things, not related to penises, that have widened the opening of their hymen: played sport, used tampons or had a medical examination. So nobody can tell (or claim) that a girl has had 'penetrative' (penis in vagina) sex, or isn't a virgin, just because her hymen is stretched, torn or can't be seen.

Some girls will bleed a little the first time, or couple of times, they have penetrative sex (from the hymen being stretched or pushed aside), but lots don't. If a girl doesn't bleed it doesn't mean she's had sex before. (If you bleed after the third time, or any time after that, pop along to a doctor.)

Whether or not you're a virgin isn't important unless you want it to be. It isn't nearly as important as many other things, including whether you're healthy, respected, educated or (on the negative side) exploited, worried, pregnant or doing something you really don't want to.

Girls are often told that their virginity is special, that they shouldn't 'give it away', and their first time must be a considered decision. This isn't a luxury

eeny, meeny, miney...

CHOOSE YOUR PARTNER... CAREFULLY!

> Don't just be with someone for the sake of it or to show off. Don't be pressured into having sex.

> Do what feels right for you and if your boyfriend doesn't like it he's not worth it! Missy, 18, McCrae, Vic.

all girls get to decide – many have 'lost' their virginity when they were affected by alcohol, or in a rather fumbling encounter that didn't feel special or romantic. When you have sex for the first time, you're not 'giving away' anything or making a guy a gift of your virginity.

'Losing' your virginity doesn't make you any less special, or mean that you now may as well have sex again, or with anybody. Being a 'virgin' isn't a special, sacred state that's tragically lost forever. What's far more important is that you feel respected and cared for each time you consider anything sexual. That includes the right to say no and, on your own terms, to say yes. Having sex or not being a virgin doesn't make you a 'slut' or 'damaged goods'. These are outdated ideas.

to avoid the 'Euwww' factor: don't go out with somebody heaps older than you

Since nobody can ever tell, even by looking at your vagina opening and hymen, whether you're a virgin or not, if you need to say you're a virgin for your own safety, then say that. But don't fool yourself – if you do other sexual things aside from penis-in-vagina sex then you're a sexual person, and you can still get a sexually transmitted disease.

Things to sort out before deciding to have sex

It's important that you choose somebody you get on really well with so that you can laugh about anything that happens during the sex; you can keep asking if the sex is okay for the other person and what they'd like you to do; and you can feel comfortable telling them what they can do to make you feel good.

It's completely wrong and illegal for anyone in a position of power to have a romantic or a sexual relationship with you or to say or do sexual things to you. This includes teachers, coaches, relatives and friends' fathers. It doesn't matter what they say, or how confused you feel, it's not okay and they are doing the wrong thing. Talk to a trusted adult.

Sex and your age

The 'right' age for sex There isn't one – instead there's just a huge range of who does what when. The most important thing is to know as much as you can before making your own decision. Depending on where you live, it's illegal for anyone to have sex with

Ways to say no to sex

'No.'

'No, I really don't want to.'

'I'm not ready for that yet.'

'I don't want to go any further than this.'

'I am happy to kiss you, but that's all.'

'Let's just kiss for a while.'

'I don't want to go any further than kissing, hugging and touching.'

'I want to slow down.'

'Slow down.'

'Stop!'

'Not now.' (That doesn't mean you have to say yes next time!)

you until you're at least 16 (or 17), but that doesn't mean you *have* to have sex then. The law also depends on how old your sexual partner is. For how to check laws in different places, see the next 'More Info' section.

Older guys, even only a year or so ahead of you, are more likely to want sex before you're ready and are probably more likely to put the pressure on. The older they are, the more likely they are to be carrying a sexually transmitted infection: so always use a condom.

Questions to ask yourself before you have sex

- Are you sure that *you* have chosen the person to have sex with and haven't been pressured? Don't just be grateful that someone has picked you. >

FACT

Sexual insults At some time in your life you'll probably be called a 'slut' or 'frigid', or both. Words that suggest you like sex but you shouldn't include 'easy', 'moll' and 'ho' (whore) as well as 'slut'. (These insults are part of a stupid 'double standard' that says men can have sex with lots of people but girls shouldn't.) Words like 'frigid' or 'cockteaser' suggest you don't want sex but you should (or that a girl should be available to a guy who wants sex). None of these insults is true. They're just designed to humiliate or manipulate you.

Things guys can say to pressure you into sex (and handy replies)

'Everyone else is doing it.'
'Well, you'd better go and have sex with everybody else then.'

'It's okay because I love you.'
'If you really love me you won't pressure me.'

'If you don't, then you don't love me.'
'That's just emotional blackmail. You wouldn't say that if you cared more about me than about having sex.'

'I'll leave you if you don't.'
'Okay then.'

'I'll tell everyone you're frigid.'
'I'll tell everyone I didn't want to, and you cried and said you'd tell everyone I was frigid.'

'You made me think you wanted to.'
'I like it when we kiss and touch, but I don't want to have sex.'

'I have to have it.'
'It's your choice to wait for me or to break up and do it with someone else.'

'It's not fair. You just get me hot and then you don't want to. You're a cockteaser.'
'No, I'm not. I've told you that I like to kiss, hug and touch but don't want to have sex.'

'It's medically bad for me to get aroused and then not have sex.'
'Is not.' (Guys are not harmed in any way by getting aroused and then not having sex.)

It's always OK to say 'NO'

But if you don't have sex with me, my testicles will fall off...

You can start a juggling act

- Have you thought about why you want to have sex? Is it because the two of you have been with each other for a while, and you think this is the right person to share a caring time with, or because you're worried about not seeming cool or getting the first time over with?
- How will you protect yourself against pregnancy and sexually transmitted infections? What would you do if either of those things happened? (See 'Safe Sex' and 'Contraception' later in this chapter, and Chapter 17, Pregnancy.)
- Do you know the reasons why the other person wants to have sex?
- Is the person kind? Do they usually listen to you? Do they want a real relationship or are they likely to 'use' you? Are they discreet or a blabbermouth?
- Can you talk to them about safe sex and contraception, and about what you need to get organised before you have sex?
- Will you feel okay talking to them afterwards about the experience?
- Do you know what sort of relationship you want? Are you just having sex or going to be a couple? Is it a 'one-night stand' or will you be having sex again soon? Every now and again or every week? Does your partner have the same understanding?

> **FACT**
>
> **You might not get to choose** Unfortunately not all girls get to choose when and how they have sex: see 'If Things Turn Scary' and 'Sex Without Consent', right at the end of this chapter.

A guy repeatedly asked and pressured me to 'give him head' [*oral sex*]. When I kept saying no he started to manipulate and blackmail me saying that if I didn't do it he would spread rumours about me. Eventually he forced me to do it. For a long time I was very confused and felt shameful and dirty. I felt like no guy would ever accept me unless I had sex with them. I realise now that what he did was wrong and not my fault. Heather, 16, Brighton, Vic.

More info on sex

likeitis.org.au
This Australian site especially for teens has info on your body, sex, contraception and pregnancy. You can call anonymously to ask questions. The site and the free info line are run by drmarie.org.au.

thetalkdvd.com.au
A DVD for parents and teens explaining how to talk about sex, produced by comedian and educator Nelly Thomas with experienced, expert medical and counselling staff. Covers STIs, unwanted sex and more.

lawstuff.org.au
Check out your state or territory's laws on the minimum legal age for having sex, and on sexting, harassment or assault.

familyplanningallianceaustralia.org.au
FPA Healthline: 1300 658 886
Sexual health and Family Planning Australia. To find a helpful clinic near you, from the main page click on the link to your state or territory organisation. The Healthline will take you to the NSW service, which can answer questions from anywhere in Australia about contraception and other sex issues.

Sex and Other Stuff: The A to Z of Everything You Need to Know by Annie Rose
Annie Rose, a consultant on *Girl Stuff 13+*, has spent years telling teens about sex and answering their questions. Her book is a dictionary of sex terms, explaining all the words, feelings and actions you might be curious about.

scarleteen.com
'Sex Education for the Real World': a US site designed for young people, with an email question service. Medical and legal info is US-only.

sexetc.org
US youth sex by and for teens. Medical and legal info is US-only.

familyplanning.org.nz
Healthline: 0800 611 116
The NZ Family Planning Association has info on the site and clinics where doctors can answer sex questions in confidence. You can attend a clinic free if you're under 22. Choose Info and Resources, then Need Help Now? or call the Healthline.

In an episode of Home and Away they were going to have sex and then didn't really know what to do and I'm afraid that will happen to me. **Clare, 13, Flagstaff Hill, SA**

I would like to talk about sex with my friends more often but most of them would be too embarrassed to even bring up the issue! Elizabeth, 14, Geelong, Vic.

We did sex-ed in year 7 (I'm in year 9), but that was just diagrams, but we need it now, and it needs to be explicit. My family don't really go there. I want to know everything there is to know really!! I want to know what to expect at my first time. **Jacquie, 14, McCrae, Vic.**

Going all the way

If you've read this chapter, and thought about it, and talked about it, and sorted out all the questions you need to answer, and you still want to have sex, you are probably ready.

When you decide to have penis-in-vagina sex for the first time, the two of you should talk beforehand about how you want it to go. Here are some essentials.

> I have done everything else except have sex. So I guess it seems like the next natural step.
> Jan, 17, Mosman, NSW

- The sex should happen in a safe place. (Even though you obviously want privacy, it's a good idea to have some people you trust very nearby.)
- A condom will be used any and every time you have sex.
- You'll organise the contraception, or he will. If it's not organised the sex won't happen.
- The guy has practised putting a condom on, and will get it off straight after he's 'come' (see the box 'How to Use a Condom' later in this chapter).
- You've talked about which things you'd like to do, and which ones you're not interested in. (Make sure your partner knows how you feel and respects your limits.)
- If you or your partner says so, everything stops immediately, that second, no matter what stage you're at. Make sure your partner understands that 'No' or 'Stop' never means 'Maybe' or 'Go ahead anyway'.
- Nobody will take or send naked, topless or sexual pictures of any kind (often known as 'sexting'). This can result in criminal charges and, obviously, major embarrassment and other trouble.
- Neither partner will be mean to the other one about anything that happens or is said.
- The details of the sex will be kept private and won't be used as gossip.

It's like a Christmas stocking for pixies!

LEARN HOW TO USE A CONDOM PROPERLY

What happens when you have sex?

Probably something like this.

- As soon as the guy's penis is erect one of you gets a condom on it (for instructions, see the box 'How to Use a Condom' coming up).
- Holding the condom on at the base, the guy then gently starts to put his penis inside you, perhaps taking a little while to find the right place to slide it in and going slowly so that the vagina stretches to fit the penis.
- Once the penis is inside your vagina you'll both usually start to move – the guy will pull his penis out slightly and then thrust forward all the way in again, creating an ongoing rhythm.
- When the guy ejaculates you probably won't be able to actually feel it happen inside you, but you will most likely be able to tell from his actions and noises that he has had an orgasm (usually you can also tell because he stops doing the in-and-out business).
- Even though it may feel nice for him to stay inside you, and he's feeling a temporary exhausted glow, you need to make sure that as soon as he has 'come' he holds the bottom of the condom around the base of his penis and pulls out – you don't want to get any of that semen near your vagina or those pesky hundreds of millions of sperm may head up to try to get you pregnant. (It only takes one to do it.)

You should have the chance to have an orgasm as well as the guy – afterwards or before he has had an orgasm – through touching or oral sex. He should want you to feel good too. This means he may have to slow down (guys tend to go too fast).

Being new to sex

Don't expect the first time to be the most amazing experience of your life. Almost everybody says the first wasn't the best time (by far). It's not going to be like it is in the movies or, thankfully, on a porn site. It's you two, in real life, and you need to be prepared to smile when things aren't perfect, try again, and understand that if it's kind of romantic and sweet then that's a bonus. A lot of people's first-time reaction is 'Huh? Is that all there is? After the big build-up?'

Don't expect to be 'good at sex' for a while. It's an intimate act and 'getting it together' can take time.

Like most things, it takes practice to know what you are doing and to be able to work out what you like. And it needs you to be able to talk about it comfortably with your partner.

The penis

A guy will be as sensitive and insecure about what his penis looks like, and how big it is, as you are about your body or girly bits. So don't laugh or point (not that you would, but you know what I'm saying).

The male genitals are a package deal of one sausage-shaped penis and two testicles (nicknamed 'balls'), which store the sperm. The testicles hang side by side behind the penis and are held away from the body by the scrotum, which looks more or less like a wrinkly, hairy sock with a pair of golf balls in it (one of the two usually hangs slightly lower than the other). Next time you're a little worried about your body image, think what it would be like to have a wrinkly, hairy sock hanging off you.

If a guy is uncircumcised that means the end of his penis is naturally covered by a little skivvy neck called the foreskin, which is pulled back when the guy wants to wee. When the penis is erect, its head pokes out of the skivvy neck. Circumcision is a surgical procedure done to baby boys in some religious and cultural groups including many Jewish and Muslim families. When a penis is circumcised the foreskin is cut away, so there is no skivvy neck for the penis head.

You may have heard, or a guy may have told you, that it's safer to have sex with him without a condom because a circumcised penis is less likely to pass on sexually transmitted infections. This isn't true. The only way to have 'safe sex' is to use a condom whether the guy is circumcised or not. Without a condom, there's a much, much greater chance of getting a disease or pregnant: circumcision is irrelevant.

Both uncircumcised and circumcised penises can be properly cleaned. Wee and sperm can never come out of a penis at the same time.

Don't forget that men and women are designed to fit together, so it's very, very rare for someone to have a penis too large for a vagina.

Don't get your idea of what a penis looks like from porn. Because, you know how there are those strange women with breasts bigger than their heads? Well, enormous penises are not exactly your everyday item either.

Erection

When a penis becomes erect, it gets bigger and harder, almost as if it had a bone in it, but it's just all the extra blood rushing to the area. An erect penis sticks out from a guy's body, angled upwards. Sometimes it bends a little to the left or the right.

Guys get an erection when they have sexual thoughts; while they're asleep; sometimes even from the vibrations in a train or bus; any time, really, if they're a teenager. They often have one when they wake up. Erections eventually go down again, whether or not a guy has come. A guy can't control when he gets an erection, and this can be really embarrassing for him.

What do all those sex words mean?

There are lots of 'slang' terms in sex you might hear and want a definition of. If I included a list of those words and their definitions, it might be out of date quickly, and it would probably stop conservative schools from having this book in their library.

Unfortunately, you may have to use a search engine to track down a term you've heard and don't understand. It can be a bit confronting: some words are so rare (used by only a very few people) and the definitions can be extreme, strangely specific or really make you go euwwwwww. Some sites like urbandictionary.com might help, but they often only deal with US or UK slang and won't cover Australian slang (like 'wristie' for a 'hand job').

Your school or home computer might have a filter that stops you from going to such websites anyway, or from receiving an email from a reputable service that answers sex questions (see the sites in 'More Info on Sex' a few pages earlier).

There's no shame in asking what a word means. And knowing about something doesn't mean you're interested in doing it. Often other teens will use a word to try to make it sound like they know something you don't. They may have seen the word on a porn site or heard others talking about it. It doesn't mean it's something lots of people do, or should do.

It doesn't really matter what some words mean, especially if you're a younger teen. All you need to know is that somebody is going on about it in a sleazy way, it's about sex and you don't need to know any details. 'I bet you've never tried a reverse teapot, ha ha ha aha harghhh' can be answered with a roll of your eyes, some dignity, and the retort: 'I bet you've never tried growing up.' (By the way, there's no such thing as a 'reverse teapot'. I *hope*, because I just made it up.)

If you're not sure what something means or you need info about sexual terms or any aspect of sex or contraception, for non-judgemental and independent info call the Dr Marie Helpline, freecall 1800 003 707, or check their teen site likeitis.org for definitions of sex terms.

Or for explanations of lots of words get the 'dictionary' *Sex and Other Stuff* by Annie Rose – for details see 'More Info on Sex' earlier.

Friends of mine are starting to have sex in short relationships and on the spur of the moment, eg, in public toilets. It's a bit feral and unromantic.   Tash, 15, Lilyfield, NSW

Foreplay   For sex to feel good, there generally needs to be more foreplay than in-and-out penetrative sex. Foreplay is all the stuff you do to get aroused beforehand: kissing, touching and perhaps licking and sucking (see 'Sexual Touching' earlier). It's for both partners to do to each other, to make them feel good on the way to having sex. It can feel great to avoid the private bits altogether and stroke the feet, fingers, arms – anywhere can be arousing if the right person is doing the touching and doing it well. You can experiment together to discover what you like.

How long will the sex take?   From the time the guy puts his penis in you until he comes could be only a few seconds or a few minutes. That's why just 'doing it', without foreplay or the guy slowing down, can be boring and disappointing for you.

After orgasm the guy's penis goes limp again, and it may take a little while for him to get another erection. If he waits until his penis gets hard again, and you want to have sex a second time, he may last longer. (You'll need to use another condom.)

Dryness during sex   When you are sexually aroused, your vagina becomes slippery with a sexual lubrication your body makes so that it's easier for the penis to go inside you. If there is no natural lubricant it probably means you are too nervous or not aroused enough to have penetrative sex, and should have more foreplay before trying again.

If you are dry during sex there will be too much friction and you will be sore and get a rash, abrasion or even a bruise. Dryness can also cause a condom to break, so if you feel dry, stop. A water-based lubricant from a chemist or supermarket (they're sold near the condoms) is good to use around your vagina opening, and on the outside of a condom. Don't use an oil-based lubricant as it can damage the condom.

Does sex hurt?   It doesn't usually hurt, although the first time the penis may stretch your hymen (see the 'Virginity' section earlier). There may be a small stab of pain, but this should only happen the first time or the first couple of times.

Sex can hurt if the guy puts his penis in too suddenly or roughly. Let him know what feels good, and if he has to change what he's doing. You're learning together. All sexual partners tell each other what's working, no matter how old they are or how many times they've done it before.

If sex is hurting, and it isn't because you're dry or the sex is rough, or you bleed after sex and it isn't the first time, see a doctor.

Sexual positions There are a number of possible sexual positions for penetrative sex. Here are some common ones.

- Both partners lie down, with the guy on top (the 'straight' or 'missionary' position).
- The girl sits on top of the guy, who's lying down – the penis should always go into the vagina slowly and gently, to make sure it doesn't hurt.
- The girl props on her hands and knees and her partner crouches over her, entering her vagina from behind. Some people call this 'doggie style'. This doesn't mean anal sex, which is when the penis is put into the anus.

Not such a good idea Many guys now want to try anal sex with girls, mainly because it's portrayed in lots of porn videos as really enjoyable for the guy and the girl. The truth is that most women don't have anal sex because not only is it much less enjoyable for them, it can really hurt. Feel free to say 'no' to anal sex – even in the midst of it almost happening, if you've started to give it a try.

Also, anal sex is often said to be 'safe' because you can't get pregnant. The truth is that it's unsafe sex in another way because it makes it much more likely that any sexual infection or disease will be transmitted. Anal sex, whether straight or gay, must involve a condom, with a lubricant, to protect against this (see the 'Safe Sex' section coming up).

> **FACT**
>
> **How you look** Lots of girls worry about how they appear during sex: whether their body is the 'right' size or shape. A good sex partner won't be concerned with possible (or imaginary) 'flaws'; they and you can concentrate on the important thing – how you both feel. And anyway guys (and girls) are sexually aroused by all sorts of shapes and sizes.

I just recently made sex with my boyfriend. It was a really special night and I don't regret it at all.

Brigette, 15, Rutherglen, Vic.

> **FACT**
>
> **Faking orgasm** Faking it? Don't bother. Better to either say, 'Oh well, I'm obviously not in the mood', or help the other person to do the things that arouse you. There's no rule that says you have to have an orgasm every time – but if you never do, and your partner always does, that's not fair.

Not enjoying sex Many girls get worried and think there's something wrong with them if they don't enjoy sex. There isn't. It's not surprising girls don't enjoy it when so many of them are involved in a quick, fumbling meeting of bodies that ends as soon as the guy has come.

There's no point continuing to have sex with somebody if you're not enjoying it and it isn't getting any better. Otherwise you get all the risks (heartbreak, chlamydia) and none of the benefits (having fun, feeling safe). It could mean you're not ready. Or it's just not the right person. Or that your partner needs to care about how it is for you (just doing what the guy wants = bad sex). It's always a good idea to stop and think whether this is what you really want or how you'd like it to be. Don't waste your life, or another minute, on settling for consistently bad sex.

> **FACT**
>
> **What do lesbians do?** I'm reliably informed that lesbians just do all the stuff guys and girls do, like kissing, touching and/or oral sex, but obviously there's no penis involvement. Many of the websites and magazines for gays and lesbians can be all about sex, even porn, but if you're a lesbian you don't have to have extreme sex. Lesbians are at lower risk of some sexually transmitted diseases but still need to have the smear tests and health checks that other girls and women do. (See Chapter 15, Love, for more on working out if you're gay, falling in love with girls, dating, emotions and groups to contact.)

I wish I'd known that letting a guy have sex with you does not mean he'll love you. Jessica, 17, NSW

Creepy porn

There's so much pornography now on the net, in films, on phones and in mags. And even music videos can look like a porn movie, with girls humping around, grinding their bottoms in a rhythmic circle as if they were having sex, and making orgasmic noises and pretending they're dying to 'do it' with the star of the video – hey, the singer pays them to act like that so he can pretend he's a magnet for sex-crazed women. If a guy wants you to look at porn pics or video, you don't have to. It's also okay to start and then say you want to stop. It's normal to feel some kind of excitement if you see porn. Having a sexual reaction doesn't mean that you want to do what you saw, or that you want to watch it again. Other common reactions (sometimes at the same time) can include embarrassment, boredom and feeling angry or offended at the way the women are treated.

Porn can give people some false and twisted ideas about sex. Here's the truth:

- Women and girls don't always want sex.
- Guys don't always want it.
- Women and girls are not just there for men to look at and to use for their own pleasure.
- It's not okay to make DIY porn, or to take pictures or record having sex, or send these pictures or video ('sexting'). Sending such pictures or recordings can result in criminal charges and a permanent criminal record, which limits your job prospects.
- Teenagers who have sex should always use at least one form of contraception and always use condoms to prevent STIs (see 'Safe Sex' coming up).
- Most guys don't go on for ages before they 'come'. In fact, teenage guys especially often come very quickly. It's not your 'fault' if they do. They may be embarrassed about this.
- Women and girls don't have to dress to look 'hot' or sexy or like they want sex.
- Sex isn't always grunty and loud and fast.
- You don't have to thrash around shrieking.
- Women don't find everything guys do, or all attempts at sex, wildly exciting.
- Few, if any, women orgasm during vaginal sex that doesn't involve the clitoris. The 'pounding-away' type sex often seen in porn can be dead boring.
- It isn't 'finished' just because the guy has ejaculated. It's not only about him.
- It's not okay for a guy to be mean or rough when you're having sex.
- It's never okay to be forced into it.
- Women and girls don't like being forced.

- Women and girls don't all want to give oral sex and swallow the semen.
- It's not okay to say or do abusive things during sex.
- Women and girls may not want a guy to ejaculate on their face, chest or elsewhere.
- Women and girls don't have to do stuff just because the guy wants to.
- Most girls and women don't like anal sex because it hurts: it's okay to say no.
- It's normal for guys to give oral sex to girls and women rather than just expect it to be done to them.

Some 'women's porn' or 'erotica' stories and films are sexy without being creepy. It's worth seeking out, when you're older.

Saying 'yes': consent

If somebody wants to kiss you, or touch you, they need to ask first, and you need to say yes. That's called 'consent'. Get your partner to read this, too. Things to know:

- You never have to say yes to any kind of sex, even if it seems embarrassing to say no. You don't have to say yes if you said yes before, even moments ago (see Going back, next page). If you feel pressured, or unsure or not quite right about it, say no.
- Guys (and girl partners) should know that silence, or being too drunk or unable to say no, is not consent. Only a firm yes is consent. If they don't get consent, they are in the wrong, and it can be judged as illegal sexual assault.
- You can discuss it first to set the ground rules of what you do and don't want. Or you can say yes and no to things as they happen.
- Questions can include: 'Where would you like me to kiss?', 'Can I touch you there?', or 'Do you want to go all the way?' (this usually is not about the last stop on the train line).
- Consent can include: 'Yes!', 'Yeeeeesssss!', 'More, please', 'I like that', or 'Keep doing that'. You can say 'stop' and 'go'.

Going back

What if you discover you weren't ready for your first experience, it was boring or it was horrible? Lots of girls have a first sexual experience that they didn't want to have, which made them feel used, or that they can't even remember because it happened when they were drunk or affected by drugs. It's a shame if that has happened to you, but you don't have to let it ruin your future experience of sex. Next time make sure you do it the way you'd like it to be.

> Wait until you've met someone you really really like and can see a future with before starting something up.
> Michelle, 17, Woolloongabba, Qld

And just because you had sex before you were ready doesn't mean you have to keep doing it. You can stop and go back to waiting until you do feel ready.

If things went further than you wanted them to, think about whether somebody pressured you or somehow took advantage of you. If they did, don't be with that person any more: they don't respect you and can't be relied on as a friend. If you were both just 'carried away', have a talk and explain that things went further than you meant them to, but that you don't want it to happen again and you need them to agree.

More info on guy and girl bits

Many pictures of penises available on the net are ridiculously large, porn-actory ones, or have symptoms of a sexually transmitted infection such as warts that will make you go euww. Most pics of girly bits are unnaturally hairless and often digitally altered to look 'neater' and less natural.

en.wikipedia.org/wiki/Penis and
en.wikipedia.org/wiki/Vulva
Pics and info.

sexualityandu.ca
Click Sexual Health, then Understanding Your Body or All About Puberty: choose Male or Female.

> I lost my virginity at 13, and don't regret it. I was in a relationship with the boy for 9 months, and I am now 16. I have had 3 sexual partners and have been in long term relationships with all of them and I don't believe in doing things with random people. Grazia, 16, Melbourne, Vic.

> I wish I had waited and I regret lots of things, but if those experiences had not happened I wouldn't be the person I am today. I respect myself so much more now, after everything that's happened. Deni, 16, Nambucca Heads, NSW

Safe sex

If you have sex of any kind – vaginal, oral or anal – with a guy, even once, then it needs to be 'safe sex'. This means finding ways to cut the risk of getting a sexually transmitted infection (also called a sexually transmitted disease – STD).

Sexually transmitted infections (STIs)

STIs are diseases passed from one person to another during sexual contact: they are caused by a variety of bacteria, viruses and parasites and can infect many parts of the body after being 'caught'. They can be passed on in blood, semen and vaginal fluids, and by skin contact. (Some girls have been told that they can't get an STI from doing oral sex on a guy – this is a lie.)

The long-term effects of some STIs can severely affect your life, or even end it (see the 'Sexually Transmitted Infections (STIs)' chart coming up). But most people with an STI don't know they have one.

In most cases using a condom during sex will hugely reduce your risk of catching an STI (see the box 'How to Use a Condom', over the page). Condoms are most effective if they are used with a water-based personal lubricant, bought from a chemist or supermarket.

Symptoms of STIs   Many of the common STIs are 'invisible': they don't have any symptoms, such as pain or outside body changes. So you can't tell who has one – or more than one – by looking.

Not all infections of the girly bits are STIs, but all symptoms need to be investigated by a doctor because the longer any infection goes on the more damage it can do (see the 'Common Infections of the Girly Bits' chart in Chapter 7, Body Health, as well as the 'Sexually Transmitted Infections (STIs)' one coming up, for details of symptoms and effects on the body).

Most sexually transmitted diseases have worse, or more complicated, problems for girls than guys (including not being able to have a baby later on), so please be careful and don't be afraid or too embarrassed to see a doctor. They see this stuff every day. Having an STI doesn't mean you are a 'slut'.

If you've had sex without a condom or had one break, *or* you show any of the following symptoms in the next days, weeks or months after sex, off you pop to your doctor or health centre, a Family Planning clinic, or an STIs clinic (see 'More Info' coming up).

Possible symptoms of STIs:
- pain during sex
- pain when weeing
- redness, soreness, warts, bumps, swelling, blisters, scabby bits, itchy bits or sores on or near the vagina or anal area
- any abnormal discharge from the vagina such as pus (yellowy or stinky) or a 'weeping' fluid
- lower 'tummy' pain, with or without a fever, that comes and goes or doesn't go away
- swelling or lumps under the skin in the groin area.

> I discovered to my horror that I had contracted an STI and I had no idea I had it. (AND I don't sleep around at all. I got it from my boyfriend.)
> Ange, 18, Greenwith, SA

If one partner is diagnosed with an STI, the other partner also needs to be checked.

Common symptoms for a guy include lumps, bumps, warts, red spots, sores, blisters, scabby bits or rashes on his penis (or around the area). If you see any of these don't have sex with him, don't touch his penis and tell him to get it checked by a doctor. The same applies if you notice any fluid coming from his penis when it's not erect, or he says he has a pain in the testicles area.

More info on how to use condoms

School and community health centre nurses can help with info on how to privately get access to condoms. Chemists and supermarkets sell condoms and 'personal lubricant', usually on shelves together. All condom packets have instructions inside the box.

getthefacts.health.wa.gov.au
Choose Condoms and Contraception, then How to Use a Condom – Animation.

More info on sexually transmitted infections

familyplanningallianceaustralia.org.au
Healthline: 1300 658 886
Click on your state or territory to find a Family Planning clinic for check-ups and free condoms.

healthdirect.gov.au
Search STIs on the home page.

thefacts.com.au and herpes.org.nz
Info on herpes.

plannedparenthood.org
US site with fact sheets. Choose STDs.

familyplanning.org.nz
Choose Advice, then Sexually Transmissible Infections.

How to use a condom

YouTube has a lot of 'How to use a condom' videos, but many of them are kind of unwatchable, at least without screaming. Warning – any of these 'how-to' illustrations and videos will show plastic models or drawings of erect penises. Or, you know, a banana. Also they tend to assume it's a 'man' and a 'woman' who want to know rather than a girl and a guy.

* Use the condom within its use-by date.

* Don't use one that's been left in extreme heat (for example, in a car glove box).

* Use a fresh one out of the packet.

* Make sure the packet and the condom are not damaged in any way.

* Don't damage the wrapper or the condom with fingernails or teeth when opening the packet (this is a common way to create holes or cuts in a condom).

* Never put one condom over another one. This is not safer – in fact it makes them both more likely to break.

* Put the condom on before the penis gets anywhere near the vagina.

* Hold the condom in one hand while squeezing the condom's tip with the other hand. The space left by the air being squeezed out will be taken up by semen when the guy ejaculates.

* While the tip is still squeezed, roll the condom down onto the erect penis – before any little drops of semen leak out of it, which can happen long before the guy ejaculates.

* Throw the condom away if it is accidentally put on inside out – use a fresh one.

* Put some water-based personal lubricant over it. Oil-based lubricants such as moisturisers and Vaseline can damage the condom, making it not as safe.

* Make sure that as soon as the guy has come, and while the penis is still hard, he holds the condom around the base of the penis and pulls out (otherwise the condom could get left behind in there). He then needs to move away so that it doesn't accidentally spill near the vagina.

* The guy should tie a knot in the used condom so the semen doesn't come out, then dispose of it in the bin, not the toilet.

* Use any condom only once.
See also 'More Info' opposite.

Sexually transmitted infections (STIs)

Teenagers who have sex without a condom run a really high risk of getting, or passing on, an STI. You can get an STI on your first or any other experience of sex. If you've ever had vaginal, oral or anal sex, get tested for STIs. Most STIs are common, not rare. All tests and treatments for STIs must be done by a doctor.

Chlamydia

What is it? Chlamydia (pronounced clam-mid-ee-yar) is caused by bacteria and is common.

How you get it Having vaginal, oral or anal sex with someone who has it.

Signs and symptoms None or an unusual vaginal fluid, stinging wee or bleeding after sex.

How you know you have it A lab analysis of a wee sample or a swab of the cervix taken by a doctor.

Effects If not treated, it can cause pelvic inflammatory disease (PID), which can result in never being able to have a baby. PID symptoms include tummy pain, pain during sex, heavy periods and fever.

Treatment Usually a single dose of an antibiotic pill.

How to prevent it Always use a condom during vaginal, oral or anal sex.

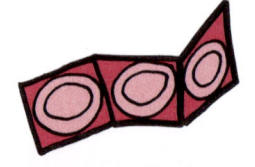

Genital herpes

What is it? A common virus that causes sores. Once you've caught it, you always carry the virus and have recurring outbreaks. Herpes is *very* common.

How you get it Spread by skin contact during vaginal, oral or anal sex. Cold sores around the mouth are not all caused by an STI, but can be transferred to sexual areas.

Signs and symptoms None, or the first outbreak may cause flu-like symptoms and small blisters around the vaginal area, which break open as painful sores.

How you know you have it A lab analysis of a swab taken from a sore, or a blood test.

Effects At first outbreak, pain and itching. Each outbreak can be less severe.

Treatment There's no vaccine or cure, but ointments and drugs can relieve the symptoms of pain and itching, and really reduce outbreaks. (A vaccine is coming.)

How to prevent it Always use a condom during sex. Don't have vaginal, oral or anal sex if a partner has sores anywhere.

Human papilloma virus (HPV), or genital warts

What is it? One of more than sixty common viruses that cause visible or invisible warts around your vagina or anus.

How you get it Skin contact during vaginal, oral or anal sex. Most people pass it on without knowing they have it. About half of all people get a wart virus within three years of first having sex.

Signs and symptoms None visible, or painless warts or bumps around the vulva, vagina and anus (or guy's penis and anus). Some cause changes to cells on the cervix.

How you know you have it A doctor may tell by looking, or lab analysis of a cervix swab.

Effects Warts will eventually disappear if treated. Some kinds of HPV that don't cause visible warts can turn into cancer of the cervix if not treated – every girl or woman who's had sex needs immunisation against HPV *and* regular smear tests (see 'Smear Tests' in Chapter 7, Body Health).

Treatment Freezing or ointments to remove visible warts. Follow-up tests to make sure nothing nasty develops.

How to prevent it Use a condom during sex. Immunisation (see 'Immunisation' in Chapter 7, Body Health: ask your doctor about it).

Gonorrhoea

What is it? A bacteria infection.

How you get it Vaginal, oral or anal sex.

Signs and symptoms None, or discharge from the vagina, tummy pain or stinging wee.

How you know you have it A lab analysis of a swab from the cervix.

Effects Untreated it can lead to pelvic inflammatory disease (see 'Chlamydia' opposite).

Treatment Usually an antibiotic pill.

How to prevent it Always use a condom.

Hepatitis B and C

What is it? Two hepatitis viruses.

How you get it Sex, sharing needles.

Signs and symptoms Often none; hunger, nausea, tiredness, vomiting, jaundice (yellow skin and eyes), and a sore, enlarged liver.

How you know you have it Blood test.

Effects Untreated it can eventually become liver cancer.

Treatment None.

How to prevent it Immunisation for Hepatitis B only. Always use a condom during sex and don't share drug needles.

→

HIV (and AIDS)

What are they? The virus known as HIV causes AIDS: the body's immune system is weakened over many years until destroyed.

How you get HIV Passed on during vaginal, oral or anal sex, sharing drug needles, breastfeeding and blood transmission.

Signs and symptoms of HIV As for flu.

How you know you have HIV Blood tests.

Effects An infection in late stages causes death.

Treatment Drugs to slow the progression from HIV to AIDS. There's no vaccine or cure.

How to prevent HIV Always use a condom during sex and don't share drug needles.

Syphilis

What is it? Syphilis (pronounced sif-il-is) is an infection caused by bacteria.

How you get it Vaginal, oral or anal sex.

Signs and symptoms Stage 1: unnoticed sores. Stage 2: red rash, maybe lumps in the groin and under arms, hair loss and tiredness.

How you know you have it A lab analysis of a swab from a sore, or a blood test.

Effects If untreated, will progress to Stage 3, with heart problems and brain damage.

Treatment Antibiotic injection.

How to prevent it Always use a condom.

Trichomoniasis

What is it? A common vaginal infection caused by a parasite, often called 'trike'.

How you get it Usually vaginal sex. Rarely, by sharing wet towels or swimwear.

Signs and symptoms None, or itching and a stinky, yellowy green, frothy, irritating discharge from the vagina. Stinging when you wee.

How you know you have it A doctor can tell, or a lab analyses a discharge sample.

Effects Untreated it can become pelvic inflammatory disease (see 'Chlamydia' earlier).

Treatment Antibiotic pills.

How to prevent it Always use a condom.

Pubic lice (crabs)

What are they? Just like hair lice and nits, but in your pubic or underarm hair.

How you get them Sexual or close body contact, or sharing sheets, towels or clothes.

Signs and symptoms Itching.

How you know you have it A doctor can tell.

Treatment Lice shampoo and nit comb. Wash clothes and bedding in hot water. Repeat in a week.

How to prevent it Condoms won't help much. Anybody itching in the pants department should be checked and treated.

Contraception

Contraception is something used to try to stop pregnancy happening: a device, medical drug or procedure. It's also called birth control. And a damned good idea: to avoid getting pregnant, everyone having sex that involves sperm and a vagina needs to use contraception.

Condoms

A condom protects against pregnancy as well as STIs – but is only very reliable when used properly. See the box 'How to Use a Condom' earlier, for all the palaver about how to use condoms. You have to use a manufactured, bought condom. What won't work: trying to make one out of cling wrap or anything else, and novelty and joke condoms.

> **FACT**
>
> **Condoms and trust** Carrying and using condoms doesn't mean you don't trust a guy to be faithful. He, or you, could have caught an STI before you met, and could now pass it on without knowing.

The Pill

The contraceptive pill is the most common reliable form of contraception that women use. The Pill uses a combination of girly hormones (oestrogen and progesterone) in certain doses to tell the body not to ovulate (release an egg) so that even if a hopeful sperm arrives in a fallopian tube there's no egg waiting to be fertilised by it.

The Pill is bought from a chemist, on prescription from a GP, a gynaecologist (girly-bits doctor) or a Family Planning clinic doctor. Sometimes doctors won't prescribe the Pill to anyone, or to girls under a certain age. If you have this problem go to a Family Planning clinic.

Good points about the Pill
- It's the most reliable method of contraception if taken properly.
- It can help reduce period pain, heavy periods and other problems because the Pill causes periods to be shorter and lighter, as well as more regular. Many girls are on the Pill to deal with problem periods or severe pimples, not for any contraceptive reason.

How to take the Pill

* Get the doctor who prescribes you the Pill to show you a packet and explain how to take it.

* The pills are in 'blister sheets', each containing twenty-eight days' worth. There are usually three sheets, meaning three months' worth, in a packet. You must take one pill every day, whether or not you have any sex.

* Each blister sheet has twenty-one hormone, or 'active', pills, followed by a clearly marked section containing some pills made from sugar. The lack of active hormones in the sugar pills will trigger your body to have a period, usually two or three days after you've started them. The sugar pills also ensure you don't get out of the habit of taking a pill every day.

* Start the pills on the first day of a period.

* You'll see that the back of the blister sheet has a clearly coloured area showing you where to start. If the first day of your period is a Wednesday, for example, take the first Wednesday (Wed) pill from this start section. The following day take the Thursday pill next to it. There are arrows on the sheet to show which way to go. They can be small and confusing, often changing direction, so be careful.

* Follow the blister-sheet arrows for the twenty-eight days. You should take all twenty-one active pills, then the seven sugar pills. Take a pill each day at about the same time – say, just before bed or at breakfast time. (To remember a pill each day, you could put your pills with your toothbrush or set a daily message or alarm on your phone.) You will not be protected against pregnancy until

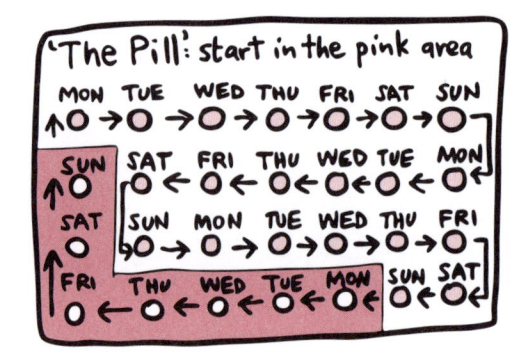

typical pill blister sheet

FACT

Contraception plus condom The contraceptive pill doesn't prevent STIs. Always use a condom, with a lubricant as well, even if you're on the Pill, so that you enormously reduce the risk of getting an STI.

Don't risk having sex. Emma, 14, Hampton, Vic.

390   HEART ♥ sex

you've taken an active hormone pill each day for at least fourteen days in a row.

* And keep using condoms whenever you have sex, to protect against STIs.

* If you forget to take an active hormone pill and it's still within twelve hours of your regular time, take it as soon as you remember, and then take another one at the usual time the next day and continue as normal.

* If you don't remember until twelve or more hours after your usual time it's called a 'missed pill', and you need to take the next active one at the usual time PLUS the one you missed: that means you take two at the same time. Use condoms or don't have sex until two weeks have gone by with you taking an active hormone pill each day at the right time.

* If you are near the end of the active pills when you miss a pill don't take the sugar pills: move on to a new sheet, beginning as usual at the start section marked on it. This means you skip a period, which won't harm you.

* If you have gastro (vomiting or diarrhoea), a pill may not be properly absorbed into your system before coming out again. Keep taking one each day and use condoms or don't have sex for the next seven days of taking the active hormone pills.

* If your doctor prescribes you antibiotics or anything else, always tell them you're 'on the Pill' because some antibiotics interfere with it working properly. Mention the Pill if a doctor asks if you're taking any 'medication'.

* Make sure when you're getting near the end of a packet that you get the prescription filled again or go back to the doctor for a new prescription so you don't have a break in taking the Pill, leaving you unprotected against pregnancy.

* If you don't get a period when you have finished the active hormone pills and started on the sugar pills, or there's something unusual about the period, get a pregnancy test (see Chapter 17, Pregnancy).

Other points about the Pill

- The side effects can include 'retaining fluid', breast tenderness, headaches, nausea, feeling bloated, mood changes and being 'down'. Some may go after the first few weeks; if not, another brand of the Pill can sometimes stop them.
- On its own, but especially combined with smoking, the Pill raises the chance of serious side effects such as blood clots. If you're on the Pill don't smoke, and tell the doctor if you have a family history of strokes or blood clots.
- It can make you put on a bit of weight, but usually only a little.
- You have to pay for it. Ask for the cheapest version.

Implant

This is a flexible white plastic rod, slightly smaller than a matchstick, which contains progesterone and provides protection against pregnancy for three years. (Progesterone causes thick mucus to form at the cervix, blocking sperm from getting through.) The rod is inserted by a doctor just under the skin of the upper arm, after a local anaesthetic. It usually can't be seen, but can be felt. Sometimes it will show up as a shape under UV light in a club, unless your sleeve covers it. It can be taken out by a doctor at any time.

Ask your local doctor or community health centre if they are experienced in placing an implant, or go to a Family Planning clinic.

> If you're not ready to be a parent don't have sex without a condom!
> Patti, 13, Bristol, UK

> Mum said if I did have sex, to tell her straight away, to use protection and to go straight on the Pill!
> Gabbie, 14, Rye, Vic.

Good points about an implant

- It's cheap, effective and can make periods less heavy and painful.
- There are not many known side effects.

Other points about an implant

- It doesn't protect against STIs: condoms must also be used.
- It often causes irregular period behaviour, such as spotting – light bleeding showing up as spots on your pants (sometimes every day), which is so annoying that up to a third of users get the implant removed after three months or so, if the spotting doesn't go away.
- Some people find their period comes more often, or less often.

Injection

A doctor injects a slow-release progesterone called Depo Provera (or 'Depo') into the upper arm or a buttock or thigh. Protection lasts for about three months, after which a user can get another injection. Depo Provera can stop periods, and often stops ovulation. The body can take quite a while to start doing ovulation and periods normally again, once protection from an injection has stopped.

> I don't need to get info. I am the sexual encyclopedia. I'm not an idiot. I know what relationships and emotions are, I learn through experience. If you have sex and are stupid enough to not use a condom, chances are you'll get pregnant. What else is there to know? Sophy, 13, Wollongong, NSW

Good points about the injection
- It's 'set and forget' for three months.
- It's very reliable as contraception.

Other points about the injection
- It doesn't protect against STIs: condoms must also be used.
- Side effects can include retained fluid, moodiness and spotting. It can also cause thinning of the bones, which usually stops after the injection wears off.
- It can't be stopped if there are nasty side effects.
- Another injection needs to be remembered every three months.

IUD

An IUD or IUS (intra-uterine device or system) is put into the uterus, under general anaesthetic, by a surgeon and can stop an egg implanting for at least five years. It's not generally recommended for teens, and gives no protection against STIs.

Diaphragm (or cap), and ring

A diaphragm (pronounced dire-fram) is a little plastic doover that looks like a tiny, flexible bowl. It goes into the vagina before sex to fit over the cervix, stopping sperm from getting into the uterus. The newer ring, which fits around the cervix and releases progesterone, can be left in for three weeks, but is expensive and has to be replaced each month. Both are fiddly to insert and remove, and unreliable. They don't protect against STIs. Give 'em a miss.

Douching

'Washing' or squirting anything into the vagina after sex will not catch up with or kill sperm and doesn't protect against pregnancy or STIs. Useless.

'Natural' methods

Grouped under the description 'natural' are a variety of methods not involving a device or a medical drug or procedure. Generally they don't work.

> I go to a Catholic school. Contraception is kind of frowned upon.
> Janonica, 15, Alexandra, Vic.

> They seriously need to give out condoms free. Most girls are too scared to buy them.
> Mia, 16, Dulwich, SA

Trying to avoid fertile days The term 'natural' contraception usually refers to women avoiding sex at a time when she *thinks* there's an egg waiting to be fertilised.

(Various forms are known as the 'rhythm method', 'Vatican roulette' and the 'Billings method'.) Girls and women are most likely to get pregnant (are at their most fertile) when they ovulate – usually about halfway between two periods. But, especially during the teenage years, a menstrual cycle can be irregular so girls can never really know if or when they have ovulated. Even women with established cycles who measure vaginal secretions and vaginal temperatures, so they can choose the 'safe' days for sex, are caught out. This is a totally unreliable form of contraception, and doesn't protect against STIs.

Withdrawal The guy tries to pull out before he ejaculates inside the vagina. This doesn't work because a guy always has a leak of semen before he ejaculates, and even if he doesn't ejaculate; and because sometimes he may not withdraw in time or may 'get carried away' and forget. It's not a form of contraception at all, and doesn't protect against STIs. Don't go there!

Sex during a period Although getting pregnant is far less likely during a period than halfway between periods, it has happened, especially to young girls whose cycle hasn't sorted itself out yet. And sperm, the sneaky stuff, can stay alive for up to seven days inside the body, so having sex at a 'safe' time might end up as a pregnancy anyway.

Sex without penetration This includes oral sex; hands-only sex; and 'dry sex', a term used to describe a guy with his clothes on having an orgasm against a clothed girl. Pregnancy is unlikely – as long as leaked or ejaculated semen doesn't accidentally go anywhere near the vagina. You can still get an STI from oral or even hands-only sex.

Abstinence The problem with abstinence (deciding not to have sex at all) is that, for almost every person who chooses it, a situation will come up in which they find themselves going ahead anyway. Often they have no condoms because they weren't expecting sex, and can end up pregnant or dealing with an STI.

Anal sex Some people use it as contraception because sperm doesn't go into the vagina. It does not protect against STIs – and in fact is an easy way to get diseases and infections because the skin inside the anus is delicate and easily torn. A condom absolutely must be used. Not a good solution. Girls usually don't like it. (It hurts.)

> The info I've been given about not getting pregnant is to not have sex when you are at this age. Emily, 15, Templestowe, Vic.

Operation

There are operations to make a guy or a woman infertile – unable to have a baby – but doctors will usually not perform these on a teenager, even if they want it.

Emergency contraception: the Morning-after Pill

This is a special dose of the hormone progesterone taken in pill form to prevent pregnancy after unprotected sex. It works by preventing that month's ovulation or, if fertilisation has already happened, by stopping the microscopic egg from implanting itself in the uterus. The fertilised egg, so tiny you can't see it, comes out in your next period or is just absorbed back into the body. (This sometimes happens to fertilised eggs naturally.)

Although it's called the Morning-after Pill, it's best taken straight away, or as soon as possible after the unprotected sex, and within 24 hours if possible – but definitely within three days. And despite being called 'a' pill, it's usually two, taken together, or one taken as soon as you can, and the other exactly twelve hours later.

There can be a bit of bleeding a couple of days afterwards, as the body cleans house with a period. You may experience PMT-type symptoms, emotional swings and nausea.

The Morning-after Pill is not 100 per cent guaranteed but the earlier it's taken after unprotected sex, the more effective it is. If you've needed to use the Morning-after Pill take a pregnancy test about three weeks later, in case it didn't work. If the test is positive go straight to a doctor. Don't delay for any reason.

The Morning-after Pill is available without a prescription at the chemist. Just ask for it at the desk where the prescriptions are taken. You can also get it from a Family Planning clinic or a women's health clinic. It may be expensive for you: up to $30 or more.

If you live in a remote area, or are using condoms as contraception, you can keep a Morning-after Pill at home for emergencies, in case a condom breaks. (Keep it in a cool, dry place.)

The Morning-after Pill prevents pregnancy from beginning. It's not the 'abortion pill' RU486 (that's explained in Chapter 17, Pregnancy), and does not cause an abortion.

More info on contraception and the Morning-after Pill

drmarie.org.au
Advisors online answer questions about contraception and STIs. Helpline: 1300 315 664.

familyplanning.org.nz
Sex info for Kiwi teens.

Don't get pregnant to a dude. Amy, 15, Ipswich, Qld

Sex and love

A lot of people believe you should only have sex with people you love. Others think you should only have sex with somebody who respects you and is kind and considerate, even if you're not in love.

One of the hardest things for girls to learn is that sex does not equal love for everybody. You may be in love, and feel that the sex makes it even more romantic, but for the guy it can be all about sex, not about love. Some girls feel that way too.

Getting swept away

Because having sex does not necessarily equal love, it is a good idea to be cautious about your feelings at first. Having sex with someone is such an intimate experience that it can make you feel very close to that person emotionally, can be overwhelming, and can give you some kooky, if temporary, thoughts:

- We're going to be together forever.
- I could never love anybody else.
- We belong together.
- It doesn't matter if I get pregnant because we love each other.
- I'd do anything for him.
- We're in a long-term relationship. (Even though you've only known each other for six days.)

No matter what you're feeling, keep using condoms and sticking to the 'essentials' of sex in 'Going All the Way' earlier. Planned sex, where you have everything ready, is just as romantic as unplanned sex – and in fact is usually better because you're not terrified of getting pregnant or getting an STI (which is really unromantic). Having condoms at home or in your bag doesn't mean that you're expecting to have sex. It means they're just there if you need them. You don't have to use them. (Unless you have sex. Then you really do have to use them!)

> **My mum thinks I'm a sex crazed teenager who has no control over my emotions ... when actually I'm more interested in love than sex.** Jessie, 15, Casuarina, NT

> It is better if they love you. As time passed, my boyfriend lost his love for me, and it became just sex. Kylie, 16, Melbourne, Vic.

If things turn scary

Sometimes a guy can be kissing or touching and then won't take 'No' or 'Stop' for an answer and keeps the pressure up, with words or even physically. A guy may even push, try to wrestle clothes off, sit on top of you or otherwise try to restrain you from getting up or walking away. If you've said no, he must stop. Try these responses:

- 'I said STOP, and I mean it!' Raise your voice and shout it.
- Fight. Yell. Don't give in or think that it's more embarrassing to make a fuss than to 'let him'. Call out to friends who are nearby.
- 'My older brothers/cousins/dad will be picking me up and they'll kill you if you don't stop.'
- 'I'm going to be sick.' Put your hand over your mouth, pretend you're going to be sick, then get away from there.
- 'I need to go to the toilet' or 'I need to take a tampon out.' Then get away from there.
- 'I've got my period and there's blood everywhere.' Then get away from there.

> I agreed when he asked, for him to penetrate my vagina, but when I told him to stop, after he first put it in, he didn't, and repeated it about four more times. It scared me that someone so close, whom I knew so well, would get so carried away so easily and would not listen when I said 'stop'.
> Jules, 16, Woodend, Vic.

If necessary, and you're not at your place, you may have to fool him by leaving your handbag or jacket behind, so that it's not obvious that you've gone. Sneak your keys, phone and money into your pockets or underwear, say, 'Mind my bag for a minute. I'll be right back', then get as far away as you can. Find somewhere private and call your emergency number to get picked up. (See Chapter 8, Confidence, for more about emergency numbers and defending yourself.)

FACT

Nobody owns you Nobody – no boyfriend, husband or anyone else – has the right to sex without consent, no matter what they think or say, or what anyone else tells you.

> A guy tried to force me once but then I dumped him. It didn't feel right. Ruby, 14, Vermont, Vic.

> I had sex but my partner, he was very mean to me. He gave me bruises. Amy, 14, Hawksburn, Vic.

Sex without consent

You need to know that:

- even if there is no physical violence, it's still sexual assault if you are forced into sex by verbal threats, name-calling, nastiness, emotional blackmail, threats that otherwise he'll tell people something mean or made up, or claims such as 'I know you want it'
- someone who does this to you after understanding that 'no means no' is NOT good boyfriend material, and you shouldn't be alone with him again
- it's okay to have agreed to do something and then have second thoughts and say no
- it's okay to have had sex with ex-boyfriends, or with a guy, and then say no. Having had sex once, or seventy times, already doesn't mean you have to say yes the next time.
- having or not having your virginity has nothing to do with consent. You still get to choose every time whether you want to have sex. You're no less special if you've had sex before.
- ugly words like 'frigid', 'bitch', 'slut' or 'whore' can be used to threaten or intimidate girls in these situations. None of these labels has anything to do with you as a person, they're just a tactic used by some guys to try to get what they want. Ignore them.

Look after yourself

Sex is supposed to be intimate, romantic or at least fun, with some respect. It should not involve abuse, insults, cruelty, restraint against your will, being ordered around, roughness, forcing, threats or violence. Although some guys see this sort of sex in porn, it's not okay. Talk with him about the need to be kind and careful of you. If he doesn't listen, it's time to be on your own or find somebody new. See Chapter 15, Love, for what to do if you're with somebody who tries to control you, or who forces you.

> **FACT**
>
> **Stranger danger?** It's much more common for women and girls to be raped by somebody they've met, or who they know, than by a complete stranger in a random attack.

FACT

No joke Rape is something that is joked about by ignorant people. Once you know what it involves, you understand why there is nothing funny about it. Don't let people make jokes about rape around you. Tell them it isn't funny.

Sexual assault

Sex without consent is a crime called rape or sexual assault. These days the crime is often referred to as sexual assault and this term can also cover other unwanted acts, including the groping of private parts or forcing somebody to do something sexual.

A guy commits rape if, against your will, he has penetrative sex with you (the penetration can be with a penis, fingers or objects, and in the vagina, the anus or the mouth). Other words used are forced sex, non-consensual sex or sex with coercion.

Legally, rape or sexual assault is about whether or not you consented – wanted it to happen. If you did not freely say yes, it's rape. It's legally rape if physical force or violence was used, and in many cases if it wasn't, if you were too drunk or out of it to give your consent, you were held down or overpowered but have no visible injuries, or if you 'gave in' because you were too scared or couldn't see a way of escaping.

In some rape cases, a woman will sustain injuries from punching, kicking and other violence, or be raped by more than one attacker. In other cases, bruising and hurt may not be visible. Multiple rapes can be committed at different times by the same person. It's rape, and illegal, if you don't consent or don't want to and you're forced by a boyfriend or husband.

If the rape happens within a social situation, some people call it 'date rape' (see 'Sex Without Consent' opposite). This is also the term some people use when a rapist gives a person drugs that make them partly or completely unconscious.

Sadly many girls drink enough voluntarily or accidentally to put themselves into a state in which they can't fight against or try to avoid a sexual assault. Some girls can believe they've secretly been drugged – say in their drink at a club or at a party – but this is actually quite rare. It's always worth making sure this doesn't happen to you by guarding against the possibility.

Being assaulted is NEVER your fault

See 'Gaining Confidence and Independence' in Chapter 8, Confidence, for tips on how to avoid other dangerous situations and how to resist an attack. Nobody deserves to be raped, or should never be blamed if it happens to them. If it happens to you, fiercely guard this knowledge: no matter what anyone else says, what you were wearing or where it happened – it's never, ever your fault, it's happened to many women, and there is help for you. If it happens to a friend, see the 'More Info' section coming up for how to help.

Getting help after an assault

Just as consenting sex can give you intense feelings of being cared for and a sense of intimacy, rape and sexual assault can often cause serious and long-lasting feelings of violation, terror, and even shame. While it's very common for girls and women to feel shame about being raped or assaulted, it's *so* important to realise as you recover that the shame is not yours – bad things can happen to good people.

The possibility of pregnancy or a sexually transmitted infection adds to the distress. It can also be very worrying for somebody if they know they were raped but can't remember what happened (perhaps because they were drunk).

You *can* get help.

- Call the police on 000 if you are in immediate danger or to report an assault straight away.
- Tell someone you trust about the assault so they can help you with the following steps.
- Get medical help and counselling: every state and territory has a sexual assault service staffed by women who can help you – whether you were assaulted by somebody you know or by a stranger, and whether or not you want to involve the police (see 'More Info' opposite). They can recommend kind doctors to help you.

> My friend got drunk and her sister's boyfriend's friend raped her. Even though she said no, she thinks that she must have done something to make him think she wanted it.
> Claire, 14, Parkside, SA

> I started dating a guy. We wagged school and he raped me. I never told anyone. He spread all sorts of shit around school about me. I went from A student to barely passing. Sex is meant to be good and fun, but that goes for both of you. Don't feel pressured – you'll just regret it later. Georgie, Qld

400   HEART ♥ sex

- As soon as possible after you have been raped, but definitely within 72 hours (three days), go to a chemist and ask for the Morning-after Pill, which should prevent pregnancy (see 'Emergency Contraception' earlier in this chapter). Do a pregnancy test three weeks later to make doubly sure. Also see a doctor to check you haven't been given any infections that could cause health problems in the future. You can go to your school nurse, GP or a Family Planning clinic.
- Think about having ongoing counselling – many people find it helps them work through their feelings after an assault. Counselling can be free on Medicare: ask your GP about it.

If the assault is ongoing   If you continue to be assaulted by a person in your family, an adult in a position of trust, a boyfriend or someone else, there are many services that will help you choose how you want to handle the situation, and help you through it. See 'More Info on Sexual Assault and Rape' below.

You can also call the police or take out a court order to make the person leave you alone and stay away from you and your home, school or work. If you are under 18 a parent or the police can take out the order for you.

More info on sexual assault and rape

Kids Helpline: 1800 55 1800

1800 RESPECT Helpline: 1800 737 732
The National Sexual Assault, Family Domestic Violence Counselling Line is free, 24-hour, anonymous, and will help you find local services such as rape crisis centres. Help and advice whether what happened to you is very recent or occurred a long time ago, with a stranger or with somebody known to you.

Escaping Control and Abuse by Kaz Cooke
My free-to-download ebook on escaping unhealthy relationships, assault and abuse.

secasa.com.au
Sexual assault help service: choose Information Sheets.

au.reachout.com
Choose Understand and Act, then Tough Times, then Abuse and Violence.

> I've been raped by 3 different males; I would like to know the best way to deal with it without having to go to the police.   Anonymous, 17, Curtin, ACT

> It's not that easy to say 'no'. You freeze. It sends you crazy inside your head and makes you wonder whether it's your fault. Tell someone what has happened.   Lou, 16, Newcastle, NSW

PREGNANCY

17

positive pregnancy test

what are your options?

There are lots of ways of saying somebody is pregnant: they've 'fallen pregnant' (as if it was caused by tripping over a crack in the footpath), 'got a bun in the oven', or 'conceived' (the traditional word); or they're 'up the duff', 'in the family way', or even 'in trouble' (the old-fashioned phrase).

Most teenage girls don't **want** to get pregnant, but thousands do each year, usually because they didn't use contraception. If you're pregnant this chapter explains your options so that you can make an **informed decision** about what to do. This is one of the most serious decisions anybody ever makes. Whatever you choose, you'll experience a mix of strong emotions, including relief, guilt and regret.

Being pregnant

You can get pregnant *only* if a guy ejaculates or a little pre-ejaculate semen leaks from the tip of his erect penis. But wait – pregnancy won't happen if he's on the other side of the room. Either his penis has to be in you at the time, or somehow his semen has to get near enough to your vagina for a sperm to wriggle up to a fallopian tube and fertilise an egg there. You'd have to be fairly unlucky for this to happen if he doesn't actually 'come' inside you, but it *is* possible, and sperm inside you can stay able to impregnate you for up to a week.

Common signs of pregnancy

Some people have no idea they're pregnant; others have a feeling there's something different. There are some early signs but not everyone has these, and some people might get certain ones and not others. Getting a bigger tummy only happens much, *much* later in a pregnancy and you'll need to know a long time before that.

Pregnancy symptoms can include:
- a period hasn't arrived (it's very rare to have periods while you're pregnant)
- instead of your period you get a light spotting of blood, which could be a signal that an egg is implanting itself in your uterus
- you've missed a couple of periods (but don't wait this long to do a pregnancy test – missing one period is enough to suggest you are pregnant)
- your breasts are sore – they might be slightly swollen and tender, and the nipples or areola (area around the nipples) could get larger or darker in colour
- you start to feel sick in the stomach (nausea) or actually throw up ('morning sickness' can affect you at any time of the day)
- you have 'stomach' cramps – many women say that the early days of pregnancy feel a lot like getting a period, which can make it hard to tell the difference
- you need to wee a lot – some women feel like weeing much more when they are pregnant
- you're more tired than usual.

How to find out if you're pregnant

Aside from getting sperm very near or in your vagina, you can't get pregnant from any other form of sex, such as thinking sexual thoughts, masturbation, kissing, sexual touching, oral sex, swallowing sperm, anal sex – or from toilet seats, wishing you were pregnant, irregular or missed periods if you've never had sex, or anything else you can imagine.

If you have one or more of the symptoms listed earlier or you suspect you may be pregnant, the best thing to do is to take a pregnancy test. Even when you have irregular periods and you're usually not worried about a missed one, do a test as soon as possible if you've had unprotected sex (without a condom or other contraception).

You can get tests from a pharmacy. These are very accurate and can sometimes show within a couple of days of the sex whether you're pregnant. If you get a 'negative' result after a missed period do another test in ten days to be sure. Most people find it hard to trust just the one test so do another one immediately to confirm the result – it's usually cheaper to buy two tests in the one packet for a bit more money than two separate tests.

These tests usually involve weeing on a plastic stick. Follow the instructions. If there's a pregnancy hormone in your urine (wee) you'll get a 'positive' result: usually a little window or line on the stick changes colour. You can also do a pregnancy test at a local GP, community health centre or Family Planning clinic.

> I often fear that I may be pregnant, possibly because I am not fully aware and educated about the ways in which one can get pregnant.
>
> Amber, 18, Mullumbimby, NSW

If the test shows you're pregnant

If the home test result is a 'positive' get to a doctor, community health centre or Family Planning clinic in the next day or so. (Anything you tell them is in confidence.) Don't delay no matter how confused or worried you feel. You may hope the problem will go away – it won't. Or believe that your parents will be angry when they find out – they may or may not be angry, but will definitely find out if you delay.

Going to a doctor, community health centre or a Family Planning clinic means you can have important questions answered. And you must go straight away to be able to choose from the full range of options available. You can also anonymously call one of the counselling services listed under 'Unbiased Pregnancy Counselling' coming up soon.

You need to make a big decision pretty quickly

Many girls who don't realise at first that they are pregnant, who are pregnant as a result of sexual assault, or who are too frightened to tell their family can end up far along in a pregnancy before they get help and won't have as many options available to them.

Your options If you are pregnant you have three options: to have the baby and be its mother; to have the baby and give it up for adoption; or to end the pregnancy by having a termination (which is also called an abortion) in a safe, professional medical way. You will have to make a decision fairly quickly because after a short time a termination is no longer possible.

There isn't one option out of the three that you 'must' choose. The important thing is to decide for yourself, with the support of others. None of the available decisions is likely to make you totally happy, and each option needs a lot of thought and talking through. To help you, the three are fully explained a bit later in this chapter.

Motherhood, which can be wonderful, isn't for everybody at every time of their life. Being a mum is too difficult, emotional,

Some things to consider

You may feel you want to be a mother now, and that you can manage whatever happens because you have full family support.

or

You may feel you're not ready to be a mum and may want to finish your education and grow up more, believing that you'll be a better mum later if you wait.

*

You may be aware that pregnancy can be a health risk for teenage girls, and think it would be better not to continue.

or

You may feel you're full of energy so you will be able to cope with a baby.

*

You may not like the idea of giving a baby up for adoption because you wouldn't be there to protect it through life.

or

You may like the idea of giving a baby to a family who wants one very much.

*

You may believe for religious or ethical reasons that anything after fertilisation of the egg is a baby, no matter how undeveloped, and should not be terminated.

or

You may believe that something so undeveloped and incapable of surviving outside the uterus is not yet a human being.

full-on and complicated a job to be compulsory, especially for a teenager. You have the right to choose when or if you have children. Nobody should ever be forced or pressured to continue a pregnancy they don't want – and nobody should ever be forced or pressured to terminate a pregnancy that they do want.

Pregnancy counselling services

Pregnancy counsellors will help you explore your options: you can get a referral to one from your doctor; or find them in 'More Info' at the end of this section; or look them up in the phone book. But you need to be very careful because many pregnancy counselling agencies deliberately don't tell you about all your options.

Biased counselling services Some pregnancy counselling agencies are affiliated with anti-abortion and church organisations. Their main aim is to stop you having a pregnancy termination even if that's what you want to do.

These services can have posters in doctors' waiting rooms and other public places, and they have 24-hour helplines partly funded by the national government. They don't say that they have religious or other biases against termination of pregnancy when you visit or call them. So if you want pregnancy counselling that lets you make up your own mind, don't continue with an agency that doesn't acknowledge all the options, and see 'More Info' coming up for unbiased helplines.

Some of the lies told by anti-abortion counsellors include claims that an abortion, whether you have surgery or take a pill, will create many physical and mental health problems for you. Let's just clear up some of those lies. Here are the facts:
- A safe, medical termination will not make it hard or impossible for you to have a baby in the future.
- Statistically, carrying a baby to full term is a much bigger health risk to the pregnant person than having a safe, medical termination.
- Termination does *not* increase your risk of getting breast cancer or any other major health problem.
- You can't get a sexually transmitted infection from a termination.
- You will not automatically develop a mental illness because you've had an abortion, although any stressful time or event can contribute to mental health problems. Statistically, *having* a baby is more likely to trigger a mental health problem – post-natal depression.

- Some girls who feel they were forced into an abortion, for example by parents, can feel great regret (often linked to feeling powerless to make their own decision), but most girls and women who have a termination don't suffer from terrible regret and grief afterwards. Most think it was the right decision at that time, even though they were saddened that they had to make it.
- Doctors and counsellors who believe in a woman's right to have an abortion do not insist on or recommend it to anybody who doesn't want one. 'Pro-choice' people want abortion to be one of the options, not compulsory.

Biased pregnancy counselling services may try to get you to see gruesome pictures or films to frighten you into not considering a pregnancy termination.

Unbiased pregnancy counselling   Go to a Family Planning clinic in your state or territory (known as a Shine clinic in South Australia), a Marie Stopes clinic near you, or contact Children By Choice in Queensland (see 'More Info' coming up).

Your GP or community health centre may also refer you to a pregnancy counselling service. Some GPs though, because of their religious convictions, will try to convince you not to include abortion in your list of options. Other doctors, while wanting you to make your own decision about the three options, may accidentally refer you to an anti-abortion counselling service.

Any clinic that offers terminations should ask you to undergo counselling first to make sure you have considered all your options.

When you're pregnant you have a right to confidential, non-judgemental care and respect for whichever option you choose. You need to decide, not be forced into it by your parents, church, teachers, friends, boyfriend or anybody else. Talking to people who care for you often helps. You could be surprised by how supportive your parents are, after the first shock.

You may feel alone. But there are lots of people who can help you...

> **FACT**
> **School chaplains and counsellors** Some may not tell girls all their pregnancy options because of their personal or religious beliefs.

More info on pregnancy counselling

Some pregnancy counselling service websites and helplines are set up primarily as anti-abortion centres run by religious or other organisations. Many of these give information (some of it false or unproven) to try to dissuade you from having a pregnancy termination. Anti-abortion campaigners have set up pregnancy advice services with mainstream-sounding names such as pregnancycounselling.com.au and Birthline. There are other, independent pregnancy-counselling services, such as Children by Choice, which will talk about and help with all options: having the baby, adoption and pregnancy termination.

familyplanningallianceaustralia.org.au
Use their site to find the nearest Family Planning Australia clinic in your state or territory.
Healthline (NSW only): 1300 658 886.

childrenbychoice.org.au
The site of Children by Choice (in Qld) has lots of useful info and a free counselling service staffed by qualified psychologists and counsellors (or email advocacy@childrenbychoice.org.au).
Helpline: 1800 177 725 (for Qld);
(07) 3357 5377 (outside Qld).

mariestopes.org
A worldwide women's reproductive health service with clinics in the ACT, NSW, Qld, Vic., and WA.

sexetc.org
This US site has stories from pregnant girls, showing each making a different decision, plus other info on being pregnant. Helplines on the site aren't relevant to Australia.

Some public women's hospitals also offer unbiased pregnancy counselling services.

familyplanning.org.nz
Your nearest Family Planning clinic will help you with info and seeing a doctor.

> The info I have been given about not getting pregnant is to keep your underwear on.
> Tara, 14, Bankstown, NSW

Pregnancy termination (abortion)

An average pregnancy lasts about forty weeks (about three school terms). The fertilised egg is known as an embryo (pronounced em-bree-o) for about the first ten weeks, after which it's often called a fetus and then a baby when it's 'viable' (able to survive outside the mum's uterus). Some very premature babies have survived after being born at about twenty-four weeks, or even earlier.

A surgical pregnancy termination or abortion happens well before that, usually between seven and twelve weeks. (How many weeks pregnant you are dates from the first day of the last period you had, not the day you 'got pregnant'). A pregnancy can also be terminated with a pill that causes the tiny embryo to come out (this looks like a period) within the first seven weeks (see 'The Abortion Pill' below).

Most pregnant teenagers choose termination. (But teenagers make up a small percentage of total abortions.) Abortion is legal in all states of Australia under certain circumstances and when done by a registered surgeon.

Having a termination is not an easy option, even if you're sure that's the best choice for you. Many people believe a termination is a decision not to be a 'bad mother', but instead to become a good mother at another time.

Although you'll probably feel a big sense of relief, other emotions after an abortion can include guilt, anger, confusion, and sadness wondering 'what might have been', or a mixture of all these, even if you're still sure you made the right decision. Hormones can be very unsettled for a week or two after a termination, which doesn't help. You may want to keep your termination a secret, or within your family. It's probably not a good idea to tell anyone who might not keep your confidence – it's your own business. If you need help sorting out your feelings, go to a community health centre or a Family Planning clinic or get a referral from your doctor to a non-judgemental counsellor.

> I have had cousins who have had babies in their teens and have seen how much hard work a baby is. Sascha, 18, Canberra, ACT

> If you get pregnant there are ways that you can deal with it and still have a good life without ruining yours. Lila, 17, Canberra, ACT

The 'abortion pill'

A non-surgical way to end a pregnancy is to take the pill called mifepristone (RU486). It may be available as an option, from your doctor or Family Planning or Marie Stopes clinic (see 'More Info on Pregnancy Counselling' earlier in this chapter).

RU486 is successful 95 per cent of the time, but needs to be taken in the first nine weeks of pregnancy. The pill works by stopping the action of the hormone progesterone, which the body needs to continue a pregnancy. It's used with another drug (misoprostal), which causes the uterus to contract and helps the fetal tissue come out (it's like having a crampy period).

It's very important that you have a friend or relative who can be with you in the days afterwards, keep in touch with the doctor, follow any after-care instructions, and have a check-up in a few days to make sure you're all okay.

RU486 is not the Morning-after Pill for emergency contraception, which has to be taken within three days of unprotected sex (see Chapter 16, Sex). The Morning-after Pill prevents a fertilised egg from implanting before it begins a pregnancy; RU486 terminates a pregnancy that's already begun.

Surgical termination

Your doctor or community health centre or a Family Planning or Marie Stopes clinic can refer you to a surgeon. If you choose confidentiality, your parents don't have to know about the termination. (In Western Australia girls under 16 who don't want their parents to know will need help from a Family Planning or Marie Stopes clinic or their GP to get the right paperwork sorted.)

Although a surgical termination is usually done up to twelve weeks of pregnancy, states and territories have different laws about the outer time limit and in certain ones it can be done later. Some Catholic hospitals refuse to do terminations for any reason.

The abortion debate

Polls done by independent organisations show most Australians are pro-choice: say it's a woman's right to choose whether or not to have an abortion before twelve weeks.

Anti-abortion groups continue to try to persuade politicians to make abortion illegal or much harder to get in Australia. Anti-abortion groups, who call themselves 'pro-life', can say hurtful things about abortion (including calling it murder) and can have some very nasty tactics, including harassing people outside clinics where terminations are performed.

Other hospitals will do them only if there is a serious abnormality in the fetus or the mother's life is threatened by the pregnancy.

Surgical termination is usually a safe, simple, low-risk procedure for the pregnant person, but the longer you've been pregnant the trickier and more confronting it can be, and most surgeons much prefer to do it in the first twelve weeks. Pregnancy terminations later than fourteen weeks are sometimes done, but are more complicated, much harder to get and more expensive.

The operation   A surgical abortion is done at a clinic or a hospital. You lie on an operating table for the procedure, with your knees apart, and are given either a light general anaesthetic, so that you are asleep, or some tablets to make you more relaxed and then a local anaesthetic so you don't feel any pain.

The most common type of surgical pregnancy termination, called a suction curette, 'vacuums' out the contents of your uterus through the vagina, using a special tube. It only takes about 15 minutes, but you'll probably need to be there for 4 hours in total.

Support before and after the operation   It helps to have someone in the waiting room to support you on the day, and to help you get home afterwards (even if you have a licence, you're not allowed to drive straight afterwards).

Before the procedure a health worker will talk you through the process and the risks – make sure you ask any questions you have then. If you're worried that you'll forget the questions, write them down beforehand and bring them along, or take a trusted adult in with you. This could also be a good time to talk about what method of contraception to use when having sex in the future.

After the op you'll be given some antibiotic pills to take for a couple of weeks, to prevent infection in your uterus, and be advised to come back in two weeks for a check-up.

The cost of pregnancy termination   Surgical and medical abortion costs are usually about the same – a few hundred dollars, with some returned to you from Medicare. (See Chapter 7, Body Health, for an explanation of Medicare.) Other factors that can change costs include location (it can be more expensive in the country than the city), how many weeks pregnant you are (it gets more expensive after twelve weeks) and whether you have private health insurance.

The operation is free in Australia at some public women's hospitals and clinics, and in New Zealand.

> **FACT**
>
> **Not an option** Trying a do-it-yourself termination can cause terrible pain and damage to you, doesn't stay secret, and very often doesn't end the pregnancy. Until legal abortion was available in Australia women's hospitals had whole wards dedicated to trying to look after women who tried to terminate their pregnancy. Many of them died. It's important for you to know that you can now end a pregnancy without harming yourself.

More info on pregnancy termination (abortion)

Family Planning Australia, Marie Stopes International and Children by Choice in Qld will help you if you decide to have a pregnancy termination (see 'More Info on Pregnancy Counselling' a few pages earlier for details about them).

mariestopes.org.au
Marie Stopes International has info about the abortion services nearest you if you live in the ACT, NSW, Qld, Vic. or WA. You can also download an info booklet and see FAQs about abortion. From the home page choose Abortion.
Helpline: 1800 003 707.

thewomens.org.au
If you're in Vic., or Tas. and can come to the mainland, the Royal Women's Hospital Pregnancy Advisory Service in Melbourne can help you.

reproductivechoiceaustralia.org.au and childrenbychoice.org.au
Info on the abortion pill RU486 and more.

🥝 abortion.gen.nz/what-to-do
A step-by-step guide if you've decided you want a termination, plus info.

Becoming a young mum

About 3 to 5 per cent of babies born in Australia have a teenage mum. Most girls who have a baby decide to stay its mum, especially after giving birth and spending time with the baby.

Making the decision

Having a baby is a responsibility that many older women feel daunted by, so it's a lot for a teenager to take on.

Good things about being a teenage mum
- You tend not to get as tired as older mums.
- Older first-time mums are just as inexperienced with babies.
- You'll be closer in age to your kid – that means you may be able to understand them better, and have more energy while they're growing up.
- Being a good teenage mum is a great achievement.

Hard things about being a teenage mum
- There's a higher risk of miscarriage and of a complicated birth in your teen years.
- Very few schools help pregnant girls or young mums.
- It can be lonely. Looking after a baby is so challenging, and takes away freedom. Most friends don't understand the relentless commitment it requires 24 hours a day, seven days a week, 365 days a year.
- Almost all teen mums are single by the time their baby turns 1 year old.
- You will probably be poor, even very poor. The 'supporting parent' benefit money from the national government is usually just enough to cover cheap rent, electricity bills and home-cooked food, without any extras.
- Unlike a pet, a baby (and older children) can't be left alone, ever. This can make you feel trapped, as you can't study, work or go out whenever you want to.
- Child care (a place that minds kids) is very expensive. And often not available.
- Being a teenage mum can mean you never get independence. Many teenage mums find that even if their family is not angry with them, the family still wants to tell them what to do and how to be a parent, especially if they're all living together.

When you've decided to become a mum

You'll need to think about telling your family and other people you're pregnant and you've decided to keep the baby; prepare for the birth; and find out how much the baby's father wants to contribute. It really helps if you have a good support network, so if that's not going to be the baby's father or your family or somebody else, you'll need to start planning how to manage, and how to finish or extend your school and training years once you're a mum (see below).

> I got pregnant at 15 and had my son at 16 and now I'm 17 and he's a darling.
> Ange, 17, Gisborne, NZ

If you're frightened of how your parents may react to your decision, think about taking somebody with you when you tell them. It would be great if you could get the support teenage mums need during and after pregnancy from your family but, if not, your local doctor, community health centre or Family Planning or Marie Stopes clinic can help you find the right social workers to help you through.

School Ask for help from your mum or dad, a school counsellor, a nice teacher, a relative or a friend's mum to help make sure your school continues to offer you the education you're legally entitled to, while you're pregnant and after your baby is born. If your school is hopeless or you feel any pressure to leave, contact your state or territory education department and insist on getting help. You may want to move to a school that has the proper supportive policies to help you. The higher your educational qualification, the better your chance of making more money later.

Pregnancy and birth You and your unborn baby will need to have regular medical check-ups to make sure you're both healthy and progressing well. And you'll need advice about what you need to eat and what you can and can't do when you're pregnant (see 'More Info' coming up).

Pregnancy and birth specialists called midwives (usually women) and obstetricians (specialist doctors) will help you during your pregnancy and when you give birth. Your GP will help you choose them or they will be part of the staff at your nearest public women's hospital.

After you've had the baby

- **Health and other costs**   If you have your baby in the public health system, instead of at a private hospital, your medical bills will be paid for by the national government (see the 'Your Medicare Card' section in Chapter 7, Body Health).
- **Government support**   The national government's Family Assistance 'supporting parent' payments start after the baby is born; at the hospital you'll be given forms to fill in. Ask what bonus or other allowance money you may be eligible for. (See 'More Info' coming up.)
- **Child care**   If you know or think you might need child care because of school or work, you need to organise it as soon as you've decided to keep the baby: call your local council and ask for the numbers of the child-care centres near you. Call the centres and put your name down on the waiting list for a place. You can always say no if you don't need it when a place comes up. Some centres have several hundred people on their waiting list. You may be eligible for government help to pay for the child care.

More info on becoming a young mum

humanservices.gov.au/individuals/families
13 61 50
The national government's Family Assistance Office will advise on what payments and allowances you're eligible for.

sexetc.org
US site by and for teens. From the home page choose Teen Pregnancy and Parenting for stories and FAQ.

Up the Duff by Kaz Cooke
My book, which takes you through a pregnancy week by week. I check it all the time to make sure medical and other info is right up to date – so don't get an old copy from the library or a friend. Make somebody buy you a new copy or borrow a new one. Do the same for any other pregnancy or child-care book.

Babies & Toddlers by Kaz Cooke
Also by me, about the first three years.

I'm a mum and the chores make me so depressed but no one else will do them, will they? I need my braces to be fixed but I have no money.
Nicola, 18, Wishart, Qld

My friends all took off and moved on when I had my baby. I don't hear from them very often at all. Aretha, 18, Glenelg, SA

QUOTE

'i've been a mum for 16 months now and i love every min of it. i'm not sayin' go out and do it, i'm sayin' if you r already pregnant and ur young don't worry what other ppl say or think. remember there's a new life growin' inside u what u have made urself outa love.'

'Rachel', posting on US website sexetc.org's teen parenting pages

Adoption

If you're sure that you want to have the baby adopted, you'll still find pregnancy and birth very big experiences physically and emotionally, and you'll need help and support throughout both (see 'Becoming a Young Mum' earlier).

How adoption is organised

Somebody who is helping you, such as a parent, relative, friend's mum, hospital social worker, your doctor or another adult, can contact your state or territory government adoption agency, which will be part of a community services or families department. A counsellor will work with you and a government-approved agency to arrange the adoption or temporary foster care.

The counsellor will discuss with you the sort of family you want your child to grow up in and will tell you a bit about the family when one is chosen. (In New Zealand you can choose the family from a list of people that gives some of their details.)

You can talk to the counsellor about meeting the family if you'd like to, as well as whether you think you will want to contact your child in the future. Most adoptions now are 'open', which means you can see your baby as it's growing up. Some girls allow their baby to be adopted by relatives or family friends.

After the adoption

You can change your mind and keep the baby when it's born. But if your baby has been legally adopted, after a certain length of time you could have no further legal rights or responsibilities.

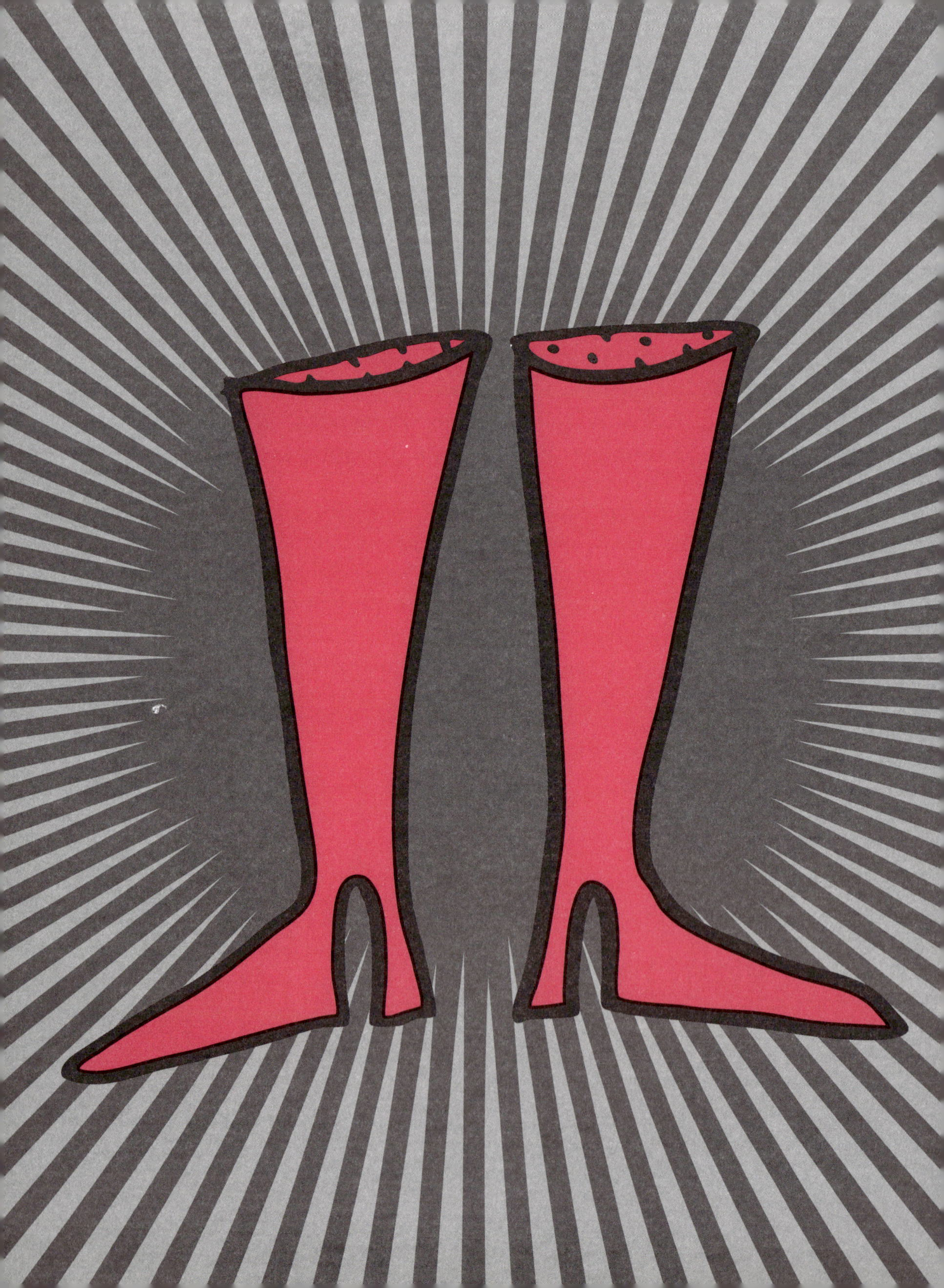

PART 4

AND THE REST

18 **SCHOOLWORK** Getting out from under **421**

19 **PAID WORK** Where's the money? **443**

20 **MONEY** Get it, spend it, use it **458**

21 **SHOPPING** Dodging the rip-offs **471**

22 **CLOTHES & MAKE-UP** Having fun with them **484**

23 **EQUALITY, FRIVOLITY** Stay strong, sister **510**

24 **CARING** Believe, belong, be you **527**

SCHOOLWORK

You're supposed to think your school years are the time of your life – as if you didn't have to deal with hormones, and negotiating every last molecule of life at home, and parents and teachers throwing hours of **homework** at you and telling you that if you don't pass your exams you'll be stuck in a dead-end job, packing toenail clippings into tiny boxes for the dodgy herbal cure market.

It's a colossal pain in the buttockular region, but whether you're in **school, college, university, a training scheme or an apprenticeship** you'll have to work at getting the study done so that one day you'll be freeeeee. And also not have to pack toenail clippings.

Homework and study

When to do homework and study? Every waking minute of your life that you're not at school, according to some parents – but that's just going to drive you nutty and won't work anyway. There's really only so much homework and study you can take.

It's dull but true that if you get the work done earlier in the night it will be easier and you'll remember more. Anything after midnight and you're wilted and not taking it in (see Chapter 12, Mind Health).

Sadly you'll need to be organised.

A homework or study plan

Keep a schedule for your homework and study so you know how much time you can spend on each subject or project. It means you don't finish up at the end of the night having completed a zillion word essay on frog spawn that's due in a week, but done nothing on the maths question that has to be in tomorrow. There's a schedule opposite, which you can photocopy or scan and print.

Work out what homework or studying you need to get through in the next few days or weeks, and how much free time you have available, then divide that time between school tasks and other things you want or have to do. It's probably something you can draw up on a Sunday night.

School stress

Don't let it get on top of you. You need to be having fun too. Don't base all your hopes for the future on one set of results, or allow yourself to feel trapped and overwhelmed by worry about studying, assessments, exams or marks. Talk to a school counsellor and/or a parent: you might need help with a strategy for more balance in your life. If you're overcommitted, you may need to cut back on a subject or drop one or two commitments that are making it all seem too much.

See the 'Feeling Worried and Stressed' section in Chapter 9, Feelings, for hints on how to feel calmer, and see Chapter 6, Move, for ideas on fun ways to stay active – a proven stress-buster. And see the 'More Info' section coming up for strategies for making homework less overwhelming.

> I can't concentrate easily, so I find if I work for slots of say 45 mins and then have a 10 min break it's easier. Because my brain absorbs only in the first 30–45 mins.
> Amelia, 17, Fish Creek, Vic.

Homework and study schedule*

Monday		dinner	
Tuesday		dinner	
Wednesday		dinner	
Thursday		dinner	
Friday		dinner	
Saturday		lunch		dinner	
Sunday		lunch		dinner	

* Remember to write in sport or other exercise time.

When homework is too hard

Your homework might be too hard because:

- your school is insisting on too much (many schools are cutting down on homework, especially before the last three years of secondary school)
- your school has misjudged what you can handle
- you're experiencing a temporary difficulty or personal stress
- you just reeeeally hate doing homework so can't get it organised
- you have a learning disability (many people do).

Talk with teachers and parents to see if you can work out your situation. Maybe it would help if they showed you another way of learning or studying the subject. Schools have to provide students with an education suited to individual needs, including help with learning difficulties. There's good specialised help available for study strategies, stress-busting and learning difficulties. See the 'More Info' sections in this chapter.

Many girls in their final years (especially year 12) have a very stressful time.

Sometimes you just feel snowed under. I do a yoga class once a week and it's a great way to relax when school gets stressful. Pia, 16

Put your plan in writing (pencil might be good so you can rub something out if your schedule has to change), then pin it above your desk or keep it in your diary.

You'll probably need to spend most time on the subjects you find hardest, which is annoying. Pencil in a fun thing for the end of each session so you have a reward.

If your schedule is so chock-a-block it's stressful and scary, talk to a teacher or parent about what you can do to ease the pressure.

> **HINT**
>
> **Back-up** Make sure, if you use a computer, that every hour or so you save your work separately (for instance, on a memory stick or disk), especially if you share the computer with somebody else.

Your homework and study spot

Some people can work in the kitchen with six brothers and sisters having a fight over the last scoop of ice-cream, but most people need a bit of quiet space somewhere. Your own bedroom is probably best, although there are usually lots of distractions (not to mention that bed just tempting you to a nap or maybe a pillow fight). Sometimes a study space can be in a corner of another room or a parent's home office; at school or the local library; or at Nanna's house – but if this is the case, you'll really have to keep it tidy.

> Make lists of homework you have to do and then stick to them. Focus on your goal. If you haven't studied and you should have and the test is happening . . . don't panic: it's too late to panic.
> Klara, 18, Fannie Bay, NT

> I wish I'd known that once you have an idea of what you want to do in the future you should only pick the subjects at school which will help you get there, with maybe some back up choices.

> I created more pressure and stress for myself by doing more than I had to . . . Monica, 17

Here are the general requirements:
- a work space that's big enough for all your stuff (and for you to be able to leave it there if possible)
- peace and quiet – some people suggest total silence, while others think a little bit of low background noise, from music or TV in another room, is probably okay if you don't find it distracting
- a chair and desk at a good work height – as a general rule you should be able to sit up straight with your feet on the floor and your hands no higher than your elbows when you're typing or writing (if your desk is too high you need to make the chair higher and use a footrest, such as a couple of old phone books taped together)
- good desk lighting and a comfortable room temperature (not too hot or too cold)
- a study area that doesn't start looking like a compost heap. Keeping it tidy will create the comforting illusion that everything is always under control (ha!).

Reliable study resources

A lot of free internet and app sources can be only relevant to the US (including US spelling, which is wrong here) and can be unreliable. Talk to your teachers about which sites might give you independent and reliable info for a project or assignment, and talk to parents about access to quality info. Some is free, some requires a subscription. Dictionary.com is free but subscribing to oed.com will give you far more amazing words and where they come from and how they've been used. Flickr and Pinterest will give you access to amateur pics, and Wikipedia provides free 'facts' on travel, the environment and science, but subscribing to *Australian* or *National Geographic* magazine sites or apps will give you professional reporting and photography. Using good 'tools' will give you an edge.

FACT

All your own work Assessors, exam markers, teachers and others now all use special software programs to check for plagiarism – work you've copied from somebody else and passed off as being your own. So don't just copy and paste stuff from websites and other sources.

More info on study and homework strategies

See also the study hints coming up in the rest of this chapter. Many schools have teachers whose job is to help with 'learning strategies' or other buzzwords that cover studying and homework. Ask a teacher you like who this is at your school. It's important to know that everyone learns differently, so try some strategies to see what helps you best to remember what's necessary, complete assignments and be well prepared for exams. If there isn't a helpful teacher at your school for this kind of stuff, try the websites below.

Here's a round-up of useful, free study and time-management info on the web that's US-based. 'Middle school' usually means years 6 to 8 and 'high school' is years 9 to 12.

studygs.net
Scroll down for an incredible list of topics.

how-to-study.com
Don't forget the hyphens in the website address.

Mind Maps for Kids: An Introduction
by Tony Buzan
Different, fun ways to organise and display info so you remember it and understand it better.

You Need good Lighting to Study

Learning stuff

What kind of learner are you? Some people remember facts better if they write them down or do, say, a science experiment for themselves rather than reading about it. Others need to talk things out. Some people like to take in a whole lot of information by reading and re-reading. Others remember it in important points. And some people have to do something new, such as essay writing, over and over again until they're used to it.

find a quiet spot to study: try Jupiter

Find out which way you learn best by talking to your parents and teachers. Then incorporate that style into your studying whenever you can.

Developing your reading skills

It's really important to be able to read pretty easily, not just because schoolwork is too hard otherwise but because, no matter what job you end up doing, it'll be more difficult if you can't read quickly. And unless you can also write reasonably well you won't be able to go for as many jobs or feel as confident about all sorts of things.

If you don't like reading, try to find written stuff in books and magazines and online about things you're interested in. The more you read writing that grabs your attention, the more you'll absorb how to spell things and put sentences together. It magically makes you a better writer as well as a better reader.

If you're having ongoing trouble with reading (and lots of people do) it is your school's responsibility to get you extra help. If your parents can afford it maybe you can have extra tutoring too.

You have a right to be able to read, write and spell by the time you leave school. If that hasn't happened and you've done your best, try not to feel ashamed. It isn't your fault; you've been let down. Bluffing your way through will be a strain, it won't work forever, and it'll restrict your life choices.

> Pay attention during the year and it's much easier at the end.
> Kirsty, 18
> Hampton, Vic.
>
> Make sure that you ask if you do not understand and keep asking until you do. Don't leave things to the last minute.
> Kate, 16
> Benalla, Vic.

You can get free lessons to boost your literacy skills as part of searching for a job (see 'More Info' at the end of this section).

Smart note-taking in class

You don't have to write down everything your teacher or lecturer says: just note the important bits.

Try to make your notes in brief but clear point form – they'll need to make sense to you later. 'Remember the thing' just isn't going to help. Jot down any questions you want to ask as they come up during the session, and raise them as soon as you can (making a note of the answer). After a class go back over the notes, and ask for help if something doesn't make sense or you can't remember what it means.

Here's a big tip: the crucial time to take stuff down in class is usually the first 10 minutes, when most teachers or lecturers summarise what they're going to be on about; and the last 10 minutes, when you're given important info such as recommended references or extra material, what you need to do for homework or when an assignment is due, and any change in class schedule, venue, or somewhere you need to be at a certain time, and anything you need to bring. So if you must zone out or have a chat about a blonde starlet's latest wardrobe malfunction, try to do it in the middle, not right at the start or the end. Of course some teachers may spring important stuff on you in the middle. Mwa ha ha! (Evil teacher laugh.)

> When you get homework do it ASAP, at the end of each class go over material learned, ensure u understand it as u go (especially at yr 11 & 12 level), prepare 4 exams slowly, don't cram study for it, ask teachers for help.
> Rachael, 17, Bendigo, Vic.

Smart note-taking as you read

You know that feeling when you get to the bottom of a page and have no idea what you've read because you've been kind of thinking about something else? It doesn't matter when you're reading the book for fun, but it's a bad way to study.

Before you start to read, think about what you need to get out of the piece of writing.

- Do you need to remember a whole bunch of facts, or just have a general idea of what the writer is on about?
- Will you need to remember which order things happened in? >

General study tips

* Don't wait until the week before an assignment or an exam, or the end of term, to get help on a tricky bit. If you don't understand something, ask.

* Don't keep putting stuff off or it will pile up – in your bag, on your desk and in your head. Aim to do a little bit every night instead of 7 hours on the weekend.

* Plan quick breaks (every half hour or so) in your schedule. Get a glass of water (not having enough water, like looking at computer screens, is a big cause of headaches). Stretch your arms, legs and back. Go to the toilet.

* Don't get sucked into the whirling vortex of a TV show or a phone call so that breaks become too long: make rules for yourself about recording the show or saving the call for a reward later.

* Don't try to boost yourself with a sugary snack or a coffee when you're flagging, even though it's really tempting: this is likely to just make it harder to sleep afterwards. Good energy snacks include almonds, fruit or fried rice with some vegies as well as protein.

* Try relaxation techniques before studying or to wind down afterwards. Do a few stretches – this can help to settle the info in your brain as you go over it in your head. Or you might like to drive everything out of your head for a while with a crazy dance.

   What can help is a fast walk for half an hour or an hour – obviously this is fine during the day, but not such a helpful tip for a winter night when your parents would be more likely to let you go out with a gang of marauding tattooed bikies than walk alone in the dark (if your family is a lovely gang of tattooed marauding bikies please change this reference to pale, blank-eyed strangers wearing floral doona covers).

Then, as you read:
- keep in mind questions set by your teacher
- underline stuff, and pencil comments and questions in the margin
- make separate notes that sum up what you've read, but don't fall into the trap of copying out the whole book
- jot key words on sticky notes and attach them to your forehead. (Or maybe not.)

> Remember that the world doesn't end if you don't get an A. You can only try your best. If you know deep down that you didn't try your best then try harder next time. If you did do your best, then be content with the grade you get.
> Melissa, 18, Perth, WA

Exams

Here are some strategies.
- Get hold of previous exam papers if possible, and do some 'under exam conditions' (such as a set time) to see how you go.
- Find out from your teachers whether questions will be multiple choice, short answers, essays or some wacky thing such as drawing a diagram of your feelings.
- Listen to your teachers' hints. They've seen lots of people go through this. Ask them for sneaky study tips and ideas, and tricky exam questions or wordings that have bamboozled students in the past.
- Before an exam ask your teacher if you should read *all* the questions before you start. It's usually a must.
- Tell yourself that you've studied hard and you're prepared (unless it's a preposterous LIE, in which case just do your best and keep everything crossed except your eyes). Tell yourself you are going to do well – and that if you don't it's not your fault, because you've done everything you could.
- Don't aim for perfection, aim to do the best you can. If you think that anything less than A+ or 99.9 per cent is a failure, then you're setting yourself up for disappointment. Exams are a small part of a long life and you'll get through this time. Failing or not getting the mark you want is NOT the end of the world.
- Don't panic cram. If you haven't given yourself time to study, studying all night before the exam won't help: you'll be too tired to make sense.
- Don't use drugs to stay awake to study or before an exam. All the drugs that make you more alert make it harder to take in and remember information. Even too much caffeine can mess you up before an exam. And any drugs,

including alcohol, that you take to relax could affect your memory and ability to co-ordinate thinking and writing, completely stuffing up your chances of passing the exam.

- At the start of an exam check out which questions are worth the most. Question One may be worth 10 per cent of the total mark and Question Two 50 per cent. Jot down how much time you'll give to each question on the basis of their importance and stick to it.
- You may need to make a quick answer plan before you start each essay-style question.
- Read exam paper instructions carefully and make like a robot, always obeying the key words in the questions such as 'List . . .' (meaning points, not complete sentences, will do); 'Imagine you are . . .' (write in the 'first person' – 'I am Prince Horatio, ruler of everything I see and also the stuff in the laundry'); 'Compare and contrast . . .' (point out the similarities and differences); 'Outline' (be brief, but not too brief); 'Describe . . .' or 'Explore . . .' (you have permission to go on a bit); 'Show how you reached the answer' (make it clear how you worked out your solution – you could get extra marks even if your final answer is not quite right); and 'Write a sentence on . . .' (faffing on for a page won't get you extra marks).
- Answer the questions you find easiest first, to get you started, if it's all a bit daunting, but keep to the time plan you've made – if you're still wrestling Question One to the ground by the end of the exam you won't have racked up enough marks.
- If you look at a question and go blank put both feet flat on the floor, close your eyes and breathe deeply a few times to calm down. Move on to the next question and come back to the curly one later.
- If the exam is not what you expected don't freak out and write nothing – trying always counts for something, especially if you have to make a complaint or appeal afterwards.
- Resist any temptation to cheat. There is no possible good outcome: you either get caught or, if you don't, you always know you cheated.
- When the exam finishes, join in a bit of screeching and pretendy fainting with friends about how hard or easy it was, and then move on. Try not to stress too much about something that you now have no control over.

> **There is life after exams.** Morley, 17, Perth, WA

Exam results And then the horrible wait . . . Sometimes it's just you but sometimes, especially in your final year, it can seem as if your parents and half the known universe wants to find out 'how you went'. Talk to your parents about how you think you did, and also about what to do if you don't get the marks you want.

Very often your marks are not just about how well you went, they're about what other students did. A score of ninety on an exam one year could end up being a seventy-eight in another year. If the results are not what you hoped for, talk to your parents and teachers (or a school careers counsellor if your school has one) about how you might improve for the next year at school or what your options are after leaving school (and see also 'More Info' at the end of this chapter).

> GAAH! I am going to finish school and spend the rest of my life living in a cardboard box deliberately not thinking academic things. Emily, 16, Florey, ACT

> **I find studying with my best friend useful because she is really motivated and if I am at her house then I am not as easily distracted!** Zoe, 17, Nunawading, Vic.

> It's so easy to get bogged down by pressure at school. I based my entire self-worth on how well I did at school, and when I got too sick to keep going, I lost sight of who I was and why I was even alive because I didn't have academic achievements to base that on. I have to fight to keep the obsession at bay.
> Amelia, 17, Reedy Creek, Qld

> You live two lives, one being yours with your family, friends, sport and spare time and the other your schooling life with homework, exams and assignments.
> Brieane, 16, Gold Coast, Qld

schoolwork AND THE REST 433

After school
Schoolies week

Schoolies (often called 'Leavers' week' in WA) is now a tradition for senior students who've finished their final year of school exams, where they go to a warm place with holiday resorts and nightclubs and get drunk and lie down in the sand and throw up. I beg your pardon, no it isn't, it's a graduation festival beloved of the tourism industry (which loves to refer to it as 'three weeks long') and a rite of passage for sensible young adults who quite frequently keep their pants on.

Many students start saving years earlier for their Schoolies accommodation and hijinks. It can be a really fun time to let off steam and enjoy some well-deserved rest. No, not rest. I mean recreation. Dancing. Shrieking. That sort of thing. In Australia, the Gold Coast is the biggest destination; in New Zealand, the Schoolies culture isn't so strong, but there are now more end-of-school adventure holidays. Many travel agents and sites offer Schoolies 'packages' or accommodation 'deals' but if it's not the 'official' weeks for Schoolies, then you won't be there for any of the arranged festivities on offer.

Unfortunately a few idiots tend to cause a lot of problems for local police and ambulance paramedics, taking risks, having 'accidents' and getting far too out-of-it to know what they're doing. Also watch out for Toolies – older men who hang out at Schoolies weeks and try to take advantage of younger girls too drunk to take care of themselves. That's why for many concerts, clubs and other events, you'll need to bring your year 12 student photo ID from your school (now ex-school) to get in, which will allow you to get a wristband for access to all the best events. No exceptions means if you have no ID, you'll have no wristband and no access.

Official volunteers also try to help Schoolies teens who might be spinning out of control and get them home safe. Try not to be a dick to them, won't you?

If you go to a Schoolies week, make sure you use all your instincts and knowledge about how to look after yourself and friends. See the info in Chapter 8, Confidence, under 'Gaining Confidence and Independence'.

Many girls choose to go somewhere quieter with just one friend, or a group of friends, who'd rather have some adventures than get pissed the whole time.

More info on schoolies

schoolies.org.au
The least commercial site, while still supported by accommodation ads, has independent info on the dates when events are planned for schoolies weeks in various places, plus lots of insider info from last year's Schoolies participants on ways to save money, and not get hurt.

schoolies.qld.gov.au/schoolies
The Queensland government has great guides for teens heading to Schoolies, and different ones to help calm your parents.

redfrogs.com.au
A volunteer organisation that helps take care of teens at Schoolies. Click on I'm a Schoolie for 'Tips to Survive Schoolies'.

A gap year

A gap year is the year after year 12 (some people call it 'year 13') (in NZ the final year of school itself is called year 13) (try and keep up), a year 'off' before starting uni or other tertiary education, or starting a job or apprenticeship. Some people use the time to work and get some money together for uni fees. Others want to have a break from study and use their savings or part-time jobs to jet off overseas. Your options are pretty much limitless. There are student exchanges, work opportunities and charity or adventuresome volunteer programs you can do to broaden your horizons and help change the world for the better.

More info on gap years

statravel.com.au/live_learn.htm
This commercial travel agency has a great hub page with links to working and volunteering gap years.

defencejobs.gov.au
Choose Education then Gap Year to see what paid Defence Force jobs you may be able to do in your gap year.

studentexchange.org.au and
🥝 **studentexchange.org.nz**
Student Exchange Australia and New Zealand has some exchange programs for school leavers who want to work, train or study overseas.

Education and careers

Even though it can seem like a good idea to leave school at 16 to get a full-time job, so you have some money and don't have to go to school any more, here's the thing: a boring, dead-end, low-wage job is worse than school because you can be stuck in it forever. If you leave school young for an unskilled job it probably won't offer you very much opportunity to either get out of the low-pay area or learn more stuff to get into a better job.

Finishing school, getting skills training or doing further education may take some more years, but will usually get you a better job, with more pay. Very few well-paying jobs involve no training or education. In fact I can't think of one. Except princess. So unless you were born with your own tiara, read on.

> It seems like everyone else has a plan and knows what uni they want to go to and what courses to do so they can have the type of career they want. I have no idea about any of those things.
> Marianne, 15, Frankston, Vic.

Choosing a career

A few people are sure from an early age about what they want to do, but most have a sorta, kinda general idea of what area they'd like to work in, or they can't make up their mind. It's always good to have a few ideas so that if you don't get into the course you want you have a couple of back-up plans. Make sure, though, that all your back-up plans have some attraction for you, or you'll probably end up dropping out of courses halfway through.

There is no one right answer to 'What am I going to do?', just a range of possibilities. Sometimes not getting into your first course choice opens up a whole lot of new opportunities that end up suiting you better. Sometimes you get your first choice but change careers later anyway. (Many people now swap between careers throughout their life, so don't feel you have to choose something and stick with it forever.) And sometimes the original idea for a career becomes a hobby, while you find a different area to earn money in.

If you do something only because it's the family business, or because it's what your parents want you to do, you may be setting yourself up for a lifetime of wishing you'd done something else.

> I don't know what I want to do with my life and I don't want pressure from family to go down a path I might not want to take. Karla, 18, Brighton, Vic.

What would suit you? Talk to your friends, parents and teachers about what jobs they see you as being suited to. Think about the talents and abilities people have complimented you on, and the hobbies and activities you like doing. Work out what sort of job would suit your personality.

- Would you prefer to work in a laboratory with exciting chemicals?
- Would you rather have a job on your own, or in a social workplace?
- Would you be happy to work a night shift for more money?
- Would you like a stable job in which you do the same thing every day, or one that throws up challenges you have to figure out?
- Do you want to travel?
- Did you spend your entire girlhood doing hairstyles for your dollies, or wanting to weld their naked, headless bodies into modernistic sculptures?
- Do you prefer talking to little kids, or old folk?

Your school may have a careers counsellor who can help you try to match your interests and talents to a potential career. Try some work experience, community involvement or volunteer work. Go to the employment section of the newspapers or one of the major job websites, make a list of all the occupations that look interesting and find out about the skills needed to do them. Wages can also be good in areas where there is a skills shortage: if, for instance, there are not enough metallurgists, being one will mean you're in big demand and can choose where you'd like to work and you'll be paid extra. Use the contacts given in 'More Info' coming up to research the areas you're interested in, and to find out whether there are subjects and levels of education you need to get into a course.

No matter what job you'd like, you'll need the best skills you can manage in English – both spoken and written – and some maths, for running your own finances for the rest of your life and making sure you don't get ripped off.

Education options

Completing year 12 isn't for everybody, but there are other good options around, including specific training or a mix of training and education (there's more on this coming up).

A lot of schools also offer a recognised Vocational Education and Training (VET) qualification, usually studied for in years 11 and 12 ('vocational' means relevant to a job). The courses can be done at school, at a local Technical and Further Education (TAFE) college or with a registered private training organisation. The most popular industry areas for VET in schools are tourism, hospitality (restaurant and hotel work), and business and computer skills (see 'More Info' coming up).

> **FACT**
>
> **Studying overseas** 'Student exchanges' are schemes that place students for one to twelve months in a 'host family' overseas – often one that has a kid about your age so you can go to school together. You need to go through a recognised scheme and be sure you'll enjoy a different life (see 'More Info' coming up). Australian students are also often able to study at an overseas university (your uni should be able to give you the info).

The main post-school qualifications you can get

- **TAFE certificates, diplomas and advanced diplomas** At a TAFE college you study for jobs such as public relations officer, chef or graphic designer.
- **Apprenticeship and traineeship certificates** You learn on the job but usually attend TAFE part-time, with a view to becoming, for example, a builder, hairdresser or mechanic.
- **University degrees** These offer the possibility of a professional career as, for instance, a doctor, lawyer, engineer, teacher, veterinarian or chemist (but going to university is not a guarantee of getting a job).
- **Private college certificates, diplomas and advanced diplomas** These qualifications prepare you for a job as, say, a hotel manager, beauty therapist or financial planner.
- **Pre-training** The police, defence forces and some private companies train their own new recruits, often in partnership with a uni or similar institution.

> I'm quitting next year and working for a year then going to TAFE because only TAFE offers me the course I need to achieve my dream job.
> Keely, 17, Narre Warren, Vic.

> I'm at university. It's wonderful – a true paradise for the likes of me.
> Min, 18, Wellington, NZ

Apprenticeships for girls Although apprentices are paid a real wage, it's usually low during the three or four years of the apprenticeship. Later it can become high – especially in some traditionally guy-dominated industries such as plumbing, electrical work, mechanics and building. There are programs that encourage girls to enter these areas.

College and university courses All big colleges, unis and other major institutions have open days so that you can wander around and get a feel for the places and what they have to offer. Most have careers counsellors or departments to help with course information and career planning (and to help students decide what to choose if they change their mind in the middle of a course).

If you're not so sure, or think you'd like to be able to change your mind easily, a general qualification focusing on business skills, science or humanities, for example, might be better than choosing a very narrow specialty such as tulip breeding. (Although, if tulip breeding is the only thing you've ever wanted to do, I reckon you could find a course at a horticultural institution, or in Holland, if you're single-minded and determined enough.)

You can finish your last year of school and go straight on to further study, or take a 'gap year' to work or travel before enrolling for more training or education.

Sometimes people who've been working for several years (either following school or after a further education course) want to get into a different type of job. This often means having a long-term goal and learning when they can, by studying part-time or at night.

Further education costs

Costs you should be aware of can include:

* fees
* student loans, with interest
* living expenses (rent, food, transport, fun).

Higher education is an expensive business, with many students forced to build up a huge debt. The debt is paid back later, when your job pays enough.

You can find out what you'll be in for, and whether you're entitled to any government benefits (money), by talking to the college or uni you want to attend (and see also the websites listed in 'More Info' coming up).

Many courses can be done part-time – even online or through distance learning (for people living away from major cities), using intranet access, printed notes, interactive websites, podcasts, apps, video lectures and all sorts of other ways. It can be hard work, and you need to be focused, and know that for you the achievements will be worth the effort and sacrifice. Just make very sure you deal with a reputable school and that your qualifications will be recognised where you'll need them.

> Should I go to the closest uni or to a better one further away? There are so many forms!
> Jessica, 16

More info on education and careers

Further education

myfuture.edu.au
Official info for senior students on post-school education and training.

training.gov.au
Info on qualifications and colleges.

openday.com.au
Full list of open days at universities and TAFE and other colleges, as well as careers days and related info.

studyassist.gov.au
Info on courses, institutions, fees and loans, and course info and advice.

🥝 **education.govt.nz**
A good starting point is the Ministry of Education site: lots of links and info.

TAFEs

For more info on Vocational Education and Training (VET) courses search for the phone number or website of the Department of Education and Training in your state or territory, or ask teachers to help.

For TAFE colleges search the name of the individual one, if you know what you want, or try your state or territory TAFE site (some TAFE colleges have a name that doesn't tell you where it is or whether it has several locations, known as campuses, so once you're on a TAFE website, from its home page choose Campuses, Where We Are or Locations for this info):

ACT: cit.edu.au

NSW: tafensw.edu.au

NT: education.nt.gov.au or cdu.edu.au/cdu-vet

Qld: tafeqld.edu.au

SA: tafesa.edu.au

Tas: tastafe.tas.edu.au

Vic: skills.vic.gov.au

WA: dtwd.wa.gov.au

Apprenticeships

Most career websites also have a section listing apprenticeship opportunities. Use your search engine to find Australian sites under Career and Job, and also see:

australianapprenticeships.gov.au
Advice and help for students and job seekers, and links to apprenticeships.
Free call for new apprenticeships info:
13 38 73.

Student exchange programs

studentexchange.org.au, yfu.com.au, rotary.org, afs.org.au and 🥝 studentexchange.org.nz
The sites of Student Exchange Australia New Zealand, the Youth for Understanding, Rotary International and the AFS Intercultural Programs (formerly the American Field Service), which are not-for-profit companies that help organise high school exchanges and can advise on scholarships and other stuff.

Financial help for students

Ask at the administration office of any college, uni or TAFE you go to about possible student assistance.

centrelink.gov.au
Centrelink has information about what government assistance you might be eligible for, in terms of youth allowance payments, student loans or benefits. Youth and Student Services: 13 24 90.

Scams

Watch out for dodgy pirate colleges and courses that may be too expensive or not give you useful or recognised qualifications. These are often pitched at students from overseas.

Career options

myfuture.edu.au
Info on careers, work and employment, training, education and funding.

youthcentral.vic.gov.au
Choose Jobs & Careers for career profiles, job descriptions and work experience ideas.

cdaa.org.au
The Career Development Association of Australia can help match you with training, education and career choices. Choose I Want Career Support to find a career practitioner near you or for useful downloads.
Advice line: 1800 222 390.

🥝 careers.govt.nz and cdanz.org.nz
Career advice from the Kiwi government.

School got too much for me. I'm in year 12 but because of my situation I've had to stop. I'm getting a job. It has been the best thing for me.   Lara, 17, Springwood, NSW

I have many interests and it's too hard to choose which one I should follow professionally. I know that whatever I choose I have to put my heart and soul into achieving a great outcome and I just don't think I am ready for that yet.
Becky, 18, Geraldton, WA

I don't feel confident about leaving school . . . school is a comfort zone and uni is out of that zone, but I'll be fine . . . I'm sure I'll work myself into it.   Monica, 16, Beechworth, Vic.

I got an apprenticeship and if I want to go to uni later I still can.   Eva, 18, Adelaide, SA

Sure I took the long way round by going to TAFE first then Uni, but I realised that through my lack of school work in high school I may never have learned some great lessons, never met these amazing and interesting people or even realised how much I want to be at Uni.   Samara, 18, Lilli Pilli, NSW

I feel confident about my job and traineeship. I know at the end I'll come out the other side with a really good qualification even if I don't ever go to university.
Lauren, 18, Cooktown, Qld

Year 12 exams are over rated. I didn't do very well but I'm making money and enjoying life.
Beth, 18, Mildura, Vic.

I feel confident that I will get into a hairdressing school when I finish high school.   Peta, 16, Deception Bay, Qld

I wish I could focus more. I took a year off to work (last year) and it was hard work, but it really screwed my head on. I used to muck around in school and hate it so much but I love it now and am doing really well.   Fran, 18, Caboolture, Qld

19
PAID WORK

today the sink, tomorrow a head chef!

No doubt you've worked out that money can't buy you love or happiness or health. But you're going to need some other stuff that money *can* buy, such as **lunches and shoes**. So unless you have a pirate treasure chest full of gold doubloons, getting money for things you want means finding work.

Nearly everyone needs a part-time job to get them through the last years of school or higher education; some even work more hours a week than they spend on their uni or TAFE course. (See Chapter 18, Schoolwork, for info about careers, and Chapter 20, Money, for how to manage your cash.)

But how do you find a part-time or full-time job? And how do you apply for it? What should you wear to the interview and to work? What do you do if the boss tries to **rip you off**? How should you behave at your job? (Out in the real world if you sulk, roll your eyes or mutter, you don't get sent to your room – you end up getting fired.)

Looking for a job

There are some things you need to consider when you're deciding which jobs (part-time or full-time) to apply for.

- What kinds of jobs are you suited to (for instance, working in the kitchen or working 'front of house' as a waiter)?
- What are you qualified for, or most likely to get?
- How many hours can you work, and on which days?
- How far can you safely travel, and at what times of the day or night?
- Will it cost too much to get there and back?
- How much will you accept as an hourly rate of pay?
- Is there a low training wage that automatically becomes a better wage later?
- When you turn a certain age, and should be paid more, will you be replaced with a new junior on a lower wage?
- Do you get a free meal?
- Is a uniform provided or do you have to buy your own work clothes?
- Is there a discount on the company's goods (and are the products the sort of stuff you'd want anyway)?

> I don't really like taking money from my parents all the time, I feel guilty. I'd like to have more independence which is why I think I'd like to get a job.
>
> Elyse, 17, Newport, Vic.

Job advertisements

Here are some good places to look for a job:

- employment websites, many of which will keep track of job ads in your chosen areas (search Career and Job in your search engine)
- Centrelink, the national government's one-stop shop for government benefits and job searching

If I can't be a mechanic, I'll be a florist!

AND THE REST — paid work

- community noticeboards at bookshops, backpacker hostels, shops and supermarkets – beware of scams (check scamwatch.gov.au)
- restaurant and shop windows (these can have notices saying they're looking for staff).

'Word of mouth' is also a good way to learn of positions coming up. Friends with jobs may hear of vacancies, and bosses are often pleased to interview or try someone out on a recommendation.

> It is so hard to have enough money to move out, especially if you are a full time student.
> Meng, 18, Lower Templestowe, Vic.

> Juniors don't earn enough.
> Melissa, 17, Moorooka, Qld

Sorting out your image and online profiles

Here's some stuff to sort out to give you a better chance of getting and keeping a job.

- Potential employers and work colleagues are likely to search your name and get access to your social media pages. Are there any embarrassing photos or other items available to public view or that could be sent on? What have you written or said that might work against you? Get rid of it if you can. Don't forget: once you post something, the company that owns the website may have copyright of the material. Check your privacy and other settings regularly.
- Make sure you have a sensible message on your home and mobile answering services. 'Hello, you've called Kelli. Please leave a message and I'll get back to you as soon as I can' is good. 'Heeyyyy, wassup? It's Kel Kel, dudes. Wanna PARRRRRTY?' is really not.
- Lose the cutesy email address. Get a simple email address that uses your first and last name, adding a middle initial or extra number if you need to. Trust me, bosses are less likely to hire someone with an email address such as horny-pantz@bigpond.com.au, slapme@yahoo, nutbag@crazyfairie or poutygurl@hotmail. Seriously, what kind of boss wants to give the keys to their building to someone who has voluntarily called themselves Dumchik?
- Don't slag off your workplace in a blog, tweet or online comments if you want to keep the job.

> When I got my job I tended to save more because I had to work hard to earn the money and you learn to be more appreciative of the money that your parents put out for you. Jess, 17

Applying for a job

Sometimes you're just expected to call a number given in a job advertisement to have a chat, perhaps followed by an interview; but often you're required to apply for the job in writing, supplying a résumé. They'll probably want you to send it by email, and maybe also a 'hard copy' (on paper).

Your résumé, or CV

A résumé (pronounced ray-zoo-may because it's French, but usually as rez-you-may by Australians), or CV (short for the Latin name *curriculum vitae*), is a summary of who you are, your relevant job qualifications and your contact details. It should always be sent, with a covering letter (see over the page), when you apply for a job.

Obviously as a teenager you're not going to have a huge résumé, and it probably won't include the Nobel Peace Prize, but even a brief one-pager helps a potential boss remember who you are and what you might be good at.

A résumé needs to be:
- brief – employers may look at hundreds
- adaptable – so that you can make small changes to it to fit a specific job application
- typed (not hand-written)
- well set out so the reader can find relevant information quickly and you look like an organised person
- checked by someone else before you send it as it's hard to pick up your own errors. Avoid spelling or typographical slips such as 'Ive always Wanted to wrok hear' (there are four mistakes in that sentence).

Teachers, job centres and many websites can help you to put together a résumé.

Setting the information out in bulleted points helps make a CV easy to read. Use the following headings to write your own.

> I wish I had a part-time job to pay my own way through life, but I just don't have the time.
>
> Becky, 18, Melbourne, Vic.

Personal details   You can give your age or date of birth if that's relevant or you want to, but always include your:
- first and last name
- address (the full address is optional – you can just put a suburb)
- email address
- contact phone numbers.

> I think having a part-time job is great. I have a bank account and a debit card set up and it helps me learn how to manage my money.
> Laura, 15,
> Mt Waverley, Vic.

Education and qualifications   List your highest educational achievements: year 11, maybe; or your further education degree or diploma. Also give details of any extra training you've done, even a two-day computer course.

Add any other specifics that could be useful, such as relevant subjects (business studies or first aid qualifications).

Work experience   List any previous jobs, including the name of the place you worked. If a job title was vague, such as 'assistant' or 'office duties', add a couple of sentences to explain what you did.

Skills and interests   Try to include anything that will make you stand out from fifty other applicants. Briefly, what makes you different? 'Member of the school debating team, years 10 and 11' can tell the reader you're persuasive, confident and can express an opinion; 'Co-organiser of field trips to a penguin rookery, fossil reserve and other sites, involving making bookings and itineraries' (shows wide interests and organising ability); 'Member of the school fundraising committee, year 12' (suggests a joiner who is not narrowly focused on schoolwork). Don't put 'I like tennis', but you could put 'Mount Galah Tennis club member since the age of 12, in charge of court maintenance for the last two years and member of the social committee.' That says you're fit, outgoing, and you take on responsibility and make time for interests.

References   Provide the names of two or three people who can give you a reference – speak on your behalf about your work and personal abilities. This makes them a 'referee', but not the sort with a whistle around their neck. A referee could be a teacher, a neighbour you've done chores for or a previous boss.

Sorry to be blindingly obvious, but if you don't know what someone thinks of you, or you know they dislike you, don't put their name down. Always ask a referee beforehand if you can add their name, and ask them what they'd say about you. (This is crucial: if you don't like what they'd say don't include them as a referee.)

The covering letter

In more formal situations an application letter, included with your résumé, lets an employer know that you have really thought about the advertised job and why you'd be suitable for it. Some employers will want this printed out, others will be happy to receive all the info in an email. Job agencies, parents, teachers and career websites can help you with this covering letter.

> It's very hard to find a part time job when you study full time at uni and don't have a car (or transport late at night).
> Katherine, 18, Dandenong, Vic.

The letter should:
- be no longer than a page or a bit over, if printed out
- be set out as a business letter and include at the top, in separate blocks, the employer's name and address, your own address and the date (have a look at one to see how this is done)
- be businesslike and to the point, not rambling
- include details that relate specifically to the particular job, such as why you think you would be good at it
- answer any specific questions or supply any information requested
- be triple-checked by somebody else for errors and sentences that don't read well, not just 'spell-checked' by the computer.

> Getting a job and making your own money gives you great independence.
> Emma, 17, Katherine, NT

The job interview

Yay for you – getting a job interview is an achievement in itself, even if you don't get the job. It means that your résumé and application letter were good.

> Job interviews – very daunting. When you have too many turn-downs, it can get you thinking, 'what's so wrong with me?'
> Loz, 18, Kiama, NSW

Some hints for job interviews

You'll need to start preparing a few days before an interview.

- Do your research so you can seem clued up at the interview. Find out a bit about the place where you've applied to work.
- Practise! Do fake interviews with family, friends or teachers.
- Check out the hints given later in this chapter on dressing for work, then organise what you're going to wear. Your potential boss doesn't want to see your navel ring (and if they do, then you don't want that job).

Just before the interview make sure you do the following things.

- Turn off your phone.
- Be on time. If you're running late call and explain why, with a sincere apology.
- Take some deep breaths while you wait.
- Read through your application letter and résumé again in case an interviewer asks you something about them – always take copies with you.

paid work AND THE REST

Possible job interview questions

Interviewer's questions

'Tell us a bit about yourself.'

'Why do you think you'd be suitable for this job?'

'Why do you want this job?'

'What experience do you have?'

'What are your strengths?'

'What are your weaknesses?'

'Where do you see yourself as being in five years' time?'

Your questions

'What would my duties be on a typical day?'

'Are there any other duties that could come up?'

'Why is the position vacant?'

'How far in advance will I know my hours, or is every shift (hours of work in a day) predictable?'

'Are there opportunities for training and advancement?'

'When will I hear back from you?'

Finally, in the interview itself, make sure you 'do yourself justice'.
- Greet your interviewers (and any office staff) with a smile, make eye contact and say 'Hello'. Try not to swear. (It's surprising what nerves will cause people to do!)
- Be aware of your body language: don't, for instance, slide down in the chair. The worst thing you can do is chew gum. Actually, the worst thing is probably to shriek and try to strangle somebody.
- Present a cheery, positive attitude and look interested.
- Be confident.
- Take your time to answer questions; don't speak too quickly.
- If you don't understand a question ask them to repeat it. If you don't know the answer say, 'I don't know, but I'd hope that either your training would prepare me or that I could ask a supervisor, to make sure I was representing company policy.'

- Always stay calm and polite. They might deliberately ask you difficult or frustrating questions to see how you handle pressure. Sometimes one person will be nice and another one a bit stern or rude, to see how you react.

> Since I got a job my self confidence has improved, because in my industry I'm forced to talk to all kinds of people and this helped me come out of my shell.
> Ash, 18, Brisbane, Qld

Finding out about pay At a job interview, wait for the interviewer to tell you what the rates of pay are, although they're more likely to do this later, when they offer you the job.

Never sign a contract at a job interview. Take it away and get help from a parent or another adult.

You'll need to know what rate of pay is standard for that job. Sometimes the ad will have said what the pay range is, or a friend who works for the company may have told you already. Contact one of the government or union websites given in 'More Info on Workers' Rights and Responsibilities' at the end of the chapter if you want to know how much pay is fair for the job.

More info on a résumé or CV and job applications

youthcentral.vic.gov.au
Search How to Write a Résumé on this Victorian government site for young people.

Knock-backs

If you don't get the job, first say, 'Thanks for letting me know. I appreciate it.' If possible, take the opportunity or ring back to politely ask:
- 'Is there anything I could have done to be a better candidate?'
- 'Could you please keep my details on file in case something else comes up?'
- 'What's the best way to know when another job comes up there?'

Getting knock-backs can make you feel lousy. But it happens to everyone. It's hard, but stay positive and don't give up. Keep reminding yourself about your good points and why you're outrageously employable – and that every 'failed' job interview is good training for that great interview you're going to do in the future for the job you really want.

Being a good employee

Getting the job may seem like the biggest hurdle, but once you're in you have to show you're serious about it and deserve to be kept on as a casual, or past the probationary period if the job is on contract. There's a bunch of skills that all bosses like and want to see displayed on the job.

The following hints may help you get noticed for the right reasons.

Show a good attitude Be positive and enthusiastic. Smile genuinely at clients and customers. Instead of saying, 'I don't know how to do that, so I can't', try 'Can you show me how so I know how to do it properly?'

When you're given a whole lot of instructions about things to do during the day, write them down and tick them off as you complete them.

> I go to work even when I'm really sick just so I know I'll have enough money to get through the next week.
> Rachelle, 17, Ferny Hills, Qld

Be grown up One of the things an employer will hate most is if you act like a little kid – this includes sulking, whingeing and treating your employer like an annoying parent.

Demonstrate communication skills Try to listen, and let people know when you understand. Speak and write clearly. If you're tied up with one customer, tell somebody waiting: 'I'll be with you in a moment.'

If you work with the public you'll have to deal with rude and slightly nutty people. Ask in advance about the company's policy on what to do. Practise some useful phrases such as: 'Let me check that for you, I'll be right back', or 'I'd be happy to take your number and have a manager call you.'

Work well in a team You'll need to get on with other people and try to reach solutions together. You need to have enough sensitivity and brains to understand that it's stupid to make sexist or racist comments that will upset co-workers.

Hold the phone Most employers will want you to keep your phone off while you're at work, unless it's part of your job to use it. Personal calls and checking texts during work time can be banned.

Be smart on the computer Most workplaces will check which sites you've visited on the computer. Accessing or checking or changing social media pages while at work can be grounds for the sack – accessing pornography almost certainly will be.

Show independence Try to handle situations and solve problems yourself, but ask for help when you need it so that time isn't wasted.

Be flexible Stay an extra 5 minutes or half an hour later to get a job finished, rather than leaving 5 minutes early each day. Bosses are more likely to let you go early one day if you've been flexible.

If your half an hour of overtime starts happening regularly you should be getting paid for it. Be wary of bosses who get you to do hours of work for free as a 'trial'. This can be a scam to get one day's work out of a different teenager each time. Unless you're on a formal work experience program, arranged through school, you have a right to be paid a minimum youth wage for any work that you do.

Be honest Some people steal from work – little things such as pens and paper, or big things such as money from the till. The basic rule should be – don't take anything away from the workplace unless you're told to. Not only do all companies have ways of tracking their stock and money (and maybe hidden cameras), but there's usually a policy to report thefts to the police.

Clothes for work

Some jobs come with a complete uniform. Others have bits: you may have to wear their shirt and baseball cap, but supply your own trousers. Being a waiter often involves wearing a white shirt and black skirt or pants. Before your first day, ask what to wear.

It's illegal for a boss to try to force you to wear any clothes that make you feel uncomfortable or exposed, such as a low-cut top or something see-through (see 'More Info on Discrimination and Sexual Harassment' later in this chapter).

If it's up to you to decide what to wear you can put together your own 'uniform' so you know it's always clean and ready for work. Something that doesn't show the dirt and looks professional may be appropriate, depending on the job. Sports shoes are not acceptable at most jobs, but required for others. One knee-length dark skirt or dark pants (not jeans) with two shirts might get you through.

Bad looks (in most cases) for work – and job interviews – include:
- grubby hair, fingernails or clothes
- pigtails (too little-girl)
- heavy obvious make-up and very dark lipstick
- visible underwear of any description – this means bra, bra straps, and the top of knickers, front or back
- mini-skirt or very short dress
- exposed cleavage (between-the-breasts area) or part of your breasts
- exposed tummy, or butt crack when bending
- thongs or thong-shaped sandals
- very high heels.

Good looks (in most cases) for work – and job interviews – include:
- clean hair tucked out of the way behind ears or in a ponytail
- clean, shortish fingernails
- natural make-up or none
- clothes that are obviously for daytime, not what you'd wear to a party or out at night – no sequins, for example
- low to mid-heel shoes
- no visible tattoos – some jobs don't allow them
- no piercing jewellery (except earrings) – again most bosses will ask you to take any out while at work, especially if it's a safety or hygiene issue. (On the other hand, if you're working in a shop that sells rubber vampire bats, looking like a full-on goth can be positively required.)

A BAD LOOK FOR WORK

454 AND THE REST paid work

Your rights as a worker

In a part-time or full-time job you have some rights protected by law, and others that are negotiated when you take the job. These rights cover things such as how long a shift can be; the possibility of holiday and sick pay; whether you can be suddenly sacked; whether your boss is required to make a superannuation contribution for you or take the government tax from your wage; the safety of the workplace and your tasks; and how a boss is allowed to treat you.

Depending on how your job is classified, you'll have different rights. 'Permanent' part-time and full-time employees usually have more rights and benefits than a casual worker employed on an hourly or daily basis, or as the work becomes available.

Youth wages and rules

In some places you'll be paid a lower, 'youth' wage, which means that until you're 21 you get paid less than an adult for the same job. (A 17-year-old gets less than an 18-year-old and so on up to 21.)

In some places you're not allowed to have a full-time job before the age of 15 or 16. In most places teenagers under 18 can't serve or sell alcohol, operate certain machinery or participate in dangerous occupations such as some petrol station jobs. If you want to get a job before or after school or on weekends before you're 15, some states require you to have a child employment certificate or other special government permission. Check out your state or territory rules (see 'More Info on Workers' Rights and Responsibilities' coming up soon).

> My bosses at work are forever trying to change me into someone else ... This makes me doubt if who I am is a good person.
> Kate, 17, Cairns, Qld

What you don't have to put up with

There are laws that protect you from being hurt or harassed, or being made to feel embarrassed or humiliated at work. They protect you against discrimination based on your religion, race, skin colour, disability and gender (whether you're male or female). It's also illegal to sexually harass somebody. Sexual harassment includes comments or inquiries about your sex life, intimidating and insulting stares, the display or sending of pornography in the workplace, and sexual touching or groping.

Leaving a job/getting sacked

Resigning from a job

Keeping a good employment reputation is important for future jobs. Stay professional, hard working and polite right up to when you leave your present job: you'll have a better chance of getting a good reference.

- Usually it's best to resign after you've found another job so you're not left without an income. And it's always easier to get a job if you already have one: you seem more employable.

- Never resign when you're angry. Don't tell the boss what you think of them. Don't shout, slam doors or behave as if they're your parent.

- Don't walk out in the middle of a bad scene (unless it involves a safety or harassment issue) or just leave one day, and never go back, without an explanation.

- Tell your immediate boss you're resigning before you inform the big boss or the employment officer.

- Put your resignation in writing and print it out or email it, with the date you're leaving, and keep it short. Don't give detailed reasons: just say it's time to move on, or another opportunity has come up. Many job search websites have sample letters and advice on how to resign with dignity.

- If you agreed when you took the job that you'd stay for, say, two weeks after resigning, you'll need to do that (it's called 'working out your notice'). Even if it's not part of your contract, it can create goodwill to stay on for at least a few days so that the company can try to fill your position.

- Talk to the pay office or boss to make sure you have the right superannuation records and other paperwork when you leave.

- Ask for a written reference to be ready when you leave.

- Return anything of the company's you still have, such as a uniform or property.

If you're fired or 'made redundant'

- Check with an independent person, such as a government or union helpline advisor, about whether your entitlements (such as 'super') have been met.

- If it's appropriate, ask for a reference. You may have been 'let go' (made redundant) just because there's no more work for that season, or so a company can avoid paying a higher wage.

It can be hard not to take it personally, even when it's not your fault. Again, job search websites often have useful info about being sacked.

To fix a work problem you can try:
- your boss (unless the boss is the problem)
- your union or a union helpline
- the Equal Employment Officer or Human Resources Manager if your workplace has one
- the Equal Opportunity Commission, or Anti-Discrimination Commission or Board, in your state or territory
- the Human Rights and Equal Opportunity Commission (HREOC), a national organisation that covers national laws.

> **HINT**
>
> **Out of there** Don't stay in a job where the atmosphere is all about fear and intimidation. You only have one life and there's no point wasting it by being around people who miss being the school bully.

More info on discrimination and sexual harassment

humanrights.gov.au
Complaints and Info Line: 1300 656 419
Find your local anti-discrimination organisation through the Australian Human Rights Commission. Info and advice on bias towards males, racism or other discrimination at work. Go to humanrights.gov.au/our-work/sex-discrimination/guides/sexual-harassment, find Publications then click on info and fact sheets including Know Your Rights, Young People at Work, and others.

More info on workers' rights and responsibilities

fwc.gov.au
Hotline: 1300 799 675
Government info on wage rates and work disputes.

worksite.actu.org.au
Young people's hotline: 1300 486 466
Union info on workers' rights for young people. Covers workplace bullying, work experience and school assignments about careers.
General workers' hotline: 1300 362 223.

moneysmart.gov.au
From this government money site, choose Information for Under 25s.

ato.gov.au
Tax Info Helpline: 13 28 61
Australian Taxation Office info for young workers, covering superannuation and tax info.

MONEY

20

You mean I'm probably NOT going to marry the next Prince of Bratislava?

There goes my financial strategy

I know, you want more. Here's how to **save** it, how to hang onto it, how to **spend** it, and how not to get into **debt**. And see Chapter 21, Shopping, to find out how to avoid becoming a crazed buying robot who's always broke.

How to hang onto money

You may get regular pocket money through your teens, but the older you get, and the more you want to choose and buy your own clothes or save for something big, the more you'll probably need an extra way to get money. The main way to get money is to work for it, and Chapter 19, Paid Work, has lots of info on part-time and full-time jobs.

I guess it's kinda good that I work for the money to pay for clothes. It teaches me that I can't get everything I want.
Louise, 13, Glenhaven, NSW

Saving

Saving is really the only way to get something major such as a car, a bond for a rented house, or a big holiday. If you're in your late teens see below for how to set up your own bank account. If you're too young to do this by yourself you can get your parents to help you.

rattle, rattle

FACT

The unavoidable truth about saving The only way to save is to spend less than you earn and put away what's left over. Even if you save only $2 a week from your pocket money that's $104 by the end of a year.

Opening a bank account

- Do some online, in person or phone research. Compare the account fees of the different banks. Will some charge you whenever you take money out, or just deduct a monthly fee for keeping your money parked with them?
- Pick a banking institution that has a branch office near your home or work. Although most banking these days is done automatically or online, which can be a lot quicker and more convenient, it can help to have a local outlet that you can go to with a query. >

money AND THE REST

Pocket money

Pocket money is traditionally just for the odd little expenses, such as going to a movie with a friend, or lip gloss, or 'just in case' money to keep in your – well, pocket (or bag).

Parents have different ideas about pocket money. Some believe their kids should do set chores in return for a fixed weekly amount so that they learn about earning money. Some feel their children should automatically have a small, regular share in the family's money, with no conditions attached. Some think pocket money is unnecessary because they look after all their children's needs and hand out money for anything special. And some believe teenagers should be given enough money each week to cover expenses such as fares, entertainment and casual clothes, so that they learn the value of handling money and budgeting.

Increasing your pocket money

- Explain to your parents why you want them to increase it. They may not know what you need, or how you're using it, or what other kids pay for. Try not to compare your pocket money with a friend's: maybe your family just can't afford more.

- Look at ways to earn more pocket money. Suggest to your parents that you do special one-off things around the house or extra chores.

At a certain point most parents will insist that you somehow earn your own extra money, usually in a part-time job (see Chapter 19, Paid Work).

- Walk into the branch you've chosen and tell someone at the inquiries desk that you'd like to find out about opening an account. They'll give you a form to fill in, and about 347 467 467 476 words explaining the bank's different accounts, fees and interest rates. You may need to bring ID next time.
- Also ask a trusted, financially clever adult or a finance or business teacher which is the best deal before you make a final decision to go with a particular institution.
- If you have a part-time or full-time job, you can organise an automatic deduction from your pay so that each week some of it goes straight into your bank account (or a special savings account): that way you don't see it and immediately spend it.

- You'll probably be given a plastic debit card you can use to withdraw money from an automatic teller machine (ATM), or to pay for things in shops (see the later 'Credit and Debit Cards' section). Check what the limits are on how much you can take out at any one time and the withdrawal fees. And keep a rough estimate of how much you have in your account after each withdrawal.
- Always check your bank account statements (you can do it online) and ATM receipts, and keep them in case there's a mistake and you need to sort it out with your bank.

Making a budget A budget is a saving and spending plan based on the money (income) you receive. See 'More Info' below for a headstart on working out what money you have 'coming in' and which essential bills you have to pay regularly; how much to save; and what to do with any money left over. You can put a budget onto a fancy phone app or even write it down on a brown paper bag: as long as you understand it.

More info on managing your money

moneysmart.gov.au
Choose Information for Under 25s for info on everything: budgeting, credit cards, prepaid debit cards, buying a mobile phone or a car, leaving home, money problems and more. Noodle around the site for extra info.

choice.com.au
The Australian Consumers' Association has info on how not to get ripped off, banking, saving, borrowing, and research on the best or cheapest item to buy, from cars to soap.

infochoice.com.au
Independent information to help you choose the best financial services. Covers banks, credit cards and loans.

FACT

Saving for a car This is a big one. Factor into the price the high cost of registration and insurance; a weekly fuel bill; maintenance (regular servicing isn't cheap but can prevent even more expensive repairs); any driving lessons; and a licence. Do as much research as you can on a car before you buy it, and don't let yourself get ripped off by smooth sales talk. Start with the roads authority in your state or territory.

Sometimes I feel guilty for having a lot but sometimes I feel that I never have enough! Holly, 14, Naremburn, NSW

Don't waste it on superficial things. Save it up. Lauren, 17, Springsure, Qld

Why is it such a big issue how much money you have? I mean, who cares?
Esme, 14, East Lindfield, NSW

Save! Begin early! Michelle, 17, Dandenong, Vic.

I think you should save up your money for something special . . . even if you don't know what you're saving up for at the time. Amanda, 13, Glenorchy, Tas.

I think getting my first job made me a lot more appreciative of the money my parents gave me when I was younger. I think I've learnt to be more frugal with my money. Bella, 16, Sydney, NSW

I hate owing money. I owe people money now. Not much but enough to make me feel guilty.
Fran, 14, Donnybrook, NSW

How to spend money and not get into debt

Watch out for common money traps, which can get you into a spiral of owing money. These include mobile phones, dodgy contracts, loans, gambling and the very devil itself – credit cards.

You can watch live wrestling on it!

'Special features' on a phone may just mean stuff you don't need

Phones

Phones can cost you heaps. Either research the best phone plan for you, or just get lots of $100 notes and start tearing them up right now.

Thousands of girls end up not being able to pay their phone bill, which can lead to legal problems; paying off a debt for years; and having their name put on a central registry of 'credit risks', which may mean it's hard for them to get a loan or a credit card later or to get another phone service provider.

Do some research before you buy.
- Look at websites or books on phone sales trickery (see 'More Info' opposite).
- Consider using a prepaid system such as phone cards (bought from newsagents and other outlets) for your calls so you can't get into debt – essentially you're buying a certain amount of phone time in advance.
- Shop around and look at different service providers, or carriers (phone companies you'll have to sign a contract with) and their deals. Compare things such as flat call rates, special offers and discounts, and terms and conditions of contracts. Ask a trusted, money-savvy adult for help.
- Shop around for a plan that gives you cheaper rates for the service you use most, whether it's text, calls or downloads.
- Know how many downloads, texts or calls you can make within the cheapest or free part of your plan.
- Consider using a second-hand phone, such as one somebody else has discarded.
- Check out specials that are available if you use the same service provider as your friends do. Make sure you won't be paying extra for calling anybody (such as a parent) who is not with that service provider.
- Check out the difference between day and night rates to work out when to make cheaper calls.
- If a parent signs the contract for you, or you do because you're over 18, it's legally binding and some can last for two or three years. This means that even if you want to change you still have to keep paying out until the contract expires. Read your contract thoroughly and make sure you understand it.
- If you're 'trapped' in the contract, and realise you're in trouble, see if a trusted adult or consumer legal service can help (see 'More Info' opposite).
- Ask your service provider to put a 'bar' on your phone, so that if you lose it or it's stolen nobody can make calls to international numbers or information or voting lines. If your phone is stolen, report it to the service provider the second you find out, so that from that moment on you're not liable for any charges on the phone.
- Go through your bills: what service is chewing up the most money? Can you cut down or do without it? Voicemail, downloads and texts can be typical money-eaters.
- Texting is not always cheaper. Check your plan and your bills. Depending on your plan, if you send six text messages to organise to meet somebody, when one 10-second phone call could have done it, you lose.

6 Find out exactly what a 'standard call cost' is with your provider, and how they define it: local call of less than 2 minutes, local call of any length, or something else.

More info on mobile phone costs

When researching mobile phone plans and costs, don't just take the service provider's word for what a great deal it is.

moneysmart.gov.au
Search Buying a Mobile.

choice.com.au
For independent consumer advice and reviews search Phones, Mobile Phone Plans, or Landline.

tio.com.au
This is where you can officially complain about your service provider.

consumeraction.org.au
The Consumer Action Law Centre. Choose Legal Assistance then Free Legal Advice, then scroll down to your nearest office contact.

Other mobile phone hints

* Mobile phones emit low-level radiation so keep them away from your head and the middle of your body (near internal organs) as much as you can. Although no link to brain tumours has been proved, long-term use may not be harmless either. Experts worry about the effects on the teenage brain because it's still growing. Use a hands-free headphones and microphone set.

* When you're old enough to drive yourself or be in cars with friends, all mobile phones should be turned off. Drivers using a mobile have killed people because they were distracted and less in control of the wheel. In some areas local laws say P-platers can't be on the phone using a hands-free device while driving, either.

* If you go overseas, check what the 'roaming' costs on your phone plan are. They can be horrendously expensive, leading to unexpected bills of tens of thousands of dollars. A cheap prepaid phone bought at your destination might be a much better idea.

Credit and debit cards

Most people under 18 can't own a credit card, but some teenage girls have a credit card that allows them access to a parent's account. Some others will apply as soon as they turn 18.

'Credit' cards are really 'debt' cards. You use a credit card to 'pay' for something, but actually you've just borrowed money from the credit card company (or department store) and they will charge you interest on the loan. That means for every $100 you borrow, you're paying back say $105 or $117 for the privilege of being able to borrow it, depending on the percentage interest rate. Some credit cards don't charge interest if you pay regularly every month, but they usually still charge fees just for having the card, or for taking more than a month to pay back everything you owe on the card.

This means that with every credit card purchase you pay more than the price on the tag: you're wasting money and possibly getting into a debt that you can't pay back.

If, after being told that the credit card is THE DEVIL, you still want one . . . do some serious research. Many of the credit contracts are a gigantic rip-off when it comes to fees and conditions. (See any of the websites earlier, under 'More Info on Managing Your Money', for info on how to choose a credit card.)

A better way of paying for things is to use a prepaid card or debit card, which just takes the money out of your bank account by the EFTPOS system (electronic funds transfer, point of sale). You can only buy something with a debit card if the cost is covered by what you've got in your savings account, so you can't rack up any debts. Some debit cards can be used online, to buy tickets to events or to shop.

> I can't spend heaps of money because I live in the middle of nowhere and I hardly ever get into town.
> Kaz, 13, Whorouly, Vic.

If I put it on credit, fairies will pay!

YOU MAY NEED A MORE GROWN-UP APPROACH TO MONEY...

Sharing finances

* Many women don't have shared finances with a boyfriend unless they're living together or married. Even then, many women choose to keep their income, credit cards and other finances separate.

* Whether you have a boyfriend, girlfriend, partner or husband, or you're financially involved with a relative, you always need to know what's happening with any shared finances.

* Have your own bank account and cards, and regularly check that you haven't overspent. You'll need a good financial reputation for your future transactions.

* If you pay off a business or housing loan together you can each pay money from your own accounts into the loan. If your partner can't help you pay the loan – whether they refuse, or lose their job or get sick – you alone will be responsible for paying back the entire debt in both your names, not just half or a part of it.

* Know your partner's debts, and don't sign on for a legal responsibility to pay these if something goes wrong. That means you don't agree to be a 'guarantor' or sign anybody else's loan document.

* Don't share a credit card with a partner. If you have a shared credit card with a partner or you're an equal signatory on a card with a parent, once you're 18 you're responsible for ALL the debt on the card if the other person can't pay – not half, or not only the things you used the card to buy.

* If you intend to get married in the future, think hard about whether to change your name. This can result in months of hassles and forms, waiting in queues, having to provide original documents, and being questioned and bombarded with paperwork from banks, the passport office and others. You don't have to change your name to be married: many women keep their family name. (See also 'Miss, Ms or Mrs?' in Chapter 23, Equality, Frivolity.)

More info on credit cards and debt

infochoice.com.au
Independent advice on credit cards. From the home page choose Credit Cards.

choice.com.au
Search Credit Cards for heaps of info.

moneysmart.gov.au
Lots on debt and credit cards here under Borrowing & Credit.

Money rules

✱ Don't spend more than you have.

✱ Don't lend money.

✱ Don't borrow money from friends.

✱ Never guarantee somebody else's loan, even if they're your boyfriend, girlfriend or relative.

✱ Don't sign anything you don't understand: that won't be an excuse in court.

✱ If you're in debt, get help.

Scams

There are a squillion email, phone and other financial scams out there. Always be suspicious of a brilliant-sounding, low-risk 'sure thing' or no-risk, high-return investment. There's no such thing.

- Don't open or reply to an attachment on an email from anybody you don't know.
- Never text, email, or give out any bank account details, PIN numbers (personal identity numbers – codes for your bank account or other financial matters) or credit card numbers unless it's on a secure site.
- Don't send money, a bank account number or a reply to someone who emails or texts or offers on a website that they'll send you money, lottery winnings or an inheritance (money left to you in a will), no matter how professional it seems.
- Always hang up on somebody who calls you on the phone and talks about this sort of stuff, and delete similar emails. This is a dodgy way in which criminals steal money – they're successful because they send out thousands of spam emails and calls, and of every 100 people maybe one person will respond and be ripped off.

Schemes designed to take money from you include all sorts of so-called money-making schemes and games, some expensive seminars and training courses, 'work from home' or 'training' jobs and calls saying you've 'won a prize'.

Getting ripped off

If you've bought something that doesn't do what it's supposed to, or it falls apart, or you feel otherwise ripped off, you may be able to get your money back or exchange it for a good one. Take a trusted adult or try to talk to the shop owner yourself (always be polite and reasonable). If that doesn't work, you may need back-up.

More info on rip-offs and scams

moneysmart.gov.au/tools-and-resources/how-to-complain
How to make a complaint (with sample letters) and how to take it further.

consumeraction.org.au
The Consumer Action Law Centre. Choose I Need Help then Consumer Action Legal Help.

scamwatch.gov.au
Check it out: some people are so devious!

consumeraffairs.govt.nz
For info on how to avoid rip-offs and financial problems, choose Scams.

consumer.org.nz
Independent, non-profit advice on your rights as a buyer.

> **HINT**
>
> **Your signature** Don't just copy your mum's signature, only substituting your initial. For business transactions you'll need to have your own professional-looking signature. Practise signing your name until it's easy for you. You'll be stuck with it for life, so don't make it little-girly or hard to do exactly the same way over and over again – no huge letters, hearts, smiley faces or elaborate swirly underlinings.

Gambling

Gambling includes playing games for money at casinos, using gaming machines ('pokies'), betting on races and other sporting events, and buying lottery tickets. Casino games and gaming machines are rigged so that the vast majority of money put into them goes to the profits of the people who own them: you can never make money if you keep betting against 'the house'.

If you enjoy gambling and spend only what you can afford on it, such as the price of a raffle ticket every now and then or $10 at the races once a year, then gambling isn't a problem. But many people feel that even a 'little' gambling can trigger a habit or addiction. Many girls develop a gambling problem once they don't stick to a set limit and start to lose money. They keep trying to win back what they've lost, losing more and more, which has a disastrous effect on their finances and relationships.

If there's a problem gambler in your family, you may see or be affected by related problems, including stress, conflict and other mental health issues.

More info on gambling

Call for yourself or if a friend or family member has the problem.

National Gambling helpline:
1800 858 858

gamblinghelponline.org.au
Support and counselling service with practical strategies.

gaaustralia.org.au
For support and recovery programs.

gamblinghelpline.co.nz
Free phone 0800 654 655 or free text 8006. A 24-hour government-backed helpline.

Every year, and sometimes twice a year (summer and winter) I get a set clothes budget, and I can only spend that money. Mum won't give me any more for all the clothes I need. Kate, 14, Hawthorn, Vic.

I never have enough. I'm scared that I won't have enough when I grow up. I won't be able to afford a car any time soon because I am going overseas.
Lisa, 17, Bilgola Plateau, NSW

Once you get in debt, it's so hard to get out of.
Elanora, 16, Albury, NSW

I want more! I don't get enough!
Erica, 14, Murrumbeena, Vic.

Too many kids are spoilt and just get what they want from their parents straight away. I have to save up for it, and it makes me appreciate it more.
Elise, 15, Penrith, NSW

I've heard you can become a millionaire in a couple of months by doubling money – how?
[*You really, really can't*]
Tessa, 14, East Doncaster, Vic.

21 SHOPPING

Everybody wants you. **Every** clothes company, every shoe company, every fast-food company, drink company, TV network, major electronics company. The companies pay advisors, have 'focus groups' and brain-storming sessions and then proceed to spend billions and billions of dollars on hype, **trying to get you to buy their stuff**. They want you to mix up the ideas of 'want' and 'need' so that you feel you must must must have something new **now now now**.

The tricky persuaders

Everybody wants you to spend money on their products – and they have some pretty clever ways of pretending that's not what they're trying to do. This section is about how to recognise marketing when the companies are trying to sneak it past you.

The big companies know that you're smarter and more cynical than your parents were in their teens – and harder to trick. So they spend heaps finding new ways to fool you. These days they've changed tactics: they don't try to get parents to buy stuff for you ('My, these are sensible, long-lasting school shoes!'), they go after *you* ('These are the coolest!').

Advertising

Advertising tries to make you feel you want or need something. Look at the ads on a billboard, in a mag, on TV or on a website to see if you can spot these obvious strategies:

- 'You deserve it, you're special, you've earnt it. We get how special you are and how hard you work. We want to reward you.'
- 'Having this product will make you look more attractive. And your life will be transformed, somewhat like Cinderella's.'
- 'We have cool-seeming people in our ad so this product is cool, and because you like it you're cool too.'
- 'We have a nerdy person in our ad who isn't using our cool product, so let's all laugh at them. Ha ha! We're mean, but cool.'
- 'Check out this really cool song/amazing visual image/piece of animation. Now we have your attention, here's what we want you to buy.'
- 'Having this product will make you happy, oh so happy, ha ha, with laughing, very white teeth.'
- 'In the world where people use this product everything is sunny and fun.'
- 'You're one of a select group getting this text.'
- 'We care about you so buy our stuff.'
- 'We care about animals/the environment/poor people so buy our stuff.'
- 'This is such a funny ad you'll remember our brand name. (You don't? That's $15 million down the drain then.)'
- 'This is such a weird ad it will intrigue you and get you talking about it.'
- 'If you buy our product you'll have an edge over competitors. In fact they will be CRUSHED.'

- 'Buy this because it's really exclusive and glamorous.'
- 'Buy this because it's really cheap.'
- 'If you have this takeaway your family will sit down together to eat and be happy.'
- 'Omigod, if you get this thing it will be so exciting. Lots of music and zoomy, colourful things will happen. And your life now is dull. And you bore the pants off everyone.'
- 'This celebrity says they use our stuff. If you want to be like them buy our stuff.'
- 'Everyone likes our stuff – don't be a left-out, sad, lonely loser.'
- 'We know you're too smart to fall for advertising and marketing. Smart people like you buy our stuff.'
- 'We have paid a lot of money for the rights to this really catchy song, so when you hear it you'll feel good and sing it, and that will remind you to buy our thing. And the ad is louder than the TV show, so don't try to ignore it.'
- 'Get a load of this scientific statistical stuff that makes it seem as if our product is proven to be the best. We paid someone to do

Brand loyalty

Companies want your brand loyalty, which means that:

- instead of just saying, 'I feel like a hamburger',
  you say 'I feel like (insert name of giant company here).'

- instead of going into a shop and saying, 'I want a sticking plaster' (Huh?),
  you say, 'Can I have a Band-Aid, please.' (Which is really a registered trademark.)

- instead of wanting any old pair of jeans,
  you only want the ones from the hot label.

Getting you early

Global corporations, local businesses and the advertising and marketing industry want to:

- grab your loyalty before you even turn 9 (in fact many companies aim to have kids telling their parents what to buy as soon as they can speak)

- get you now, as a teenage consumer, so they can keep you for life as a 'L'Oréal lipstick girl' or a 'Target undies buyer' – someone who always buys one brand rather than any other.

the research and come up with those results.' (And don't you love an ad where cartoon arrows bounce off the skin, because that proves . . . um . . . wait . . . yes, that proves that cartoon arrows bounce off cartoon skin.)

- 'This ad is on high rotation. It's on TV, on radio, on public transport, on billboards and at the movies, so you can't get away from our message. You can't hide from us.'

'Aspirational appeal' This is a term used by marketers and advertisers for the feeling they wish to create in you – the feeling that you want the same kind of life/face/body/boyfriend/hairstyle/acting career as the person in their ad – so that you'll buy the product. The theory is that you aspire to the image, so the product appeals to you. Basically it's creating envy.

Misleading advertising Although there are laws that are supposed to protect us against fibbing ads, they're not always enforced. And ads can also be legal but misleading. Models in ads are not legally required to have used the stuff being advertised. That's right: Glossy Hair Model doesn't even use that shampoo. She just has nice hair.

The picture of a body used in an ad for cosmetic surgery usually belongs to a person who's never been in the same room as a surgeon. And here's a 'shocking secret' (der): the person in the white coat isn't really a doctor/scientist/researcher – they're an actor.

glossy hair model

> **FACT**
>
> **Thought association** Sometimes mere association is enough to create a reminder of a product. A big, curvy yellow M makes you think hamburgers – McDonald's hamburgers. The colour purple makes you think chocolate – Cadbury's chocolate. (Cadbury has even taken court action, saying that no other company should be allowed to use purple packaging on cakes, lollies or chocolates.)

When is an ad not an ad?

Ads are always ads, it's just that sometimes they come in the form of a 'marketing campaign' that doesn't use the ad spaces you expect, such as in magazines and on websites, billboards, bus stop shelters, TV and radio. Here are some ads that don't always look like ads.

'Reports' An article in a magazine or on a website can look as if it is written by a reporter, and be printed in the same style as the other articles, but can actually be a paid ad. Often an article – especially in free local magazines, but also in some of the fancy expensive ones – will mention products from companies that regularly advertise in the magazine. It works on TV shows too. Did that travel reporter get a free trip? Then she's not likely to say the pool smelled like cheese, is she?

'Trend watchers' Magazine pages called things like What's In, What's Cool or New Products are often really unpaid ads cobbled together by a reporter whose job it is to go through all the press releases of the magazine's advertisers to keep them happy.

'Direct marketing' Companies make contact with you via mail, pamphlets, emails and phone calls you never asked for.

Videos, pics, texts, signing up for website 'membership', various other messages, social media page 'likes', emails Access to your phone and your computer is now used by companies as part of selling campaigns.

'Viral marketing' Companies try to spread their message like a virus. It looks like 'word of mouth' – people telling each other about it – but it's really company employees using phone messages, websites, meeting sites, blogs, fake blogs ('flogs') and short films. The ads can look like an animation, a joke, inside info, a cute picture, a recommendation from a friend, a filmed romance story – anything but an ad.

Product placements It's no accident that the cute guy in your favourite new movie is wearing that particular brand of watch or going into that particular restaurant chain in one scene – it's 'product placement'. This partly involves getting the brand name seen, and partly associating it with something cool such as a TV star or a hit film. Companies pay (sometimes several million dollars) for their drink to be the one poured at the table, or their cars to be the ones in the chase scene.

Girl-friendly, smart media

* Magazines are expensive to produce – the price every reader pays for a copy isn't enough to pay for the printing and distribution – so their profits come from advertising (and other clever ideas such as phone-in competitions).

* The money to produce a magazine or website comes from advertisers, so an editor who writes a story criticising an advertiser's product, or any other aspect of the business, won't last long.

* Magazines, websites and social media posting accounts have some fantastic stories and some great things to look at. But question why they want you to read what you're reading. Is the beauty editor influenced by all her freebies? Is the woman in the Insta post paid to wear that stuff? Or did she get it supplied for free?

* The Australian media scene has been brutal to independent media for girls, because we have a relatively small population compared to the rest of the world. So when you see something good, share it!

* Try these media outlets for girl-friendly, inspiring stuff:

teenbreathe.com.au
Teen Breathe is a mag with a mindfulness vibe, available in hard copy. Order or buy from a newsagent or supermarket.

expressmedia.org.au
Express Media's *Voiceworks* magazine for young people comes out four times a year with stuff from writers and illustrators under 25. Plus much more for young creative folk. Try here, too: express-media.tumblr.com.

shadezine.com
An online magazine for and by women and girls of colour.

bitchmedia.org
A US feminist website that pushes back against accusation of being a 'bitch' by stealing the word. Lots of articles and ideas.

bust.com
Another US site for girls and women, with some serious and some fun celebrity stuff, all with the philosophy of women – and the magazine site – being independent and real.

sistermagazine.co.uk
Online mag from England with theme issues including Strong, Space, Size and Sad.

Some singers have even been paid to mention brand names in their songs. Luckily most singers, writers and other artists, and a few movie makers, reject being bribed to compromise their artistic vision. Just for fun, next time you watch a movie or TV show see how many product placements you can spot.

'Membership plans' and 'loyalty programs' You get a tiny discount or 'reward'. They get all your contact details, and to bombard you with 'ads'.

Freebies Companies often give you a free sample of a product: you'll find it in your letterbox, stuck to the front of a magazine, in a 'show bag' from a launch, or at a youth festival or careers night. It feels like a gift, but actually it's a small, cheap sample to persuade you to buy a (much bigger) packet or bottle.

Companies also send heaps of free products to people with 'influence' – writers on newspapers and magazines, radio and TV show hosts, celebrities – to get free mentions here and there.

Targeting Companies often target a particular group for freebies: for instance, they go to schools, clubs and hangouts, identify the 'cool kids' there and give them free new stuff to wear or use, and samples to give to friends. Suddenly everyone wants the product.

Endorsements Endorsement ranges from celebrities paid to be in ads pretending they use the products, to radio hosts who are influenced by freebies faffing on about how yummy the donuts are from the bakery that just delivered them a boxful.

Celebrity handouts Film and TV stars, models, singers, radio hosts, sporting 'heroes' and all sorts of celebrities have stuff given to them by companies that want their products to be associated with glamour and fame. When the celebrities are photographed wearing an obvious label, holding a certain kind of drink or attending the opening of a certain club, assume they could have been paid to do it.

'Push marketing' Girls with not a lot of clothes on, except high heels, hand out samples, or even pretend to be bar customers ordering a new drink, to get people talking about a product to create a buzz.

Merchandising A company gets people to be walking ads by putting their name or logo on T-shirts, hats, matchbooks, lighters, stickers, pens, food or even cute toys.

Sponsorships Companies can get their brand name everywhere by sponsoring an event such as a concert, sporting contest, festival or even a charity fundraiser. The idea is that the more you see a product associated with something you like, the more you'll like the product.

Competition prizes A contest says, 'To win a pack of Twang cosmetics worth $200, write down in twenty-five words or less why you need our stuff, and send it to . . .' So 10 000 girls write down how great the product is (and think about buying Twang), and the company has only had to pay $200, for stuff that they get out of the back room. And then they can even use the competition entries as unpaid 'endorsements' of their products.

Donated prizes Say a company donates a motorcycle as a prize for a competition in which you have to collect coupons from five packets of chips. The company gets ads for their motorcycle on millions of chips packets for the cost of only one motorcycle. The prizes you can win on radio, in magazines and on websites are all donated by companies to get their product mentioned and 'out there'.

Social conscience donations Many companies say they are helping good causes and charities by donating a percentage of their profits. And they may be. It's just that the percentage of profit may be less than 1 per cent, while the percentage they marked up on the price of their items was 5 per cent. You'd be better off donating money directly to the charity and buying a cheaper product. Be careful when companies claim to be doing something out of the goodness of their hearts. Look closely and there's usually a profit.

More info on ads

adiosbarbie.com
A site born from the idea that advertisers were using sexist, violent and anti-woman imagery to sell their products.

choice.com.au
The Australian Consumers' Association has info on dodgy ads. Search Ads.

Going shopping

Have you ever had that sinking feeling of arriving home with something in a shopping bag, knowing you shouldn't have bought it, you'll never use it, it's a waste of money, it doesn't look like it did in the shop, and now you can't even afford to buy a lolly snake? That's because shopping lures in the twenty-first century are very clever and hard to resist (or even see).

Sales techniques

Assistants who sell in shops and over the phone have often been trained in sales techniques. Somebody I know who used to sell gym memberships says, 'I asked them what it was about their body they would change if they could, and then in different words I told them the gym could do that for them.'

Here are some common sales techniques. The salesperson:

- is friendly, asks how you are, chats about something other than the product (actually they're finding out things about you so they can work out the best way to persuade you to buy)
- gets you to test or handle the product so you picture yourself having it and using it
- tells you stories about 'real' people, including 'other customers', who are so happy with their product ('I have one and it's great', 'My friend has one of these and she's never had so many handsome, rich chappies wanting to take her to Hollywood')
- informs you the price or the great bonus is only available for another day or while the boss is out to lunch (they're trying to get you to hand over money or a signature in a hurry)
- makes you feel in charge, but pushes you by saying things such as, 'It's up to you of course, but this is the last model available at this price.'

Always remember that a salesperson wants to sell you something, no matter how nice they seem. So if you want a really honest opinion don't ask Flossy behind the counter – take your mum or a friend shopping with you.

Shop atmosphere

Malls, department stores and smaller shops (sometimes called boutiques) spend thousands of dollars on consultants to create the right vibe to get customers in and keep them there (yes, that's why half the time you can't find your way out).

- Music is picked carefully, decor is artfully arranged, little things are temptingly left on counters, the assistants are wearing clothes that are on sale. Some shops even have perfumed candles. Others look like bargain basements, with stuff seemingly chucked into cardboard boxes with hand-lettered signs so that the items look more like a bargain than perhaps they really are.
- Lighting is kept low in changing rooms and near mirrors so you can't see any faults in the clothes.
- Mirrors may be angled to make you look thinner.
- A big, attractive display in a shop suggests the products shown are the best or the cheapest, but in reality it could mean the owner wants to get rid of the stuff quickly or a manufacturer paid for that spot in the store. (Drinks companies supply fridges to shops and don't let other companies put their drinks in them.)

Online shopping

Buying online from overseas avoids some taxes and the inconvenience of leaving the house, but drawbacks can include: getting ripped off by a dodgy site, high shipping costs, clothes and shoes don't fit and the quality of other stuff isn't what you expected, and the company uses your personal details and history for marketing. The retailer should have a good returns policy, a solid reputation with customers and a customer service department or person and, crucially, a 'secure server' for you to send your credit card or debit card details. If you're under 18, ask a clever adult to help you buy anything online: in any case you'll probably need their credit card or special debit card to do it. (See the previous chapter, Money, for details on credit and other cards.)

Online prices can vary for the same item in different countries, as taxes are deducted or added at the 'checkout' point, and currency exchange and delivery fees can change. Consumer complaint sources in Australia don't have much power over the foreign companies operating without a physical local presence. After you've done your research, always check whether a local supplier or producer can match a price, as this can keep jobs in your community.

More info on shopping online

choice.com.au
The Australian Consumers' Association details the advantages and traps of shopping, and how to research purchases online. Search Shopping Online Buying Guide, Online Shopping or Shopping Comparison Site Guide.

consumerprotection.govt.nz
On this Kiwi ministry site, search Online Shopping for info on the basics.

accc.gov.au
Infoline: 1300 302 502
On the national government's Australian Competition and Consumer Commission site, choose Online Shopping for a safety checklist and more; see also the sister site scamwatch.gov.au.

Spending

Your great-grandma would hardly recognise the way we go shopping now. She would always have gone out with a list of what she needed, and that's all she would have bought. She would have taken a purse full of cash to buy the things on that list, or to pay off a short-term debt at the local store. She probably had an everyday handbag, and if she was very lucky another one for 'best'. Most people had one or two work outfits and a pair of work shoes, plus one 'good' outfit including shoes. Back then most shops were almost all full of things you needed, not wanted. Only the super-rich could afford pretty but non-essential things, or extra clothes.

These days a handbag shop in a mall has more beautiful things in it than most major museums had a hundred years ago. We now have a huge choice of things to look at and buy – in one department store there is probably more

'You deserve it'

Don't ask, 'Do I deserve this?', because of course you do. You deserve an emerald tiara and a holiday house in the Caribbean, but they're probably not going to happen. Instead ask yourself:

* 'Can I afford it?'
* 'Can I do without it?'
* 'Is there a cheaper option?'
* 'Would a laugh with a friend cheer me up just as much?'
* 'Should I think about it for a couple of days?'
* 'Do I want lots of small things now, or can I wait and save up for one really big, wonderful thing?'

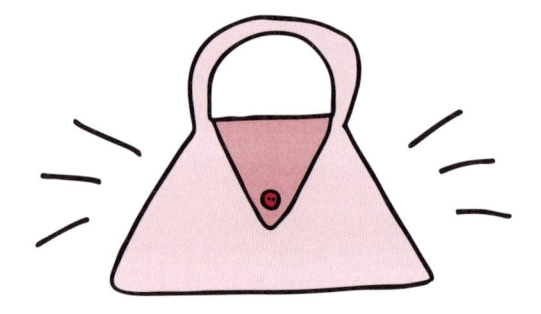

pretty stuff than great-grandma saw in her whole lifetime.

Shopping centres today are places where we can choose from lots of shops, hang out with friends, eat, go to the loo, and stay dry, cool or warm. It's entertainment just to walk around and look at nice things, even if you can't afford them.

Shopping as therapy Armed with a bunch of research about how girls and women use shopping as a social event and a kind of compensation for having a tough week at school, home or work, companies like the idea of 'retail therapy': shopping as a feel-good activity. They've come up with advertising slogans and shop-assistant chat along the lines of 'Because you're worth it', 'Treat yourself', 'You've earnt it' and 'Reward yourself'. The rise of salons, spas and home-grooming treatments is part of this self-pampering idea.

Staying in control of spending Whether you 'deserve it' or not, you may not be able to afford it. Be careful not to get giddy with wanting, and instead be happy with just looking. Buying what you want can be a great way to celebrate having your own money from a part-time job, or your first real job. But it can be easy to blow all your money if you let yourself be manipulated by marketing.

Don't get hypnotised by the shiny-shiny and forget that you need money for necessities. See the previous chapter, Money, for hints on how not to get yourself into trouble with cash and, even worse, credit cards.

'Shopaholics' Some psychologists think that being a 'shopaholic' – always needing something new, and getting into debt – may be part of trying to fill up an emptiness people feel inside.

Shopping for some people has become a compulsion. If this sounds like you, have a think about your shopping habits.

- Are you going shopping every week, or more, and spending more than you should?
- Do you think it's become a habit or an addiction that you need to break?

Instead of shopping try:
- visiting a gallery, an interesting place or a park
- going on a nature walk
- staying at home and creating something with a friend so you don't need to buy stuff
- seeing how long you can go not buying anything except absolute necessities such as public transport fares.

And don't forget all the other ways of feeling good without spending . . .

mmmm shiny, shiny

don't get HYPNOtiseD! Remember your budget!

shopping AND THE REST   483

22 CLOTHES & MAKE-UP

Do you spend an hour in the morning handpainting every eyelash? Are you a **'fashion tragic'**, with the attention span of a tadpole, who has to have something new every four days and wear the latest thing even if it makes you look like a colour-blind magician's assistant in a bubble skirt, gumboots and orange lipstick? Or do you wear the **same pair of jeans** until they are a bunch of threads held up by habit and hope? Are you totally baffled by the idea of self-decoration, or wish you could have fun with it?

In this chapter we'll check out the good and bad aspects of clothes, style, fashion, accessories and make-up, and explain why reeeeeally high heels are officially the **stupidest** things ever.

Clothes

Even if you don't walk around covered in labels, or pop on a T-shirt saying 'My Boss Sucks', you're saying something about yourself and the life you live with your clothes. If it was just about keeping warm, Tasmanians would wear sleeping-bag suits and people in Darwin would wear hats and toenail polish and nothing in between. A school or work uniform sends a message. Wearing army pants and a black singlet says something different from a flouncy pink dress with ballet slippers.

Fashion

At any one time fashion can mean something quite different for different groups of people. For someone with $8000 to spare on a skirt, fashion may be what a starving, blank-eyed, flouncy model is wearing on the catwalk in Milan or Paris. To people who love reading about the lives of celebrities, fashion is what's worn by a Hollywood starlet on the red carpet on Oscars night. To some teenagers it's the zillion clothes they see in magazines and online. For you it's probably also what's popular at your school or in your group of friends – and what you can afford.

CLOTHES CAN MAKE A POLITICAL STATEMENT

The one thing that's true for every kind of fashion is that it changes all the time. Check out some of the 'costume movies' in the list later in this chapter – it's a great way to see how fashions have changed, what was fashionable when, what still looks good and what an art form clothes can be. ('Vintage' is the fancy name given to old clothes kept long enough to have come back into fashion.)

Possible reasons for fashion always changing are:
- fashion can be heaps of fun
- companies make more money if people think they need new clothes all the time, even when they've stopped growing out of them >

I like having something girly and fashionable to wear.
Jess, 15, Toowoomba, Qld

I like comfort and quite baggy clothing.
Alex, 14, Alexandria, NSW

- fashion pages and TV shows are often put together by grown-ups who have their own money, and also get so much free stuff from the fashion and make-up companies as 'samples' (or bribes) that it's easy for them to keep changing what they wear all the time
- fashion writers keep advertisers happy by featuring new clothes and looks and claiming that some things are 'essential' when they're really optional extras
- some people in the fashion world have very short attention spans.

> I am a model so that makes me feel very bad about my self esteem.
> Tamara, 17, Pinnaroo, SA

What magazines and websites tell you about fashion Here's why they tell you that this winter it's all chocolate brown and aubergine (fancy talk for purple) whereas last winter it was all lime and orange: they want you to buy NEW clothes. Look carefully and you'll see that many of the 'must-have' items are made by companies who already advertise in the magazine.

When magazines have a shot of a famous actress in an outfit and tell you 'How You Can Recreate the Look', then show you all the stuff you can buy that looks like hers – skirt, top, shoes, earrings, handbag, jacket, belt (complete with brand names, stockists and prices) – that's at least seven ways on one page to make you envious, suggest you need to look like someone else and spend your money.

Fashion websites and magazines tell you to buy what's 'in fashion', not what suits you. It's hard to give individual tips so, apart from including the odd advice column and a few articles about 'hiding your figure flaws' (as if everybody is some kind of biological error), what most magazines tend to do is tell you to buy what's in the shops – in other words, what the fashion companies have made and want you to buy, whether or not it looks good on you.

> **Brand names make people feel poor.** Kelly, 17, country WA

> **FACT**
>
> **Models** Models are not role models. You don't want to be one. Really you don't. Only one in thousands makes good money, and most of them spend heaps of time being hungry and feeling that they're never right – never beautiful or thin or tall enough. Almost all of them have had experience with eating disorders and with obsessing about parts of their body.

Labels

You probably know what the hot jeans label is at the moment, and the names of another couple of 'must-have' labels. When you are paying for that sort of temporary cool, you're paying what's called a premium – a higher price for an item that's exactly the same as a cheaper one in another shop or with another label on it.

A 'label queen' is a fashion tragic who has to wear the right label, even if the item is ugly, wrong or just plain stupidly expensive.

It doesn't make sense to buy madly expensive clothes while you're still growing. And if you're just buying an item for the name on its label, not for its high quality or timeless style, then you're buying something that will look outdated in a flash.

Label traps

- A lot of clothes, handbags and shoes are made cheaply in Asia, India or the Pacific islands, then chain stores pay to have their own label sewn into them.
- Some 'designers' create what's called a knock-off: they copy ideas from the genuine designer collections shown at fashion weeks. Sometimes a fake big-name label is just sewn onto stuff sold in a market for a fraction of the price (and usually the quality).
- The items in a clothing range with a celebrity label, which ties in with an actress, a singer or a TV show, are usually the same ones you can buy in most chain stores – but you pay more for the name. And if you believe that the actress really designed all the clothes herself then . . . well, okaaay.

Most models are NOT role models

Style

Style is not the same as fashion, although 'in style' is another way of saying 'in fashion'. Fashions come and go and are largely aimed at people who care about what other people think and who want to fit in, not look different from everyone else. Style is something more personal: a look that suits your personality, creativity and body shape. It's 'you' – what *you* like, no matter what's in the shops.

During our teens and twenties most of us experiment with styles until we find one or maybe a handful that we like, that say what we want to say, and that are comfortable to wear. Many people eventually develop a 'signature style' and stick with it – a way of dressing that's always around the same theme. It could be arty or sporty, tight and short or baggy, op-shoppy or girly.

> **QUOTE**
> 'Most people wear 20 per cent of their clothes 80 per cent of the time.' **Widely accepted fashion saying**

> **MORE**
> **Sizes** See Chapter 4, Body Image, for why you shouldn't panic about the numbers on your clothes labels. And see the 'Breasts' section in Chapter 1, Change, for info on bra fittings and sizes.

How to have style

Style isn't something you're born with. It takes some experiments and disasters along the way before you find your signature style. Here are a few hints.

* Don't buy clothes when you're hungry and light-headed, or exhausted but desperate to 'get something'.

* Don't buy clothes *just* because they're cheap.

* Don't buy this season's colour if it doesn't look good on you – blondes can look sickly in a yellow top, for example.

* Go for something you look great in – don't buy what's in fashion if it doesn't suit you.

* Dress for yourself. Don't worry too much about what you think others may or may not like – if you're confident, you'll look great.

* Make sure that even your 'good' clothes are comfortable. If you wear a skirt so short you're always tugging it down and can't bend over, you're going to feel – and therefore look – uncomfortable and 'wrong'.

* Try a new kind of shop, check out a second-hand place, go shopping with an adult whose style you like.

Dressing to be noticed

These things say 'look at me' (not that there's anything wrong with that):
- big hairstyles
- flashy jewellery (from swinging, sparkly bling to battery-operated earrings)
- shiny fabrics
- moving bits such as beads and tassels
- bright colours
- busy patterns.

Clothes that are very shiny, shimmery and glittery are best left to the over-eighteens at night, unless they're for a school Formal.

Dressing to 'attract' guys

Some girls pile on the make-up, fake tan and tight and revealing clothes they think will make them look older or more 'sexy'. In fact it can just look 'try hard' and a bit sad. If a guy really likes you he'll like you whether you're wearing tracky daks or a dress with heels.

Problem looks
- Visible underwear, including G-strings, undies and bras: these always look like you didn't mean to show them, which is embarrassing, or like you did mean it, which is tacky. >

Fashion bullies

Watch out for mean girls masquerading as fashion experts (some of them work for magazines and are 47 years old). It can be secretly fun to hear: 'Oh my god, what is she WEARING?' if it's directed at some goddess or other on the red carpet and not at some mere mortal like ourselves. We've all done it. But it's nice to 'live and let live', complimenting somebody when they look good, and not tying it to weight or weight loss, or size. It's best to say nothing when somebody looks like a victim of circuspantses. It's easy to be snobby and snide, but it's also easy to train yourself out of it.

Wear what you like, live and let live, wear and let wear. Those crazy pants/shoes/hats (whatever) that people think are old-fashioned this week will be 'back in fashion' in about 86 seconds.

I love experimenting, finding things and dressing up a bit to get noticed. I have an eclectic style that's not really 'in' but I love finding things and co-ordinating.
Maddy, 15,
Rozelle, NSW

> **HINT**
>
> **Free advertising** You know how some clothes manufacturers give themselves an advertising bonus by emblazoning their label's name or logo across bums, the front of T-shirts, the back of jackets and the side of shoes? Don't become a 'walking billboard' advertising their stuff.

- Clothes that look like strippers' or sex workers' outfits, worn with heaps of dark make-up: these include anything that shows lots of skin, breast-revealing tops, really tiny skirts and way high heels. While some people promote this image as glamorous, and many male rock stars require the look for women in their videos, most strippers and sex workers come from an abusive past and many are working to feed a drug habit.
- Clothes with sex images or slogans such as 'Porn Star', or the Playboy bunny logo. (The logo is from *Playboy*, one of the exploitative 'men's' magazines, with pictures of often topless or nude women in suggestive poses.)

Looking and acting as if they're sexually available to guys doesn't make girls strong and independent, or popular. Instead of appearing grown up, girls can seem manipulated into presenting themselves as sexual objects whose brains, thoughts and feelings don't matter.

While a girl might be horrified that a 40-year-old guy is trying to pick her up, he might think her clothes are sending an unspoken invitation. A lot of guys don't know what's in fashion: they just think girls in revealing clothes are more likely to have sex with them. There is never an excuse for boorish, rude behaviour or sexual harassment or assault, no matter what you are wearing. No woman or girl is 'asking for it'.

All this doesn't mean you have to dress in a bag. You have a right to dress in whatever way you like. (After all, some people think bathers on the beach are too raunchy.) Just be aware of why you're presenting yourself the way you do, and what various icons, outfits and messages can mean to other people.

> I'm not the kind of person to be alternative. I go along with the trends.   Lucy, 18, Bendigo, Vic.

Dressing to suit a religion

Some girls wear certain items or a type of clothes because of their religion. Some Christian girls wear a cross; others always have long hair. Some Muslim girls cover their hair with a hijab, or scarf. In Australia most Muslim women who wear the hijab say it's their own choice, as part of their personal dedication to Islam, but in some countries where Muslim religious leaders form the government women are forced to wear a veil. Many Muslim girls also wear sports uniforms or swimsuits that cover more of their body than the other players' clothes do. It's okay to ask a girl about her religion and her choice of clothes, but it's obviously not okay to be part of any bullying or mean, rude commenting about it (see Chapter 14, Friends).

> For the love of GOD people, keep your privates for private times. Some of us have eyes.
> Chloe, 17, East Doncaster, Vic.

> Seriously girls, be your own person.
> Siobhan, 14, Clontarf, Qld

Shopping for clothes

You'd think, given they want us to hand over money, that all sales assistants would be nice. But sometimes they're snotty, snide, deceitful and more interested in talking on the phone than helping you.

Go back to shops where the sales assistants are helpful, don't try to pressure you, and say if something isn't right for you. Never let an assistant persuade you to buy something you're not sure of. First instincts are usually pretty good. You can always come back later and have another look. Just say, 'I'm going to think about it, thanks.' (See also 'Going Shopping' in Chapter 21, Shopping.)

Sales It's smart to wonder why something is on sale.
- Badly cut?
- Badly made?
- A colour that hardly suits anybody?
- Nobody wanted it so there are heaps left?
- It's an 'over-run' – meaning there's already a lot of it out there?

You can't return clothes that are on sale (or second-hand), so always try things on: never assume it will look okay because it's 'your' size. The cut may be bad, leaving it gaping at the waist, or it could be too tight across the shoulders or around your bot. Lots of clothes are fine in theory but look shocking on. And it's not your body's fault.

> **HINT**
> **If something doesn't fit** Don't buy it. There's nothing wrong with you – there's something wrong with the clothes.

> Get a job if you want to buy expensive brand name clothes.
> Leanne, 18, Mackay, Qld
>
> Why can't mum pay for them?
> Samantha, 16, Canungra, Qld

Accessories

You don't have to take any notice of them, but here are some accepted shoe and handbag 'rules'.

Shoes

- If you're not comfortable and able to walk confidently in your shoes, don't wear them. Many of us just look like a drunken trainee drag queen in high heels.
- Don't wear really high heels or high heels every day: they damage your feet and toes, resulting in bunions and eventually even deformities, and cause foot and ankle injuries (from falling or 'going over' on your ankle). At the very least don't wear them for more than a couple of hours, or if you're going to be standing up or dancing, or if you need to get home from a party or club and might need to walk more than a few steps. And don't wear them because you think all guys love them. They don't. And the ones who do love them can try them for themselves.
- The shorter the skirt, the flatter the heel should be (a fashion 'rule' you don't have to listen to).

> I only wear black and I love it. Anica, 16, Geelong, Vic.

> I can't live without clothes, and my career is going to be a fashion designer. Nicole, 14, East Melbourne, Vic.

Handbags

- Handbags generally need to kind of match the feel of what you're wearing. That means a heavy, shiny black backpack won't look quite right with a pale, flowery cotton dress. But when you're young you really can get away with anything – including lots of mixing and matching.
- Don't get tricked into thinking it's worth paying heaps for a handbag. A handbag is not an investment. It's actually . . . a handbag.
- Any handbag should be secured, with a zip or magnets, so that important things like phones can't fall out or be easily stolen. Big, open tote bags are only good for the beach, but even those should have a zipper compartment for keys, period kit and money.

Basic handbag contents

- House keys
- Purse or wallet
- Phone
- Tissues
- Emergency period kit
- Lip gloss
- Sunscreen
- Sunglasses
- Emergency public transport or taxi money
- Phone numbers written down in case your phone goes missing or has no battery power
- NOT your home address because you don't want someone getting that *and* your house keys if your bag is lost or stolen.

> I have my own eccentric bohemian style, and I'm proud to be different.
> Jessie, 15, Alice Springs, NT

> It's important these days to feel you fit in with the fashions otherwise you feel left out.
> Mel, 15, Valley View, SA

Costume movies

Here's a list of films and TV shows that showcase fashion from different eras. The period given refers to the era of the costumes. Check ratings to see if they're suitable for your age.

- **Ancient Egypt**   *Cleopatra*
- **Tang Dynasty**   (China, 859) *House of Flying Daggers*
- **1500s**   *Elizabeth, Orlando, Shakespeare in Love*
- **1700s**   *Marie Antoinette*
- **Qing Dynasty**   (China, 1770s) *Crouching Tiger, Hidden Dragon*
- **1800s**   All the movies and TV series based on Jane Austen novels (*Pride and Prejudice, Sense and Sensibility, Emma, Persuasion*), many Charles Dickens books (*Little Dorritt, Great Expectations, Bleak House*), Charlotte Brontë's *Jane Eyre*, Elizabeth Gaskell's *Cranford* and Louisa May Alcott's *Little Women*
- **Around 1900**   *My Fair Lady, Picnic at Hanging Rock, My Brilliant Career, The Getting of Wisdom*
- **Early 1900s**   *Downton Abbey, Titanic*
- **1920s**   *Chicago, Bullets Over Broadway, Thoroughly Modern Millie, Miss Fisher's Murder Mysteries, The Great Gatsby*
- **1930s**   *Gosford Park, Cold Comfort Farm, The Cotton Club, Cabaret, The Aviator, Caddie, Tea with Mussolini, His Girl Friday, The Women*
- **1940s**   *Come in Spinner, Land Girls, Charlotte Gray, All About Eve*
- **1950s**   *Funny Face, The Talented Mr Ripley, Children of the Revolution, Pleasantville, Designing Woman, Far from Heaven, 8 Women, Gentlemen Prefer Blondes*
- **1960s**   *What a Way to Go!, Walk the Line*, the Austin Powers movies, *Down with Love, The Avengers* (not the movie), *The Dish, The Year My Voice Broke, Breakfast at Tiffany's, Don's Party*
- **1970s**   *The Night We Called It a Day, Saturday Night Fever, Dick, Puberty Blues, Annie Hall*
- **1980s**   *Working Girl, Desperately Seeking Susan, Heathers, Romy and Michelle's High School Reunion, Muriel's Wedding, Valley Girl*
- **1990s**   *Clueless, Buffy the Vampire Slayer, Spiceworld*
- **2000s**   *Josie and the Pussycats, Mean Girls, The Devil Wears Prada, Material Girls, Kath & Kim* (TV and film)
- **Futuristic**   *Barbarella, Star Trek, Blade Runner, The Fifth Element, Serenity*
- **Fantasy or crossover worlds** *Mad Max*, Baz Luhrmann and Catherine Martin's *Romeo + Juliet* and *Moulin Rouge, Amélie.*

> I wish we could wear costumes to school.   Nami, 13, Kula, Hawaii, US

494   AND THE REST clothes and make-up

Clothes disasters

You can wear any of the stuff on this list if you like. Just be aware that, whatever your intentions, others will consider them fashion mistakes.

* Clothes that are too tight, so they look and feel uncomfortable.

* Anything that shows bum crack, girly bits or undies when you bend over, stretch or get out of a car.

* Boob tubes: they look like some sort of bandage and create bulges over the top.

* Slippers outside the house – this includes moccasins and ugg boots.

* Platform shoes: not unless you want to seem like you're walking on bricks.

* Socks or stockings with non-school sandals – especially dark socks.

Don't forget: it's fun to break the rules sometimes. Don't take fashion 'laws' too seriously.

More info on clothes and fashion

Anything you read on a fashion site may be an ad, or there to keep an advertiser happy. It's not always independent advice. Be aware that if you make a habit of looking at fashion sites and magazines, you can end up with a very wrong idea about what looks 'normal' for a woman, as all the images are digitally altered.

blogchicks.com.au
Find some local fashion bloggers.

heartifb.com
This site helps independent fashion bloggers run their own blog with style.

thesartorialist.com and **video.nytimes.com** (search On the Street or Bill Cunningham)
Places to see photos of street fashion worn by real people.

fairwear.org, **cleanclothes.org** and **ethicalclothingaustralia.org.au**
Campaigners to stop clothes workers being ripped off and mistreated. Find out which labels you should and shouldn't buy.

Search the fashion or 'costume' departments of these museum sites:

collections.artscentremelbourne.com.au
The Performing Arts Museum in Melbourne.

maas.museum
Museum of Applied Arts and Sciences.

vam.ac.uk
London's Victoria and Albert Museum.

metmuseum.org
The Metropolitan Museum of Art, New York.

Liking clothes does not necessarily mean you are materialistic. I love clothes but it's because I love the fabric, I love making them, I love putting them together, I love the look of things. I think the way you present yourself is important. Emma, 15, Brisbane, Qld

I love to look different from everyone else. Zoe, 16, Ballarat, Vic.

I feel confident about the way I dress, although it's different and a little 'out there'. It's who I am. If people don't like it, they can deal with it.
Carla, 17, Gladesville, NSW

Yeah, I get really annoyed at the chicks who insist on wearing a brand – that is not style! All their clothes are the same, they are really boring and really expensive.
Rhiana, 16, Mandurah, WA

What's with all the popular girls dressing exactly the same? They're like an ARMY!!
Jess and Bree, 15, Woodend, Vic.

I like bargain hunting.
Isabelle, 13, Sydney, NSW

The average size in Australia for women is 14, yet most of the clothes in shops are size 8-12. It's basically a slap in the face. Catherine, 16, Pascoe Vale South, Vic.

Why are there no clothes for young, short people? Why is everything in traffic-cone bloody orange? Why are there no pants for anyone with an arse?
Anna, 17, Traralgon, Vic.

Once someone buys it everyone gets it. Emma, 14, Doncaster, Vic.

Unfortunately the majority of clothing promotes 'thin is best'. It's hard to find clothing made for real women with bums and hips and a waist. Lyndsie, 18, Canberra, ACT

AND THE REST ≡○ **clothes and make-up**

I do judge people a lot by their clothes, like how high their pants are and stuff.

Hannah, 13, Epping, NSW

Making your own clothes like a skirt or something isn't daggy or anything. If you get a good pattern and material, no one will be able to tell the difference and it'll be unique.

Shana, 14, Blue Mountains, NSW

I'm a ladies' size in a lot of shops and I'm only 13 and all the ladies' clothes are dull and boring.

Claire, 13, Bairnsdale, Vic.

Why is stuff only made in a certain 'common' size? Everyone likes groovy clothes.

Ashlee, 16, Dapto, NSW

I get them for my birthday and Christmas generally and they last me the year.

Tracy, 17, Footscray, Vic.

I get bored clothes shopping.

Hannah, 18, Isaacs, ACT

My fave items are my toe socks, my bowler hat I bought from an op shop and my Dunlop shoes with skulls on.

Lucy, 13, Cleveland, Qld

Why can't we all just go around in the nuddy? Ruby, 14, Gawler, SA

I like clothes but it really pisses me off that your status in groups is defined by what labels you wear.

Amber, 15, Padbury, WA

Clothes are my life. That is a bad thing. Charlotte, 14, Sydney, NSW

I hate it when girls analyse what you are wearing and decide what kind of person you are from that. It is so shallow.

Vanessa, 14, Sydney, NSW

clothes and make-up ✪ AND THE REST

Make-up

We'll get to what to do with your eyebrows (ignore them or plait them?) later, but first here's the word on make-up. Make-up isn't supposed to hide your face. It's for accentuating and showing off the nice things about it such as your eyes, your lips, your teeth and your natural rosy cheeks. But make-up is basically used a lot by older women trying to look more like teenagers (minus the spotty moments).

Make-up should be something you use as a bit of fun, or not at all. It's not compulsory. Lots of people never wear it. Some people only ever wear lipstick. Others only wear make-up on special occasions.

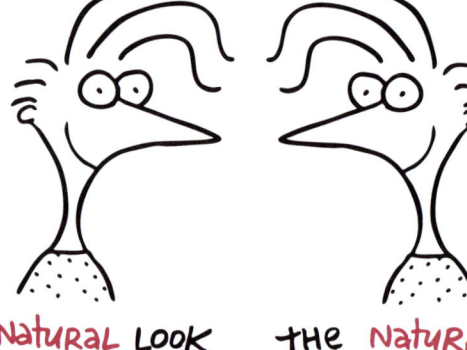

the Natural Look (USING HEAPS OF Make-up)

the Natural Look (NO MAKE-UP at ALL)

Make-up products

The following stuff has been described as 'essentials' by beauty magazines. If you really needed it all you'd have to have a suitcase on wheels and a fortune to fill it.

> I can't work out how to use eyeliner. Anyone I see wearing it has it smudged all around their eyes, it looks awful.
>
> Kate, 15, Jerrabomberra, NSW

For skin

- **Primer**   This is a ridiculous 'pre-foundation foundation' invented simply to sell more make-up. A waste of time and money for girls.
- **Foundation**   It's used to make your face look exactly the same shade all over. It comes as a thick, skin-coloured fluid, applied with fingers or a sponge, or as a creamy stick that you use like a big crayon to draw the foundation on your face before blending it all over. Teenagers don't need it. If you have a tinted oil-free moisturiser it will do the job.

- **Powder** Face-coloured powder is usually brushed or patted on over foundation to create a matt (non-shiny) look. It's available in a tub and brushed on with a make-up brush, or as pressed powder in an (easier to transport) compact and patted on with the compact's pad. Powder doesn't work without foundation because it doesn't stick easily or smoothly, so it's a way of making you buy two things. Teenagers don't need it.

- **Combined foundation and powder** This comes in a compact or a stick, with a semi-matt finish. Teenagers don't need it.

- **Concealer** This is mainly used to 'cover' dark circles under the eyes of older women so it's usually the wrong tint to cover red pimples on girls. It comes in a tube, like a lipstick, or as a soft pencil. To hide a spot it's better to carefully dab on some foundation that matches your complexion.

- **Blusher** This is either brushed, in powder form, or rubbed, in cream form, onto the roundest bit of your cheeks and up your cheek bones. It's hard to avoid looking as if you have patchy sunburn, severe embarrassment or a strange rash, so use only a little, if any. Teenagers don't need it.

- **Bronzer** Too much of this glittery or shimmery powder or lotion and you'll look like you've been rolling around in your little sister's fairy costume.

> I only wear lip gloss to school and only wear eyeshadow and foundation when going out.
> Shona, 14, Cobar, NSW

For lips

- **Lipliner** Older women whose lip line is starting to get less distinct, because of ageing skin, use a pencil to outline their lips. The inside area is then coloured in with the pencil or with lipstick (sometimes using a lip-brush). Lipliner should be the colour of the lipstick: lighter or darker looks odd. Teenagers don't need it.

- **Lip gloss** Cheaper than lipstick, this is a clear, shiny or tinted lip ointment in a tube. Teenage girls have enough colour in their lips already so a clear gloss is fine.

- **Lipstick** Sheer, pale and neutral colours look best on young faces. Don't wear lipstick or lip gloss if, like most girls, you're doing something active or being a normal teenager at school – you just end up with it everywhere else, such as on your teeth, your sleeve and the basketball.

For eyes

- **Eyeliner** This is basically a pencil (or sometimes a liquid or paste applied with a little brush) that is used to outline the eyes and make them look bigger. Always put it outside, not inside, the line of your lashes. Eyeliner (especially the liquid version) is best left to professionals or the very experienced. It's generally considered a dramatic, night-time make-up and not a good look for young teenagers.

- **Mascara** Because it makes the eyelashes look darker, it can give the illusion of more length and thickness, and is a way of drawing attention to your eyes. If you have light-coloured eyelashes, black can look too heavy, so go for a brown instead. It comes as goop in a tube, which you apply with a small 'wand'. When it smudges or runs it can make you look like a sad panda (and stain your clothes). Waterproof mascara must be removed with special eye-make-up remover every night, so that adds more trouble and expense.

- **False eyelashes** Definitely best left to the professionals. Dangers include getting the glue in your eye, looking totally ludicrous, and having the eyelashes peel off and flap in the breeze.

- **Eyeshadow** A temporary stain for your eyelids, it often looks unnatural and over-dramatic. It's generally considered to be for night-time, special-occasion or theatrical wear. Usually a neutral tone looks best. A shade close to your eye colour may make your eyes look dull in comparison, and most eyeshadow is best left to professionals to apply unless they've been drinking.

- **Eyebrow pencil** Used to make eyebrows look thicker or darker, it's almost impossible to get right unless you're a professional. Sketched-on eyebrows tend to look like a 4-year-old's drawing. Give them a miss. (See also the 'Eyebrows' section coming up.)

Safe make-up

If we didn't have preservatives in some make-up we'd be very likely to get bacterial infections from it. Cosmetics usually contain preservatives and other laboratory-made chemicals. Any ingredients can cause eye problems and skin rashes. Natural ingredients can also cause skin reactions and problems.

Beware of ads claiming that make-up is 'toxic' or has 'cancer-causing ingredients'. It's illegal to sell make-up with dangerous ingredients. Most of these claims are made by people selling or supporting 'organic' or 'natural' make-up. Organic make-up may or may not be better for the environment. Non-organic doesn't necessarily mean it's dangerous. 'Organic' can still cause skin reactions in some people: and for some people there's no such thing as 'allergy-free'.

Choose a reputable brand from a supermarket or chemist – not a cheap import shop, which may have cheap stuff from overseas that doesn't comply with our safety regulations.

You can choose 'organic' as a pro-environment stance and choose make-up that's 'not tested on animals'. Most make-up isn't tested on animals any more anyway, because most ingredients have already been established as safe. In most places in the world it's illegal to test cosmetics on animals. According to manufacturers, no make-up manufactured in Australia is tested on animals. See the websites below for more.

beautypedia.com/animal-testing
Make-up brands not tested on animals.

austorganic.com
See the Australian organic logo.

cosmeticsinfo.org
US industry's take on why chemicals and preservatives are necessary in make-up.

Professional make-up artists also use lots of sponges and brushes, but you don't need to. Eyeshadow and blusher can be applied with clean fingertips or a cotton bud, then blended and rubbed in gently with the fingertips.

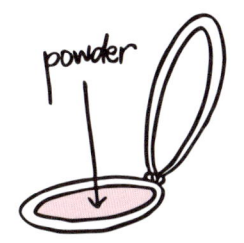

The selling of make-up

If you buy make-up keep in mind that, like clothes and skin-care and hair-care products, it's big business, worth billions, and companies will use lots of tricks to convince you to buy loads of products.

Make-up is a fashion This means that, like clothes, it's subject to trends – new season's colours are brought out to try to encourage you to ditch last month's pale lipstick and go for the 'dramatic colours' now all the rage. Or shiny. Or matt. Or autumn colours. Or bold shimmery stuff. Or purple and green (which together can make it look like you have two 'black eyes').

So if what's hot one season is out a couple of months later, the only questions really are:
- 'Do I like it? Why?'
- 'Does it suit me?'
- 'When would I use it?'
- 'Can I afford it?'

Make-up is expensive It's worth knowing that really expensive make-up isn't any better than less expensive make-up: you're just paying extra for packaging design, the label name and the companies' big advertising campaigns.

Even medium-quality make-up costs a lot: the total cost of buying most of the items for skin, lips and eyes listed earlier in 'Make-up Products' would be easily $200 to 400.

false eyelashes are a drag

73.6 per cent nonsense Don't ever believe the make-up ads. No matter what they say, make-up can't actually physically change any of your features. It's not possible for a lipstick to make your lips 40 per cent plumper or for a mascara to make your lashes 20 per cent longer or 'three times thicker'.

As with skin and hair products, watch out for silly claims and pretendy science-speak.

Brand loyalty   Cosmetics companies would like you to buy all your items from their brand range, but you don't have to. One brand may have the eyeshadow colour you like, while another has the SPF 15 you want in a tinted moisturiser that's oil free.

Hard sell   Also watch out for make-up sales staff. They often get more money if they sell more stuff, so don't fall for being told that you're too pale or too dark and 'need' certain things to 'fix' yourself (and see Chapter 21, Shopping).

> Make-up costs a lot of money if you use it daily.
> Dejah, 18, Ocean Grove, Vic.
>
> It's too expensive.
> Savannah, 16, Yelgun, NSW

Too much make-up

Heavy make-up in the movies, on stage and in photos looks good because there's a whole team of skilled and experienced make-up artists, lighting technicians and other professionals working on it. But in real life it looks waaaay overdone to anyone nearby.

Obvious make-up on anyone is a bad move because it:
- can look as if they've put on fancy dress or they've got into a crayon box and started drawing on their face
- can send a message that they want to look sexual when really they're just trying to look older
- would take less time and be easier to pop out for a few hours and do a bit of coal mining every morning than put on all the products the magazine beauty pages say we should.

So don't waste heaps of valuable sleeping, eating and activity time doing your make-up and hair. Many schools have rules against make-up anyway, and parents will probably want to have their say, too, about when it's okay to wear make-up. Dads can be more horrified than mums: it's one of those 'Oh, my god, my little girl is growing up' things. Maybe a bit of sensible conversation is a good idea before you try to bounce out the door with bright red lipstick and spider-flappy false eyelashes.

too MUCH make-up

clothes and make-up ⚬ AND THE REST   503

Whether or not you care what guys think, it's worth knowing that most of them say they don't like it when a girl wears a lot of make-up. And it's also worth wondering why *guys* aren't expected to wear make-up to 'look better'.

> **FACT**
>
> **Inside info** When an Oscar-winning American actress appeared on an Australian talk show, the producers agreed, as a condition of the 10-minute interview, to pay US$4000 to her hair and make-up artist just to joosh her up.

28.7% more radiant than last Thursday...

blusher

> **QUOTE**
>
> 'In sixth grade, wear lip gloss, some mascara, and maybe a little bit of pale eye shadow. In seventh grade . . . you might want to try curling your hair a few days a week [and] you might want to try eyeliner. In high school you might want to wear your usual make-up during the day, and as you start to go out with friends and boys at night, add a darker shade of eyeliner, or jazz up your lips . . .'
> **Insane advice from a US website offering 'free beauty tips for teen girls'**

AND THE REST ⇒○ clothes and make-up

If you want to use make-up

Here are some make-up hints you can adopt, or ignore.

* Any face make-up (foundation, powder or tinted moisturiser) should have a sunscreen of SPF 15, or higher (rare).

* If you have sensitive skin try hypo-allergenic make-up brands. Test any make-up on a bit of skin and wait 24 hours, to check that you don't get a reaction, before putting it on your face. Oil-free and 'non-comedogenic' make-up is best for teenage skin prone to spots (see Chapter 2, Skin).

* Use make-up that's close to your skin's natural colouring – pale and neutrals for pale skin, bolder colours for darker skin. Black eyebrows on a blonde look simply bizarre, like stuck-on fuzzy felt. Blondes look more natural with light brown or dark brown lashes and eyebrows. Girls with dark skin and very pale lipstick can look a bit like extras in a 1963 science fiction movie.

* Add colour gently, little by little. Experiment so you know what looks bad. Always use your face's natural shapes as a guide. In other words, don't draw outside the natural line of your lips; and only put eyeshadow on your eyelid, not up to your eyebrow. No, actually, do that so you can see how wrong it looks.

* Go outside and look at the make-up in a mirror. How does it look?

* Go to a department-store make-up counter and get the person to make you up with a natural look and then a party one. See how subtle changes can make you look a little different. Don't feel you have to buy the products.

* If you're really keen maybe you could ask for an hour's session with a make-up artist as a late-teens birthday present. Having a session at a department store may be free, but a make-up artist attached to a brand counter will only recommend what they're trying to sell at the moment rather than concentrating on what suits you, the person.

* You could have a make-up party for which a group of friends pitch in to hire a make-up artist.

* Always wash off all make-up before bed. You may need to buy a make-up remover.

I think boys look very nice in make-up and it's a shame it's so socially unaccepted.

Bron, 16, Gympie, Qld

I like to use it to cover up pimples and things, but find that using too much just causes more because all of it blocks the skin.

Jacqui, 13, Kaleen, ACT

I will never leave the house without wearing a face full of make-up.

Jessica, 16, Taylors Hill, Vic.

I'm not allowed to wear it to school, so I get into the habit of not wearing it.

Kristin, 16, Brisbane, Qld

I have 2 words to say to you – liquid eyeliner. Not a good look if you don't know what you're doing. I didn't know what I was doing! Anna, 13, Darwin, NT

REMOVE IT BEFORE YOU SLEEP!!! MY SKIN IS ICKY FROM NEVER REMOVING IT!!

Shelley, 16, Happy Valley, SA

I dye my hair black, and I wear black eye make-up, and if I can be bothered black lipstick. It's not all that hard to put it on, but it takes a while to get it off.

Polly, 15, St Kilda, Vic.

I hate make-up. HATE HATE HATE. The concept of it disgusts me.

Soph, 16, Bondi, NSW

I went through a stage where I used a make-up base on my face every day at school and on weekends. This lasted about 3 weeks. It completely ruined my skin, I was breaking out. It's better now but not completely. Em, 14, Tarragindi, Qld

I got into Mum's make-up when I was about 4. Our family cat and I looked stunning.

Sarah, 14, Creswick, Vic.

Once I bruised my eyelid because I pinched it really hard accidentally with my eye lash curler. Lil, 13, Lysterfield, Vic.

AND THE REST ⇒ clothes and make-up

I think some girls wear too much makeup EVERY DAY. I think it's stupid coz on a special occasion when you do get dressed up you look the same as you do every day.

Holly, 13, Mooloolaba, Qld

Fake eyelashes are tools of the devil. Bethn, 17, Rutherglen, Vic.

I can't be bothered. I hate make up. As soon as I put it on I want to scratch it off.

Katharine, 18, Wantirna, Vic.

Have a day when you're alone to just experiment with different make-up because if you leave the experimentation to just before you leave home, it won't look good or you'll stab your eye.

Louise, 17, Doonside, NSW

I love make-up. I would die without it. Eff, 15, Margaret River, WA

I used to hide behind big gothic make-up, but now my boyfriend who tells me I'm beautiful without any makes it easier for me to go out a lot of the time without any make-up on.

Alyssa, 16, Perth, WA

DON'T OVERPLUCK!!!
Laura, 17, Lane Cove, NSW

I absolutely LOVE make-up, without it I would probably die. I wear make-up nearly every day because I would not be seen in public without it. I think make-up, for me, is like a mask that I put on so no one will have to see the real me which I hate and I think that others won't accept. I'm very self-conscious and make-up lets me be this other person who I want to be.

Mollie, 16, Springfield, Qld

Make-up is for fun and for looking and feeling spesh at times, but I think it should never be compulsory. That's just crappy! Keda, 13, Adelaide, SA

clothes and make-up AND THE REST

Eyebrows

Eyebrows can frame and draw attention to the eyes, but most fiddling about ends up making them look much worse than natural, never-touched ones. Disasters include eyebrows looking too thin, too straggly, too unnaturally shaped, too drawn on or too different from your natural skin and hair tones.

Most women who shape their eyebrows pluck them at home, or have someone at a beauty salon do it by plucking or waxing. (Yes, both ways hurt.) Unless you have the time and money to go to a professional every month (which, let's be honest, is a little obsessive for a teenager), it's best to leave your eyebrows alone in case you ruin them for life. Please don't just wade in – some eyebrow hair may not grow back because the hair follicles get damaged.

eyebrow monthly magazine

If you want to change your eyebrows

- Go to a popular beauty salon and talk to the beauty therapist about what you'd like and how to achieve it. Ask them to be conservative and take off less rather than more, so that you can assess the look and have a second go if it's needed. Don't stay if the eyebrow-shaper likes a thin eyebrow. Tell them you'll think about it, then run, run, run awaaaaay.
- Once they've created the shape you want by waxing or plucking, you can try to follow the line when you're plucking your eyebrows at home.
- Never pluck until your eyebrows look thin. The thinner the eyebrows, the more they look unnatural and strangely balding. The very worst are mean-looking, skinny eyebrows actually painted or drawn on.
- Never shape your eyebrows into a sharp arch – it will make you look constantly astonished.
- When you're plucking, use good tweezers that get a firm grip on individual hairs. Just remove a few hairs at a time or you'll go too far.

- Never pluck hairs from the top of your brows, always just hairs underneath, outside the main shape.
- Never shave or bleach your eyebrow hair. Sharp stubble quickly follows shaving, and bleaching can cause skin conditions or eye damage.
- Only a professional should wax your eyebrows: hot goo can damage your eyes.

More info on make-up and eyebrows

Most make-up websites are full of ads disguised as advice and gushing faff instead of a real independent review of a product. Some brands have site videos on how to apply make-up, or you can scan in a photo of yourself and play with pretend make-up on screen. YouTube has a squillion how-to videos of make-up application and eyebrow shaping. Make your own judgement about how bonkers they are.

> I plucked all my eyebrows out and only about half ever grew back. I wish I had left them alone!
> Mel, Cairns.

EQUALITY, FRIVOLITY

23

Equality, freedom, women's rights, feminism, **girlpower**: lots of ways to describe a simple idea. It's the belief that girls and women should have as many **opportunities** as guys. It's the hope that girls everywhere should be able to celebrate their human rights, and their achievements.

It's the idea that we deserve the right to be **respected**, choose our own path in life, and enjoy life (that's where frivolity comes in). We need feminism to make life more **fun**. This chapter's all about how to change the world, one girl at a time. Check out how far we've come and where we need to go, and the Top 10 lists of the best books, movies, and TV shows for girls: weepies, comedies, triumphs and action adventures.

Why we had to fight for our rights

And not just our right to parrrrrrty. Feminists and strong women through history have struggled hard to get rights and benefits for us women and girls, and wow, have we come a long way. The right to go to school, vote, to choose a partner, control our own finances, choose whether to get pregnant, get a properly paid job, have legal protection from violence – many rights have largely been 'awarded' to us only in the last few decades. And let's not forget the women in other countries who are still fighting for rights we take for granted.

> 'Feminism has gorn too far.'
> Every old pain in the arse who thinks girls and women should just be quiet – and decorative.

What girls and women have gained

It's because feminists fought hard, against strong opposition each time, that we have so much freedom now. Until relatively recently, we women weren't allowed to:

- earn, keep and spend our own money
- get help if a partner abused or hit us
- vote, or be a politician
- choose our own job
- train to be a doctor, lawyer, builder, racing driver, tradesperson (and lots more)
- be paid at least a minimum wage
- get as much money as a man for doing exactly the same job (until 1972 Australian law said women could only earn 75 per cent of a man's wage)
- be legally protected from sexual harassment at work or in another public place, and from discrimination because we're female
- own and sell property
- as adults, ignore what our father – or our partner or husband – tells us to do
- participate in the Olympics
- study at a college or university
- be on a jury, or be made a judge
- keep working while we're pregnant, and get our job back later, instead of being sacked immediately >

- have legal access to safe contraception and termination of pregnancy
- be a single parent and keep our children if we're not married or helped by a man, and get some government financial assistance
- decide to have medical treatment without the permission of our partner or husband
- legally stop our partner or husband from raping us
- not be accused of past 'sluttish' behaviour during a rape trial.

FACT

Did you know? Your great-great-grandmother wasn't allowed to vote, and in her time having paid work was considered not respectable. And your grandmother, who *could* work – usually for low pay in a 'woman's job' – was probably automatically sacked when she got married.

FACT

Being strong You don't have to yell or even make a fuss about what you believe. Strong and shy works just fine. You can quietly speak up and say what you think is right – sometimes that can be just as powerful. Just make sure you're not silent when somebody, or something, needs to be defended and supported. See Chapter 8, Confidence, for more.

FACT

Did you know? Traditionally, the reason you take your husband's name when you get married is that you're being passed on – as a possession – from your father's control to your husband's control.

> I'd like girls to become more aware about gender issues. I'm doing sexual politics at university, but I am often dismissed or called strange for insisting girls stick up for themselves, or that they do not take labels such as slut/bitch/whore. Melissa, 18, Carlton, Vic.

Why we still need women's rights

Women are still discriminated against here. And in some countries women still don't have any of the rights just listed, and are brutally oppressed. If the number of years humans have been around was expressed as a kilometre, we've had women's rights for about a millimetre. Unless we keep fighting, even the rights we've won recently can be taken away.

So if somebody tells you that all the fights are over, and nobody needs to bother about being a feminist any more, think about these questions. >

> Boys aren't superior to you! The world doesn't revolve around them like I used to think!
>
> Girls are more than half the population of Australia. Hell, we even live longer! We can make things happen!
>
> Marcella, 18, Launceston, Tas.

- How come, on average, girls do much better than boys at school and uni, yet women are more likely to be in the lower paid part-time or casual jobs with fewer benefits and worse conditions?
- Why are most managers, bosses and politicians men?
- How come the average full-time wage for women is still less than the average weekly earnings for men? (In most cases, less than or around 80 per cent of the man's wage.)
- What is the 'glass ceiling' – and why do women keep talking about it?
- Why is it that in many countries women who have been raped are arrested and punished because they are no longer 'virgins'?
- Why is it that in some cultures girls' genitals are mutilated? And why are girls in some countries forced to cover themselves entirely with fabric or risk being insulted or assaulted in public or legally punished?
- Why is it that in many cultures young girls are 'promised' to older men and forced to marry against their wishes?
- How come so many guys in our own society don't respect girls and women or their achievements?
- Why do some people persist in behaving as if girls are just toys for guys?
- Why do some girls feel they need to know 'What guys want' and 'Will guys like it if I . . .'? Wouldn't it be nice if girls more often thought, 'What would a guy have to do to impress *me*'?
- Why is it that radio stations and music channels play songs in which guys call girls 'hos', bitches and other brutal, disrespectful things, as if it was nothing – as if it was okay to do that?
- How come more girl singers can't sing their own songs dressed the way they want, instead of having to look as if they're practically in a porn video?
- Why do some religious leaders say that women who have their period can't enter a place of worship? Or have to sit at the back?
- Why is a teenage girl who gets pregnant sometimes asked or pressured to leave school, but the father of the baby isn't?

> Girls (especially younger girls) need to know how important it is to believe in yourself and be your own person . . . it really does make life a lot easier.
> Portia, 18, Christchurch, NZ

- How come most of the sports reports (and sponsorships) are for men's sports?
- Why do large corporations sponsor only (or mainly) men's sports, not women's?
- Why do so many radio and TV shows have lots of men but only one woman, never the other way round?
- How come male newsreaders and actors can get old and look 'distinguished', but the women have to try to 'look younger' by using cosmetic surgery?
- How come teachers can stand there straight-faced and talk about the history of 'modern man' or 'man's achievements'? How hard is it to include the other 50 per cent of the world by saying 'humanity'?
- How come the mostly male politicians in the national government, many of them with a religious bias, make the rules about abortion when they will never be pregnant? And when most male politicians leave the raising of their families to their wives and disappear for weeks at a time?
- How come even the women who work full-time with children usually do a lot more of the housework than their partners?
- Why do most children's films have male heroes, rather than female ones?
- How come women writers often write dramas and comedies with equal roles for guys and women, while most male writers tend to write interesting roles for guys but not so many good roles or lines for women? (Of course girls and women aren't always portrayed as just the passive, decorative or sexual interest in a story: see the lists of 'Feisty Girls and Heroines' coming up.)

More info for girls and women

hoydenabouttown.com and **thedawnchorus.wordpress.com**
Smart sites by feisty Aussie women.

girlsinc.org, rookiemag.com and **bust.com**
Online US mag sites with good links. See page 476 for other girl mags.

pinkstinks.org.uk
Bad name for a good idea – pointing out all the ways girls are told to restrict themselves to certain colours, toys and behaviours.

about-face.org
A great media-awareness site showing sexist ads and attitudes. See the Gallery of Shame.

> Why the bloody hell can't there be coverage of WOMEN'S sports on prime time television?
>
> Toula, 17, Erskine Park, NSW

Equality FAQs

What's the difference between feminist and feminine? *Feminine*: Something that's obviously girly or frilly, flouncy, associated with being a woman and unmanly. *Feminism*: The belief in equal rights and opportunities for girls and women, and against disadvantages on the basis of being female.

Are feminists all man-hating hairy lesbians? No. Just as not all men are Neanderthal women-hating creeps with disconcerting goatees and a love of Bulgarian disco.

Are feminists just a bunch of strident Feminazis? Ahem. Do you know what the real Nazis did? Please reserve this word for them. There *are* some extremist feminists who would prefer a world without men – at last count I think there were about two of them, worldwide. But there are far, far fewer nutty edge-of-the-world feminists than there are conservative, religious and bonkers extremists who believe women are good only for child-rearing and as sexual objects. Most of the rest of us are huddled in the middle, nervously eating our sandwiches and keeping an eye on the lunatic fringe in both directions, thank you very much.

Did feminism lie to us by promising everything? It isn't feminism that lied to you, it's advertising. Feminism doesn't mean having it all. Nobody can have it all: a fabulously well-paid job, six kids, a yacht, a tiara and a pet monkey called Ferdie. There isn't enough time. Feminism means freedom to choose which things to *try* to have. It means you shouldn't be forced to have one child, or any children, or a job, or no job. But you have the freedom to choose whether to concentrate on family or career, or somehow try to manage both. (There's no guarantee you'll be able to have kids, or get a job you love, of course. Life's a lottery.) It's up to us to try to work out how we choose to put together our available options and make a life.

Can't I just call myself an 'equalist' or humanist instead of or as well as a feminist? Yep. You can be an advocate for other people's rights as well as women's rights. You can like peanut butter AND Vegemite. One moment please, I have a pressing urge to make some toast.

Do you call yourself a feminist?

A lot of girls say they don't want to call themselves a feminist because there's no need for it, or it means they don't like guys, or because they don't really know what it means. Being a feminist just means you support girls and women having opportunities and equal rights with guys. Whatever you call yourself, some people will still try to discriminate against you because you're female.

You're a feminist woman if you want to be paid a fair wage for your work, if you want to vote, if you want to use contraception so you're not pregnant all the time, if you don't want a male boss to be able to put his hand up your skirt at work, if you want to choose your own job, boyfriend and friends or make any financial decisions. Otherwise, you could accept the non-feminist option that women should wear what they're told, do all the cooking and cleaning, stay hidden and behave like a robot mother or a sex object.

If you want to take advantage of all that feminists have won for you, but then say you don't like the sound of 'feminism', oookaaaaay. All we ask is that when you say 'I'm not a feminist', you add, 'I don't like the word, but I think there's still a long way to go in the world to get equality for everybody.' Or 'I think I have all the rights I need but a lot of women don't.' For the sake of women all over the world, and the younger girls coming after us, please make it clear what you *do* believe in. Just saying 'I'm not a feminist' sounds like you're happy for girls and women to be second-class citizens.

So it's time to pick a side. It's not about women versus men. It's women and men who believe in a fair go for women versus the people who think girls and women are second-best. Call yourself whatever you want, but it's time to choose. Are you with us in our fight for equal rights for all girls and women across the world? Because if we don't keep speaking out, we'll lose all the gains we've made over the past hundred years or so. When it comes to equal rights for women, it's choose it or lose it.

Can't I just stay at home? I don't want to be a feminist. Feminism doesn't say you can't stay at home – it says you should have the choice. It says you shouldn't be forced to stay at home.

So of course you can stay at home. But you can still be a feminist in case your circumstances change – or you change your mind. Feminism isn't just for you – it's for your mum and your eventual daughters and the lady next door and the women of Nigeria and Asia, and Natasha Tediumskya, who works in a factory in Siberia. She could probably do with some more.

A day in the life of women's rights

Recognisable humans have been on the earth for about 200 000 years or so. Imagine that those 200 000 years have been compressed into a 24-hour day. Right now, this year, it's the end of the 24 hours – midnight. That means:

* Neanderthals became extinct at about 3.07 this afternoon.

* Aboriginal people arrived in Australia about 20 minutes later.

* Greeks invented democracy (only for men, who weren't slaves) about quarter of an hour ago.

* Most New Zealand women got the vote about 50 seconds ago.

* Non-Indigenous Australian women were given the vote 44 seconds ago.

* Women got the vote in Greece about 25 seconds ago.

* Indigenous women got the vote in Australia about 20 seconds ago.

* Swiss women got the vote about 5 seconds ago.

(Still not allowing women to have a full vote: Saudi Arabia and the Catholic 'state' in Rome, Vatican City.)

Miss, Ms or Mrs?

To avoid saying Miss or Mrs, 'Ms' was born, pronounced like a cross between Muz and Miz, or Mzz. It didn't really catch on until the 1960s, when women pushed hard for it to be included as an option on official forms. Women said it wasn't fair that men were called 'Mister' whereas women had to reveal whether or not they were married. Married women were even addressed by their husband's name – an Emma Smith would become 'Mrs John Brown'.

Women wanted to be seen as independent people, with their own name. Also, they knew that 'Misses' were expected to cheerfully endure sexual harassment at work, while those called 'Mrs' were often sacked or forced to resign as soon as they were married.

Since the 1970s, the more common habit of using first names at work means we don't often get to use these formal 'honorifics'. It's still pretty common in some medical situations, hotel bookings and lots of schools. If you don't know whether a woman is married, and it's irrelevant, always use the option of 'Ms'. But be a bit careful with elderly and old-fashioned women who like being called Mrs or Miss and are offended by strangers using their first name. Ask politely, 'Would you like me to call you Mrs Suchansuch?' and then they can correct you, as their name probably isn't Suchansuch, for a start.

More info on feminism

whoneedsfeminism.tumblr.com
Contribute your own idea and see pics and comments from others.

finallyfeminism101.wordpress.com
Aussie founding editor of this blog presents Top Posts for answers to feminism FAQs.

thefword.org.uk
Up-to-the-minute feminism commentary from the UK.

feminist.com and **feministing.com**
US sites with ideas, info, inspiration and links.

globalfundforwomen.org
Inspiring projects to help girls and women worldwide.

cwaa.org.au
The Country Women's Association is an independent lobby group, scholarship source and support network in country and remote areas of Australia.

change.org
Browse petitions, or start your own.

ywca.org.au
This Aussie organisation is run entirely by and for young women. It campaigns for women's rights, and runs community projects and classes for girls in communication and other skills.

ywca.org.nz
More programs for girls and women in NZ.

Too damn hot

Girls and women spend so much time worrying about their appearance now. For some, the pressure they feel is to look 'hot', in other words sexy, from the age of 12 (far too early) until they're about 80. (Are you kidding me? Can't we just have a cup of tea and lie down by the time we get there?) Girls and women are pressured by relentless, imposed definitions of what supposedly looks 'hot' – from fashion industries, media empires and, sadly, sometimes other women.

They'd like us to spend all our energies – and money – on make-up and other cosmetic products and clothes. The big commercial companies don't care about our ideas, achievements and inner selves, or our future financial security or independence. They don't care who we are, only what we look like and how much of our money they can get. Well, it's time for girls to decide for themselves who they are and how to present themselves, and it doesn't have to be looking like a pitiable and demented sex worker who seems to have accidentally bought stilts instead of shoes.

In any case, it's a safety issue. One day I'm going to throw something at the TV screen and break it because there are only two women in any given movie I'm watching – and one's a long-suffering wife who's supposed to look like a supermodel and the other is advancing the plot by accidentally falling out of her pants.

Pop-porn

If you like pop music you're forced to swallow a load of exploitative and disrespectful imagery with almost every video. There's nothing enviable about looking 'like a porn star'. In any case, there's really no such thing as a 'porn star' any more, just thousands of sad women, often with low self-esteem and a history of being sexually abused, who think it might be more glamorous to be in porn videos. The bump and grind, simulated oral sex, pole-dancing moves and gestures from so many women in pop videos come directly from the tawdry junior fantasies of rock industry identities.

You may need to search a little wider for interesting music and videos. Ask around to find out more about women singers, songwriters and musicians who are all about the song, the performance, a strong image and having something to say.

More info on women in music

sbs.com.au/rockwiz
The Aussie show on SBS features local and global singers of all ages and both genders. See some great duets and other performances.

bbc.co.uk/later
Try to catch repeats or get DVDs of the show *Later With Jools Holland*, which features world-class music artists, women as well as men. Videocasts available.

Some useful hashtags about the rights of girls and women include #likeagirl #everydaysexism #misogyny #feminism #IWD #heforshe and #girleffect.

I feel confident about my ability to assert myself, my ability to see reason, responsibility, rationality, positivity and both sides in any situation. I feel confident about what I want and what I am passionate about. I am confident that I know who I am and how I feel. Sascha, 18, Mullumbimby, NSW

I would like to read why it is okay for guys to sleep with as many girls as they want and get congratulated for it, while girls get called sluts. [*Actually it's not okay.*]
Janne, 17, Mount Barker, SA

Put girls in power!!! Man, we need to kick these old men out of parliament! Who says they have the right to decide on such things as abortion!?! Girls need to realise their potential! And not be afraid of things such as law or maths simply because 'boys are naturally better' – that's crap and we know it! Amy, 17, Boorowa, NSW

There are always going to be things you want to change about yourself, that's just the way a girl's mind works. But I like to think that everything about you makes you special and unique. Jessica, 14, Casino, NSW

You have to be strong to love yourself for who you are, especially when today's media is so strongly focused on beauty and image.
Ruby, 16, Orange, NSW

If a boy treats you badly you are too good for him and you should leave.
Marianne, 18, Brisbane, Qld

equality, frivolity AND THE REST

Feisty fun

Feisty means bold and sassy. Here are some lists (in no particular order) of feisty female heroines, and interesting girls and women in movies, TV series and books. Add your own favourites to the lists. Check film and TV ratings for age suitability. Teen-book specialist Rebecca Hutcheson from my local bookshop and some other pals helped make the book lists. Ask your librarian or local bookseller which ones are right for your age (and reading level). Order them at your local bookshop or from an Aussie online bookshop.

10 great book series for girls

Ask for help at your library or local bookshop, or check with an Australian online bookshop to make sure you start with the first book in a series and read them in order.

Noughts and Crosses Trilogy by Malorie Blackman. Noughts are downtrodden former slaves, and the Crosses are dominant; a Cross girl has a daughter with a Nought boy.

The Tomorrow Series by John Marsden. Australia is invaded but some country kids get away and hide. Will they make a difference? Will they live?

The Hunger Games Trilogy by Suzanne Collins. Survival of the fittest, corrupt officials, and a teenage girl fighting for what's right.

The Uglies Series by Scott Westerfeld. An adventure story with themes of body image, loyalty and more, all set in the future.

Skulduggery Pleasant Series by Derek Landy. Stephanie Edgley aka Valkyrie Cain ably assists a skeleton detective.

Little Women Series by Louisa May Alcott. Four different sisters in a very close family grow up in this historical American story.

Tale of the Otori Series by Lian Hearn. Set in feudal Japan with an awesome heroine.

Little Fur Series by Isobel Carmody. Starring an elf troll healer in a forest world.

Emily the Strange Series by Rob Reger, illustrated by Buzz Parker. She's sassy, quirky and, well, strange. Now a merchandising phenomenon.

Harry Potter Series by J. K. Rowling. Oh Hermione, you seemed to grow up so fast. Possibly because we watched all the movies in a marathon.

(Also see the 'Costume Movies' list in Chapter 22, Clothes and Make-up, and for falling-in-love and heartbreak songs and movies see the 'Lists for Every Stage of Love' in Chapter 15, Love.)

10 amazing books for girls

Beauty Queens by Libba Bray. Hilarious. Teen beauty contest meets reality show on an island.
The Illustrated Mum by Jacqueline Wilson. Dolphin loves her mum being so colourful, but her sister, Star, doesn't.
Hoot (and also **Chomp**) by Carl Hiaasen. Teens to the rescue of the environment; lots of fun.
Why We Broke Up by Daniel Handler, illustrated by Maira Kalman. A box full of bittersweet memories: about first love, hope and being different . . . or not.
The Whale Rider by Witi Ihimaera. Pai needs to prove she has what it takes to be a Maori chieftain, despite being 'just' a girl.
I Capture the Castle by Dodie Smith. Mature themes in a much-loved classic.
The Fault in Our Stars by John Green. Hazel's experience with cancer, love and other feelings.
The Book Thief by Marcus Zusak. A young girl's experience of World War 2 in Germany, narrated by 'Death'. Sounds bleak, but is a popular book that's won many awards.
Chinese Cinderella by Adeline Yen Mah. The true story of an unwanted daughter.
Speak by Laurie Halse Anderson. Melinda is forced into doing something sexual: she spirals down, then puts her life back together and fights for justice.

10 great Aussie books for teens

Does My Head Look Big in This? by Randa Abdel-Fattah. Amal, a 16-year-old Australian-Palestinian Muslim, tries for a 'normal' life.
How to Make a Bird by Martine Murray. Mannie runs away to the city.
Take 3 Girls by Fiona Wood, Simmone Howell and Cath Crowley. Three authors write about three friends, who are dealing with finding their true selves, bullying and gossip.
Growing Up Aboriginal in Australia edited by Anita Heiss. **Growing Up Asian in Australia** edited by Alice Pung. Different voices tell their own stories.
Looking for Alibrandi by Melina Marchetta. Josie searches for the freedom to be herself.
Queen Kat, Carmel and St Jude Get a Life by Maureen McCarthy. Three girls from the same town move to the city after high school and take different paths.
My Brilliant Career by Miles Franklin. A historical Australian story about a bold girl who follows her dream to be a writer.
All I Ever Wanted by Vikki Wakefield. A thriller involving a girl who may be trapped in a crime family and the suburbs . . . or just be somebody working out how to live.
This Is Shyness by Leanne Hall. Wolfboy meets Wolfgirl in Shyness (the suburb). Then it gets weirder.
Graffiti Moon by Cath Crowley. Romance in the world of graffiti art: for older teens.

Top 10 girlfriends'-night-in movies

All About Eve   Sisterhood versus scheming. The first stalker movie.
Beaches   Cry, cry, cry.
Rabbit Proof Fence   Oh, have another cry.
A League of Their Own   Girls play their own game.
The Women   Gossip and gowns.
Charlie's Angels   Ultra-groomed action nonsense.
Jane Eyre   The latest remake is the best, they say. Or read the book!
Bend It Like Beckham   A girl from a strict family wants to play soccer.
Funny Face   Audrey Hepburn, mad cozzies and dancing.
Whip It   Dramedy about all teen problems, triumphs and, um, rollerderby.

Top 10 teen romance movies

Also check out any original book versions of these movies.
Angus, Thongs and Perfect Snogging   Fourteen, funny and freaking out.
Miss Congeniality   Puts clever above glamour.
Muriel's Wedding   About deciding to be yourself.
Nick and Norah's Infinite Playlist   Romance and confusion.
Say Anything   Teen romance from a teen perspective.
Puberty Blues   Aussie surfer teens grow up in the 1970s.
Riding in Cars with Boys   A young mum grows up.
Ghost World   About two girls who aren't like everybody else.
Pride and Prejudice or Emma or Sense and Sensibility   Or any other Jane Austen novel made into a film or TV show. Eighteenth-century heroines modern girls can identify with.
My Days of Mercy   Two young women in love fight the death penalty.

Top 10 ladies' night comedies

Mean Girls   Beating the bullies.
Freaky Friday   A mum and her teenage daughter swap bodies – and lives.
Suddenly 30   A 13-year-old wakes up 30 years old and isn't the woman she'd planned to be.
Romy and Michelle's High School Reunion   High-larious.
Bridesmaids   US comedy ladies write, star and shine.
Kath & Kim   Aussie comedy ladies write, star and whine. (TV and movie.)
10 Things I Hate about You   A Shakespeare comedy in an American high school.
Clueless   Hollywood does Jane Austen's *Emma*, with shopping.
Gilmore Girls   Single mother and daughter talk quickly. (TV series.)
His Girl Friday   Old, wonderful black-and-white movie with wise-crackin' reporter babe.

Top 10 movies with a heroine

Erin Brockovich   A 'lowly' law-office assistant takes on corporate bad guys.
Mermaids   Single mother Cher makes her own fun.
Norma Rae   A woman takes on the bosses.
North Country   Women take on sexual harassment.
The Prime of Miss Jean Brodie   English school movie.
Silkwood   A woman takes on the nuclear industry.
Run Lola Run   An unusual girl gets fast and furious.
Tangled   Animated reimagining of the Rapunzel legend, for teens.
Thelma and Louise   The ultimate girlpower road movie.
Wonder Woman   Patty Jenkins directs, comic book heroine lives!

Top 10 TV shows for girls

Most of these are available in boxed DVD sets, in reruns or on cable TV.
Buffy the Vampire Slayer   Buffy takes on demons, vampires and worse, at high school.
Dance Academy   Aussie teen drama series set in a ballet school.
Daria   Animated teen queen of irony.
Freaks and Geeks   Classic TV series about not fitting in but finding your people.
Friday Night Lights   Great girl characters: this show's not really about US football, it's about life as a teen.
Glee   Gay-friendly comedy-drama you can sing along to.
Misfits   UK teens with special powers go to school together.
My So-called Life   US teen trying to deal with friends, school and home: it was so good, they cancelled it.
Skins   Controversial and hard-hitting British teen drama series.
Veronica Mars   Teen private investigator mixes school and sleuth stuff.

Top 10 female action-adventure characters

Katniss Everdeen in *The Hunger Games*.
Sydney Bristow in the TV series *Alias*.
Buffy in the TV series *Buffy the Vampire Slayer*.
Guinevere in *King Arthur*.
Ellie Linton in *Tomorrow, When the War Began* (read the great Aussie book series, too!).
Mulan in, you guessed it, *Mulan*.
Zoë Washburne in the movie *Serenity* and the TV series *Firefly*.
Ripley in *Alien* and *Aliens*.
Yu Shu Lien in *Crouching Tiger, Hidden Dragon*.
Natasha Romanoff/The Black Widow in *The Avengers*.

Girls and women we admire

I'm sure there have been wonderful women in every place on earth, in every age. But now we get to hear about more of them, and there are more opportunities for women to stretch their wings. All over the world in the last hundred years or so, women have been powering up.

There are heaps of options when it comes to finding splendid examples of the sisterhood. We have women running the State Department (foreign relations) of the US, mums of all kinds, Indigenous activists; we have women running farms and being judges and doing a bersquillion other fascinating, useful, ordinary and extraordinary things. Here are some role models, heroines and women of note nominated by other women for my book *Women's Stuff*: sailors, politicians, architects, artists, activists, scientists, 'everyday' admirable folk, spies, athletes, professors, judges, doctors, global-power pivots, comedians, leaders, explorers and writers.

Eva Zeisel ❋ Lady Gaga ❋ Ellen Johnson Sirleaf ❋ Jenny Blokland ❋ Leymah Gbowee ❋ Christine Lagarde ❋ Tawakkul Karman ❋ Missy Higgins ❋ Waris Dirie ❋ Anna Bligh ❋ Judith Lucy ❋ Layne Beachley ❋ Aruna Roy ❋ Marjorie Bligh ❋ Eva Crane ❋ Zaha Hadid ❋ Queenie McKenzie ❋ Madeleine Albright ❋ Quentin Bryce ❋ Vivian Bullwinkel ❋ Rosa Parks ❋ Meryl Streep ❋ Hillary Clinton ❋ Nancy Bird Walton ❋ Marcia Langton ❋ One of the girls I work with; she's a geologist and has no fear of being in the middle of nowhere alone ❋ My great-grandmother ❋ Lorde ❋ Queens Elizabeth I and II ❋ Stella Rimington ❋ Zali Steggall ❋ Miles Franklin ❋ Zelda D'Aprano ❋ Bindi Irwin ❋ Lisa Simpson ❋ Germaine Greer ❋ Lillian Hellman ❋ Greta Thunberg ❋ Virginia Bell ❋ Oodgeroo Noonuccal ❋ Alice Pung ❋ Edna Ryan ❋ Beryl Beaurepaire ❋ Emma Goldman ❋ My cousin Sandra ❋ Maggie Beer ❋ Joan of Arc ❋ An engineer where I work ❋ Nina Simone ❋ Bessie Smyth ❋ PJ Harvey ❋ Penny Wong ❋ Lucinda Smith ❋ Helen Clark ❋ My grandmother – she gave birth to fourteen children ❋ Evonne Goolagong Cawley ❋ Sue Fear ❋ Katharine Hepburn ❋ Naomi Wolf ❋ Rosalie Gascoigne ❋ Temple Grandin ❋ Kay Cottee ❋ Those thousands of pioneer women 200 years ago ❋ Leah Purcell ❋ Elizabeth Bennet ❋ Julia Gillard ❋ Pink ❋ Jo Rowling ❋ Nigella Lawson ❋ Catherine Hamlin ❋ Zoë Bell ❋ Stevie Smith ❋ Fiona Wood ❋ Rell Sunn ❋ Mary Herring ❋ Oprah Winfrey ❋ The Pankhurst sisters ❋ Virginia Woolf ❋ Jane Austen ❋ Patti Smith ❋ My sister ❋ Elisabeth Murdoch ❋ Marie Curie ❋ Barbara Cummings ❋ Nakkia Lui ❋ My great-aunt Vera ❋ Benazir Bhutto ❋ Björk ❋ Eleanor Roosevelt ❋ Feminist bloggers ❋ Cate Blanchett ❋ Kim Deal ❋ Sabine Schmitz ❋ The Topp Twins ❋ Phoolan Devi ❋ Ayaan Hirsi Ali ❋ Whina Cooper ❋ Women who foster children ❋ My daughter, who dropped out of school at 15 but later went back to uni.

CARING

24 the environment

When you're a teenager you sometimes ask yourself the **big** philosophical questions such as 'Why am I here?', 'What's the meaning of life?', 'What should I believe in?', 'What's the **right way** to live?', 'Why should I do the right thing when so many people seem to get away with doing the wrong thing?' and 'How can I help to fix things in the world so it could be better?'

Discoveries in science and increased knowledge have disproved many previously accepted religious ideas, but we all still need to have a personal set of beliefs and to decide what's **important** and what's the right way to live.

What people believe in

Most people have been taught a certain religious faith or set of values from birth because it's the religion or philosophy of their family. There isn't a day when you turn 18 and get to tick the box for 'Zoroastrian', 'Greek Orthodox Christian' or 'Huh? Still Confused'. What god or belief system you have is usually an accident of where you were born, and into which family.

Religious beliefs

Most religions attempt to answer those big questions about how people got here, what our purpose is on earth, how we should live, and what happens when we die.

All cultures in the world have creation stories that try to explain how we got here. Most religions revere a specific god, several gods or a force of nature, said to have created the world and to control it; recognise key prophets (interpreters of a god's will), teachers or elders; and follow a set of morals or a book based on an interpretation of the wishes of gods or prophets.

Depending on your family's religious tradition, you could be brought up to believe in the teachings of the Prophet Mohammed, an earth goddess, the Jewish or Christian God, Buddha, a giant crow who made the world, or aliens who came to earth and gave a set of rules to somebody who was standing in a paddock.

Religion also fulfils a basic human need for a sense of belonging and community: for a support group, a meeting place, celebrations to mark important occasions, and a ready-made set of rules to follow. Most religions have observances and religious holidays; examples include Christmas and Easter for Christians, and the holy month of Ramadan for Muslims.

Common forms of observance include gatherings (often in a special place), prayer, song, and food, incense or other offerings made to the shrines of a god or gods or ancestors. There are often rules about what you can eat, or how the food is to be prepared and stored, and which days or times must be set aside for worship or prayer.

Most believers think their religion requires them to live a moral life and do good in the world. Many religious organisations are involved in charitable works such as helping the poor and disadvantaged.

Often religions want the children within their organisation to be educated at a religious school, mixing only with other people of the same beliefs. Many religious schools teach their own version of history, morals and even science (for example, 'intelligent design' or 'creationism' instead of evolutionary science). This can mean that students miss out on essential scientific information, sex and contraception education, and knowing about other views of life.

Many of the basic principles of old religions remain in place today – it's wrong to kill, you must treat others with kindness, do not steal – but often religions struggle to remain relevant, given the ever-increasing scientific explanations of the world, the pace of technology, and the vast difference between life now and hundreds or thousands of years ago when the holy books were written (for instance, many religions still teach that women are inferior to men).

New Age beliefs

Although the major religions of the world offer supernatural answers to the questions about the 'meaning of life', many accept that in the everyday world other factors – economics, science, politics, psychology – influence people's lives. But there are still some ancient or traditional ideas around that have been recycled as what's often called New Age beliefs. These include astrology, clairvoyancy, 'healing' and other crystals, and witchcraft and spells.

Astrology Astrologers continue to say, as they have done for thousands of years, that the stars determine a person's personality and their future. Constellations (combinations) of stars are said to resemble, say, a bull (Taurus) or an archer (Sagittarius), and people are sorted into one of twelve 'star signs', which are believed to have certain characteristics. Astrologers draw up individual 'horoscopes', using charts 'connecting the dots' of the stars visible in the sky when a particular person was born, to decide the person's star sign and predict what they'll feel and do.

Indigenous people looked at the same stars in the same sky and imagined different pictures, and scientific advances in astronomy since then have proved that stars are really giant gaseous balls in space, and that stars that look like they're near each other can actually be light years apart. So think of your horoscope as one-size-fits-all advice that could apply to just about anybody, and just read the astrology columns for fun.

I was a Pisces. Then the stars moved. Now I'm a small asteroid

'Types' Some books and articles divide people up according to ancient ideas such as the earth, fire, air and water 'signs', or types. Newer versions sort people according to their birth date, their numerology, their body shape or their blood type.

People who see the world in this way often say that your personality, your future, who you choose as a partner, how you relate to your parents and even what you eat should be dictated by which type you are. This is harmless fun – unless you take it seriously and follow it.

Now that we understand so much more about science and psychology, we know that people are individual and complex, and it's not helpful to label them in this way or tell them to run their life solely according to old superstitions.

Clairvoyants, psychics, fortune tellers and mediums Clairvoyants and psychics are people who claim to be able to see hidden things – sometimes in the 'spirit world'. They can have good intuition and can be surprisingly accurate at guessing, or knowing, what's important to somebody; others have lots of stage tricks to make them seem as if they know stuff.

There's no harm in having a fortune teller or psychic read your palm or tell your fortune – unless you run your life by it, or take everything as a definite. Mediums, who claim they can recognise 'messages' from the dead, are best left where they belong – in movies and TV shows. See also Chapter 7, Body Health, for why homeopathic 'medicine' doesn't work.

> **FACT**
>
> **'Karma'** Karma is the Buddhist, Hindu and Jain religious belief that being a good person will be rewarded with a better status when you are reincarnated (take on a new form after death), while bad behaviour will be punished by you being reborn as, say, an insect. It's often used by non-members of these religions as a warning: 'Don't do that, you'll have bad karma.' Don't interpret this to mean that if you have bad luck, or get sick, it's your fault. It isn't.

Humanist (non-religious) ethics

Lots of people are atheists: they don't believe in a god. Others are agnostics: they're not convinced either way.

Many atheists are humanists: people who try to live morally, although not for religious reasons. Humanists say they reject religious answers that are not based on logic or evidence. They disagree with the way that some churches resist change and discourage or even punish questioning. They place their faith in the laws of science, reasonable behaviour, social rules, and independence of mind.

Humanists believe that you don't have to be religious to have rules about kindness and not hurting others, or to do good in the world. They (like most religious people) oppose wars and terrorism carried out in the name of religion.

Tolerance

It's not possible to accept or agree with somebody's religion or value system if you are not convinced by it – every religion and culture has rituals or beliefs that are inexplicable to others – but one of the principles of a democratic society is that people agree to tolerate each other's beliefs: in other words, to respect another person's right to believe. While there are laws against trying to create hatred or violence based on religious (or racial or other discriminatory) grounds, everyone is allowed to discuss and question religious beliefs. It's part of the democratic concept of freedom of speech.

It's also each person's right not to have to live by someone else's religious rules. In secular democracies such as Australia and New Zealand religion and government are separate: religion is a matter of private choice, whereas governments are elected to protect and promote the social wellbeing of everyone.

People of strong religious (or minority) beliefs are expected not to interfere in the lives of the rest of the community, although some try to make the country's laws follow their views – say, by trying to make pregnancy termination illegal, or by refusing to allow gay people the civil right to marry.

Religious discrimination   It's illegal to discriminate against somebody at work or any other place because of religious differences. Some people look different because of their religion. For example, some Muslim girls wear a headscarf or veil, some Jewish guys wear special kinds of caps, and men of the Sikh religion wear turbans.

It's a sign of maturity not to make fun of somebody just because they look or dress differently. There's no reason why you can't quietly and politely ask someone why they

Take some time

Most religions and many non-religious people set aside a time each day for something they might call prayer, meditation, reflection, 'having some space', 'communing with nature', or thinking.

Taking 20 (or even a few) minutes in the day to walk or sit in a peaceful way and think, without your phone, music, TV or another distraction, can help you:

❋ become a calmer person

❋ come up with useful ideas and solutions

❋ work out what you hope for and how you could make things happen.

wear or do certain things because of their religion, if you are genuinely interested, but it's wrong to do it in a way that might embarrass the person.

And if you're the person being asked, even though it may be the fifty-sixth time that week, try to be patient. The more people learn about each other the easier it is to make friends, instead of feeling alienated from each other.

Fanaticism and extremism Fanaticism is when someone holds to their set of beliefs – religious or non-religious – so passionately that they try to make everybody else live by what they believe.

All the major religions have minority offshoots, including smaller, stricter and often weirder versions (there are some US Christians who interpret the Bible to suggest they should cavort with bitey, poisonous rattlesnakes). And most religions have some members who are fanatical.

Many fanatics want the religion to be the same as it was thousands or hundreds of years ago, and demand that strict rules or the words of a holy book be followed exactly – as interpreted by them. Because old holy books have nothing to say about recent inventions such as mobile phones or popular music or a million other things, extremists tend to think most aspects of modern life are evil but ignore obvious evils that weren't mentioned back then, such as child abuse and racism.

A frank exchange of views

Beliefs round-up

Some religions with one god
Christianity, Islam (Muslim), Judaism (Jewish), Sikh, Mormon (Church of Jesus Christ of Latter Day Saints).

Some religions with several gods
Hinduism, Hare Krishna (Krishna as the supreme god), Jain, Yoruba, Shintoism.

Some religions with teachers, prophets or gurus
Christianity, Islam, Sikh, Mormon, Confucianism, Buddhism, Baha'i, Zoroastrianism.

Some indigenous belief systems
Various Aboriginal, Torres Strait Islander, Maori, various Pacific Islander, Native American, various African.

Some New Age religions
Nature worship, Wicca (modern witchcraft), goddess and earth worship.

Other spiritual movements
Taoism, yoga and meditation.

Some other belief systems and philosophies
Capitalism, Communism, Fascism, social Darwinism (dominance by the rich and strong, survival of the fittest), nihilism (nothing matters), humanism, scientific approach – acceptance of explanations based solely on verifiable data and research (such as evolution) to explain life, green living, plus too many other non-religious beliefs to list here!

Most extremists hold that they must convert others to their views and insist that their beliefs alone should be legally enforced. Some use violence or threats to try to impose their ideas. Some animal rights fanatics in England dug up the dead body of a man's mother-in-law, and threatened the grandchildren of his cleaner, because he worked for a place that sold guinea pigs to scientific researchers. Some Christian anti-abortion fanatics bomb clinics that offer pregnancy termination. Some Muslim fanatics kill innocent people at random.

Obviously it's best not to engage with fanatics, and to try not to have anything to do with them personally. You can express your concern publicly and use the political system to oppose fanatics who want to destroy the democratic, tolerant way of life our society has chosen (see the 'How to Change the World' section coming up).

Cults A cult is the name given to a secretive organisation that tends to recruit members; to use psychological tricks to try to control the way members think, including lack of sleep, granting and withdrawal of affection and approval, and isolation from friends and family; and to teach that those outside the cult are bad people and the only world needed is the church or organisation.

Many cults are based on interpretations of the Christian Bible; others are presented as New Age studies or as 'personal development' style courses about how to be more 'successful'; and some are commercial ventures teaching you how to sell or market products. Examples of cults include the Exclusive Brethren, the Jehovah's Witnesses, Scientology (one of the many based on ideas about aliens), and Landmark Forum and Enterprises. Most cults somehow involve asking you to donate lots of money.

More info on religion, philosophy and ideas

askphilosophers.org
Email questions on moral issues to a panel of philosophers at this US site, or see what's already been discussed in the archives.

youthinterfaith.org
This US site was founded by a Muslim girl and with Jewish and Christian leadership too. This site is all about education and understanding between faiths.

nswccl.org.au, libertyvictoria.org.au and **qccl.org.au**
NSW, Vic. and Qld councils for civil liberties, which have a philosophy of human rights, equal justice for all and free speech.

abc.net.au/religion
ABC TV's religious program pages.

theinterfaithobserver.org
Another US website dedicated to interfaith, with articles about aspects of different religions.

jcma.org.au
The Jewish Christian Muslim Association of Australia is all about working to end religious intolerance.

Ideas That Changed the World by Felipe Fernandez Armesto
Brilliant overview of old and new spiritual ideas, political movements, and different ethical and philosophical ways of thinking.

FACT

'Gurus' These are 'teachers' who pass on their 'wisdom'. It can be dangerous to put all your faith in only one teacher (or friend or coach). Nobody, no matter how much older and more experienced than you, has all the answers for you or should isolate you from family and friends.

Positive values

Here's an adapted round-up of some ideas from the sequel to this book for adults, *Women's Stuff*. They're probably even more useful for teens.

Seeking knowledge Many people find purpose and peace in extending their knowledge, particularly through reading. Many find great solace in the classics of literature or in reading about things that are important to them. For some people, their sacred object is their library card. Other people might just love film, or feel totally different when they're outdoors or listening to music – find the one thing, or the few things, you love and extend your knowledge. It won't feel like work, it'll feel like freedom.

Congratulating yourself Any completed task can make you feel good – from a clean bedroom to academic and trade qualifications, schoolwork, sport, artistic ventures, or simple recognition and compliments from friends and adults. Shared achievements also count, of course. If you hate your school or feel trapped in your lifestyle, identify the positives – it's temporary, it's a stepping stone, it's laying the foundations for something else.

Tick off the achievements you've already made and acknowledge what the next one might be. You can count off small increments or keep pushing for the one big goal. Smaller and multiple aims (doing your homework tonight, saving $10 a week, sewing a little bit more on that project each week) can give you more landmark achievements, though.

Being flexible Plan B is always a good idea so you're not pinning all your chances for happiness on something possibly elusive, like only one course, or one job, or one gold medal. A lot of grown-ups have already been through plans B, C, and D up to about plan W, so don't feel your life has only one possible path. Be as kind to yourself as you would be to a friend who's adjusting their goals or beliefs about the future.

Feeling gratitude A lot of religions and spiritual programs build in 'thankyous' and gratefulness as prayers or meditations. Whether or not you're religious, try sitting down for half an hour (turn off the TV, the computer and the phone) (yes, the phone) and make a list of what you're grateful for. You may be surprised at what you come up with.

If you're stuck, start with some you take for granted, perhaps: I have running water; I had the chance to go to school; my legs work. Obviously you don't have to be grateful for everything or deny setbacks and whatever sucks at the moment. Think about how other people live, or friends in a worse situation. A bit of perspective is a lovely accessory to have, and cheaper than jewellery.

Count your blessings, say thanks to people, tell somebody you really like them, pay a compliment. Before every complaint, ask yourself, 'Really?' And gently detach yourself from whingers. See Chapter 14, Friends, for how.

Avoiding burnout Almost everyone has a time (or times) in their life when they find it hard to see meaning, to get enthused, to feel free and joyous. If it isn't a normal down followed by an up in life's road, it might be burnout. Burnout means you need some spiritual and brain rest and recuperation: it's time to jettison some worries and take a chill pill. (No, no, I'm not telling you to take drugs. It's an imaginary chill pill. Okay, think of it as a chill muffin.) If necessary, cut back and throw some responsibilities over the side of your metaphorical boat (make it a nice imaginary yacht with a timber deck and rather handsome, jaunty chappies in striped shirts).

Sit down and write a list of the things you can STOP doing. They have to be responsibilities that weigh on you or things you feel obliged to do. Resign from the committee. Give up the competitive thing you were aiming for that you weren't sure you could fit in. Stop shaving your legs every day, for heaven's sake. Make sure you're not doing a go-slow on your homework. Find time to stick some headphones on and dance, or go for a walk in the fresh air with some mates. Remind yourself who you are and what you like doing, then elbow yourself some space to be that and do that. See Chapter 9, Feelings, for some more stress-busting ideas.

Gaining grit Even the most talented world-beating sports champion has to have more than talent. They need to be able to knuckle down and work really, really hard, for a long time. They need to be able to take setbacks and keep going. They need to be able to allow themselves to 'fail', and keep striving and practising and changing their habits and their brain patterns by sheer will, day after day.

Perseverance and resilience are not often mentioned in a world where it's more fashionable to talk about 'gifts' or 'talents', as if success falls from the sky or springs, fully formed, from a genetic recipe. I mean, you just have to look at, I mean listen to, some of the poor souls who want to be famous singers but sound a bit like a cat trying to get out of a set of bagpipes in the dark.

Part of the skill of grit, tenacity and perseverance is knowing when to quit, cut your losses and move on. Life's too short to stay in a miserable relationship or keep studying something you haaaate to get a soul-sucking job (unless you have a plan to get you to the end of the tunnel and the destination is worth it). And life's too short to finish a book you hate or watch a TV show that's stupid or boring. Or to live out somebody else's idea of who you should be or what kind of work you should do. It's so much easier to work hard at your own dreams than somebody else's.

Standing up for what's right   It's harder to stand up and be counted when you're scared of being picked on, or of being noticed at all. It can be nerve-racking to speak your mind. It's hard enough getting out the door with your underpants not showing, let alone popping along to a street march before lunch. But if you join a group, it can lobby on your behalf and be your 'voice' on things you feel strongly about.

It's not just election votes that count. Think about how to volunteer or support various causes: lots of schools have special fundraising days or even camps that involve helping others. This makes you feel good and can add to your sense of purpose and self-esteem.

More info on philosophy, ethics and the meaning of life

Sophie's World by Jostein Gaarder
Teenage Sophie learns about philosophy in this wildly popular novel.

thisibelieve.org and *This I Believe: The Personal Philosophies of Remarkable Men and Women* edited by Jay Allison & Dan Gediman
Responses to the US National Public Radio series broadcasting the philosophies of famous and 'ordinary' people.

> Many times my parents do not take my ideas on society seriously. I am consistently labelled as going through 'a stage' when I question what we are told through the media, and present my views on such things as religion, abortion, pollution, and world conflict. I have very different views to my parents but I don't think that a difference in opinion should equate to being categorised as going through 'a stage'.   Eloise, 17, Woden, ACT

How to change the world

Your religion or philosophy can make you think not just about yourself, but about the bigger world and what you can do to make a difference (apart from having green hair). Heaps of young people are trying to change things for the better. Others would like to but don't know how they can help.

Being active in politics, protests, social justice causes and charity can make you feel you're involved in something important, that you're doing a good thing. And getting involved is just a phone call or a click away.

Voting

In a democracy everyone has the right and responsibility to vote for the people they want to represent them in government. In Australia you get fined if you don't vote, so you may as well vote for people who share your views. You can't vote until you've turned 18 but you need to register (enrol) to vote when you turn 17 in case a government calls a snap election, because often there's not enough time to register then. Maybe you could make the form a part of a seventeenth birthday present to yourself or a friend.

You can register at most post offices by filling in a form, or go to the Australian Electoral Commission website (see 'More Info' at the end of this chapter). Or drop into an Australian Electoral Commission office – there are hundreds across Australia (addresses are on the website).

Activism

Activism is about having a say in the issues that affect your life and the lives of others – even if you're not old enough to vote. An activist is someone who seeks to create positive change, often by influencing decision makers or taking action in a social or political way.

Some ways to be an activist

- Join a charity, a church or an issue-focused group.
- Write letters, make phone calls and send emails to your local member of parliament or a minister heading a department to ask the government (state or national) to change or make a law.
- Contact the media, from local papers to radio and TV shows, to express your view.
- Protest peacefully by going to meetings, rallies and marches about an issue that matters to you.
- Help organise or go to fundraising events and concerts.
- Collect money for special projects (such as building a school in another country).
- Participate in a boycott (a campaign convincing people not to buy a product such as animal fur, or products made by a company that you feel exploits workers or the environment).
- Invent publicity stunts (legal ones that don't harm yourself or other people).
- Get involved in global campaigns and petitions (for instance, against ocean pollution) – or choose a small, local volunteer program such as visiting old people to cheer them up.

What activism has won   It's young people who have almost always been a major part, if not the leaders, of social movements and social change, and not always just ones concerned with youth issues.

Successful activism has led in many places to the vote for women; equal rights for people with dark skin; workers having the weekend or a day off each week; children not being forced to work, for no or little pay; democratic governments in countries where there were dictators; large fines for polluters; governments signing global agreements on human rights and environmental issues.

The cynical may say the world is in bad shape – but it would be in much worse shape, or no shape at all, if it were not for activists and young people who care.

'Think global, act local'   This means that because we think about the effects on the wider world we will make small changes in our own lives – and if that encourages everyone else to do the same all the little changes will add up to a great big change. For example, actions that are good for the environment include persuading your family to buy a car that uses less petrol, taking a shopping bag instead of getting plastic bags, conserving water and recycling your rubbish.

Pick a cause Don't be bamboozled by the range of possibilities. The important thing is to pick just one cause, and start to do something.

This could range from asking your grandparents to buy you a membership of a group that tries to save animals and their habitats (such as the Australian Conservation Foundation or the World Wide Fund for Nature), to finding out about each Australian political party and joining a youth organisation affiliated to the one you think most reflects your own beliefs and values.

Fundraising

Teenagers tend to have lots of enthusiasm and energy, and they like to help others, so it's often young people shaking the cans and door-knocking to collect money for charities. It's not really the right thing to do unless most or all of the money is going directly to a charity. Many charities have their own shops and websites, and they give all the profit to the good cause, not a tiny percentage.

Although 'philanthropist' (pronounced fill-an-thro-pist) is a word used to describe rich people or organisations that donate lots of money, you're being a philanthropist every time you drop a coin in a collection bucket; buy a raffle ticket when the money raised goes to a good cause; or give your old (but still good) clothes to the local opportunity shop that raises money for, say, programs providing emergency shelter for homeless people.

There are lots of ways you can be involved in fundraising.

- Talk to your family about making an automatic small monthly contribution from a bank account to a major charity on behalf of the family.
- Ask your parents what you can donate (in addition to old clothes) if you can't give money. Maybe blankets or toys.
- Try to use services or buy products that give a percentage of their proceeds to charities, but don't be sucked in: ask for the details. It may be better to buy elsewhere, cheaper, and donate money directly to the charity.
- At Christmas and birthday times remember the charities that sell cards and donation presents (such as a certificate saying a goat has been bought for a village in the name of the person receiving the gift).
- Shake a can for your local children's hospital.
- Join in readathons, walkathons and other fundraising campaigns (except ones that mean you can't eat for a period of time – donate money instead and keep eating to have energy for the cause).

Volunteering

Volunteering means you're performing a service, but not getting paid in money. Nearly 5 million Australians do some sort of volunteer work, just using the time they can spare, even if they're busy. It can also be a fun way of regularly meeting up with friends.

Some common volunteering ideas include:
- dog-walking for elderly or disabled people, or a local animal shelter
- tree planting for conservation projects
- teaching computer skills to older people
- helping people improve their reading and writing skills
- helping refugees and migrants to learn English
- working in a charity shop or an organisation's office.

It's best to do your volunteer work through an accredited organisation, and to make sure your parents are on hand to help with any problem. Always let people know where you are going when you do your volunteer work.

Although you don't get paid for volunteering, other benefits include work experience and other skills; a more impressive résumé for schools, colleges or jobs; impressing your parents with your maturity and independence; useful social and organisational skills; increased confidence; and new friends.

Being active in the world gives you a new perspective on life and makes you realise you can get things done.

More info on staying informed

abc.net.au
Be informed on what's happening locally and globally. The ABC, along with ABCTV and the JJJ radio network, also has an Australia-wide radio station called Radio National, which has programs and podcasts about sport, science, music, world events, philosophy and religion, rural and regional issues, politics and other areas.

unyouth.org.au
The United Nations Youth Association of Australia on international issues.

amnesty.org.au
Amnesty International campaigns for human rights in every country.

More info on getting involved

Australian politics

aec.gov.au
From the Australian Electoral Commission's site choose Enrol to Vote.

alp.org.au, liberal.org.au, nationals.org.au and **greens.org.au**
Sites of the major Australian political parties.

Aboriginal and Islander issues

indigenousliteracyfoundation.org.au
The Indigenous Literacy Foundation gives books to kids in remote communities who may otherwise never have books of their own. You can help by having simple fundraisers at your school, like a gold-coin day.

antar.org.au
Australians for Native Title and Reconciliation: Aboriginal and Islander issues in Australia.

Young people's groups

reach.org.au
The Reach organisation helps 13- to 18-year-olds gain more confidence and a voice in the community, network with other young people, and deal with teen issues.

girlguides.org.au and **scouts.com.au**
As well as community service, guides and scouts do lots of outdoorsy stuff and travel. Scouts now has girls as well as guys.

Environmental groups

acfonline.org.au, greenpeace.org.au, wilderness.org.au, wwf.org.au and **conservationvolunteers.com.au**
Sites for environmental groups: the Australian Conservation Foundation, Greenpeace, the Wilderness Society, the World Wide Fund for Nature and Conservation Volunteers.

Charities

ourcommunity.com.au
Fundraising ideas and guidelines for charities and community groups.

hollows.org.au, care.org.au, oxfam.org.au, worldvision.com.au and **unicef.org.au**
Aid organisations that fund practical development projects for communities in Australia and elsewhere.

thesmithfamily.com.au, salvos.org.au and **redcross.org.au**
Charities helping disadvantaged Australians and others in disaster zones.

Surf Lifesaving

Thanks for reading *Girl Stuff 13+*...

that's quite enough book...
Now it's OVER to you!

Have fun out there, in the great, big, wonderful, exciting, sometimes scary, but generally excellent WORLD!

Need a girl-friendly organisation to donate to for a school fundraiser?

Girls at the Shree Gyangfedi School in Nepal, funded by Adara Group.

Please consider donating to Adara Group, which works with girls and their communities in Uganda and Nepal, providing them with menstrual products, healthcare, and the opportunity to go to school and university. Adara is an Australian organisation and every year it helps more than 50,000 people who live in poverty.

Find out about Kaz's
other books here:

kazcooke.com.au

New edition and reprint acknowledgements

Well, there's no point flouncing about pretending I did it all by myself.

These wonderful and clever people helped with chapter checking and other advice:

Feelings and mental health: Jayashri Kulkarni, Professor and Director, Monash Alfred Psychiatry Research Centre.

Drinking and drugs: Paul Dillon, Head, Drug and Alcohol Research and Training Australia (DARTA).

Puberty changes and pregnancy: Dr Melissa Cameron, specialist paediatrician and IVF consultant.

Body maintenance: Professor Susan Sawyer, Director, Adolescent School of Health, Royal Children's Hospital (RCH), Melbourne.

Food and body image: Dr Zoe McCallum, consultant paediatrician, Department of Gastroenterology and Clinical Nutrition, RCH, Melbourne; Stephanie Campbell, clinical nurse consultant for eating disorders, Adolescent School of Health, RCH.

Exercise and activity: Dr Geraldine Naughton, Professor in Paediatric Exercise Science and Director, Centre for Physical Activity Across the Lifespan, Australian Catholic University.

Brain: Professor Vicky Anderson, Theme Director of Critical Care and Neurosciences, Group Head Child Neuropsychology, Murdoch Childrens Research Institute.

Family: Shelley Atkins, National Manager Policy and Projects, Relationships Australia.

Friends: Helen McGrath, Senior Lecturer in Psychology, Deakin University, author of books and programs about bullying.

Skin: Dr Rod Philips, RCH.

Hair: Dermatologist Belinda Welsh.

Sex: Annie Rose, sex educator of teens, author.

Gender and identity: Michelle Telford, Associate Professor and paediatrician; Rebekah Robertson, author; The Gender Centre.

Perceptions of vulva appearance: Emma Barnard, researcher and sociologist, University of Melbourne School of Population and Global Health, and her project on girls' concerns.

Online safety and other issues: Susan McLean, Director of Cyber Safety Solutions; Mary Lou O'Brien, Director, eLearning, Melbourne Girls Grammar School; Michelle Blanchard, Youth and Sector Engagement Manager, Young and Well Cooperative Research Centre.

Work: Amanda Nguyen, Communications and Media Project Manager, ACTU.

Money and shopping: Delia Rickard, Deputy Chair of the ACCC.

National health policy and related issues: Neil Branch, Federal Department of Health and Ageing.

Participating students from Rockhampton High School (and Jacalean Wines, Head of English), Melbourne Girls Grammar School (and teachers Mary Ross-Volk and Faye Crossman, Head of English) and Albury High School (and Denis Haynes, Head of English).

At Penguin Random House

Grayce Arlov, Clive Hebard, Rachel Scully and Rosie Pearce: Editorial changes management.
Gordon McKenzie: Online Content Manager.
Nicola Young: Patient and meticulous editing.
Tracey Jarrett: Senior Production Controller.
Evi O: Design modifying and new cover.
Julie Gibbs: Commissioning publisher.
Lesley Dunt: Original edition editor.
Adam Laszczuk: Original edition designer.
Rockin' Ron Eady: Typesetting.

Other helpers

Rebecca Hutcheson, Fiona Wood. More Info section: checks by the splendid Greer Clemens.

Original edition acknowledgements

The Survey

The Girl Stuff Survey produced just over 4000 responses. Thanks to each person who sent in their answers to the website questionnaires, which were divided into age groups (10–12, 13–15, 16–18 and 18+). All quotes used from the Survey are from girls who were aged 13 to 18. I changed names on the quotes whenever I thought somebody might need, or want, privacy. Answers from other responses to the Survey provided ideas and info for the book.

The web service technician at Penguin Australia, Brendan Barlow, set up the site, managed it, collated the responses and statistically analysed them, co-ordinated email notifications, ensured the privacy of respondents and printed out approximately 67 gerzillion pages of quotes, all sorted by age and subject. He is a whiz and a wonder.

All hard copies of questionnaire answers have been destroyed. The electronic version of these and the database will be deleted one year after publication, without being used for any other purpose.

The Researcher

Emma Moss worked full-time for three months, finding expert helpers and fact checkers, asking impertinent questions on my behalf, and compiling the information for each chapter. Her efficient work laid the solid foundations for the book, even as she was knitting eyebrows inside for baby Eve, who arrived between the first and second drafts.

The Experts

A great many people lent me their hard-won expertise for this book. I was cheered and sustained by their generosity and dedication, and I would very much like to thank them. (Annoyingly, I cannot blame any of them for mistakes in the book, nor hold them responsible for my opinions, conclusions or emphases.)

Professor Susan Sawyer, head of the Adolescent School of Health at the Royal Children's Hospital, Melbourne, supported *Girl Stuff 13+* from the time it was an idea, bringing her vast medical knowledge and understanding of girls to a close reading of the manuscript. She is, frankly, marvellous.

The Skin chapter is adorned with the suggestions of Dr Tanya Gilmour, dermatologist, surgeon and Fellow of the Australasian College of Dermatologists, and of Dr Josephine Yeatman, dermatologist and query-wrangler of notable stamina. Dr Belinda Welsh, also a dermatologist, was the full bottle on the Hair chapter. Dr Ruth Morley, Senior Research Fellow at the University of Melbourne, advised on sun protection, and dark skin.

I am grateful to the Drugs chapter go-to guru, Paul Dillon, the Information/Media Liaison Manager of the National Drug and Alcohol Research Centre, University of New South Wales.

Thanks also for comments from Geoff Munro, Director of the Community Alcohol Action Network, Renée Otmar, Publishing Manager, and Cindy Van Rooy, Information Officer, all of the Australian Drug Foundation. Others who helped at the research stage were Anita Lal, Research Officer at the VicHealth Centre for Tobacco Control; Jane Martin, Policy and Information Manager, Quit Victoria; the Victoria Police Traffic and Alcohol Division; and Dr David Caldicott, Emergency Research Fellow, Department of Emergency Medicine and Trauma, Royal Adelaide Hospital.

Dr Louise Newman, Director of the New South Wales Institute of Psychiatry, was bombarded with, and commented on, several chapters relating to the mind. Barbara Hocking at SANE Australia, and Monica Hadges, Mental Health Co-ordinator at the Centre for Adolescent Health, Melbourne, were similarly bothered, without saying so.

Maureen Humphrey, clinical specialist dietician at the Royal Children's Hospital, Melbourne, read and commented on the Food chapter more than once, and answered queries, as did Dr Rick Kausman, the Australian Medical Association representative on eating behaviours (who also commented on the Shape chapter). I thought it kind of him not to mention I'd stolen some of his ideas. The National Health and Medical Research Council helped me navigate their online eating guidelines. Dr Zoe McCallum, paediatrician, Senior Lecturer and Co-ordinator of the Child and Adolescent Health Course, Department of Paediatrics, University of Melbourne, had a helpful squiz at the Shape chapter.

The very excellent Dr Melissa Cameron, Adolescent Gynaecology Fellow at the Centre for Adolescent Health, Melbourne, provided info, read the Change and Sex chapters and answered many ludicrous queries.

I'm indebted to sexual health specialists Dr Susan Bagshaw, Fellow of the Australasian Chapter of Sexual Health Medicine, College of Sexual Health Physicians, Chief Resident at the 198 Youth Health Centre, Christchurch, and Senior Lecturer in Adolescent Health, Christchurch School of Medicine, New Zealand; and the splendid Annie Rose, sexual and reproductive health educator and consultant. Donna Tilley at Family Planning Australia helped out with info on the most common questions posed to the FPA Healthline. Advisors on young mums included Angela Steele, Manager of the Young Women's Health Program at the Royal Women's Hospital, Melbourne, and Kylie Houltham, a peer support worker at that hospital's Young Mums Clinic.

Readers of the Family and Friends chapters included Anne Hollands, CEO of Relationships Australia, Lorraine Rose, consultant psychotherapist, and Antony Gleeson, psychotherapist and consultant psychologist, all of New South Wales.

For several useful contributions to the Friends chapter I thank Dr Helen McGrath, counselling psychologist, Senior Lecturer in Education and Psychology in the Faculty of Education at Deakin University and member of the National Coalition Against Bullying.

Brain chapter helpers and readers included Gerald Edmunds, National and New South Wales Executive Director of Brain Australia; Professor Michael Halmagyi, Professor of Neurology, Prince Alfred Hospital, Sydney; Dr Kathryn Strasser, a Sydney GP who's worked in general practice and psychiatry; and Professor Andrew Kornberg, neurologist, Children's Neuroscience Unit, Royal Children's Hospital, Melbourne.

I thank the legal 'team' of James McDougall (Director), Elizabeth Mifsud and Kate Fenessy of the National Children's and Youth Law Centre at the University of New South Wales. And the Shopping chapter helpers Dr Michael Beverland, from the Faculty of Economics and Commerce, Department of Management, University of Melbourne; Jane Roberts, President of Young Media Australia (at the research stage); and especially Dr Teresa Davis, Senior Lecturer, Discipline of Marketing, School of Business, University of Sydney (for reading an early draft of the chapter).

Finance honcho Alan Kohler, publisher of the Eureka Report and ABC TV finance reporter, had smart things to say about the Money chapter. David Elia, CEO of Hostplus Superfund, helped with queries. Advice on study and work was taken from Marcia Devlin, psychologist, higher education consultant and Associate Professor of Higher Education at the University of Melbourne; Julie Farthing, career and life–work consultant; and Cath Bowtell, industrial lawyer and Industrial Officer for the Australian Council of Trade Unions.

Various information was kindly provided by Dr Andrew Kennedy of the Centre for Adolescent Health, and Dr Frederike Veit, clinician at the centre's

Obesity Clinic; Pam Garcia and Dr Bill Cockburn at the Australian Society of Plastic Surgeons; Professor Anthony Smith, Deputy Director of the Australian Centre in Sex, Health and Society, who drew on data from the Australian Longitudinal Study of Health and Relationships; Colin Batrouney, Manager of the Health Promotions Program of the Victorian AIDS Council; Dot Henning, Co-ordinator of the Young People's Health Service (Centre for Adolescent Health) centres; Dr Kathy McNamee, Senior Medical Officer, Family Planning Victoria; Lisa Daniels, Director of the Melbourne Queer Film Festival; Ruth Trickey, herbalist; the National Health and Medical Research Council's Nigel Harding and Dr Katrine Baghurst; Dr Leslie Cannold of Reproductive Choice Australia; Cait Calcutt, Co-ordinator of Children by Choice, Queensland; Rebecca Smith at Family Planning Western Australia; Neil Branch at the federal Department of Health and Ageing; Peter Clifton, Team Leader, Obesity at the CSIRO; Marcus Chen from the Melbourne Sexual Health Centre; Susan Spence, a Tasmanian Ambulance Service paramedic and my lovely cousin; the Melbourne Market Authority; the Media and Marketing department of the federal Department of Education, Science and Training; and the Australian Federal Police.

Kitty Stuckey, wardrobe mistress, adjudicated on the best costume movies. Imogen Lamport, image consultant, contributed to the research on clothes.

Helpers

Consultants on the movie, TV, song and book lists included Rebecca Hutcheson (so helpful she got her own list), Stephanie Bunbury, Philippa Hawker, Greer Clemens, Emma Tom and Dioni Melis. Dee Mason of Diva Data gave good network. Alan Brough prevented a discomfiting omission.

Important friends of the book during research and writing included the incomparable Frank Prain from The Age newspaper's editorial library; Penny Hueston and Julia Heyward; Fiona and Zoe Wood; Patty Ring; Louise Inglis; Lyndal Thorne; Rebecca Lamoin; Michael Koller; Kevin Whyte and Token Artists staff, especially Veronica Barton and Norma Chidichimo; Annie Alderson; Peg McColl; Kristin Otto and other Avenue Bookstore folk; Judith Lucy; Gabrielle Coyne; and most of all TLG and VMCL.

Production and Publishing

Kate Chisholm and Lee Floyd keyed in corrections and, along with Kate Dunlop, isolated chosen quotes from tens of thousands of others. Cath Nicholson lashed her keyboard to mine and helped to make a bridge to the first draft. Jessica Crouch checked ALL the websites (yes), did more photocopying than should be legally allowed and, assisted by Jo Rosenberg, kept the couriers running. The indispensable Jane Drury supplied her customary meticulous queries and crucial editing assistance.

Blessings upon Rockin' Ron Eady, typesetter from Post Pre-press Group, whose job on this project was not unlike crocheting a dictionary while wearing boxing gloves. And all hail Sue Van Velsen, Senior Production Controller, and Anyez Lindop, Publicity Manager.

'More Info' sections (suggested websites and books)

Abusive families 287
Abusive relationship 357
Ads 478
Alcohol 201
Alcohol problems, help with 212
Anger 182
Anxiety and stress 188
Apprenticeships 441
Avoiding diets 93
Becoming a young mum 416
Being attracted to girls 347
Bipolar disorder 258
Body changes 14
Body hair 77
Body image 101
Bra sizes 20
Breast health 145
Career options 441
Careers and education 440–1
Clothes and fashion 495
Contraception and the Morning-after Pill 395
Credit cards and debt 467
Crisis helplines 357
Depression 257
Discrimination and sexual harassment 457
Drinking water 109
Drugs and help with drug problems 235
Eating disorders 265
Education and careers 440–1
Family abuse 357
Fast food, additives and labels 122
Feeling angry 182
Feeling anxiety and stress 188
Feeling optimistic and strong 194
Feminism 519
Financial help for students 442
Finding your own activity 132
Food allergies and intolerances 123
Further education 440
Gambling 470
Gap years 435
Getting involved 542
Girls and women, more info 515
Good eating and recipe books 115
Good friends 298
Grief 190
Guy and girl bits 382
How to use condoms 384
Immunisation 141
Job applications 451
Kids Helpline 357

Legal drugs 222
Looking after your face 44
Looking after your hair 71
Looking for a job 451
Make-up and eyebrows 509
Managing your money 461
Meanness and bullying, dealing with 330
Mental health problems 253
Mobile phone costs 465
Not-so-happy families 285
Optimism 194
Organic products 43
Parties 177
Periods 38
Philosophy, ethics and the meaning of life 537
Piercing and tattoos 62
Pimples and blackheads 51
Pregnancy counselling 408
Pregnancy termination (abortion) 412
Psychosis and schizophrenia 269
Relationships 358
Religion, philosophy and ideas 534
Résumé or CV 451
Rip-offs and scams 469
Scams 441
Schoolies 435
Self-confidence 164
Self-harm 259
Severe anxiety 255
Sex 372
Sexual assault and rape 401
Sexually transmitted diseases 384
Shopping online 481
Skin marks 57
Sleep 247
Smear tests 147
Smoking 220
Social media and phones 304
Staying informed 541
Step or blended families 295
Student exchange programs 441
Study and homework strategies 427
Suicide 267
Sun protection 55
Sweating 59
TAFEs 440
When families break up 290
Women in music 520
Workers' rights and responsibilities 457
Your brain 243
Your girly bits 24

550 **index**

Index

A

abdominal muscles 134
abortion (pregnancy termination)
   'abortion pill' (RU486) 395, 409, 410
   antiabortion versus prochoice debate 406, 410
   surgical 405, 409, 410–12
above healthy weight
   getting a healthier life 86–7
   going to a doctor 85, 86
   'obesity' 85
   patches or gels no help 92
   smoking no help 91
   see also dieting
abstinence 366–8, 394
abusive relationships
   boyfriends and girlfriends 355, 356–7
   family 177, 284, 286–7
   how to get out of 356–7
accessories 58, 492, 493, 495
acne 45
acquired immune deficiency syndrome (AIDS) 388
   from piercing and tattoos 60
activism 538–9
activity *see* physical activity
adoption
   finding out about 292
   finding your birth parents 292
   for your own baby 405, 417
adrenaline 180
advertising 472–4, 490, 502–3
   when is an ad not an ad? 475–8
affirmations 193
AIDS *see* acquired immune deficiency syndrome
alcohol
   advertisements 200
   bubbly drinks 200, 215
   causing dehydration 30, 197
   and depression 257
   effect on body 197, 200, 201
   effect on brain 199, 204, 241
   girls more affected 199–201
   legal age for buying 196
   mixing with illegal drugs 207, 214, 224
   mixing with legal drugs 214, 222
   no recommended amount 200
   percentages in different drinks 197
   pre-mixed drinks 198, 199–200, 215
   in a standard drink 198, 200
   and violence 208
   and weight gain 201
   see also drinking; drunkenness
alcohol addiction and dependence 195, 199, 202, 211
alcohol poisoning 210
'alternative' remedies 142
ambulance, calling for
   for drug reaction 233
   for out-of-control drunkenness 210
anal sex 378, 381, 386, 387, 394, 399
   condoms for 378
androgen 46, 50, 59
anger 182–3, 189
anorexia 251, 261–2
antiabortion versus prochoice debate 406, 410
antibiotics and contraceptive pill 391
Anti-Discrimination Commission 457
antiperspirants 59
anxiety
   and brain health 241
   and eating 112
   as a grief reaction 189
   hints for handling 184–5, 188, 255
   severe 250, 254–5
   symptoms 184
   talking to someone 187
   treatment for 255
   what girls worry about 186
   see also stress
apologising 159, 275, 308
applying for a job 445, 446–8, 451
apprenticeships 438
   for girls 439
areola 15, 403
arguments, family
   body language (unhelpful) 283
   dumb things to say 283
   setting guidelines 281
   taking the heat out of 281–2
   useful things to say 284
armpits
   shaving 72, 73, 75
   sweating from 58
arms, hair on 11, 72, 73
asexual 347
'aspirational appeal' in marketing 474
assertiveness 158, 323
asthma and exercise 130
astringents 41–2, 51
astrology 529
atheists 531
ATM (automatic teller machine) 461
attention deficit disorder 238
attraction to certain people 332, 333–5
Australian Consumers' Association 111
Australian Dental Association 60
Australian Electoral Commission 538
Australian Natural Therapists Association 31, 48
Australian Society of Plastic Surgeons 57, 95
autism 238

B

back, hair on 72
backhanded compliments 162, 164
backing up your computer 425
bacterial vaginosis 148
bad breath 143
'bad fats' 118
'baked not fried' 121
bank account 459–61
banking online 459
'barn-raised' food 121
becoming a sexual person 360–2
becoming a young mum
   after you've had the baby 415
   good things about 413
   hard things about 413
   making the decision 413
   pregnancy and birth 414
   support network 414, 415
beer 197, 198
being single is fine 355
being thin is okay 81
belief systems 528–37
bikini wax 74
binge drinking 195, 199
binge eating 89, 262–3
bipolar disorder 250, 258
birth control *see* contraception
birth parents, finding 292
birthmarks 56–7, 95
bisexuality 333, 344
blackheads 40, 41, 45–6, 51
bleaching body hair 77
blended families 293–5
blood alcohol content 196, 207–8
'blue light' for pimples 50
blusher 499, 501
blushing 180–1
BO (body odour) 59

index 551

body changes
  body hair 9, 11–12, 23, 56, 63
  order of changes 13–14
  what to expect 11–14
  when they start 9, 13
body confidence 154
body fat 80–1
  assessing yourself 81–4
body hair
  in moles 56
  purpose 63
  removal 72–7
  and starvation 72
  when it starts 9, 11–12, 14
  where it develops 11, 23, 73
body image
  accepting compliments 101
  assessing yourself 81–4
  cosmetic procedure problems 95–7
  and mirrors 95, 100
  not liking your bits 79, 95–7
  obsessing about 88, 100, 250
body language (unhelpful) 283
Body Mass Index calculation 82
body moisturiser 41
body types 79
bones
  stress fractures 92
boob tubes 495
books for girls 522–3
boredom and eating 112
Botox injections 96
bottom, hair on 73
boyfriend violence 286
brain
  being proud of 242–3
  exercising 241–2
  girls' brains 238
  guys' brains 238
  main bits 239–40
brain chemicals 125, 179, 240, 241, 251, 257, 268
brain health
  and depression 241, 256, 257
  effect of alcohol 199, 204, 241
  effect of drugs 223, 226, 228, 241
  injury to 241
  looking after 107, 241
  sleep for 241, 244, 246
brand loyalty 473, 503
bras
  alternatives 15–16, 19
  for big bosoms 17
  cleavage 16
  fitting 17, 20
  padded 16
  reason for 18
  working out your size 19

bread 106, 111, 113
breakfast 110, 111
breakfast bars 110
breaking up
  being the dumpee 354–5
  being the dumper 354
  of families 288–90
  heartbreak 358
breasts
  before a period 16, 30
  big 17
  bouncing 16, 18
  changes to look out for 13, 145
  changing your shape 16
  getting bigger 13, 14, 15
  jiggling 18, 19
  little 16
  lumpy 16, 145
  no milk until pregnant 15
  one bigger than the other 16
  painful in pregnancy 403
  rude comments about 12, 16, 18
  sagging 18
  swollen and tender 403
  touching or kissing 363
breast checks 16, 139, 145
breast enlargement surgery 95
breast reduction surgery 17, 95, 96
breathing to relax 185
bronzer 499
brothers 279
bruises, treating 134
budget, making a 461
bulimia 262–3
bulk–billing doctors 139, 144
bullying
  changing the feelings caused by 328
  dealing with 313, 323–4
  different from meanness 313
  getting backup 325–6
  how to stop being a bully 321
  Intentional Freezeout 314, 316–17
  keeping evidence of 324
  on phone and computer 301, 313, 324
  reasons (not excuses) for 319
  snappy comebacks 327
  standing up for somebody else 322
  taking a break from 329
  types of 314
  what is it? 313, 314
  who the bullies are 317–19
  whom to tell 315, 324, 325–6
  workplace 455, 457
bum crack, revealing 495
burnout, avoiding 536

C

caffeine 30, 121, 185
  and sleep 120, 245
cakey things 117
calcium 32, 108, 109, 113
camisole tops 19
candida (thrush) 148
cannabis 223, 224, 225, 228, 268
carbohydrates 107
career choices 436–7
cars
  drink drivers 207–8
  personal safety 174–5
  saving for 462
catastrophisers 192
causes (beliefs and values) 540
  social conscience donation 478
celebrity crush 332, 335
celebrity handouts 477
celebrity labels 487
celibacy 366–8, 394
'cellulite' 80–1
Centrelink 444
cereals 106, 111, 113, 117
cerebellum 239
cervical cancer
  and human papilloma virus (HPV) 141, 387
  immunisation against some forms of HPV 141, 387
  smear (or pap) test for 146
cervix 22, 146
changing the world 538–41
cheering yourself up 193
'chemical-free' products 43
chewing gum 143
child care 413, 415
children, legal rights 177, 287
chips 106, 113, 118
chlamydia 386
chocolate 30, 45, 120, 245
cigarette smoke 47
cigarettes
  herbal 219
  'light' or 'mild' 219
  menthol 219
  stuff the cigarette companies don't tell you 219
  see also smoking
circumcision of penis 375
clairvoyants 530
clear or white secretion on undies 12, 13, 25
cleavage 16
clinical (major) depression 191, 150, 256–7

clitoris 24
    clitoral hood 24
    stimulated in orgasm 362, 380
    touching in masturbation 360, 361
clothes
    accessories 58, 492–3, 495
    advertising on 490
    disasters 491–2, 495
    dressing to 'attract' guys 489–90
    dressing to be noticed 489
    dressing to suit a religion 491
    labels 83, 487
    problem looks 489–90
    returning to shop 491–2
    sales 491–2
    second-hand 488
    shopping for 488, 491–2
    signature style 488
    sizes 83, 488
    style 488
    vintage 485
    for work 453–4
    see also fashion
clubbing or dancing
    dehydration 215, 233
cocaine 223, 232
cocktails 197, 198, 200
coffee 30, 120, 121, 245, 430
cognitive therapy 250, 255
cola drinks 30, 120, 185, 245
cold sores 386
colleges 439
'colloidal silver' dangers 48
'coming' (orgasm) 362, 380
'coming out' (sexuality) 346, 347
community health centres 14, 38, 138,
    144, 184, 383, 384, 392, 404, 414
competition prizes in marketing 478
complementary medicines 123, 142
compliments
    accepting 101
    backhanded 162, 164
computer, backing up 425
computer bullying 321, 324
concealer (make-up) 499
conditioner
    action 64
    claims on the label 66
    combined with shampoo 64
    for dandruff 70
    facts about 65
    for oily hair 65
condoms
    for anal sex 378
    as contraception 367, 369, 373,
        387, 389
    disposing of 385
    guys practising to put on 373

how to use 385
    with lubricant 383, 385
    protection against STIs 369, 380,
        383, 389
    putting on before sex 374, 385
    removing 385
    using with contraceptive Pill
        390, 391
confidence
    being assertive 158, 323
    being cool 153, 160–1
    changing the family rules 170–1
    'cool group' 160–1
    getting confident 155–64
    knowing who you are 165–7
    not feeling confident 154
    overcoming shyness 159–60
    practising 157
    responding to horrible
        comments 161–4
    security and stranger danger
        172–6, 398
    what girls do feel confident
        about 168–9
    what girls don't feel confident
        about 154
congratulating yourself 535
contraception 21, 207, 367, 371, 380
    emergencies 395, 401, 410
    methods 389–95
    see also condoms
contraceptive pill (Pill)
    antibiotics interfere with 391
    a combination of hormones 389
    using condom as well 390, 391
    effect on periods 389
    doesn't prevent STIs 390
    good points about 388–9
    how to take 390–1
    missing 391
    for period pain 31, 32
    for pimples 50, 389
    for PMS 31, 32
    on prescription 389, 391
    side effects 389, 391
contract of employment 451
controlling behaviour 286–7
cooking 111
cool 153, 160–1
    what's not cool 160
'cool group' 160–1
cordial 143
corpus callosum 239
cosmetic centres 57
cosmetic physician 57
cosmetic procedure problems 95–7
cosmetic surgeon 46, 57, 77
cosmetic surgery

birthmarks 56–7
    breast reduction 17, 95
    downsides and dangers 96
    only in special circumstances
        95, 96
cosmetics companies' claims 42–4
'costume movies' 485, 494
counselling (talking therapy) 250,
    259, 292
counsellors, seeing for
    abusive relationship 356
    anxiety 184, 187, 255
    body image problem 95
    drinking problem 211
    drug problem 234
    family conflict and breakdown
        282, 288–9
    grief 190
    mental health problems 249, 250,
        255, 257, 259, 266
    rape 400
    see also gay and lesbian
        counsellors; school
        counsellors; pregnancy
        counselling services
counting your blessings 535–6
'cover sticks' 48
covering letter for job application 448
crabs (pubic lice) 388
cramps with period 31–2
credit cards 466, 467, 483
'credit risks' 463
creeps online 303–4
crisis lines 357
crop-tops 15–16, 19, 30
crushes 332, 335, 344, 360
crying in grief 189
cults 534
curling tongs 67
curriculum vitae (CV) 446–8, 456
custody arrangements 288
cyberbullying 313
cystitis 149
cysts 46

D

dairy foods 108
dandruff 70
'date rape' 399
dating
    asking and being asked 338–9
    blabbing about 341
    first date hints 340–2
    give up if he's not interested 340
    group date 338

index   553

kissing 342–3, 362
paying the bill 341
rejection 339–40
second date 342
daydreaming 242
debit cards 461, 466
dehydration
    from alcohol 30, 197
    when clubbing or dancing 215, 233
    when exercising 133
    headaches from 430
delusions 240
denial in grief 189
dental floss 143
dentist, seeing 143
deodorants 59
depilatories 76
Depo Provera injection 392–3
depression
    and alcohol 257
    and brain health 241, 256, 257
    can be caused by dieting 90
    clinical (major) depression 191, 150, 256–7
    feeling a bit down 189–91
    a grief reaction 189
    and sadness 191
    severe 191, 250, 256
    and stress 257
    treatment 257
dermatologist 46, 50
diaphragm (or cap) 393
diet
    and hair 65
    and skin health 43
diet pills 91
'diet' drinks 88, 119, 121
dieticians 86, 114, 263
dieting
    blame the diet not yourself 91
    cause of depression 90
    diets tried that didn't work 94
    'don'ts' 90–1
    and exercise 90, 92
    fad diets 89, 90
    fasting 90–1
    low-carb 107, 143
    risk factor for eating disorders 87, 89, 90, 261
    short-term 87–8, 89, 90
    smoking no help 91
    why diets don't work 89–90
    why you shouldn't diet 88, 90
    'yo-yo' dieting 88, 90
direct marketing 475
dirt not a cause of pimples 45

discharge from vagina 12, 13, 25, 148
discrimination
    religious 531–2
    at work 455
distance learning 440
divorce 289
doctor, going to the
    before becoming vegetarian or vegan 114
    before taking a supplement 109, 114
    for changes in moles 56
    checking for breast lumps 139
    for contraception 389, 392
    for drinking or other drug problem 211, 234
    for a mental health problem 184, 187, 249, 250, 251
    for painful sex 377
    for period problems 27, 28, 32, 34, 35
    for persistent dandruff 70
    for pimples 48, 50–1
    about pregnancy 404
    for regular checks 138–9
    for smear (or pap) test 139
    for snoring 246
    for STI symptoms 383–4
    for STI tests and treatments 396
    for weight problems 85, 86
    taking someone with you 139
    things you should tell them 139
'domestic' violence 286
donated prizes (marketing) 478
dopamine 179, 240
douching 148, 149, 393
dreams 244, 246
drinking
    deciding whether or not to drink 202
    and driving 207–8
    getting drunk quicker than you meant to 200–1
    glass sizes 198, 200
    legal age to start 196
    making rules for 213
    in pregnancy 200
    reasons for 202
    safe environment for 213–14
    a sneaky strategy for not drinking 202
    spiked drinks 208, 230, 399
    taking control 213–15
    taking it slowly and carefully 214
    things to say when you're not drinking 203
    see also alcohol; drunkenness

drinking problem 195, 199, 202, 211
driving
    and drinking 207–8
    mobile phones turned off 465
drugs
    to keep awake when studying 431–2
    see also alcohol; cigarettes; illegal drugs; legal drugs, over-the-counter and prescription
drunkenness
    binge drinking 195, 199, 262–3
    coping with drunk person 209
    getting drunk quicker than you meant to 200–1
    girls more affected 199–200
    hospitalisation for 210
    risks associated with 207–9, 214
    stages of 204–5
    throwing up 205
    waiting for an ambulance 210
    warning signs 197
    when to call an ambulance 210
'dry sex' 394
dry skin 40, 41, 43
dryness during sex 377
dyslexia 238

E

ear plugs for noisy places 142
earphones and hearing loss 142
ears, pinning back 95
eating
    before bed 245
    and boredom 112
    breakfast 110, 111
    changing family habits 122
    don't ban foods, just ration them 112
    don't eat alone 112
    don't obsess about measuring 112
    eating quickly 110
    hints for enjoying food 105
    non-hungry 'reasons' for 112
    portion size 107, 112
    and skin health 43
    stop when you're full 112
    try something new 112
    what you don't need much of 116–21
    what you need 105–9
    when you're hungry 105, 112

554   index

eating disorders 82
  anorexia nervosa 251, 261–2
  binge eating 89, 263
  bulimia nervosa 262–3
  guys 262
  helping someone with 264
  risk factors 87, 89, 90, 261
  steps to recovery 263–4
  weird behaviour 260
Eating Disorder Not Otherwise Specified 261
eating plans 105
'eating program' 92
ecstasy 223, 230, 231, 268
eczema 40, 149
education options 41, 437, 438–40
EFTPOS (Electronic Funds Transfer Point of Sale) 466
eggs (in ovaries) 14, 21, 26, 395
ejaculation of semen 362, 374, 380, 381
electrolysis for hair removal 76
e-mail
  bullying 313
  flirting and sexy talk 335
  safety 468
  scams 468
embarrassment 180–1
  handy recovery lines 181
emergency contraception 395
emergency rescue crew 174
emotional abuse 286
emotional blackmail 335
'emotional intelligence' 243
emphysema 218
employment websites 444
endometrium 26, 27
endorphins 125, 240
endorsements in marketing 477
energy drinks 30, 117, 120, 121, 185, 245
energy snacks 430
Equal Opportunity Commission 457
erection 362, 375
exams
  cheating 432
  results 431, 433
  strategies 431–2
exercise
  and asthma 130
  before bedtime 245
  for your brain health 241
  before period 31
  dehydration 133
  and diet 106
  and dieting 90, 92
  family involvement in 135–6
  first aid for injuries 134
  overdoing it 92
  and skin health 43
  stretching before 130
  see also physical activity
exercise plan 130
exercising your brain 241–2
extremism with beliefs 532–3
eye make-up 500, 501
eyebrows
  changing shape of 508–9
  dandruff 70
  waxing or plucking 72, 73, 76, 508–9
eyebrow pencil 500, 505
eyelashes
  false 500
  no dye jobs 70
eyeliner 500
eyeshadow 500, 501, 505

F

facial cleansers 40–1, 49
facial hair 72
facial skin
  acne 45
  birthmarks 56–7, 95
  blackheads 40, 41, 45–6, 51
  freckles 54
  hints for health 43
  inherited 40
  moles 56, 95
  pimples 45–51
  scars 56
  soap on 40, 49
fad diets 89, 90
fair-weather friendship 332
fake tans 55
falling in love
  attraction 332, 333–5
  crushes 332, 335, 344, 360
  dating 338–43
  guys to avoid 336–7
  how to make him like you 337
  keeping your friends 352–3
  kinds of love 332
  movies for every stage 348–51
  relationships 331–58
  songs for every stage 348–51
  symptoms 334
  see also sex
fallopian tubes 21, 26
false eyelashes 500
family
  being adopted 292
  arguments 281–4
  changing the rules 170–1
  different combos 291–5
  eating habits 122
  happy 274–9
  helping deal with meanness and bullying 324, 325
  involvement in exercise 135–6
  not-so-happy 281–5
  'partner parade' 292–3
  sole parent 292
  step or blended 293–5
  telling about pregnancy 405
  violence *see* family abuse
family, breaking up
  adjusting to 289, 292–3
  custody arrangements 288
  living arrangements 288–9
  sharing the parenting 288
  talking it through with parents 288–9
  things to know about separation and divorce 289, 292
  understanding 288
  upside of separation 290
family, happy
  brothers and sisters 279
  conversation starters with a parent 276
  family rules 277–8, 279, 280
  getting to know a parent 275
  getting on with a parent 274–6
  what girls say are the strict rules 280
  when a parent isn't there for you 276
family, not-so-happy
  conflict between partners 282
  dumb things to say in an argument 283
  not feeling safe in 282
  taking the heat out of arguments 281–2
  tension-breakers 282
  useful things to say in arguments 284
  when parents are hopeless 282, 284
  your body language 283
family abuse 284
  crisis lines 357
  emotional abuse 286
  legal rights of children and young people 177, 287
  physical abuse 286
  sexual abuse 286–7
  what to do about it 286–7
family arguments 281–4
family counselling services 282
Family Court 288

index 555

family love 332
Family Planning Clinics 24, 38, 144,
    389, 392, 404, 407, 410, 414
    SHINE clinics, SA 407
family rules 170–1, 277–8, 279, 280
fanaticism (beliefs) 532–3
'farm-raised' food 121
fashion 492
    changes in 485–6
    in 'costume movies' 485, 494
    'knock-offs' 487
    labels 83, 487
    meaning 485
    models 84, 487
    'vintage' clothes 485
    websites and magazines 486
    'tips' 486
fashion bullies 489
fashion mistakes 495
fashion shows 486
fast food 112, 116, 118
fasting 90–1
'fat-free' food 118, 121
fat-pinch caliper test 82–3
fats and oils 108, 118
feelings
    anger 182–3, 189
    anxiety and stress 112, 184–8,
        189, 250, 254–5
    embarrassment 180–1
    and food 112
    getting strong 192–3, 194
    moodiness 12, 179
    optimism 192, 193
    see also confidence
feeling down 189–91
    ten things to avoid 190
feet 11, 13, 16
feisty women
    10 amazing books for girls 523
    10 great Aussie books for teens 523
    10 great book series for girls 522
    top 10 female action-adventure
        characters 525
    top 10 girlfriends'-night-in
        movies 524
    top 10 ladies' night comedies 524
    top 10 movies with a heroine 525
    top 10 teen romance movies 524
    top 10 TV shows for girls 525
female reproductive system
    see girly bits
feminine hygiene products
    see pads; tampons
feminism
    calling yourself a feminist 517
    frequently asked questions
        about 516–17

what women fought for 511–12
    see also feisty women
fibre in food 106
finances, sharing 467
financial scams 468
fired from job 456
first aid for exercise injuries 134
first aid courses 141
first date hints 340–2
first time sex
    doesn't usually hurt 377
    dryness during 377
    faking orgasm 379
    foreplay 363–4, 377
    how long it takes 377
    how you look 378
    lubricant 377
    not enjoying it 379, 382
    reaction to 374
    sexual positions 378
    talking about 377
fish 111
fizzy (bubbly, soft) drinks 119, 143
flashbacks 255
flexibility in life 535
fluid retention 30
fluoride 109, 143
food
    for the brain 107
    enjoying 105
    and feelings 112
    'natural' 121
    takeaway 112, 116, 118, 122
    what you don't need much of
        116–21
    what you need 105–15
    see also eating disorders;
        healthy eating
food allergies 123
food intolerances 123
food labels 117, 118, 119,
    120, 121
foreplay 363–4, 377
foreskin 375
Formal, school 338, 346–7
fortified wines 197, 198
fortune tellers 530
foster care for your baby 417
foundation (make-up)
    498, 499
freckles 54
'free range' 121
freebies 477, 486
freezing out (being mean)
    314, 316–17
French kissing 343
frenemies 308
'fresh' food 111, 121

friends
    choosing 299
    fair-weather 332
    fixing a friendship 306
    frenemies 308
    friendship going bad 305–7
    gay 346
    good friends 297–300, 332
    with guys 300, 336
    helping deal with meanness and
        bullying 324, 326
    jealous kind 306
    keeping during relationship 352–3
    leaving a bad friendship 306–7
    making new 307–8, 309
    mean 329
    meeting an online 'friend' 304
    on social media and your phone
        301–4
    reassuring friends if you're
        gay 345
    saying it face-to-face 307
    saying sorry 308
    stopping friendship cold 307
    starter sentences with someone
        new 307, 309
    taking sides 313
friendship groups
    fitting in 310
    moving to a new group 309, 312
    peer group 310
    'peer pressure' 310–11
frontal cortex 239, 240
fruit 106, 111
fruit drinks and juices 109, 119, 143
fundraising 540
further education 437–41

G

gambling 469
gap year 435, 439
gardnerella infection 148
gay friends 346
gay guys 337, 344
gay parents 291
gay relationships see lesbian
    relationships; bisexuality;
    homosexuality
gay rights 344, 531
gay and lesbian counsellors 346, 347
general practitioners (GPs) see doctor,
    going to the
genital herpes 386
genital warts (HPV) 141, 146, 387

556   index

genitals (your outsidey bits) 21, 22–3, 97
getting involved 538–41
'getting over' grief 190
getting strong 192–3, 194
   things to cheer you up 192
GHB (illegal drug) 230
giant carrot, looking like 55
girl brains 238
Girl Stuff survey 68, 72, 73, 94, 154, 168–9, 186, 207, 277, 280, 313, 314, 319, 326
girlfriend violence 286
girly bits (inside)
   cervix 22, 146
   fallopian tubes 21, 26
   ovaries 13, 14, 21, 26, 50
   uterus 22, 26
   see also vagina
girly bits (outside)
   clitoris 24, 360, 361, 362, 380
   hymen 23, 367, 368, 377
   labia majora 23, 74
   labia minora 23
   looking at 22–3
   shaving 74
   vaginal opening 23
   vulva 23, 35, 149
   worries if they're normal 79
girly bits, infections
   and body-piercing 60
   common non-STIs 47, 148–9
   tests for 147
   see also sexually transmitted infections (STIs)
glass ceiling 514
GLBT (gay, lesbian, bisexual and transgender) 346
going all the way (penis-in-vagina sex)
   condoms 367, 369, 373, 387, 389
   doesn't usually hurt 277
   dryness during 377
   ejaculation 362
   first time 373, 374
   foreplay 363–4
   going back 382
   how long it takes 377
   orgasm 374
   positions 378
   talking about it beforehand 373
   what happens 374
going to a community health centre
   see community health centres
gonorrhoea 387
good friends 297–300, 332
'good mood' brain chemicals 125
good relationships 352–3
gossip 314, 315, 355

GPs see doctor, going to the
grains (food) 106–7
gratitude for what you have 535–6
grief 189
   'getting over it' 190
   reactions to 189–90
'grit' 536–7
group date 338
groups
   fitting in 310
   Intentional Freezeout 314, 316–17
   moving on to new 312
   'peer pressure' 310–11
growth spurt 13, 57, 244
guarana drinks 30, 120
'gurus' 534
'gut reactions' 239
guys
   abusive 356–7
   to avoid 336–7
   brains 238
   don't like too much make-up 504
   dressing to 'attract' 489–90
   eating disorders 262
   as friends 300, 336
   gay 337, 344
   giving up if he's not interested 340
   going through similar changes 336
   hints that a guy might be a good one 337
   hormones 21
   how to make him like you 337
   mean 336
   older guys and STIs 369
   rejects you on a date 339–40
   stuff to know 336
   see also dating; falling in love
guys' bits
   scrotum 375
   testicles 375, 384
   see also penis
guys and sex
   ejaculation 362, 374, 380, 381
   going too fast 374
   older guys 369
   orgasm ('coming') 362, 363, 364, 374, 380
   practising putting on condom 373
   putting condom on before sex 374, 385
   removing condom 385
   symptoms of STIs 384
   what guys can say to pressure you into sex 370
gyms 134
gynaecologists 144

H

hair, body see body hair
hair, head
   chlorine from pools 65
   colour 64
   composition 64
   curly or kinky 67
   dandruff 70
   and diet 65
   dry 64
   dyed 68, 70
   frizzy 68
   keeping it looking good 65
   keeping off face and neck 47
   oily 12, 64, 65
   straight 67
   straightening 67, 68
   untangling wet hair 65
   washing every few days 65
hair dryers 65
hair dye 68, 70
hair products
   conditioner 64–5, 66, 68
   labels 66
   shampoo 64–5, 66
hairstyles 68–9
halitosis 143
hallucinations 268
handbags 493
hands 11, 13, 181
hands-only sex 394
happy families 274–9
harassment see bullying
having a baby see becoming a young mum
'having sex' 363
head injuries or knocks 134
headaches
   from big heavy breasts 17
   from dehydration 430
   from looking at computer screens 430
health
   girls' and women's 144–9
   healthy weight range 80, 81, 85, 86–7, 116
   managing 138–43
   support groups 140
   when above healthy weight 84
   see also doctor, going to the
'health' products 92, 116
health websites 140
healthy eating
   avoiding pimples 47
   breakfast 110, 111
   changing family habits 122

index   557

healthy weight range 80, 81, 85, 86–7, 116
hearing problems 142
heartbreak after breakup 358
height changes 11, 12, 13
helplines see Kids Helpline; pregnancy counselling services; and also 'More Info Sections' (list of helplines) 550
hepatitis B and C 387
herbal cigarettes 219
herbal remedies
    for period pain 32
    for PMS 31
    prescribers 48
    telling your doctor 139, 142
herbalists 31
heroin 223, 230
heterosexuality 333, 346
'hickeys' 343
high heels 492
hippocampus 239
hitchhiking (not safe) 175
HIV (human immunodeficiency virus) 60, 61, 388
home alone, security tips 172
homeopathy 31, 141, 142
homework and study
    backing up computer 426
    note-taking 429, 431
    no plagiarism 426
    reliable resources 426
    schedule 422–3, 425
    study space 425–6
    study tips 430
    when it's too hard 424
homosexuality 333, 344, 346
hopelessness, feeling of 191
hormones
    androgen 46, 50, 59
    and facial hair 72
    guys 21
    melatonin 244
    and moodiness 179
    oestrogen 21, 26, 50, 179
    produced in ovaries 13
    progesterone 21, 179, 392, 395
    testosterone 21
    triggering puberty 12, 21
horoscopes 529
HPV (human papilloma virus) 141, 146, 387
human immunodeficiency virus (HIV) 60, 61, 388
human papilloma virus (HPV) 141, 146, 387
Human Rights and Equal Opportunity Commission 457

humanist (non-religious) ethics 531
hymen 24, 377
    not always present 23
    and periods 23
    and virginity 367, 368
'hypo-allergenic' skin products 40, 42

I

ice (illegal drug) 229, 268
icing an injury 134
'ideal' body shape 79
illegal drugs
    addiction and dependence 223, 227
    adverse reactions 223, 233
    with alcohol 207, 214, 224
    and brain health 223, 226, 228, 241
    chart of commonly used 228–32
    deciding whether to take 226–7
    drinking water 233
    downsides 223
    helping someone with a problem 234
    legal risk (penalties) 224, 225
    minimising harm 233
    no safe dose 224
    overdoses 223, 224, 233
    possession and trafficking 224, 225
    postal screening for 226
    and psychosis (severe mental illness) 223, 224, 268, 269
    random roadside testing 226
    reactions to 224
    reasons not to take 226–7
    risks of use 224, 234
    when to call an ambulance 233
    when travelling 224, 225
    why people take 223
immune system 138, 184
immunisation 140, 142
    before piercing 60
    before tattoos 61
    before travelling 140
    boosters 140–1
implant for contraception 392
ingrown hairs from shaving 74, 76
inhalants (for illegal purpose) 232
injection for contraception 392–3
injuries, icing 134
inner labia 23
Intentional Freezeout 314, 316–17
intersex 347
intrauterine device (IUD) 393

Invisible Cloak of Dignity 315
iron supplements 108, 113
isotretinoin (pimple medication), dangers of 50–1
IUD (intrauterine device) 393

J

jealous friends 306
job advertisements 444–5
job application 446–8
job interview 449–51, 454
jogging 131
juices see fruit drinks and juices

K

karma 530
keratin 51, 64
Kids Helpline 282, 313, 325, 357
kissing 342–3, 362
knock-off designs 487

L

labels
    fashion 83, 487
    food products 117, 118, 119, 120, 121
    salt content 120
    shampoos and conditioners 66
    sugar content 117
    traps (clothes) 487
'label queen' 487
labia majora (outer labia) 23, 74
labia minora (smaller labia) 23
laser treatment
    hair removal 76–7
    skin marks 57
laxatives 91
learning
    extra tutoring 428–9
    listening to the teacher 429, 431
    note-taking 429, 431
    reading skills 428–9
    your learning style 428
    see also exams; homework and study
leg hair 11
    shaving 72, 73, 75
    waxing 76

legal drugs, over-the-counter
    and prescription
        addiction to 222
        with alcohol 214, 222
        emergency help 210, 222
        illegal overseas 225
        painkillers 220
        taking more than prescribed 221
        taking someone else's drug 221
        see also alcohol; cigarettes;
            illegal drugs
legal rights of children and
    young people 177, 287
lesbian relationships
    being a lesbian 345–7
    'coming out' 346
    health checks 379
    how do you know you're
        gay? 344–5
    reassuring your friends 345
    sex 379
    your sexuality is up to you 345
lice (crabs, pubic lice) 388
light beer 197
'light' cigarettes 219
'light' foods 121
lip gloss 499, 500
lip make-up 499–500
lip piercing 60
lipliner 499
liposuction 95
lipstick 499–500
liqueurs 197
'lite' foods 121
loneliness in grief 189
looking 'hot' 519–20
looking for a job 444–5
lopsidedness 102
love
    different kinds of 332
    falling in 333–7
    movies and songs for every stage
        of 348–51
    relationships 352–8
    and sex 396–7
    sexting dangers 335
lovebites 343
'low fat' foods 118
low self-esteem 261
low-carb diets 107, 143
low-fat fizzy drinks 119
'loyalty programs' 477
lubricant 360, 377, 383, 385
lung damage from cigarettes
    217, 218
lust 332

M

magazines
    and advertising 476
    and fashion 486
    good ones for teens 476
    and their websites 476
magnesium supplements 32
make-up
    advertisements 501, 502
    brand loyalty 503
    cost 502
    'essentials' 498–501
    hints for using 505
    hypoallergenic 505
    'not tested on animals' 501
    'organic' 501
    removing 505
    safe 501
    school rules 503, 504
    selling 502–3
    with sunscreen 505
    too much 58, 503–4
    see also specific products
make-up artist 505
manic depression (bipolar disorder)
    250, 258
'map of Tassie' 13, 73
Marie Stopes clinics 407, 410, 414
marketing
    'aspirational appeal' 474
    brand loyalty 473, 503
    direct 475
    industry tricks 92, 474, 475,
        477–8
    magazines and their websites 476
    see also advertising
mascara 500
masturbation 360–1, 363, 364
meal 'replacements' or
    'supplements' 92
meanness
    bad excuses for 318
    different from bullying 313
    in friends 329
    gossip and rumours 314, 315
    in guys 336
    how to stop being mean 321
    the Intentional Freezeout
        314, 316–17
    mean things 314
    nasty tactics 315
    real reasons for 319
    to those who are 'different' 314
    why it happens 317–18
    when you're the mean one
        319, 321

meanness, dealing with
    DIY tactics 323–4
    friends helping 324, 326
    keeping evidence of 324
    help from home 325
    Kids Helpline 325
    last resort help 326
    protecting yourself 324
    responding to horrible
        comments 161–4
    snappy comebacks 327
    speaking up when you see it 322
    taking a break 329
Medicare 96, 411
Medicare card 139
meeting an online 'friend' 304
melanin 54
melatonin 244
memory centre 239
menarche 13
menstrual cups 34
menstrual cycle 28–30, 392, 394
menstrual period see periods
mental (mind) health 138
    affirmations to say to yourself 248
    getting help with problems
        249–50
    living with someone with
        an illness 252
    problems 249–50
    self-help tips 248
    treatment options 250
    website advice 249
    see also feelings
mental illness
    bipolar disorder 250, 258
    causes 251–2
    diagnosing 250, 252
    eating disorders 260–5
    effects of illegal drugs 223, 224, 226
    facts about 250
    family history of 251–2
    living with someone with
        a problem 252
    psychosis 223, 224, 240,
        250, 268–9
    schizophrenia 268–9
    self-harm 250, 259
    predisposition 224, 251–2
    severe anxiety 250, 254–5
    suicide 266–7
    treatment options 249–50, 268
    who to tell about 249, 251
    see also depression
merchandising 478
methamphetamines
    223, 229
midwives 414

index 559

mind health *see* mental (mind) health
mini-naps 246
missionary position (sex) 378
mobile phones
    bullying 301, 313, 324
    cost control 463–5
    on a date 341
    prank calls 301
    radiation from 465
    roaming costs 465
    running costs 463
    safety 301, 302
    scams 468
    texting 335, 464–5
    when driving 465
models
    fashion 84, 487
    role models 165–6
moisturisers 41, 498
moles 56, 95
money management 459–61, 468
money rules 468
money traps 463–6
money-making schemes 468
mood disorders 258
mood swings 239, 248, 258
moodiness 12, 179
'morning sickness' 403
Morning-after Pill 395, 401, 410
Mother Nature 9
mouth piercing 60
movies
    costume movies 485, 494
    for every stage of love 348–51
    for feisty women 524, 525
    top 10 female action-adventure characters 525
    top 10 girlfriends 'night-in' movies 524
    top 10 ladies' night comedies 524
    top 10 movies for girls 525
    top 10 movies with a heroine 525
    top 10 teen romances 524
music
    to help sleep 245
    in shops 480
    women in 520
mutual masturbation 364

N

names
    changing on marriage 467, 512
    Miss, Ms or Mrs? 518
    your signature 469

National Herbalists Association of Australia 31, 48
National Sexual Assault, Domestic Family Violence Counselling Service 357
natural health practitioner 123
natural therapies 142
    as complementary medicine 123
    for pimples 48, 389
    for PMS 31
'natural' contraception 393–4
'natural' food 121
'natural' skin products 43
negative body image 79
New Age beliefs 529–30, 534
new friends 307–8
nicotine 217, 221
    see also smoking
nightmares 246
nipples
    areola 15, 403
    being seen 15, 19
    change colour in pregnancy 15
    changes to watch out for 145
    erect 15
    hairs 73, 145
    in sexual arousal 362
    start to develop 13, 14
    sticking out 13, 15
    tender 15–16
    turned in (inverted) 15
'no added chemicals' 121
'no added sugar' 117
non-binary 347
'non-comedogenic' 40, 47, 505
'normal' skin 40
'nose jobs' 95
note-taking
    in class 429
    as you read 429, 431

O

'obesity' 85
obsessions 250
obsessive compulsive disorder 254
obstetricians 414
oestrogen 21, 26, 50, 179
oily foods 45, 47
oily hair 12, 64, 65
oily skin 40
omega 3 fatty acids 32, 108, 241
online 'friend', meeting 304
online banking 459
online creeps 303–4

online pics 302
    see also sexting 335
online safety 301–4, 321, 324, 335, 468
online shopping 303, 480–1
optimism 192
    10 things to cheer you up 193
oral sex 363
    as contraception 378
    and pregnancy 394
    and STIs 364, 383, 387
    swallowing semen 364, 381
organic make-up 501
'organic' products 43, 66, 121
orgasm
    faking 379
    for girls 362, 363, 364, 374, 380
    for guys 362, 363, 364, 374, 380
out and about security tips 172–5
outer labia 23, 74
ovaries 13, 14, 21, 26, 50
overdose (drugs) 223, 224, 233
over-exercising for weight loss 92
overseas study 438
overtired 246
over-training 133
ovulation 21, 25, 394
ovum 14, 21, 26, 395

P

pads for period 32–3, 34, 36, 37–8
paid work *see* jobs
painkillers, dangers of 221
palms, sweating 181
panic attacks 184, 254
panty liners 25, 33
pap smear 146
parents
    birth parents 292
    conflict between 282
    conversation starters with 276
    discussing family breakup with 288–90
    divorcing 289
    dumb things to say in argument 283
    gay 291
    getting on with 274–6
    getting to know 275
    hopeless parents 282, 284
    and your make-up 503
    with mental illness 252
'partner parade' 292–3
supporting your pregnancy 414
separating 288–90
training 279

telling about meanness and
  bullying 315, 324, 325
telling about porn stuff and
  sexting 303, 304
useful things to say in
  argument 284
when they're not there for you 276
how they use alcohol 213
partying
  dehydration 215, 233
  personal safety 175–6
pash rash 343
'pashing' 343
passive smoking 218, 219
patches for weight loss 92
paying the bill on a date 341
peer group 310
'peer pressure' 310–11
  how not to be controlled 311
pelvic inflammatory disease
  386, 387
penetrative vaginal sex 363, 399
penis 22
  circumcised 375
  cleaning 375
  during erection 362, 375
  guys' sensitivity about 375
  limp after orgasm 377
  rarely too large 375
  STI symptoms 384
  uncircumcised 375
  waiting to get hard again 377
penis-in-vagina sex see going all
  the way
perfectionism 188
perineum 24
period calendar 28–29
period pants 34
periods
  age they start 12, 13, 14, 26, 35
  amount of blood 27, 35
  attitudes to 28
  bleeding between 35
  and body fat 80
  clots in blood 27
  colour of blood 27
  cramps 31–2
  effect of Pill on 389
  emergencies 36–8
  exercising before 31
  feeling crabby before 12, 179
  'heavy' days 32
  hiding bloodstains 37
  how long they last 26, 35
  how often they come 26
  irregular or stopped 35, 92
  kit for 36
  missed when pregnant 403

other names for 27
pads for 32–3, 34, 36, 37–8
pain 31–2, 35, 389
premenstrual syndrome
  (PMS) 30–1
reason for 26
reasons to see a doctor 27, 30,
  32, 34, 35
regularity 30
sex during 394
'spotting' between 35
stain etiquette 38
tampons 32, 33–4, 35,
  36, 37
what to expect 11–14
worrying about smell 27
see also menstrual cycle
perseverance 536–7
personal safety 172–6
  emergency contacts 174
pesco-vegetarians 113
pessaries 148
pet love 332
pheromones 334
philanthropy 540
phones see mobile phones
physical abuse 286
physical activity
  amount you need 125–6
  downsides of 133–6
  exercises 134
  family involvement 135–6
  finding the right one 128–32
  group activities 128
  gyms 134
  helps with stress 184
  hints for starting 129–31
  huffy-puffery 126
  increasing 86
  injuries 134
  the lone mover 131
  making you feel good 125
  moderate exercise 126
  screen time in the way 134
  and sleep 245
  stretching before 130
  vigorous exercise 126
  what girls do 127
  what to avoid 133–5
  when it's hard 131–2
  why you feel good 124, 125
piercing
  facts about 60–1
  infection 60–1
  jewellery 454
  scars 61
Pilates 134
Pill see contraceptive pill

pimples 39, 40, 43, 72
  advice from chemist 48
  bacteria in 46
  blind 46
  on body 46
  causes 41, 45–6, 47, 55
  covering up 48
  dangers of isotretinoin
    medication 50–1
  doctors' treatments for 48, 50–1
  facial cleansers 48
  fighting 47
  herbal remedies for 48
  natural therapies for 48, 389
  Pill for treatment of 50, 389
  pus in 46
  scars from 46, 47
  squeezing 47
  and stress 46
  from upperlip waxing 76
  washes and creams 48–50
  what's not a cause 45
pimple creams 49–50
PIN 301
plastic surgery 95, 96
platform shoes 495
plucking (hair removal) 72, 73,
  76, 508–9
PMS (premenstrual syndrome) 30–1
pocket money 459, 460
polycystic ovaries 50, 72
pop videos 520
popcorn 114
pores, blocked 45, 47
porn 380–1
porn stars 520
porn stuff and sexting 302–4, 335,
  373, 380
  reporting 303–4
positions for sex 378
positive values 535–7
post-school qualifications 438–40
post-traumatic stress disorder 255
powder (make-up) 499
pregnancy
  common signs of 403
  confirming 403–4
  danger of pimple medication
    isotretinoin 50–1
  Family Planning Clinics 24, 38,
    144, 389, 404, 407, 410, 414
  fear of telling the family 405
  illegal drug use during 229
  no alcohol 200
  options 405–6
  after rape 400
  and smoking 217
  what to do 404–6

index 561

pregnancy counselling services
    biased 406–7, 408
    unbiased 407
pregnancy termination (abortion)
    see surgical pregnancy
      termination
pregnancy test 403, 404
    after rape 401
premenstrual syndrome (PMS) 30–1
pre-mixed drinks 198, 199–200, 215
prescription drugs 221–2, 224, 225
primer (make-up) 498
private college certificates and
    diplomas 438
problem relationships 353–4
problem skin 40
processed foods 116, 121
product placement (marketing)
    475, 477
progesterone 21, 179, 392, 395
protein 107–8, 240
psychiatrists 250, 252, 268
psychics 530
psychologists 250
psychosis 240, 250, 268–9
    and illegal drugs 223, 224,
      268, 269
puberty
    age it starts 9, 11
    becoming a sexual person 360–2
    common worries 10
    hormones trigger 12, 21
    what to expect 11–14
pubic hair
    shaving 74, 149
    total removal 74
    waxing 74, 75, 149
    when it starts 11, 13
    where it comes 11, 13
pubic lice (crabs) 388
pubic mound 11, 22, 73, 74
public transport safety 172
'push marketing' 477

Q
queer 347

R
rape 207, 208, 214, 223, 398–401
    getting help after 400–1
reading skills 428–9
real friends 297

'recommended serve' (food) 121
redundancy, job 456
referees for job 447–8
references (for résumé) 447–8, 456
regular meals 110
rejection
    by friends 192
    by guy you're dating 339–40
relationships
    abusive 284, 286–7, 356–7
    break-ups 354–5, 358
    good 352–3
    having sex 353
    keeping your friends 352–3
    love 332, 352–8
    problem 353–4
    same-sex 344–7
relaxation
    before and after studying 430
    breathing to relax 185
    helps mind health 248
religions
    beliefs 528–9
    dressing to suit 491
religious discrimination 531–2
resigning from job 456
resilience 192, 536—6
résumé (CV) 446–8, 456
rhythm method of
    contraception 393–4
rights
    as a worker 455
    see also women's rights
rip-offs 468
risk-taking 207, 239, 240
    in guys 336
Roaccutane 50
role models 165–6
romantic love 332
rules
    in the family 170–1, 277–8,
      279, 280
    money 468
    your rules for drinking 213
rumours 314, 315

S
sacked from a job 456
sadness 189, 191
safe sex 375
    how to use a condom 385
    sexually transmitted infections
      379, 383–8
safety
    in not-so-happy family 282

    online 301–4, 321, 324, 335, 468
    personal 172–5
same-sex marriages 344
same-sex relationships 344–7
    see also lesbian relationships
saving money 459–61
    for car 462
saying no
    to alcohol 202
    being confident about 158
    to cigarettes 220
    to sex 366–8
    ways to say it 158
saying sorry 159, 275, 308
scams 303, 441, 468
scars
    on the face 56
    from piercing and tattoos 61
    from pimples 46
schizophrenia 268–9
school
    advice on pregnancy 408
    being gay 346–7
    bullying policy 326
    careers counselling 437
    changing 329
    'cool group' at 160–1
    and electronic bullying 313
    exams 431–2, 433
    after final year exams 434–5
    Formal 338, 346–7
    gay students 346–7
    homework and study
      422–6, 430
    learning 428–9, 431
    and pregnant girls and young
      mums 414, 415
    religious 528–9
    rules about make-up 503
    VET qualification 438
    see also friends
school counsellors 10, 37, 187, 313,
    408, 433, 437, 414, 415
school nurses 10, 37
school stress 422
Schoolies ('Leavers') week
    175, 434–5
schoolwork
    exams 431–3
    homework and study 422–31
    learning stuff 428–31
'scientific' cosmetic claims 44
scrotum 375
scrubs 41, 51
sebaceous glands 45–6, 47
'seborrhoeic dermatitis' 70
sebum 45–6, 47, 51, 70
second date 342

second-hand clothes 488
secretions, vaginal
    abnormal 384
    clear or white 12, 13, 25
    panty pads for 25
    thick and lumpy 148
security tips 172–6
seeing a doctor
    see doctor, going to the
self-blame in grief 189
self-confidence see confidence
self-consciousness 12, 180
self-defence training 176
self-esteem 261
self-harm 250, 259
semen 362
    ejaculation of 362, 374, 380, 381
    and STIs 383
    swallowing in oral sex 364, 381
sensitive skin 40, 41, 46
separating parents 288–90
serotonin 125, 240
'serving size' (food) 121
severe acne 45
severe anxiety 250, 254–5
severe depression 191, 250, 256
sex 359
    anal sex 378, 381, 386, 387, 394, 399
    bad reasons for having 366, 371
    deciding to have 366
    deciding not to have 366–8
    does it hurt? 377
    dryness during 377
    during a period 394
    hands-only 394
    how long does it take? 377
    how you look 378
    if things turn scary 397
    and love 396–7
    meaning 363, 365–6
    not always enjoying 379, 380
    not ready for 365–6
    with older guys 369
    orgasm 362, 363, 364, 374, 379, 380
    porn not a true picture 380–1
    positions for 378
    rape 207, 208, 214, 223, 397–401
    right age for 365, 368–9
    sexual touching 363–4
    unwanted, when drunk 207
    ways to say no 369
    what lesbians do 379
    without consent (rape) 207, 208, 214, 223, 380–1, 398–401

without penetration 394
    see also contraception; first-time sex; going all the way; safe sex
sex words (slang) 376
sexting 302–3, 335, 373, 380
sexual abuse in the family 286–7
sexual arousal
    doesn't mean having sex 360–2, 363
    foreplay 363–4, 377
    through masturbation 360, 361
    signs of 362
sexual assault 214, 223, 397–400
    getting help after 400–1
    National Sexual Assault, Domestic Family Violence Counselling Service 357
    never the girl's fault 207, 208
    ongoing 401
sexual harassment at work 455
sexual insults 314, 369
sexual person, stages in development 361
sexual stimulation 362
sexual thoughts 360, 375
sexual touching
    not being comfortable with 365–6
    oral sex 363, 364, 378, 381, 383, 387, 394
    part of foreplay 363–4
    and STIs 364, 383
    stroking 364, 374, 377
    taking your time 363–4
sexuality
    coming out 346, 347
    gay students 346–7
    who's who and what's what 346
sexually transmitted diseases (STD)
    see sexually transmitted infections
sexually transmitted infections (STIs) 47, 148–9
    from anal sex 378
    catching during sex 364
    causes 383
    chart of common ones 386–8
    contraceptive pill no help against 390
    long-term effects 383
    more likely in older guys 369
    from oral sex 364, 383, 394
    after rape 400
    symptoms in girls and women 383–4
    symptoms in guys 384
    tests for 386
    see also condoms
shampoo
    claims on label 66

and conditioner combos 64
cost and quality 64
for dandruff 70
facts about 64–5
shared finances 467
shaving body hair 72, 73, 74, 75, 76
SHINE clinics, SA 407
shoes
    disasters 495
    high heels 492
    and skirt length 492
    without socks 58
'shopaholics' 483
shopping
    brand loyalty 473, 503
    clothes 485, 488, 491–2
    with credit cards 483
    industry tricks 472–8
    non-essentials 481–2
    online 303, 480–1
    sales assistants 482
    sales techniques 479
    shop atmosphere 480
    staying in control 482–3
    as therapy 482
    'you deserve it' 482
    see also make-up
shopping centres 482
shyness
    about big breasts 17
    socially 159–60
signature, creating your own 469
signature style (clothes) 488
single girls 355
sisters 279
skills and interests (in CV) 447
skin
    allergies and rashes 42
    becoming oiler 12, 47
    and diet 43
    dry 40, 41, 43
    and exercise 43
    facial 41–4
    healthy skin hints 43
    make-up 'essentials' 498–9
    marks on 56–7
    'normal' 40
    piercing and tattoos 60–2
    problem 40
    sun protection 41, 53, 54
    sweating 58–9, 180, 181
    tanning 54–5
    wrinkles 43, 54, 218
    see also blackheads; pimples
skin cancer
    and moles 56

index 563

and sunburn 52, 54–5
skin irritations and allergies
    42, 43, 70
skin marks 56–7
skin products 38–40, 498–9
    cosmetic companies' claims
        40, 42–4
    'hypo-allergenic' 40, 42
    'natural' 43
skin types 40
skipping meals (why not to) 122
sleep
    and brain health 241, 244,
        246, 248
    'broken' 246
    and caffeine 120, 245
    dreams 244, 246
    and exercise 245
    how much you need 244
    ideas to help you sleep 245
    nightmares 246
    and severe depression 256
    why you need it 244
sleep apnoea 246
sleep debt 246
sleep deprivation 244, 246
sleeping tablets 245
smaller labia 23
smear test 139, 146–7
smells
    BO (sweat) 59
    menstruation (periods) 27
smoking
    addiction 218, 219
    causes cancer 218
    causes early wrinkles 43, 218
    effects 217–18
    how to give up 219
    lung damage 217, 218
    passive smoking 218, 219
    and pimple formation 47
    things to say when you don't
        want to smoke 220
    and weight 91, 219
smoothies (food) 110
snacks 110
    energy snacks 430
    healthy 30
snail trail (body hair) 73
snoring 246
soap, drying 40
soap substitute 49
social conscience donation 478
social media and friendship sites
    301–4, 326
solariums 54–5
sole-parent families 292

songs for every stage of love 348–51
soy products 108, 112
speed (illegal drug) 229, 268
spending 481–3
sperm 375
    in ejaculate 362, 374, 380, 381
    fertilising egg 21, 26
spiked drinks 208, 230, 399
spirits (drinks) 197, 198
sponsorships 478
sports drinks 117, 120
spotting of blood 392, 403
sprains, treating 134
spray-on tans 55
stalking 357
standard alcoholic drinks 198, 200
standing up for what's right 537
starvation and body hair 72
STDs see sexually transmitted
    infections
stepfamilies 293–5
    ups and downs of 294
STIs see sexually transmitted
    infections
stomach 'cramps' 403
straight (sexuality) 346
stranger danger (rape) 172–6, 398
stress fractures 92
stress
    and brain health 241
    dealing with 184–5
    and depression 257
    hints for handling 187, 188
    homework and study 422
    and pimples 46
    stress-busting 536
    and sweating 58
    taking a break from 329
stretch marks 57
stretching before exercise 130
stroking (foreplay) 364, 377
student exchanges 438
study see homework and study
studying
    distance learning 440
    overseas 438
    post-school 438
style (clothes) 488
sugary things 116–17, 119, 420
    'no added sugar' 117
suicide 266–7
sun protection 41, 53, 54
sunburn and skin cancer 54–5
sunhats 53, 58
sunscreens 41, 53, 505
sunshine 53, 54
supporting parent benefit 413, 415
surgery 17, 58–9, 95, 96

surgical termination of pregnancy
    405, 409, 410, 411, 412
sweat glands 58–9
sweating
    BO 59
    feet 58
    hands 184
    more in teenage years 12, 58,
        180, 181
    treatment options 58–9
    underarm 58
swimming 132
    and alcohol 208
    chlorinated pools 65
    period pain 31
syphilis 388

T

TAFE (Technical and Further
    Education) colleges 438
takeaway food 112, 116, 118, 122
talking therapy (counselling)
    250, 259, 292
    see also counsellors
tampons
    can't be pushed too far 36
    changing 32, 34, 35, 36
    disposing of 36, 37
    emergency cleanups 37
    forgetting to take out before
        new one 35
    inserting 34, 36
    'natural' alternatives 32
    no effect on virginity 32
    string 33, 36
    swimming with 34
    toxic shock syndrome 34, 35
    types 32, 34
    what are they? 33–4
    where to buy 32
tanning 54–5
tattoos 60, 61–2
taxi safety 173
teachers, supportive 303, 304, 315,
    324, 325, 326
tearfulness before a period 30
teenagers
    becoming a young mum 413–16
    blending in or standing out 166
    brain 237–43
    deciding whether or not to
        drink 202
    effect of alcohol 197–200, 201
    employment restrictions 455
    erections 375

564   index

mental health problems 249
need more fuel 105, 107, 114
need more sleep 244
obsessing about your bits 95–101, 102
risk-taking 207, 239, 240
sexual abuse of 286
skeleton size doubles 83
skin 40
sleep needs 244
using a condom 386
using contraceptives 380
see also becoming a young mum; puberty
teeth
    bad breath 143
    causes of decay 143
    cigarette stains 218
    daily care 143
    dental floss 143
    dentists 143
    fluoridated water
    holes 117, 143
    whitening 97
television
    action heroines 525
    girl-friendly shows 525
    suggestions for watching less 135
    see also movies
termination of pregnancy 404
    'abortion pill' (RU486) 395, 409, 410
    feelings about 409
    never try to do it yourself 412
    support before and after 411
    surgical 405, 409, 410–12
testicles 375, 384
testosterone 21
'think global, act local' 539
thought association in advertising 474
threading (hair removal) 76
threats 314
throwing up when drunk 205
thrush (candida) 148
toilet paper, how to use to avoid infections 148
toners (for skin) 41–2, 51
tongue piercing 60
Tongue Thing (kissing) 343
'toolies' 175
top lip hair 73, 76
toxic shock syndrome 34, 35
traineeships 438
trans 4, 347
transgender *see* trans
travelling
    with illegal drugs 224, 225

immunisation 140
    with prescription drugs 225
'trend watchers' 475
trichomoniasis 388
trichotillomania 255
'trike' 388
trophy boy 337
trophy girlfriend 337
tummy
    flat or rounded 11
    hair on 73
'types' of people 530

U

ultrathin pads 33
under a healthy weight 81
underarm hair
    shaving 72, 73, 75
    starts growing 11, 13
    waxing 76
underarm sweating 58, 59
underwear
    changing 25
    visible 489
unhealthy fats 118
'unhealthy' weight 80
United Nations Convention on the Rights of the Child 287
university
    career counselling 439
    degrees 438
    open days 439
unprocessed food 111
unrequited love 332
upper lip hair 73, 76
urethra 24, 149
urinary infections 149
uterus (womb)
    changes size with baby 22
    endometrium breakdown becomes period 26
    monthly preparation for fertilised egg 26

V

vaccination *see* immunisation
vagina
    clear or white stuff on undies 12, 13, 25
    dryness during sex 377
    no sprays or deodorants 58
    opening covered by hymen 23

passage for baby 22
passage for period blood 22
place for penis during sex 22
putting objects in during masturbation 361
in sexual arousal 362
symptoms and signs of infection 147, 148, 383–4, 386–8
using tampons 13, 34, 36
thick and clumpy discharge 148
values *see* positive values
'Vatican roulette' 394
vegans 113, 114
vegetables 106, 109, 111, 113–14
vegetarians 113–14
VET (Vocational Education and Training) qualification 438
vibrators 361
vintage clothes 485
violence
    and alcohol 208
    boyfriend 357
    family 357
    girlfriend 357
viral marketing 475
virginity 367–8
vitamins and minerals
    for PMS 31
    supplements 109, 113, 248
    vitamin A medication 48, 50
Vocational Education and Training (VET) qualification 438
volunteering 538, 541
voting 538
vulva
    hair on 23
    itching, burning 25, 149
    problems 149
    what it looks like 23

W

walking
    for exercise 129, 131
    for period pain 31
    safety 172–3, 174
water
    before bed 245
    when clubbing or dancing 215, 233
    daily needs 109
    when exercising 133
    fluoride in 109, 143
    at parties and clubs 215, 232
    and skin health 43
waxing body hair 75–6
wee-hole (urethra) 24

weeing
    with burning 149
    a lot when pregnant 403
weight
    and alcohol 201
    answering comments about 12, 82, 84
    assessing yourself 81–4
    don't compare yourself with others 83–4
    healthy range 80, 81, 85, 86–7, 116
    no perfect weight 116
    people shouldn't comment about 84
    too heavy 84–7, 89
    weight gain and stretch marks 57
'weight cycling' 88
weight loss
    laxatives (to be avoided) 91
    over-exercising 92
    patches for 92
    support groups 86
    tips 86
    weight-for-height chart 82
    weight-loss industry 88
    when to call an ambulance 210, 233
whiteheads 51
whitening teeth 97
who am I? 165
    role models 165–6
    questionnaire 167

wine 197, 198, 200
withdrawal (not a contraceptive method) 394
womb *see* uterus
women
    in music 520
    smoking 219
    women we admire 526
women's health clinics 144, 146
women's rights
    a day in the life of 518
    discrimination lives on 511–13
    honorifics 518
    looking 'hot' 519–20
    porn stars 520
    why we still need them 513–21
    see also feisty women; feminism
work experience (for résumé) 447
work *see* jobs
working
    basic business skills 452–3
    being a good employee 452–4
    banking your pay 460
    clothes 453–4
    what feminists fought for 511–12
    fired or made redundant 456
    fixing a work problem 457
    laws to protect you 455
    part-time when studying 443
    resigning 456
    rules 455

sacked 456
wages 455
your rights as a worker 455, 457
workplace
    bullying 455, 457
    discrimination 455
    sexual harassment 455
worrying *see* anxiety
wrinkles 43, 54, 218

Y

year 13 (gap year) 435, 439
yoga 32, 134, 185, 250
young people's legal rights 177, 287
youth wages and rules 455
'yo-yo' dieting 88, 90

Z

zinc 108

While every care has been taken in researching and compiling the medical information in this book, it is in no way intended to replace or supersede professional medical advice. Neither the author nor the publisher may be held responsible for any action or any claim howsoever resulting from the use of this book or anything contained in it. Readers must obtain their own professional medical advice before relying or otherwise making use of the medical information contained in this book.

Contact details for organisations and website addresses frequently change: those included in this book were correct at the time of going to press.

VIKING

UK | USA | Canada | Ireland | Australia
India | New Zealand | South Africa | China

Penguin Books is part of the Penguin Random House group of companies whose addresses can be found at global.penguinrandomhouse.com.

Penguin Random House Australia

First published by Penguin Australia Pty Ltd, 2007
This revised edition published by Penguin Australia Pty Ltd, 2020

Reprinted and updated in 2020

Text and illustrations copyright © Kaz Cooke 2007, 2013, 2017, 2018, 2019, 2020

The moral right of the author has been asserted.

All rights reserved. Without limiting the rights under copyright reserved above, no part of this publication may be reproduced, stored in or introduced into a retrieval system, or transmitted, in any form or by any means (electronic, mechanical, photocopying, recording or otherwise), without the prior written permission of both the copyright owner and the above publisher of this book.

Designed by Adam Laszczuk © Penguin Australia Pty Ltd
Cover design and design coordination by Evi O. © Penguin Australia Pty Ltd
Typeset in 9.5/15 Stone Serif by Post Pre-press Group, Brisbane, Queensland
Colour reproduction by Splitting Image Colour Studio, Clayton, Victoria
Printed in China by RR Donnelley Asia Printing Solutions Ltd

A catalogue record for this book is available from the National Library of Australia

978 0 67007 666 6

penguin.com.au

Kaz Cooke is an Australian author, a mum, and a former teenage girl. She began her career as a reporter, sashayed into cartooning, and has written several bestselling books including *Girl Stuff 8-12*, *Up the Duff*, *Babies & Toddlers* – all updated each year; *Women's Stuff,* the children's picture books *Wanda Linda Goes Beserk* and *The Terrible Underpants*, and the novel, *Ada*. Kaz is a rabid feminist who enjoys toast and dancing on the couch.

kazcooke.com.au